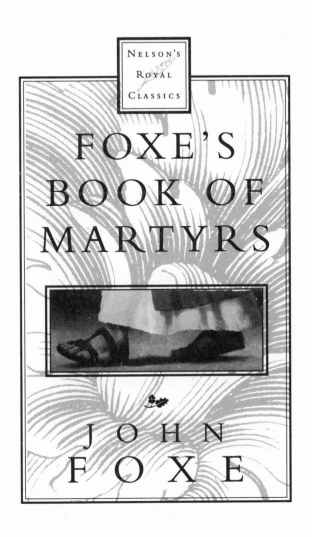

NELSON'S
ROYAL
CLASSICS

FOXE'S BOOK OF MARTYRS

JOHN FOXE

THOMAS NELSON PUBLISHERS
Nashville

Published in Nashville, Tennessee, by Thomas Nelson, Inc.

Library of Congress Cataloging-in-Publication Data

Foxe, John, 1516–1587.
  [Book of martyrs]
  Foxe's Book of martyrs / John Foxe.—[Rev. ed.].
     p.   cm.
  ISBN 0-7852-4262-7
     1. Christian martyrs—Biography.   2. Persecution—History.
  3. Church history.   4. Christian martyrs—Great Britain—Biography.
  5. Persecution—Great Britain—History.   6. Great Britain—Church
  history.   I. Title: Book of martyrs.   II. Title.
  BR1601.2.F68   2000
  272—dc21   99-045888
                                                                 CIP

Printed in the United States of America
3 4 5 6 7 — 04 03 02 01

PUBLISHER'S PREFACE

S ince the birth of the Christian church, thousands of writers have examined the teachings of the church and chronicled the experience of faith. Yet only a few of these works stand out as true classics—books that had and continue to have a significant impact on the church and the everyday lives of believers. They describe the core of our beliefs and capture the essence of our Christian experience. They remain an essential part of every Christian's library, and they continue to challenge the way we conceive our faith and our world.

Welcome to Nelson's Royal Classics—our commitment to preserving these treasures and presenting them to a new generation of believers. Every book contains an introduction that will detail the life and faith of the author and define why these works have such an important place in the history of our faith. As you read, you'll find that the timeless wisdom of the writers in this series is not only encouraging and enlightening but also very stimulating. These rich resources will strengthen your spiritual growth and show you ways to grow ever closer to God.

Each volume, such as Sheldon's *In His Steps*, Bunyan's *Pilgrim's Progress*, or St. Augustine's *Confessions*, is a treasure to be read and cherished. As a series, they become an heirloom library of invaluable worth. Read them now, and share them with others as a way to pass on the heart of Christianity.

JOHN FOXE, 1516–1587

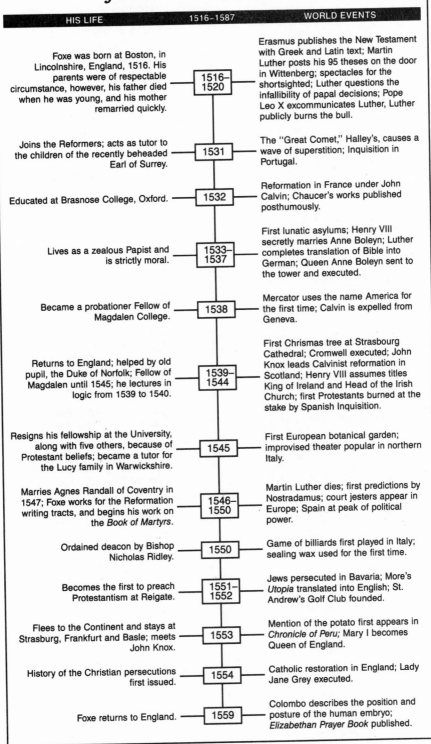

HIS LIFE	1516–1587	WORLD EVENTS
Foxe was born at Boston, in Lincolnshire, England, 1516. His parents were of respectable circumstance, however, his father died when he was young, and his mother remarried quickly.	1516–1520	Erasmus publishes the New Testament with Greek and Latin text; Martin Luther posts his 95 theses on the door in Wittenberg; spectacles for the shortsighted; Luther questions the infallibility of papal decisions; Pope Leo X excommunicates Luther, Luther publicly burns the bull.
Joins the Reformers; acts as tutor to the children of the recently beheaded Earl of Surrey.	1531	The "Great Comet," Halley's, causes a wave of superstition; Inquisition in Portugal.
Educated at Brasnose College, Oxford.	1532	Reformation in France under John Calvin; Chaucer's works published posthumously.
Lives as a zealous Papist and is strictly moral.	1533–1537	First lunatic asylums; Henry VIII secretly marries Anne Boleyn; Luther completes translation of Bible into German; Queen Anne Boleyn sent to the tower and executed.
Became a probationer Fellow of Magdalen College.	1538	Mercator uses the name America for the first time; Calvin is expelled from Geneva.
Returns to England; helped by old pupil, the Duke of Norfolk; Fellow of Magdalen until 1545; he lectures in logic from 1539 to 1540.	1539–1544	First Chrismas tree at Strasbourg Cathedral; Cromwell executed; John Knox leads Calvinist reformation in Scotland; Henry VIII assumes titles King of Ireland and Head of the Irish Church; first Protestants burned at the stake by Spanish Inquisition.
Resigns his fellowship at the University, along with five others, because of Protestant beliefs; became a tutor for the Lucy family in Warwickshire.	1545	First European botanical garden; improvised theater popular in northern Italy.
Marries Agnes Randall of Coventry in 1547; Foxe works for the Reformation writing tracts, and begins his work on the Book of Martyrs.	1546–1550	Martin Luther dies; first predictions by Nostradamus; court jesters appear in Europe; Spain at peak of political power.
Ordained deacon by Bishop Nicholas Ridley.	1550	Game of billiards first played in Italy; sealing wax used for the first time.
Becomes the first to preach Protestantism at Reigate.	1551–1552	Jews persecuted in Bavaria; More's Utopia translated into English; St. Andrew's Golf Club founded.
Flees to the Continent and stays at Strasburg, Frankfurt and Basle; meets John Knox.	1553	Mention of the potato first appears in Chronicle of Peru; Mary I becomes Queen of England.
History of the Christian persecutions first issued.	1554	Catholic restoration in England; Lady Jane Grey executed.
Foxe returns to England.	1559	Colombo describes the position and posture of the human embryo; Elizabethan Prayer Book published.

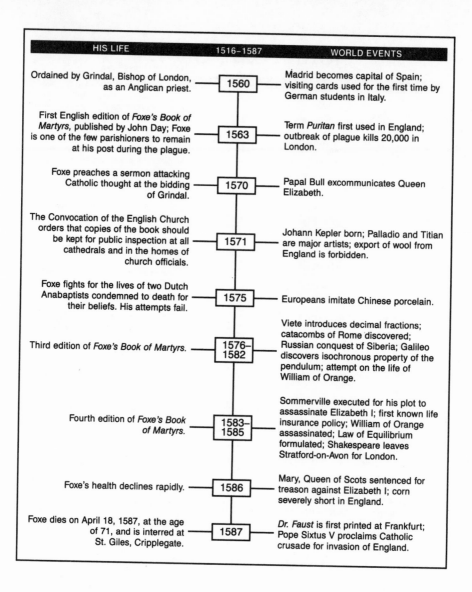

HIS LIFE	1516–1587	WORLD EVENTS
Ordained by Grindal, Bishop of London, as an Anglican priest.	1560	Madrid becomes capital of Spain; visiting cards used for the first time by German students in Italy.
First English edition of *Foxe's Book of Martyrs*, published by John Day; Foxe is one of the few parishioners to remain at his post during the plague.	1563	Term *Puritan* first used in England; outbreak of plague kills 20,000 in London.
Foxe preaches a sermon attacking Catholic thought at the bidding of Grindal.	1570	Papal Bull excommunicates Queen Elizabeth.
The Convocation of the English Church orders that copies of the book should be kept for public inspection at all cathedrals and in the homes of church officials.	1571	Johann Kepler born; Palladio and Titian are major artists; export of wool from England is forbidden.
Foxe fights for the lives of two Dutch Anabaptists condemned to death for their beliefs. His attempts fail.	1575	Europeans imitate Chinese porcelain.
Third edition of *Foxe's Book of Martyrs*.	1576–1582	Viete introduces decimal fractions; catacombs of Rome discovered; Russian conquest of Siberia; Galileo discovers isochronous property of the pendulum; attempt on the life of William of Orange.
Fourth edition of *Foxe's Book of Martyrs*.	1583–1585	Sommerville executed for his plot to assassinate Elizabeth I; first known life insurance policy; William of Orange assassinated; Law of Equilibrium formulated; Shakespeare leaves Stratford-on-Avon for London.
Foxe's health declines rapidly.	1586	Mary, Queen of Scots sentenced for treason against Elizabeth I; corn severely short in England.
Foxe dies on April 18, 1587, at the age of 71, and is interred at St. Giles, Cripplegate.	1587	*Dr. Faust* is first printed at Frankfurt; Pope Sixtus V proclaims Catholic crusade for invasion of England.

INTRODUCTION

His friends were worried. Each night they could wander by the secluded grove of trees near the university, where the young man had recently been appointed to a prestigious fellowship, and hear him sobbing and praying aloud, pleading with God to help him with the torment in his soul. They could see him pacing and raising his arms toward heaven. Finally, they reported his behavior to the university officials, unaware that they were setting events in motion that would change the face of the English church and Christianity worldwide.

The young man was John Foxe, who had come to Oxford University very early in life, after showing himself to be highly intelligent and very adept in his studies. He had unprecedented gifts for poetry and languages, especially Greek and Latin, and he soon gained the admiration of his colleagues at Oxford. He was chosen a fellow of Magdalen College in 1538, and he completed his M.A. in 1543. At the encouragement of his friends William Tyndale and Hugh Latimer, Foxe then turned his attentions to the study of Scripture and church history.

That was when his troubles began. Foxe's studies in church history began to distress him as he saw more and more evidence that church doctrine stood in opposition to Scripture. He started his studies over again, beginning with the earliest church documents, in an effort to prove his own conclusions to be incorrect. He could not, and found himself even more on the side of the Protestant reformers, much to his dismay. Thus began the nightly excursions to the grove, in hopes that God Himself would come to his aid.

Called before the university officials to explain his behavior, Foxe could have lied and saved his career, but he did not, and in 1545, he was requested to leave. His friends, who had supported him financially as well as emotionally, were stunned by his departure from the Catholic church and abandoned him. Foxe took a position as a tutor in the home of Sir Thomas Lucy, and he married in 1547. The persecution of the reformers, however, made it difficult for his employers to retain him, and Foxe moved to London in 1548.

In London, Foxe almost starved to death. Weak and desperate, he sought refuge at St. Paul's. As he prayed, a stranger approached him and handed him a significant amount of money. Quietly, the stranger explained that Foxe would soon find employment and that these funds would sustain him until then. With no other word, the stranger left. Three days later, Fox was hired to tutor the three grandchildren of the Duke of Norfolk. The oldest, Thomas, would later take his grandfather's place as Duke and would remain a lifelong friend of Foxe.

These were good times for Foxe and his family, and they continued until Mary became queen of England in 1553. A staunch supporter of the Catholic church, Mary endorsed and promoted the persecution of the Protestant Reformers. Foxe fled England for Germany, where he found work at a printing house. Using information sent to him from friends still in England, he began writing a short treatise on the English persecutions, beginning with Wycliffe. Entitled *The Acts and Monuments of These Latter and Perilous Days,* the first Latin draft of the book was printed in 1554. Foxe continued to gather information on the persecutions and, encouraged by the quick success of his small book, he began research into martyrs throughout church history.

When Elizabeth I came to the throne following Mary's death, Thomas of Norfolk encouraged Fox to return to England along with a great number of fellow Protestant exiles. In 1560, the Bishop of London ordained John Foxe, and Elizabeth appointed him to a position in the cathedral at Salisbury. Foxe took the position reluctantly, but it gave him the time and resources to continue his work on *The Acts and Monuments.*

This work became the makings of a local legend. Because he was determined not to neglect his regular duties, neighbors told stories of how Foxe diligently tended to the spiritual and material needs of his flock during the day, then labored over the manuscript late into every night, writing each line by hand, and praying aloud and pacing when troubled over some part of the text. His health began to fail, and he became thin and pale. Yet no one could persuade him to leave the manuscript.

The English edition of the book was finally published in 1563, and it was an immediate success and was soon called *Foxe's Book of Martyrs* by everyone. Foxe continued to work on the book, and new editions were released in 1570, 1576, and 1583. The book affected anyone who read it—Queen Elizabeth even commented on it, and Sir Francis Drake was so moved by the stories that he sought out John Foxe and became a close and valued friend. The Anglican church declared that a copy of the book be placed in every church, and wealthy parishioners were encouraged to have it in their homes.

The Book of Martyrs secured John Foxe's name in history, and the book rightly retains a place among the great works of Christian literature. Yet upon his death in 1587, Foxe was remembered by his friends and neighbors not as a writer but as a compassionate, loyal, and trusted man who sought most of all to follow God's will for his own life and to help others do the same.

TABLE OF CONTENTS

CHAPTER ONE

The First Persecutions

Containing a history of the first Persecutions of the Primitive Church, from the year of our Lord, 67, and the reign of Nero Domitius, until the time of Constantine the Great:[1] in which are detailed the lives and actions of the principal Christian martyrs of both sexes, who suffered for their faith in Europe and in Africa.

The dreadful martyrdoms we are now about to describe arose from the persecutions of the Christians by pagan fury in the primitive ages of the church during the space of three hundred years until the time of Constantine the Great.

It is both wonderful and horrible to peruse the descriptions of the sufferings of those godly martyrs as they are described by ancient historians. Their torments were as various as the ingenuity of man, excited by the devil, could devise, and their numbers were truly incredible. "Some," says Robanus, "were slain with the sword, some burnt with fire, some scourged with whips, some stabbed with forks of iron, some fastened to the cross or gibbet, some drowned in the sea, some had their skins plucked off, some their tongues cut out, some were stoned to death, some frozen with cold, some starved with hunger, some with their hands cut off, or otherwise dismembered, were left naked to the

---

[1] Eusebius was the principal historian who has transmitted to us an account of the sufferings of these blessed martyrs, and to his works we are indebted for many valuable anecdotes not to be found in any other writer.

open shame of the world." Augustine, speaking of these martyrs, says that, though their punishments were various, yet the constancy in all was the same. And notwithstanding the sharpness of so many torments, and cruelty of the tormentors, such was the number of these faithful saints, that as Hierome, in his epistle to Cromatius and Heliodorus, observes, "There is no day in the whole year, unto which the number of five thousand martyrs cannot be ascribed, except only the first day of January."

The first martyr to our holy religion was its Blessed Founder himself.[2] His history is sufficiently known, as it has been handed down to us in the New Testament; nevertheless it will be proper here to give an outline of his sufferings, and more particularly as they will be followed by those of the apostles and evangelists. (A.D. 1 to 18.) The persecutions by the emperors took place long after the death of our Savior.

It is known that in the reign of Herod, the angel Gabriel was sent by divine command to the Virgin Mary. This maiden was betrothed to a carpenter named Joseph, who resided at Nazareth, a city of Galilee; but the marriage had not then taken place; for it was the custom of the eastern nations to contact persons of each sex from their childhood, though the alliance was not permitted until years of maturity. The angel informed Mary how highly she was favoured of God, and that she should conceive a son by the Holy Spirit, which happened accordingly; for traveling to Bethlehem to pay the capitation-tax then levied, the town was so crowded that they could get lodgings only in a stable, where the Holy Virgin gave birth to our Blessed Redeemer, which was announced to the world by a star and an angel: the wise men of the East saw the former, and the shepherds the latter.

After Jesus had been circumcised, He was presented in the temple by the Holy Virgin; upon which occasion Simeon exclaimed in the celebrated words mentioned in the liturgy: "Lord, now lettest thou thy servant depart in peace, according to thy word: for mine eyes have seen thy salvation." Luke ii. 29, 30.

Jesus, in his youth, conversed with the most learned doctors in the temple, and soon after was baptized by John in the river Jordan, when the Holy Ghost descended upon Him in the form of a dove, and a voice was heard audibly to pronounce these words: "This is my beloved Son, in whom I am well pleased."

After this Christ fasted forty days and nights in the wilderness, where He was tempted by the devil, but resisted all his allurements. He performed His first miracle at Cana, in Galilee; He likewise conversed with the good Samaritan, and restored to life a nobleman's dead child. While traveling through

---

[2] A reverend editor of an edition of the Book of Christian Martyrs, published some years since, with a pompous title-page, and announced as the only "complete and original History of Martyrdom," has absurdly described as martyrs, Noah, Lot, Joseph, the Children of Israel, Shadrach, Meshach, Abednego. It is, nevertheless, evident, that these characters, who sustained with all becoming fortitude, as we learn from Scripture, the malignity of their persecutors, ought not to be classed amongst the blessed martyrs, whose lives were sacrificed for the perseverance in the doctrines of Christianity. As well might be recorded in a history of martyrs every man who had been in danger of perishing by the hand of an assassin.

Galilee He restored the blind to sight, He cured the lame and the lepers. Among other benevolent actions, He cured at the pool of Bethseda, a paralytic man who had been lame thirty-eight years, bidding him take up his bed and walk; and He afterwards cured a man whose right hand was shrunk up and withered, with many acts of a similar nature.

When He had chosen His twelve apostles, He preached the celebrated sermon on the Mount; after which He performed several miracles, particularly the feeding of the multitude, and the walking on the surface of the sea.

On the celebration of the passover, Jesus supped with His disciples; He informed them that one of them would betray Him, and another deny Him: in short He preached His farewell sermon. A multitude of armed men soon afterwards surrounded Him, and Judas kissed Him, in order to point him out to the soldiers, who were not acquainted with His person. In the conflict occasioned by the apprehension of Jesus, Peter cut off the ear of Malchus, the servant of the high-priest, for which Jesus reproved him, and, by touching the wound, healed it. (A.D. 34.) Peter and John followed Jesus to the house of Annas, who refusing to judge Him, sent Him bound to Caiaphas, in whose house Peter denied Christ, as He had predicted; but, on Christ reminding him of his perfidy, the apostle went out and wept bitterly.

When the council had assembled in the morning, the Jews mocked Jesus, and the elders suborned false witnesses against Him: the principal accusation being, that He had said, "I will destroy this temple made with hands, and within three days I will build another made without hands." Caiaphas then asked Him if He was Christ the Son of God, or not; being answered in the affirmative he accused Him of blasphemy, and condemned Him to death by Pontius Pilate, the Roman governor, who, though conscious of His innocence, yielded to the solicitations of the Jews, and condemned Him to be crucified. His remarkable expression at the time of passing sentence proved how much he was convinced that the Lord was persecuted.

Previous to the crucifixion, the Jews, by way of derision, clothed Christ in a regal robe, put a crown of thorns upon His head, and a reed, for a sceptre, in his hand; they then mocked Him with ironical compliments, spat in His face, smote His cheeks, and taking the reed out of His hand, they struck Him with it upon the head. Pilate would have released Him, but the general cry was, "Crucify him, crucify him," which occasioned the governor to call for a basin of water, and having washed his hands, he declared himself innocent of the blood of Christ, whom he termed a just person. But the Jews said, "Let His blood be upon us, and our children": and the governor found himself obliged to comply with their wishes. Their imprecation, too, has manifestly taken place, as they have ever since been a people scattered and cursed.[3]

---

[3] A similar example of punishment is to be noted amongst the Romans; for when Tiberius Caesar, having received accounts from Pontius Pilate, of the doings of Christ, of his miracles, resurrection, and ascension into Heaven, and how he was received as a divine messenger, was himself also moved with belief, and conferred with the whole senate of Rome to have Christ adored as God:

While they were leading Christ to the place of crucifixion, He was obliged to bear the cross, which being unable long to sustain, his enemies compelled one Simon, a native of Cyrene, to carry it the rest of the way. Mount Calvary was fixed on for the place of execution, where, having arrived, the soldiers offered Christ a mixture of gall and vinegar to drink, which He refused. Having stripped Him, they nailed Him to the cross, and crucified Him between two malefactors. On being fastened to the cross, He uttered this benevolent prayer for his enemies: "Father, forgive them, for they know not what they do." Four soldiers who crucified Him, now cut His mantle to pieces, and divided it between them; but His coat being without seam, they cast lots for it. While Christ remained in the agonies of death, the Jews mocked Him, and said, "If Thou art the son of God, come down from the cross." The chief priests and scribes also reviled Him, and said, "He saved others, but cannot save Himself." One of the criminals who was crucified with Him, also cried out, and said, "If Thou art the Messiah, save Thyself and us;" but the other malefactor, having great faith, exclaimed, "Lord, remember me when Thou comest into Thy kingdom." To which Christ replied, "This day shalt thou be with Me in Paradise."

When Christ was upon the cross, the earth was covered with darkness, and the stars appeared at noon-day, which struck the people and even the Jews with terror. In the midst of His tortures, He cried out, "My God, my God, why hast Thou forsaken Me!" and then expressed a desire to drink, when one of the soldiers gave Him, upon the point of a reed, a sponge dipped in vinegar, which however He refused. About three o'clock in the afternoon He gave up the ghost, and at that moment a violent earthquake commenced, when the rocks were rent, the mountains trembled, and the dead emerged from the graves. These and other prodigies attended the death of Christ, and such was the mortal end of the Redeemer of mankind. It is not a subject of wonder that the heathens who lived so long after Him, endeavoured by persecution and the

---

they refused, because that, contrary to the law of the Romans, he was consecrated for God, before the senate of Rome had so decreed and approved him. Tertul. Apol. cap.5. Thus the senate following rather the law of a man than of God, the permission of God stirred up their own emperors against them in such a degree, that the senators were almost all destroyed, and the whole city horribly afflicted for the space of three hundred subsequent years. Tiberius, who for a great part of his reign was a moderate prince, was afterwards a severe tyrant, who neither favoured his own mother, spared his own nephews, nor the princes of the city, nor such as were his own counsellors, of whom, to the number of twenty, he left only two or three alive. History relates him to have been so tyrannical, that in his reign many were accused, and condemned with their wives and children. In one day, according to Suetonius, he ordered twenty persons to be drawn to the place of execution. By him, also, Pilate, under whom Christ was crucified, was apprehended and accused at Rome, deposed, then banished to the town of Lyons, and at length committed suicide. Herod and Caiaphas also did not long escape. We shall here, combining historical facts with our narrative, inform the reader, that it was in the reign of Tiberius, that Jesus, the Son of God, in the four-and-thirtieth year of his age, which was the seventeenth of this emperor, suffered martyrdom. After this, Tiberius lived six years, during which time no persecution had begun in Rome against the Christians. It was in the reign of this emperor that St. Paul was converted to the faith.

most horrid cruelties, to prevent the propagation of that source of comfort and happiness in all affliction, which has resulted from the blessed system of faith that our Savior confirmed with His blood.

ACCOUNT OF THE LIVES, SUFFERINGS, AND MARTYRDOM OF THE APOSTLES, EVANGELISTS, ETC.

I. St. Stephen

This early martyr was elected, with six others, as a deacon of the first Christian church. He was also an able and successful preacher. The principal persons belonging to five Jewish synagogues entered into dispute with him; but he, by the soundness of his doctrine, and the strength of his arguments, overcame them all, which so much irritated them, that they bribed false witnesses to accuse him of blaspheming God and Moses. On being carried before the council, he made a noble defence; but this so much exasperated his judges, that they resolved to condemn him. At the instant Stephen saw a vision from heaven, representing Jesus, in his glorified state, sitting at the right hand of God. This vision so enraptured him, that he exclaimed, "Behold I see the heavens open, and the Son of Man standing on the right hand of God." This caused him to be condemned, and having dragged him out of the city they stoned him to death. On the spot where he was martyred, Eudocia, the empress of Theodosius, erected a superb church, and the memory of the martyr is annually celebrated on the 26th day of December.

The death of Stephen was succeeded by a severe persecution in Jerusalem, in which 2000 Christians, with Nicanor the deacon, were martyred, and many others obliged to leave their country.[4]

II. St. James The Great

He was a Galilean, and the son of Zebedee, a fisherman, the elder brother of St. John, and related to Christ himself; for his mother Salome was cousin to the Virgin Mary. Being one day with his father fishing in the sea of Galilee, he and his brother John were called by the Saviour to become his disciples. They cheerfully obeyed the mandate, and leaving their father, followed Jesus. It is to be observed, that Christ placed greater confidence in them than in any other of the apostles, Peter excepted. Christ called these brothers Boanerges, or sons of thunder, on account of their vigorous minds and zealous spirits.

When Herod Agrippa was made governor of Judea by the emperor Caligula, he raised a persecution against the Christians, and particularly selected

---

[4]Dorotheus, in his Synopsis, asserts, apparently upon good authority, that Nicanor, one of the seven deacons, with two thousand others, who believed in Christ, suffered on the same day when Stephen was martyred. He also adds, that Simon, another of the deacons, afterwards bishop of Bostrum, in Arabia, was there burned. Parmenas, another of the deacons, suffered at the same time.

James as an object of his vengeance. This martyr, on being condemned to death, showed such intrepidity and constancy of mind, that even his accuser was struck with admiration, and became a convert to christianity. This transition so enraged the people in power, that they condemned him likewise to death; when the apostle, and his penitent accuser, were both beheaded on the same day and with the same sword. These events took place in the year of Christ 44; and the 25th of July was fixed by the church for the commemoration of James's martyrdom. About the same period, Timon and Parmenas, two of the seven deacons, suffered martyrdom, the former at Corinth, and the latter at Philippi, in Macedonia.

III. St. Philip

This apostle and martyr was born at Bethsaida, in Galilee, and was the first called by the name of disciple. He was employed in several important missions by Christ, and being deputed to preach in Upper Asia, laboured very diligently in his apostleship. He then travelled into Phrygia, and arriving at Heliopolis, found the inhabitants so sunk in idolatry, as to worship a large serpent. St. Philip, however, was the means of converting many of them to christianity, and even procured the death of the serpent. This so enraged the magistrates, that they committed him to prison, had him severely scourged, and afterwards crucified. His friend, St. Bartholomew, found an opportunity of taking down the body, and burying it; for which, however, he was very near suffering the same fate. The martyrdom of Philip happened eight years after that of James the Great, A.D. 52; and his name, together with that of St. James the Less, is commemorated on the 1st of May.

IV. St. Matthew

This evangelist, apostle, and martyr, was born at Nazareth, in Galilee; but resided chiefly in Capernaum, on account of his business, which was that of a tax-gatherer, to collect tribute of such as had to pass the sea of Galilee. On being called as a disciple, he immediately complied, and left every thing to follow Christ. After the ascension of his Lord, he continued preaching the gospel in Judea about nine years. Intending to leave Judea, to go and preach among the Gentiles, he wrote his gospel in Hebrew, for the use of the Jewish converts; but it was afterwards translated into Greek by St. James the Less. He then went to Ethiopia, ordained preachers, settled churches, and made many converts. He afterwards proceeded to Parthia, where he had the same success; but returning to Ethiopia, he was slain by a halberd in the city of Nadabar, about the year of Christ 60; and his festival is kept by the church on the 21st day of September. He was inoffensive in his conduct, and remarkably temperate in his mode of living.

V. St. Mark

This evangelist and martyr was born of Jewish parents of the tribe of Levi. It is supposed that he was converted to christianity by St. Peter, whom he served as an amanuensis, and whom he attended in all his travels. Being entreated by the converts at Rome to commit to writing the admirable discourses they had heard from St. Peter and himself, he complied with their request, and composed his gospel in the Greek language. He then went to Egypt, and constituted a bishopric at Alexandria: afterwards he proceeded to Lybia, where he made many converts. On returning to Alexandria, some of the Egyptians, exasperated at his success, determined on his death. They tied his feet, dragged him through the streets, left him bruised in a dungeon all night, and the next day burned his body. This took place on the 25th of April, on which day the church commemorates his martyrdom. His bones were carefully gathered up by the Christians, decently interred, and afterwards removed to Venice, where he is honoured as the tutelar saint and patron of the state.

VI. St. James The Less

This apostle and martyr was so called to distinguish him from St. James the Great. He was the son of Joseph, the reputed father of Christ; and after the Lord's ascension was elected bishop of Jerusalem. He wrote his general epistles to all Christians and converts whatever, to suppress a dangerous error then propagating, viz. "That faith in Christ was alone sufficient for salvation, without good works." The Jews, being at this time greatly enraged that St. Paul had escaped their fury, by appealing to Rome, determined to wreak their vengeance on James, who was now ninety-four years of age: they accordingly threw him down, beat, bruised, and stoned him; and then dashed out his brains with a club, such as was used by fullers in dressing cloths. His festival, together with that of St. Philip, is kept on the first of May.[5]

---

[5] Egissippus in his commentaries, gives the following interesting account of this martyr—"James, the brother of our Lord, took in hand to govern the church after the apostles, being counted of all men, from the time of Christ, to be a just and perfect man. There were many other of the name; but this was born holy: he drank no wine nor any strong drink, neither did he eat any living creature, the razor never came upon his head, he was not anointed with oil, neither did he use bath; to him only was it lawful to enter into the holy place; neither was he clothed with woollen cloth, but with silk; and he entered into the temple, always upon his knees, asking remission for the people, so that his knees, by constant use, lost the sense of feeling, being benumbed and hardened like the knees of a camel. He was (for worshipping God, and craving forgiveness for the people), called the Just, and for the excellency of his life named Oblias, which is the safeguard and justice of the people, as the prophets declare of him: therefore, when many of the heretics which were among the people asked him what manner of man Jesus should be, he answered, that he was the Saviour. But the aforesaid heretics, neither believe the resurrection, nor that one shall come, who shall render unto every man according to his works; but as many as believe, they believe in James's faith. When some, therefore, of the princes did, there was a tumult made of the Scribes, Jews, and Pharisees, saying, it is dangerous lest that all the people do look for this Jesus as for Christ. Therefore, they gathered themselves together, and said, to James—'We beseech thee restrain the people, for they believe in Jesus as though he were Christ; we pray thee persuade them all which come unto the feast of the passover of Jesus; for we are all obedient unto thee, and all the people do testify of thee that thou art just, neither that thou dost accept the person of any man; therefore persuade the people that they be not deceived in Jesus, and all the people and we will obey thee; therefore stand upon the pillar of the temple, that thou mayest be seen from above, and that thy words may be perceived of all the people, for to his

VII. St. Matthias

This martyr was called to the apostleship after the death of Christ, to supply the vacant place of Judas, who had betrayed his master. He was also one of the seventy disciples. He was martyred at Jerusalem, by being first stoned, and then beheaded; and the 24th of February is observed for the celebration of his festival.

VIII. St. Andrew

This apostle and martyr was the brother of St. Peter, and preached the gospel to many Asiatic nations. On arriving at Edessa, the governor of the country, named Egeas, threatened him for preaching against the idols they worshipped. St. Andrew, persisting in the propagation of his doctrines, was ordered to be crucified, two ends of the cross being fixed transversely in the ground. He boldly told his accusers, that he would not have preached the glory of the cross, had he feared to die on it. And again, when they came to crucify him, he said that he coveted the cross, and longed to embrace it. He was fastened to the cross, not with nails, but cords; that his death might be more slow. In this situation he continued two days, preaching the greatest part of the time to the people; and expired on the 30th of November, which is commemorated as his festival.

IX. St. Peter

This great apostle and martyr was born at Bethsaida in Galilee, being the son of Jonas, a fisherman, which employment St. Peter himself followed. He was persuaded by his brother to turn Christian, when Christ gave him the name of Cephas, implying, in the Syriac language, a rock. He was called, at the same time as his brother, to be an apostle, gave uncommon proofs of his zeal for the service of Christ, and always appeared as the principal speaker among the apostles. He had, however, the weakness to deny his Master after his apprehension, though he defended him at the time; but the sincerity of his repentance proved that he soon became deeply convinced of the greatness of his crime. After the death of Christ, the Jews still continued to persecute the Christians, and ordered several of the apostles, among whom was Peter, to be scourged. This punishment they bore with the greatest fortitude, and rejoiced that they were thought worthy to suffer for the sake of their Redeemer.

When Herod Agrippa caused St. James the Great to be put to death, and found that it pleased the Jews, he resolved, in order to ingratiate himself with

---

passover all the tribes do come with all the country.' And thus the Scribes and Pharisees did set James upon the battlements of the church, and they cried unto him and said, 'Thou just man, whom we all ought to obey, because this people is led after Jesus, who is crucified, tell what is Jesus crucified?' And he answered with a great voice, 'What do you ask me of Jesus the Son of Man, seeing that he sitteth on the right hand of God, and shall come in the clouds of Heaven.' When many were persuaded of this, they glorified God upon the witness of James, and said, 'Hosanna in the highest to the Son of David.'"

the people, that Peter should be the next sacrifice. He was accordingly appre-hended, and thrown into prison; but an angel of the Lord released him, which so enraged Herod, that he ordered the sentinels who guarded the dungeon in which he had been confined, to be put to death. St. Peter, after various miracles, retired to Rome, where he defeated the artifices, and confounded the magic of Simon Magus, a great favourite of the emperor Nero: he likewise converted to christianity one of the concubines of that monarch, which so exasperated the tyrant, that he ordered both St. Peter and St. Paul to be apprehended. During the time of their confinement, they converted two of the captains of the guard, and forty-seven other persons to christianity. Having been nine months in prison, Peter was brought from thence for execution, when after being severely scourged, he was crucified with his head downwards; which position, however, was at his own request.[6] His festival is observed on the 29th of June, on which day he as well as Paul suffered. His body being taken down, embalmed, and buried in the Vatican, a church was erected on the spot; but this being destroyed by the emperor Heliogabalus, the body was concealed until the 20th bishop of Rome, Cornelius, conveyed it again to the Vatican; afterwards Constantine the Great erected one of the most stately churches in the universe over the place. Before we quit this article, it is requisite to observe, that previous to the death of St. Peter, his wife suffered martyrdom for the faith of Christ, when he exhorted her, as she was going to be put to death, to remember her Saviour.

X. St. Paul

This apostle and martyr was a Jew of the tribe of Benjamin, born at Tarsus in Cilicia. He was at first a great enemy to, and persecutor of the Christians; but after his miraculous conversion, he became a devout follower of the Lord. At Iconium, St. Paul and St. Barnabas were near being stoned to death by the enraged Jews; after which they fled to Lyconia. At Lystra, St. Paul was stoned, dragged out of the city, and left for dead. He, however, happily revived, and escaped to Derbe. At Philippi, Paul and Silas were imprisoned and whipped; and both were again persecuted at Thessalonica. Being afterwards taken at Jerusalem, he was sent to Cesarea, but appealed to Caesar at Rome. Here he continued a prisoner at large for two years; and at length being released, he visited the churches of Greece and Rome and preached in France and Spain.

---

[6] As to the cause and manner of his death there are many who describe them, as Hierome, Egissip-pus, Eusebius, Abdias, and others, although they do not all precisely agree in the time. The words of Hierome are these, "Simon Peter the son of Jonas, of the province of Galilee, and of the town of Bethsaida, the brother of Andrew, after he had been bishop of the church of Antioch, and had preached to the dispersed of them that believed of the circumcision, in Pontus, Galatia, Cappado-cia, Asia, and Bithynia, in the second year of Claudius the emperor (which was about the year of our Lord 44) came to Rome to withstand Simon Magus and there kept the priestly chair the space of five-and-twenty years, until the last year of the aforesaid Nero, which was the fourteenth year of his reign, in which he was crucified, his head being down, and his feet upward, himself so requiring, because he was, he said, unworthy to be crucified after the same form and manner as the Lord Jesus.

Returning to Rome, he was again apprehended and, by the order of Nero, martyred, by beheading. Two days are dedicated to the commemoration of this apostle; the one to his conversion, which is on the 25th of January, and the other to his martyrdom, which is on the 29th of June, A.D. 72.

XI. St. Jude

This apostle and martyr, the brother of James, was commonly called Thaddaeus. Being sent to Edessa, he wrought many miracles, and made many converts, which exciting the resentment of people in power, he was crucified, A.D. 72; and the 28th of October is, by the church, dedicated to his memory.

XII. St. Bartholomew

This apostle and martyr preached in several countries, performed many miracles, and healed various diseases. He translated St. Matthew's gospel into the Indian language, and propagated it in that country; but at length, the idolators growing impatient with his doctrines, severely beat and crucified him. He was scarcely alive when taken down and beheaded. The anniversary of his martyrdom is on the 24th of August.

XIII. St. Thomas

He was called by this name in Syriac, but Didymus in Greek; he was an apostle and martyr, and preached in Parthia and India, where displeasing the pagan priests, he was martyred by being thrust through with a spear. His death is commemorated on the 21st of December.

XIV. St. Luke the Evangelist

This martyr was the author of the third most excellent gospel; and also of the Acts of the Apostles. He travelled with St. Paul to Rome and preached to divers barbarous nations until the priests of Greece hanged him on an olive-tree. The anniversary of his martyrdom is on the 18th of October.

XV. St. Simon

This apostle and martyr was distinguished for his zeal by the name of Zelotes. He preached with great success in Mauritania and other parts of Africa, and even in Britain, where, though he made many converts, he was crucified, A.D. 74; and the church, joining him with St. Jude, commemorates his festival on the 28th of October.

XVI. St. John

He was distinguished as a prophet, an apostle, a divine, an evangelist, and a martyr. He is called the beloved disciple and was brother to James the Great. He was previously a disciple of John the baptist and afterwards not only one of the twelve apostles, but one of the three to whom Christ communicated the most secret passages of his life. He founded churches at Smyrna, Pergamos, Sardis, Philadelphia, Laodicea, and Thyatria, to which he directs his book of

Revelation. Being at Ephesus, he was ordered by the emperor Domitian to be sent bound to Rome, where he was condemned to be cast into a caldron of boiling oil.[7] But here a miracle was wrought in his favour, the oil did him no injury; and Domitian, not being able to put him to death, banished him to Patmos to labour in the mines, A.D. 73. He was, however, recalled by Nerva, who succeeded Domitian but was deemed a martyr on account of his having undergone an execution, though it did not take effect. He wrote his epistles, gospel, and Revelation, each in a different style; but they are all equally admired. He was the only apostle who escaped a violent death and lived the longest of any, he being nearly 100 years of age at the time of his death. The church devotes the 27th of December to his memory.

XVII. St. Barnabas

He was a native of Cyprus, but of Jewish parents: the time of his death is uncertain; but it is supposed to have been about the year of Christ 73; and his festival is kept on the 11th of June.

---

[7] With respect to this punishment the Legend and Perionius say, it took place at Rome, Isidorus also writing of him, declared that he turned certain places of wood into gold, and stones by the sea-side into pearls, to satisfy the desire of those whom he had persuaded to renounce their riches; and they afterwards repenting that for worldly treasure they had lost Heaven, the apostle again changed the same into their former substance. It is said by Eusebius that he raised a widow and a young man from death to life. That he drank poison and it hurt him not. These and other miracles, though they may be true, and are found in several writers, yet are not mentioned in the sacred books, and may therefore be considered at best as apocryphal.

CHAPTER TWO

The Ten Primitive Persecutions

THE FIRST PERSECUTION,
UNDER NERO, A.D. 67

The first persecution of the Church took place in the year 67, under Nero, the sixth emperor of Rome. This monarch reigned for the space of five years, with tolerable credit to himself, but then gave way to the greatest extravagancy of temper, and to the most atrocious barbarities. Among other diabolical whims, he ordered that the city of Rome should be set on fire, which order was executed by his officers, guards, and servants. While the imperial city was in flames, he went up to the tower of Macaenas, played upon his harp, sung the song of the burning of Troy, and openly declared that "he wished the ruin of all things before his death." Besides the noble pile, called the Circus, many other palaces and houses were consumed; several thousands perished in the flames, were smothered in the smoke, or were buried beneath the ruins.

This dreadful conflagration continued nine days; when Nero, finding that his conduct was greatly blamed, and a severe odium cast upon him, determined to lay the whole upon the Christians, at once to excuse himself, and have an opportunity of glutting his sight with new cruelties. This was the occasion of the first persecution; and the barbarities exercised on the Christians were such as even excited the commiseration of the Romans themselves. Nero even refined upon cruelty, and contrived all manner of punishments for the Christians that the most infernal imagination could design. In particular, he had some sewed up in skins of wild beasts, and then worried by dogs until they expired; and others dressed in shirts made stiff with wax, fixed to axletrees, and set on fire in his gardens, in order to illuminate them. This persecution was general throughout the whole Roman Empire; but it rather increased than diminished the spirit of Christianity. In the course of it, St. Paul and St. Peter were martyred.

To their names may be added, Erastus, chamberlain of Corinth; Aristarchus, the Macedonian, and Trophimus, an Ephesian, converted by St. Paul, and fellow-laborer with him, Joseph, commonly called Barsabas, and Ananias, bishop of Damascus; each of the Seventy.

THE SECOND PERSECUTION,
UNDER DOMITIAN, A.D. 81

The emperor Domitian, who was naturally inclined to cruelty, first slew his brother, and then raised the second persecution against the Christians. In his rage he put to death some of the Roman senators, some through malice; and others to confiscate their estates. He then commanded all the lineage of David be put to death.

Among the numerous martyrs that suffered during this persecution was Simeon, bishop of Jerusalem, who was crucified; and St. John, who was boiled in oil, and afterward banished to Patmos. Flavia, the daughter of a Roman senator, was likewise banished to Pontus; and a law was made, "That no Christian, once brought before the tribunal, should be exempted from punishment without renouncing his religion."

A variety of fabricated tales were, during this reign, composed in order to injure the Christians. Such was the infatuation of the pagans, that, if famine, pestilence, or earthquakes afflicted any of the Roman provinces, it was laid upon the Christians. These persecutions among the Christians increased the number of informers and many, for the sake of gain, swore away the lives of the innocent.

Another hardship was, that, when any Christians were brought before the magistrates, a test oath was proposed, when, if they refused to take it, death was pronounced against them; and if they confessed themselves Christians, the sentence was the same.

The following were the most remarkable among the numerous martyrs who suffered during this persecution.

Dionysius, the Areopagite, was an Athenian by birth, and educated in all the useful and ornamental literature of Greece. He then travelled to Egypt to study astronomy, and made very particular observations on the great and supernatural eclipse, which happened at the time of our Savior's crucifixion.

The sanctity of his conversation and the purity of his manners recommended him so strongly to the Christians in general, that he was appointed bishop of Athens.

Nicodemus, a benevolent Christian of some distinction, suffered at Rome during the rage of Domitian's persecution.

Protasius and Gervasius were martyred at Milan.

Timothy was the celebrated disciple of St. Paul, and bishop of Ephesus, where he zealously governed the Church until A.D. 97. At this period, as the pagans were about to celebrate a feast called Catagogion, Timothy, meeting the procession, severely reproved them for their ridiculous idolatry, which so exasperated the people that they fell upon him with their clubs, and beat him in so dreadful a manner that he expired of the bruises two days later.

THE THIRD PERSECUTION, UNDER TRAJAN, A.D. 108

In the third persecution Pliny the Second, a man learned and famous, seeing the lamentable slaughter of Christians, and moved therewith to pity, wrote to Trajan, certifying him that there were many thousands of them daily put to death, of which none did any thing contrary to the Roman laws worthy of persecution. "The whole account they gave of their crime or error (whichever it is to be called) amounted only to this—viz. that they were accustomed on a stated day to meet before daylight, and to repeat together a set form of prayer to Christ as a God, and to bind themselves by an obligation—not indeed to commit wickedness; but, on the contrary—never to commit theft, robbery, or adultery, never to falsify their word, never to defraud any man: after which it was their custom to separate, and reassemble to partake in common of a harmless meal."

In this persecution suffered the blessed martyr, Ignatius, who is held in famous reverence among very many. This Ignatius was appointed to the bishopric of Antioch next after Peter in succession. Some do say, that he, being sent from Syria to Rome, because he professed Christ, was given to the wild beasts to be devoured. It is also said of him, that when he passed through Asia, being under the most strict custody of his keepers, he strengthened and confirmed the churches through all the cities as he went, both with his exhortations and preaching of the Word of God. Accordingly, having come to Smyrna, he wrote to the Church at Rome, exhorting them not to use means for his deliverance from martyrdom, lest they should deprive him of that which he most longed and hoped for. "Now I begin to be a disciple. I care for nothing, of visible or invisible things, so that I may but win Christ. Let fire and the cross, let the companies of wild beasts, let breaking of bones and tearing of limbs, let the grinding of the whole body, and all the malice of the devil, come upon me; be it so, only may I win Christ Jesus!" And even when he was sentenced to be thrown to the beasts, such as the burning desire that he had to suffer, that he spake, what time he heard the lions roaring, saying: "I am the wheat of Christ: I am going to be ground with the teeth of wild beasts, that I may be found pure bread."

Trajan being succeeded by Adrian, the latter continued this third persecution with as much severity as his predecessor. About this time Alexander, bishop of Rome, with his two deacons, were martyred; as were Quirinus and Hernes, with their families;

Zenon, a Roman nobleman, and about ten thousand other Christians.

In Mount Ararat many were crucified, crowned with thorns, and spears run into their sides, in imitation of Christ's passion. Eustachius, a brave and successful Roman commander, was by the emperor ordered to join in an idolatrous sacrifice to celebrate some of his own victories; but his faith (being a Christian in his heart) was so much greater than his vanity, that he nobly refused it. Enraged at the denial, the ungrateful emperor forgot the service of this skilful commander, and ordered him and his whole family to be martyred.

At the martyrdom of Faustines and Jovita, brothers and citizens of Brescia, their torments were so many, and their patience so great, that Calocerius, a pagan, beholding them, was struck with admiration, and exclaimed in a kind of ecstasy, "Great is the God of the Christians!" for which he was apprehended, and suffered a similar fate.

Many other similar cruelties and rigors were exercised against the Christians, until Quadratus, bishop of Athens, made a learned apology in their favor before the emperor, who happened to be there and Aristides, a philosopher of the same city, wrote an elegant epistle, which caused Adrian to relax in his severities, and relent in their favor.

Adrian dying A.D. 138, was succeeded by Antoninus Pius, one of the most amiable monarchs that ever reigned, and who stayed the persecutions against the Christians.

THE FOURTH PERSECUTION, UNDER MARCUS AURELIUS ANTONINUS, A.D. 162

Marcus Aurelius, followed about the year of our Lord 161, a man of nature more stern and severe; and, although in study of philosophy and in civil government no less commendable, yet, toward the Christians sharp and fierce; by whom was moved the fourth persecution.

The cruelties used in this persecution were such that many of the spectators shuddered with horror at the sight, and were astonished at the intrepidity of the sufferers. Some of the martyrs were obliged to pass, with their already wounded feet, over thorns, nails, sharp shells, etc. upon their points, others were scourged until their sinews and veins lay bare, and after suffering the most excruciating tortures that could be devised, they were destroyed by the most terrible deaths.

Germanicus, a young man, but a true Christian, being delivered to the wild beasts on account of his faith, behaved with such astonishing courage that several pagans became converts to a faith which inspired such fortitude.

Polycarp, the venerable bishop of Smyrna, hearing that persons were seeking for him, escaped, but was discovered by a child. After feasting the guards who apprehended him, he desired an hour in prayer, which being allowed, he prayed with such fervency, that his guards repented that they had been instrumental in taking him. He was, however, carried before the proconsul, condemned, and burnt in the market place.

The proconsul then urged him, saying, "Swear, and I will release thee;—reproach Christ."

Polycarp answered, "Eighty and six years have I served him, and he never once wronged me; how then shall I blaspheme my King, Who hath saved me?" At the stake to which he was only tied, but not nailed as usual, as he assured them he should stand immovable, the flames, on their kindling the fagots, encircled his body, like an arch, without touching him; and the executioner, on seeing this, was ordered to pierce him with a sword, when so great a quantity of blood flowed out as extinguished the fire. But his body, at the instigation of the enemies of the Gospel, especially Jews, was ordered to be consumed in the pile, and the request of his friends, who wished to give it Christian burial, rejected. They nevertheless collected his bones and as much of his remains as possible, and caused them to be decently interred.

Metrodorus, a minister, who preached boldly, and Pionius, who made some excellent apologies for the Christian faith, were likewise burnt. Carpus and Papilus, two worthy Christians, and Agatonica, a pious woman, suffered martyrdom at Pergamopolis, in Asia.

Felicitatis, an illustrious Roman lady, of a considerable family, and the most shining virtues, was a devout Christian. She had seven sons, whom she had educated with the most exemplary piety.

Januarius, the eldest, was scourged, and pressed to death with weights; Felix and Philip, the two next had their brains dashed out with clubs; Silvanus, the fourth, was murdered by being thrown from a precipice; and the three younger sons, Alexander, Vitalis, and Martial, were beheaded. The mother was beheaded with the same sword as the three latter.

Justin, the celebrated philosopher, fell a martyr in this persecution. He was a native of Neapolis, in Samaria, and was born A.D. 103. Justin was a great lover of truth, and a universal scholar; he investigated the Stoic and Peripatetic philosophy, and attempted the Pythagorean; but the behavior of its professors disgusting him, he applied himself to the Platonic, in which he took great delight. About the year 133, when he was thirty years of age, he became a convert to Christianity, and then, for the first time, perceived the real nature of truth.

He wrote an elegant epistle to the Gentiles, and employed his talents in convincing the Jews of the truth of the Christian rites; spending a great deal of time in travelling, until he took up his abode in Rome, and fixed his habitation upon the Viminal mount.

He kept a public school, taught many who afterward became great men, and wrote a treatise to confuse heresies of all kinds. As the pagans began to treat the Christians with great severity, Justin wrote his first apology in their favor. This piece displays great learning and genius, and occasioned the emperor to publish an edict in favor of the Christians.

Soon after, he entered into frequent contests with Crescens, a person of a vicious life and conversation, but a celebrated cynic philosopher; and his arguments appeared so powerful, yet disgusting to the cynic, that he resolved on, and in the sequel accomplished, his destruction.

The second apology of Justin, upon certain severities, gave Crescens the cynic an opportunity of prejudicing the emperor against the writer of it; upon which Justin, and six of his companions, were apprehended. Being commanded to sacrifice to the pagan idols, they refused, and were condemned to be scourged, and then beheaded; which sentence was executed with all imaginable severity.

Several were beheaded for refusing to sacrifice to the image of Jupiter; in particular Concordus, a deacon of the city of Spolito.

Some of the restless northern nations having risen in arms against Rome, the emperor marched to encounter them. He was, however, drawn into an ambuscade, and dreaded the loss of his whole army. Enveloped with mountains, surrounded by enemies, and perishing with thirst, the pagan deities were invoked in vain; when the men belonging to the militine, or thundering legion, who were all Christians, were commanded to call upon their God for succor. A miraculous deliverance immediately ensued; a prodigious quantity of rain fell, which, being caught by the men, and filling their dykes, afforded a sudden and astonishing relief. It appears that the storm which miraculously flashed in the face of the enemy so intimidated them, that part deserted to the Roman army; the rest were defeated, and the revolted provinces entirely recovered.

This affair occasioned the persecution to subside for some time, at least in those parts immediately under the inspection of the emperor; but we find that it soon after raged in France, particularly at Lyons, where the tortures to which many of the Christians were put, almost exceed the powers of description.

The principal of these martyrs were Vetius Agathus, a young man; Blandina, a Christian lady, of a weak constitution; Sanctus, a deacon of Vienna; red hot plates of brass were placed upon the tenderest parts of his body; Biblias, a weak woman, once an apostate. Attalus, of Pergamus; and Pothinus, the venerable bishop of Lyons, who was ninety years of age. Blandina, on the day when she and the three other champions were first brought into the amphitheater, she was suspended on a piece of wood fixed in the ground, and exposed as food for the wild beasts; at which time, by her earnest prayers, she encouraged others. But none of the wild beasts would touch her, so that she was remanded to prison. When she was again produced for the third and last time, she was accompanied by Ponticus, a youth of fifteen, and the constancy of their faith so enraged the multitude that neither the sex of the one nor the youth of the other were respected, being exposed to all manner of punishments and tortures. Being strengthened by Blandina, he persevered unto death; and she, after enduring all the torments heretofore mentioned, was at length slain with the sword.

When the Christians, upon these occasions, received martyrdom, they were ornamented, and crowned with garlands of flowers; for which they, in heaven, received eternal crowns of glory.

It has been said that the lives of the early Christians consisted of "persecution above ground and prayer below ground." Their lives are expressed by the Coliseum and the catacombs. Beneath Rome are the excavations which we call the catacombs, which were at once temples and tombs. The early Church of Rome might well be called the Church of the Catacombs. There are some sixty catacombs near Rome, in which some six hundred miles of galleries have been traced, and these are not all. These galleries are about eight feet high and from three to five feet wide, containing on either side several rows of long, low, horizontal recesses, one above another like berths in a ship. In these the dead bodies were placed and the front closed, either by a single marble slab or several great tiles laid in mortar. On these slabs or tiles, epitaphs or symbols are graved or painted. Both pagans and Christians buried their dead in these catacombs. When the Christian graves have been opened the skeletons tell their own terrible tale. Heads are found severed from the body, ribs and shoulder blades are broken, bones are often calcined from fire. But despite the awful story of persecution that we may read here, the inscriptions breathe forth peace and joy and triumph. Here are a few:

Here lies Marcia, put to rest in a dream of peace.

Lawrence to his sweetest son, borne away of angels.

Victorious in peace and in Christ.

Being called away, he went in peace.

Remember when reading these inscriptions the story the skeletons tell of persecution, of torture, and of fire.

But the full force of these epitaphs is seen when we contrast them with the pagan epitaphs, such as:

Live for the present hour, since we are sure of nothing else.

I lift my hands against the gods who took me away
at the age of twenty though I had done no harm.

Once I was not. Now I am not. I know nothing
about it, and it is no concern of mine.

Traveler, curse me not as you pass, for I am
in darkness and cannot answer.

The most frequent Christian symbols on the walls of the catacombs, are, the good shepherd with the lamb on his shoulder, a ship under full sail, harps, anchors, crowns, vines, and above all the fish.

THE FIFTH PERSECUTION, COMMENCING WITH SEVERUS, A.D. 192

Severus, having been recovered from a severe fit of sickness by a Christian, became a great favorer of the Christians in general; but the prejudice and fury of the ignorant multitude prevailing, obsolete laws were put in execution against the Christians. The progress of Christianity alarmed the pagans, and they revived the stale calumny of placing accidental misfortunes to the account of its professors, A.D. 192.

But, though persecuting malice raged, yet the Gospel shone with resplendent brightness; and, firm as an impregnable rock, withstood the attacks of its boisterous enemies with success. Tertullian, who lived in this age, informs us that if the Christians had collectively withdrawn themselves from the Roman territories, the empire would have been greatly depopulated.

Victor, bishop of Rome, suffered martyrdom in the first year of the third century, A.D. 201. Leonidus, the father of the celebrated Origen, was beheaded for being a Christian. Many of Origen's hearers likewise suffered martyrdom; particularly two brothers, named Plutarchus and Serenus; another Serenus, Heron, and Heraclides, were beheaded. Rhais had boiled pitch poured upon her head, and was then burnt, as was Marcella her mother. Potainiena, the sister of Rhais, was executed in the same manner as Rhais had been; but Basilides, an officer belonging to the army, and ordered to attend her execution, became her convert.

Basilides being, as an officer, required to take a certain oath, refused, saying, that he could not swear by the Roman idols, as he was a Christian. Struck with surprise, the people could not, at first, believe what they heard; but he had no sooner confirmed the same, than he was dragged before the judge, committed to prison, and speedily afterward beheaded.

Irenaeus, bishop of Lyons, was born in Greece, and received both a polite and a Christian education. It is generally supposed that the account of the persecutions at Lyons was written by himself. He succeeded the martyr Pothinus as bishop of Lyons, and ruled his diocese with great propriety; he was a zealous opposer of heresies in general, and, about A.D. 187, he wrote a celebrated tract against heresy. Victor, the bishop of Rome, wanting to impose the keeping of Easter there, in preference to other places, it occasioned some disorders among the Christians. In particular, Irenaeus wrote him a synodical epistle, in the name of the Gallic churches. This zeal, in favor of Christianity, pointed him out as an object of resentment to the emperor; and in A.D. 202, he was beheaded.

The persecutions now extending to Africa, many were martyred in that quarter of the globe; the most particular of whom we shall mention.

Perpetua, a married lady, of about twenty-two years. Those who suffered with her were, Felicitas, a married lady, big with child at the time of her being apprehended, and Revocatus, catechumen of Carthage, and a slave. The names of the other prisoners, destined to suffer upon this occasion, were Saturninus, Secundulus, and Satur. On the day appointed for their execution, they were led to the amphitheater. Satur, Saturninus, and Revocatus were ordered to run the gauntlet between the hunters, or such as had the care of the wild beasts. The hunters being drawn up in two ranks, they ran between, and were severely lashed as they passed. Felicitas and Perpetua were stripped, in order to be thrown to a mad bull, which made his first attack upon Perpetua, and stunned her; he then darted at Felicitas, and gored her dreadfully; but not killing them, the executioner did that office with a sword. Revocatus and Satur were destroyed by wild beasts; Saturninus was beheaded; and Secundulus died in prison. These executions were in A.D. 205, on the eighth day of March.

Speratus and twelve others were likewise beheaded; as was Andocles in France. Asclepiades, bishop of Antioch, suffered many tortures, but his life was spared.

Cecilia, a young lady of good family in Rome, was married to a gentleman named Valerian. She converted her husband and brother, who were beheaded; and the maximus, or officer, who led them to execution, becoming their convert, suffered the same fate. The lady was placed naked in a scalding bath, and having continued there a considerable time, her head was struck off with a sword, A.D. 222.

Calistus, bishop of Rome, was martyred, A.D. 224; but the manner of his death is not recorded; and Urban, bishop of Rome, met the same fate A.D. 232.

THE SIXTH PERSECUTION,
UNDER MAXIMUS, A.D. 235

A.D. 235, was in the time of Maximinus. In Cappadocia, the president, Seremianus, did all he could to exterminate the Christians from that province.

The principal persons who perished under this reign were Pontianus, bishop of Rome; Anteros, a Grecian, his successor, who gave offence to the government by collecting the acts of the martyrs, Pammachius and Quiritus, Roman senators, with all their families, and many other Christians; Simplicius, senator;

Calepodius, a Christian minister, thrown into the Tyber; Martina, a noble and beautiful virgin; and Hippolitus, a Christian prelate, tied to a wild horse, and dragged until he expired.

During this persecution, raised by Maximinus, numberless Christians were slain without trial, and buried indiscriminately in heaps, sometimes fifty or sixty being cast into a pit together, without the least decency.

The tyrant Maximinus dying, A.D. 238, was succeeded by Gordian, during whose reign, and that of his successor Philip, the Church was free from persecution for the space of more than ten years; but in A.D. 249, a violent persecution broke out in Alexandria, at the instigation of a pagan priest, without the knowledge of the emperor.

THE SEVENTH PERSECUTION,
UNDER DECIUS, A.D. 249

This was occasioned partly by the hatred he bore to his predecessor Philip, who was deemed a Christian and was partly by his jealousy concerning the amazing increase of Christianity; for the heathen temples began to be forsaken, and the Christian churches thronged.

These reasons stimulated Decius to attempt the very extirpation of the name of Christian; and it was unfortunate for the Gospel, that many errors had, about this time, crept into the Church: the Christians were at variance with each other; self-interest divided those whom social love ought to have united; and the virulence of pride occasioned a variety of factions.

The heathens in general were ambitious to enforce the imperial decrees upon this occasion, and looked upon the murder of a Christian as a merit to themselves. The martyrs, upon this occasion, were innumerable; but the principal we shall give some account of.

Fabian, the bishop of Rome, was the first person of eminence who felt the severity of this persecution. The deceased emperor, Philip, had, on account of his integrity, committed his treasure to the care of this good man. But Decius, not finding as much as his avarice made him expect, determined to wreak his vengeance on the good prelate. He was accordingly seized; and on January 20, A.D. 250, he suffered decapitation.

Julian, a native of Cilicia, as we are informed by St. Chrysostom, was seized upon for being a Christian. He was put into a leather bag, together with a number of serpents and scorpions, and in that condition thrown into the sea.

Peter, a young man, amiable for the superior qualities of his body and mind, was beheaded for refusing to sacrifice to Venus. He said, "I am astonished you should sacrifice to an infamous woman, whose debaucheries even your own historians record, and whose life consisted of such actions as your laws would punish. No, I shall offer the true God the acceptable sacrifice of praises and prayers." Optimus, the proconsul of Asia, on hearing this, ordered the prisoner to be stretched upon a wheel, by which all his bones were broken, and then he was sent to be beheaded.

Nichomachus, being brought before the proconsul as a Christian, was ordered to sacrifice to the pagan idols. Nichomachus replied, "I cannot pay that respect to devils, which is only due to the Almighty." This speech so much enraged the proconsul that Nichomachus was put to the rack. After enduring the torments for a time, he recanted; but scarcely had he given this proof of his frailty, than he fell into the greatest agonies, dropped down on the ground, and expired immediately.

Denisa, a young woman of only sixteen years of age, who beheld this terrible judgment, suddenly exclaimed, "O unhappy wretch, why would you buy a moment's ease at the expense of a miserable eternity!" Optimus, hearing this, called to her, and Denisa avowing herself to be a Christian, she was beheaded, by his order, soon after.

Andrew and Paul, two companions of Nichomachus, the martyr, A.D. 251, suffered martyrdom by stoning, and expired, calling on their blessed Redeemer.

Alexander and Epimachus, of Alexandria, were apprehended for being Christians: and, confessing the accusation, were beat with staves, torn with hooks, and at length burnt in the fire; and we are informed, in a fragment preserved by Eusebius, that four female martyrs suffered on the same day, and at the same place, but not in the same manner; for these were beheaded.

Lucian and Marcian, two wicked pagans, though skilful magicians, becoming converts to Christianity, to make amends for their former errors, lived the lives of hermits, and subsisted upon bread and water only. After some time spent in this manner, they became zealous preachers, and made many converts. The persecution, however, raging at this time, they were seized upon, and carried before Sabinus, the governor of Bithynia. On being asked by what authority they took upon themselves to preach, Lucian answered, "That the laws of charity and humanity obliged all men to endeavor the conversion of their neighbors, and to do everything in their power to rescue them from the snares of the devil."

Lucian having answered in this manner, Marcian said, "Their conversion was by the same grace which was given to St. Paul, who, from a zealous persecutor of the Church, became a preacher of the Gospel."

The proconsul, finding that he could not prevail with them to renounce their faith, condemned them to be burnt alive, which sentence was soon after executed.

Trypho and Respicius, two eminent men, were seized as Christians, and imprisoned at Nice. Their feet were pierced with nails; they were dragged through the streets, scourged, torn with iron hooks, scorched with lighted torches, and at length beheaded, February 1, A.D. 251.

Agatha, a Sicilian lady, was not more remarkable for her personal and acquired endowments, than her piety; her beauty was such, that Quintian, governor of Sicily, became enamored of her, and made many attempts upon her chastity without success. In order to gratify his passions with the greater conveniency, he put the virtuous lady into the hands of Aphrodica, a very infamous and licentious woman. This wretch tried every artifice to win her to the desired prostitution; but found all her efforts were vain; for her chastity was impregnable, and she well knew that virtue alone could procure true happiness. Aphrodica acquainted Quintian with the inefficacy of her endeavors, who, enaged to be foiled in his designs, changed his lust into resentment. On her confessing that she was a Christian, he determined to gratify his revenge, as he could not his passion. Pursuant to his orders, she was scourged, burnt with red-hot irons, and torn with sharp hooks. Having borne these torments with admirable fortitude, she was next laid naked upon live coals, intermingled with glass, and then being carried back to prison, she there expired on February 5, 251.

Cyril, bishop of Gortyna, was seized by order of Lucius, the governor of that place, who, nevertheless, exhorted him to obey the imperial mandate, perform the sacrifices, and save his venerable person from destruction; for he was now eighty-four years of age. The good prelate replied that as he had long taught others to save their souls, he should only think now of his own salvation. The worthy prelate heard his fiery sentence without emotion, walked cheerfully to the place of execution, and underwent his martyrdom with great fortitude.

The persecution raged in no place more than the Island of Crete; for the governor, being exceedingly active in executing the imperial decrees, that place streamed with pious blood.

Babylas, a Christian of a liberal education, became bishop of Antioch, A.D. 237, on the demise of Zebinus. He acted with inimitable zeal, and governed the Church with admirable prudence during the most tempestuous times.

The first misfortune that happened to Antioch during his mission, was the siege of it by Sapor, king of Persia; who, having overrun all Syria, took and plundered this city among others, and used the Christian inhabitants with greater severity than the rest, but was soon totally defeated by Gordian.

After Gordian's death, in the reign of Decius, that emperor came to Antioch, where, having a desire to visit an assembly of Christians, Babylas opposed him, and absolutely refused to let him come in. The emperor dissembled his anger at that time; but soon sending for the bishop, he sharply reproved him for his insolence, and then ordered him to sacrifice to the pagan deities as an expiation for his ofence. This being refused, he was committed to prison, loaded with chains, treated with great severities, and then beheaded, together with three young men who had been his pupils. A.D. 251.

Alexander, bishop of Jerusalem, about this time was cast into prison on account of his religion, where he died through the severity of his confinement.

Julianus, an old man, lame with the gout, and Cronion, another Christian, were bound on the backs of camels, severely scourged, and then thrown into a fire and consumed. Also forty virgins, at Antioch, after being imprisoned, and scourged, were burnt.

In the year of our Lord 251, the emperor Decius having erected a pagan temple at Ephesus, he commanded all who were in that city to sacrifice to the idols. This order was nobly refused by seven of his own soldiers, viz. Maximianus, Martianus, Joannes, Malchus, Dionysius, Seraion, and Constantinus. The emperor wishing to win these soldiers to renounce their faith by his entreaties and lenity, gave them a considerable respite until he returned from an expedition. During the emperor's absence, they escaped, and hid themselves in a cavern; which the emperor being informed of at his return, the mouth of the cave was closed up, and they all perished with hunger.

Theodora, a beautiful young lady of Antioch, on refusing to sacrifice to the Roman idols, was condemned to the stews, that her virtue might be sacrificed to the brutality of lust. Didymus, a Christian, disguised himself in the habit of a Roman soldier, went to the house, informed Theodora who he was, and advised her to make her escape in his clothes. This being effected, and a man found in the brothel instead of a beautiful lady, Didymus was taken before the president, to whom confessing the truth, and owning that he was a Christian the sentence of death was immediately pronounced against him. Theodora, hearing that her deliverer was likely to suffer, came to the judge, threw herself at his feet, and begged that the sentence might fall on her as the guilty person; but, deaf to the cries of the innocent, and insensible to the calls of justice, the inflexible judge condemned both; when they were executed accordingly, being first beheaded, and their bodies afterward burnt.

Secundianus, having been accused as a Christian, was conveyed to prison by some soldiers. On the way, Verianus and Marcellinus said, "Where are you carrying the innocent?" This interrogatory occasioned them to be seized, and all three, after having been tortured, were hanged and decapitated.

Origen, the celebrated presbyter and catechist of Alexandria, at the age of sixty-four, was seized, thrown into a loathsome prison, laden with fetters, his feet placed in the stocks, and his legs extended to the utmost for several successive days. He was threatened with fire, and tormented by every lingering means the most infernal imaginations could suggest. During this cruel temporizing, the emperor Decius died, and Gallus, who succeeded him, engaging in a war with the Goths, the Christians met with a respite. In this interim, Origen obtained his enlargement, and, retiring to Tyre, he there remained until his death, which happened when he was in the sixty-ninth year of his age.

Gallus, the emperor, having concluded his wars, a plague broke out in the empire: sacrifices to the pagan deities were ordered by the emperor, and persecutions spread from the interior to the extreme parts of the empire, and many fell martyrs to the impetuosity of the rabble, as well as the prejudice of the magistrates. Among these were Cornelius, the Christian bishop of Rome, and Lucius, his successor, in 253.

Most of the errors which crept into the Church at this time arose from placing human reason in competition with revelation; but the fallacy of such arguments being proved by the most able divines, the opinions they had created vanished away like the stars before the sun.

THE EIGHTH PERSECUTION,
UNDER VALERIAN, A.D. 257

Began under Valerian, in the month of April, 257, and continued for three years and six months. The martyrs that fell in this persecution were innumerable, and their tortures and deaths as various and painful. The most eminent martyrs were the following, though neither rank, sex, nor age were regarded.

Rufina and Secunda were two beautiful and accomplished ladies, daughters of Asterius, a gentleman of eminence in Rome. Rufina, the elder, was designed in marriage for Armentarius, a young nobleman; Secunda, the younger, for Verinus, a person of rank and opulence. The suitors, at the time of the persecution's commencing, were both Christians; but when danger appeared, to save their fortunes, they renounced their faith. They took great pains to persuade the ladies to do the same, but, disappointed in their purpose, the lovers were base enough to inform against the ladies, who, being apprehended as Christians, were brought before Junius Donatus, governor of Rome, where, A.D. 257, they sealed their martyrdom with their blood.

Stephen, bishop of Rome, was beheaded in the same year, and about that time Saturninus, the pious orthodox bishop of Toulouse, refusing to sacrifice to idols, was treated with all the barbarous indignities imaginable, and fastened by the feet to the tail of a bull. Upon a signal given, the enraged animal was driven down the steps of the temple, by which the worthy martyr's brains were dashed out.

Sextus succeeded Stephen as bishop of Rome. He is supposed to have been a Greek by birth or by extraction, and had for some time served in the capacity of a deacon under Stephen. His great fidelity, singular wisdom, and uncommon courage distinguished him upon many occasions; and the happy conclusion of a controversy with some heretics is generally ascribed to his piety and prudence. In the year 258, Marcianus, who had the management of the Roman government, procured an order from the emperor Valerian, to put to death all the Christian clergy in Rome, and hence the bishop with six of his deacons, suffered martyrdom in 258.

Let us draw near to the fire of martyred Lawrence, that our cold hearts may be warmed thereby. The merciless tyrant, understanding him to be not only a minister of the sacraments, but a distributor also of the Church riches, promised to himself a double prey, by the apprehension of one soul. First, with the rake of avarice to scrape to himself the treasure of poor Christians; then with the fiery fork of tyranny, so to toss and turmoil them, that they should wax weary of their profession. With furious face and cruel countenance, the greedy wolf demanded where this Lawrence had bestowed the substance of the Church: who, craving three days' respite, promised to declare where the treasure might be had. In the meantime, he caused a good number of poor Christians to be congregated. So, when the day of his answer was come, the persecutor strictly charged him to stand to his promise. Then valiant Lawrence, stretching out his arms over the poor, said: "These are the precious treasure of the Church; these are the treasure indeed, in whom the faith of Christ reigneth, in whom Jesus Christ hath His mansion-place. What more precious jewels can Christ have, than those in whom He hath promised to dwell? For so it is written, 'I was an hungered, and ye gave me meat: I was thirsty, and ye gave me drink: I was a stranger, and ye took me in.' And again, 'Inasmuch as ye have done it unto one of the least of these my brethren, ye have done it unto me.' What greater riches can Christ our Master possess, than the poor people in whom He loveth to be seen?"

O, what tongue is able to express the fury and madness of the tyrant's heart! Now he stamped, he stared, he ramped, he fared as one out of his wits: his eyes like fire glowed, his mouth like a boar formed, his teeth like a hellhound grinned. Now, not a reasonable man, but a roaring lion, he might be called.

"Kindle the fire (he cried)—of wood make no spare. Hath this villain deluded the emperor? Away with him, away with him: whip him with scourges, jerk him with rods, buffet him with fists, brain him with clubs. Jesteth the traitor with the emperor? Pinch him with fiery tongs, gird him with burning plates, bring out the strongest chains, and the fire-forks, and the grated bed of iron: on the fire with it; bind the rebel hand and foot; and when the bed is fire-hot, on with him: roast him, broil him, toss him, turn him: on pain of our high displeasure do every man his office, O ye tormentors."

The word was no sooner spoken, but all was done. After many cruel handlings, this meek lamb was laid, I will not say on his fiery bed of iron, but on his soft bed of down. So mightily God wrought with his martyr Lawrence, so miraculously God tempered His element the fire; that it became not a bed of consuming pain, but a pallet of nourishing rest.

In Africa the persecution raged with peculiar violence; many thousands received the crown of martyrdom, among whom the following were the most distinguished characters:

Cyprian, bishop of Carthage, an eminent prelate, and a pious ornament of the Church. The brightness of his genius was tempered by the solidity of his judgment; and with all the accomplishments of the gentleman, he blended the virtues of a Christian. His doctrines were orthodox and pure; his language easy and elegant; and his manners graceful and winning: in fine, he was both the pious and polite preacher. In his youth he was educated in the principles of Gentilism, and having a considerable fortune, he lived in the very extravagance of splendor, and all the dignity of pomp.

About the year 246, Coecilius, a Christian minister of Carthage, became the happy instrument of Cyprian's conversion: on which account, and for the great love that he always afterward bore for the author of his conversion, he was termed Coecilius Cyprian. Previous to his baptism, he studied the Scriptures with care and being struck with the beauties of the truths they contained, he determined to practise the virtues therein recommended. Subsequent to his baptism, he sold his estate, distributed the money among the poor, dressed himself in plain attire, and commenced a life of austerity. He was soon after made a presbyter; and, being greatly admired for his virtues and works, on the death of Donatus, in A.D. 248, he was almost unanimously elected bishop of Carthage.

Cyprian's care not only extended over Carthage, but to Numidia and Mauritania. In all his transactions he took great care to ask the advice of his clergy, knowing that unanimity alone could be of service to the Church, this being one of his maxims, "That the bishop was in the church, and the church in the bishop; so that unity can only be preserved by a close connexion between the pastor and his flock."

In A.D. 250, Cyprian was publicly proscribed by the emperor Decius, under the appellation of Coecilius Cyprian, bishop of the Christians; and the universal cry of the pagans was, "Cyprian to the lions, Cyprian to the beasts." The bishop, however, withdrew from the rage of the populace, and his effects were immediately confiscated. During his retirement, he wrote thirty pious and elegant letters to his flock; but several schisms that then crept into the Church gave him great uneasiness. The rigor of the persecution abating, he returned to Carthage, and did everything in his power to expunge erroneous opinions. A terrible plague breaking out in Carthage, it was, as usual, laid to the charge of the Christians; and the magistrates began to persecute accordingly, which occasioned an epistle from them to Cyprian, in answer to which he vindicates the cause of Christianity. A.D. 257, Cyprian was brought before the proconsul Aspasius Paturnus, who exiled him to a little city on the Lybian sea. On the death of this proconsul, he returned to Carthage, but was soon after seized, and carried before the new governor, who condemned him to be beheaded; which sentence was executed on the fourteenth of September, A.D. 258.

The disciples of Cyprian, martyred in this persecution, were Lucius, Flavian, Victoricus, Remus, Montanus, Julian, Primelus, and Donatian.

At Utica, a most terrible tragedy was exhibited: three hundred Christians were, by the orders of the proconsul, placed round a burning limekiln. A pan of coals and incense being prepared, they were commanded either to sacrifice to Jupiter, or to be thrown into the kiln. Unanimously refusing, they bravely jumped into the pit, and were immediately suffocated.

Fructuosus, bishop of Tarragon, in Spain, and his two deacons, Augurius and Eulogius, were burnt for being Christians.

Alexander, Malchus, and Priscus, three Christians of Palestine, with a woman of the same place, voluntarily accused themselves of being Christians; on which account they were sentenced to be devoured by tigers, which sentence was executed accordingly.

Maxima, Donatilla, and Secunda, three virgins of Tuburga, had gall and vinegar given them to drink, were then severely scourged, tormented on a gibbet, rubbed with lime, scorched on a gridiron, worried by wild beasts, and at length beheaded.

It is here proper to take notice of the singular but miserable fate of the emperor Valerian, who had so long and so terribly persecuted the Christians. This tyrant, by a strategem, was taken prisoner by Sapor, emperor of Persia, who carried him into his own country, and there treated him with the most unexampled indignity, making him kneel down as the meanest slave, and treading upon him as a footstool when he mounted his horse. After having kept him for the space of seven years in this abject state of slavery, he caused his eyes to be put out, though he was then eighty-three years of age. This not satiating his desire of revenge, he soon after ordered his body to be flayed alive, and rubbed with salt, under which torments he expired; and thus fell one of the most tyrannical emperors of Rome, and one of the greatest persecutors of the Christians.

A.D. 260, Gallienus, the son of Valerian, succeeded him, and during his reign (a few martyrs excepted) the Church enjoyed peace for some years.

THE NINTH PERSECUTION
UNDER AURELIAN, A.D. 274

The principal sufferers were: Felix, bishop of Rome. This prelate was advanced to the Roman see in 274. He was the first martyr to Aurelian's petulancy, being beheaded on the twenty-second of December, in the same year.

Agapetus, a young gentleman, who sold his estate, and gave the money to the poor, was seized as a Christian, tortured, and then beheaded at Praeneste, a city within a day's journey of Rome.

These are the only martyrs left upon record during this reign, as it was soon put to a stop by the emperor's being murdered by his own domestics, at Byzantium.

Aurelian was succeeded by Tacitus, who was followed by Probus, as the latter was by Carus: this emperor being killed by a thunder storm, his sons, Carnious and Numerian, succeeded him, and during all these reigns the Church had peace.

Diocletian mounted the imperial throne, A.D. 284; at first he showed great favor to the Christians. In the year 286, he associated Maximian with him in the empire; and some Christians were put to death before any general persecution broke out. Among these were Felician and Primus, two brothers.

Marcus and Marcellianus were twins, natives of Rome, and of noble descent. Their parents were heathens, but the tutors, to whom the education of the children was intrusted, brought them up as Christians. Their constancy at length subdued those who wished them to become pagans, and their parents and whole family became converts to a faith they had before reprobated. They were martyred by being tied to posts, and having their feet pierced with nails. After remaining in this situation for a day and a night, their sufferings were put an end to by thrusting lances through their bodies.

Zoe, the wife of the jailer, who had the care of the before-mentioned martyrs, was also converted by them, and hung upon a tree, with a fire of straw lighted under her. When her body was taken down, it was thrown into a river, with a large stone tied to it, in order to sink it.

In the year of Christ 286, a most remarkable affair occurred; a legion of soldiers, consisting of six thousand six hundred and sixty-six men, contained none but Christians. This legion was called the Theban Legion, because the men had been raised in Thebias: they were quartered in the east until the emperor Maximian ordered them to march to Gaul, to assist him against the rebels of Burgundy. They passed the Alps into Gaul, under the command of Mauritius, Candidus, and Exupernis, their worthy commanders, and at length joined the emperor. Maximian, about this time, ordered a general sacrifice, at which the whole army was to assist; and likewise he commanded that they should take the oath of allegiance and swear, at the same time, to assist in the extirpation of Christianity in Gaul. Alarmed at these orders, each individual of the Theban Legion absolutely refused either to sacrifice or take the oaths prescribed. This so greatly enraged Maximian, that he ordered the legion to be decimated, that is, every tenth man to be selected from the rest, and put to the sword. This bloody order having been put in execution, those who remained alive were still inflexible, when a second decimation took place, and every tenth man of those living was put to death. This second severity made no more impression than the first had done; the soldiers preserved their fortitude and their principles, but by the advice of their officers they drew up a loyal remonstrance to the emperor. This, it might have been presumed, would have softened the emperor, but it had a contrary effect: for, enraged at their perseverance and unanimity, he commanded that the whole legion should be put to death, which was accordingly executed by the other troops, who cut them to pieces with their swords, September 22, 286.

Alban, from whom St. Alban's, in Hertfordshire, received its name, was the first British martyr. Great Britain had received the Gospel of Christ from Lucius, the first Christian king, but did not suffer from the rage of persecution for many years after. He was originally a pagan, but converted by a Christian ecclesiastic, named Amphibalus, whom he sheltered on account of his religion. The enemies of Amphibalus, having intelligence of the place where he was secreted, came to the house of Alban; in order to facilitate his escape, when the soldiers came, he offered himself up as the person they were seeking for. The deceit being detected, the governor ordered him to be scourged, and then he was sentenced to be beheaded, June 22, A.D. 287.

The venerable Bede assures us, that, upon this occasion, the executioner suddenly became a convert to Christianity, and entreated permission to die for Alban, or with him. Obtaining the latter request, they were beheaded by a soldier, who voluntarily undertook the task of executioner. This happened on the twenty-second of June, A.D. 287, at Verulam, now St. Alban's, in Hertfordshire, where a magnificent church was erected to his memory about the time of Constantine the Great. The edifice, being destroyed in the Saxon wars, was rebuilt by Offa, king of Mercia, and a monastery erected adjoining to it, some remains of which are still visible, and the church is a noble Gothic structure.

Faith, a Christian female, of Acquitain, in France, was ordered to be broiled upon a gridiron, and then beheaded; A.D. 287.

Quintin was a Christian, and a native of Rome, but determined to attempt the propagation of the Gospel in Gaul, with one Lucian, they preached together in Amiens; after which Lucian went to Beaumaris, where he was martyred. Quintin remained in Picardy, and was very zealous in his ministry. Being seized upon as a Christian, he was stretched with pullies until his joints were dislocated; his body was then torn with wire scourges, and boiling oil and pitch poured on his naked flesh; lighted torches were applied to his sides and armpits; and after he had been thus tortured, he was remanded back to prison, and died of the barbarities he had suffered, October 31, A.D. 287. His body was sunk in the Somme.

THE TENTH PERSECUTION, UNDER DIOCLETIAN, A.D. 303

Under the Roman emperors, commonly called the Era of the Martyrs, was occasioned partly by the increasing number and luxury of the Christians, and the hatred of Galerius, the adopted son of Diocletian, who, being stimulated by his mother, a bigoted pagan, never ceased persuading the emperor to enter upon the persecution, until he had accomplished his purpose.

The fatal day fixed upon to commence the bloody work, was the twenty-third of February, A.D. 303, that being the day in which the Terminalia were celebrated, and on which, as the cruel pagans boasted, they hoped to put a termination to Christianity. On the appointed day, the persecution began in Nicomedia, on the morning of which the prefect of that city repaired, with a great number of officers and assistants, to the church of the Christians, where, having forced open the doors, they seized upon all the sacred books, and committed them to the flames.

The whole of this transaction was in the presence of Diocletian and Galerius, who, not contented with burning the books, had the church levelled with the ground. This was followed by a severe edict, commanding the destruction of all other Christian churches and books; and an order soon succeeded, to render Christians of all denomination outlaws.

The publication of this edict occasioned an immediate martyrdom, for a bold Christian not only tore it down from the place to which it was affixed, but execrated the name of the emperor for his injustice. A provocation like this was sufficient to call down pagan vengeance upon his head; he was accordingly seized, severely tortured, and then burned alive.

All the Christians were apprehended and imprisoned; and Galerius privately ordered the imperial palace to be set on fire, that the Christians might be charged as the incendiaries, and a plausible pretence given for carrying on the persecution with the greater severities. A general sacrifice was commenced, which occasioned various martyrdoms. No distinction was made of age or sex; the name of Christian was so obnoxious to the pagans that all indiscriminately fell sacrifices to their opinions. Many houses were set on fire, and whole Christian families perished in the flames; and others had stones fastened about their necks, and being tied together were driven into the sea. The persecution became general in all the Roman provinces, but more particularly in the east; and as it lasted ten years, it is impossible to ascertain the numbers martyred, or to enumerate the various modes of martyrdom.

Racks, scourges, swords, daggers, crosses, poison, and famine, were made use of in various parts to dispatch the Christians; and invention was exhausted to devise tortures against such as had no crime, but thinking differently from the votaries of superstition.

A city of Phrygia, consisting entirely of Christians, was burnt, and all the inhabitants perished in the flames.

Tired with slaughter, at length, several governors of provinces represented to the imperial court, the impropriety of such conduct. Hence many were respited from execution, but, though they were not put to death, as much as possible was done to render their lives miserable, many of them having their ears cut off, their noses slit, their right eyes put out, their limbs rendered useless by dreadful dislocations, and their flesh seared in conspicuous places with red-hot irons.

It is necessary now to particularize the most conspicuous persons who laid down their lives in martyrdom in this bloody persecution.

Sebastian, a celebrated martyr, was born at Narbonne, in Gaul, instructed in the principles of Christianity at Milan, and afterward became an officer of the emperor's guard at Rome. He remained a true Christian in the midst of idolatry; unallured by the splendors of a court, untainted by evil examples, and uncontaminated by the hopes of preferment. Refusing to be a pagan, the emperor ordered him to be taken to a field near the city, termed the Campus Martius, and there to be shot to death with arrows; which sentence was executed accordingly. Some pious Christians coming to the place of execution, in order to give his body burial, perceived signs of life in him, and immediately moving him to a place of security, they, in a short time effected his recovery, and prepared him for a second martyrdom; for, as soon as he was able to go out, he placed himself intentionally in the emperor's way as he was going to the temple, and reprehended him for his various cruelties and unreasonable prejudices against Christianity. As soon as Diocletian had overcome his surprise, he ordered Sebastian to be seized, and carried to a place near the palace, and beaten to death; and, that the Christians should not either use means again to recover or bury his body, he ordered that it should be thrown into the common sewer. Nevertheless, a Christian lady named Lucina, found means to remove it from the sewer, and bury it in the catacombs, or repositories of the dead.

The Christians, about this time, upon mature consideration, thought it unlawful to bear arms under a heathen emperor. Maximilian, the son of Fabius Victor, was the first beheaded under this regulation.

Vitus, a Sicilian of considerable family, was brought up a Christian; when his virtues increased with his years, his constancy supported him under all afflictions, and his faith was superior to the most dangerous perils. His father, Hylas, who was a pagan, finding that he had been instructed in the principles of Christianity by the nurse who brought him up, used all his endeavors to bring him back to paganism, and at length sacrificed his son to the idols, June 14, A.D. 303.

Victor was a Christian of a good family at Marseilles, in France; he spent a great part of the night in visiting the afflicted, and confirming the weak; which pious work he could not, consistently with his own safety, perform in the daytime; and his fortune he spent in relieving the distresses of poor Christians. He was at length, however, seized by the emperor Maximian's decree, who ordered him to be bound, and dragged through the streets. During the execution of this order, he was treated with all manner of cruelties and indignities by the enraged populace. Remaining still inflexible, his courage was deemed obstinacy. Being by order stretched upon the rack, he turned his eyes toward heaven, and prayed to God to endue him with patience, after which he underwent the tortures with most admirable fortitude. After the executioners were tired with inflicting torments on him, he was conveyed to a dungeon. In his confinement, he converted his jailers, named Alexander, Felician, and Longinus. This affair coming to the ears of the emperor, he ordered them immediately to be put to death, and the jailers were accordingly beheaded. Victor was then again put to the rack, unmercifully beaten with batoons, and again sent to prison. Being a third time examined concerning his religion, he persevered in his principles; a small altar was then brought, and he was commanded to offer incense upon it immediately. Fired with indignation at the request, he boldly stepped forward, and with his foot overthrew both altar and idol. This so enraged the emperor Maximian, who was present, that he ordered the foot with which he had kicked the altar to be immediately cut off; and Victor was thrown into a mill, and crushed to pieces with the stones, A.D. 303.

Maximus, governor of Cilicia, being at Tarsus, three Christians were brought before him; their names were Tarachus, an aged man, Probus, and Andronicus. After repeated tortures and exhortations to recant, they, at length, were ordered for execution.

Being brought to the amphitheater, several beasts were let loose upon them; but none of the animals, though hungry, would touch them. The keeper then brought out a large bear, that had that very day destroyed three men; but this voracious creature and a fierce lioness both refused to touch the prisoners. Finding the design of destroying them by the means of wild beasts ineffectual, Maximus ordered them to be slain by the sword, on October 11, A.D. 303.

Romanus, a native of Palestine, was deacon of the church of Caesarea at the time of the commencement of Diocletian's persecution. Being condemned for his faith at Antioch, he was scourged, put to the rack, his body torn with hooks, his flesh cut with knives, his face scarified, his teeth beaten from their sockets, and his hair plucked up by the roots. Soon after he was ordered to be strangled, November 17, A.D. 303.

Susanna, the niece of Caius, bishop of Rome, was pressed by the emperor Diocletian to marry a noble pagan, who was nearly related to him. Refusing the honor intended her, she was beheaded by the emperor's order.

Dorotheus, the high chamberlain of the household to Diocletian, was a Christian, and took great pains to make converts. In his religious labors, he was joined by Gorgonius, another Christian, and one belonging to the palace. They were first tortured and then strangled.

Peter, a eunuch belonging to the emperor, was a Christian of singular modesty and humility. He was laid on a gridiron, and broiled over a slow fire until he expired.

Cyprian, known by the title of the magician, to distinguish him from Cyprian, bishop of Carthage, was a native of Natioch. He received a liberal education in his youth, and particularly applied himself to astrology; after which he traveled for improvement through Greece, Egypt, India, etc. In the course of time he became acquainted with Justina, a young lady of Antioch, whose birth, beauty, and accomplishments, rendered her the admiration of all who knew her. A pagan gentleman applied to Cyprian, to promote his suit with the beautiful Justina; this he undertook, but soon himself became converted, burnt his books of astrology and magic, received baptism, and felt animated with a powerful spirit of grace. The conversion of Cyprian had a great effect on the pagan gentleman who paid his addresses to Justina, and he in a short time embraced Christianity. During the persecutions of Diocletian, Cyprian and Justina were seized upon as Christians, the former was torn with pincers, and the latter chastised; and, after suffering other torments, both were beheaded.

Eulalia, a Spanish lady of a Christian family, was remarkable in her youth for sweetness of temper, and solidity of understanding seldom found in the capriciousness of juvenile years. Being apprehended as a Christian, the magistrate attempted by the mildest means, to bring her over to paganism, but she ridiculed the pagan deities with such asperity, that the judge, incensed at her behavior, ordered her to be tortured. Her sides were accordingly torn by hooks, and her breasts burnt in the most shocking manner, until she expired by the violence of the flames, December, A.D. 303.

In the year 304, when the persecution reached Spain, Dacian, the governor of Terragona, ordered Valerius the bishop, and Vincent the deacon, to be seized, loaded with irons, and imprisoned. The prisoners being firm in their resolution, Valerius was banished, and Vincent was racked, his limbs dislocated, his flesh torn with hooks, and he was laid on a gridiron, which had not only a fire placed under it, but spikes at the top, which ran into his flesh. These torments neither destroying him, nor changing his resolutions, he was remanded to prison, and confined in a small, loathsome, dark dungeon, strewed with sharp flints, and pieces of broken glass, where he died, January 22, 304. His body was thrown into the river.

The persecution of Diocletian began particularly to rage in A.D. 304, when many Christians were put to cruel tortures and the most painful and ignominious deaths; the most eminent and particular of whom we shall enumerate.

Saturninus, a priest of Albitina, a town of Africa, after being tortured, was remanded to prison, and there starved to death. His four children, after being variously tormented, shared the same fate with their father.

Dativas, a noble Roman senator; Thelico, a pious Christian;

Victoria, a young lady of considerable family and fortune, with some others of less consideration, all auditors of Saturninus, were tortured in a similar manner, and perished by the same means.

Agrape, Chionia, and Irene, three sisters, were seized upon at Thessalonica, when Diocletian's persecution reached Greece. They were burnt, and received the crown of martyrdom in the flames, March 25, A.D. 304. The governor, finding that he could make no impression on Irene, ordered her to be exposed naked in the streets, which shameful order having been executed, a fire was kindled near the city wall, amidst whose flames her spirit ascended beyond the reach of man's cruelty.

Agatho, a man of a pious turn of mind, with Cassice, Philippa, and Eutychia, were martyred about the same time; but the particulars have not been transmitted to us.

Marcellinus, bishop of Rome, who succeeded Caius in that see, having strongly opposed paying divine honors to Diocletian, suffered martyrdom, by a variety of tortures, in the year 324, conforting his soul until he expired with the prospect of these glorious rewards it would receive by the tortures suffered in the body.

Victorius, Carpophorus, Severus, and Severianus, were brothers, and all four employed in places of great trust and honor in the city of Rome. Having exclaimed against the worship of idols, they were apprehended, and scourged, with the plumbetae, or scourges, to the ends of which were fastened leaden balls. This punishment was exercised with such excess of cruelty that the pious brothers fell martyrs to its severity.

Timothy, a deacon of Mauritania, and Maura his wife, had not been united together by the bands of wedlock above three weeks, when they were separated from each other by the persecution. Timothy, being apprehended, as a Christian, was carried before Arrianus, the governor of Thebais, who, knowing that he had the keeping of the Holy Scriptures, commanded him to deliver them up to be burnt; to which he answered, "Had I children, I would sooner deliver them up to be sacrificed, than part with the Word of God." The governor being much incensed at this reply, ordered his eyes to be put out, with red-hot irons, saying, "The books shall at least be useless to you, for you shall not see to read them." His patience under the operation was so great that the governor grew more exasperated; he, therefore, in order, if possible, to overcome his fortitude, ordered him to be hung up by the feet, with a weight tied about his neck, and a gag in his mouth. In this state, Maura his wife, tenderly urged him for her sake to recant; but, when the gag was taken out of his mouth, instead of consenting to his wife's entreaties, he greatly blamed her mistaken love, and declared his resolution of dying for the faith. The consequence was, that Maura resolved to imitate his courage and fidelity and either to accompany or follow him to glory. The governor, after trying in vain to alter her resolution, ordered her to be tortured, which was executed with great severity. After this, Timothy and Maura were crucified near each other, A.D. 304.

Sabinus, bishop of Assisium, refusing to sacrifice to Jupiter, and pushing the idol from him, had his hand cut off by the order of the governor of Tuscany. While in prison, he converted the governor and his family, all of whom suffered martyrdom for the faith. Soon after their execution, Sabinus himself was scourged to death, December, A.D. 304.

Tired with the farce of state and public business, the emperor Diocletian resigned the imperial diadem, and was succeeded by Constantius and Galerius; the former a prince of the most mild and humane disposition and the latter equally remarkable for his cruelty and tyranny. These divided the empire into two equal governments, Galerius ruling in the east, and Constantius in the west; and the people in the two governments felt the effects of the dispositions of the two emperors; for those in the west were governed in the mildest manner, but such as resided in the east felt all the miseries of oppression and lengthened tortures.

Among the many martyred by the order of Galerius, we shall enumerate the most eminent.

Amphianus was a gentleman of eminence in Lucia, and a scholar of Eusebius; Julitta, a Lycaonian of royal descent, but more celebrated for her virtues than noble blood. While on the rack, her child was killed before her face. Julitta, of Cappadocia, was a lady of distinguished capacity, great virtue, and uncommon courage. To complete the execution, Julitta had boiling pitch poured on her feet, her sides torn with hooks, and received the conclusion of her martyrdom, by being beheaded, April 16, A.D. 305.

Hermolaus, a venerable and pious Christian, of a great age, and an intimate acquaintance of Panteleon's, suffered martyrdom for the faith on the same day, and in the same manner as Panteleon.

Eustratius, secretary to the governor of Armina, was thrown into a fiery furnace for exhorting some Christians who had been apprehended, to persevere in their faith.

Nicander and Marcian, two eminent Roman military officers, were apprehended on account of their faith. As they were both men of great abilities in their profession, the utmost means were used to induce them to renounce Christianity; but these endeavors being found ineffectual, they were beheaded.

In the kingdom of Naples, several martyrdoms took place, in particular, Januaries, bishop of Beneventum; Sosius, deacon of Misene; Proculus, another deacon; Eutyches and Acutius, two laymen; Festus, a deacon; and Desiderius, a reader; all, on account of being Christians, were condemned by the governor of Campania to be devoured by the wild beasts. The savage animals, however, would not touch them, and so they were beheaded.

Quirinus, bishop of Siscia, being carried before Matenius, the governor, was ordered to sacrifice to the pagan deities, agreeably to the edicts of various Roman emperors. The governor, perceiving his constancy, sent him to jail, and ordered him to be heavily ironed; flattering himself, that the hardships of a jail, some occasional tortures and the weight of chains, might overcome his resolution. Being decided in his principles, he was sent to Amantius, the principal governor of Pannonia, now Hungary, who loaded him with chains, and carried him through the principal towns of the Danube, exposing him to ridicule wherever he went. Arriving at length at Sabaria, and finding that Quirinus would not renounce his faith, he ordered him to be cast into a river, with a stone fastened about his neck. This sentence being put into execution, Quirinus floated about for some time, and, exhorting the people in the most pious terms, concluded his admonitions with this prayer: "It is no new thing, O all-powerful Jesus, for Thee to stop the course of rivers, or to cause a man to walk upon the water, as Thou didst Thy servant Peter; the people have already seen the proof of Thy power in me; grant me now to lay down my life for Thy sake, O my God." On pronouncing the last words he immediately sank, and died, June 4, A.D. 308. His body was afterwards taken up, and buried by some pious Christians.

Pamphilus, a native of Phoenicia, of a considerable family, was a man of such extensive learning that he was called a second Origen. He was received into the body of the clergy at Caesarea, where he established a public library and spent his time in the practice of every Christian virtue. He copied the greatest part of the works of Origen with his own hand, and, assisted by Eusebius, gave a correct copy of the Old Testament, which had suffered greatly by the ignorance or negligence of former transcribers. In the year 307, he was apprehended, and suffered torture and martyrdom.

Marcellus, bishop of Rome, being banished on account of his faith, fell a martyr to the miseries he suffered in exile, January 16, A.D. 310.

Peter, the sixteenth bishop of Alexandria, was martyred November 25, A.D. 311, by order of Maximus Caesar, who reigned in the east.

Agnes, a virgin of only thirteen years of age, was beheaded for being a Christian; as was Serene, the empress of Diocletian. Valentine, a priest, suffered the same fate at Rome; and Erasmus, a bishop, was martyred in Campania.

Soon after this the persecution abated in the middle parts of the empire, as well as in the west; and Providence at length began to manifest vengeance on the persecutors. Maximian endeavored to corrupt his daughter Fausta to murder Constantine her husband; which she discovered, and Constantine forced him to choose his own death, when he preferred the ignominious death of hanging after being an emperor near twenty years.

Constantine was the good and virtuous child of a good and virtuous father, born in Britain. His mother was named Helena, daughter of King Coilus. He was a most bountiful and gracious prince, having a desire to nourish learning and good arts, and did oftentimes use to read, write, and study himself. He had marvellous good success and prosperous achieving of all things he took in hand, which then was (and truly) supposed to proceed of this, for that he was so great a favorer of the Christian faith. Which faith when he had once embraced, he did ever after most devoutly and religiously reverence.

Thus Constantine, sufficiently appointed with strength of men but especially with strength of God, entered his journey coming towards Italy, which was about the last year of the persecution, A.D. 313. Maxentius, understanding of the coming of Constantine, and trusting more to his devilish art of magic than to the good will of his subjects, which he little deserved, durst not show himself out of the city, nor encounter him in the open field, but with privy garrisons laid wait for him by the way in sundry straits, as he should come; with whom Constantine had divers skirmishes, and by the power of the Lord did ever vanquish them and put them to flight.

Notwithstanding, Constantine yet was in no great comfort, but in great care and dread in his mind (approaching now near unto Rome) for the magical charms and sorceries of Maxentius, wherewith he had vanquished before Severus, sent by Galerius against him. Wherefore, being in great doubt and perplexity in himself, and revolving many things in his mind, what help he might have against the operations of his charming, Constantine, in his journey drawing toward the city, and casting up his eyes many times to heaven, in the south part, about the going down of the sun, saw a great brightness in heaven, appearing in the similitude of a cross, giving this inscription, *In hoc vince,* that is, "In this overcome."

Eusebius Pamphilus doth witness that he had heard the said Constantine himself oftentimes report, and also to swear this to be true and certain, which he did see with his own eyes in heaven, and also his soldiers about him. At the sight whereof when he was greatly astonished, and consulting with his men upon the meaning thereof, behold, in the night season in his sleep, Christ appeared to him with the sign of the same cross which he had seen before, bidding him to make the figuration thereof, and to carry it in his wars before him, and so should we have the victory.

Constantine so established the peace of the Church that for the space of a thousand years we read of no set persecution against the Christians, unto the time of John Wickliffe.

So happy, so glorious was this victory of Constantine, surnamed the Great! For the joy and gladness whereof, the citizens who had sent for him before, with exceeding triumph brought him into the city of Rome, where he was most honorably received, and celebrated the space of seven days together; having, moreover, in the market place, his image set up, holding in his right hand the sign of the cross, with this inscription:

> *With this wholesome sign, the true token of fortitude, I have rescued and delivered our city from the yoke of the tyrant.*

We shall conclude our account of the tenth and last general persecution with the death of St. George, the titular saint and patron of England. St. George was born in Cappadocia, of Christian parents; and giving proofs of his courage, was promoted in the army of the emperor Diocletian. During the persecution, St. George threw up his command, went boldly to the senate house, and avowed his being a Christian, taking occasion at the same time to remonstrate against paganism, and point out the absurdity of worshipping idols. This freedom so greatly provoked the senate that St. George was ordered to be tortured, and by the emperor's orders was dragged through the streets, and beheaded the next day.

The legend of the dragon, which is associated with this martyr, is usually illustrated by representing St. George seated upon a charging horse and trans-fixing the monster with his spear. This fiery dragon symbolizes the devil, who was vanquished by St. George's steadfast faith in Christ, which remained unshaken in spite of torture and death.

CHAPTER THREE

An Account of the Inquisition

When the reformed religion began to diffuse the Gospel light throughout Europe, Pope Innocent III entertained great fear for the Romish Church. He accordingly instituted a number of inquisitors, or persons who were to make inquiry after, apprehend, and punish, heretics, as the reformed were called by the papists.

At the head of these inquisitors was one Dominic, who had been canonized by the pope, in order to render his authority the more respectable. Dominic, and the other inquisitors, spread themselves into various Roman Catholic countries, and treated the Protestants with the utmost severity. In process of time, the pope, not finding these roving inquisitors so useful as he had imagined, resolved upon the establishment of fixed and regular courts of Inquisition. After the order for these regular courts, the first office of Inquisition was established in the city of Toulouse, and Dominic became the first regular inquisitor, as he had before been the first roving inquisitor.

Courts of Inquisition were now erected in several countries; but the Spanish Inquisition became the most powerful, and the most dreaded of any. Even the kings of Spain themselves, though arbitrary in all other respects, were taught to dread the power of the lords of the Inquisition; and the horrid cruelties they exercised compelled multitudes, who differed in opinion from the Roman Catholics, carefully to conceal their sentiments.

The most zealous of all the popish monks, and those who most implicitly obeyed the Church of Rome, were the Dominicans and Franciscans: these, therefore, the pope thought proper to invest with an exclusive right of presiding over the different courts of Inquisition, and gave them the most unlimited powers, as judges delegated by him, and immediately representing his person: they were permitted to excommunicate, or sentence to death whom they thought proper, upon the most slight information of heresy. They were allowed to publish crusades against all whom they deemed heretics, and enter into leagues with sovereign princes, to join their crusades with their forces.

In 1244, their power was further increased by the emperor Frederic II, who declared himself the protector and friend of all the inquisitors, and published the cruel edicts, viz., 1. That all heretics who continue obstinate, should be burnt. 2. That all heretics who repented, should be imprisoned for life.

This zeal in the emperor, for the inquisitors of the Roman Catholic persuasion, arose from a report which had been propagated throughout Europe, that he intended to renounce Christianity, and turn Mahometan; the emperor therefore, attempted, by the height of bigotry, to contradict the report, and to show his attachment to popery by cruelty.

The officers of the Inquisition are three inquisitors, or judges, a fiscal proctor, two secretaries, a magistrate, a messenger, a receiver, a jailer, an agent of confiscated possessions; several assessors, counsellors, executioners, physicians, surgeons, doorkeepers, familiars, and visitors, who are sworn to secrecy.

The principal accusation against those who are subject to this tribunal is heresy, which comprises all that is spoken, or written, against any of the articles of the creed, or the traditions of the Roman Church. The inquisition likewise takes cognizance of such as are accused of being magicians, and of such who read the Bible in the common language, the Talmud of the Jews, or the Alcoran of the Mahometans.

Upon all occasions the inquisitors carry on their processes with the utmost severity, and punish those who offend them with the most unparalleled cruelty. A Protestant has seldom any mercy shown him, and a Jew, who turns Christian, is far from being secure.

A defence in the Inquisition is of little use to the prisoner, for a suspicion only is deemed sufficient cause of condemnation, and the greater his wealth the greater his danger. The principal part of the inquisitors' cruelties is owing to their rapacity: they destroy the life to possess the property; and, under the pretence of zeal, plunder each obnoxious individual.

A prisoner in the Inquisition is never allowed to see the face of his accuser, or of the witnesses against him, but every method is taken by threats and tortures, to oblige him to accuse himself, and by that means corroborate their evidence. If the jurisdiction of the Inquisition is not fully allowed, vengeance is denounced against such as call it in question for if any of its officers are opposed, those who oppose them are almost certain to be sufferers for the temerity; the maxim of the Inquisition being to strike terror, and awe those who are the objects of its power into obedience. High birth, distinguished rank, great dignity, or eminent employments, are no protection from its severities; and the lowest officers of the Inquisition can make the highest characters tremble.

When the person impeached is condemned, he is either severely whipped, violently tortured, sent to the galleys, or sentenced to death; and in either case the effects are confiscated. After judgment, a procession is performed to the place of execution, which ceremony is called an auto da fe, or act of faith.

The following is an account of an auto da fe, performed at Madrid in the year 1682.

The officers of the Inquisition, preceded by trumpets, kettledrums, and their banner, marched on the thirtieth of May, in cavalcade, to the palace of the great square, where they declared by proclamation, that, on the thirtieth of June, the sentence of the prisoners would be put in execution.

Of these prisoners, twenty men and women, with one renegade Mahometan, were ordered to be burned; fifty Jews and Jewesses, having never before been imprisoned, and repenting of their crimes, were sentenced to a long confinement, and to wear a yellow cap. The whole court of Spain was present on this occasion. The grand inquisitor's chair was placed in a sort of tribunal far above that of the king.

Among those who were to suffer, was a young Jewess of exquisite beauty, and but seventeen years of age. Being on the same side of the scaffold where the queen was seated, she addressed her, in hopes of obtaining a pardon, in the following pathetic speech: "Great queen, will not your royal presence be of some service to me in my miserable condition? Have regard to my youth; and, oh! consider, that I am about to die for professing a religion imbibed from my earliest infancy!" Her majesty seemed greatly to pity her distress, but turned away her eyes, as she did not dare to speak a word in behalf of a person who had been declared a heretic.

Now Mass began, in the midst of which the priest came from the altar, placed himself near the scaffold, and seated himself in a chair prepared for that purpose.

The chief inquisitor then descended from the amphitheater, dressed in his cope, and having a miter on his head. After having bowed to the altar, he advanced towards the king's balcony, and went up to it, attended by some of his officers, carrying a cross and the Gospels, with a book containing the oath by which the kings of Spain oblige themselves to protect the Catholic faith, to extirpate heretics, and to support with all their power and force the prosecutions and decrees of the Inquisition: a like oath was administered to the counsellors and whole assembly. The Mass was begun about twelve at noon, and did not end until nine in the evening, being protracted by a proclamation of the sentence of the several criminals, which were already separately rehearsed aloud one after the other.

After this followed the burnings of the twenty-one men and women, whose intrepidity in suffering that horrid death was truly astonishing. The king's near situation to the criminals rendered their dying groans very audible to him; he could not, however, be absent from this dreadful scene, as it is esteemed a religious one; and his coronation oath obliged him to give a sanction by his presence to all the acts of the tribunal.

What we have already said may be applied to inquisitions in general, as well as to that of Spain in particular. The Inquisition belonging to Portugal is exactly upon a similar plan to that of Spain, having been instituted much about the same time, and put under the same regulations. The inquisitors allow the torture to be used only three times, but during those times it is so severely inflicted, that the prisoner either dies under it, or continues always after a cripple, and suffers the severest pains upon every change of weather. We shall give an ample description of the severe torments occasioned by the torture, from the account of one who suffered it the three respective times, but happily survived the cruelties he underwent.

At the first time of torturing, six executioners entered, stripped him naked to his drawers, and laid him upon his back on a kind of stand, elevated a few feet from the floor. The operation commenced by putting an iron collar round his neck, and a ring to each foot, which fastened him to the stand. His limbs being thus stretched out, they wound two ropes round each thigh; which ropes being passed under the scaffold, through holes made for that purpose, were all drawn tight at the same instant of time, by four of the men, on a given signal.

It is easy to conceive that the pains which immediately succeeded were intolerable; the ropes, which were of a small size, cut through the prisoner's flesh to the bone, making the blood to gush out at eight different places thus bound at a time. As the prisoner persisted in not making any confession of what the inquisitors required, the ropes were drawn in this manner four times successively.

The manner of inflicting the second torture was as follows: they forced his arms backwards so that the palms of his hands were turned outward behind him; when, by means of a rope that fastened them together at the wrists, and which was turned by an engine, they drew them by degrees nearer each other, in such a manner that the back of each hand touched, and stood exactly parallel to each other. In consequence of this violent contortion, both his shoulders became dislocated, and a considerable quantity of blood issued from his mouth. This torture was repeated thrice; after which he was again taken to the dungeon, and the surgeon set the dislocated bones.

Two months after the second torture, the prisoner being a little recovered, was again ordered to the torture room, and there, for the last time, made to undergo another kind of punishment, which was inflicted twice without any intermission. The executioners fastened a thick iron chain round his body, which crossing at the breast, terminated at the wrists. They then placed him with his back against a thick board, at each extremity whereof was a pulley, through which there ran a rope that caught the end of the chain at his wrists. The executioner then, stretching the end of his rope by means of a roller, placed at a distance behind him, pressed or bruised his stomach in proportion as the ends of the chains were drawn tighter. They tortured him in this manner to such a degree, that his wrists, as well as his shoulders, were quite dislocated. They were, however, soon set by the surgeons; but the barbarians, not yet satisfied with this species of cruelty, made him immediately undergo the like torture a second time, which he sustained (though, if possible, attended with keener pains) with equal constancy and resolution. After this, he was again remanded to the dungeon, attended by the surgeon to dress his bruises and adjust the part dislocated, and here he continued until their auto da 'fe, or jail delivery, when he was discharged, crippled and diseased for life.

AN ACCOUNT OF THE CRUEL HANDLING AND BURNING OF NICHOLAS BURTON, AN ENGLISH MERCHANT, IN SPAIN

The fifth day of November, about the year of our Lord 1560, Mr. Nicholas Burton, citizen sometime of London, and merchant, dwelling in the parish of Little St. Bartholomew, peaceably and quietly, following his traffic in the trade of merchandise, and being in the city of Cadiz, in the party of Andalusia, in Spain, there came into his lodging a Judas, or, as they term them, a familiar of the fathers of Inquisition; who asking for the said Nicholas Burton, feigned that he had a letter to deliver into his own hands; by which means he spake with him immediately. And having no letter to deliver to him, then the said promoter, or familiar, at the motion of the devil his master, whose messenger he was, invented another lie, and said he would take lading for London in such ships as the said Nicholas Burton had freighted to lade, if he would let any; which was partly to know where he loaded his goods, that they might attach them, and chiefly to protract the time until the sergeant of the Inquisition might come and apprehend the body of the said Nicholas Burton; which they did incontinently.

He then well perceiving that they were not able to burden or charge him that he had written, spoken, or done any thing there in that country against the ecclesiastical or temporal laws of the same realm, boldly asked them what they had to lay to his charge that they did so arrest him, and bade them to declare the cause, and he would answer them. Notwithstanding they answered nothing, but commanded him with threatening words to hold his peace, and not speak one word to them.

And so they carried him to the filthy common prison of the town of Cadiz where he remained in irons fourteen days amongst thieves.

All which time he so instructed the poor prisoners in the Word of God, according to the good talent which God had given him in that behalf, and also in the Spanish tongue to utter the same, that in that short space he had well reclaimed several of those superstitiuous and ignorant Spaniards to embrace the Word of God, and to reject their popish traditions.

Which being known unto the officers of the Inquisition, they conveyed him laden with irons from thence to a city called Seville, into a more cruel and straiter prison called Triana, where the said fathers of the Inquisition proceeded against him secretly according to their accustomable cruel tyranny, that never after he could be suffered to write or speak to any of his nation: so that to this day it is unknown who was his accuser.

Afterward, the twentieth of December, they brought the said Nicholas Burton, with a great number of other prisoners, for professing the true Christian religion, into the city of Seville, to a place where the said inquisitors sat in judgment which they called auto, with a canvas coat, whereupon in divers parts was painted the figure of a huge devil, tormenting a soul in a flame of fire, and on his head a copping tank of the same work.

His tongue was forced out of his mouth with a cloven stick fastened upon it, that he should not utter his conscience and faith to the people, and so he was set with another Englishman of Southampton, and divers other condemned men for religion, as well Frenchmen as Spaniards, upon a scaffold over against the said Inquisition, where their sentences and judgments were read and pronounced against them.

And immediately after the said sentences given, they were carried from there to the place of execution without the city, where they most cruelly burned them, for whose constant faith, God is praised.

This Nicholas Burton by the way, and in the flames of fire, had so cheerful a countenance, embracing death with all patience and gladness, that the tormentors and enemies which stood by, said, that the devil had his soul before he came to the fire; and therefore they said his senses of feeling were past him.

It happened that after the arrest of Nicholas Burton aforesaid, immediately all the goods and merchandise which he brought with him into Spain by the way of traffic, were (according to their common usage) seized, and taken into the sequester; among which they also rolled up much that appertained to another English merchant, wherewith he was credited as factor. Whereof as soon as news was brought to the merchant as well of the imprisonment of his factor, as of the arrest made upon his goods, he sent his attorney into Spain, with authority from him to make claim to his goods, and to demand them; whose name was John Fronton, citizen of Bristol.

When his attorney was landed at Seville, and had shown all his letters and writings to the holy house, requiring them that such goods might be delivered into his possession, answer was made to him that he must sue by bill, and retain an advocate (but all was doubtless to delay him) and they forsooth of courtesy assigned him one to frame his supplication for him, and other such bills of petition, as he had to exhibit into their holy court, demanding for each bill eight reals, albeit they stood him in no more stead than if he had put up none at all. And for the space of three or four months this fellow missed not twice a day attending every morning and afternoon at the inquisitors' palace, suing unto them upon his knees for his despatch, but especially to the bishop of Tarracon, who was at that very time chief of the Inquisition at Seville, that he of his absolute authority would command restitution to be made thereof; but the booty was so good and great that it was very hard to come by it again.

At length, after he had spent four whole months in suits and requests, and also to no purpose, he received this answer from them, that he must show better evidence, and bring more sufficient certificates out of England for proof of this matter, than those which he had already presented to the court. Whereupon the party forthwith posted to London, and with all speed returned to Seville again with more ample and large letters testimonial, and certificates, according to their requests, and exhibited them to the court.

Notwithstanding, the inquisitors still shifted him off, excusing themselves by lack of leisure, and for that they were occupied in more weighty affairs, and with such answers put him off, four months after.

At last, when the party had well nigh spent all his money, and therefore sued the more earnestly for his despatch, they referred the matter wholly to the bishop, of whom, when he repaired unto him, he made answer, 'That for himself, he knew what he had to do, howbeit he was but one man, and the determination appertained to the other commissioners as well as unto him;' and thus by posting and passing it from one to another, the party could obtain no end of his suit. Yet for his importunity's sake, they were resolved to despatch him: it was on this sort: one of the inquisitors, called Gasco, a man very well experienced in these practices, willed the party to resort unto him after dinner.

The fellow being glad to hear this news, and supposing that his goods should be restored unto him, and that he was called in for that purpose to talk with the other that was in prison to confer with him about their accounts, rather through a little misunderstanding, hearing the inquisitors cast out a word, that it should be needful for him to talk with the prisoner, and being thereupon more than half persuaded, that at length they meant good faith, did so, and repaired thither about the evening. Immediately upon his coming, the jailer was forthwith charged with him, to shut him up close in such a prison where they appointed him.

The party, hoping at the first that he had been called for about some other matter, and seeing himself, contrary to his expectation, cast into a dark dungeon, perceived at length that the world went with him far otherwise than he supposed it would have done.

But within two or three days after, he was brought into the court, where he began to demand his goods: and because it was a device that well served their turn without any more circumstance, they bid him say his Ave Maria: Ave Maria, gratia plena, Dominus tecum, benedicta tu in mulieribus, et benedictus fructus ventris tui Jesus Amen.

The same was written word by word as he spake it, and without any more talk of claiming his goods, because it was needless, they commanded him to prison again, and entered an action against him as a heretic, forasmuch as he did not say his Ave Maria after the Romish fashion, but ended it very suspiciously, for he should have added moreover; Sancta Maria mater Dei, ora pro nobis peccatoribus: by abbreviating whereof, it was evident enough (said they) that he did not allow the mediation of saints.

Thus they picked a quarrel to detain him in prison a longer season, and afterward brought him forth upon their stage disguised after their manner;

where sentence was given, that he should lose all the goods which he sued for, though they were not his own, and besides this, suffer a year's imprisonment.

Mark Brughes, an Englishman, master of an English ship called the *Minion,* was burned in a city in Portugal.

William Hoker, a young man about the age of sixteen years, being an Englishman, was stoned to death by certain young men in the city of Seville, for the same righteous cause.

SOME PRIVATE ENORMITIES OF THE INQUISITION LAID OPEN, BY A VERY SINGULAR OCCURRENCE

When the crown of Spain was contested for in the beginning of the present century, by two princes, who equally pretended to the sovereignty, France espoused the cause of one competitor, and England of the other.

The duke of Berwick, a natural son of James II who abdicated England, commanded the Spanish and French forces, and defeated the English at the celebrated battle of Almanza. The army was then divided into two parts; the one consisting of Spaniards and French, headed by the duke of Berwick, advanced towards Catalonia; the other body, consisting of French troops only, commanded by the duke of Orleans, proceeded to the conquest of Arragon.

As the troops drew near to the city of Arragon, the magistrates came to offer the keys to the duke of Orleans; but he told them haughtily that they were rebels, and that he would not accept the keys, for he had orders to enter the city through a breach.

He accordingly made a breach in the walls with his cannon, and then entered the city through it, together with his whole army. When he had made every necessary regulation here, he departed to subdue other places, leaving a strong garrison at once to overawe and defend, under the command of his lieutenant-general M. de Legal. This gentleman, though brought up a Roman Catholic, was totally free from superstition; he united great talents with great bravery; and was the skilful officer, and accomplished gentleman.

The duke, before his departure, had ordered that heavy contributions should be levied upon the city in the following manner:

- That the magistrates and principal inhabitants should pay a thousand crowns per month for the duke's table.
- That every house should pay one pistole, which would monthly amount to 18,000 pistoles.
- That every convent and monastery should pay a donative, proportionable to its riches and rents.
- The two last contributions to be appropriated to the maintenance of the army.
- The money levied upon the magistrates and principal inhabitants, and upon every house, was paid as soon as demanded; but when the persons

applied to the heads of convents and monasteries, they found that the ecclesiastics were not so willing, as other people, to part with their cash.

Of the donatives to be raised by the clergy:

- The College of Jesuits to pay—2000 pistoles.
- Carmelites—1000
- Augustins—1000
- Dominicans—1000

M. de Legal sent to the Jesuits a peremptory order to pay the money immediately. The superior of the Jesuits returned for answer that for the clergy to pay money for the army was against all ecclesiastical immunities; and that he knew of no argument which could authorize such a procedure. M. de Legal then sent four companies of dragoons to quarter themselves in the college, with this sarcastic message. "To convince you of the necessity of paying the money, I have sent four substantial arguments to your college, drawn from the system of military logic; and, therefore, hope you will not need any further admonition to direct your conduct."

These proceedings greatly perplexed the Jesuits, who despatched an express to court to the king's confessor, who was of their order; but the dragoons were much more expeditious in plundering and doing mischief, than the courier in his journey: so that the Jesuits, seeing everything going to wreck and ruin, thought proper to adjust the matter amicably, and paid the money before the return of their messenger. The Augustins and Carmelites, taking warning by what had happened to the Jesuits, prudently went and paid the money, and by that means escaped the study of military arguments, and of being taught logic by dragoons.

But the Dominicans, who were all familiars of, or agents dependent on, the Inquisition, imagined that that very circumstance would be their protection; but they were mistaken, for M. de Legal neither feared nor respected the Inquisition. The chief of the Dominicans sent word to the military commander that his order was poor, and had not any money whatever to pay the donative; for, says he, "The whole wealth of the Dominicans consists only in the silver images of the apostles and saints, as large as life, which are placed in our church, and which it would be sacrilege to remove."

This insinuation was meant to terrify the French commander, whom the inquisitors imagined would not dare to be so profane as to wish for the possession of the precious idols.

He, however, sent word that the silver images would make admirable substitutes for money, and would be more in character in his possession, than in that of the Dominicans themselves, "For [said he] while you possess them in the manner you do at present, they stand up in niches, useless and motionless, without being of the least benefit to mankind in general, or even to yourselves; but, when they come into my possession, they shall be useful; I will put them in motion; for I intend to have them coined, when they may travel like the apostles, be beneficial in various places, and circulate for the universal service of mankind."

The inquisitors were astonished at this treatment, which they never expected to receive, even from crowned heads; they therefore determined to deliver their precious images in a solemn procession, that they might excite the people to an insurrection. The Dominican friars were accordingly ordered to march to de Legal's house, with the silver apostles and saints, in a mournful manner, having lighted tapers with them and bitterly crying all the way, "heresy, heresy."

M. de Legal, hearing these proceedings, ordered four companies of grenadiers to line the street which led to his house; each grenadier was ordered to have his loaded fuzee in one hand, and a lighted taper in the other; so that the troops might either repel force with force, or do honor to the farcical solemnity.

The friars did all they could to raise the tumult, but the common people were too much afraid of the troops under arms to obey them; the silver images were, therefore, of necessity delivered up to M. de Legal, who sent them to the mint, and ordered them to be coined immediately.

The project of raising an insurrection having failed, the inquisitors determined to excommunicate M. de Legal, unless he would release their precious silver saints from imprisonment in the mint, before they were melted down, or otherwise mutilated. The French commander absolutely refused to release the images, but said they should certainly travel and do good; upon which the inquisitors drew up the form of excommunication, and ordered their secretary to go and read it to M. de Legal.

The secretary punctually performed his commission, and read the excommunication deliberately and distinctly. The French commander heard it with great patience, and politely told the secretary that he would answer it the next day.

When the secretary of the Inquisition was gone, M. de Legal ordered his own secretary to prepare a form of excommunication, exactly like that sent by the Inquisition; but to make this alteration, instead of his name to put in those of the inquisitors.

The next morning he ordered four regiments under arms, and commanded them to accompany his secretary, and act as he directed.

The secretary went to the Inquisition, and insisted upon admittance, which, after a great deal of altercation, was granted. As soon as he entered, he read, in an audible voice, the excommunication sent by M. de Legal against the inquisitors. The inquisitors were all present, and heard it with astonishment, never having before met with any individual who dared to behave so boldly. They loudly cried out against de Legal, as a heretic; and said, "This was a most daring insult against the Catholic faith." But to surprise them still more, the French secretary told them that they must remove from their present lodgings; for the French commander wanted to quarter the troops in the Inquisition, as it was the most commodious place in the whole city.

The inquisitors exclaimed loudly upon this occasion, when the secretary put them under a strong guard, and sent them to a place appointed by M. de Legal to receive them. The inquisitors, finding how things went, begged that they might be permitted to take their private property, which was granted; and they immediately set out for Madrid, where they made the most bitter complaints to the king; but the monarch told them that he could not grant them any redress, as the injuries they had received were from his grandfather, the king of France's troops, by whose assistance alone he could be firmly established in his kingdom. "Had it been my own troops, [said he] I would have punished them; but as it is, I cannot pretend to exert any authority."

In the mean time, M. de Legal's secretary set open all the doors of the Inquisition, and released the prisoners, who amounted in the whole to four hundred; and among these were sixty beautiful young women, who appeared to form a seraglio for the three principal inquisitors.

This discovery, which laid the enormity of the inquisitors so open, greatly alarmed the archbishop, who desired M. de Legal to send the women to his palace, and he would take proper care of them; and at the same time he published an ecclesiastical censure against all such as should ridicule, or blame, the holy office of the Inquisition.

The French commander sent word to the archbishop, that the prisoners had either run away, or were so securely concealed by their friends, or even by his own officers, that it was impossible for him to send them back again; and, therefore, the Inquisition having committed such atrocious actions, must now put up with their exposure.

Some may suggest, that it is strange crowned heads and eminent nobles did not attempt to crush the power of the Inquisition, and reduce the authority of those ecclesiastical tyrants, from whose merciless fangs neither their families nor themselves were secure.

But astonishing as it is, superstition hath, in this case, always overcome common sense, and custom operated against reason. One prince, indeed, intended to abolish the Inquisition, but he lost his life before he became king, and consequently before he had the power so to do; for the very intimation of his design procured his destruction.

This was that amiable prince Don Carlos, son of Philip the Second, king of Spain, and grandson of the celebrated emperor Charles V. Don Carlos possessed all the good qualities of his grandfather, without any of the bad ones of his father; and was a prince of great vivacity, admirable learning, and the most amiable disposition. He had sense enough to see into the errors of popery, and abhorred the very name of the Inquisition. He inveighed publicly against the institution, ridiculed the affected piety of the inquisitors, did all he could to expose their atrocious deeds, and even declared, that if he ever came to the crown, he would abolish the Inquisition, and exterminate its agents.

These things were sufficient to irritate the inquisitors against the prince: they, accordingly, bent their minds to vengeance, and determined on his destruction.

The inquisitors now employed all their agents and emissaries to spread abroad the most artful insinuations against the prince; and, at length raised such a spirit of discontent among the people that the king was under the necessity of removing Don Carlos from court. Not content with this, they pursued even his friends, and obliged the king likewise to banish Don John, duke of Austria, his own brother, and consequently uncle to the prince; together with the prince of Parma, nephew to the king, and cousin to the prince, because they well knew that both the duke of Austria, and the prince of Parma, had a most sincere and inviolable attachment to Don Carlos.

Some few years after, the prince having shown great lenity and favor to the Protestants in the Netherlands, the Inquisition loudly exclaimed against him, declaring, that as the persons in question were heretics, the prince himself must necessarily be one, since he gave them countenance. In short, they gained so great an ascendency over the mind of the king, who was absolutely a slave to superstition, that, shocking to relate, he sacrificed the feelings of nature to the force of bigotry, and, for fear of incurring the anger of the Inquisition, gave up his only son, passing the sentence of death on him himself.

The prince, indeed, had what was termed an indulgence; that is, he was permitted to choose the manner of his death. Roman-like, the unfortunate young hero chose bleeding and the hot bath; when the veins of his arms and legs were opened, he expired gradually, falling a martyr to the malice of the inquisitors, and the stupid bigotry of his father.

THE PERSECUTION OF DR. AEGIDIO

Dr. Aegidio was educated at the university of Alcala, where he took his several degrees, and particularly applied himself to the study of the sacred Scriptures and school divinity. When the professor of theology died, he was elected into his place, and acted so much to the satisfaction of every one that his reputation for learning and piety was circulated throughout Europe.

Aegidio, however, had his enemies, and these laid a complaint against him to the inquisitors, who sent him a citation, and when he appeared to it, cast him into a dungeon.

As the greatest part of those who belonged to the cathedral church at Seville, and many persons belonging to the bishopric of Dortois highly approved of the doctrines of Aegidio, which they thought perfectly consonant with true religion, they petitioned the emperor in his behalf. Though the monarch had been educated a Roman Catholic, he had too much sense to be a bigot, and therefore sent an immediate order for his enlargement.

He soon after visited the church of Valladolid, and did every thing he could to promote the cause of religion. Returning home he soon after fell sick, and died in an extreme old age.

The inquisitors having been disappointed of gratifying their malice against him while living, determined (as the emperor's whole thoughts were engrossed by a military expedition) to wreak their vengeance on him when dead. Therefore, soon after he was buried, they ordered his remains to be dug out of the grave; and a legal process being carried on, they were condemned to be burnt, which was executed accordingly.

THE PERSECUTION OF DR. CONSTANTINE

Dr. Constantine, an intimate acquaintance of the already mentioned Dr. Aegidio, was a man of uncommon natural abilities and profound learning; exclusive of several modern tongues, he was acquainted with the Latin, Greek, and Hebrew languages, and perfectly well knew not only the sciences called abstruse, but those arts which come under the denomination of polite literature.

His eloquence rendered him pleasing, and the soundness of his doctrines a profitable preacher; and he was so popular that he never preached but to a crowded audience. He had many opportunities of rising in the Church, but never would take advantage of them; for if a living of greater value than his own was offered him, he would refuse it, saying, "I am content with what I have"; and he frequently preached so forcibly against simony, that many of his superiors, who were not so delicate upon the subject, took umbrage at his doctrines upon that head.

Having been fully confirmed in Protestantism by Dr. Aegidio, he preached boldly such doctrines only as were agreeable to Gospel purity, and uncontaminated by the errors which had at various times crept into the Romish Church. For these reasons he had many enemies among the Roman Catholics, and some of them were fully determined on his destruction.

A worthy gentleman named Scobaria, having erected a school for divinity lectures, appointed Dr. Constantine to be reader therein. He immediately undertook the task, and read lectures, by portions, on the Proverbs, Ecclesiastes, and Canticles; and was beginning to expound the Book of Job, when he was seized by the inquisitors.

Being brought to examination, he answered with such precaution that they could not find any explicit charge against him, but remained doubtful in what manner to proceed, when the following circumstances occurred to determine them.

Dr. Constantine had deposited with a woman named Isabella Martin, several books, which to him were very valuable, but which he knew, in the eyes of the Inquisition, were exceptionable.

This woman having been informed against as a Protestant, was apprehended, and, after a small process, her goods were ordered to be confiscated. Previous, however, to the officers coming to her house, the woman's son had removed away several chests full of the most valuable articles; among these were Dr. Constantine's books.

A treacherous servant gave intelligence of this to the inquisitors, and an officer was despatched to the son to demand the chests. The son, supposing the officer only came for Constantine's books, said, "I know what you come for, and I will fetch them to you immediately." He then fetched Dr. Constantine's books and papers, when the officer was greatly surprised to find what he did not look for. He, however, told the young man that he was glad these books and papers were produced, but nevertheless he must fulfill the end of his commission, which was to carry him and the goods he had embezzled before the inquisitors, which he did accordingly; for the young man knew it would be in vain to expostulate, or resist, and therefore quietly submitted to his fate.

The inquisitors being thus possessed of Constantine's books and writings, now found matter sufficient to form charges against him. When he was brought to a re-examination, they presented one of his papers, and asked him if he knew the handwriting? Perceiving it was his own, he guessed the whole matter, confessed the writing, and justified the doctrine it contained: saying, "In that, and all my other writings, I have never departed from the truth of the Gospel, but have always kept in view the pure precepts of Christ, as He delivered them to mankind."

After being detained upwards of two years in prison, Dr. Constantine was seized with a bloody flux, which put an end to his miseries in this world. The process, however, was carried on against his body, which, at the ensuing auto da fe, was publicly burnt.

THE LIFE OF WILLIAM GARDINER

William Gardiner was born at Bristol, received a tolerable education, and was, at a proper age, placed under the care of a merchant, named Paget.

At the age of twenty-six years, he was, by his master, sent to Lisbon to act as factor. Here he applied himself to the study of the Portuguese language, executed his business with assiduity and despatch, and behaved with the most engaging affability to all persons with whom he had the least concern. He conversed privately with a few, whom he knew to be zealous Protestants; and, at the same time cautiously avoided giving the least offence to any who were Roman Catholics; he had not, however, hitherto gone into any of the popish churches.

A marriage being concluded between the king of Portugal's son, and the Infanta of Spain, upon the wedding-day the bridegroom, bride, and the whole court went to the cathedral church, attended by multitudes of all ranks of people, and among the rest William Gardiner, who stayed during the whole ceremony, and was greatly shocked at the superstitions he saw.

The erroneous worship which he had seen ran strongly in his mind; he was miserable to see a whole country sunk into such idolatry, when the truth of the Gospel might be so easily obtained. He, therefore, took the inconsiderate, though laudable design, into his head, of making a reform in Portugal, or perishing in the attempt; and determined to sacrifice his prudence to his zeal, though he became a martyr upon the occasion.

To this end, he settled all his worldly affairs, paid his debts, closed his books, and consigned over his merchandise. On the ensuing Sunday he went again to the cathedral church, with a New Testament in his hand, and placed himself near the altar.

The king and the court soon appeared, and a cardinal began Mass, at that part of the ceremony in which the people adore the wafer. Gardiner could hold out no longer, but springing towards the cardinal, he snatched the host from him, and trampled it under his feet.

This action amazed the whole congregation, and one person, drawing a dagger, wounded Gardiner in the shoulder, and would, by repeating the blow, have finished him, had not the king called to him to desist.

Gardiner, being carried before the king, the monarch asked him what countryman he was: to which he replied, "I am an Englishman by birth, a Protestant by religion, and a merchant by occupation. What I have done is not out of contempt to your royal person, God forbid it should, but out of an honest indignation, to see the ridiculous superstitious and gross idolatries practiced here."

The king, thinking that he had been stimulated by some other person to act as he had done, demanded who was his abetter, to which he replied, "My own conscience alone. I would not hazard what I have done for any man living, but I owe that and all other services to God."

Gardiner was sent to prison, and a general order issued to apprehend all Englishmen in Lisbon. This order was in a great measure put into execution, (some few escaping) and many innocent persons were tortured to make them confess if they knew any thing of the matter; in particular, a person who resided in the same house with Gardiner was treated with unparalleled barbarity to make him confess something which might throw a light upon the affair.

Gardiner himself was then tormented in the most excruciating manner; but in the midst of all his torments he gloried in the deed. Being ordered for death, a large fire was kindled near a gibbet, Gardiner was drawn up to the gibbet by pulleys, and then let down near the fire, but not so close as to touch it; for they burnt or rather roasted him by slow degrees. Yet he bore his sufferings patiently and resigned his soul to the Lord cheerfully.

It is observable that some of the sparks that were blown from the fire, (which consumed Gardiner) towards the haven, burnt one of the king's ships of war, and did other considerable damage. The Englishmen who were taken up on this occasion were, soon after Gardiner's death, all discharged, except the person who resided in the same house with him, who was detained two years before he could procure his liberty.

AN ACCOUNT OF THE LIFE AND SUFFERINGS OF MR. WILLIAM LITHGOW, A NATIVE OF SCOTLAND

This gentleman was descended from a good family, and having a natural propensity for travelling, he rambled, when very young, over the northern and western islands; after which he visited France, Germany, Switzerland, and

Spain. He set out on his travels in the month of March, 1609, and the first place he went to was Paris, where he stayed for some time. He then prosecuted his travels through Germany and other parts, and at length arrived at Malaga, in Spain, the seat of all his misfortunes.

During his residence here, he contracted with the master of a French ship for his passage to Alexandria, but was prevented from going by the following circumstances. In the evening of the seventeenth of October, 1620, the English fleet, at that time on a cruise against the Algerine rovers, came to anchor before Malaga, which threw the people of the town into the greatest consternation, as they imagined them to be Turks. The morning, however, discovered the mistake, and the governor of Malaga, perceiving the cross of England in their colors, went on board Sir Robert Mansel's ship, who commanded on that expedition, and after staying some time returned, and silenced the fears of the people.

The next day many persons from on board the fleet came ashore. Among these were several well known by Mr. Lithgow, who, after reciprocal compliments, spent some days together in festivity and the amusements of the town. They then invited Mr. Lithgow to go on board, and pay his respects to the admiral. He accordingly accepted the invitation, was kindly received by him, and detained until the next day when the fleet sailed. The admiral would willingly have taken Mr. Lithgow with him to Algiers; but having contracted for his passage to Alexandria, and his baggage, etc., being in the town, he could not accept the offer.

As soon as Mr. Lithgow got on shore, he proceeded towards his lodgings by a private way, (being to embark the same night for Alexandria) when, in passing through a narrow uninhabited street, he found himself suddenly surrounded by nine sergeants, or officers, who threw a black cloak over him, and forcibly conducted him to the governor's house. After some little time the governor appeared when Mr. Lithgow earnestly begged he might be informed of the cause of such violent treatment. The governor only answered by shaking his head, and gave orders that the prisoner should be strictly watched until he (the governor) returned from his devotions; directing, at the same time, that the captain of the town, the alcade major, and town notary, should be summoned to appear at his examination, and that all this should be done with the greatest secrecy, to prevent the knowledge reaching the ears of the English merchants then residing in the town.

These orders were strictly discharged, and on the governor's return, he, with the officers, having seated themselves, Mr. Lithgow was brought before them for examination. The governor began by asking several questions, namely, of what country he was, whither bound, and how long he had been in Spain. The prisoner, after answering these and other questions, was conducted to a closet, where, in a short space of time, he was visited by the town captain, who inquired whether he had ever been at Seville, or was lately come from thence; and patting his cheeks with an air of friendship, conjured him to tell the truth, "For (said he) your very countenance shows there is some hidden matter in your mind, which prudence should direct you to disclose." Finding himself, however, unable to extort any thing from the prisoner, he left him, and reported the same to the governor and the other officers; on which Mr. Lithgow was again brought before them, a general accusation was laid against him, and he was compelled to swear that he would give true answers to such questions as should be asked him.

The governor proceeded to inquire the quality of the English commander, and the prisoner's opinion what were the motives that prevented his accepting an invitation from him to come on shore. He demanded, likewise, the names of the English captains in the squadron, and what knowledge he had of the embarkation, or preparation for it before his departure from England. The answers given to the several questions asked were set down in writing by the notary; but the junto seemed surprised at his denying any knowledge of the fitting out of the fleet, particularly the governor, who said he lied; that he was a traitor and a spy, and came directly from England to favor and assist the designs that were projected against Spain, and that he had been for that purpose nine months in Seville, in order to procure intelligence of the time the Spanish navy was expected from the Indies. They exclaimed against his familiarity with the officers of the fleet, and many other English gentlemen, between whom, they said, unusual civilities had passed, but all these transactions had been carefully noticed.

Besides to sum up the whole, and put the truth past all doubt, they said he came from a council of war, held that morning on board the admiral's ship, in order to put in execution the orders assigned him. They upbraided him with being accessory to the burning of the island of St. Thomas, in the West Indies. "Wherefore (said they) these Lutherans, and sons of the devil, ought to have no credit given to what they say or swear."

In vain did Mr. Lithgow endeavor to obviate every accusation laid against him, and to obtain belief from his prejudiced judges. He begged permission to send for his cloak bag which contained his papers, and might serve to show his innocence. This request they complied with, thinking it would discover some things of which they were ignorant. The cloak bag was accordingly brought, and being opened, among other things, was found a license from King James the First, under the sign manual, setting forth the bearer's intention to travel into Egypt; which was treated by the haughty Spaniards with great contempt. The other papers consisted of passports, testimonials, etc., of persons of quality. All these credentials, however, seemed rather to confirm than abate the suspicions of these prejudiced judges, who, after seizing all the prisoner's papers, ordered him again to withdraw.

In the meantime a consultation was held to fix the place where the prisoner should be confined. The alcade, or chief judge, was for putting him into the town prison; but this was objected to, particularly by the corregidor, who said, in Spanish, "In order to prevent the knowledge of his confinement from reaching his countrymen, I will take the matter on myself, and be answerable for the consequences"; upon which it was agreed that he should be confined in the governor's house with the greatest secrecy.

This matter being determined, one of the sergeants went to Mr. Lithgow, and begged his money, with liberty to search him. As it was needless to make any resistance, the prisoner quietly complied, when the sergeant (after rifling his pockets of eleven ducatoons) stripped him to his shirt; and searching his breeches he found, inclosed in the waistland, two canvass bags, containing one hundred and thirty-seven pieces of gold. The sergeant immediately took the money to the corregidor, who, after having told it over, ordered him to clothe the prisoner, and shut him up close until after supper.

About midnight, the sergeant and two Turkish slaves released Mr. Lithgow from his then confinement, but it was to introduce him to one much more horrible. They conducted him through several passages, to a chamber in a remote part of the palace, towards the garden, where they loaded him with irons, and extended his legs by means of an iron bar above a yard long, the weight of which was so great that he could neither stand nor sit, but was obliged to lie continually on his back. They left him in this condition for some time, when they returned with a refreshment of food, consisting of a pound of boiled mutton and a loaf, together with a small quantity of wine; which was not only the first, but the best and last of the kind, during his confinement in this place. After delivering these articles, the sergeant locked the door, and left Mr. Lithgow to his own private contemplations.

The next day he received a visit from the governor, who promised him his liberty, with many other advantages, if he would confess being a spy; but on his protesting that he was entirely innocent, the governor left him in a rage, saying, "He should see him no more until further torments constrained him to confess"; commanding the keeper, to whose care he was committed, that he should permit no person whatever to have access to, or commune with him; that his sustenance should not exceed three ounces of musty bread, and a pint of water every second day; that he shall be allowed neither bed, pillow, nor coverlid. "Close up (said he) this window in his room with lime and stone, stop up the holes of the door with double mats: let him have nothing that bears any likeness to comfort." These, and several orders of the like severity, were given to render it impossible for his condition to be known to those of the English nation.

In this wretched and melancholy state did poor Lithgow continue without seeing any person for several days, in which time the governor received an answer to a letter he had written, relative to the prisoner, from Madrid; and, pursuant to the instructions given him, began to put in practice the cruelties devised, which were hastened, because Christmas holy-days approached, it being then the forty-seventh day since his imprisonment.

About two o'clock in the morning, he heard the noise of a coach in the street, and sometime after heard the opening of the prison doors, not having had any sleep for two nights; hunger, pain, and melancholy reflections having prevented him from taking any repose.

Soon after the prison doors were opened, the nine sergeants, who had first seized him, entered the place where he lay, and without uttering a word, conducted him in his irons through the house into the street, where a coach waited, and into which they laid him at the bottom on his back, not being able to sit. Two of the sergeants rode with him, and the rest walked by the coach side, but all observed the most profound silence. They drove him to a vinepress house, about a league from the town, to which place a rack had been privately conveyed before; and here they shut him up for that night.

At daybreak the next morning, arrived the governor and the alcade, into whose presence Mr. Lithgow was immediately brought to undergo another examination. The prisoner desired he might have an interpreter, which was allowed to strangers by the laws of that country, but this was refused, nor would they permit him to appeal to Madrid, the superior court of judicature. After a long examination, which lasted from morning until night, there appeared in all his answers so exact a conformity with what he had before said, that they declared he had learned them by heart, there not being the least prevarication. They, however, pressed him again to make a full discovery; that is, to accuse himself of crimes never committed, the governor adding, "You are still in my power; I can set you free if you comply, if not, I must deliver you to the alcade." Mr. Lithgow still persisting in his innocence, the governor ordered the notary to draw up a warrant for delivering him to the alcade to be tortured.

In consequence of this he was conducted by the sergeants to the end of a stone gallery, where the rack was placed. The encarouador, or executioner, immediately struck off his irons, which put him to very great pains, the bolts being so closely riveted that the sledge hammer tore away half an inch of his heel, in forcing off the bolt; the anguish of which, together with his weak condition, (not having the least sustenance for three days) occasioned him to groan bitterly; upon which the merciless alcade said, "Villain, traitor, this is but the earnest of what you shall endure."

When his irons were off, he fell on his knees, uttering a short prayer, that God would be pleased to enable him to be steadfast, and undergo courageously the grievous trial he had to encounter. The alcade and notary having placed themselves in chairs, he was stripped naked, and fixed upon the rack, the office of these gentlemen being to be witness of, and set down the confessions and tortures endured by the delinquent.

It is impossible to describe all the various tortures inflicted upon him.

Suffice it to say that he lay on the rack for above five hours, during which time he received above sixty different tortures of the most hellish nature; and had they continued them a few minutes longer, he must have inevitably perished.

These cruel persecutors being satisfied for the present, the prisoner was taken from the rack, and his irons being again put on, he was conducted to his former dungeon, having received no other nourishment than a little warm wine, which was given him rather to prevent his dying, and reserve him for future punishments, than from any principle of charity or compassion.

As a confirmation of this, orders were given for a coach to pass every morning before day by the prison, that the noise made by it might give fresh terrors and alarms to the unhappy prisoner, and deprive him of all possibility of obtaining the least repose.

He continued in this horrid situation, almost starved for want of the common necessaries to preserve his wretched existence, until Christmas day, when he received some relief from Mariane, waiting-woman to the governor's lady. This woman having obtained leave to visit him, carried with her some refreshments, consisting of honey, sugar, raisins, and other articles; and so affected was she at beholding his situation that she wept bitterly, and at her departure expressed the greatest concern at not being able to give him further assistance.

In this loathsome prison was poor Mr. Lithgow kept until he was almost devoured by vermin. They crawled about his beard, lips, eyebrows, etc., so that he could scarce open his eyes; and his mortification was increased by not having the use of his hands or legs to defend himself, from his being so miserably maimed by the tortures. So cruel was the governor, that he even ordered the vermin to be swept on him twice in every eight days. He, however, obtained some little mitigation of this part of his punishment, from the humanity of a Turkish slave that attended him, who, when he could do it with safety, destroyed the vermin, and contributed every refreshment to him that laid in his power.

From this slave Mr. Lithgow at length received information which gave him little hopes of ever being released, but, on the contrary, that he should finish his life under new tortures. The substance of this information was that an English seminary priest, and a Scotch cooper, had been for some time employed by the governor to translate from the English into the Spanish language, all his books and observations; and that it was commonly said in the governor's house, that he was an arch-heretic.

This information greatly alarmed him, and he began, not without reason, to fear that they would soon finish him, more especially as they could neither by torture or any other means, bring him to vary from what he had all along said at his different examinations.

Two days after he had received the above information, the governor, an inquisitor, and a canonical priest, accompanied by two Jesuits, entered his dungeon, and being seated, after several idle questions, the inquisitor asked Mr. Lithgow if he was a Roman Catholic, and acknowledged the pope's supremacy? He answered that he neither was the one nor did the other, adding that he was surprised at being asked such questions, since it was expressly stipulated by the articles of peace between England and Spain that none of the English subjects should be liable to the Inquisition, or any way molested by them on account of diversity in religion, etc. In the bitterness of his soul he made use of some warm expressions not suited to his circumstances: "As you have almost murdered me (said he) for pretended treason, so now you intend to make a martyr of me for my religion." He also expostulated with the governor on the ill return he made to the king of England, (whose subject he was) for the princely humanity exercised towards the Spaniards in 1588, when their armada was shipwrecked on the Scotch coast, and thousands of the Spaniards found relief, who must otherwise have miserably perished.

The governor admitted the truth of what Mr. Lithgow said, but replied with a haughty air that the king, who then only ruled Scotland, was actuated more by fear than love, and therefore did not deserve any thanks. One of the Jesuits said there was no faith to be kept with heretics. The inquisitor then rising, addressed himself to Mr. Lithgow in the following words: "You have been taken up as a spy, accused of treachery, and tortured, as we acknowledge, innocently: (which appears by the account lately received from Madrid of the intentions of the English) yet it was the divine power that brought those judgments upon you, for presumptuously treating the blessed miracle of Loretto with ridicule, and expressing yourself in your writings irreverently of his holiness, the great agent and Christ's vicar upon earth; therefore you are justly fallen into our hands by their special appointment: thy books and papers are miraculously translated by the assistance of Providence influencing thy own countrymen."

This trumpery being ended, they gave the prisoner eight days to consider and resolve whether he would become a convert to their religion; during which time the inquisitor told him he, with other religious orders, would attend, to give him such assistance thereto as he might want. One of the Jesuits said, (first making the sign of the cross upon his breast), "My son, behold, you deserve to be burnt alive; but by the grace of our lady of Loretto, whom you have blasphemed we will both save your soul and body."

In the morning the inquisitor, with three other ecclesiastics, returned, when the former asked the prisoner what difficulties he had on his conscience that retarded his conversion; to which he answered, "he had not any doubts in his mind, being confident in the promises of Christ, and assuredly believing his revealed will signified in the Gospels, as professed in the reformed Catholic Church, being confirmed by grace, and having infallible assurance thereby of the Christian faith." To these words the inquisitor replied, "Thou art no Christian, but an absurd heretic, and without conversion a member of perdition." The prisoner then told him that it was not consistent with the nature and essence of religion and charity to convince by opprobrious speeches, racks, and torments, but by arguments deduced from the Scriptures; and that all other methods would with him be totally ineffectual.

The inquisitor was so enraged at the replies made by the prisoner, that he struck him on the face, used many abusive speeches, and attempted to stab him, which he had certainly done had he not been prevented by the Jesuits; and from this time he never again visited the prisoner.

The next day the two Jesuits returned, and putting on a very grave, supercilious air, the superior asked him what resolution he had taken. To which Mr. Lithgow replied that he was already resolved, unless he could show substantial reasons to make him alter his opinion. The superior, after a pedantic display of their seven sacraments, the intercession of saints, transubstantiation, etc., boasted greatly of their Church, her antiquity, universality, and uniformity; all of which Mr. Lithgow denied: "For (said he) the profession of the faith I hold hath been ever since the first days of the apostles, and Christ had ever his own Church (however obscure) in the greatest time of your darkness."

The Jesuits, finding their arguments had not the desired effect, that torments could not shake his constancy, nor even the fear of the cruel sentence he had reason to expect would be pronounced and executed on him, after severe menaces, left him. On the eighth day after, being the last of their Inquisition, when sentence is pronounced, they returned again, but quite altered both in their words and behavior after repeating much of the same kind of arguments as before, they with seeming tears in their eyes, pretended they were sorry from their heart he must be obliged to undergo a terrible death, but above all, for the loss of his most precious soul; and falling on their knees, cried out, "Convert, convert, O dear brother, for our blessed Lady's sake convert!" To which he answered, "I fear neither death nor fire, being prepared for both."

The first effects Mr. Lithgow felt of the determination of this bloody tribunal was, a sentence to receive that night eleven different tortures, and if he did not die in the execution of them, (which might be reasonably expected from the maimed and disjointed condition he was in) he was, after Easter holy-days, to be carried to Grenada, and there burnt to ashes. The first part of this sentence was executed with great barbarity that night; and it pleased God to give him strength both of body and mind, to stand fast to the truth, and to survive the horrid punishments inflicted on him.

After these barbarians had glutted themselves for the present, with exercising on the unhappy prisoner the most distinguished cruelties, they again put irons on, and conveyed him to his former dungeon. The next morning he received some little comfort from the Turkish slave before mentioned, who secretly brought him, in his shirt sleeve, some raisins and figs, which he licked up in the best manner his strength would permit with his tongue. It was to this slave Mr. Lithgow attributed his surviving so long in such a wretched situation; for he found means to convey some of these fruits to him twice every week. It is very extraordinary, and worthy of note, that this poor slave, bred up from his infancy, according to the maxims of his prophet and parents, in the greatest detestation of Christians, should be so affected at the miserable situation of Mr. Lithgow that he fell ill, and continued so for upwards of forty days. During this period Mr. Lithgow was attended by a negro woman, a slave, who found means to furnish him with refreshments still more amply than the Turk, being conversant in the house and family. She brought him every day some victuals, and with it some wine in a bottle.

The time was now so far elapsed, and the horrid situation so truly loathsome, that Mr. Lithgow waited with anxious expectation for the day, which, by putting an end to his life, would also end his torments. But his melancholy expectations were, by the interposition of Providence, happily rendered abortive, and his deliverance obtained from the following circumstances.

It happened that a Spanish gentleman of quality came from Grenada to Malaga, who being invited to an entertainment by the governor, informed him of what had befallen Mr. Lithgow from the time of his being apprehended as a spy, and described the various sufferings he had endured. He likewise told him that after it was known the prisoner was innocent, it gave him great concern. That on this account he would gladly have released him, restored his money and papers, and made some atonement for the injuries he had received, but that, upon an inspection into his writings, several were found of a very blasphemous nature, highly reflecting on their religion, that on his refusing to abjure these heretical opinions, he was turned over to the Inquisition, by whom he was finally condemned.

While the governor was relating this tragical tale, a Flemish youth (servant to the Spanish gentleman) who waited at the table, was struck with amazement and pity at the sufferings of the stranger described. On his return to his master's lodgings he began to revolve in his mind what he had heard, which made such an impression on him that he could not rest in his bed. In the short slumbers he had, his imagination pointed to him the person described, on the rack, and burning in the fire. In this anxiety he passed the night; and when the morning came, without disclosing his intentions to any person whatever, he went into the town, and inquired for an English factor. He was directed to the house of a Mr. Wild, to whom he related the whole of what he had heard pass the preceding evening, between his master and the governor, but could not tell Mr. Lithgow's name. Mr. Wild, however, conjectured it was he, by the servant's remembering the circumstance of his being a traveller, and his having had some acquaintance with him.

On the departure of the Flemish servant, Mr. Wild immediately sent for the other English factors, to whom he related all the particulars relative to their unfortunate countryman. After a short consultation it was agreed that an information of the whole affair should be sent, by express, to Sir Walter Aston, the English ambassador to the king of Spain, then at Madrid. This was accordingly done, and the ambassador having presented a memorial to the king and council of Spain, obtained an order for Mr. Lithgow's enlargement, and his delivery to the English factor. This order was directed to the governor of Malaga; and was received with great dislike and surprise by the whole assembly of the bloody Inquisition.

Mr. Lithgow was released from his confinement on the eve of Easter Sunday, when he was carried from his dungeon on the back of the slave who had attended him, to the house of one Mr. Bosbich, where all proper comforts were given him. It fortunately happened that there was at this time a squadron of English ships in the road, commanded by Sir Richard Hawkins, who being informed of the past sufferings and present situation of Mr. Lithgow, came the next day ashore, with a proper guard, and received him from the merchants. He was instantly carried in blankets on board the *Vanguard,* and three days after was removed to another ship, by direction of the general Sir Robert Mansel, who ordered that he should have proper care taken of him. The factor presented him with clothes, and all necessary provisions, besides which they gave him two hundred reals in silver; and Sir Richard Hawkins sent him two double pistoles.

Before his departure from the Spanish coast, Sir Richard Hawkins demanded the delivery of his papers, money, books, etc., but could not obtain any satisfactory answer on that head.

We cannot help making a pause here to reflect how manifestly Providence interfered in behalf of this poor man, when he was just on the brink of destruction; for by his sentence, from which there was no appeal, he would have been taken, in a few days, to Grenada, and burnt to ashes; and that a poor ordinary servant, who had not the least knowledge of him, nor was any ways interested in his preservation, should risk the displeasure of his master, and hazard his own life, to disclose a thing of so momentous and perilous a nature, to a strange gentleman, on whose secrecy depended his own existence. By such secondary means does Providence frequently interfere in behalf of the virtuous and oppressed; of which this is a most distinguished example.

After lying twelve days in the road, the ship weighed anchor, and in about two months arrived safe at Deptford. The next morning, Mr. Lithgow was carried on a feather bed to Theobalds, in Hertfordshire, where at that time was the king and royal family. His majesty happened to be that day engaged in hunting, but on his return in the evening, Mr. Lithgow was presented to him, and related the particulars of his sufferings, and his happy delivery. The king was so affected at the narrative, that he expressed the deepest concern, and gave orders that he should be sent to Bath, and his wants properly supplied from his royal munificence. By these means, under God, after some time, Mr. Lithgow was restored from the most wretched spectacle, to a great share of health and strength; but he lost the use of his left arm and several of the smaller bones were so crushed and broken, as to be ever after rendered useless.

Notwithstanding that every effort was used, Mr. Lithgow could never obtain any part of his money or effects, although his majesty and the ministers of state interested themselves in his behalf. Gondamore, the Spanish ambassador, indeed, promised that all his effects should be restored, with the addition of 1000 pounds English money, as some atonement for the tortures he had undergone, which last was to be paid him by the governor of Malaga. These engagements, however, were but mere promises; and although the king was a kind of guarantee for the well performance of them, the cunning Spaniard found means to elude the same. He had, indeed, too great a share of influence in the English council during the time of that pacific reign, when England suffered herself to be bullied into slavish compliance by most of the states and kings in Europe.

THE STORY OF GALILEO

The most eminent men of science and philosophy of the day did not escape the watchful eye of this cruel despotism. Galileo, the chief astronomer and mathematician of his age, was the first who used the telescope successfully in solving the movements of the heavenly bodies. He discovered that the sun is the center of motion around which the earth and various planets revolve. For making this great discovery Galileo was brought before the Inquisition, and for a while was in great danger of being put to death.

After a long and bitter review of Galileo's writings, in which many of his most important discoveries were condemned as errors, the charge of the inquisitors went on to declare, "That you, Galileo, have upon account of those things which you have written and confessed, subjected yourself to a strong suspicion of heresy in this Holy Office, by believing, and holding to be true, a doctrine which is false, and contrary to the sacred and divine Scripture—viz., that the sun is the center of the orb of the earth, and does not move from the east to the west; and that the earth moves, and is not the center of the world."

In order to save his life. Galileo admitted that he was wrong in thinking that the earth revolved around the sun, and swore that—"For the future, I will never more say, or assert, either by word or writing, anything that shall give occasion for a like suspicion." But immediately after taking this forced oath he is said to have whispered to a friend standing near, "The earth moves, for all that."

SUMMARY OF THE INQUISITION

Of the multitudes who perished by the Inquisition throughout the world, no authentic record is now discoverable. But wherever popery had power, there was the tribunal. It had been planted even in the east, and the Portuguese Inquisition of Goa was, until within these few years, fed with many an agony. South America was partitioned into provinces of the Inquisition; and with a ghastly mimickry of the crimes of the mother state, the arrivals of viceroys, and the other popular celebrations were thought imperfect without an auto da fe. The Netherlands were one scene of slaughter from the time of the decree which planted the Inquisition among them. In Spain the calculation is more attainable. Each of the seventeen tribunals during a long period burned annually, on an average, ten miserable beings! We are to recollect that this number was in a country where persecution had for ages abolished all religious differences, and where the difficulty was not to find the stake, but the offering. Yet, even in Spain, thus gleaned of all heresy, the Inquisition could still swell its lists of murders to thirty-two thousand! The numbers burned in effigy, or condemned to penance, punishments generally equivalent to exile, confiscation, and taint of blood, to all ruin but the mere loss of worthless life, amounted to three hundred and nine thousand. But the crowds who perished in dungeons of torture, of confinement, and of broken hearts, the millions of dependent lives made utterly helpless, or hurried to the grave by the death of the victims, are beyond all register; or recorded only before HIM, who has sworn that "He that leadeth into captivity, shall go into captivity: he that killeth with the sword must be killed with the sword."

Such was the Inquisition, declared by the Spirit of God to be at once the offspring and the image of the popedom. To feel the force of the parentage, we must look to the time. In the thirteenth century, the popedom was at the summit of mortal dominion; it was independent of all kingdoms; it ruled with a rank of influence never before or since possessed by a human scepter; it was the acknowledged sovereign of body and soul; to all earthly intents its power was immeasurable for good or evil. It might have spread literature, peace, freedom, and Christianity to the ends of Europe, or the world. But its nature was hostile; its fuller triumph only disclosed its fuller evil; and, to the shame of human reason, and the terror and suffering of human virtue, Rome, in the hour of its consummate grandeur, teemed with the monstrous and horrid birth of the INQUISITION!

CHAPTER FOUR

An Account of the Life and Persecutions of John Wickliffe

It will not be inappropriate to devote a few pages of this work to a brief detail of the lives of some of those men who first stepped forward, regardless of the bigoted power which opposed all reformation, to stem the tide of papal corruption, and to seal the pure doctrines of the Gospel with their blood.

Among these, Great Britain has the honor of taking the lead, and first maintaining that freedom in religious controversy which astonished Europe, and demonstrated that political and religious liberty are equally the growth of that favored island. Among the earliest of these eminent persons was

JOHN WICKLIFFE

This celebrated reformer, denominated the "Morning Star of the Reformation," was born about the year 1324, in the reign of Edward II. Of his extraction we have no certain account. His parents designing him for the Church, sent him to Queen's College, Oxford, about that period founded by Robert Eaglesfield, confessor to Queen Philippa. But not meeting with the advantages for study in that newly established house which he expected, he removed to Merton College, which was then esteemed one of the most learned societies in Europe.

The first thing which drew him into public notice was his defence of the university against the begging friars, who about this time, from their settlement in Oxford in 1230, had been troublesome neighbors to the university. Feuds were continually fomented; the friars appealing to the pope, the scholars to the civil power; and sometimes one party, and sometimes, the other, prevailed. The friars became very fond of a notion that Christ was a common beggar; that his disciples were beggars also; and that begging was of Gospel institution. This doctrine they urged from the pulpit and wherever they had access.

Wickliffe had long held these religious friars in contempt for the laziness of their lives, and had now a fair opportunity of exposing them. He published a treatise against able beggary, in which he lashed the friars, and proved that they were not only a reproach to religion, but also to human society. The university began to consider him one of their first champions, and he was soon promoted to the mastership of Baliol College.

About this time, Archbishop Islip founded Canterbury Hall, in Oxford, where he established a warden and eleven scholars. To this wardenship Wickliffe was elected by the archbishop, but upon his demise, he was displaced by his successor, Stephen Langham, bishop of Ely. As there was a degree of flagrant injustice in the affair, Wickliffe appealed to the pope, who subsequently gave it against him from the following cause: Edward III, then king of England, had withdrawn the tribune, which from the time of King John had been paid to the pope. The pope menaced; Edward called a parliament. The parliament resolved that King John had done an illegal thing, and given up the rights of the nation, and advised the king not to submit, whatever consequences might follow.

The clergy now began to write in favor of the pope, and a learned monk published a spirited and plausible treatise, which had many advocates. Wickliffe, irritated at seeing so bad a cause so well defended, opposed the monk, and did it in so masterly a way that he was considered no longer as unanswerable. His suit at Rome was immediately determined against him; and nobody doubted but his opposition to the pope, at so critical a period, was the true cause of his being non-suited at Rome.

Wickliffe was afterward elected to the chair of the divinity professor: and now fully convinced of the errors of the Romish Church, and the vileness of its monastic agents, he determined to expose them. In public lectures he lashed their vices and opposed their follies. He unfolded a variety of abuses covered by the darkness of superstition. At first he began to loosen the prejudices of the vulgar, and proceeded by slow advances; with the metaphysical disquisitions of the age, he mingled opinions in divinity apparently novel. The usurpations of the court of Rome was a favorite topic. On these he expatiated with all the keenness of argument, joined to logical reasoning. This soon procured him the clamor of the clergy, who, with the archbishop of Canterbury, deprived him of his office.

At this time the administration of affairs was in the hands of the duke of Lancaster, well known by the name of John of Gaunt. This prince had very free notions of religion, and was at enmity with the clergy. The exactions of the court of Rome having become very burdensome, he determined to send the bishop of Bangor and Wickliffe to remonstrate against these abuses, and it was agreed that the pope should no longer dispose of any benefices belonging to the Church of England. In this embassy, Wickliffe's observant mind penetrated into the constitution and policy of Rome, and he returned more strongly than ever determined to expose its avarice and ambition.

Having recovered his former situation, he inveighed, in his lectures, against the pope—his usurpation—his infallibility—his pride—his avarice—and his tyranny. He was the first who termed the pope Antichrist. From the pope, he would turn to the pomp, the luxury, and trappings of the bishops, and compared them with the simplicity of primitive bishops. Their superstitions and deceptions were topics that he urged with energy of mind and logical precision.

From the patronage of the duke of Lancaster, Wickliffe received a good benefice; but he was no sooner settled in his parish, than his enemies and the bishops began to persecute him with renewed vigor. The duke of Lancaster was his friend in this persecution, and by his presence and that of Lord Percy, earl marshal of England, he so overawed the trial, that the whole ended in disorder.

After the death of Edward III his grandson Richard II succeeded, in the eleventh year of his age. The duke of Lancaster not obtaining to be the sole regent, as he expected, his power began to decline, and the enemies of Wickliffe, taking advantage of the circumstance, renewed their articles of accusation against him. Five bulls were despatched in consequence by the pope to the king and certain bishops, but the regency and the people manifested a spirit of contempt at the haughty proceedings of the pontiff, and the former at that time wanting money to oppose an expected invasion of the French, proposed to apply a large sum, collected for the use of the pope, to that purpose. The question was submitted to the decision of Wickliffe. The bishops, however, supported by the papal authority, insisted upon bringing Wickliffe to trial, and he was actually undergoing examination at Lambeth, when, from the riotous behavior of the populace without, and awed by the command of Sir Lewis Clifford, a gentleman of the court, that they should not proceed to any definitive sentence, they terminated the whole affair in a prohibition to Wickliffe, not to preach those doctrines which were obnoxious to the pope; but this was laughed at by our reformer, who, going about barefoot, and in a long frieze gown, preached more vehemently than before.

In the year 1378, a contest arose between two popes, Urban VI and Clement VII which was the lawful pope, and true vicegerent of God. This was a favorable period for the exertion of Wickliffe's talents: he soon produced a tract against popery, which was eagerly read by all sorts of people.

About the end of the year, Wickliffe was seized with a violent disorder, which it was feared might prove fatal. The begging friars, accompanied by four of the most eminent citizens of Oxford, gained admittance to his bed chamber, and begged of him to retract, for his soul's sake, the unjust things he had asserted of their order. Wickliffe, surprised at the solemn message, raised himself in his bed, and with a stern countenance replied, "I shall not die, but live to declare the evil deeds of the friars."

When Wickliffe recovered, he set about a most important work, the translation of the Bible into English. Before this work appeared, he published a tract, wherein he showed the necessity of it. The zeal of the bishops to suppress the Scriptures greatly promoted its sale, and they who were not able to purchase copies, procured transcripts of particular Gospels or Epistles. Afterward, when Lollardy increased, and the flames kindled, it was a common practice to fasten about the neck of the condemned heretic such of these scraps of Scripture as were found in his possession, which generally shared his fate.

Immediately after this transaction, Wickliffe ventured a step further, and affected the doctrine of transubstantiation. This strange opinion was invented by Paschade Radbert, and asserted with amazing boldness. Wickliffe, in his lecture before the University of Oxford, 1381, attacked this doctrine, and published a treatise on the subject. Dr. Barton, at this time vice-chancellor of Oxford, calling together the heads of the university, condemned Wickliffe's doctrines as heretical, and threatened their author with excommunication. Wickliffe could now derive no support from the duke of Lancaster, and being cited to appear before his former adversary, William Courteney, now made archbishop of Canterbury, he sheltered himself under the plea, that, as a member of the university, he was exempt from episcopal jurisdiction. This plea was admitted, as the university were determined to support their member.

The court met at the appointed time, determined, at least to sit in judgment upon his opinions, and some they condemned as erroneous, others as heretical. The publication on this subject was immediately answered by Wickliffe, who had become a subject of the archbishop's determined malice. The king, solicited by the archbishop, granted a license to imprison the teacher of heresy, but the commons made the king revoke this act as illegal. The primate, however, obtained letters from the king, directing the head of the University of Oxford to search for all heresies and books published by Wickliffe; in consequence of which order, the university became a scene of tumult. Wickliffe is supposed to have retired from the storm, into an obscure part of the kingdom. The seeds, however, were scattered, and Wickliffe's opinions were so prevalent that it was said if you met two persons upon the road, you might be sure that one was a Lollard. At this period, the disputes between the two popes continued. Urban published a bull, in which he earnestly called upon all who had any regard for religion, to exert themselves in its cause; and to take up arms against Clement and his adherents in defence of the holy see.

A war, in which the name of religion was so vilely prostituted, roused Wickliffe's inclination, even in his declining years. He took up his pen once more, and wrote against it with the greatest acrimony. He expostulated with the pope in a very free manner, and asks him boldly: "How he durst make the token of Christ on the cross (which is the token of peace, mercy and charity) a banner to lead us to slay Christian men, for the love of two false priests, and to oppress Christendom worse than Christ and his apostles were oppressed by the Jews? 'When,' said he, 'will the proud priest of Rome grant indulgences to mankind to live in peace and charity, as he now does to fight and slay one another?'"

This severe piece drew upon him the resentment of Urban, and was likely to have involved him in greater troubles than he had before experienced, but providentially he was delivered out of their hands. He was struck with the palsy, and though he lived some time, yet it was in such a way that his enemies considered him as a person below their resentment.

Wickliffe returning within short space, either from his banishment, or from some other place where he was secretly kept, repaired to his parish of Lutterworth, where he was parson; and there, quietly departing this mortal life, slept in peace in the Lord, in the end of the year 1384, upon Silvester's day. It appeared that he was well aged before he departed, "and that the same thing pleased him in his old age, which did please him being young."

Wickliffe had some cause to give them thanks, that they would at least spare him until he was dead, and also give him so long respite after his death, forty-one years to rest in his sepulchre before they ungraved him, and turned him from earth to ashes; which ashes they also took and threw into the river. And so was he resolved into three elements, earth, fire, and water, thinking thereby utterly to extinguish and abolish both the name and doctrine of Wickliffe forever. Not much unlike the example of the old Pharisees and sepulchre knights, who, when they had brought the Lord unto the grave, thought to make him sure never to rise again. But these and all others must know that, as there is no counsel against the Lord, so there is no keeping down of verity, but it will spring up and come out of dust and ashes, as appeared right well in this man; for though they dug up his body, burned his bones, and drowned his ashes, yet the Word of God and the truth of his doctrine, with the fruit and success thereof, they could not burn.

CHAPTER FIVE

An Account of the Life and Persecutions of Martin Luther

This illustrious German divine and reformer of the Church was the son of John Luther and Margaret Ziegler, and born at Isleben, a town of Saxony, in the county of Mansfield, November 10, 1483. His father's extraction and condition were originally but mean, and his occupation that of a miner; it is probable, however, that by his application and industry he improved the fortunes of his family, as he afterward became a magistrate of rank and dignity. Luther was early initiated into letters, and at the age of thirteen was sent to school at Magdeburg, and thence to Eisenach, in Thuringia, where he remained four years, producing the early indications of his future eminence.

In 1501 he was sent to the University of Erfurt, where he went through the usual courses of logic and philosophy. When twenty, he took a master's degree, and then lectured on Aristotle's physics, ethics, and other parts of philosophy. Afterward, at the instigation of his parents, he turned himself to the civil law, with a view of advancing himself to the bar, but was diverted from this pursuit by the following accident. Walking out into the fields one day, he was struck by lightning so as to fall to the ground, while a companion was killed by his side; and this affected him so sensibly, that, without communicating his purpose to any of his friends, he withdrew himself from the world, and retired into the order of the hermits of St. Augustine.

Here he employed himself in reading St. Augustine and the schoolmen; but in turning over the leaves of the library, he accidentally found a copy of the Latin Bible, which he had never seen before. This raised his curiosity to a high degree: he read it over very greedily, and was amazed to find what a small portion of the Scriptures was rehearsed to the people.

He made his profession in the monastery of Erfurt, after he had been a novice one year; and he took priest's orders, and celebrated his first Mass in 1507. The year after, he was removed from the convent of Erfurt to the University of Wittenberg; for this university being just founded, nothing was thought more likely to bring it into immediate repute and credit, than the authority and presence of a man so celebrated, for his great parts and learning, as Luther.

In this University of Erfurt, there was a certain aged man in the convent of the Augustines with whom Luther, being then of the same order, a friar Augustine, had conference upon divers things, especially touching remission of sins; which article the said aged father opened unto Luther; declaring that God's express commandment is that every man should particularly believe his sins to be forgiven him in Christ: and further said that this interpretation was confirmed by St. Bernard: "This is the testimony that the Holy Ghost giveth thee in thy heart, saying, thy sins are forgiven thee. For this is the opinion of the apostle, that man is freely justified by faith."

By these words Luther was not only strengthened, but was also instructed of the full meaning of St. Paul, who repeateth so many times this sentence, "We are justified by faith." And having read the expositions of many upon this place, he then perceived, as well by the discourse of the old man, as by the comfort he received in his spirit, the vanity of those interpretations, which he had read before, of the schoolmen. And so, by little and little, reading and comparing the sayings and examples of the prophets and apostles, with continual invocation of God, and the excitation of faith by force of prayer, he perceived that doctrine most evidently. Thus continued he his study at Erfurt the space of four years in the convent of the Augustines.

In 1512, seven convents of his order having a quarrel with their vicar-general, Luther was chosen to go to Rome to maintain their cause. At Rome he saw the pope and the court, and had an opportunity of observing also the manners of the clergy, whose hasty, superficial, and impious way of celebrating Mass, he has severely noted. As soon as he had adjusted the dispute which was the business of his journey, he returned to Wittenberg, and was created doctor of divinity, at the expense of Frederic, elector of Saxony; who had often heard him preach, was perfectly acquainted with his merit, and reverenced him highly.

He continued in the University of Wittenberg, where, as professor of divinity, he employed himself in the business of his calling. Here then he began in the most earnest manner to read lectures upon the sacred books: he explained the Epistle to the Romans, and the Psalms, which he cleared up and illustrated in a manner so entirely new, and so different from what had been pursued by former commentators, that "there seemed, after a long and dark night, a new day to arise, in the judgment of all pious and prudent men."

Luther diligently reduced the minds of men to the Son of God: as John the Baptist demonstrated the Lamb of God that took away the sins of the world, even so Luther, shining in the Church as the bright daylight after a long and dark night, expressly showed that sins are freely remitted for the love of the Son of God, and that we ought faithfully to embrace this bountiful gift.

His life was correspondent to his profession; and it plainly appeared that his words were no lip-labor, but proceeded from the very heart. This admiration of his holy life much allured the hearts of his auditors.

The better to qualify himself for the task he had undertaken, he had applied himself attentively to the Greek and Hebrew languages; and in this manner was he employed, when the general indulgences were published in 1517.

Leo X who succeeded Julius II in March, 1513, formed a design of building the magnificent Church of St. Peter's at Rome, which was, indeed, begun by Julius, but still required very large sums to be finished. Leo, therefore, in 1517 published general indulgences throughout all Europe, in favor of those who contribute any sum to the building of St. Peter's; and appointed persons in different countries to preach up these indulgences, and to receive money for them. These strange proceedings gave vast offence at Wittenberg, and particularly inflamed the pious zeal of Luther; who, being naturally warm and active, and in the present case unable to contain himself, was determined to declare against them at all adventures.

Upon the eve of All-saints, therefore, in 1517, he publicly fixed up, at the church next to the castle of that town, a thesis upon indulgences; in the beginning of which he challenged any one to oppose it either by writing or disputation. Luther's propositions about indulgences were no sooner published, than Tetzel, the Dominican friar, and commissioner for selling them, maintained and published at Frankfort, a thesis, containing a set of propositions directly contrary to them. He did more; he stirred up the clergy of his order against Luther; anathematized him from the pulpit, as a most damnable heretic; and burnt his thesis publicly at Frankfort. Tetzel's thesis was also burnt, in return, by the Lutherans at Wittenberg; but Luther himself disowned having had any hand in that procedure.

In 1518, Luther, though dissuaded from it by his friends, yet, to show obedience to authority, went to the monastery of St. Augustine, at Heidelberg, while the chapter was held; and here maintained, April 26, a dispute concerning "justification by faith"; which Bucer, who was present at, took down in writing, and afterward communicated to Beatus Rhenanus, not without the highest commendations.

In the meantime, the zeal of his adversaries grew every day more and more active against him; and he was at length accused to Leo X as a heretic. As soon as he returned therefore from Heidelberg, he wrote a letter to that pope, in the most submissive terms; and sent him, at the same time, an explication of his propositions about indulgences. This letter is dated on Trinity Sunday, 1518, and was accompanied with a protestation, wherein he declared that he did not pretend to advance or defend anything contrary to the Holy Scriptures, or to the doctrine of the fathers, received and observed by the Church of Rome, or to the canons and decretals of the popes: nevertheless, he thought he had the liberty either to approve or disapprove the opinions of St. Thomas, Bonaventure, and other schoolmen and canonists, which are not grounded upon any text.

The emperor Maximilian was equally solicitous with the pope about putting a stop to the propagation of Luther's opinions in Saxony; troublesome both to the Church and empire. Maximilian, therefore, applied to Leo, in a letter dated August 5, 1518, and begged him to forbid, by his authority, these useless, rash, and dangerous disputes; assuring him also that he would strictly execute in the empire whatever his holiness should enjoin.

In the meantime Luther, as soon as he understood what was transacting about him at Rome, used all imaginable means to prevent his being carried thither, and to obtain a hearing of his cause in Germany. The elector was also against Luther's going to Rome, and desired of Cardinal Cajetan, that he might be heard before him, as the pope's legate in Germany. Upon these addresses, the pope consented that the cause should be tried before Cardinal Cajetan, to whom he had given power to decide it.

Luther, therefore, set off immediately for Augsburg, and carried with him letters from the elector. He arrived here in October, 1518, and, upon an assurance of his safety, was admitted into the cardinal's presence. But Luther was soon convinced that he had more to fear from the cardinal's power than from disputations of any kind; and, therefore, apprehensive of being seized if he did not submit, withdrew from Augsburg upon the twentieth. But, before his departure, he published a formal appeal to the pope, and finding himself protected by the elector, continued to teach the same doctrines at Wittenberg, and sent a challenge to all the inquisitors to come and dispute with him.

As to Luther, Miltitius, the pope's chamberlain, had orders to require the elector to oblige him to retract, or to deny him his protection: but things were not now to be carried with so high a hand, Luther's credit being too firmly established. Besides, the emperor Maximilian happened to die upon the twelfth of this month, whose death greatly altered the face of affairs, and made the elector more able to determine Luther's fate. Miltitius thought it best, therefore, to try what could be done by fair and gentle means, and to that end came to some conference with Luther.

During all these treaties, the doctrine of Luther spread, and prevailed greatly; and he himself received great encouragement at home and abroad. The Bohemians about this time sent him a book of the celebrated John Huss, who had fallen a martyr in the work of reformation; and also letters, in which they exhorted him to constancy and perseverance, owning that the divinity which he taught was the pure, sound, and orthodox divinity. Many great and learned men had joined themselves to him.

In 1519, he had a famous dispute at Leipsic with John Eccius. But this dispute ended at length like all others, the parties not the least nearer in opinion, but more at enmity with each other's persons.

About the end of this year, Luther published a book, in which he contended for the Communion being celebrated in both kinds; which was condemned by the bishop of Misnia, January 24, 1520.

While Luther was laboring to excuse himself to the new emperor and the bishops of Germany, Eccius had gone to Rome, to solicit his condemnation; which, it may easily be conceived, was now become not difficult to be attained. Indeed the continual importunities of Luther's adversaries with Leo, caused him at length to publish a formal condemnation of him, and he did so accordingly, in a bull, dated June 15, 1520. This was carried into Germany, and published there by Eccius, who had solicited it at Rome; and who, together with Jerome Alexander, a person eminent for his learning and eloquence, was intrusted by the pope with the execution of it. In the meantime, Charles V of Spain, after he had set things to rights in the Low Countries, went into Germany, and was crowned emperor, October the twenty-first at Aix-la-Chapelle.

Martin Luther, after he had been first accused at Rome upon Maunday Thursday by the pope's censure, shortly after Easter speedeth his journey toward Worms, where the said Luther, appearing before the emperor and all the states of Germany, constantly stuck to the truth, defended himself, and answered his adversaries.

Luther was lodged, well entertained, and visited by many earls, barons, knights of the order, gentlemen, priests, and the commonalty, who frequented his lodging until night.

He came, contrary to the expectation of many, as well adversaries as others. His friends deliberated together, and many persuaded him not to adventure himself to such a present danger, considering how these beginnings answered not the faith of promise made. Who, when he had heard their whole persuasion and advice, answered in this wise: "As touching me, since I am sent for, I am resolved and certainly determined to enter Worms, in the name of our Lord Jesus Christ; yea, although I knew there were as many devils to resist me as there are tiles to cover the houses in Worms."

The next day, the herald brought him from his lodging to the emperor's court, where he abode until six o'clock, for that the princes were occupied in grave consultations; abiding there, and being environed with a great number of people, and almost smothered for the press that was there. Then after, when the princes were set, and Luther entered, Eccius, the official, spake in this manner: "Answer now to the Emperor's demand. Wilt thout maintain all thy books which thou hast acknowledged, or revoke any part of them, and submit thyself?"

Martin Luther answered modestly and lowly, and yet not without some stoutness of stomach, and Christian constancy. "Considering your sovereign majesty, and your honors, require a plain answer; this I say and profess as resolutely as I may, without doubting or sophistication, that if I be not convinced by testimonies of the Scriptures (for I believe not the pope, neither his general Councils, which have erred many times, and have been contrary to themselves), my conscience is so bound and captivated in these Scriptures and the Word of God, that I will not, nor may not revoke any manner of thing; considering it is not godly or lawful to do anything against conscience. Hereupon I stand and rest: I have not what else to say. God have mercy upon me!"

The princes consulted together upon this answer given by Luther; and when they had diligently examined the same, the prolucutor began to repel him thus:

"The Emperor's majesty requireth of thee a simple answer, either negative or affirmative, whether thou mindest to defend all thy works as Christian, or no?"

Then Luther, turning to the emperor and the nobles, besought them not to force or compel him to yield against his conscience, confirmed with the Holy Scriptures, without manifest arguments alleged to the contrary by his adversaries. "I am tied by the Scriptures."

Before the Diet of Worms was dissolved, Charles V caused an edict to be drawn up, which was dated the eighth of May, and decreed that Martin Luther be, agreeably to the sentence of the pope, henceforward looked upon as a member separated from the Church, a schismatic, and an obstinate and notorious heretic. While the bull of Leo X executed by Charles V was thundering throughout the empire, Luther was safely shut up in the castle of Wittenberg; but weary at length of his retirement, he appeared publicly again at Wittenberg, March 6, 1522, after he had been absent about ten months.

Luther now made open war with the pope and bishops; and, that he might make the people despise their authority as much as possible, he wrote one book against the pope's bull, and another against the order falsely called "The Order of Bishops." He published also a translation of the New Testament in the German tongue, which was afterward corrected by himself and Melancthon.

Affairs were now in great confusion in Germany; and they were not less so in Italy, for a quarrel arose between the pope and the emperor, during which Rome was twice taken, and the pope imprisoned. While the princes were thus employed in quarrelling with each other, Luther persisted in carrying on the work of the Reformation, as well by opposing the papists, as by combating the Anabaptists and other fanatical sects; which, having taken the advantage of his contest with the Church of Rome, had sprung up and established themselves in several places.

In 1527, Luther was suddenly seized with a coagulation of the blood about the heart, which had like to have put an end to his life. The troubles of Germany being not likely to have any end, the emperor was forced to call a diet at Spires, in 1529, to require the assistance of the princes of the empire against the Turks. Fourteen cities, viz., Strassburg, Nuremberg, Ulm, Constance, Retlingen, Windsheim, Memmingen, Lindow, Kempten, Hailbron, Isny, Weissemburg, Nortlingen, S. Gal, joined against the decree of the Diet protestation, which was put into writing, and published April, 1529. This was the famous protestation, which gave the name of "Protestants" to the reformers in Germany.

After this, the Protestant princes labored to make a firm league and enjoined the elector of Saxony and his allies to approve of what the Diet had done; but the deputies drew up an appeal, and the Protestants afterwards presented an apology for their "Confession"—that famous confession which was drawn up by the temperate Melancthon, as also the apology. These were signed by a variety of princes, and Luther had now nothing else to do, but to sit down and contemplate the mighty work he had finished: for that a single monk should be able to give the Church of Rome so rude a shock, that there needed but such another entirely to overthrow it, may be well esteemed a mighty work.

In 1533, Luther wrote a consolatory epistle to the citizens of Oschatz, who had suffered some hardships for adhering to the Augsburg confession of faith: and in 1534, the Bible translated by him into German was first printed, as the old privilege, dated at Bibliopolis, under the elector's own hand, shows; and it was published in the year after. He also published this year a book, "Against Masses and the Consecration of Priests."

In February, 1537, an assembly was held at Smalkald about matters of religion, to which Luther and Melancthon were called. At this meeting Luther was seized with so grievous an illness that there was no hope of his recovery. As he was carried along he made his will, in which he bequeathed his detestation of popery to his friends and brethren. In this manner was he employed until his death, which happened in 1546.

That year, accompanied by Melancthon, he paid a visit to his own country, which he had not seen for many years, and returned again in safety. But soon after, he was called thither again by the earls of Manfelt, to compose some differences which had arisen about their boundaries, where he was received by one hundred horsemen, or more, and conducted in a very honorable manner; but was at the same time so very ill that it was feared he would die. He said that these fits of sickness often came upon him, when he had any great business to undertake. Of this, however, he did not recover, but died in February 18, in his sixty-third year. A little before he expired, he admonished those that were about him to pray to God for the propagation of the Gospel, "Because," said he, "the Council of Trent, which had set once or twice, and the pope, will devise strange things against it." Feeling his fatal hour to approach, before nine o'clock in the morning, he commended himself to God with this devout prayer:

My heavenly Father, eternal and merciful God! Thou hast manifested unto me Thy dear Son, our Lord Jesus Christ. I have taught Him, I have known Him; I love Him as my life, my health and my redemption; Whom the wicked have persecuted, maligned, and with injury afflicted. Draw my soul to Thee.

After this he said as ensueth, thrice: "I commend my spirit into Thy hands, Thou hast redeemed me, O God of Truth! 'God so loved the world, that He gave His only begotten Son, that whosoever believeth in Him should not perish, but have life everlasting.'" Having repeated oftentimes his prayers, he was called to God. So praying, his innocent ghost peaceably was separated from the earthly body.

CHAPTER SIX

The Life and Story of the True Servant and Martyr of God, William Tyndale

We have now to enter into the story of the good martyr of God, William Tyndale; which William Tyndale, as he was a special organ of the Lord appointed, and as God's mattock to shake the inward roots and foundation of the pope's proud prelacy, so the great prince of darkness, with his impious imps, having a special malice against him, left no way unsought how craftily to entrap him, and falsely to betray him, and maliciously to spill his life, as by the process of his story here following may appear.

William Tyndale, the faithful minister of Christ, was born about the borders of Wales, and brought up from a child in the University of Oxford, where he, by long continuance, increased as well in the knowledge of tongues, and other liberal arts, as especially in the knowledge of the Scriptures, whereunto his mind was singularly addicted; insomuch that he, lying then in Magdalen Hall, read privily to certain students and fellows of Magdalen College some parcel of divinity; instructing them in the knowledge and truth of the Scriptures. His manners and conversation being correspondent to the same, were such that all they that knew him reputed him to be a man of most virtuous disposition, and of life unspotted.

Thus he, in the University of Oxford, increasing more and more in learning, and proceeding in degrees of the schools, spying his time, removed from thence to the University of Cambridge, where he likewise made his abode a certain space. Being now further ripened in the knowledge of God's Word, leaving that university, he resorted to one Master Welch, a knight of Gloucestershire, and was there schoolmaster to his children, and in good favor with his master. As this gentleman kept a good ordinary commonly at his table, there resorted to him many times sundry abbots, deans, archdeacons, with divers other doctors, and great beneficed men; who there, together with Master Tyndale sitting at the same table, did use many times to enter communication, and talk of learned men, as of Luther and of Erasmus; also of divers other controversies and questions upon the Scripture.

Then Master Tyndale, as he was learned and well practiced in God's matters, spared not to show unto them simply and plainly his judgment, and when they at any time did vary from Tyndale in opinions, he would show them in the Book, and lay plainly before them the open and manifest places of the Scriptures, to confute their errors, and confirm his sayings. And thus continued they for a certain season, reasoning and contending together divers times, until at length they waxed weary, and bare a secret grudge in their hearts against him.

As this grew on, the priests of the country, clustering together, began to grudge and storm against Tyndale, railing against him in alehouses and other places, affirming that his sayings were heresy; and accused him secretly to the chancellor, and others of the bishop's officers.

It followed not long after this that there was a sitting of the bishop's chancellor appointed, and warning was given to the priests to appear, amongst whom Master Tyndale was also warned to be there. And whether he had any misdoubt by their threatenings, or knowledge given him that they would lay some things to his charge, it is uncertain; but certain this is (as he himself declared), that he doubted their privy accusations; so that he by the way, in going thitherwards, cried in his mind heartily to God, to give him strength fast to stand in the truth of His Word.

When the time came for his appearance before the chancellor, he threatened him grievously, reviling and rating him as though he had been a dog, and laid to his charge many things whereof no accuser could be brought forth, notwithstanding that the priests of the country were there present. Thus Master Tyndale, escaping out of their hands, departed home, and returned to his master again.

There dwelt not far off a certain doctor, that he been chancellor to a bishop, who had been of old, familiar acquaintance with Master Tyndale, and favored him well; unto whom Master Tyndale went and opened his mind upon divers questions of the Scripture: for to him he durst be bold to disclose his heart. Unto whom the doctor said, "Do you not know that the pope is very Antichrist, whom the Scripture speaketh of? But beware what you say; for if you shall be perceived to be of that opinion, it will cost you your life."

Not long after, Master Tyndale happened to be in the company of a certain divine, recounted for a learned man, and, in communing and disputing with him, he drove him to that issue, that the said great doctor burst out into these blasphemous words, "We were better to be without God's laws than the pope's." Master Tyndale, hearing this, full of godly zeal, and not bearing that blasphemous saying, replied, "I defy the pope, and all his laws;" and added,

"If God spared him life, ere many years he would cause a boy that driveth the plough to know more of the Scripture than he did."

The grudge of the priests increasing still more and more against Tyndale, they never ceased barking and rating at him, and laid many things sorely to his charge, saying that he was a heretic. Being so molested and vexed, he was constrained to leave that country, and to seek another place; and so coming to Master Welch, he desired him, of his good will, that he might depart from him, saying: "Sir, I perceive that I shall not be suffered to tarry long here in this country, neither shall you be able, though you would, to keep me out of the hands of the spirituality; what displeasure might grow to you by keeping me, God knoweth; for the which I should be right sorry."

So that in fine, Master Tyndale, with the good will of his master, departed, and eftsoons came up to London, and there preached a while, as he had done in the country.

Bethinking himself of Cuthbert Tonstal, then bishop of London, and especially of the great commendation of Erasmus, who, in his annotations, so extolleth the said Tonstal for his learning, Tyndale thus cast with himself, that if he might attain unto his service, he were a happy man. Coming to Sir Henry Guilford, the king's comptroller, and bringing with him an oration of Isocrates, which he had translated out of Greek into English, he desired him to speak to the said bishop of London for him; which he also did; and willed him moreover to write an epistle to the bishop, and to go himself with him. This he did, and delivered his epistle to a servant of his, named William Hebilthwait, a man of his old acquaintance. But God, who secretly disposeth the course of things, saw that was not best for Tyndale's purpose, nor for the profit of His Church, and therefore gave him to find little favor in the bishop's sight; the answer of whom was this: his house was full; he had more than he could well find: and he advised him to seek in London abroad, where, he said, he could lack no service.

Being refused of the bishop he came to Humphrey Mummuth, alderman of London, and besought him to help him: who the same time took him into his house, where the said Tyndale lived (as Mummuth said) like a good priest, studying both night and day. He would eat but sodden meat by his good will, nor drink but small single beer. He was never seen in the house to wear linen about him, all the space of his being there.

And so remained Master Tyndale in London almost a year, marking with himself the course of the world, and especially the demeanor of the preachers, how they boasted themselves, and set up their authority; beholding also the pomp of the prelates, with other things more, which greatly misliked him; insomuch that he understood not only that there was no room in the bishop's house for him to translate the New Testament, but also that there was no place to do it in all England.

Therefore, having by God's providence some aid ministered unto him by Humphrey Mummuth, and certain other good men, he took his leave of the realm, and departed into Germany, where the good man, being inflamed with a tender care and zeal of his country, refused no travail nor diligence, how, by all means possible, to reduce his brethren and countrymen of England to the same taste and understanding of God's holy Word and verity, which the Lord had endued him withal. Whereupon, considering in his mind, and conferring also with John Frith, Tyndale thought with himself no way more to conduce thereunto, than if the Scripture were turned into the vulgar speech, that the poor people might read and see the simple plain Word of God. He perceived that it was not possible to establish the lay people in any truth, except the Scriptures were so plainly laid before their eyes in their mother tongue that they might see the meaning of the text; for else, whatsoever truth should be taught them, the enemies of the truth would quench it, either with reasons of sophistry, and traditions of their own making, founded without all ground of Scripture; or else juggling with the text, expounding it in such a sense as it were impossible to gather of the text, if the right meaning thereof were seen.

Master Tyndale considered this only, or most chiefly, to be the cause of all mischief in the Church, that the Scriptures of God were hidden from the people's eyes; for so long the abominable doings and idolatries maintained by the pharisaical clergy could not be espied; and therefore all their labor was with might and main to keep it down, so that either it should not be read at all, or if it were, they would darken the right sense with the mist of their sophistry, and so entangle those who rebuked or despised their abominations; wresting the Scripture unto their own purpose, contrary unto the meaning of the text, they would so delude the unlearned lay people, that though thou felt in thy heart, and wert sure that all were false that they said, yet couldst thou not solve their subtle riddles.

For these and such other considerations this good man was stirred up of God to translate the Scripture into his mother tongue, for the profit of the simple people of his country; first setting in hand with the New Testament, which came forth in print about A.D. 1525. Cuthbert Tonstal, bishop of London, with Sir Thomas More, being sore aggrieved, despised how to destroy that false erroneous translation, as they called it.

It happened that one Augustine Packington, a mercer, was then at Antwerp, where the bishop was. This man favored Tyndale, but showed the contrary unto the bishop. The bishop, being desirous to bring his purpose to pass, communed how that he would gladly buy the New Testaments. Packington hearing him say so, said, "My lord! I can do more in this matter than most merchants that be here, if it be your pleasure; for I know the Dutchmen and strangers that have brought them of Tyndale, and have them here to sell; so that if it be your lordship's pleasure, I must disburse money to pay for them, or else I cannot have them: and so I will assure you to have every book of them that is printed and unsold." The bishop, thinking he had God "by the toe," said, "Do your diligence, gentle Master Packington! get them for me, and I will pay whatsoever they cost; for I intend to burn and destroy them all at Paul's Cross." This Augustine Packington went unto William Tyndale, and declared the whole matter, and so, upon compact made between them, the bishop of London had the books, Packington had the thanks, and Tyndale had the money.

After this, Tyndale corrected the same New Testaments again, and caused them to be newly imprinted, so that they came thick and threefold over into England. When the bishop perceived that, he sent for Packington, and said to him, "How cometh this, that there are so many New Testaments abroad? You promised me that you would buy them all." Then answered Packington, "Surely, I bought all that were to be had, but I perceive they have printed more since. I see it will never be better so long as they have letters and stamps: wherefore you were best to buy the stamps too, and so you shall be sure," at which answer the bishop smiled, and so the matter ended.

In short space after, it fortuned that George Constantine was apprehended by Sir Thomas More, who was then chancellor of England, as suspected of certain heresies. Master More asked of him, saying, "Constantine! I would have thee be plain with me in one thing that I will ask; and I promise thee I will show thee favor in all other things whereof thou art accused. There is beyond the sea, Tyndale, Joye, and a great many of you: I know they cannot live without help. There are some that succor them with money; and thou, being one of them, hadst thy part thereof, and therefore knowest whence it came. I pray thee, tell me, who be they that help them thus?" "My lord," quoth Constantine, "I will tell you truly: it is the bishop of London that hath holpen us, for he hath bestowed among us a great deal of money upon New Testaments to burn them; and that hath been, and yet is, our only succor and comfort." "Now by my troth," quoth More, "I think even the same; for so much I told the bishop before he went about it."

After that, Master Tyndale took in hand to translate the Old Testament, finishing the five books of Moses, with sundry most learned and godly prologues most worthy to be read and read again by all good Christians. These books being sent over into England, it cannot be spoken what a door of light they opened to the eyes of the whole English nation, which before were shut up in darkness.

At his first departing out of the realm he took his journey into Germany, where he had conference with Luther and other learned men; after he had continued there a certain season he came down into the Netherlands, and had his most abiding in the town of Antwerp.

The godly books of Tyndale, and especially the New Testament of his translation, after that they began to come into men's hands, and to spread abroad, wrought great and singular profit to the godly; but the ungodly (envying and disdaining that the people should be anything wiser than they and, fearing lest by the shining beams of truth, their works of darkness should be discerned) began to stir with no small ado.

At what time Tyndale had translated Deuteronomy, minding to print the same at Hamburg, he sailed thitherward; upon the coast of Holland he suffered shipwreck, by which he lost all his books, writings, and copies, his money and his time, and so was compelled to begin all again. He came in another ship to

Hamburg, where, at his appointment, Master Coverdale tarried for him, and helped him in the translating of the whole five books of Moses, from Easter until December, in the house of a worshipful widow, Mistress Margaret Van Emmerson, A.D. 1529; a great sweating sickness being at the same time in the town. So, having dispatched his business at Hamburg, he returned to Antwerp.

When God's will was, that the New Testament in the common tongue should come abroad, Tyndale, the translator thereof, added to the latter end a certain epistle, wherein he desired them that were learned to amend, if ought were found amiss. Wherefore if there had been any such default deserving correction, it had been the part of courtesy and gentleness, for men of knowledge and judgment to have showed their learning therein, and to have redressed what was to be amended. But the clergy, not willing to have that book prosper, cried out upon it, that there were a thousand heresies in it, and that it was not to be corrected, but utterly to be suppressed. Some said it was not possible to translate the Scriptures into English; some that it was not lawful for the lay people to have it in their mother tongue; some, that it would make them all heretics. And to the intent to induce the temporal rulers unto their purpose, they said it would make the people to rebel against the king.

All this Tyndale himself, in his prologue before the first book of Moses, declareth; showing further what great pains were taken in examining that translation, and comparing it with their own imaginations, that with less labor, he supposeth, they might have translated a great part of the Bible; showing moreover that they scanned and examined every title and point in such sort, and so narrowly, that there was not one *i* therein, but if it lacked a prick over his head, they did note it, and numbered it unto the ignorant people for a heresy.

So great were then the froward devices of the English clergy (who should have been the guides of light unto the people), to drive the people from the knowledge of the Scripture, which neither they would translate themselves, nor yet abide it to be translated of others; to the intent (as Tyndale saith) that the world being kept still in darkness, they might sit in the consciences of the people through vain superstition and false doctrine, to satisfy their ambition, and insatiable covetousness, and to exalt their own honor above king and emperor.

The bishops and prelates never rested before they had brought the king to their consent; by reason whereof, a proclamation in all haste was devised and set forth under public authority, that the Testament of Tyndale's translation was inhibited—which was about A.D. 1537. And not content herewith, they proceeded further, how to entangle him in their nets, and to bereave him of his life; which how they brought to pass, now it remaineth to be declared.

In the registers of London it appeareth manifest how that the bishops and Sir Thomas More having before them such as had been at Antwerp, most studiously would search and examine all things belonging to Tyndale, where and with whom he hosted, whereabouts stood the house, what was his stature, in what apparel he went, what resort he had; all which things when they had diligently learned then began they to work their feats.

William Tyndale, being in the town of Antwerp, had been lodged about one whole year in the house of Thomas Pointz, an Englishman, who kept a house of English merchants. Came thither one out of England, whose name was Henry Philips, his father being customer of Poole, a comely fellow, like as he had been a gentleman having a servant with him: but wherefore he came, or for what purpose he was sent thither, no man could tell.

Master Tyndale divers times was desired forth to dinner and support amongst merchants; by means whereof this Henry Philips became acquainted with him, so that within short space Master Tyndale had a great confidence in him, and brought him to his lodging, to the house of Thomas Pointz; and had him also once or twice with him to dinner and supper, and further entered such friendship with him, that through his procurement he lay in the same house of the said Pointz; to whom he showed moreover his books, and other secrets of his study, so little did Tyndale then mistrust this traitor.

But Pointz, having no great confidence in the fellow, asked Master Tyndale how he came acquainted with this Philips. Master Tyndale answered, that he was an honest man, handsomely learned, and very conformable. Pointz, perceiving that he bare such favor to him, said no more, thinking that he was brought acquainted with him by some friend of his. The said Philips, being in the town three or four days, upon a time desired Pointz to walk with him forth of the town to show him the commodities thereof, and in walking together without the town, had communication of divers things, and some of the king's affairs; by which talk Pointz as yet suspected nothing. But after, when the time was past, Pointz perceived this to be the mind of Philips, to feel whether the said Pointz might, for lucre of money, help him to his purpose, for he perceived before that Philips was monied, and would that Pointz should think no less. For he had desired Pointz before to help him to divers things; and such things as he named, he required might be of the best, "for," said he, "I have money enough."

Philips went from Antwerp to the court of Brussels, which is from thence twenty-four English miles, whence he brought with him to Antwerp, the procurator-general, who is the emperor's attorney, with certain other officers.

Within three or four days, Pointz went forth to the town of Barois, being eighteen English miles from Antwerp, where he had business to do for the space of a month or six weeks; and in the time of his absence Henry Philips came again to Antwerp, to the house of Pointz, and coming in, spake with his wife, asking whether Master Tyndale were within. Then went he forth again and set the officers whom he had brought with him from Brussels, in the street, and about the door. About noon he came again, and went to Master Tyndale, and desired him to lend him forty shillings; "for," said he, "I lost my purse this morning, coming over at the passage between this and Mechlin." So Master Tyndale took him forty shillings, which was easy to be had of him, if he had it; for in the wily subtleties of this world he was simple and inexpert.

Then said Philips, "Master Tyndale! you shall be my guest here this day." "No," said Master Tyndale, "I go forth this day to dinner, and you shall go with me, and be my guest, where you shall be welcome."

So when it was dinner time, Master Tyndale went forth with Philips, and at the going forth of Pointz's house, was a long narrow entry, so that two could not go in front. Master Tyndale would have put Philips before him, but Philips would in no wise, but put Master Tyndale before, for that he pretended to show great humanity. So Master Tyndale, being a man of no great stature, went before, and Philips, a tall, comely person, followed behind him; who had set officers on either side of the door upon two seats, who might see who came in the entry. Philips pointed with his finger over Master Tyndale's head down to him, that the officers might see that it was he whom they should take. The officers afterwards told Pointz, when they had laid him in prison, that they pitied to see his simplicity. They brought him to the emperor's attorney, where he dined. Then came the procurator-general to the house of Pointz, and sent away all that was there of Master Tyndale's, as well his books as other things; and from thence Tyndale was had to the castle of Vilvorde, eighteen English miles from Antwerp.

Master Tyndale, remaining in prison, was proffered an advocate and a procurator; the which he refused, saying that he would make answer for himself. He had so preached to them who had him in charge, and such as was there conversant with him in the Castle that they reported of him, that if he were not a good Christian man, they knew not whom they might take to be one.

At last, after much reasoning, when no reason would serve, although he deserved no death, he was condemned by virtue of the emperor's decree, made in the assembly at Augsburg. Brought forth to the place of execution, he was tied to the stake, strangled by the hangman, and afterwards consumed with fire, at the town of Vilvorde, A.D. 1536; crying at the stake with a fervent zeal, and a loud voice, "Lord! open the king of England's eyes."

Such was the power of his doctrine, and the sincerity of his life, that during the time of his imprisonment (which endured a year and a half), he converted, it is said, his keeper, the keeper's daughter, and others of his household.

As touching his translation of the New Testament, because his enemies did so much carp at it, pretending it to be full of heresies, he wrote to John Frith, as followeth, "I call God to record against the day we shall appear before our Lord Jesus, that I never altered one syllable of God's Word against my conscience, nor would do this day, if all that is in earth, whether it be honor, pleasure, or riches, might be given me."

CHAPTER SEVEN

An Account of the Life of John Calvin

This reformer was born at Noyon in Picardy, July 10, 1509. He was instructed in grammar, learning at Paris under Maturinus Corderius, and studied philosophy in the College of Montaign under a Spanish professor.

His father, who discovered many marks of his early piety, particularly in his reprehensions of the vices of his companions, designed him at first for the Church, and got him presented, May 21, 1521, to the chapel of Notre Dame de la Gesine, in the Church of Noyon. In 1527 he was presented to the rectory of Marseille, which he exchanged in 1529 for the rectory of Pont l'Eveque, near Noyon. His father afterward changed his resolution, and would have him study law; to which Calvin, who, by reading the Scriptures, had conceived a dislike to the superstitions of popery, readily consented, and resigned the chapel of Gesine and the rectory of Pont l'Eveque, in 1534. He made a great progress in that science, and improved no less in the knowledge of divinity by his private studies. At Bourges he applied to the Greek tongue, under the direction of Professor Wolmar.

His father's death having called him back to Noyon, he stayed there a short time, and then went to Paris, where a speech of Nicholas Cop, rector of the University of Paris, of which Calvin furnished the materials, having greatly displeased the Sorbonne and the parliament, gave rise to a persecution against the Protestants, and Calvin, who narrowly escaped being taken in the College of Forteret, was forced to retire to Xaintonge, after having had the honor to be introduced to the queen of Navarre, who had raised this first storm against the Protestants.

Calvin returned to Paris in 1534. This year the reformed met with severe treatment, which determined him to leave France, after publishing a treatise against those who believed that departed souls are in a kind of sleep. He retired to Basel, where he studied Hebrew: at this time he published his Institutions of the Christian Religion; a work well adapted to spread his fame, though he himself was desirous of living in obscurity. It is dedicated to the French king, Francis I. Calvin next wrote an apology for the Protestants who were burnt for their religion in France. After the publication of this work, Calvin went to Italy to pay a visit to the duchess of Ferrara, a lady of eminent piety, by whom he was very kindly received.

From Italy he came back to France, and having settled his private affairs, he proposed to go to Strassburg or Basel, in company with his sole surviving brother, Antony Calvin; but as the roads were not safe on account of the war, except through the duke of Savoy's territories, he chose that road. "This was a particular direction of Providence," says Bayle; "it was his destiny that he should settle at Geneva, and when he was wholly intent upon going farther, he found himself detained by an order from heaven, if I may so speak."

At Geneva, Calvin therefore was obliged to comply with the choice which the consistory and magistrates made of him, with the consent of the people, to be one of their ministers, and professor of divinity. He wanted to undertake only this last office, and not the other; but in the end he was obliged to take both upon him, in August, 1536. The year following, he made all the people declare, upon oath, their assent to the confession of faith, which contained a renunciation of popery. He next intimated that he could not submit to a regula-tion which the canton of Berne had lately made. Whereupon the syndics of Geneva summoned an assembly of the people; and it was ordered that Calvin, Farel, and another minister should leave the town in a few days, for refusing to administer the Sacrament.

Calvin retired to Strassburg, and established a French church in that city, of which he was the first minister: he was also appointed to be professor of divinity there. Meanwhile the people of Geneva entreated him so earnestly to return to them that at last he consented, and arrived September 13, 1541, to the great satisfaction both of the people and the magistrates; and the first thing he did, after his arrival, was to establish a form of church discipline, and a consistorial jurisdiction, invested with power of inflicting censures and canoni-cal punishments, as far as excommunication, inclusively.

It has long been the delight of both infidels and some professed Christians, when they wish to bring odium upon the opinions of Calvin, to refer to his agency in the death of Michael Servetus. This action is used on all occasions by those who have been unable to overthrow his opinions, as a conclusive argument against his whole system. "Calvin burnt Servetus!—Calvin burnt Servetus!" is a good proof with a certain class of reasoners, that the doctrine of the Trinity is not true—that divine sovereignty is Antiscriptural,—and Christianity a cheat.

We have no wish to palliate any act of Calvin's which is manifestly wrong.

All his proceedings, in relation to the unhappy affair of Servetus, we think, cannot be defended. Still it should be remembered that the true principles of religious toleration were very little understood in the time of Calvin. All the other reformers then living approved of Calvin's conduct. Even the gentle and amiable Melancthon expressed himself in relation to this affair, in the following manner. In a letter addressed to Bullinger, he says, "I have read your statement respecting the blasphemy of Servetus, and praise your piety and judgment; and am persuaded that the Council of Geneva has done right in putting to death this obstinate man, who would never have ceased his blasphemies. I am astonished that any one can be found to disapprove of this proceeding." Farel expressly says, that "Servetus deserved a capital punishment." Bucer did not hesitate to declare, that "Servetus deserved something worse than death."

The truth is, although Calvin had some hand in the arrest and imprisonment of Servetus, he was unwilling that he should be burnt at all. "I desire," says he, "that the severity of the punishment should be remitted." "We endeavored to commute the kind of death, but in vain." "By wishing to mitigate the severity of the punishment," says Farel to Calvin, "you discharge the office of a friend towards your greatest enemy." "That Calvin was the instigator of the magistrates that Servetus might be burned," says Turritine, "historians neither anywhere affirm, nor does it appear from any considerations. Nay, it is certain, that he, with the college of pastors, dissuaded from that kind of punishment."

It has been often asserted, that Calvin possessed so much influence with the magistrates of Geneva that he might have obtained the release of Servetus, had he not been desirous of his destruction. This however, is not true. So far from it, that Calvin was himself once banished from Geneva, by these very magistrates, and often opposed their arbitrary measures in vain. So little desirous was Calvin of procuring the death of Servetus that he warned him of his danger, and suffered him to remain several weeks at Geneva, before he was arrested. But his language, which was then accounted blasphemous, was the cause of his imprisonment. When in prison, Calvin visited him, and used every argument to persuade him to retract his horrible blasphemies, without reference to his peculiar sentiments. This was the extent of Calvin's agency in this unhappy affair.

It cannot, however, be denied, that in this instance, Calvin acted contrary to the benignant spirit of the Gospel. It is better to drop a tear over the inconsistency of human nature, and to bewail those infirmities which cannot be justified. He declared he acted conscientiously, and publicly justified the act.

It was the opinion, that erroneous religious principles are punishable by the civil magistrate, that did the mischief, whether at Geneva, in Transylvania, or in Britain; and to this, rather than to Trinitarianism, or Unitarianism, it ought to be imputed.

After the death of Luther, Calvin exerted great sway over the men of that notable period. He was influential in France, Italy, Germany, Holland, England, and Scotland. Two thousand one hundred and fifty reformed congregations were organized, receiving from him their preachers.

Calvin, triumphant over all his enemies, felt his death drawing near. Yet he continued to exert himself in every way with youthful energy. When about to lie down in rest, he drew up his will, saying: "I do testify that I live and purpose to die in this faith which God has given me through His Gospel, and that I have no other dependence for salvation than the free choice which is made of me by Him. With my whole heart I embrace His mercy, through which all my sins are covered, for Christ's sake, and for the sake of His death and sufferings. According to the measure of grace granted unto me, I have taught this pure, simple Word, by sermons, by deeds, and by expositions of this Scripture. In all my battles with the enemies of the truth I have not used sophistry, but have fought the good fight squarely and directly."

May 27, 1564, was the day of his release and blessed journey home. He was in his fifty-fifth year.

That a man who had acquired so great a reputation and such an authority, should have had but a salary of one hundred crowns, and refuse to accept more; and after living fifty-five years with the utmost frugality should leave but three hundred crowns to his heirs, including the value of his library, which sold very dear, is something so heroical, that one must have lost all feeling not to admire. When Calvin took his leave of Strassburg, to return to Geneva, they wanted to continue to him the privileges of a freeman of their town, and the revenues of a prebend, which had been assigned to him; the former he accepted, but absolutely refused the other. He carried one of the brothers with him to Geneva, but he never took any pains to get him preferred to an honorable post, as any other possessed of his credit would have done. He took care indeed of the honor of his brother's family, by getting him freed from an adultress, and obtaining leave to him to marry again; but even his enemies relate that he made him learn the trade of a bookbinder, which he followed all his life after.

CALVIN AS A FRIEND OF CIVIL LIBERTY

The Rev. Dr. Wisner, in his late discourse at Plymouth, on the anniversary of the landing of the Pilgrims, made the following assertion: "Much as the name of Calvin has been scoffed at and loaded with reproach by many sons of freedom, there is not an historical proposition more susceptible of complete demonstration than this, that no man has lived to whom the world is under greater obligations for the freedom it now enjoys, than John Calvin."

CHAPTER EIGHT

*An Account of the Persecutions in Scotland
During the Reign of King Henry the Eighth*

L ike as there was no place, either of Germany, Italy, or France, wherein there were not some branches sprung out of that most fruitful root of Luther; so likewise was not this isle of Britain without his fruit and branches. Amongst whom was Patrick Hamilton, a Scotchman born of high and noble stock, and of the king's blood, of excellent towardness, twenty-three years of age, called abbot of Ferne. Coming out of his country with three companions to seek godly learning, he went to the University of Marburg in Germany, which university was then newly erected by Philip, Landgrave of Hesse.

During his residence here, he became intimately acquainted with those eminent lights of the Gospel, Martin Luther and Philip Melancthon; from whose writings and doctrines he strongly attached himself to the Protestant religion.

The archbishop of St. Andrews (who was a rigid papist) learning of Mr. Hamilton's proceedings, caused him to be seized, and being brought before him, after a short examination relative to his religious principles, he committed him a prisoner to the castle, at the same time ordering him to be confined in the most loathsome part of the prison.

The next morning Mr. Hamilton was brought before the bishop, and several others, for examination, when the principal articles exhibited against him were, his publicly disapproving of pilgrimages, purgatory, prayers to saints, for the dead, etc.

These articles Mr. Hamilton acknowledged to be true, in consequence of which he was immediately condemned to be burnt; and that his condemnation might have the greater authority, they caused it to be subscribed by all those of any note who were present, and to make the number as considerable as possible, even admitted the subscription of boys who were sons of the nobility.

So anxious was this bigoted and persecuting prelate for the destruction of Mr. Hamilton, that he ordered his sentence to be put in execution on the afternoon of the very day it was pronounced. He was accordingly led to the place appointed for the horrid tragedy, and was attended by a prodigious number of spectators. The greatest part of the multitude would not believe it was intended he should be put to death, but that it was only done to frighten him, and thereby bring him over to embrace the principles of the Romish religion.

When he arrived at the stake, he kneeled down, and, for some time prayed with great fervency. After this he was fastened to the stake, and the fagots placed round him. A quantity of gunpowder having been placed under his arms was first set on fire which scorched his left hand and one side of his face, but did no material injury, neither did it communicate with the fagots. In consequence of this, more powder and combustible matter were brought, which being set on fire took effect, and the fagots being kindled, he called out, with an audible voice: "Lord Jesus, receive my spirit! How long shall darkness overwhelm this realm? And how long wilt Thou suffer the tyranny of these men?"

The fire burning slow put him to great torment; but he bore it with Christian magnanimity. What gave him the greatest pain was, the clamor of some wicked men set on by the friars, who frequently cried, "Turn, thou heretic; call upon our Lady; say, Salve Regina, etc." To whom he replied, "Depart from me, and trouble me not, ye messengers of Satan." One Campbell, a friar, who was the ringleader, still continuing to interrupt him by opprobrious language; he said to him, "Wicked man, God forgive thee." After which, being prevented from further speech by the violence of the smoke, and the rapidity of the flames, he resigned up his soul into the hands of Him who gave it.

This steadfast believer in Christ suffered martyrdom in the year 1527.

One Henry Forest, a young inoffensive Benedictine, being charged with speaking respectfully of the above Patrick Hamilton, was thrown into prison; and, in confessing himself to a friar, owned that he thought Hamilton a good man; and that the articles for which he was sentenced to die, might be defended. This being revealed by the friar, it was received as evidence; and the poor Benedictine was sentenced to be burnt.

Whilst consultation was held, with regard to the manner of his execution, John Lindsay, one of the archbishop's gentlemen, offered his advice, to burn Friar Forest in some cellar; "for," said he, "the smoke of Patrick Hamilton hath infected all those on whom it blew."

This advice was taken, and the poor victim was rather suffocated, than burnt.

The next who fell victims for professing the truth of the Gospel, were David Stratton and Norman Gourlay.

When they arrived at the fatal spot, they both kneeled down, and prayed for some time with great fervency. They then arose, when Stratton, addressing himself to the spectators, exhorted them to lay aside their superstitious and idolatrous notions, and employ their time in seeking the true light of the Gospel. He would have said more, but was prevented by the officers who attended.

Their sentence was then put into execution, and they cheerfully resigned up their souls to that God who gave them, hoping, through the merits of the great Redeemer, for a glorious resurrection to life immortal. They suffered in the year 1534.

The martyrdoms of the two before-mentioned persons, were soon followed by that of Mr. Thomas Forret, who, for a considerable time, had been dean of the Romish Church; Killor and Beverage, two blacksmiths; Duncan Simson, a priest; and Robert Forrester, a gentleman. They were all burnt together, on the Castle-hill at Edinburgh, the last day of February, 1538.

The year following the martyrdoms of the before-mentioned persons, viz. 1539, two others were apprehended on a suspicion of heresy; namely, Jerome Russell and Alexander Kennedy, a youth about eighteen years of age.

These two persons, after being some time confined in prison, were brought before the archbishop for examination. In the course of which Russell, being a very sensible man, reasoned learnedly against his accusers; while they in return made use of very opprobrious language.

The examination being over, and both of them deemed heretics, the archbishop pronounced the dreadful sentence of death, and they were immediately delivered over to the secular power in order for execution.

The next day they were led to the place appointed for them to suffer; in their way to which, Russell, seeing his fellow-sufferer have the appearance of timidity in his countenance, thus addressed him: "Brother, fear not; greater is He that is in us, than He that is in the world. The pain that we are to suffer is short, and shall be light; but our joy and consolation shall never have an end. Let us, therefore, strive to enter into our Master and Savior's joy, by the same straight way which He hath taken before us. Death cannot hurt us, for it is already destroyed by Him, for whose sake we are now going to suffer."

When they arrived at the fatal spot, they both kneeled down and prayed for some time; after which being fastened to the stake, and the fagots lighted, they cheerfully resigned their souls into the hands of Him who gave them, in full hopes of an everlasting reward in the heavenly mansions.

AN ACCOUNT OF THE LIFE, SUFFERINGS, AND DEATH OF MR. GEORGE WISHART, WHO WAS STRANGLED AND AFTERWARD BURNED, IN SCOTLAND, FOR PROFESSING THE TRUTH OF THE GOSPEL

About the year of our Lord 1543, there was, in the University of Cambridge, one Master George Wishart, commonly called Master George of Be-net's College, a man of tall stature, polled-headed, and on the same a round French cap of the best; judged to be of melancholy complexion by his physiognomy, black-haired, long-bearded, comely of personage, well spoken after his country of Scotland, courteous, lowly, lovely, glad to teach, desirous to learn, and well travelled; having on him for his clothing a frieze gown to the shoes, a black millian fustian doublet, and plain black hosen, coarse new canvas for his shirts, and white falling bands and cuffs at his hands.

He was a man modest, temperate, fearing God, hating covetousness; for his charity had never end, night, noon, nor day; he forbare one meal in three, one day in four for the most part, except something to comfort nature. He lay hard upon a puff of straw and coarse, new canvas sheets, which, when he changed, he gave away. He had commonly by his bedside a tub of water, in the which (his people being in bed, the candle put out and all quiet) he used to bathe himself. He loved me tenderly, and I him. He taught with great modesty and gravity, so that some of his people thought him severe, and would have slain him; but the Lord was his defence. And he, after due correction for their malice, by good exhortation amended them and went his way. Oh, that the Lord had left him to me, his poor boy, that he might have finished what he had begun! for he went into Scotland with divers of the nobility, that came for a treaty to King Henry.

In 1543, the archbishop of St. Andrews made a visitation into various parts of his diocese, where several persons were informed against at Perth for heresy. Among those the following were condemned to die, viz. William Anderson, Robert Lamb, James Finlayson, James Hunter, James Raveleson, and Helen Stark.

The accusations laid against these respective persons were as follow: The four first were accused of having hung up the image of St. Francis, nailing ram's horns on his head, and fastening a cow's tail to his rump; but the principal matter on which they were condemned was having regaled themselves with a goose on fast day.

James Reveleson was accused of having ornamented his house with the three crowned diadem of Peter, carved in wood, which the archbishop conceived to be done in mockery to his cardinal's cap.

Helen Stark was accused of not having accustomed herself to pray to the Virgin Mary, more especially during the time she was in childbed.

On these respective accusations they were all found guilty, and immediately received sentence of death; the four men, for eating the goose, to be hanged; James Raveleson to be burnt; and the woman, with her sucking infant, to be put into a sack and drowned.

The four men, with the woman and the child, suffered at the same time, but James Raveleson was not executed until some days after.

The martyrs were carried by a great band of armed men (for they feared rebellion in the town except they had their men of war) to the place of execution, which was common to all thieves, and that to make their cause appear more odious to the people. Every one comforting another, and assuring themselves that they should sup together in the Kingdom of Heaven that night, they commended themselves to God, and died constantly in the Lord.

The woman desired earnestly to die with her husband, but she was not suffered; yet, following him to the place of execution, she gave him comfort, exhorting him to perseverance and patience for Christ's sake, and, parting from him with a kiss, said, "Husband, rejoice, for we have lived together many joyful days; but this day, in which we must die, ought to be most joyful unto us both, because we must have joy forever; therefore I will not bid you good night, for we shall suddenly meet with joy in the Kingdom of Heaven." The woman, after that, was taken to a place to be drowned, and albeit she had a child sucking on her breast, yet this moved nothing in the unmerciful hearts of the enemies. So, after she had commended her children to the neighbors of the town for God's sake, and the sucking bairn was given to the nurse, she sealed up the truth by her death.

Being desirous of propagating the true Gospel in his own country George Wishart left Cambridge in 1544, and on his arrival in Scotland he first preached at Montrose, and afterwards at Dundee. In this last place he made a public exposition of the Epistle to the Romans, which he went through with such grace and freedom, as greatly alarmed the papists.

In consequence of this, (at the instigation of Cardinal Beaton, the arch-bishop of St. Andrews) one Robert Miln, a principal man at Dundee, went to the church where Wishart preached, and in the middle of his discourse publicly told him not to trouble the town any more, for he was determined not to suffer it.

This sudden rebuff greatly surprised Wishart, who, after a short pause, looking sorrowfully on the speaker and the audience, said: "God is my witness, that I never minded your trouble but your comfort; yea, your trouble is more grievous to me than it is to yourselves: but I am assured to refuse God's Word, and to chase from you His messenger, shall not preserve you from trouble, but shall bring you into it: for God shall send you ministers that shall fear neither burning nor banishment. I have offered you the Word of salvation. With the hazard of my life I have remained among you; now you yourselves refuse me; and I must leave my innocence to be declared by my God. If it be long prosperous with you, I am not led by the Spirit of truth; but if unlooked-for troubles come upon you, acknowledge the cause and turn to God, who is gracious and merciful. But if you turn not at the first warning, He will visit you with fire and sword." At the close of this speech he left the pulpit, and retired.

After this he went into the west of Scotland, where he preached God's Word, which was gladly received by many.

A short time after this Mr. Wishart received intelligence that the plague had broken out in Dundee. It began four days after he was prohibited from preaching there, and raged so extremely that it was almost beyond credit how many died in the space of twenty-four hours. This being related to him, he, notwithstanding the importunity of his friends to detain him, determined to go there, saying: "They are now in troubles, and need comfort. Perhaps this hand of God will make them now to magnify and reverence the Word of God, which before they lightly esteemed."

Here he was with joy received by the godly. He chose the east gate for the place of his preaching; so that the healthy were within, and the sick without the gate. He took his text from these words, "He sent His word and healed them," etc. In this sermon he chiefly dwelt upon the advantage and comfort of God's Word, the judgments that ensue upon the contempt or rejection of it, the freedom of God's grace to all His people, and the happiness of those of His elect, whom He takes to Himself out of this miserable world. The hearts of his hearers were so raised by the divine force of this discourse, as not to regard death, but to judge them the more happy who should then be called, not knowing whether he should have such comfort again with them.

After this the plague abated; though, in the midst of it, Wishart constantly visited those that lay in the greatest extremity, and comforted them by his exhortations.

When he took his leave of the people of Dundee, he said that God had almost put an end to that plague, and that he was now called to another place. He went from thence to Montrose; where he sometimes preached, but he spent most of his time in private meditation and prayer.

It is said that before he left Dundee, and while he was engaged in the labors of love to the bodies as well as to the souls of those poor afflicted people, Cardinal Beaton engaged a desperate popish priest, called John Weighton, to kill him; the attempt to execute which was as follows: one day, after Wishart had finished his sermon, and the people departed, a priest stood waiting at the bottom of the stairs, with a naked dagger in his hand under his gown. But Mr. Wishart, having a sharp, piercing eye, and seeing the priest as he came from the pulpit, said to him, "My friend, what would you have?" and immediately clapping his hand upon the dagger, took it from him. The priest being terrified, fell to his knees, confessed his intention, and craved pardon. A noise was hereupon raised, and it coming to the ears of those who were sick, they cried, "Deliver the traitor to us, we will take him by force"; and they burst in at the gate. But Wishart, taking the priest in his arms, said, "Whatsoever hurts him shall hurt me; for he hath done me no mischief, but much good, by teaching more heedfulness for the time to come." By this conduct he appeased the people and saved the life of the wicked priest.

Soon after his return to Montrose, the cardinal again conspired his death, causing a letter to be sent him as if it had been from his familiar friend, the laird of Kennier, in which it was desired with all possible speed to come to him, as he was taken with a sudden sickness. In the meantime the cardinal had provided sixty men armed to lie in wait within a mile and a half of Montrose, in order to murder him as he passed that way.

The letter came to Wishart's hand by a boy, who also brought him a horse for the journey. Wishart, accompanied by some honest men, his friends, set forward; but something particular striking his mind by the way, he returned, which they wondering at, asked him the cause; to whom he said, "I will not go; I am forbidden of God; I am assured there is treason. Let some of you go to yonder place, and tell me what you find." Which doing, they made the discovery; and hastily returning, they told Mr. Wishart; whereupon he said, "I know I shall end my life by that bloodthirsty man's hands, but it will not be in this manner."

A short time after this he left Montrose, and proceeded to Edinburgh, in order to propagate the Gospel in that city. By the way he lodged with a faithful brother, called James Watson of Inner-Goury. In the middle of the night he got up, and went into the yard, which two men hearing they privately followed him. While in the yard, he fell on his knees, and prayed for some time with the greatest fervency, after which he arose, and returned to his bed. Those who attended him, appearing as though they were ignorant of all, came and asked him where he had been. But he would not answer them. The next day they importuned him to tell them, saying "Be plain with us, for we heard your mourning, and saw your gestures."

On this he with a dejected countenance, said, "I had rather you had been in your beds." But they still pressing upon him to know something, he said, "I will tell you; I am assured that my warfare is near at an end, and therefore pray to God with me, that I shrink not when the battle waxeth most hot."

Soon after, Cardinal Beaton, archbishop of St. Andrews, being informed that Mr. Wishart was at the house of Mr. Cockburn, of Ormistohn, in East Lothian, applied to the regent to cause him to be apprehended; with which, after great persuasion, and much against his will, he complied.

In consequence of this the cardinal immediately proceeded to the trial of Wishart, against whom no less than eighteen articles were exhibited. Mr. Wishart answered the respective articles with great composure of mind, and in so learned and clear a manner as greatly surprised most of those who were present.

After the examination was finished, the archbishop endeavored to prevail on Mr. Wishart to recant; but he was too firmly fixed in his religious principles and too much enlightened with the truth of the Gospel, to be in the least moved.

On the morning of his execution there came to him two friars from the cardinal; one of whom put on him a black linen coat, and the other brought several bags of gunpowder, which they tied about different parts of his body.

As soon as he arrived at the stake, the executioner put a rope round his neck and a chain about his middle, upon which he fell on his knees and thus exclaimed:

"O thou Savior of the world, have mercy upon me! Father of heaven, I commend my spirit into Thy holy hands."

After this he prayed for his accusers, saying, "I beseech thee, Father of heaven, forgive them that have, from ignorance or an evil mind, forged lies of me: I forgive them with all my heart. I beseech Christ to forgive them that have ignorantly condemned me."

He was then fastened to the stake, and the fagots being lighted immediately set fire to the powder that was tied about him, which blew into a flame and smoke.

The governor of the castle, who stood so near that he was singed with the flame, exhorted the martyr, in a few words, to be of good cheer, and to ask the pardon of God for his offences. To which he replied, "This flame occasions trouble to my body, indeed, but it hath in nowise broken my spirit. But he who now so proudly looks down upon me from yonder lofty place (pointing to the cardinal) shall, ere long, be ignominiously thrown down, as now he proudly lolls at his ease." Which prediction was soon after fulfilled.

The hangman, that was his tormentor, sat down upon his knees, and said, "Sir, I pray you to forgive me, for I am not guilty of your death." To whom he answered, "Come hither to me." When that he was come to him, he kissed his cheek, and said: "Lo, here is a token that I forgive thee. My heart, do thine office." And then he was put upon the gibbet and hanged, and burned to powder. When that the people beheld the great tormenting, they might not withhold from piteous mourning and complaining of this innocent lamb's slaughter.

It was not long after the martyrdom of this blessed man of God, Master George Wishart, who was put to death by David Beaton, the bloody archbishop and cardinal of Scotland, A.D. 1546, the first day of March, that the said David Beaton, by the just revenge of God's mighty judgment, was slain within his own castle of St. Andrews, by the hands of one Leslie and other gentlemen, who, by the Lord stirred up, brake in suddenly upon him, and in his bed murdered him the said year, the last day of May, crying out, "Alas! alas! slay me not! I am a priest!" And so, like a butcher he lived, and like a butcher he died, and lay seven months and more unburied, and at last like a carrion was buried in a dunghill.

THE LAST WHO SUFFERED MARTYRDOM IN SCOTLAND, FOR THE CAUSE OF CHRIST, WAS ONE WALTER MILL, WHO WAS BURNT AT EDINBURGH IN THE YEAR 1558

This person, in his younger years, had travelled in Germany, and on his return was installed a priest of the Church of Lunan in Angus, but, on an information of heresy, in the time of Cardinal Beaton, he was forced to abandon his charge and abscond. But he was soon apprehended, and committed to prison.

Being interrogated by Sir Andrew Oliphant, whether he would recant his opinions, he answered in the negative, saying that he would "sooner forfeit ten thousand lives, than relinquish a particle of those heavenly principles he had received from the suffrages of his blessed Redeemer."

In consequence of this, sentence of condemnation was immediately passed on him, and he was conducted to prison in order for execution the following day.

This steadfast believer in Christ was eighty-two years of age, and exceedingly infirm; whence it was supposed that he could scarcely be heard. However, when he was taken to the place of execution, he expressed his religious sentiments with such courage, and at the same time composure of mind, as astonished even his enemies. As soon as he was fastened to the stake and the fagots lighted, he addressed the spectators as follows: "The cause why I suffer this day is not for any crime, (though I acknowledge myself a miserable sinner) but only for the defence of the truth as it is in Jesus Christ; and I praise God who hath called me, by His mercy, to seal the truth with my life; which, as I received it from Him, so I willingly and joyfully offer it up to His glory. Therefore, as you would escape eternal death, be no longer seduced by the lies of the seat of Antichrist: but depend solely on Jesus Christ, and His mercy, that you may be delivered from condemnation." And then added that he trusted he should be the last who would suffer death in Scotland upon a religious account.

Thus did this pious Christian cheerfully give up his life in defence of the truth of Christ's Gospel, not doubting but he should be made partaker of his heavenly Kingdom.

CHAPTER NINE

Persecutions in England During the Reign of Queen Mary

The premature death of that celebrated young monarch, Edward VI, occasioned the most extraordinary and wonderful occurrences, which had ever existed from the times of our blessed Lord and Savior's incarnation in human shape. This melancholy event became speedily a subject of general regret. The succession to the British throne was soon made a matter of contention; and the scenes which ensued were a demonstration of the serious affliction in which the kingdom was involved. As his loss to the nation was more and more unfolded, the remembrance of his government was more and more the basis of grateful recollection. The very awful prospect, which was soon presented to the friends of Edward's administration, under the direction of his counsellors and servants, was a contemplation which the reflecting mind was compelled to regard with most alarming apprehensions. The rapid approaches which were made towards a total reversion of the proceedings of the young king's reign, denoted the advances which were thereby represented to an entire resolution in the management of public affairs both in Church and state.

Alarmed for the condition in which the kingdom was likely to be involved by the king's death, an endeavor to prevent the consequences, which were but too plainly foreseen, was productive of the most serious and fatal effects. The king, in his long and lingering affliction, was induced to make a will, by which he bequeathed the English crown to Lady Jane, the daughter of the duke of Suffolk, who had been married to Lord Guilford, the son of the duke of Northumberland, and was the granddaughter of the second sister of King Henry, by Charles, duke of Suffolk. By this will, the succession of Mary and

97

Elizabeth, his two sisters, was entirely superseded, from an apprehension of the returning system of popery; and the king's council, with the chief of the nobility, the lord-mayor of the city of London, and almost all the judges and the principal lawyers of the realm, subscribed their names to this regulation, as a sanction to the measure. Lord Chief Justice Hale, though a true Protestant and an upright judge, alone declined to unite his name in favor of the Lady Jane, because he had already signified his opinion that Mary was entitled to assume the reins of government. Others objected to Mary's being placed on the throne, on account of their fears that she might marry a foreigner, and thereby bring the crown into considerable danger. Her partiality to popery also left little doubt on the minds of any, that she would be induced to revive the dormant interests of the pope, and change the religion which had been used both in the days of her father, King Henry, and in those of her brother Edward: for in all his time she had manifested the greatest stubbornness and inflexibility of temper, as must be obvious from her letter to the lords of the council, whereby she put in her claim to the crown, on her brother's decease.

When this happened, the nobles, who had associated to prevent Mary's succession, and had been instrumental in promoting, and, perhaps, advising the measures of Edward, speedily proceeded to proclaim Lady Jane Gray, to be queen of England, in the city of London and various other populous cities of the realm. Though young, she possessed talents of a very superior nature, and her improvements under a most excellent tutor had given her many very great advantages.

Her reign was of only five days' continuance, for Mary, having succeeded by false promises in obtaining the crown, speedily commenced the execution of her avowed intention of extirpating and burning every Protestant. She was crowned at Westminster in the usual form, and her elevation was the signal for the commencement of the bloody persecution which followed.

Having obtained the sword of authority, she was not sparing in its exercise. The supporters of Lady Jane Gray were destined to feel its force. The duke of Northumberland was the first who experienced her savage resentment. Within a month after his confinement in the Tower, he was condemned, and brought to the scaffold, to suffer as a traitor. From his varied crimes, resulting out of a sordid and inordinate ambition, he died unpitied and unlamented.

The changes, which followed with rapidity, unequivocally declared that the queen was disaffected to the present state of religion. Dr. Poynet was displaced to make room for Gardiner to be bishop of Winchester, to whom she also gave the important office of lord-chancellor. Dr. Ridley was dismissed from the see of London, and Bonne introduced. J. Story was put out of the bishopric of Chichester, to admit Dr. Day. J. Hooper was sent prisoner to the Fleet, and Dr. Heath put into the see of Worcestor. Miles Coverdale was also excluded from Exeter, and Dr. Vesie placed in that diocese. Dr. Tonstall was also promoted to the see of Durham. These things being marked and perceived, great heaviness and discomfort grew more and more to all good men's hearts; but to the wicked great rejoicing. They that could dissemble took no great care how the matter went; but such, whose consciences were joined with the truth, perceived already coals to be kindled, which after should be the destruction of many a true Christian.

THE WORDS AND BEHAVIOR OF THE LADY JANE UPON THE SCAFFOLD

The next victim was the amiable Lady Jane Grey, who, by her acceptance of the crown at the earnest solicitations of her friends, incurred the implacable resentment of the bloody Mary. When she first mounted the scaffold, she spoke to the spectators in this manner: "Good people, I am come hither to die, and by a law I am condemned to the same. The fact against the queen's highness was unlawful, and the consenting thereunto by me: but, touching the procurement and desire thereof by me, or on my behalf, I do wash my hands thereof in innocency before God, and the face of you, good Christian people, this day:" and therewith she wrung her hands, wherein she had her book. Then said she, "I pray you all, good Christian people, to bear me witness, that I die a good Christian woman, and that I do look to be saved by no other mean, but only by the mercy of God in the blood of His only Son Jesus Christ: and I confess that when I did know the Word of God, I neglected the same, loved myself and the world, and therefore this plague and punishment is happily and worthily happened unto me for my sins; and yet I thank God, that of His goodness He hath thus given me a time and a respite to repent. And now, good people, while I am alive, I pray you assist me with your prayers." And then, kneeling down, she turned to Feckenham, saying, "Shall I say this Psalm?" and he said, "Yea." Then she said the Psalm of Miserere mei Deus, in English, in a most devout manner throughout to the end; and then she stood up, and gave her maid, Mrs. Ellen, her gloves and handkerchief, and her book to Mr. Bruges; and then she untied her gown, and the executioner pressed upon her to help her off with it: but she, desiring him to let her alone, turned towards her two gentlewomen, who helped her off therewith, and also with her frowes, paaft, and neckerchief, giving to her a fair handkerchief to put about her eyes.

Then the executioner kneeled down, and asked her forgiveness, whom she forgave most willingly. Then he desired her to stand upon the straw, which doing, she saw the block. Then she said, "I pray you, despatch me quickly." Then she kneeled down, saying, "Will you take it off before I lay me down?" And the executioner said, "No, madam." Then she tied a handkerchief about her eyes, and feeling for the block, she said, "What shall I do? Where is it? Where is it?" One of the standers-by guiding her therunto, she laid her head upon the block, and then stretched forth her body, and said, "Lord, into Thy hands I commend my spirit;" and so finished her life, in the year of our Lord 1554, the twelfth day of February, about the seventeenth year of her age.

Thus died Lady Jane; and on the same day Lord Guilford, her husband, one of the duke of Northumberland's sons, was likewise beheaded, two innocents in comparison with them that sat upon them. For they were both very young, and ignorantly accepted that which others had contrived, and by open proclamation consented to take from others, and give to them.

Touching the condemnation of this pious lady, it is to be noted that Judge Morgan, who gave sentence against her, soon after he had condemned her, fell mad, and in his raving cried out continually to have the Lady Jane taken away from him, and so he ended his life.

On the twenty-first day of the same month, Henry, duke of Suffolk, was beheaded on Tower-hill, the fourth day after his condemnation: about which time many gentlemen and yeomen were condemned, whereof some were executed at London, and some in the country. In the number of whom was Lord Thomas Grey, brother to the said duke, being apprehended not long after in North Wales, and executed for the same. Sir Nicholas Throgmorton, also, very narrowly escaped.

JOHN ROGERS, VICAR OF ST. SEPULCHRE'S, AND READER OF ST. PAUL'S, LONDON

John Rogers was educated at Cambridge, and was afterward many years chaplain to the merchant adventurers at Antwerp in Brabant. Here he met with the celebrated martyr William Tyndale, and Miles Coverdale, both voluntary exiles from their country for their aversion to popish superstition and idolatry. They were the instruments of his conversion; and he united with them in that translation of the Bible into English, entitled "The Translation of Thomas Matthew." From the Scriptures he knew that unlawful vows may be lawfully broken; hence he married, and removed to Wittenberg in Saxony, for the improvement of learning; and he there learned the Dutch language, and received the charge of a congregation, which he faithfully executed for many years. On King Edward's accession, he left Saxony to promote the work of reformation in England; and, after some time, Nicholas Ridley, then bishop of London, gave him a prebend in St. Paul's Cathedral, and the dean and chapter appointed him reader of the divinity lesson there. Here he continued until Queen Mary's succession to the throne, when the Gospel and true religion were banished, and the Antichrist of Rome, with his superstition and idolatry, introduced.

The circumstance of Mr. Rogers having preached at Paul's cross, after Queen Mary arrived at the Tower, has been already stated. He confirmed in his sermon the true doctrine taught in King Edward's time, and exhorted the people to beware of the pestilence of popery, idolatry, and superstition. For this he was called to account, but so ably defended himself that, for that time, he was dismissed. The proclamation of the queen, however, to prohibit true preaching, gave his enemies a new handle against him. Hence he was again summoned before the council, and commanded to keep his house. He did so, though he might have escaped; and though he perceived the state of the true religion to be desperate. He knew he could not want a living in Germany; and he could not forget a wife and ten children, and to seek means to succor them.

But all these things were insufficient to induce him to depart, and, when once called to answer in Christ's cause, he stoutly defended it, and hazarded his life for that purpose.

After long imprisonment in his own house, the restless Bonner, bishop of London, caused him to be committed to Newgate, there to be lodged among thieves and murderers.

After Mr. Rogers had been long and straitly imprisoned, and lodged in Newgate among thieves, often examined, and very uncharitably entreated, and at length unjustly and most cruelly condemned by Stephen Gardiner, bishop of Winchester, the fourth day of February, in the year of our Lord 1555, being Monday in the morning, he was suddenly warned by the keeper of Newgate's wife, to prepare himself for the fire; who, being then sound asleep, could scarce be awaked. At length being raised and awaked, and bid to make haste, then said he, "If it be so, I need not tie my points." And so was had down, first to Bishop Bonner to be degraded: which being done, he craved of Bonner but one petition; and Bonner asked what that should be. Mr. Rogers replied that he might speak a few words with his wife before his burning, but that could not be obtained of him.

When the time came that he should be brought out of Newgate to Smithfield, the place of his execution, Mr. Woodroofe, one of the sheriffs, first came to Mr. Rogers, and asked him if he would revoke his abominable doctrine, and the evil opinion of the Sacrament of the altar. Mr. Rogers answered, "That which I have preached I will seal with my blood." Then Mr. Woodroofe said, "Thou art an heretic." "That shall be known," quoth Mr. Rogers, "at the Day of Judgment." "Well," said Mr. Woodroofe, "I will never pray for thee." "But I will pray for you," said Mr. Rogers; and so was brought the same day, the fourth of February, by the sheriffs, towards Smithfield, saying the Psalm Miserere by the way, all the people wonderfully rejoicing at his constancy; with great praises and thanks to God for the same. And there in the presence of Mr. Rochester, comptroller of the queen's household, Sir Richard Southwell, both the sheriffs, and a great number of people, he was burnt to ashes, washing his hands in the flame as he was burning. A little before his burning, his pardon was brought, if he would have recanted; but he utterly refused it. He was the first martyr of all the blessed company that suffered in Queen Mary's time that gave the first adventure upon the fire. His wife and children, being eleven in number, ten able to go, and one sucking at her breast, met him by the way, as he went towards Smithfield. This sorrowful sight of his own flesh and blood could nothing move him, but that he constantly and cheerfully took his death with wonderful patience, in the defence and quarrel of the Gospel of Christ."

THE REV. LAWRENCE SAUNDERS

Mr. Saunders, after passing some time in the school of Eaton, was chosen to go to King's College in Cambridge, where he continued three years, and profited in knowledge and learning very much for that time. Shortly after he quitted the university, and went to his parents, but soon returned to Cambridge again to his study, where he began to add to the knowledge of the Latin, the study of the Greek and Hebrew tongues, and gave himself up to the study of the Holy Scriptures, the better to qualify himself for the office of preacher.

In the beginning of King Edward's reign, when God's true religion was introduced, after license obtained, he began to preach, and was so well liked of them who then had authority that they appointed him to read a divinity lecture in the College of Forthringham. The College of Fothringham being dissolved he was placed to be a reader in the minster at Litchfield. After a certain space, he departed from Litchfield to a benefice in Leicestershire, called Church-langton, where he held a residence, taught diligently, and kept a liberal house. Thence he was orderly called to take a benefice in the city of London, namely, All-hallows in Bread-street. After this he preached at Northhampton, nothing meddling with the state, but boldly uttering his conscience against the popish doctrines which were likely to spring up again in England, as a just plague for the little love which the English nation then bore to the blessed Word of God, which had been so plentifully offered unto them.

The queen's party who were there, and heard him, were highly displeased with him for his sermon, and for it kept him among them as a prisoner. But partly for love of his brethren and friends, who were chief actors for the queen among them, and partly because there was no law broken by his preaching, they dismissed him.

Some of his friends, perceiving such fearful menacing, counselled him to fly out of the realm, which he refused to do. But seeing he was with violence kept from doing good in that place, he returned towards London, to visit his flock.

In the afternoon of Sunday, October 15, 1554, as he was reading in his church to exhort his people, the bishop of London interrupted him, by sending an officer for him.

His treason and sedition the bishop's charity was content to let slip until another time, but a heretic he meant to prove him, and all those, he said, who taught and believed that the administration of the Sacraments, and all orders of the Church, are the most pure, which come the nearest to the order of the primitive Church.

After much talk concerning this matter, the bishop desired him to write what he believed of transubstantiation. Lawrence Saunders did so, saying, "My Lord, you seek my blood, and you shall have it: I pray God that you may be so baptized in it that you may ever after loathe blood-sucking, and become a better man." Upon being closely charged with contumacy, the severe replies of Mr. Saunders to the bishop, (who had before, to get the favor of Henry VIII written and set forth in print, a book of true obedience, wherein he had openly declared Queen Mary to be a bastard) so irritated him that he exclaimed, "Carry away this frenzied fool to prison."

After this good and faithful martyr had been kept in prison one year and a quarter, the bishops at length called him, as they did his fellow-prisoners, openly to be examined before the queen's council.

His examination being ended, the officers led him out of the place, and stayed until the rest of his fellow-prisoners were likewise examined, that they might lead them all together to prison.

After his excommunication and delivery over to the secular power, he was brought by the sheriff of London to the Compter, a prison in his own parish of Bread-street, at which he rejoiced greatly, both because he found there a fellow-prisoner, Mr. Cardmaker, with whom he had much Christian and comfortable discourse; and because out of prison, as before in his pulpit, he might have an opportunity of preaching to his parishioners. On the fourth of February, Bonner, bishop of London, came to the prison to degrade him; the day following, in the morning the sheriff of London delivered him to certain of the queen's guard, who were appointed to carry him to the city of Coventry, there to be burnt.

When they had arrived at Coventry, a poor shoemaker, who used to serve him with shoes, came to him, and said, "O my good master, God strengthen and comfort you." "Good shoemaker," Mr. Saunders replied, "I desire thee to pray for me, for I am the most unfit man for this high office, that ever was appointed to it; but my gracious God and dear Father is able to make me strong enough." The next day, being the eighth of February, 1555, he was led to the place of execution, in the park, without the city. He went in an old gown and a shirt, barefooted, and oftentimes fell flat on the ground, and prayed. When he was come nigh to the place, the officer, appointed to see the execution done, said to Mr. Saunders that he was one of them who marred the queen's realm, but if he would recant, there was pardon for him. "Not I," replied the holy martyr, "but such as you have injured the realm. The blessed Gospel of Christ is what I hold; that do I believe, that have I taught, and that will I never revoke!" Mr. Saunders then slowly moved towards the fire, sank to the earth and prayed; he then rose up, embraced the stake, and frequently said, "Welcome, thou cross of Christ! welcome everlasting life!" Fire was then put to the fagots, and, he was overwhelmed by the dreadful flames, and sweetly slept in the Lord Jesus.

MARTYRDOM OF WILLIAM HUNTER

William Hunter had been trained to the doctrines of the Reformation from his earliest youth, being descended from religious parents, who carefully instructed him in the principles of true religion.

Hunter, then nineteen years of age, refusing to receive the communion at Mass, was threatened to be brought before the bishop; to whom this valiant young martyr was conducted by a constable.

Bonner caused William to be brought into a chamber, where he began to reason with him, promising him security and pardon if he would recant. Nay, he would have been content if he would have gone only to receive and to confession, but William would not do so for all the world.

Upon this the bishop commanded his men to put William in the stocks in his gate house, where he sat two days and nights, with a crust of brown bread and a cup of water only, which he did not touch.

At the two days' end, the bishop came to him, and finding him steadfast in the faith, sent him to the convict prison, and commanded the keeper to lay irons upon him as many as he could bear. He continued in prison three quarters of a year, during which time he had been before the bishop five times, besides the time when he was condemned in the consistory in St. Paul's, February 9, at which time his brother, Robert Hunter, was present.

Then the bishop, calling William, asked him if he would recant, and finding he was unchangeable, pronounced sentence upon him, that he should go from that place to Newgate for a time, and thence to Brentwood, there to be burned.

About a month afterward, William was sent down to Brentwood, where he was to be executed. On coming to the stake, he knelt down and read the Fifty-first Psalm, until he came to these words, "The sacrifices of God are a broken spirit; a broken and a contrite heart, O God, Thou wilt not despise." Steadfast in refusing the queen's pardon, if he would become an apostate, at length one Richard Ponde, a bailiff, came, and made the chain fast about him.

William now cast his psalter into his brother's hand, who said, "William, think on the holy passion of Christ, and be not afraid of death." "Behold," answered William, "I am not afraid." Then he lifted up his hands to heaven, and said, "Lord, Lord, Lord, receive my spirit;" and casting down his head again into the smothering smoke, he yielded up his life for the truth, sealing it with his blood to the praise of God.

DR. ROBERT FARRAR

This worthy and learned prelate, the bishop of St. David's in Wales, having in the former reign, as well as since the accession of Mary, been remarkably zealous in promoting the reformed doctrines, and exploding the errors of popish idolatry, was summoned, among others, before the persecuting bishop of Winchester, and other commissioners set apart for the abominable work of devastation and massacre.

His principal accusers and persecutors, on a charge of praemunire in the reign of Edward VI were George Constantine Walter, his servant; Thomas Young, chanter of the cathedral, afterward bishop of Bangor, etc. Dr. Farrar ably replied to the copies of information laid against him, consisting of fifty-six articles. The whole process of this trial was long and tedious. Delay succeeded delay, and after that Dr. Farrar had been long unjustly detained in custody under sureties, in the reign of King Edward, because he had been promoted by the duke of Somerset, whence after his fall he found fewer friends to support him against such as wanted his bishopric by the coming in of Queen Mary, he was accused and examined not for any matter of praemunire, but for his faith and doctrine; for which he was called before the bishop of Winchester with Bishop Hooper, Mr. Rogers, Mr. Bradford, Mr. Saunders, and others, February 4, 1555; on which day he would also with them have been condemned, but his condemnation was deferred, and he sent to prison again, where he continued until February 14, and then was sent into Wales to receive sentence. He was six times brought up before Henry Morgan, bishop of St. David's, who demanded if he would abjure; from which he zealously dissented, and appealed to Cardinal Pole; notwithstanding which, the bishop, proceeding in his rage, pronounced him a heretic excommunicate, and surrendered him to the secular power.

Dr. Farrar, being condemned and degraded, was not long after brought to the place of execution in the town of Carmathen, in the market-place of which, on the south side of the market-cross, March 30, 1555, being Saturday next before Passion Sunday, he most constantly sustained the torments of the fire.

Concerning his constancy, it is said that one Richard Jones, a knight's son, coming to Dr. Farrar a little before his death, seemed to lament the painfulness of the death he had to suffer; to whom the bishop answered that if he saw him once stir in the pains of his burning, he might then give no credit to his doctrine; and as he said, so did he maintain his promise, patiently standing without emotion, until one Richard Gravell with a staff struck him down.

MARTYRDOM OF RAWLINS WHITE

Rawlins White was by his calling and occupation a fisherman, living and continuing in the said trade for the space of twenty years at least, in the town of Cardiff, where he bore a very good name amongst his neighbors.

Though the good man was altogether unlearned, and withal very simple, yet it pleased God to remove him from error and idolatry to a knowledge of the truth, through the blessed Reformation in Edward's reign. He had his son taught to read English, and after the little boy could read pretty well, his father every night after supper, summer and winter, made the boy read a portion of the Holy Scriptures, and now and then a part of some other good book.

When he had continued in his profession the space of five years, King Edward died, upon whose decease Queen Mary succeeded and with her all kinds of superstition crept in. White was taken by the officers of the town, as a man suspected of heresy, brought before the Bishop Llandaff, and committed to prison in Chepstow, and at last removed to the castle of Cardiff, where he continued for the space of one whole year. Being brought before the bishop in his chapel, he counselled him by threats and promises. But as Rawlins would in no wise recant his opinions, the bishop told him plainly that he must proceed against him by law, and condemn him as a heretic.

Before they proceeded to this extremity, the bishop proposed that prayer should be said for his conversion. "This," said White, "is like a godly bishop, and if your request be godly and right, and you pray as you ought, no doubt God will hear you; pray you, therefore, to your God, and I will pray to my

God." After the bishop and his party had done praying, he asked Rawlins if he would now revoke. "You find," said the latter, "your prayer is not granted, for I remain the same; and God will strengthen me in support of this truth." After this, the bishop tried what saying Mass would do; but Rawlins called all the people to witness that he did not bow down to the host. Mass being ended, Rawlins was called for again; to whom the bishop used many persuasions; but the blessed man continued so steadfast in his former profession that the bishop's discourse was to no purpose. The bishop now caused the definitive sentence to be read, which being ended, Rawlins was carried again to Cardiff, to a loathsome prison in the town, called Cockmarel, where he passed his time in prayer, and in the singing of Psalms. In about three weeks the order came from town for his execution.

When he came to the place, where his poor wife and children stood weeping, the sudden sight of them so pierced his heart, that the tears trickled down his face. Being come to the altar of his sacrifice, in going toward the stake, he fell down upon his knees, and kissed the ground; and in rising again, a little earth sticking on his face, he said these words. "Earth unto earth, and dust unto dust; thou art my mother, and unto thee I shall return."

When all things were ready, directly over against the stake, in the face of Rawlins White, there was a stand erected, whereon stepped up a priest, addressing himself to the people, but, as he spoke of the Romish doctrines of the Sacraments, Rawlins cried out, "Ah! thou wicked hypocrite, dost thou presume to prove thy false doctrine by Scripture? Look in the text that followeth; did not Christ say, 'Do this in remembrance of me?'"

Then some that stood by cried out, "Put fire! set on fire!" which being done, the straw and reeds cast up a great and sudden flame. In which flame this good man bathed his hands so long, until such time as the sinews shrank, and the fat dropped away, saving that once he did, as it were, wipe his face with one of them. All this while, which was somewhat long, he cried with a loud voice, "O Lord, receive my spirit!" until he could not open his mouth. At last the extremity of the fire was so vehement against his legs that they were consumed almost before the rest of his body was hurt, which made the whole body fall over the chains into the fire sooner than it would have done. Thus died this good old man for his testimony of God's truth, and is now rewarded, no doubt, with the crown of eternal life.

THE REV. GEORGE MARSH

George Marsh, born in the parish of Deane, in the county of Lancaster, received a good education and trade from his parents; about his twenty-fifth year he married, and lived, blessed with several children, on his farm until his wife died. He then went to study at Cambridge, and became the curate of Rev. Lawrence Saunders, in which duty he constantly and zealously set forth the truth of God's Word, and the false doctrines of the modern Antichrist.

Being confined by Dr. Coles, the bishop of Chester, within the precincts of his own house, he was kept from any intercourse with his friends during four months; his friends and mother, earnestly wished him to have flown from "the wrath to come;" but Mr. Marsh thought that such a step would ill agree with that profession he had during nine years openly made. He, however, secreted himself, but he had much struggling, and in secret prayer begged that God would direct him, through the advice of his best friends, for his own glory and to what was best. At length, determined by a letter he received, boldly to confess the faith of Christ, he took leave of his mother-in-law and other friends, recommending his children to their care and departed for Smethehills, whence he was, with others, conducted to Lathum, to undergo examination before the earl of Derby, Sir William Nores, Mr. Sherburn, the parson of Garpnal, and others. The various questions put to him he answered with a good conscience, but when Mr. Sherburn interrogated him upon his belief of the Sacrament of the altar, Mr. Marsh answered like a true Protestant that the essence of the bread and wine was not at all changed, hence, after receiving dreadful threats from some, and fair words from others, for his opinions, he was remanded to ward, where he lay two nights without any bed.

On Palm Sunday he underwent a second examination, and Mr. Marsh much lamented that his fear should at all have induced him to prevaricate, and to seek his safety, as long as he did not openly deny Christ; and he again cried more earnestly to God for strength that he might not be overcome by the subtleties of those who strove to overrule the purity of his faith. He underwent three examinations before Dr. Coles, who, finding him steadfast in the Protestant faith, began to read his sentence; but he was interrupted by the chancellor, who prayed the bishop to stay before it was too late. The priest then prayed for Mr. Marsh, but the latter, upon being again solicited to recant, said he durst not deny his Savior Christ, lest he lose His everlasting mercy, and so obtain eternal death. The bishop then proceeded in the sentence. He was committed to a dark dungeon, and lay deprived of the consolation of any one (for all were afraid to relieve or communicate with him) until the day appointed came that he should suffer. The sheriffs of the city, Amry and Couper, with their officers, went to the north gate, and took out Mr. George Marsh, who walked all the way with the Book in his hand, looking upon the same, whence the people said, "This man does not go to his death as a thief, nor as one that deserveth to die."

When he came to the place of execution without the city, near Spittal-Boughton, Mr. Cawdry, deputy chamberlain of Chester, showed Mr. Marsh a writing under a great seal, saying that it was a pardon for him if he would recant. He answered that he would gladly accept the same did it not tend to pluck him from God.

After that, he began to speak to the people showing the cause of his death, and would have exhorted them to stick unto Christ, but one of the sheriffs prevented him. Kneeling down, he then said his prayers, put off his clothes unto his shirt, and was chained to the post, having a number of fagots under him, and a thing made like a firkin, with pitch and tar in it, over his head. The fire being unskilfully made, and the wind driving it in eddies, he suffered great extremity, which notwithstanding he bore with Christian fortitude.

When he had been a long time tormented in the fire without moving, having his flesh so broiled and puffed up that they who stood before him could not see the chain wherewith he was fastened, and therefore supposed that he had been dead, suddenly he spread abroad his arms, saying, "Father of heaven have mercy upon me!" and so yielded his spirit into the hands of the Lord. Upon this, many of the people said he was a martyr, and died gloriously patient. This caused the bishop shortly after to make a sermon in the cathedral church, and therein he affirmed, that the said "Marsh was a heretic, burnt as such, and is a firebrand in hell." Mr. Marsh suffered April 24, 1555.

WILLIAM FLOWER

William Flower, otherwise Branch, was born at Snow-hill, in the county of Cambridge, where he went to school some years, and then came to the abby of Ely. After he had remained a while he became a professed monk, was made a priest in the same house, and there celebrated and sang Mass. After that, by reason of a visitation, and certain injunctions by the authority of Henry VIII he took upon him the habit of a secular priest, and returned to Snow-hill, where he was born, and taught children about half a year.

He then went to Ludgate, in Suffolk, and served as a secular priest about a quarter of a year; from thence to Stoniland; at length to Tewksbury, where he married a wife, with whom he ever after faithfully and honestly continued. After marriage he resided at Tewksbury about two years, and thence went to Brosley, where he practiced physic and surgery; but departing from those parts he came to London, and finally settled at Lambeth, where he and his wife dwelt together. However, he was generally abroad, excepting once or twice in a month, to visit and see his wife. Being at home upon Easter Sunday morning, he came over the water from Lambeth into St. Margaret's Church at Westminster; when seeing a priest, named John Celtham, administering and giving the Sacrament of the altar to the people, and being greatly offended in his conscience with the priest for the same, he struck and wounded him upon the head, and also upon the arm and hand, with his wood knife, the priest having at the same time in his hand a chalice with the consecrated host therein, which became sprinkled with blood.

Mr. Flower, for this injudicious zeal, was heavily ironed, and put into the gatehouse at Westminster; and afterward summoned before bishop Bonner and his ordinary, where the bishop, after he had sworn him upon a Book, ministered articles and interrogatories to him.

After examination, the bishop began to exhort him again to return to the unity of his mother the Catholic Church, with many fair promises. These Mr. Flower steadfastly rejecting, the bishop ordered him to appear in the same place in the afternoon, and in the meantime to consider well his former answer; but he, neither apologizing for having struck the priest, nor swerving from his faith, the bishop assigned him the next day, April 20, to receive sentence if he would not recant. The next morning, the bishop accordingly proceeded to the sentence, condemning and excommunicating him for a heretic, and after pronouncing him to be degraded, committed him to the secular power.

On April 24, St. Mark's eve, he was brought to the place of martyrdom, in St. Margaret's churchyard, Westminster, where the fact was committed: and there coming to the stake, he prayed to Almighty God, made a confession of his faith, and forgave all the world.

This done, his hand was held up against the stake, and struck off, his left hand being fastened behind him. Fire was then set to him, and he burning therein, cried with a loud voice, "O Thou Son of God receive my soul!" three times. His speech being now taken from him, he spoke no more, but notwithstanding he lifted up the stump with his other arm as long as he could.

Thus he endured the extremity of the fire, and was cruelly tortured, for the few fagots that were brought being insufficient to burn him they were compelled to strike him down into the fire, where lying along upon the ground, his lower part was consumed in the fire, whilst his upper part was little injured, his tongue moving in his mouth for a considerable time.

THE REV. JOHN CARDMAKER AND JOHN WARNE

May 30, 1555, the Rev. John Cardmaker, otherwise called Taylor, prebendary of the Church of Wells, and John Warne, upholsterer, of St. John's, Walbrook, suffered together in Smithfield. Mr. Cardmaker, who first was an observant friar before the dissolution of the abbeys, afterward was a married minister, and in King Edward's time appointed to be a reader in St. Paul's; being apprehended in the beginning of Queen Mary's reign, with Dr. Barlow, bishop of Bath, he was brought to London, and put in the Fleet prison, King Edward's laws being yet in force. In Mary's reign, when brought before the bishop of Winchester, the latter offered them the queen's mercy, if they would recant.

Articles having been preferred against Mr. John Warne, he was examined upon them by Bonner, who earnestly exhorted him to recant his opinions, to whom he answered, "I am persuaded that I am in the right opinion, and I see no cause to recant; for all the filthiness and idolatry lies in the Church of Rome."

The bishop then, seeing that all his fair promises and terrible threatenings could not prevail, pronounced the definitive sentence of condemnation, and ordered May 30, 1555, for the execution of John Cardmaker and John Warne, who were brought by the sheriffs to Smithfield. Being come to the stake, the sheriffs called Mr. Cardmaker aside, and talked with him secretly, during which Mr. Warne prayed, was chained to the stake, and had wood and reeds set about him.

The people were greatly afflicted, thinking that Mr. Cardmaker would recant at the burning of Mr. Warne. At length Mr. Cardmaker departed from the sheriffs, and came towards the stake, knelt down, and made a long prayer in silence to himself. He then rose up, put off his clothes to his shirt, and went with a bold courage unto the stake and kissed it; and taking Mr. Warne by the hand, he heartily comforted him, and was bound to the stake, rejoicing. The people seeing this so suddenly done, contrary to their previous expectation, cried out, "God be praised! the Lord strengthen thee, Cardmaker! the Lord Jesus receive thy spirit!" And this continued while the executioner put fire to them, and both had passed through the fire to the blessed rest and peace among God's holy saints and martyrs, to enjoy the crown of triumph and victory prepared for the elect soldiers and warriors of Christ Jesus in His blessed Kingdom, to whom be glory and majesty forever. Amen.

JOHN SIMPSON AND JOHN ARDELEY

John Simpson and John Ardeley were condemned on the same day with Mr. Cardmaker and John Warne, which was the twenty-fifth of May. They were shortly after sent down from London to Essex, where they were burnt in one day, John Simpson at Rochford, and John Ardeley at Railey, glorifying God in His beloved Son, and rejoicing that they were accounted worthy to suffer.

THOMAS HAUKES, THOMAS WATTS, AND ANNE ASKEW

Thomas Haukes, with six others, was condemned on the ninth of February, 1555. In education he was erudite; in person, comely, and of good stature; in manners, a gentleman, and a sincere Christian. A little before death, several of Mr. Haukes' friends, terrified by the sharpness of the punishment he was going to suffer, privately desired that in the midst of the flames he should show them some token, whether the pains of burning were so great that a man might not collectedly endure it. This he promised to do; and it was agreed that if the rage of the pain might be suffered, then he should lift up his hands above his head towards heaven, before he gave up the ghost.

Not long after, Mr. Haukes was led away to the place appointed for slaughter by Lord Rich, and being come to the stake, mildly and patiently prepared himself for the fire, having a strong chain cast about his middle, with a multitude of people on every side compassing him about, unto whom after he had spoken many things, and poured out his soul unto God, the fire was kindled.

When he had continued long in it, and his speech was taken away by violence of the flame, his skin drawn together, and his fingers consumed with the fire, so that it was thought that he was gone, suddenly and contrary to all expectation, this good man being mindful of his promise, reached up his hands burning in flames over his head to the living God, and with great rejoicings as it seemed, struck or clapped them three times together. A great shout followed this wonderful circumstance, and then this blessed martyr of Christ, sinking down in the fire, gave up his spirit, June 10, 1555.

Thomas Watts, of Billerica, in Essex, of the diocese of London, was a linen draper. He had daily expected to be taken by God's adversaries, and this came to pass on the fifth of April, 1555, when he was brought before Lord Rich, and other commissioners at Chelmsford, and accused for not coming to the church.

Being consigned over to the bloody bishop, who gave him several hearings, and, as usual, many arguments, with much entreaty, that he would be a disciple of Antichrist, but his preaching availed not, and he resorted to his last revenge—that of condemnation.

At the stake, after he had kissed it, he spake to Lord Rich, charging him to repent, for the Lord would revenge his death. Thus did this good martyr offer his body to the fire, in defence of the true Gospel of the Savior.

Thomas Osmond, William Bamford, and Nicholas Chamberlain, all of the town of Coxhall, being sent up to be examined, Bonner, after several hearings, pronounced them obstinate heretics, and delivered them to the sheriffs, in whose custody they remained until they were delivered to the sheriff of Essex county, and by him were executed, Chamberlain at Colchester, the fourteenth of June; Thomas Osmond at Maningtree, and William Bamford, alias Butler, at Harwich, the fifteenth of June, 1555; all dying full of the glorious hope of immortality.

Then Wriotheseley, lord chancellor, offered Anne Askew the king's pardon if she would recant; who made this answer, that she came not thither to deny her Lord and Master. And thus the good Anne Askew, being compassed in with flames of fire, as a blessed sacrifice unto God, slept in the Lord, A.D. 1546, leaving behind her a singular example of Christian constancy for all men to follow.

REV. JOHN BRADFORD, AND JOHN LEAF, AN APPRENTICE

Rev. John Bradford was born at Manchester, in Lancashire; he was a good Latin scholar, and afterward became a servant of Sir John Harrington, knight.

He continued several years in an honest and thriving way; but the Lord had elected him to a better function. Hence he departed from his master, quitting the Temple, at London, for the University of Cambridge, to learn, by God's law, how to further the building of the Lord's temple. In a few years after, the university gave him the degree of master of arts, and he became a fellow of Pembroke Hall.

Martin Bucer first urged him to preach, and when he modestly doubted his ability, Bucer was wont to reply, "If thou hast not fine wheat bread, yet give the poor people barley bread, or whatsoever else the Lord hath committed unto thee." Dr. Ridley, that worthy bishop of London, and glorious martyr of Christ, first called him to take the degree of a deacon and gave him a prebend in his cathedral Church of St. Paul.

In this preaching office Mr. Bradford diligently labored for the space of three years. Sharply he reproved sin, sweetly he preached Christ crucified, ably he disproved heresies and errors, earnestly he persuaded to godly life. After the death of blessed King Edward VI, Mr. Bradford still continued diligent in preaching, until he was suppressed by Queen Mary.

An act now followed of the blackest ingratitude, and at which a pagan would blush. It has been recited, that a tumult was occasioned by Mr. Bourne's (then bishop of Bath) preaching at St. Paul's Cross; the indignation of the people placed his life in imminent danger; indeed a dagger was thrown at him. In this situation he entreated Mr. Bradford, who stood behind him, to speak in his place, and assuage the tumult. The people welcomed Mr. Bradford, and the latter afterward kept close to him, that his presence might prevent the populace from renewing their assaults.

The same Sunday in the afternoon, Mr. Bradford preached at Bow Church in Cheapside, and reproved the people sharply for their seditious misdemeanor. Notwithstanding this conduct, within three days after, he was sent for to the Tower of London, where the queen then was, to appear before the Council. There he was charged with this act of saving Mr. Bourne, which was called seditious, and they also objected against him for preaching. Thus he was committed, first to the Tower, then to other prisons, and, after his condemnation, to the Poultry Compter, where he preached twice a day continually, unless sickness hindered him. Such was his credit with the keeper of the king's Bench, that he permitted him in an evening to visit a poor, sick person near the steel-yard, upon his promise to return in time, and in this he never failed.

The night before he was sent to Newgate, he was troubled in his sleep by foreboding dreams, that on Monday after he should be burned in Smithfield. In the afternoon the keeper's wife came up and announced this dreadful news to him, but in him it excited only thankfulness to God. At night half a dozen friends came, with whom he spent all the evening in prayer and godly exercises.

When he was removed to Newgate, a weeping crowd accompanied him, and a rumor having been spread that he was to suffer at four the next morning, an immense multitude attended. At nine o'clock Mr. Bradford was brought into Smithfield. The cruelty of the sheriff deserves notice; for his brother-in-law, Roger Beswick, having taken him by the hand as he passed, Mr. Woodroffe, with his staff, cut his head open.

Mr. Bradford, being come to the place, fell flat on the ground, and putting off his clothes unto the shirt, he went to the stake, and there suffered with a young man of twenty years of age, whose name was John Leaf, an apprentice to Mr. Humphrey Gaudy, tallow-chandler, of Christ-church, London. Upon Friday before Palm Sunday, he was committed to the Compter in Bread-street, and afterward examined and condemned by the bloody bishop.

It is reported of him, that, when the bill of his confession was read unto him, instead of pen, he took a pin, and pricking his hand, sprinkled the blood upon the said bill, desiring the reader thereof to show the bishop that he had sealed the same bill with his blood already.

They both ended this mortal life, July 12, 1555, like two lambs, without any alteration of their countenances, hoping to obtain that prize they had long run for; to which may Almighty God conduct us all, through the merits of Christ our Savior!

We shall conclude this article with mentioning that Mr. Sheriff Woodroffe, it is said, within half a year after, was struck on the right side with a palsy, and for the space of eight years after, (until his dying day,) he was unable to turn himself in his bed; thus he became at last a fearful object to behold.

The day after Mr. Bradford and John Leaf suffered in Smithfield, William Minge, priest, died in prison at Maidstone. With as great constancy and boldness he yielded up his life in prison, as if it had pleased God to have called him to suffer by fire, as other godly men had done before at the stake, and as he himself was ready to do, had it pleased God to have called him to this trial.

REV. JOHN BLAND, REV. JOHN FRANKESH, NICHOLAS SHETTERDEN, AND HUMPHREY MIDDLETON

These Christian persons were all burnt at Canterbury for the same cause. Frankesh and Bland were ministers and preachers of the Word of God, the one being parson of Adesham, and the other vicar of Rolvenden. Mr. Bland was cited to answer for his opposition to antichristianism, and underwent several examinations before Dr. Harpsfield, archdeacon of Canterbury, and finally on the twenty-fifth of June, 1555, again withstanding the power of the pope, he was condemned, and delivered to the secular arm. On the same day were condemned John Frankesh, Nicholas Shetterden, Humphrey Middleton, Thacker, and Crocker, of whom Thacker only recanted.

Being delivered to the secular power, Mr. Bland, with the three former, were all burnt together at Canterbury, July 12, 1555, at two several stakes, but in one fire, when they, in the sight of God and His angels, and before men, like true soldiers of Jesus Christ, gave a constant testimony to the truth of His holy Gospel.

DIRICK CARVER AND JOHN LAUNDER

The twenty-second of July, 1555, Dirick Carver, brewer, of Brighthelmstone, aged forty, was burnt at Lewes. And the day following John Launder, husbandman, aged twenty-five, of Godstone, Surrey, was burnt at Stening.

Dirick Carver was a man whom the Lord had blessed as well with temporal riches as with his spiritual treasures. At his coming into the town of Lewes to be burnt, the people called to him, beseeching God to strengthen him in the faith of Jesus Christ; and, as he came to the stake, he knelt down, and prayed earnestly. Then his Book was thrown into the barrel, and when he had stripped himself, he too, went into a barrel. As soon as he was in, he took the Book, and threw it among the people, upon which the sheriff commanded, in the name of the king and queen, on pain of death, to throw in the Book again.

And immediately the holy martyr began to address the people. After he had prayed a while, he said, "O Lord my God, Thou hast written, he that will not forsake wife, children, house, and every thing that he hath, and take up Thy cross and follow Thee, is not worthy of Thee! but Thou, Lord, knowest that I have forsaken all to come unto Thee. Lord, have mercy upon me, for unto Thee I commend my spirit! and my soul doth rejoice in Thee!" These were the last words of this faithful servant of Christ before enduring the fire. And when the fire came to him, he cried, "O Lord, have mercy upon me!" and sprang up in the fire, calling upon the name of Jesus, until he gave up the ghost.

James Abbes. This young man wandered about to escape apprehension, but was at last informed against, and brought before the bishop of Norwich, who influenced him to recant; to secure him further in apostasy, the bishop afterward gave him a piece of money; but the interference of Providence is here remarkable. This bribe lay so heavily upon his conscience, that he returned, threw back the money, and repented of his conduct. Like Peter, he was contrite, steadfast in the faith, and sealed it with his blood at Bury, August 2, 1555, praising and glorifying God.

JOHN DENLEY, JOHN NEWMAN, AND PATRICK PACKINGHAM

Mr. Denley and Newman were returning one day to Maidstone, the place of their abode, when they were met by E. Tyrrel, Esq., a bigoted justice of the peace in Essex, and a cruel persecutor of the Protestants. He apprehended them merely on suspicion. On the fifth of July, 1555, they were condemned, and consigned to the sheriffs, who sent Mr. Denley to Uxbridge, where he perished, August eighth, 1555. While suffering in agony, and singing a Psalm, Dr. Story inhumanly ordered one of the tormentors to throw a fagot at him, which cut his face severely, caused him to cease singing, and to raise his hands to his face. Just as Dr. Story was remarking in jest that he had spoiled a good song, the pious martyr again changed, spread his hands abroad in the flames, and through Christ Jesus resigned his soul into the hands of his Maker.

Mr. Packingham suffered at the same town on the twenty-eighth of the same month.

Mr. Newman, pewterer, was burnt at Saffron Waldon, in Essex, August 31, for the same cause, and Richard Hook about the same time perished at Chichester.

W. COKER, W. HOOPER, H. LAURENCE, R. COLLIAR, R. WRIGHT AND W. STERE

These persons all of Kent, were examined at the same time with Mr. Bland and Shetterden, by Thornton, bishop of Dover, Dr. Harpsfield, and others.

These six martyrs and witnesses of the truth were consigned to the flames in Canterbury, at the end of August, 1555.

Elizabeth Warne, widow of John Warne, upholsterer, martyr, was burnt at Stratford-le-bow, near London, at the end of August, 1555.

George Tankerfield, of London, cook, born at York, aged twenty-seven, in the reign of Edward VI had been a papist; but the cruelty of bloody Mary made him suspect the truth of those doctrines which were enforced by fire and torture. Tankerfield was imprisoned in Newgate about the end of February, 1555, and on August 26, at St. Alban's, he braved the excruciating fire, and joyfully died for the glory of his Redeemer.

Rev. Robert Smith was first in the service of Sir T. Smith, provost of Eton; and was afterward removed to Windsor, where he had a clerkship of ten pounds a year. He was condemned, July 12, 1555, and suffered August 8, at Uxbridge. He doubted not but that God would give the spectators some token in support of his own cause; this actually happened; for, when he was nearly half burnt, and supposed to be dead, he suddenly rose up, moved the remaining parts of his arms and praised God, then, hanging over the fire, he sweetly slept in the Lord Jesus.

Mr. Stephen Harwood and Mr. Thomas Fust suffered about the same time with Smith and Tankerfield, with whom they were condemned. Mr. William Hale also, of Thorp, in Essex, was sent to Barnet, where about the same time he joined the ever-blessed company of martyrs.

George King, Thomas Leyes, and John Wade, falling sick in Lollard's Tower, were removed to different houses, and died. Their bodies were thrown out in the common fields as unworthy of burial, and lay until the faithful conveyed them away at night.

Mr. William Andrew of Horseley, Essex, was imprisoned in Newgate for heresy; but God chose to call him to himself by the severe treatment he endured in Newgate, and thus to mock the sanguinary expectations of his Catholic persecutors. His body was thrown into the open air, but his soul was received into the everlasting mansions of his heavenly Creator.

THE REV. ROBERT SAMUEL

This gentleman was minister of Bradford, Suffolk, where he industriously taught the flock committed to his charge, while he was openly permitted to discharge his duty. He was first persecuted by Mr. Foster, of Copdock, near Ipswich, a severe and bigoted persecutor of the followers of Christ, according to the truth in the Gospel. Notwithstanding Mr. Samuel was ejected from his living, he continued to exhort and instruct privately; nor would he obey the order for putting away his wife, whom he had married in King Edward's reign; but kept her at Ipswich, where Foster, by warrant, surprised him by night with her. After being imprisoned in Ipswich jail, he was taken before Dr. Hopton, bishop of Norwich, and Dr. Dunnings, his chancellor, two of the most sanguinary among the bigots of those days. To intimidate the worthy pastor, he was in prison chained to a post in such a manner that the weight of his body was supported by the points of his toes: added to this his allowance of provision was reduced to a quantity so insufficient to sustain nature that he was almost ready to devour his own flesh. From this dreadful extremity there was even a degree of mercy in ordering him to the fire. Mr. Samuel suffered August 31, 1555.

BISHOP RIDLEY AND BISHOP LATIMER

These reverend prelates suffered October 17, 1555, at Oxford, on the same day Wolsey and Pygot perished at Ely. Pillars of the Church and accomplished ornaments of human nature, they were the admiration of the realm, amiably conspicuous in their lives, and glorious in their deaths.

Dr. Ridley was born in Northumberland, was first taught grammar at Newcastle, and afterward removed to Cambridge, where his aptitude in education raised him gradually until he came to be the head of Pembroke College, where he received the title of Doctor of Divinity. Having returned from a trip to Paris, he was appointed chaplain by Henry VIII and bishop of Rochester, and was afterwards translated to the see of London in the time of Edward VI.

To his sermons the people resorted, swarming about him like bees, coveting the sweet flowers and wholesome juice of the fruitful doctrine, which he did not only preach, but showed the same by his life, as a glittering lanthorn to the eyes and senses of the blind, in such pure order that his very enemies could not reprove him in any one jot.

His tender treatment of Dr. Heath, who was a prisoner with him during one year, in Edward's reign, evidently proves that he had no Catholic cruelty in his disposition. In person he was erect and well proportioned; in temper forgiving; in self-mortification severe. His first duty in the morning was private prayer: he remained in his study until ten o'clock, and then attended the daily prayer used in his house. Dinner being done, he sat about an hour, conversing pleasantly, or playing at chess. His study next engaged his attention, unless business or visits occurred; about five o'clock prayers followed; and after he would recreate himself at chess for about an hour, then retire to his study until eleven o'clock, and pray on his knees as in the morning. In brief, he was a pattern of godliness and virtue, and such he endeavored to make men wherever he came.

His attentive kindness was displayed particularly to old Mrs. Bonner, mother of Dr. Bonner, the cruel bishop of London. Dr. Ridley, when at his manor at Fulham, always invited her to his house, placed her at the head of his table, and treated her like his own mother; he did the same by Bonner's sister and other relatives; but when Dr. Ridley was under persecution, Bonner pursued a conduct diametrically opposite, and would have sacrificed Dr. Ridley's sister and her husband, Mr. George Shipside, had not Providence delivered him by the means of Dr. Heath, bishop of Worcester.

Dr. Ridley was first in part converted by reading Bertram's book on the Sacrament, and by his conferences with archbishop Cranmer and Peter Martyr.

When Edward VI was removed from the throne, and the bloody Mary succeeded, Bishop Ridley was immediately marked as an object of slaughter. He was first sent to the Tower, and afterward, at Oxford, was consigned to the common prison of Bocardo, with archbishop Cranmer and Mr. Latimer. Being separated from them, he was placed in the house of one Irish, where he remained until the day of his martyrdom, from 1554, until October 16, 1555.

It will easily be supposed that the conversations of these chiefs of the martyrs were elaborate, learned, and instructive. Such indeed they were, and equally beneficial to all their spiritual comforts. Bishop Ridley's letters to various Christian brethren in bonds in all parts, and his disputations with the mitred enemies of Christ, alike proved the clearness of his head and the integrity of his heart. In a letter to Mr. Grindal, (afterwards archbishop of Canterbury,) he mentions with affection those who had preceded him in dying for the faith, and those who were expected to suffer; he regrets that popery is re-established in its full abomination, which he attributes to the wrath of God, made manifest in return for the lukewarmness of the clergy and the people in justly appreciating the blessed light of the Reformation.

This old practiced soldier of Christ, Master Hugh Latimer, was the son of one Hugh Latimer, of Thurkesson in the county of Leicester, a husbandman, of a good and wealthy estimation; where also he was born and brought up until he was four years of age, or thereabout: at which time his parents, having him as then left for their only son, with six daughters, seeing his ready, prompt, and sharp wit, purposed to train him up in erudition, and knowledge of good literature; wherein he so profited in his youth at the common schools of his own country, that at the age of fourteen years, he was sent to the University of Cambridge; where he entered into the study of the school divinity of that day, and was from principle a zealous observer of the Romish superstitions of the time. In his oration when he commenced bachelor of divinity, he inveighed against the reformer Melancthon, and openly declaimed against good Mr. Stafford, divinity lecturer in Cambridge.

Mr. Thomas Bilney, moved by a brotherly pity towards Mr. Latimer, begged to wait upon him in his study, and to explain to him the groundwork of his (Mr. Bilney's) faith. This blessed interview effected his conversion: the persecutor of Christ became his zealous advocate, and before Dr. Stafford died he became reconciled to him.

Once converted, he became eager for the conversion of others, and commenced to be public preacher, and private instructor in the university. His sermons were so pointed against the absurdity of praying in the Latin tongue, and withholding the oracles of salvation from the people who were to be saved by belief in them, that he drew upon himself the pulpit animadversions of several of the resident friars and heads of houses, whom he subsequently silenced by his severe criticisms and eloquent arguments. This was at Christmas, 1529. At length Dr. West preached against Mr. Latimer at Barwell Abbey, and prohibited him from preaching again in the churches of the university, notwithstanding which, he continued during three years to advocate openly the cause of Christ, and even his enemies confessed the power of those talents he possessed. Mr. Bilney remained here some time with Mr. Latimer, and thus the place where they frequently walked together obtained the name of Heretics' Hill.

Mr. Latimer at this time traced out the innocence of a poor woman, accused by her husband of the murder of her child. Having preached before King Henry VIII at Windsor, he obtained the unfortunate mother's pardon. This, with many other benevolent acts, served only to excite the spleen of his adversaries. He was summoned before Cardinal Wolsey for heresy, but being a strenuous supporter of the king's supremacy, in opposition to the pope's, by favor of Lord Cromwell and Dr. Buts, (the king's physician), he obtained the living of West Kingston, in Wiltshire. For his sermons here against purgatory, the immaculacy of the Virgin, and the worship of images, he was cited to appear before Warham, archbishop of Canterbury, and John, bishop of London. He was required to subscribe certain articles, expressive of his conformity to the accustomed usages; and there is reason to think, after repeated weekly examinations, that he did subscribe, as they did not seem to involve any important article of belief.

Guided by Providence, he escaped the subtle nets of his persecutors, and at length, through the powerful friends before mentioned, became bishop of Worcester, in which function he qualified or explained away most of the papal ceremonies he was for form's sake under the necessity of complying with. He continued in this active and dignified employment some years.

Beginning afresh to set forth his plow he labored in the Lord's harvest most fruitfully, discharging his talent as well in divers places of this realm, as before the king at the court. In the same place of the inward garden, which was before applied to lascivious and courtly pastimes, there he dispensed the fruitful Word of the glorious Gospel of Jesus Christ, preaching there before the king and his whole court, to the edification of many.

He remained a prisoner in the Tower until the coronation of Edward VI, when he was again called to the Lord's harvest in Stamford, and many other places: he also preached at London in the convocation house, and before the young king; indeed he lectured twice every Sunday, regardless of his great age (then above sixty-seven years,) and his weakness through a bruise received from the fall of a tree. Indefatigable in his private studies, he rose to them in winter and in summer at two o'clock in the morning.

By the strength of his own mind, or of some inward light from above, he had a prophetic view of what was to happen to the Church in Mary's reign, asserting that he was doomed to suffer for the truth, and that Winchester, then in the Tower, was preserved for that purpose. Soon after Queen Mary was proclaimed, a messenger was sent to summon Mr. Latimer to town, and there is reason to believe it was wished that he should make his escape.

Thus Master Latimer coming up to London, through Smithfield (where merrily he said that Smithfield had long groaned for him), was brought before the Council, where he patiently bore all the mocks and taunts given him by the scornful papists. He was cast into the Tower, where he, being assisted with the heavenly grace of Christ, sustained imprisonment a long time, notwithstanding the cruel and unmerciful handling of the lordly papists, which thought then their kingdom would never fall; he showed himself not only patient, but also cheerful in and above all that which they could or would work against him. Yea, such a valiant spirit the Lord gave him, that he was able not only to despise the terribleness of prisons and torments, but also to laugh to scorn the doings of his enemies.

Mr. Latimer, after remaining a long time in the Tower, was transported to Oxford, with Cranmer and Ridley, the disputations at which place have been already mentioned in a former part of this work. He remained imprisoned until October, and the principal objects of all his prayers were three—that he might stand faithful to the doctrine he had professed, that God would restore his Gospel to England once again, and preserve the Lady Elizabeth to be queen; all of which happened. When he stood at the stake without the Bocardo gate, Oxford, with Dr. Ridley, and fire was putting to the pile of fagots, he raised his eyes benignantly towards heaven, and said, "God is faithful, who will not suffer you to be tempted above that ye are able." His body was forcibly penetrated by the fire, and the blood flowed abundantly from the heart; as if to verify his constant desire that his heart's blood might be shed in defence of the Gospel. His polemical and friendly letters are lasting monuments of his integrity and talents. It has been before said, that public disputation took place in April, 1554, new examinations took place in October, 1555, previous to the degradation and condemnation of Cranmer, Ridley, and Latimer. We now draw to the conclusion of the lives of the two last.

Dr. Ridley, the night before execution, was very facetious, had himself shaved, and called his supper a marriage feast; he remarked upon seeing Mrs. Irish (the keeper's wife) weep, "Though my breakfast will be somewhat sharp, my supper will be more pleasant and sweet."

The place of death was on the northside of the town, opposite Baliol College. Dr. Ridley was dressed in a black gown furred, and Mr. Latimer had a long shroud on, hanging down to his feet. Dr. Ridley, as he passed Bocardo, looked up to see Dr. Cranmer, but the latter was then engaged in disputation with a friar. When they came to the stake, Mr. Ridley embraced Latimer fervently, and bid him: "Be of good heart, brother, for God will either assuage the fury of the flame, or else strengthen us to abide it." He then knelt by the stake, and after earnestly praying together, they had a short private conversation. Dr. Smith then preached a short sermon against the martyrs, who would have answered him, but were prevented by Dr. Marshal, the vice-chancellor. Dr. Ridley then took off his gown and tippet, and gave them to his brother-in-law, Mr. Shipside. He gave away also many trifles to his weeping friends, and the populace were anxious to get even a fragment of his garments. Mr. Latimer gave nothing, and from the poverty of his garb, was soon stripped to his shroud, and stood venerable and erect, fearless of death.

Dr. Ridley being unclothed to his shirt, the smith placed an iron chain about their waists, and Dr. Ridley bid him fasten it securely; his brother having tied a bag of gunpowder about his neck, gave some also to Mr. Latimer.

Dr. Ridley then requested of Lord Williams, of Fame, to advocate with the queen the cause of some poor men to whom he had, when bishop, granted leases, but which the present bishop refused to confirm. A lighted fagot was now laid at Dr. Ridley's feet, which caused Mr. Latimer to say: "Be of good cheer, Ridley; and play the man. We shall this day, by God's grace, light up such a candle in England, as I trust, will never be put out."

When Dr. Ridley saw the fire flaming up towards him, he cried with a wonderful loud voice, "Lord, Lord, receive my spirit." Master Latimer, crying as vehemently on the other side, "O Father of heaven, receive my soul!" received the flame as it were embracing of it. After that he had stroked his face with his hands, and as it were, bathed them a little in the fire, he soon died (as it appeareth) with very little pain or none.

Well! dead they are, and the reward of this world they have already. What reward remaineth for them in heaven, the day of the Lord's glory, when he cometh with His saints, shall declare.

In the following month died Stephen Gardiner, bishop of Winchester and lord chancellor of England. This papistical monster was born at Bury, in Suffolk, and partly educated at Cambridge. Ambitious, cruel, and bigoted, he served any cause; he first espoused the king's part in the affair of Anne Boleyn: upon the establishment of the Reformation he declared the supremacy of the pope an execrable tenet; and when Queen Mary came to the crown, he entered into all her papistical bigoted views, and became a second time bishop of Winchester. It is conjectured it was his intention to have moved the sacrifice of Lady Elizabeth, but when he arrived at this point, it pleased God to remove him.

It was on the afternoon of the day when those faithful soldiers of Christ, Ridley and Latimer, perished, that Gardiner sat down with a joyful heart to dinner. Scarcely had he taken a few mouthfuls, when he was seized with illness, and carried to his bed, where he lingered fifteen days in great torment, unable in any wise to evacuate, and burnt with a devouring fever, that terminated in death. Execrated by all good Christians, we pray the Father of mercies, that he may receive that mercy above he never imparted below.

MR. JOHN PHILPOT

This martyr was the son of a knight, born in Hampshire, and brought up at New College, Oxford, where for several years he studied the civil law, and became eminent in the Hebrew tongue. He was a scholar and a gentleman, zealous in religion, fearless in disposition, and a detester of flattery. After visiting Italy, he returned to England, affairs in King Edward's days wearing a more promising aspect. During this reign he continued to be archdeacon of Winchester under Dr. Poinet, who succeeded Gardiner. Upon the accession of Mary, a convocation was summoned, in which Mr. Philpot defended the Reformation against his ordinary, Gardiner, again made bishop of Winchester, and soon was conducted to Bonner and other commissioners for examination, October 2, 1555, after being eighteen months' imprisoned. Upon his demanding to see the commission, Dr. Story cruelly observed, "I will spend both my gown and my coat, but I will burn thee! Let him be in Lollard's tower, (a wretched prison,) for I will sweep the king's Bench and all other prisons of these heretics!"

Upon Mr. Philpot's second examination, it was intimated to him that Dr. Story had said that the lord chancellor had commanded that he should be made away with. It is easy to foretell the result of this inquiry. He was committed to Bonner's coal house, where he joined company with a zealous minister of Essex, who had been induced to sign a bill of recantation; but afterward, stung by his conscience, he asked the bishop to let him see the instrument again, when he tore it to pieces; which induced Bonner in a fury to strike him repeatedly, and tear away part of his beard. Mr. Philpot had a private interview with Bonner the same night, and was then remanded to his bed of straw like other prisoners, in the coal house. After seven examinations, Bonner ordered him to be set in the stocks, and on the following Sunday separated him from his fellow-prisoners as a sower of heresy, and ordered him up to a room near the battlements of St. Paul's, eight feet by thirteen, on the other side of Lollard's tower, and which could be overlooked by any one in the bishop's outer gallery. Here Mr. Philpot was searched, but happily he was successful in secreting some letters containing his examinations.

In the eleventh investigation before various bishops, and Mr. Morgan, of Oxford, the latter was so driven into a corner by the close pressure of Mr. Philpot's arguments, that he said to him, "Instead of the spirit of the Gospel which you boast to possess, I think it is the spirit of the buttery, which your fellows have had, who were drunk before their death, and went, I believe, drunken to it." To this unfounded and brutish remark, Mr. Philpot indignantly replied, "It appeareth by your communication that you are better acquainted with that spirit than the Spirit of God; wherefore I tell thee, thou painted wall and hypocrite, in the name of the living God, whose truth I have told thee, that God shall rain fire and brimstone upon such blasphemers as thou art!" He was then remanded by Bonner, with an order not to allow him his Bible nor candlelight.

On December 4, Mr. Philpot had his next hearing, and this was followed by two more, making in all, fourteen conferences, previous to the final examination in which he was condemned; such were the perseverance and anxiety of the Catholics, aided by the argumentative abilities of the most distinguished of the papal bishops, to bring him into the pale of their Church. Those examinations, which were very long and learned, were all written down by Mr.

Philpot, and a stronger proof of the imbecility of the Catholic doctors, cannot, to an unbiased mind, be exhibited.

On December 16, in the consistory of St. Paul's Bishop Bonner, after laying some trifling accusations to his charge, such as secreting powder to make ink, writing some private letters, etc., proceeded to pass the awful sentence upon him, after he and the other bishops had urged him by every inducement to recant. He was afterward conducted to Newgate, where the avaricious Catholic keeper loaded him with heavy irons, which by the humanity of Mr. Macham were ordered to be taken off. On December 17, Mr. Philpot received intimation that he was to die next day, and the next morning about eight o'clock, he joyfully met the sheriffs, who were to attend him to the place of execution.

Upon entering Smithfield, the ground was so muddy that two officers offered to carry him to the stake, but he replied:

"Would you make me a pope? I am content to finish my journey on foot." Arriving at the stake, he said, "Shall I disdain to suffer at the stake, when my Redeemer did not refuse to suffer the most vile death upon the cross for me?" He then meekly recited the One hundred and seventh and One hundred and eighth Psalms, and when he had finished his prayers, was bound to the post, and fire applied to the pile. On December 18, 1555, perished this illustrious martyr, reverenced by man, and glorified in heaven!

JOHN LOMAS, AGNES SNOTH, ANNE WRIGHT, JOAN SOLE, AND JOAN CATMER

These five martyrs suffered together, January 31, 1556. John Lomas was a young man of Tenterden. He was cited to appear at Canterbury, and was examined January 17. His answers being adverse to the idolatrous doctrine of the papacy, he was condemned on the following day, and suffered January 31.

Agnes Snoth, widow, of Smarden Parish, was several times summoned before the Catholic Pharisees, and rejecting absolution, indulgences, transubstantiation, and auricular confession, she was adjudged worthy to suffer death, and endured martyrdom, January 31, with Anne Wright and Joan Sole, who were placed in similar circumstances, and perished at the same time, with equal resignation. Joan Catmer, the last of this heavenly company, of the parish Hithe, was the wife of the martyr George Catmer.

Seldom in any country, for political controversy, have four women been led to execution, whose lives were irreproachable, and whom the pity of savages would have spared. We cannot but remark here that, when the Protestant power first gained the ascendency over the Catholic superstition, and some degree of force in the laws was necessary to enforce uniformity, whence some bigoted people suffered privation in their person or goods, we read of few burnings, savage cruelties, or poor women brought to the stake, but it is the nature of error to resort to force instead of argument, and to silence truth by taking away existence, of which the Redeemer himself is an instance.

The above five persons were burnt at two stakes in one fire, singing ho-sannahs to the glorified Savior, until the breath of life was extinct. Sir John Norton, who was present, wept bitterly at their unmerited sufferings.

ARCHBISHOP CRANMER

Dr. Thomas Cranmer was descended from an ancient family, and was born at the village of Arselacton, in the county of Northampton. After the usual school education he was sent to Cambridge, and was chosen a fellow of Jesus College. Here he married a gentleman's daughter, by which he forfeited his fellowship, and became a reader in Buckingham College, placing his wife at the Dolphin Inn, the landlady of which was a relation of hers, whence arose the idle report that he was an ostler. His lady shortly after dying in childbed; to his credit he was re-chosen a fellow of the college before mentioned. In a few years after, he was promoted to be Divinity Lecturer, and appointed one of the examiners over those who were ripe to become Bachelors or Doctors in Divinity. It was his principle to judge of their qualifications by the knowledge they possessed of the Scriptures, rather than of the ancient fathers, and hence many popish priests were rejected, and others rendered much improved.

He was strongly solicited by Dr. Capon to be one of the fellows on the foundation of Cardinal Wolsey's college, Oxford, of which he hazarded the refusal. While he continued in Cambridge, the question of Henry VIII's divorce with Catharine was agitated. At that time, on account of the plague, Dr. Cranmer removed to the house of a Mr. Cressy, at Waltham Abbey, whose two sons were then educating under him. The affair of divorce, contrary to the king's approbation, had remained undecided above two or three years, from the intrigues of the canonists and civilians, and though the cardinals Campeius and Wolsey were commissioned from Rome to decide the question, they purposely protracted the sentence.

It happened that Dr. Gardiner (secretary) and Dr. Fox, defenders of the king in the above suit, came to the house of Mr. Cressy to lodge, while the king removed to Greenwich. At supper, a conversation ensued with Dr. Cranmer, who suggested that the question whether a man may marry his brother's wife or not, could be easily and speedily decided by the Word of God, and this as well in the English courts as in those of any foreign nation. The king, uneasy at the delay, sent for Dr. Gardiner and Dr. Fox to consult them, regretting that a new commission must be sent to Rome, and the suit be endlessly protracted. Upon relating to the king the conversation which had passed on the previous evening with Dr. Cranmer, his majesty sent for him, and opened the tenderness of conscience upon the near affinity of the queen. Dr. Cranmer advised that the matter should be referred to the most learned divines of Cambridge and Oxford, as he was unwilling to meddle in an affair of such weight; but the king enjoined him to deliver his sentiments in writing, and to repair for that purpose to the earl of Wiltshire's, who would accommo-date him with books, and everything requisite for the occasion.

This Dr. Cranmer immediately did, and in his declaration not only quoted the authority of the Scriptures, of general councils, and the ancient writers, but maintained that the bishop of Rome had no authority whatever to dispense with the Word of God. The king asked him if he would stand by this bold declaration, to which replying in the affirmative, he was deputed ambassador to Rome, in conjunction with the earl of Wiltshire, Dr. Stokesley, Dr. Carne, Dr. Bennet, and others, previous to which, the marriage was discussed in most of the universities of Christendom and at home.

When the pope presented his toe to be kissed, as customary, the earl of Wiltshire and his party refused. Indeed, it is affirmed that a spaniel of the earl's attracted by the littler of the pope's toe, made a snap at it, whence his holiness drew in his sacred foot, and kicked at the offender with the other.

Upon the pope demanding the cause of their embassy, the earl presented Dr. Cranmer's book, declaring that his learned friends had come to defend it. The pope treated the embassy honorably, and appointed a day for the discussion, which he delayed, as if afraid of the issue of the investigation. The earl returned, and Dr. Cranmer, by the king's desire, visited the emperor, and was successful in bringing him over to his opinion. Upon the doctor's return to England, Dr. Warham, archbishop of Canterbury, having quitted this transitory life, Dr. Cranmer was deservedly, and by Dr. Warham's desire, elevated to that eminent station.

In this function, it may be said that he followed closely the charge of St. Paul. Diligent in duty, he rose at five in the morning, and continued in study and prayer until nine: between then and dinner, he devoted to temporal affairs. After dinner, if any suitors wanted hearing, he would determine their business with such an affability that even the defaulters were scarcely displeased. Then he would play at chess for an hour, or see others play, and at five o'clock he heard the Common Prayer read, and from this until supper he took the recreation of walking. At supper his conversation was lively and entertaining; again he walked or amused himself until nine o'clock, and then entered his study.

He ranked high in favor with King Henry, and even had the purity and the interest of the English Church deeply at heart. His mild and forgiving disposition is recorded in the following instance. An ignorant priest, in the country, had called Cranmer an ostler, and spoken very derogatory of his learning. Lord Cromwell receiving information of it, the man was sent to the Fleet, and his case was told to the archbishop by a Mr. Chertsey, a grocer, and a relation of the priest's. His grace, having sent for the offender, reasoned with him, and solicited the priest to question him on any learned subject. This the man, overcome by the bishop's good nature, and knowing his own glaring incapacity, declined, and entreated his forgiveness, which was immediately granted, with a charge to employ his time better when he returned to his parish. Cromwell was much vexed at the lenity displayed, but the bishop was ever more ready to receive injury than to retaliate in any other manner than by good advice and good offices.

At the time that Cranmer was raised to be archbishop, he was king's chaplain, and archdeacon of Taunton; he was also constituted by the pope the penitentiary general of England. It was considered by the king that Cranmer would be obsequious; hence the latter married the king to Anne Boleyn, performed her coronation, stood godfather to Elizabeth, the first child, and divorced the king from Catharine. Though Cranmer received a confirmation of his dignity from the pope, he always protested against acknowledging any other authority than the king's, and he persisted in the same independent sentiments when before Mary's commissioners in 1555.

One of the first steps after the divorce was to prevent preaching throughout his diocese, but this narrow measure had rather a political view than a religious one, as there were many who inveighed against the king's conduct. In his new dignity Cranmer agitated the question of supremacy, and by his powerful and just arguments induced the parliament to "render to Caesar the things that are Caesar's." During Cranmer's residence in Germany, 1531, he became acquainted with Ossiander, at Nuremberg, and married his niece, but left her with him while on his return to England. After a season he sent for her privately, and she remained with him until the year 1539, when the Six Articles compelled him to return her to her friends for a time.

It should be remembered that Ossiander, having obtained the approbation of his friend Cranmer, published the laborious work of the Harmony of the Gospels in 1537. In 1534 the archbishop completed the dearest wish of his heart, the removal of every obstacle to the perfection of the Reformation, by the subscription of the nobles and bishops to the king's sole supremacy. Only Bishop Fisher and Sir Thomas More made objection; and their agreement not to oppose the succession Cranmer was willing to consider as sufficient, but the monarch would have no other than an entire concession.

Not long after, Gardiner, in a private interview with the king, spoke inimically of Cranmer, (whom he maliciously hated) for assuming the title of primate of all England, as derogatory to the supremacy of the king. This created much jealousy against Cranmer, and his translation of the Bible was strongly opposed by Stokesley, bishop of London. It is said, upon the demise of Queen Catharine, that her successor Anne Boleyn rejoiced—a lesson this to show how shallow is the human judgment! since her own execution took place in the spring of the following year, and the king, on the day following the beheading of this sacrificed lady, married the beautiful Jane Seymour, a maid of honor to the late queen. Cranmer was ever the friend of Anne Boleyn, but it was dangerous to oppose the will of the carnal tyrannical monarch.

In 1538, the Holy Scriptures were openly exposed to sale; and the places of worship overflowed everywhere to hear its holy doctrines expounded. Upon the king's passing into a law the famous Six Articles, which went nearly again to establish the essential tenets of the Romish creed, Cranmer shone forth with all the luster of a Christian patiot, in resisting the doctrines they contained, and in which he was supported by the bishops of Sarum, Worcester, Ely, and Rochester, the two former of whom resigned their bishoprics. The king, though now in opposition to Cranmer, still revered the sincerity that marked his conduct. The death of Lord Cromwell in the Tower, in 1540, the good friend of Cranmer, was a severe blow to the wavering Protestant cause, but even now Cranmer, when he saw the tide directly adverse to the truth, boldly waited on the king in person, and by his manly and heartfelt pleading, caused the Book of Articles to be passed on his side, to the great confusion of his enemies, who had contemplated his fall as inevitable.

Cranmer now lived in as secluded a manner as possible, until the rancor of Winchester preferred some articles against him, relative to the dangerous opinion he taught in his family, joined to other treasonable charges. These the king himself delivered to Cranmer, and believing firmly the fidelity and assertions of innocence of the accused prelate, he caused the matter to be deeply investigated, and Winchester and Dr. Lenden, with Thornton and Barber, of the bishop's household, were found by the papers to be the real conspirators. The mild, forgiving Cranmer would have interceded for all remission of publishment, had not Henry, pleased with the subsidy voted by parliament, let them be discharged. These nefarious men, however, again renewing their plots against Cranmer, fell victims to Henry's resentment, and Gardiner forever lost his confidence. Sir G. Gostwick soon after laid charges against the archbishop, which Henry quashed, and the primate was willing to forgive.

In 1544, the archbishop's palace at Canterbury was burnt, and his brother-in-law with others perished in it. These various afflictions may serve to reconcile us to a humble state; for of what happiness could this great and good man boast, since his life was constantly harassed either by political, religious, or natural crosses? Again the inveterate Gardiner laid high charges against the meek archbishop and would have sent him to the Tower; but the king was his friend, gave him his signet that he might defend him, and in the Council not only declared the bishop one of the best affected men in his realm, but sharply rebuked his accusers for their calumny.

A peace having been made, Henry, and the French king, Henry the Great, were unanimous to have the Mass abolished in their kingdom, and Cranmer set about this great work; but the death of the English monarch, in 1546, suspended the precedure, and King Edward his successor continued Cranmer in the same functions, upon whose coronation he delivered a charge that will ever honor his memory, for its purity, freedom, and truth. During this reign he prosecuted the glorious Reformation with unabated zeal, even in the year 1552, when he was seized with a severe ague, from which it pleased God to restore him that he might testify by his death the truth of that seed he had diligently sown.

The death of Edward, in 1553, exposed Cranmer to all the rage of his enemies. Though the archbishop was among those who supported Mary's accession, he was attainted at the meeting of parliament, and in November adjudged guilty of high treason at Guildhall, and degraded from his dignities. He sent a humble letter to Mary, explaining the cause of his signing the will in favor of Edward, and in 1554 he wrote to the Council, whom he pressed to obtain a pardon from the queen, by a letter delivered to Dr. Weston, but which the letter opened, and on seeing its contents, basely returned.

Treason was a charge quite inapplicable to Cranmer, who supported the queen's right; while others, who had favored Lady Jane were dismissed upon paying a small fine. A calumny was now spread against Cranmer that he complied with some of the popish ceremonies to ingratiate himself with the queen, which he dared publicly to disavow, and justified his articles of faith. The active part which the prelate had taken in the divorce of Mary's mother had ever rankled deeply in the heart of the queen, and revenge formed a prominent feature in the death of Cranmer.

We have in this work noticed the public disputations at Oxford, in which the talents of Cranmer, Ridley, and Latimer shone so conspicuously, and tended to their condemnation. The first sentence was illegal, inasmuch as the usurped power of the pope had not yet been re-established by law.

Being kept in prison until this was effected, a commission was despatched from Rome, appointing Dr. Brooks to sit as the representative of his holiness, and Drs. Story and Martin as those of the queen. Cranmer was willing to bow to the authority of Drs. Story and Martin, but against that of Dr. Brooks he protested. Such were the remarks and replies of Cranmer, after a long examination, that Dr. Brooks observed, "We come to examine you, and methinks you examine us."

Being sent back to confinement, he received a citation to appear at Rome within eighteen days, but this was impracticable, as he was imprisoned in England; and as he stated, even had he been at liberty, he was too poor to employ an advocate. Absurd as it must appear, Cranmer was condemned at Rome, and on February 14, 1556, a new commission was appointed, by which, Thirlby, bishop of Ely, and Bonner, of London, were deputed to sit in judgment at Christ-church, Oxford. By virtue of this instrument, Cranmer was gradually degraded, by putting mere rags on him to represent the dress of an archbishop; then stripping him of his attire, they took off his own gown, and put an old worn one upon him instead. This he bore unmoved, and his enemies, finding that severity only rendered him more determined, tried the opposite course, and placed him in the house of the dean of Christ-church, where he was treated with every indulgence.

This presented such a contrast to the three years' hard imprisonment he had received, that it threw him off his guard. His open, generous nature was more easily to be seduced by a liberal conduct than by threats and fetters. When Satan finds the Christian proof against one mode of attack, he tries another; and what form is so seductive as smiles, rewards, and power, after a long, painful imprisonment? Thus it was with Cranmer: his enemies promised him his former greatness if he would but recant, as well as the queen's favor, and this at the very time they knew that his death was determined in council. To soften the path to apostasy, the first paper brought for his signature was conceived in general terms; this once signed, five others were obtained as explanatory of the first, until finally he put his hand to the following detestable instrument:

I, Thomas Cranmer, late archbishop of Canterbury, do renounce, abhor, and detest all manner of heresies and errors of Luther and Zuinglius, and all other teachings which are contrary to sound and true doctrine. And I believe most constantly in my heart, and with my mouth I confess one holy and Catholic Church visible, without which there is no salvation; and therefore I acknowledge the Bishop of Rome to be supreme head on earth, whom I acknowledge to be the highest bishop and pope, and Christ's vicar, unto whom all Christian people ought to be subject.

And as concerning the sacraments, I believe and worship in the sacrament of the altar the body and blood of Christ, being contained most truly under the forms of bread and wine; the bread, through the mighty power of God being turned into the body of our Savior Jesus Christ, and the wine into his blood.

And in the other six sacraments, also, (alike as in this) I believe and hold as the universal Church holdeth, and the Church of Rome judgeth and determineth.

Furthermore, I believe that there is a place of purgatory, where souls departed be punished for a time, for whom the Church doth godily and wholesomely pray, like as it doth honor saints and make prayers to them.

Finally, in all things I profess, that I do not otherwise believe than the Catholic Church and the Church of Rome holdeth and teacheth. I am sorry that I ever held or thought otherwise. And I beseech Almighty God, that of His mercy He will vouchsafe to forgive me whatsoever I have offended against God or His Church, and also I desire and beseech all Christian people to pray for me.

And all such as have been deceived either by mine example or doctrine, I require them by the blood of Jesus Christ that they will return to the unity of the Church, that we may be all of one mind, without schism or division.

And to conclude, as I submit myself to the Catholic Church of Christ, and to the supreme head thereof, so I submit myself unto the most excellent majesties of Philip and Mary, king and queen of this realm of England, etc., and to all other their laws and ordinances, being ready always as a faithful subject ever to obey them. And God is my witness, that I have not done this for favor or fear of any person, but willingly and of mine own conscience, as to the instruction of others.

"Let him that standeth take heed lest he fall!" said the apostle, and here was a falling off indeed! The papists now triumphed in their turn: they had acquired all they wanted short of his life. His recantation was immediately printed and dispersed, that it might have its due effect upon the astonished Protestants. But God counter worked all the designs of the Catholics by the extent to which they carried the implacable persecution of their prey. Doubtless, the love of life induced Cranmer to sign the above declaration: yet death may be said to have been preferable to life to him who lay under the stings of a goaded conscience and the contempt of every Gospel Christian; this principle he strongly felt in all its force and anguish.

The queen's revenge was only to be satiated by Cranmer's blood, and therefore she wrote an order to Dr. Pole, to prepare a sermon to be preached March 21, directly before his martyrdom, at St. Mary's, Oxford. Dr. Pole visited him the day previous, and was induced to believe that he would publicly deliver his sentiments in confirmation of the articles to which he had subscribed. About nine in the morning of the day of sacrifice, the queen's commissioners, attended by the magistrates, conducted the amiable unfortunate to St. Mary's Church. His torn, dirty garb, the same in which they habited him upon his degradation, excited the commiseration of the people. In the church he found a low mean stage, erected opposite to the pulpit, on which being placed, he turned his face, and fervently prayed to God.

The church was crowded with persons of both persuasions, expecting to hear the justification of the late apostasy: the Catholics rejoicing, and the Protestants deeply wounded in spirit at the deceit of the human heart. Dr. Pole, in his sermon, represented Cranmer as having been guilty of the most atrocious crimes; encouraged the deluded sufferer not to fear death, not to doubt the support of God in his torments, nor that Masses would be said in all the churches of Oxford for the repose of his soul. The doctor then noticed his conversion, and which he ascribed to the evident working of Almighty power and in order that the people might be convinced of its reality, asked the prisoner to give them a sign. This Cranmer did, and begged the congregation to pray for him, for he had committed many and grievous sins; but, of all, there was one which awfully lay upon his mind, of which he would speak shortly.

During the sermon Cranmer wept bitter tears: lifting up his hands and eyes to heaven, and letting them fall, as if unworthy to live: his grief now found vent in words: before his confession he fell upon his knees, and, in the following words unveiled the deep contrition and agitation which harrowed up his soul.

O Father of heaven! O Son of God, Redeemer of the world! O Holy Ghost, three persons all one God! have mercy on me, most wretched caitiff and miserable sinner. I have offended both against heaven and earth, more than my tongue can express. Whither then may I go, or whither may I flee? To heaven I may be ashamed to lift up mine eyes and in earth I find no place of refuge or succor. To Thee, therefore, O Lord, do I run; to Thee do I humble myself, saying, O Lord, my God, my sins be great, but yet have mercy upon me for Thy great mercy. The great mystery that God became man, was not wrought for little or few offences. Thou didst not give Thy Son, O Heavenly Father, unto death for small sins only, but for all the greatest sins of the world, so that the sinner return to Thee with his whole heart, as I do at present. Wherefore, have mercy on me, O God, whose property is always to have mercy, have mercy upon me, O Lord, for Thy great mercy. I crave nothing for my own merits, but for Thy name's sake, that it may be hallowed thereby, and for Thy dear Son, Jesus Christ's sake. And now therefore, O Father of Heaven, hallowed be Thy name, etc.

Then rising, he said he was desirous before his death to give them some pious exhortations by which God might be glorified and themselves edified. He then descanted upon the danger of a love for the world, the duty of obedience to their majesties, of love to one another and the necessity of the rich administering to the wants of the poor. He quoted the three verses of the fifth chapter of James, and then proceeded,

Let them that be rich ponder well these three sentences: for if they ever had occasion to show their charity, they have it now at this present, the poor people being so many, and victual so dear.

And now forasmuch as I am come to the last end of my life, whereupon hangeth all my life past, and all my life to come, either to live with my master Christ for ever in joy, or else to be in pain for ever with the wicked in hell, and I see before mine eyes presently, either heaven ready to receive me, or else hell ready to swallow me up; I shall therefore declare unto you my very faith how I believe, without any color of dissimulation: for now is no time to dissemble, whatsoever I have said or written in times past.

First, I believe in God the Father Almighty, Maker of heaven and earth, etc. And I believe every article of the Catholic faith, every word and sentence taught by our Savior Jesus Christ, His apostles and prophets, in the New and Old Testament.

And now I come to the great thing which so much troubleth my conscience, more than any thing that ever I did or said in my whole life, and that is the setting abroad of a writing contrary to the truth, which now here I renounce and refuse, as things written with my hand contrary to the truth which I thought in my heart, and written for fear of death, and to save my life, if it might be; and that is, all such bills or papers which I have written or signed with my hand since my degradation, wherein I have written many things untrue. And forasmuch as my hand hath offended, writing contrary to my heart, therefore my hand shall first be punished; for when I come to the fire it shall first be burned.

And as for the pope, I refuse him as Christ's enemy, and Antichrist, with all his false doctrine.

Upon the conclusion of this unexpected declaration, amazement and indignation were conspicuous in every part of the church. The Catholics were completely foiled, their object being frustrated, Cranmer, like Samson, having completed a greater ruin upon his enemies in the hour of death, than he did in his life.

Cranmer would have proceeded in the exposure of the popish doctrines, but the murmurs of the idolaters drowned his voice, and the preacher gave an order to "lead the heretic away!" The savage command was directly obeyed, and the lamb about to suffer was torn from his stand to the place of slaughter, insulted all the way by the revilings and taunts of the pestilent monks and friars.

With thoughts intent upon a far higher object than the empty threats of man, he reached the spot dyed with the blood of Ridley and Latimer. There he knelt for a short time in earnest devotion, and then arose, that he might undress and prepare for the fire. Two friars who had been parties in prevailing upon him to abjure, now endeavored to draw him off again from the truth, but he was steadfast and immovable in what he had just professed, and publicly taught. A chain was provided to bind him to the stake, and after it had tightly encircled him, fire was put to the fuel, and the flames began soon to ascend.

Then were the glorious sentiments of the martyr made manifest; then it was, that stretching out his right hand, he held it unshrinkingly in the fire until it was burnt to a cinder, even before his body was injured, frequently exclaiming, "This unworthy right hand."

His body did abide the burning with such steadfastness that he seemed to have no more than the stake to which he was bound; his eyes were lifted up to heaven, and he repeated "this unworthy right hand," as long as his voice would suffer him; and using often the words of Stephen, "Lord Jesus, receive my spirit," in the greatness of the flame, he gave up the ghost.

THE VISION OF THREE LADDERS

When Robert Samuel was brought forth to be burned, certain there were that heard him declare what strange things had happened unto him during the time of his imprisonment; to wit, that after he had famished or pined with hunger two or three days together, he then fell into a sleep, as it were one half in a slumber, at which time one clad all in white seemed to stand before him, who ministered comfort unto him by these words:

"Samuel, Samuel, be of good cheer, and take a good heart unto thee: for after this day shalt thou never be either hungry or thirsty."

No less memorable it is, and worthy to be noted, concerning the three ladders which he told to divers he saw in his sleep, set up toward heaven; of the which there was one somewhat longer than the rest, but yet at length they became one, joining (as it were) all three together.

As this godly martyr was going to the fire, there came a certain maid to him, which took him about the neck, and kissed him, who, being marked by them that were present, was sought for the next day after, to be had to prison and burned, as the very party herself informed me: howbeit, as God of His goodness would have it, she escaped their fiery hands, keeping herself secret in the town a good while after.

But as this maid, called Rose Nottingham, was marvellously preserved by the providence of God, so there were other two honest women who did fall into the rage and fury of that time. The one was a brewer's wife, the other was a shoemaker's wife, but both together now espoused to a new husband, Christ.

With these two was this maid aforesaid very familiar and well acquainted, who, on a time giving counsel to the one of them, that she should convey herself away while she had time and space, had this answer at her hand again: "I know well," saith she, "that it is lawful enough to fly away; which remedy you may use, if you list. But my case standeth otherwise. I am tied to a husband, and have besides young children at home; therefore I am minded, for the love of Christ and His truth, to stand to the extremity of the matter."

And so the next day after Samuel suffered, these two godly wives, the one called Anne Potten, the other called Joan Trunchfield, the wife of Michael Trunchfield, shoemaker, of Ipswich, were apprehended, and had both into one prison together. As they were both by sex and nature somewhat tender, so were they at first less able to endure the straitness of the prison; and especially the brewer's wife was cast into marvellous great agonies and troubles of mind thereby. But Christ, beholding the weak infirmity of His servant, did not fail to help her when she was in this necessity; so at the length they both suffered after Samuel, in 1556, February 19. And these, no doubt, were those two ladders, which, being joined with the third, Samuel saw stretched up into heaven. This blessed Samuel, the servant of Christ, suffered the thirty-first of August, 1555.

The report goeth among some that were there present, and saw him burn, that his body in burning did shine in the eyes of them that stood by, as bright and white as new-tried silver.

When Agnes Bongeor saw herself separated from her prison-fellows, what piteous moan that good woman made, how bitterly she wept, what strange thoughts came into her mind, how naked and desolate she esteemed herself, and into what plunge of despair and care her poor soul was brought, it was piteous and wonderful to see; which all came because she went not with them to give her life in the defence of her Christ; for of all things in the world, life was least looked for at her hands.

For that morning in which she was kept back from burning, had she put on a smock, that she had prepared only for that purpose. And also having a child, a little young infant sucking on her, whom she kept with her tenderly all the time that she was in prison, against that day likewise did she send away to another nurse, and prepared herself presently to give herself for the testimony of the glorious Gospel of Jesus Christ. So little did she look for life, and so greatly did God's gifts work in her above nature, that death seemed a great deal better welcome than life. After which, she began a little to stay herself, and gave her whole exercise to reading and prayer, wherein she found no little comfort.

In a short time came a writ from London for the burning, which according to the effect thereof, was executed.

HUGH LAVERICK AND JOHN APRICE

Here we perceive that neither the impotence of age nor the affliction of blindness, could turn aside the murdering fangs of these Babylonish monsters.

The first of these unfortunates was of the parish of Barking, aged sixty-eight, a painter and a cripple. The other was blind, dark indeed in his visual faculties, but intellectually illuminated with the radiance of the everlasting Gospel of truth. Inoffensive objects like these were informed against by some of the sons of bigotry, and dragged before the prelatical shark of London, where they underwent examination, and replied to the articles propounded to them, as other Christian martyrs had done before. On the ninth day of May, in the consistory of St. Paul's, they were entreated to recant, and upon refusal, were sent to Fulham, where Bonner, by way of a dessert after dinner, condemned them to the agonies of the fire. Being consigned to the secular officers, May 15, 1556, they were taken in a cart from Newgate to Stratford-le-Bow, where they were fastened to the stake. When Hugh Laverick was secured by the chain, having no further occasion for his crutch, he threw it away saying to his fellow-martyr, while consoling him, "Be of good cheer my brother; for my lord of London is our good physician; he will heal us both shortly—thee of thy blindness, and me of my lameness." They sank down in the fire, to rise to immortality!

The day after the above martyrdoms, *Catharine Hut,* of Bocking, widow; *Joan Horns,* spinster, of Billerica; *Elizabeth Thackwel,* spinster, of Great Burstead, suffered death in Smithfield.

THOMAS DOWRY

We have again to record an act of unpitying cruelty, exercised on this lad, whom Bishop Hooper, had confirmed in the Lord and the knowledge of his Word. How long this poor sufferer remained in prison is uncertain.

By the testimony of one John Paylor, register of Gloucester, we learn that when Dowry was brought before Dr. Williams, then chancellor of Gloucester, the usual articles were presented him for subscription. From these he dissented; and, upon the doctor's demanding of whom and where he had learned his heresies, the youth replied, "Indeed, Mr. Chancellor, I learned from you in that very pulpit. On such a day (naming the day) you said, in preaching upon the Sacrament, that it was to be exercised spiritually by faith, and not carnally and really, as taught by the papists." Dr. Williams then bid him recant, as he had done; but Dowry had not so learned his duty. "Though you," said he, "can so easily mock God, the world, and your own conscience, yet will I not do so."

PRESERVATION OF GEORGE CROW
AND HIS TESTAMENT

This poor man, of Malden, May 26, 1556, put to sea, to lade in Lent with fuller's earth, but the boat, being driven on land, filled with water, and everything was washed out of her; Crow, however, saved his Testament, and coveted nothing else. With Crow was a man and a boy, whose awful situation became every minute more alarming, as the boat was useless, and they were ten miles from land, expecting the tide should in a few hours set in upon them. After prayer to God, they got upon the mast, and hung there for the space of ten hours, when the poor boy, overcome by cold and exhaustion, fell off, and was drowned. The tide having abated, Crow proposed to take down the masts, and float upon them, which they did; and at ten o'clock at night they were borne away at the mercy of the waves. On Wednesday, in the night, Crow's companion died through the fatigue and hunger, and he was left alone, calling upon God for succor. At length he was picked up by a Captain Morse, bound to Antwerp, who had nearly steered away, taking him for some fisherman's buoy floating in the sea. As soon as Crow was got on board, he put his hand in his bosom, and drew out his Testament, which indeed was wet, but not otherwise injured. At Antwerp he was well received, and the money he had lost was more than made good to him.

EXECUTIONS AT STRATFORD-LE-BOW

At this sacrifice, which we are about to detail no less than thirteen were doomed to the fire.

Each one refusing to subscribe contrary to conscience, they were condemned, and the twenty-seventh of June, 1556, was appointed for their execution at Stratford-le-Bow. Their constancy and faith glorified their Redeemer, equally in life and in death.

REV. JULIUS PALMER

This gentleman's life presents a singular instance of error and conversion. In the time of Edward, he was a rigid and obstinate papist, so adverse to godly and sincere preaching, that he was even despised by his own party; that this frame of mind should be changed, and he suffer persecution and death in Queen Mary's reign, are among those events of omnipotence at which we wonder and admire.

Mr. Palmer was born at Coventry, where his father had been mayor. Being afterward removed to Oxford, he became, under Mr. Harley, of Magdalen College, an elegant Latin and Greek scholar. He was fond of useful disputation, possessed of a lively wit, and a strong memory. Indefatigable in private study, he rose at four in the morning, and by this practice qualified himself to become reader in logic in Magdalen College. The times of Edward, however, favoring the Reformation, Mr. Palmer became frequently punished for his contempt of prayer and orderly behavior, and was at length expelled the house.

He afterwards embraced the doctrines of the Reformation, which occasioned his arrest and final condemnation.

A certain nobleman offered him his life if he would recant.

"If so," said he, "thou wilt dwell with me. And if thou wilt set thy mind to marriage, I will procure thee a wife and a farm, and help to stuff and fit thy farm for thee. How sayst thou?"

Palmer thanked him very courteously, but very modestly and reverently concluded that as he had already in two places renounced his living for Christ's sake, so he would with God's grace be ready to surrender and yield up his life also for the same, when God should send time.

When Sir Richard perceived that he would by no means relent: "Well, Palmer," saith he, "then I perceive one of us twain shall be damned: for we be of two faiths, and certain I am there is but one faith that leadeth to life and salvation."

Palmer: "O sir, I hope that we both shall be saved."

Sir Richard: "How may that be?"

Palmer: "Right well, sir. For as it hath pleased our merciful Savior, according to the Gospel's parable, to call me at the third hour of the day, even in my flowers, at the age of four and twenty years, even so I trust He hath called, and will call you, at the eleventh hour of this your old age, and give you everlasting life for your portion."

Sir Richard: "Sayest thou so? Well, Palmer, well, I would I might have thee but one month in my house: I doubt not but I would convert thee, or thou shouldst convert me."

Then said Master Winchcomb, "Take pity on thy golden years, and pleasant flowers of lusty youth, before it be too late."

Palmer: "Sir, I long for those springing flowers that shall never fade away."

He was tried on the fifteenth of July, 1556, together with one Thomas Askin, fellow prisoner. Askin and one John Guin had been sentenced the day before, and Mr. Palmer, on the fifteenth, was brought up for final judgment. Execution was ordered to follow the sentence, and at five o'clock in the same afternoon, at a place called the Sand-pits, these three martyrs were fastened to a stake. After devoutly praying together, they sung the Thirty-first Psalm.

When the fire was kindled, and it had seized their bodies, without an appearance of enduring pain, they continued to cry, "Lord Jesus, strengthen us! Lord Jesus receive our souls!" until animation was suspended and human suffering was past. It is remarkable, that, when their heads had fallen together in a mass as it were by the force of the flames, and the spectators thought Palmer as lifeless, his tongue and lips again moved, and were heard to pronounce the name of Jesus, to whom be glory and honor forever!

JOAN WASTE AND OTHERS

This poor, honest woman, blind from her birth, and unmarried, aged twenty-two, was of the parish of Allhallows, Derby. Her father was a barber, and also made ropes for a living: in which she assisted him, and also learned to knit several articles of apparel. Refusing to communicate with those who maintained doctrines contrary to those she had learned in the days of the pious Edward, she was called before Dr. Draicot, the chancellor of Bishop Blaine, and Peter Finch, official of Derby.

With sophistical arguments and threats they endeavored to confound the poor girl; but she proffered to yield to the bishop's doctrine, if he would answer for her at the Day of Judgment, (as pious Dr. Taylor had done in his sermons) that his belief of the real presence of the Sacrament was true. The bishop at first answered that he would; but Dr. Draicot reminding him that he might not in any way answer for a heretic, he withdrew his confirmation of his own tenets; and she replied that if their consciences would not permit them to answer at God's bar for that truth they wished her to subscribe to, she would answer no more questions. Sentence was then adjudged, and Dr. Draicot appointed to preach her condemned sermon, which took place August 1, 1556, the day of her martyrdom. His fulminating discourse being finished, the poor, sightless object was taken to a place called Windmill Pit, near the town, where she for a time held her brother by the hand, and then prepared herself for the fire, calling upon the pitying multitude to pray with her, and upon Christ to have mercy upon her, until the glorious light of the everlasting Sun of righteousness beamed upon her departed spirit.

In November, fifteen martyrs were imprisoned in Canterbury castle, of whom all were either burnt or famished. Among the latter were J. Clark, D. Chittenden, W. Foster of Stonc, Alice Potkins, and J. Archer, of Cranbrooke, weaver. The two first of these had not received condemnation, but the others were sentenced to the fire. Foster, at his examination, observed upon the utility of carrying lighted candles about on Candlemas-day, that he might as well carry a pitchfork; and that a gibbet would have as good an effect as the cross.

We have now brought to a close the sanguinary proscriptions of the merciless Mary, in the year 1556, the number of which amounted to above EIGHTY-FOUR!

The beginning of the year 1557, was remarkable for the visit of Cardinal Pole to the University of Cambridge, which seemed to stand in need of much cleansing from heretical preachers and reformed doctrines. One object was also to play the popish farce of trying Martin Bucer and Paulus Phagius, who had been buried about three or four years; for which purpose the churches of St. Mary and St. Michael, where they lay, were interdicted as vile and unholy places, unfit to worship God in, until they were perfumed and washed with the pope's holy water, etc., etc. The trumpery act of citing these dead reformers to appear, not having had the least effect upon them, on January 26, sentence of condemnation was passed, part of which ran in this manner, and may serve as a specimen of proceedings of this nature: "We therefore pronounce the said Martin Bucer and Paulus Phagius excommunicated and anathematized, as well by the common law, as by letters of process; and that their memory be condemned, we also condemn their bodies and bones (which in that wicked time of schism, and other heresies flourishing in this kingdom, were rashly buried in holy ground) to be dug up, and cast far from the bodies and bones of the faithful, according to the holy canons, and we command that they and their writings, if any be there found, be publicly burnt; and we interdict all persons whatsoever of this university, town, or places adjacent, who shall read or conceal their heretical book, as well by the common law, as by our letters of process!"

After the sentence thus read, the bishop commanded their bodies to be dug out of their graves, and being degraded from holy orders, delivered them into the hands of the secular power; for it was not lawful for such innocent persons as they were, abhorring all bloodshed, and detesting all desire of murder, to put any man to death.

February 6, the bodies, enclosed as they were in chests, were carried into the midst of the market place at Cambridge, accompanied by a vast concourse of people. A great post was set fast in the ground, to which the chests were affixed with a large iron chain, and bound round their centers, in the same manner as if the dead bodies had been alive. When the fire began to ascend, and caught the coffins, a number of condemned books were also launched into the flames, and burnt. Justice, however, was done to the memories of these pious and learned men in Queen Elizabeth's reign, when Mr. Ackworth, orator of the university, and Mr. J. Pilkington, pronounced orations in honor of their memory, and in reprobation of their Catholic persecutors.

Cardinal Pole also inflicted his harmless rage upon the dead body of Peter Martyr's wife, who, by his command, was dug out of her grave, and buried on a distant dunghill, partly because her bones lay near St. Fridewide's relics, held once in great esteem in that college, and partly because he wished to purify Oxford of heretical remains as well as Cambridge. In the succeeding reign, however, her remains were restored to their former cemetery, and even intermingled with those of the Catholic saint, to the utter astonishment and mortification of the disciples of his holiness the pope.

Cardinal Pole published a list of fifty-four articles, containing instructions to the clergy of his diocese of Canterbury, some of which are too ludicrous and puerile to excite any other sentiment than laughter in these days.

PERSECUTIONS IN THE DIOCESE OF CANTERBURY

In the month of February, the following persons were committed to prison: R. Coleman, of Waldon, laborer; Joan Winseley, of Horsley Magna, spinster; S. Glover, of Rayley; R. Clerk, of Much Holland, mariner; W. Munt, of Much Bentley, sawyer; Marg. Field, of Ramsey, spinster; R. Bongeor, currier; R. Jolley, mariner;

Allen Simpson, Helen Ewire, C. Pepper, widow; Alice Walley (who recanted), W. Bongeor, glazier, all of Colchester; R. Atkin, of Halstead, weaver; R. Barcock, of Wilton, carpenter; R. George, of Westbarhonlt, laborer; R. Debnam of Debenham, weaver; C. Warren, of Cocksall, spinster; Agnes Whitlock, of Dover-court, spinster;

ROSE ALLEN, SPINSTER; AND
T. FERESANNES, MINOR; BOTH OF COLCHESTER

These persons were brought before Bonner, who would have immediately sent them to execution, but Cardinal Pole was for more merciful measures, and Bonner, in a letter of his to the cardinal, seems to be sensible that he had displeased him, for he has this expression: "I thought to have them all hither to Fulham, and to have given sentence against them; nevertheless, perceiving by my last doing that your grace was offended, I thought it my duty, before I proceeded further, to inform your grace." This circumstance verifies the account that the cardinal was a humane man; and though a zealous Catholic, we, as Protestants, are willing to render him that honor which his merciful character deserves. Some of the bitter persecutors denounced him to the pope as a favorer of heretics, and he was summoned to Rome, but Queen Mary, by particular entreaty, procured his stay. However, before his latter end, and a little before his last journey from Rome to England, he was strongly suspected of favoring the doctrine of Luther.

As in the last sacrifice four women did honor to the truth, so in the following auto da fe we have the like number of females and males, who suffered June 30, 1557, at Canterbury, and were J. Fishcock, F. White, N. Pardue, Barbary Final, widow, Bardbridge's widow, Wilson's wife, and Benden's wife.

Of this group we shall more particularly notice Alice Benden, wife of Edward Benden, of Staplehurst, Kent. She had been taken up in October, 1556, for non-attendance, and released upon a strong injunction to mind her conduct. Her husband was a bigoted Catholic, and publicly speaking of his wife's contumacy, she was conveyed to Canterbury castle, where knowing, when she should be removed to the bishop's prison, she should be almost starved upon three farthings a day, she endeavored to prepare herself for this suffering by living upon twopence halfpenny per day.

On January 22, 1557, her husband wrote to the bishop that if his wife's brother, Roger Hall, were to be kept from consoling and relieving her, she might turn; on this account, she was moved to a prison called Monday's Hole. Her brother sought diligently for her, and at the end of five weeks providentially heard her voice in the dungeon, but could not otherwise relieve her, than by putting some money in a loaf, and sticking it on a long pole. Dreadful must have been the situation of this poor victim, lying on straw, between stone walls, without a change of apparel, or the meanest requisites of cleanliness, during a period of nine weeks!

On March 25 she was summoned before the bishop, who, with rewards, offered her liberty if she would go home and be comfortable; but Mrs. Benden had been inured to suffering, and, showing him her contracted limbs and emaciated appearance, refused to swerve from the truth. She was however removed from this black hole to the West Gate, whence, about the end of April, she was taken out to be condemned, and then committed to the castle prison until the nineteenth of June, the day of her burning. At the stake, she gave her handkerchief to one John Banks, as a memorial; and from her waist she drew a white lace, desiring him to give it to her brother, and tell him that it was the last band that had bound her, except the chain; and to her father she returned a shilling he had sent her.

The whole of these seven martyrs undressed themselves with alacrity, and, being prepared, knelt down, and prayed with an earnestness and Christian spirit that even the enemies of the cross were affected. After invocation made together, they were secured to the stake, and, being encompassed with the unsparing flames, they yielded their souls into the hands of the living Lord.

Matthew Plaise, weaver, a sincere and shrewd Christian, of Stone, Kent, was brought before Thomas, bishop of Dover, and other inquisitors, whom he ingeniously teased by his indirect answers, of which the following is a specimen.

Dr. Harpsfield. Christ called the bread His body; what dost thou say it is?
Plaise. I do believe it was that which He gave them.
Dr. H. What was that?
P. That which He brake.
Dr. H. What did He brake?
P. That which He took.
Dr. H. What did He take?
P. I say, what He gave them, that did they eat indeed.
Dr. H. Well, then, thou sayest it was but bread which the disciples did eat.
P. I say, what He gave them, that did they eat indeed.

A very long disputation followed, in which Plaise was desired to humble himself to the bishop; but this he refused. Whether this zealous person died in prison, was executed, or delivered, history does not mention.

REV. JOHN HULLIER

Rev. John Hullier was brought up at Eton College, and in process of time became curate of Babram, three miles from Cambridge, and went afterward to Lynn; where, opposing the superstition of the papists, he was carried before Dr. Thirlby, bishop of Ely, and sent to Cambridge castle: here he lay for a time, and was then sent to Tolbooth prison, where, after three months, he was brought to St. Mary's Church, and condemned by Dr. Fuller. On Maunday Thursday he was brought to the stake: while undressing, he told the people to bear witness that he was about to suffer in a just cause, and exhorted them to believe that there was no other rock than Jesus Christ to build upon. A priest named Boyes, then desired the mayor to silence him. After praying, he went meekly to the stake, and being bound with a chain, and placed in a pitch barrel, fire was applied to the reeds and wood; but the wind drove the fire directly to his back, which caused him under the severe agony to pray the more fervently.

His friends directed the executioner to fire the pile to windward of his face, which was immediately done.

A quantity of books were now thrown into the fire, one of which (the Communion Service) he caught, opened it, and joyfully continued to read it, until the fire and smoke deprived him of sight; then even, in earnest prayer, he pressed the book to his heart, thanking God for bestowing on him in his last moments this precious gift.

The day being hot, the fire burnt fiercely; and at a time when the spectators supposed he was no more, he suddenly exclaimed, "Lord Jesus, receive my spirit," and meekly resigned his life. He was burnt on Jesus Green, not far from Jesus College. He had gunpowder given him, but he was dead before it became ignited. This pious sufferer afforded a singular spectacle; for his flesh was so burnt from the bones, which continued erect, that he presented the idea of a skeleton figure chained to the stake. His remains were eagerly seized by the multitude, and venerated by all who admired his piety or detested inhuman bigotry.

SIMON MILLER AND ELIZABETH COOPER

In the following month of July, received the crown of martyrdom. Miller dwelt at Lynn, and came to Norwich, where, planting himself at the door of one of the churches, as the people came out, he requested to know of them where he could go to receive the Communion. For this a priest brought him before Dr. Dunning, who committed him to ward; but he was suffered to go home, and arrange his affairs; after which he returned to the bishop's house, and to his prison, where he remained until the thirteenth of July, the day of his burning.

Elizabeth Cooper, wife of a pewterer, of St. Andrews, Norwich, had recanted; but tortured for what she had done by the worm which dieth not, she shortly after voluntarily entered her parish church during the time of the popish service, and standing up, audibly proclaimed that she revoked her former recantation, and cautioned the people to avoid her unworthy example. She was taken from her own house by Mr. Sutton the sheriff, who very reluctantly complied with the letter of the law, as they had been servants and in friendship together. At the stake, the poor sufferer, feeling the fire, uttered the cry of "Oh!" upon which Mr. Miller, putting his hand behind him towards her, desired her to be of a good courage, "for (said he) good sister, we shall have a joyful and a sweet supper." Encouraged by this example and exhortation, she stood the fiery ordeal without flinching, and, with him, proved the power of faith over the flesh.

EXECUTIONS AT COLCHESTER

It was before mentioned that twenty-two persons had been sent up from Colchester, who upon a slight submission, were afterward released. Of these, William Munt, of Much Bentley, husbandman, with Alice, his wife, and Rose

Allin, her daughter, upon their return home, abstained from church, which induced the bigoted priest secretly to write to Bonner. For a short time they absconded, but returning again, March 7, one Edmund Tyrrel, (a relation of the Tyrrel who murdered King Edward V and his brother) with the officers, entered the house while Munt and his wife were in bed, and informed them that they must go to Colchester castle. Mrs. Munt at that time being very ill, requested her daughter to get her some drink; leave being permitted, Rose took a candle and a mug; and in returning through the house was met by Tyrrel, who cautioned her to advise her parents to become good Catholics. Rose briefly informed him that they had the Holy Ghost for their adviser; and that she was ready to lay down her own life for the same cause. Turning to his company, he remarked that she was willing to burn; and one of them told him to prove her, and see what she would do by and by. The unfeeling wretch immediately executed this project; and, seizing the young woman by the wrist, he held the lighted candle under her hand, burning it crosswise on the back, until the tendons divided from the flesh, during which he loaded her with many opprobrious epithets. She endured his rage unmoved, and then, when he had ceased the torture, she asked him to begin at her feet or head, for he need not fear that his employer would one day repay him. After this she took the drink to her mother.

This cruel act of torture does not stand alone on record.

Bonner had served a poor blind harper in nearly the same manner, who had steadily maintained a hope that if every joint of him were to be burnt, he should not fly from the faith. Bonner, upon this, privately made a signal to his men, to bring a burning coal, which they placed in the poor man's hand, and then by force held it closed, until it burnt into the flesh deeply.

George Eagles, tailor, was indicted for having prayed that "God would turn Queen Mary's heart, or take her away"; the ostensible cause of his death was his religion, for treason could hardly be imagined in praying for the reformation of such an execrable soul as that of Mary. Being condemned for this crime, he was drawn to the place of execution upon a sledge, with two robbers, who were executed with him. After Eagles had mounted the ladder, and been turned off a short time, he was cut down before he was at all insensible; a bailiff, named William Swallow, then dragged him to the sledge, and with a common blunt cleaver, hacked off the head; in a manner equally clumsy and cruel, he opened his body and tore out the heart.

In all this suffering the poor martyr repined not, but to the last called upon his Savior. The fury of these bigots did not end here; the intestines were burnt, and the body was quartered, the four parts being sent to Colchester, Harwich, Chelmsford, and St. Rouse's. Chelmsford had the honor of retaining his head, which was affixed to a long pole in the market place. In time it was blown down, and lay several days in the street, until it was buried at night in the churchyard. God's judgment not long after fell upon Swallow, who in his old age became a beggar, and who was affected with a leprosy that made him obnoxious even to the animal creation; nor did Richard Potts, who troubled Eagles in his dying moments, escape the visiting hand of God.

MRS. JOYCE LEWES

This lady was the wife of Mr. T. Lewes, of Manchester. She had received the Romish religion as true, until the burning of that pious martyr, Mr. Saunders, at Coventry. Understanding that his death arose from a refusal to receive the Mass, she began to inquire into the ground of his refusal, and her conscience, as it began to be enlightened, became restless and alarmed. In this inquietude, she resorted to Mr. John Glover, who lived near, and requested that he would unfold those rich sources of Gospel knowledge he possessed, particularly upon the subject of transubstantiation. He easily succeeded in convincing her that the mummery of popery and the Mass were at variance with God's most holy Word, and honestly reproved her for following too much the vanities of a wicked world. It was to her indeed a word in season, for she soon became weary of her former sinful life and resolved to abandon the Mass and dilatrous worship. Though compelled by her husband's violence to go to church, her contempt of the holy water and other ceremonies was so manifest, that she was accused before the bishop for despising the sacramentals.

A citation, addressed to her, immediately followed, which was given to Mr. Lewes, who, in a fit of passion, held a dagger to the throat of the officer, and made him eat it, after which he caused him to drink it down, and then sent him away. But for this the bishop summoned Mr. Lewes before him as well as his wife; the former readily submitted, but the latter resolutely affirmed, that, in refusing holy water, she neither offended God, nor any part of his laws. She was sent home for a month, her husband being bound for her appearance, during which time Mr. Glover impressed upon her the necessity of doing what she did, not from self-vanity, but for the honor and glory of God.

Mr. Glover and others earnestly exhorted Lewes to forfeit the money he was bound in, rather than subject his wife to certain death; but he was deaf to the voice of humanity, and delivered her over to the bishop, who soon found sufficient cause to consign her to a loathsome prison, whence she was several times brought for examination. At the last time the bishop reasoned with her upon the fitness of her coming to Mass, and receiving as sacred the Sacrament and sacramentals of the Holy Ghost. "If these things were in the Word of God," said Mrs. Lewes, "I would with all my heart receive, believe, and esteem them." The bishop, with the most ignorant and impious effrontery, replied, "If thou wilt believe no more than what is warranted by Scriptures, thou art in a state of damnation!" Astonished at such a declaration, this worthy sufferer ably rejoined that his words were as impure as they were profane.

After condemnation, she lay a twelve-month in prison, the sheriff not being willing to put her to death in his time, though he had been but just chosen. When her death warrant came from London, she sent for some friends, whom she consulted in what manner her death might be more glorious to the name of God, and injurious to the cause of God's enemies. Smilingly, she said: "As for death, I think but lightly of. When I know that I shall behold the amiable countenance of Christ my dear Savior, the ugly face of death does not much trouble me." The evening before she suffered, two priests were anxious to visit her, but she refused both their confession and absolution, when she could hold a better communication with the High Priest of souls. About three o'clock in the morning, Satan began to shoot his fiery darts, by putting into her mind to doubt whether she was chosen to eternal life, and Christ died for her. Her friends readily pointed out to her those consolatory passages of Scripture which comfort the fainting heart, and treat of the Redeemer who taketh away the sins of the world.

About eight o'clock the sheriff announced to her that she had but an hour to live; she was at first cast down, but this soon passed away, and she thanked God that her life was about to be devoted to His service. The sheriff granted permission for two friends to accompany her to the stake—an indulgence for which he was afterward severely handled. Mr. Reniger and Mr. Bernher led her to the place of execution; in going to which, from its distance, her great weakness, and the press of the people, she had nearly fainted. Three times she prayed fervently that God would deliver the land from popery and the idolatrous Mass; and the people for the most part, as well as the sheriff, said Amen.

When she had prayed, she took the cup, (which had been filled with water to refresh her,) and said, "I drink to all them that unfeignedly love the Gospel of Christ, and wish for the abolition of popery." Her friends, and a great many women of the place, drank with her, for which most of them afterward were enjoined penance.

When chained to the stake, her countenance was cheerful, and the roses of her cheeks were not abated. Her hands were extended towards heaven until the fire rendered them powerless, when her soul was received into the arms of the Creator. The duration of her agony was but short, as the under-sheriff, at the request of her friends, had prepared such excellent fuel that she was in a few minutes overwhelmed with smoke and flame. The case of this lady drew a tear of pity from everyone who had a heart not callous to humanity.

EXECUTIONS AT ISLINGTON

About the seventeenth of September, suffered at Islington the following four professors of Christ: Ralph Allerton, James Austoo, Margery Austoo, and Richard Roth.

James Austoo and his wife, of St. Allhallows, Barking, London, were sentenced for not believing in the presence. Richard Roth rejected the seven Sacraments, and was accused of comforting the heretics by the following letter written in his own blood, and intended to have been sent to his friends at Colchester:

O dear Brethren and Sisters,

How much reason have you to rejoice in God, that He hath given you such faith to overcome this bloodthirsty tyrant thus far! And no doubt He that hath begun that good work in you, will fulfill it unto the end. O dear hearts in Christ, what a crown of glory shall ye receive with Christ in the kingdom of God! O that it had been the good will of God that I had been ready to have gone with you; for I lie in my lord's Little-ease by day, and in the night I lie in the Coalhouse, apart from Ralph Allerton, or any other; and we look every day when we shall be condemned; for he said that I should be burned within ten days before Easter; but I lie still at the pool's brink, and every man goeth in before me; but we abide patiently the Lord's leisure, with many bonds, in fetters and stocks, by which we have received great joy of God. And now fare you well, dear brethren and sisters, in this world, but I trust to see you in the heavens face to face.

O brother Munt, with your wife and my sister Rose, how blessed are you in the Lord, that God hath found you worthy to suffer for His sake! with all the rest of my dear brethren and sisters known and unknown. O be joyful even unto death. Fear it not, saith Christ, for I have overcome death. O dear heart, seeing that Jesus Christ will be our help, O tarry you the Lord's leisure. Be strong, let your hearts be of good comfort, and wait you still for the Lord. He is at hand. Yea, the angel of the Lord pitcheth his tent round about them that fear him, and delivereth them which way he seeth best. For our lives are in the Lord's hands; and they can do nothing unto us before God suffer them. Therefore give all thanks to God.

O dear hearts, you shall be clothed in long white garments upon the mount of Sion, with the multitude of saints, and with Jesus Christ our Savior, who will never forsake us. O blessed virgins, ye have played the wise virgins' part, in that ye have taken oil in your lamps that ye may go in with the Bridegroom, when he cometh, into the everlasting joy with Him. But as for the foolish, they shall be shut out, because they made not themselves ready to suffer with Christ, neither go about to take up His cross. O dear hearts, how precious shall your death be in the sight of the Lord! for dear is the death of His saints. O fare you well, and pray. The grace of our Lord Jesus Christ be with you all. Amen, Amen. Pray, pray, pray!

Written by me, with my own blood,
RICHARD ROTH

This letter, so justly denominating Bonner the "bloodthirsty tyrant," was not likely to excite his compassion. Roth accused him of bringing them to secret examination by night, because he was afraid of the people by day. Resisting every temptation to recant, he was condemned, and on September 17, 1557, these four martyrs perished at Islington, for the testimony of the Lamb, who was slain that they might be of the redeemed of God.

John Noyes, a shoemaker, of Laxfield, Suffolk, was taken to Eye, and at midnight, September 21, 1557, he was brought from Eye to Laxfield to be burned. On the following morning he was led to the stake, prepared for the horrid sacrifice. Mr. Noyes, on coming to the fatal spot, knelt down, prayed, and rehearsed the Fiftieth Psalm. When the chain enveloped him, he said, "Fear not them that kill the body, but fear him that can kill both body and soul, and cast it into everlasting fire!" As one Cadman placed a fagot against him, he blessed the hour in which he was born to die for the truth; and while trusting only upon the all-sufficient merits of the Redeemer, fire was set to the pile, and the blazing fagots in a short time stifled his last words, "Lord, have mercy on me! Christ, have mercy upon me!" The ashes of the body were buried in a pit, and with them one of his feet, whole to the ankle, with the stocking on.

MRS. CICELY ORMES

This young martyr, aged twenty-two, was the wife of Mr. Edmund Ormes, worsted weaver of St. Lawrence, Norwich. At the death of Miller and Elizabeth Cooper, before mentioned, she had said that she would pledge them of the same cup they drank of. For these words she was brought to the chancellor, who would have discharged her upon promising to go to church, and to keep her belief to herself. As she would not consent to this, the chancellor urged that he had shown more lenity to her than any other person, and was unwilling to condemn her, because she was an ignorant foolish woman; to this she replied, (perhaps with more shrewdness than he expected), that however great his desire might be to spare her sinful flesh, it could not equal her inclination to surrender it up in so great a quarrel. The chancellor then pronounced the fiery sentence, and September 23, 1557, she was brought to the stake, at eight o'clock in the morning.

After declaring her faith to the people, she laid her hand on the stake, and said, "Welcome, thou cross of Christ." Her hand was sooted in doing this, (for it was the same stake at which Miller and Cooper were burnt), and she at first wiped it; but directly after again welcomed and embraced it as the "sweet cross of Christ." After the tormentors had kindled the fire, she said, "My soul doth magnify the Lord, and my spirit doth rejoice in God my Savior." Then crossing her hands upon her breast, and looking upwards with the utmost serenity, she stood the fiery furnace. Her hands continued gradually to rise until the sinews were dried, and then they fell. She uttered no sigh of pain, but yielded her life, an emblem of that celestial paradise in which is the presence of God, blessed forever.

It might be contended that this martyr voluntarily sought her own death, as the chancellor scarcely exacted any other penance of her than to keep her belief to herself; yet it should seem in this instance as if God had chosen her to be a shining light, for a twelve-month before she was taken, she had recanted; but she was wretched until the chancellor was informed, by letter, that she repented of her recantation from the bottom of her heart. As if to compensate for her former apostasy, and to convince the Catholics that she meant no more to compromise for her personal security, she boldly refused his friendly offer of permitting her to temporize. Her courage in such a cause deserves commendation—the cause of Him who has said, "Whoever is ashamed of me on earth, of such will I be ashamed in heaven."

REV. JOHN ROUGH

This pious martyr was a Scotchman. At the age of seventeen, he entered himself as one of the order of Black Friars, at Stirling, in Scotland. He had been kept out of an inheritance by his friends, and he took this step in revenge for their conduct to him. After being there sixteen years, Lord Hamilton, earl of Arran, taking a liking to him, the archbishop of St. Andrew's induced the provincial of the house to dispense with his habit and order; and he thus became the earl's chaplain. He remained in this spiritual employment a year, and in that time God wrought in him a saving knowledge of the truth; for which reason the earl sent him to preach in the freedom of Ayr, where he remained four years; but finding danger there from the religious complexion of the times, and learning that there was much Gospel freedom in England, he travelled up to the duke of Somerset, then Lord Protector of England, who gave him a yearly salary of twenty pounds, and authorized him, to preach at Carlisle, Berwick, and Newcastle, where he married. He was afterward removed to a benefice at Hull, in which he remained until the death of Edward VI.

In consequence of the tide of persecution then setting in, he fled with his wife to Friesland, and at Nordon they followed the occupation of knitting hose, caps, etc., for subsistence. Impeded in his business by the want of yarn, he came over to England to procure a quantity, and on November 10, arrived in London, where he soon heard of a secret society of the faithful, to whom he joined himself, and was in a short time elected their minister, in which occupation he strengthened them in every good resolution.

On December 12, through the information of one Taylor, a member of the society, Mr. Rough, with Cuthbert Symson and others, was taken up in the Saracen's Head, Islington, where, under the pretext of coming to see a play, their religious exercises were holden. The queen's vice-chamberlain conducted Rough and Symson before the Council, in whose presence they were charged with meeting to celebrate the Communion. The Council wrote to Bonner and he lost no time in this affair of blood. In three days he had him up, and on the next (the twentieth) resolved to condemn him. The charges laid against him were, that he, being a priest, was married, and that he had rejected the service in the Latin tongue. Rough wanted not arguments to reply to these flimsy tenets. In short, he was degraded and condemned.

Mr. Rough, it should be noticed, when in the north, in Edward VI's reign, had saved Dr. Watson's life, who afterward sat with Bishop Bonner on the bench. This ungrateful prelate, in return for the kind act he had received, boldly accused Mr. Rough of being the most pernicious heretic in the country. The godly minister reproved him for his malicious spirit; he affirmed that, during the thirty years he had lived, he had never bowed the knee to Baal; and that twice at Rome he had seen the pope borne about on men's shoulders with the false-named Sacrament carried before him, presenting a true picture of the very Antichrist; yet was more reverence shown to him than to the wafer, which they accounted to be their God. "Ah?" said Bonner, rising, and making towards him, as if he would have torn his garment, "Hast thou been at Rome, and seen our holy father the pope, and dost thou blaspheme him after this sort?" This said, he fell upon him, tore off a piece of his beard, and that the day might begin to his own satisfaction, he ordered the object of his rage to be burnt by half-past five the following morning.

CUTHBERT SYMSON

Few professors of Christ possessed more activity and zeal than this excellent person. He not only labored to preserve his friends from the contagion of popery, but he labored to guard them against the terrors of persecution. He was deacon of the little congregation over which Mr. Rough presided as minister.

Mr. Symson has written an account of his own sufferings, which he cannot detail better than in his own words:

On the thirteenth of December, 1557, I was committed by the Council to the Tower of London. On the following Thursday, I was called into the ward-room, before the constable of the Tower, and the recorder of London, Mr. Cholmly, who commanded me to inform them of the names of those who came to the English service. I answered that I would declare nothing; in consequence of my refusal, I was set upon a rack of iron, as I judge for the space of three hours!

They then asked me if I would confess: I answered as before.

After being unbound, I was carried back to my lodging. The Sunday after I was brought to the same place again, before the lieutenant and recorder of London, and they examined me. As I had answered before, so I answered now. Then the lieutenant swore by God I should tell; after which my two forefingers were bound together, and a small arrow placed between them, they drew it through so fast that the blood followed, and the arrow brake.

After enduring the rack twice again, I was retaken to my lodging, and ten days after the lieutenant asked me if I would not now confess that which they had before asked of me. I answered, that I had already said as much as I would. Three weeks after I was sent to the priest, where I was greatly assaulted, and at whose hand I received the pope's curse, for bearing witness of the resurrection of Christ. And thus I commend you to God, and to the Word of His grace, with all those who unfeignedly call upon the name of Jesus; desiring God of His endless mercy, through the merits of His dear Son Jesus Christ, to bring us all to His everlasting Kingdom, Amen. I praise God for His great mercy shown upon us. Sing Hosanna to the Highest with me, Cuthbert Symson. God forgive my sins!

I ask forgiveness of all the world, and I forgive all the world, and thus I leave the world, in the hope of a joyful resurrection!

If this account be duly considered, what a picture of repeated tortures does it present! But even the cruelty of the narration is exceeded by the patient meekness with which it was endured. Here are no expressions of malice, no invocations even of God's retributive justice, not a complaint of suffering wrongfully! On the contrary, praise to God, forgiveness of sin, and a forgiving all the world, concludes this unaffected interesting narrative.

Bonner's admiration was excited by the steadfast coolness of this martyr. Speaking of Mr. Symson in the consistory, he said, "You see what a personable man he is, and then of his patience, I affirm, that, if he were not a heretic, he is a man of the greatest patience that ever came before me. Thrice in one day has he been racked in the Tower; in my house also he has felt sorrow, and yet never have I seen his patience broken."

The day before this pious deacon was to be condemned, while in the stocks in the bishop's coal-house, he had the vision of a glorified form, which much encouraged him. This he certainly attested to his wife, to Mr. Austen, and others, before his death.

With this ornament of the Christian Reformation were apprehended Mr. Hugh Foxe and John Devinish; the three were brought before Bonner, March 19, 1558, and the papistical articles tendered. They rejected them, and were all condemned. As they worshipped together in the same society, at Islington, so they suffered together in Smithfield, March 28; in whose death the God of Grace was glorified, and true believers confirmed!

THOMAS HUDSON, THOMAS CARMAN, AND WILLIAM SEAMEN

Were condemned by a bigoted vicar of Aylesbury, named Berry.

The spot of execution was called Lollard's Pit, without Bishopsgate, at Norwich. After joining together in humble petition to the throne of grace, they rose, went to the stake, and were encircled with their chains. To the great surprise of the spectators, Hudson slipped from under his chains, and came forward. A great opinion prevailed that he was about to recant; others thought that he wanted further time. In the meantime, his companions at the stake urged every promise and exhortation to support him. The hopes of the enemies of the cross, however, were disappointed: the good man, far from fearing the smallest personal terror at the approaching pangs of death, was only alarmed that his Savior's face seemed to be hidden from him. Falling upon his knees, his spirit wrestled with God, and God verified the words of His Son, "Ask, and it shall be given." The martyr rose in an ecstasy of joy, and exclaimed, "Now, I thank God, I am strong! and care not what man can do to me!" With an unruffled countenance he replaced himself under the chain, joined his fellow-sufferers, and with them suffered death, to the comfort of the godly, and the confusion of Antichrist.

Berry, unsatiated with this demoniacal act, summoned up two hundred persons in the town of Aylesham, whom he compelled to kneel to the cross at Pentecost, and inflicted other punishments. He struck a poor man for a trifling word, with a flail, which proved fatal to the unoffending object. He also gave a woman named Alice Oxes, so heavy a blow with his fist, as she met him entering the hall when he was in an ill-humor, that she died with the violence. This priest was rich, and possessed great authority; he was a reprobate, and, like the priesthood, he abstained from marriage, to enjoy the more a debauched and licentious life. The Sunday after the death of Queen Mary, he was revelling with one of his concubines, before vespers; he then went to church, administered baptism, and in his return to his lascivious pastime, he was smitten by the hand of God. Without a moment given for repentance, he fell to the ground, and a groan was the only articulation permitted him. In him we may behold the difference between the end of a martyr and a persecutor.

THE STORY OF ROGER HOLLAND

In a retired close near a field, in Islington, a company of decent persons had assembled, to the number of forty. While they were religiously engaged in praying and expounding the Scripture, twenty-seven of them were carried before Sir Roger Cholmly. Some of the women made their escape, twenty-two were committed to Newgate, who continued in prison seven weeks. Previous to their examination, they were informed by the keeper, Alexander, that nothing more was requisite to procure their discharge, than to hear Mass. Easy as this condition may seem, these martyrs valued their purity of conscience more than loss of life or property; hence, thirteen were burnt, seven in Smithfield, and six at Brentford; two died in prison, and the other seven were providentially preserved. The names of the seven who suffered were, H. Pond, R. Estland, R. Southain, M. Ricarby, J. Floyd, J. Holiday, and Roger Holland. They were sent to Newgate, June 16, 1558, and executed on the twenty-seventh.

This Roger Holland, a merchant-tailor of London, was first an apprentice with one Master Kemption, at the Black Boy in Watling Street, giving himself to dancing, fencing, gaming, banqueting, and wanton company. He had received for his master certain money, to the sum of thirty pounds; and lost every groat at dice. Therefore he purposed to convey himself away beyond the seas, either into France or into Flanders.

With this resolution, he called early in the morning on a discreet servant in the house, named Elizabeth, who professed the Gospel, and lived a life that did honor to her profession. To her he revealed the loss his folly had occasioned, regretted that he had not followed her advice, and begged her to give his master a note of hand from him acknowledging the debt, which he would repay if ever it were in his power; he also entreated his disgraceful conduct might be kept secret, lest it would bring the gray hairs to his father with sorrow to a premature grave.

The maid, with a generosity and Christian principle rarely surpassed, conscious that his imprudence might be his ruin, brought him the thirty pounds, which was part of a sum of money recently left her by legacy. "Here," said she, "is the sum requisite: you shall take the money, and I will keep the note; but expressly on this condition, that you abandon all lewd and vicious company; that you neither swear nor talk immodestly, and game no more; for, should I learn that you do, I will immediately show this note to your master. I also require, that you shall promise me to attend the daily lecture at Allhallows, and the sermon at St. Paul's every Sunday; that you cast away all your books of popery, and in their place substitute the Testament and the Book of Service, and that you read the Scriptures with reverence and fear, calling upon God for his grace to direct you in his truth. Pray also fervently to God, to pardon your former offences, and not to remember the sins of your youth, and would you obtain his favor ever dread to break his laws or offend his majesty. So shall God have you in His keeping, and grant you your heart's desire." We must honor the memory of this excellent domestic, whose pious endeavors were equally directed to benefit the thoughtless youth in this life and that which is to come. God did not suffer the wish of this excellent domestic to be thrown upon a barren soil; within half a year after the licentious Holland became a zealous professor of the Gospel, and was an instrument of conversion to his father and others whom he visited in Lancashire, to their spiritual comfort and reformation from popery.

His father, pleased with his change of conduct, gave him forty pounds to commence business with in London.

Then Roger repaired to London again, and came to the maid that lent him the money to pay his master withal, and said unto her, "Elizabeth, here is thy money I borrowed of thee; and for the friendship, good will, and the good counsel I have received at thy hands, to recompense thee I am not able, otherwise than to make thee my wife." And soon after they were married, which was in the first year of Queen Mary.

After this he remained in the congregations of the faithful, until, the last year of Queen Mary, he, with the six others aforesaid, were taken.

And after Roger Holland there was none suffered in Smithfield for the testimony of the Gospel, God be thanked.

FLAGELLATIONS BY BONNER

When this Catholic hyena found that neither persuasions, threats, nor imprisonment, could produce any alteration in the mind of a youth named Thomas Hinshaw, he sent him to Fulham, and during the first night set him in the stocks, with no other allowance than bread and water. The following morning he came to see if this punishment had worked any change in his mind, and finding none, he sent Dr. Harpsfield, his archdeacon, to converse with him. The doctor was soon out of humor at his replies, called him peevish boy, and asked him if he thought he went about to damn his soul? "I am persuaded," said Thomas, "that you labor to promote the dark kingdom of the devil, not for the love of the truth." These words the doctor conveyed to the bishop, who, in a passion that almost prevented articulation, came to Thomas, and said, "Dost thou answer my archdeacon thus, thou naughty boy? But I'll soon handle thee well enough for it, be assured!" Two willow twigs were then brought him, and causing the unresisting youth to kneel against a long bench, in an arbor in his garden, he scourged him until he was compelled to cease for want of breath and fatigue. One of the rods was worn quite away.

Many other conflicts did Hinsaw undergo from the bishop; who, at length, to remove him effectually, procured false witnesses to lay articles against him, all of which the young man denied, and, in short, refused to answer any interrogatories administered to him. A fortnight after this, the young man was attacked by a burning ague, and at the request of his master. Mr. Pugson, of St. Paul's church-yard, he was removed, the bishop not doubting that he had given him his death in the natural way; he however remained ill above a year, and in the mean time Queen Mary died, by which act of providence he escaped Bonner's rage.

John Willes was another faithful person, on whom the scourging hand of Bonner fell. He was the brother of Richard Willes, before mentioned, burnt at Brentford. Hinshaw and Willes were confined in Bonner's coal house together, and afterward removed to Fulham, where he and Hinshaw remained during eight or ten days, in the stocks. Bonner's persecuting spirit betrayed itself in his treatment of Willes during his examinations, often striking him on the head with a stick, seizing him by the ears, and filliping him under the chin, saying he held down his head like a thief. This producing no signs of recantation, he took him into his orchard, and in a small arbor there he flogged him first with a willow rod, and then with birch, until he was exhausted. This cruel ferocity arose from the answer of the poor sufferer, who, upon being asked how long it was since he had crept to the cross, replied, "Not since he had come to years of discretion, nor would he, though he should be torn to pieces by wild horses." Bonner then bade him make the sign of the cross on his forehead, which he refused to do, and thus was led to the orchard.

One day, when in the stocks, Bonner asked him how he liked his lodging and fare. "Well enough," said Willes, "might I have a little straw to sit or lie upon." Just at this time came in Willes' wife, then largely pregnant, and entreated the bishop for her husband, boldly declaring that she would be delivered in the house, if he were not suffered to go with her. To get rid of the good wife's importunity, and the trouble of a lying-in woman in his palace, he bade Willes make the sign of the cross, and say, In nomine Patris, et Filii, et Spiritus Sancti, Amen. Willes omitted the sign, and repeated the words, "in the name of the Father, and of the Son, and of the Holy Ghost, Amen." Bonner would have the words repeated in Latin, to which Willes made no objection, knowing the meaning of the words. He was then permitted to go home with his wife, his kinsman Robert Rouze being charged to bring him to St. Paul's the next day, whither he himself went, and subscribing to a Latin instrument of little importance, was liberated. This is the last of the twenty-two taken at Islington.

REV. RICHARD YEOMAN

This devout aged person was curate to Dr. Taylor, at Hadley, and eminently qualified for his sacred function. Dr. Taylor left him the curacy at his departure, but no sooner had Mr. Newall gotten the benefice, than he removed Mr. Yeoman, and substituted a Romish priest. After this he wandered from place to place, exhorting all men to stand faithfully to God's Word, earnestly to give themselves unto prayer, with patience to bear the cross now laid upon them for their trial, with boldness to confess the truth before their adversaries, and with an undoubted hope to wait for the crown and reward of eternal felicity. But when he perceived his adversaries lay wait for him, he went into Kent, and with a little packet of laces, pins, points, etc., he travelled from village to village, selling such things, and in this manner subsisted himself, his wife, and children.

At last Justice Moile, of Kent, took Mr. Yeoman, and set him in the stocks a day and a night; but, having no evident matter to charge him with, he let him go again. Coming secretly again to Hadley, he tarried with his poor wife, who kept him privately, in a chamber of the town house, commonly called the Guildhall, more than a year. During this time the good old father abode in a chamber locked up all the day, spending his time in devout prayer, in reading the Scriptures, and in carding the wool which his wife spun. His wife also begged bread for herself and her children, by which precarious means they supported themselves. Thus the saints of God sustained hunger and misery, while the prophets of Baal lived in festivity, and were costily pampered at Jezebel's table.

Information being at length given to Newall, that Yeoman was secreted by his wife, he came, attended by the constables, and broke into the room where the object of his search lay in bed with his wife. He reproached the poor woman with being a whore, and would have indecently pulled the clothes off, but Yeoman resisted both this act of violence and the attack upon his wife's character, adding that he defied the pope and popery. He was then taken out, and set in stocks until day.

In the cage also with him was an old man, named John Dale, who had sat there three or four days, for exhorting the people during the time service was performing by Newall and his curate. His words were, "O miserable and blind guides, will ye ever be blind leaders of the blind? Will ye never amend? Will ye never see the truth of God's Word? Will neither God's threats nor promises enter into your hearts? Will the blood of the martyrs nothing mollify your stony stomachs? O obdurate, hard-hearted, perverse, and crooked generation! to whom nothing can do good."

These words he spake in fervency of spirit against the superstitious religion of Rome; wherefore Newall caused him forthwith to be attached, and set in the stocks in a cage, where he was kept until Sir Henry Doile, a justice, came to Hadley.

When Yeoman was taken, the parson called earnestly upon Sir Henry Doile to send them both to prison. Sir Henry Doile as earnestly entreated the parson to consider the age of the men, and their mean condition; they were neither persons of note nor preachers; wherefore he proposed to let them be punished a day or two and to dismiss them, at least John Dale, who was no priest, and therefore, as he had so long sat in the cage, he thought it punishment enough for this time. When the parson heard this, he was exceedingly mad, and in a great rage called them pestilent heretics, unfit to live in the commonwealth of Christians.

Sir Henry, fearing to appear too merciful, Yeoman and Dale were pinioned, bound like thieves with their legs under the horses' bellies, and carried to Bury jail, where they were laid in irons; and because they continually rebuked popery, they were carried into the lowest dungeon, where John Dale, through the jail-sickness and evil-keeping, died soon after: his body was thrown out, and buried in the fields. He was a man of sixty-six years of age, a weaver by occupation, well learned in the holy Scriptures, steadfast in his confession of the true doctrines of Christ as set forth in King Edward's time; for which he joyfully suffered prison and chains, and from this worldly dungeon he departed in Christ to eternal glory, and the blessed paradise of everlasting felicity.

After Dale's death, Yeoman was removed to Norwich prison, where, after strait and evil keeping, he was examined upon his faith and religion, and required to submit himself to his holy father the pope. "I defy him, (quoth he), and all his detestable abomination: I will in no wise have to do with him." The chief articles objected to him, were his marriage and the Mass sacrifice. Finding he continued steadfast in the truth, he was condemned, degraded, and not only burnt, but most cruelly tormented in the fire. Thus he ended this poor and miserable life, and entered into that blessed bosom of Abraham, enjoying with Lazarus that rest which God has prepared for His elect.

THOMAS BENBRIDGE

Mr. Benbridge was a single gentleman, in the diocese of Winchester. He might have lived a gentleman's life, in the wealthy possessions of this world; but he chose rather to enter through the strait gate of persecution to the heavenly possession of life in the Lord's Kingdom, than to enjoy present pleasure with disquietude of conscience. Manfully standing against the papists for the defence of the sincere doctrine of Christ's Gospel, he was apprehended as an adversary to the Romish religion, and led for examination before the bishop of Winchester, where he underwent several conflicts for the truth against the bishop and his colleague; for which he was condemned, and some time after brought to the place of martyrdom by Sir Richard Pecksal, sheriff.

When standing at the stake he began to untie his points, and to prepare himself; then he gave his gown to the keeper, by way of fee. His jerkin was trimmed with gold lace, which he gave to Sir Richard Pecksal, the high sheriff. His cap of velvet he took from his head, and threw away. Then, lifting his mind to the Lord, he engaged in prayer.

When fastened to the stake, Dr. Seaton begged him to recant, and he should have his pardon; but when he saw that nothing availed, he told the people not to pray for him unless he would recant, no more than they would pray for a dog.

Mr. Benbridge, standing at the stake with his hands together in such a manner as the priest holds his hands in his Memento, Dr. Seaton came to him again, and exhorted him to recant, to whom he said, "Away, Babylon, away!" One that stood by said, "Sir, cut his tongue out"; another, a temporal man, railed at him worse than Dr. Seaton had done.

When they saw he would not yield, they bade the tormentors to light the pile, before he was in any way covered with fagots. The fire first took away a piece of his beard, at which he did not shrink. Then it came on the other side and took his legs, and the nether stockings of his hose being leather, they made the fire pierce the sharper, so that the intolerable heat made him exclaim, "I recant!" and suddenly he thrust the fire from him. Two or three of his friends being by, wished to save him; they stepped to the fire to help remove it, for which kindness they were sent to jail. The sheriff also of his own authority took him from the stake, and remitted him to prison, for which he was sent to the Fleet, and lay there sometime. Before, however, he was taken from the stake, Dr. Seaton wrote articles for him to subscribe to. To these Mr. Benbridge made so many objections that Dr. Seaton ordered them to set fire again to the pile. Then with much pain and grief of heart he subscribed to them upon a man's back.

This done, his gown was given him again, and he was led to prison. While there, he wrote a letter to Dr. Seaton, recanting those words he had spoken at the stake, and the articles which he had subscribed, for he was grieved that he had ever signed them. The same day he was again brought to the stake, where the vile tormentors rather broiled than burnt him. The Lord give his enemies repentance!

MRS. PREST

From the number condemned in this fanatical reign, it is almost impossible to obtain the name of every martyr, or to embellish the history of all with anecdotes and exemplifications of Christian conduct. Thanks be to Providence, our cruel task begins to draw towards a conclusion, with the end of the reign of papal terror and bloodshed. Monarchs, who sit upon thrones possessed by hereditary right, should, of all others, consider that the laws of nature are the laws of God, and hence that the first law of nature is the preservation of their subjects. Maxims of persecutions, of torture, and of death, they should leave to those who have effected sovereignty by fraud or by sword; but where, except among a few miscreant emperors of Rome, and the Roman pontiffs, shall we find one whose memory is so "damned to everlasting fame" as that of Queen Mary? Nations bewail the hour which separates them forever from a beloved governor, but, with respect to that of Mary, it was the most blessed time of her whole reign. Heaven has ordained three great scourges for national sins—plague, pestilence, and famine. It was the will of God in Mary's reign to bring a fourth upon this kingdom, under the form of papistical persecution. It was sharp, but glorious; the fire which consumed the martyrs has undermined the popedom; and the Catholic states, at present the most bigoted and unenlightened, are those which are sunk lowest in the scale of moral dignity and political consequence. May they remain so, until the pure light of the Gospel shall dissipate the darkness of fanaticism and superstition! But to return.

Mrs. Prest for some time lived about Cornwall, where she had a husband and children, whose bigotry compelled her to frequent the abominations of the Church of Rome. Resolving to act as her conscience dictated, she quitted them, and made a living by spinning. After some time, returning home, she was accused by her neighbors, and brought to Exeter, to be examined before Dr. Troubleville, and his chancellor Blackston. As this martyr was accounted of inferior intellect, we shall put her in competition with the bishop, and let the reader judge which had the most of that knowledge conducive to everlasting life. The bishop bringing the question to issue, respecting the bread and wine being flesh and blood, Mrs. Prest said, "I will demand of you whether you can deny your creed, which says, that Christ doth perpetually sit at the right hand of His Father, both body and soul, until He come again; or whether He be there in heaven our Advocate, and to make prayer for us unto God His Father? If He be so, He is not here on earth in a piece of bread. If He be not here, and if He do not dwell in temples made with hands, but in heaven, what! shall we seek Him here? If He did not offer His body once for all, why make you a new offering? If with one offering He made all perfect, why do you with a false offering make all imperfect? If He be to be worshipped in spirit and in truth, why do you worship a piece of bread? If He be eaten and drunken in faith and truth, if His flesh be not profitable to be among us, why do you say you make His flesh and blood, and say it is profitable for body and soul? Alas! I am a poor woman, but rather than to do as you do, I would live no longer. I have said, Sir."

Bishop. I promise you, you are a jolly Protestant. I pray you in what school have you been brought up?

Mrs. Prest. I have upon the Sundays visited the sermons, and there have I learned such things as are so fixed in my breast, that death shall not separate them.

B. O foolish woman, who will waste his breath upon thee, or such as thou art? But how chanceth it that thou wentest away from thy husband? If thou wert an honest woman, thou wouldst not have left thy husband and children, and run about the country like a fugitive.

Mrs. P. Sir, I labored for my living; and as my Master Christ counselleth me, when I was persecuted in one city, I fled into another.

B. Who persecuted thee?

Mrs. P. My husband and my children. For when I would have them to leave idolatry, and to worship God in heaven, he would not hear me, but he with his children rebuked me, and troubled me. I fled not for whoredom, nor for theft, but because I would be no partaker with him and his of that foul idol the Mass; and wheresoever I was, as oft as I could, upon Sundays and holydays. I made excuses not to go to the popish Church.

B. Belike then you are a good housewife, to fly from your husband the Church.

Mrs. P. My housewifery is but small; but God gave me grace to go to the true Church.

B. The true Church, what dost thou mean?

Mrs. P. Not your popish Church, full of idols and abominations, but where two or three are gathered together in the name of God, to that Church will I go as long as I live.

B. Belike then you have a church of your own. Well, let this mad woman be put down to prison until we send for her husband.

Mrs. P. No, I have but one husband, who is here already in this city, and in prison with me, from whom I will never depart.

Some persons present endeavoring to convince the bishop she was not in her right senses, she was permitted to depart. The keeper of the bishop's prisons took her into his house, where she either spun, worked as a servant, or walked about the city, discoursing upon the Sacrament of the altar. Her husband was sent for to take her home, but this she refused while the cause of religion could be served. She was too active to be idle, and her conversation, simple as they affected to think her, excited the attention of several Catholic priests and friars. They teased her with questions, until she answered them angrily, and this excited a laugh at her warmth.

"Nay," said she, "you have more need to weep than to laugh, and to be sorry that ever you were born, to be the chaplains of that whore of Babylon. I defy him and all his falsehood; and get you away from me, you do but trouble my conscience. You would have me follow your doings; I will first lose my life. I pray you depart."

"Why, thou foolish woman," said they, "we come to thee for thy profit and soul's health." To which she replied, "What profit ariseth by you, that teach nothing but lies for truth? how save you souls, when you preach nothing but lies, and destroy souls?"

"How provest thou that?" said they.

"Do you not destroy your souls, when you teach the people to worship idols, stocks, and stones, the works of men's hands? and to worship a false God of your own making of a piece of bread, and teach that the pope is God's vicar, and hath power to forgive sins? and that there is a purgatory, when God's

Son hath by His passion purged all? and say you make God and sacrifice Him, when Christ's body was a sacrifice once for all? Do you not teach the people to number their sins in your ears, and say they will be damned if they confess not all; when God's Word saith, Who can number his sins? Do you not promise them trentals and dirges and Masses for souls, and sell your prayers for money, and make them buy pardons, and trust to such foolish inventions of your imaginations? Do you not altogether act against God? Do you not teach us to pray upon beads, and to pray unto saints, and say they can pray for us? Do you not make holy water and holy bread to fray devils? Do you not do a thousand more abominations? And yet you say, you come for my profit, and to save my soul. No, no, one hath saved me. Farewell, you with your salvation."

During the liberty granted her by the bishop, before-mentioned, she went into St. Peter's Church, and there found a skilful Dutchman, who was affixing new noses to certain fine images which had been disfigured in King Edward's time; to whom she said, "What a madman art thou, to make them new noses, which within a few days shall all lose their heads?" The Dutchman accused her and laid it hard to her charge. And she said unto him, "Thou art accursed, and so are thy images." He called her a whore. "Nay," said she, "thy images are whores, and thou art a whore-hunter; for doth not God say, 'You go a whoring after strange gods, figures of your own making? and thou art one of them.'" After this she was ordered to be confined, and had no more liberty.

During the time of her imprisonment, many visited her, some sent by the bishop, and some of their own will, among these was one Daniel, a great preacher of the Gospel, in the days of King Edward, about Cornwall and Devonshire, but who, through the grievous persecution he had sustained, had fallen off. Earnestly did she exhort him to repent with Peter, and to be more constant in his profession.

Mrs. Walter Rauley and Mr. William and John Kede, persons of great respectability, bore ample testimony of her godly conversation, declaring, that unless God were with her, it were impossible she could have so ably defended the cause of Christ. Indeed, to sum up the character of this poor woman, she united the serpent and the dove, abounding in the highest wisdom joined to the greatest simplicity. She endured imprisonment, threatenings, taunts, and the vilest epithets, but nothing could induce her to swerve; her heart was fixed; she had cast anchor; nor could all the wounds of persecution remove her from the rock on which her hopes of felicity were built.

Such was her memory, that, without learning, she could tell in what chapter any text of Scripture was contained: on account of this singular property, one Gregory Basset, a rank papist, said she was deranged, and talked as a parrot, wild without meaning. At length, having tried every manner without effect to make her nominally a Catholic, they condemned her. After this, one exhorted her to leave her opinions, and go home to her family, as she was poor and illiterate. "True, (said she) though I am not learned, I am content to be a witness of Christ's death, and I pray you make no longer delay with me; for my heart is fixed, and I will never say otherwise, nor turn to your superstitious doing."

To the disgrace of Mr. Blackston, treasurer of the church, he would often send for this poor martyr from prison, to make sport for him and a woman whom he kept; putting religious questions to her, and turning her answers into ridicule. This done, he sent her back to her wretched dungeon, while he battened upon the good things of this world.

There was perhaps something simply ludicrous in the form of Mrs. Prest, as she was of a very short stature, thick set, and about fifty-four years of age; but her countenance was cheerful and lively, as if prepared for the day of her marriage with the Lamb. To mock at her form was an indirect accusation of her Creator, who framed her after the fashion He liked best, and gave her a mind that far excelled the transient endowments of perishable flesh. When she was offered money, she rejected it, "because (said she) I am going to a city where money bears no mastery, and while I am here God has promised to feed me."

When sentence was read, condemning her to the flames, she lifted up her voice and praised God, adding, "This day have I found that which I have long sought." When they tempted her to recant, "That will I not, (said she) God forbid that I should lose the life eternal, for this carnal and short life. I will never turn from my heavenly husband to my earthly husband; from the fellowship of angels to mortal children; and if my husband and children be faithful, then am I theirs. God is my father, God is my mother, God is my sister, my brother, my kinsman; God is my friend, most faithful."

Being delivered to the sheriff, she was led by the officer to the place of execution, without the walls of Exeter, called Sothenhey, where again the superstitious priests assaulted her. While they were tying her to the stake, she continued earnestly to exclaim "God be merciful to me, a sinner!" Patiently enduring the devouring conflagration, she was consumed to ashes, and thus ended a life which in unshaken fidelity to the cause of Christ, was not surpassed by that of any preceding martyr.

RICHARD SHARPE, THOMAS BANION, AND THOMAS HALE

Mr. Sharpe, weaver, of Bristol, was brought the ninth day of March, 1556, before Dr. Dalby, chancellor of the city of Bristol, and after examination concerning the Sacrament of the altar, was persuaded to recant; and on the twenty-ninth, he was enjoined to make his recantation in the parish church. But, scarcely had he publicly avowed his backsliding, before he felt in his conscience such a tormenting fiend, that he was unable to work at his occupation; hence, shortly after, one Sunday, he came into the parish church, called Temple, and after high Mass, stood up in the choir door, and said with a loud voice, "Neighbors, bear me record that yonder idol (pointing to the altar) is the greatest and most abominable that ever was; and I am sorry that ever I denied my Lord God!" Notwithstanding the constables were ordered to apprehend him, he was suffered to go out of the church; but at night he was apprehended and carried to Newgate. Shortly after, before the chancellor, denying the Sacrament of the altar to be the body and blood of Christ, he was condemned to be burned by Mr. Dalby. He was burnt the seventh of May, 1558, and died godly, patiently, and constantly, confessing the Protestant articles of faith. With him suffered Thomas Hale, shoemaker, of Bristol, who was condemned by Chancellor Dalby. These martyrs were bound back to back.

Thomas Banion, a weaver, was burnt on August 27, of the same year, and died for the sake of the evangelical cause of his Savior.

J. CORNEFORD, OF WORTHAM; C. BROWNE, OF MAIDSTONE; J. HERST, OF ASHFORD; ALICE SNOTH, AND CATHARINE KNIGHT, AN AGED WOMAN

With pleasure we have to record that these five martyrs were the last who suffered in the reign of Mary for the sake of the Protestant cause; but the malice of the papists was conspicuous in hastening their martyrdom, which might have been delayed until the event of the queen's illness was decided. It is reported that the archdeacon of Canterbury, judging that the sudden death of the queen would suspend the execution, travelled post from London, to have the satisfaction of adding another page to the black list of papistical sacrifices.

The articles against them were, as usual, the Sacramental elements and the idolatry of bending to images. They quoted St. John's words, "Beware of images!" and respecting the real presence, they urged according to St. Paul, "the things which are seen are temporal." When sentence was about to be read against them, and excommunication to take place in the regular form, John Corneford, illuminated by the Holy Spirit, awfully turned the latter proceeding against themselves, and in a solemn impressive manner, recriminated their excommunication in the following words:

In the name of our Lord Jesus Christ, the Son of the most mighty God, and by the power of His Holy Spirit, and the authority of His holy Catholic and apostolic Church, we do here give into the hands of Satan to be destroyed, the bodies of all those blasphemers and heretics that maintain any error against His most holy Word, or do condemn His most holy truth for heresy, to the maintenance of any false church or foreign religion, so that by this Thy just judgment, O most mighty God, against Thy adversaries, Thy true religion may be known to Thy great glory and our comfort and to the edifying of all our nation. Good Lord, so be it. Amen.

This sentence was openly pronounced and registered, and, as if Providence had awarded that it should not be delivered in vain, within six days after, Queen Mary died, detested by all good men and accursed of God!

Though acquainted with these circumstances, the archdeacon's implacability exceeded that of his great exemplary, Bonner, who, though he had several persons at that time under his fiery grasp, did not urge their deaths hastily, by which delay he certainly afforded them an opportunity of escape. At the queen's decease, many were in bonds: some just taken, some examined, and others condemned. The writs indeed were issued for several burnings, but by the death of the three instigators of Protestant murder—the chancellor, the bishop, and the queen, who fell nearly together, the condemned sheep were liberated, and lived many years to praise God for their happy deliverance.

These five martyrs, when at the stake, earnestly prayed that their blood might be the last shed, nor did they pray in vain. They died gloriously, and perfected the number God had selected to bear witness of the truth in this dreadful reign, whose names are recorded in the Book of Life; though last, not least among the saints made meet for immortality through the redeeming blood of the Lamb!

Catharine Finlay, alias Knight, was first converted by her son's expounding the Scriptures to her, which wrought in her a perfect work that terminated in martyrdom. *Alice Snoth* at the stake sent for her grandmother and godfather, and rehearsed to them the articles of her faith, and the Commandments of God, thereby convincing the world that she knew her duty. She died calling upon the spectators to bear witness that she was a Christian woman, and suffered joyfully for the testimony of Christ's Gospel.

Among the numberless enormities committed by the merciless and unfeeling Bonner, the murder of this innocent and unoffending child may be ranged as the most horrid. His father, John Fetty, of the parish of Clerkenwell, by trade a tailor, and only twenty-four years of age, had made blessed election; he was fixed secure in eternal hope, and depended on Him who so builds His Church that the gates of hell shall not prevail against it. But alas! the very wife of his bosom, whose heart was hardened against the truth, and whose mind was influenced by the teachers of false doctrine, became his accuser. Brokenbery, a creature of the pope, and parson of the parish, received the information of this wedded Delilah, in consequence of which the poor man was apprehended. But here the awful judgment of an ever-righteous God, who is "of purer eyes than to behold evil," fell upon this stone-hearted and perfidious woman; for no sooner was the injured husband captured by her wicked contriving, than she also was suddenly seized with madness, and exhibited an awful and awakening instance of God's power to punish the evil-doer. This dreadful circumstance had some effect upon the hearts of the ungodly hunters who had eagerly grasped their prey; but, in a relenting moment, they suffered him to remain with his unworthy wife, to return her good for evil, and to comfort two children, who, on his being sent to prison, would have been left without a protector, or have become a burden to the parish. As bad men act from little motives, we may place the indulgence shown him to the latter account.

We have noticed in the former part of our narratives of the martyrs, some whose affection would have led them even to sacrifice their own lives, to preserve their husbands; but here, agreeable to Scripture language, a mother proves, indeed, a monster in nature! Neither conjugal nor maternal affection could impress the heart of this disgraceful woman.

Although our afflicted Christian had experienced so much cruelty and falsehood from the woman who was bound to him by every tie both human and divine, yet, with a mild and forbearing spirit, he overlooked her misdeeds, during her calamity endeavoring all he could to procure relief for her malady, and soothing her by every possible expression of tenderness: thus she became in a few weeks nearly restored to her senses. But, alas! she returned again to her sin, "as a dog returneth to his vomit." Malice against the saints of the Most High was seated in her heart too firmly to be removed; and as her strength returned, her inclination to work wickedness returned with it. Her heart was hardened by the prince of darkness; and to her may be applied these afflicting and soul-harrowing words, "Can the Ethiopian change his skin, or the leopard his spots? then may ye also do good, that are accustomed to do evil." Weighing this text duly with another, "I will have mercy on whom I will have mercy," how shall we presume to refine away the sovereignty of God by arranging Jehovah at the bar of human reason, which, in religious matters, is too often opposed by infinite wisdom? "Broad is the way, that leadeth to destruction, and many there be which go in thereat. Narrow is the way, which leadeth unto life, and few there be that find it." The ways of heaven are indeed inscrutable, and it is our bounden duty to walk ever dependent on God, looking up to Him with humble confidence, and hope in His goodness, and ever confess His justice; and where we "cannot unravel, there learn to trust." This wretched woman, pursuing the horrid dictates of a heart hardened and depraved, was scarcely confirmed in her recovery, when, stifling the dictates of honor, gratitude, and every natural affection, she again accused her husband, who was once more apprehended, and taken before Sir John Mordant, knight, and one of Queen Mary's commissioners.

Upon examination, his judge finding him fixed in opinions which militated against those nursed by superstition and maintained by cruelty, he was sentenced to confinement and torture in Lollard's Tower. Here he was put into the painful stocks, and had a dish of water set by him, with a stone put into it, to what purpose God knoweth, except it were to show that he should look for little other subsistence: which is credible enough, if we consider their like practices upon divers before mentioned in this history; as, among others, upon Richard Smith, who died through their cruel imprisonment touching whom, when a godly woman came to Dr. Story to have leave she might bury him, he asked her if he had any straw or blood in his mouth; but what he means thereby, I leave to the judgment of the wise.

On the first day of the third week of our martyr's sufferings, an object presented itself to his view, which made him indeed feel his tortures with all their force, and to execrate, with bitterness only short of cursing, the author of his misery. To mark and punish the proceedings of his tormentors, remained with the Most High, who noteth even the fall of a sparrow, and in whose sacred Word it is written, "Vengeance is mine; I will repay." This object was his own son, a child of the tender age of eight years. For fifteen days, had its hapless father been suspended by his tormentor by the right arm and left leg, and sometimes by both, shifting his positions for the purpose of giving him strength to bear and to lengthen the date of his sufferings. When the unoffending innocent, desirous of seeing and speaking to its parent, applied to Bonner for permission to do so, the poor child being asked by the bishop's chaplain the purport of his errand, he replied he wished to see his father. "Who is thy father?" said the chaplain. "John Fetty," returned the boy, at the same time pointing to the place where he was confined. The interrogating miscreant on this said, "Why, thy father is a heretic!" The little champion again rejoined, with energy sufficient to raise admiration in any breast, except that of this unprincipled and unfeeling wretch—this miscreant, eager to execute the behests of a remoseless queen—"My father is no heretic: for you have Balaam's mark."

Irritated by reproach so aptly applied, the indignant and mortified priest concealed his resentment for a moment, and took the undaunted boy into the house, where having him secure, he presented him to others, whose baseness and cruelty being equal to his own, they stripped him to the skin, and applied their scourges to so violent a degree, that, fainting beneath the stripes inflicted on his tender frame, and covered with the blood that flowed from them, the victim of their ungodly wrath was ready to expire under his heavy and unmerited punishment.

In this bleeding and helpless state was the suffering infant, covered only with his shirt, taken to his father by one of the actors in the horrid tragedy, who, while he exhibited the heart-rending spectacle, made use of the vilest taunts, and exulted in what he had done. The dutiful child, as if recovering strength at the sight of his father, on his knees implored his blessing. "Alas! Will," said the afflicted parent, in trembling amazement, "who hath done this to thee!" the artless innocent related the circumstances that led to the merciless correction which had been so basely inflicted on him; but when he repeated the reproof bestowed on the chaplain, and which was prompted by an undaunted spirit, he was torn from his weeping parent, and conveyed again to the house, where he remained a close prisoner.

Bonner, somewhat fearful that what had been done could not be justified even among the bloodhounds of his own voracious pack, concluded in his dark and wicked mind, to release John Fetty, for a time at least, from the severities he was enduring in the glorious cause of everlasting truth! whose bright rewards are fixed beyond the boundaries of time, within the confines of eternity; where the arrow of the wicked cannot wound, even "where there shall be no more sorrowing for the blessed, who, in the mansion of eternal bliss shall glorify the Lamb forever and ever." He was accordingly by order of Bonner, (how disgraceful to all dignity, to say bishop!) liberated from the painful bonds, and led from Lollard's Tower, to the chamber of that ungodly and infamous butcher, where he found the bishop bathing himself before a great fire; and at his first entering the chamber, Fetty said, "God be here and peace!" "God be here and peace, (said Bonner,) that is neither God speed nor good morrow!" "If ye kick against this peace, (said Fetty), then this is not the place that I seek for."

A chaplain of the bishop, standing by, turned the poor man about, and thinking to abash him, said, in mocking wise, "What have we here—a player!" While Fetty was thus standing in the bishop's chamber, he espied, hanging about the bishop's bed, a pair of great black beads, whereupon he said, "My Lord, I think the hangman is not far off: for the halter (pointing to the beads) is here already!" At which words the bishop was in a marvellous rage. Then he immediately after espied also, standing in the bishop's chamber, in the window, a little crucifix. Then he asked the bishop what it was, and he answered, that it was Christ. "Was He handled as cruelly as He is here pictured!" said Fetty. "Yea, that He was," said the bishop. "And even so cruelly will you handle such as come before you; for you are unto God's people as Caiaphas was unto Christ!" The bishop, being in a great fury, said, "Thou art a vile heretic, and I will burn thee, or else I will spend all I have, unto my gown." "Nay, my Lord, (said Fetty) you were better to give it to some poor body, that he may pray for you." Bonner, notwithstanding his passion, which was raised to the utmost by the calm and pointed remarks of this observing Christian, thought it most prudent to dismiss the father, on account of the nearly murdered child. His coward soul trembled for the consequences which might ensue; fear is inseparable from little minds; and this dastardly pampered priest experienced its effects so far as to induce him to assume the appearance of that he was an utter stranger to, namely, MERCY.

The father, on being dismissed, by the tyrant Bonner, went home with a heavy heart, with his dying child, who did not survive many days the cruelties which had been inflicted on him.

How contrary to the will of our great King and Prophet, who mildly taught His followers, was the conduct of this sanguinary and false teacher, this vile apostate from his God to Satan! But the archfiend had taken entire possession of his heart, and guided every action of the sinner he had hardened; who, given up to terrible destruction, was running the race of the wicked, marking his footsteps with the blood of the saints, as if eager to arrive at the goal of eternal death.

DELIVERANCE OF DR. SANDS

This eminent prelate, vice-chancellor of Cambridge, at the request of the duke of Northumberland, when he came down to Cambridge in support of Lady Jane Grey's claim to the throne, undertook at a few hours' notice, to preach before the duke and the university. The text he took was such as presented itself in opening the Bible, and a more appropriate one he could not have chosen, namely, the three last verses of Joshua. As God gave him the text, so He gave him also such order and utterance that it excited the most lively emotions in his numerous auditors. The sermon was about to be sent to London to be printed, when news arrived that the duke had returned and Queen Mary was proclaimed.

The duke was immediately arrested, and Dr. Sands was compelled by the university to give up his office. He was arrested by the queen's order, and when Mr. Mildmay wondered that so learned a man could wilfully incur danger, and speak against so good a princess as Mary, the doctor replied, "If I would do as Mr. Mildmay has done, I need not fear bonds. He came down armed against Queen Mary; before a traitor—now a great friend. I cannot with one mouth blow hot and cold in this manner." A general plunder of Dr. Sands' property ensued, and he was brought to London upon a wretched horse. Various insults he met on the way from the bigoted Catholics, and as he passed through Bishopsgate-street, a stone struck him to the ground. He was the first prisoner that entered the Tower, in that day, on a religious account; his man was admitted with his Bible, but his shirts and other articles were taken from him.

On Mary's coronation day the doors of the dungeon were so laxly guarded that it was easy to escape. A Mr. Mitchell, like a true friend, came to him, afforded him his own clothes as a disguise, and was willing to abide the consequence of being found in his place. This was a rare friendship: but he refused the offer; saying, "I know no cause why I should be in prison. To do thus were to make myself guilty. I will expect God's good will, yet do I think myself much obliged to you"; and so Mr. Mitchell departed.

With Doctor Sands was imprisoned Mr. Bradford; they were kept close in prison twenty-nine weeks. John Fowler, their keeper, was a perverse papist, yet, by often persuading him, at length he began to favor the Gospel, and was so persuaded in the true religion, that on a Sunday, when they had Mass in the chapel, Dr. Sands administered the Communion to Bradford and to Fowler. Thus Fowler was their son begotten in bonds. To make room for Wyat and his accomplices, Dr. Sands and nine other preachers were sent to the Marshalsea.

The keeper of the Marshalsea appointed to every preacher a man to lead him in the street; he caused them to go on before, and he and Dr. Sands followed conversing together. By this time popery began to be unsavory. After they had passed the bridge, the keeper said to Dr. Sands: "I perceive the vain people would set you forward to the fire. You are as vain as they, if you, being a young man, will stand in your own conceit, and prefer your own judgment before that of so many worthy prelates, ancient, learned, and grave men as be in this realm. If you do so, you shall find me a severe keeper, and one that utterly dislikes your religion." Dr. Sands answered, "I know my years to be young, and my learning but small; it is enough to know Christ crucified, and he hath learned nothing who seeth not the great blasphemy that is in popery. I will yield unto God, and not unto man; I have read in the Scriptures of many godly and courteous keepers: may God make you one! if not, I trust He will give me strength and patience to bear your hard usage." Then said the keeper, "Are you resolved to stand to your religion?" "Yes," quoth the doctor, "by God's grace!" "Truly," said the keeper, "I love you the better for it; I did but tempt you: what favor I can show you, you shall be assured of; and I shall think myself happy if I might die at the stake with you."

He was as good as his word, for he trusted the doctor to walk in the fields alone, where he met with Mr. Bradford, who was also a prisoner in the King's

Bench, and had found the same favor from his keeper. At his request, he put Mr. Saunders in along with him, to be his bedfellow, and the Communion was administered to a great number of communicants.

When Wyat with his army came to Southwark, he offered to liberate all the imprisoned Protestants, but Dr. Sands and the rest of the preachers refused to accept freedom on such terms.

After Dr. Sands had been nine weeks prisoner in the Marshalsea, by the mediation of Sir Thomas Holcroft, knight marshal, he was set at liberty. Though Mr. Holcroft had the queen's warrant, the bishop commanded him not to set Dr. Sands at liberty, until he had taken sureties of two gentlemen with him, each one bound in £500, that Dr. Sands should not depart out of the realm without license. Mr. Holcroft immediately after met with two gentlemen of the north, friends and cousins to Dr. Sands, who offered to be bound for him.

After dinner, the same day, Sir Thomas Holcroft sent for Dr. Sands to his lodgings at Westminster, to communicate to him all he had done. Dr. Sands answered: "I give God thanks, who hath moved your heart to mind me so well, that I think myself most bound unto you. God shall requite you, nor shall I ever be found unthankful. But as you have dealt friendly with me, I will also deal plainly with you. I came a freeman into prison; I will not go forth a bondman. As I cannot benefit my friends, so will I not hurt them. And if I be set at liberty, I will not tarry six days in this realm, if I may get out. If therefore I may not get free forth, send me to the Marshalsea again, and there you shall be sure of me."

This answer Mr. Holcroft much disapproved of; but like a true friend he replied: "Seeing you cannot be altered, I will change my purpose, and yield unto you. Come of it what will, I will set you at liberty; and seeing you have a mind to go over sea, get you gone as quick as you can. One thing I require of you, that, while you are there, you write nothing to me hither, for this may undo me."

Dr. Sands having taken an affectionate farewell of him and his other friends in bonds, departed. He went by Winchester house, and there took boat, and came to a friend's house in London, called William Banks, and tarried there one night. The next night he went to another friend's house, and there he heard that strict search was making for him, by Gardiner's express order.

Dr. Sands now conveyed himself by night to one Mr. Berty's house, a stranger who was in the Marshalsea prison with him a while; he was a good Protestant and dwelt in Mark-lane. There he was six days, and then removed to one of his acquaintances in Cornhill; he caused his man Quinton to provide two geldings for him, resolved on the morrow to ride into Essex, to Mr. Sands, his father-in-law, where his wife was, which, after a narrow escape, he effected. He had not been there two hours, before Mr. Sands was told that two of the guards would that night apprehend Dr. Sands.

That night Dr. Sands was guided to an honest farmer's near the sea, where he tarried two days and two nights in a chamber without company. After that he removed to one James Mower's, a shipmaster, who dwelt at Milton-Shore, where he waited for a wind to Flanders. While he was there, James Mower brought to him forty or fifty mariners, to whom he gave an exhortation; they liked him so well that they promised to die rather than he should be apprehended.

The sixth of May, Sunday, the wind served. In taking leave of his hostess, who had been married eight years without having a child, he gave her a fine handkerchief and an old royal of gold, and said, "Be of good comfort; before that one whole year be past, God shall give you a child, a boy." This came to pass, for, that day twelve-month, wanting one day, God gave her a son.

Scarcely had he arrived at Antwerp, when he learned that King Philip had sent to apprehend him. He next flew to Augsburg, in Cleveland, where Dr. Sands tarried fourteen days, and then travelled towards Strassburg, where, after he had lived one year, his wife came to him. He was sick of a flux nine months, and had a child which died of the plague. His amiable wife at length fell into a consumption, and died in his arms. When his wife was dead, he went to Zurich, and there was in Peter Martyr's house for the space of five weeks.

As they sat at dinner one day, word was suddenly brought that Queen Mary was dead, and Dr. Sands was sent for by his friends at Strassburg, where he preached. Mr. Grindal and he came over to England, and arrived in London the same day that Queen Elizabeth was crowned. This faithful servant of Christ, under Queen Elizabeth, rose to the highest distinction in the Church, being successively bishop of Worcester, bishop of London, and archbishop of York.

QUEEN MARY'S TREATMENT OF HER SISTER, THE PRINCESS ELIZABETH

The preservation of Princess Elizabeth may be reckoned a remarkable instance of the watchful eye which Christ had over His Church. The bigotry of Mary regarded not the ties of consanguinity, of natural affection, of national succession. Her mind, physically morose, was under the dominion of men who possessed not the milk of human kindness, and whose principles were sanctioned and enjoined by the idolatrous tenets of the Romish pontiff. Could they have foreseen the short date of Mary's reign, they would have imbrued their hands in the Protestant blood of Elizabeth, and, as a sine qua non of the queen's salvation, have compelled her to bequeath the kingdom to some Catholic prince. The contest might have been attended with the horrors incidental to a religious civil war, and calamities might have been felt in England similar to those under Henry the Great in France, whom Queen Elizabeth assisted in opposing his priest-ridden Catholic subjects. As if Providence had the perpetual establishment of the Protestant faith in view, the difference of the duration of the two reigns is worthy of notice. Mary might have reigned many years in the course of nature, but the course of grace willed it otherwise. Five years and four months was the time of persecution allotted to this weak, disgraceful reign, while that of Elizabeth reckoned a number of years among the highest of those who have sat on the English throne, almost nine times that of her merciless sister!

Before Mary attained the crown, she treated Elizabeth with a sisterly kindness, but from that period her conduct was altered, and the most imperious distance substituted. Though Elizabeth had no concern in the rebellion of Sir Thomas Wyat, yet she was apprehended, and treated as a culprit in that commotion. The manner too of her arrest was similar to the mind that dictated it: the three cabinet members, whom she deputed to see the arrest executed, rudely entered the chamber at ten o'clock at night, and, though she was extremely ill, they could scarcely be induced to let her remain until the following morning. Her enfeebled state permitted her to be moved only by short stages in a journey of such length to London; but the princess, though afflicted in person, had a consolation in mind which her sister never could purchase: the people, through whom she passed on her way pitied her, and put up their prayers for her preservation.

Arrived at court, she was made a close prisoner for a fortnight, without knowing who was her accuser, or seeing anyone who could console or advise her. The charge, however, was at length unmasked by Gardiner, who, with nineteen of the Council, accused her of abetting Wyat's conspiracy, which she religiously affirmed to be false. Failing in this, they placed against her the transactions of Sir Peter Carew in the west, in which they were as unsuccessful as in the former. The queen now signified that it was her pleasure she should be committed to the Tower, a step which overwhelmed the princess with the greatest alarm and uneasiness. In vain she hoped the queen's majesty would not commit her to such a place; but there was no lenity to be expected; her attendants were limited, and a hundred northern soldiers appointed to guard her day and night.

On Palm Sunday she was conducted to the Tower. When she came to the palace garden, she cast her eyes towards the windows, eagerly anxious to meet those of the queen, but she was disappointed. A strict order was given in London that every one should go to church, and carry palms, that she might be conveyed without clamor or commiseration to her prison.

At the time of passing under London Bridge the fall of the tide made it very dangerous, and the barge some time stuck fast against the starlings. To mortify her the more, she was landed at Traitors' Stairs. As it rained fast, and she was obliged to step in the water to land, she hesitated; but this excited no complaisance in the lord in waiting. When she set her foot on the steps, she exclaimed, "Here lands as true a subject, being prisoner, as ever landed at these stairs; and before Thee, O God, I speak it, having no friend but Thee alone!"

A large number of the wardens and servants of the Tower were arranged in order between whom the princess had to pass. Upon inquiring the use of this parade, she was informed it was customary to do so. "If," said she, "it is on account of me, I beseech you that they may be dismissed." On this the poor men knelt down, and prayed that God would preserve her grace, for which they were the next day turned out of their employments. The tragic scene must have been deeply interesting, to see an amiable and irreproachable princess sent like a lamb to languish in expectation of cruelty and death; against whom there was no other charge than her superiority in Christian virtues and acquired endowments. Her attendants openly wept as she proceeded with a dignified step to the frowning battlements of her destination. "Alas!" said Elizabeth, "what do you mean? I took you to comfort, not to dismay me; for my truth is such that no one shall have cause to weep for me."

The next step of her enemies was to procure evidence by means which, in the present day, are accounted detestable. Many poor prisoners were racked, to extract, if possible, any matters of accusation which might affect her life, and thereby gratify Gardiner's sanguinary disposition. He himself came to examine her, respecting her removal from her house at Ashbridge to Dunnington castle a long while before. The princess had quite forgotten this trivial circumstance, and Lord Arundel, after the investigation, kneeling down, apologized for having troubled her in such a frivolous matter. "You sift me narrowly," replied the princess, "but of this I am assured, that God has appointed a limit to your proceedings; and so God forgive you all."

Her own gentlemen, who ought to have been her purveyors, and served her provision, were compelled to give place to the common soldiers, at the command of the constable of the Tower, who was in every respect a servile tool of Gardiner; her grace's friends, however, procured an order of Council which regulated this petty tyranny more to her satisfaction.

After having been a whole month in close confinement, she sent for the lord chamberlain and Lord Chandois, to whom she represented the ill state of her health from a want of proper air and exercise. Application being made to the Council, Elizabeth was with some difficulty admitted to walk in the queen's lodgings, and afterwards in the garden, at which time the prisoners on that side were attended by their keepers, and not suffered to look down upon her. Their jealousy was excited by a child of four years, who daily brought flowers to the princess. The child was threatened with a whipping, and the father ordered to keep him from the princess's chambers.

On the fifth of May the constable was discharged from his office, and Sir Henry Benifield appointed in his room, accompanied by a hundred ruffian-looking soldiers in blue. This measure created considerable alarm in the mind of the princess, who imagined it was preparatory to her undergoing the same fate as Lady Jane Grey, upon the same block. Assured that this project was not in agitation, she entertained an idea that the new keeper of the Tower was commissioned to make away with her privately, as his equivocal character was in conformity with the ferocious inclination of those by whom he was appointed.

A report now obtained that her Grace was to be taken away by the new constable and his soldiers, which in the sequel proved to be true. An order of Council was made for her removal to the manor Woodstock, which took place on Trinity Sunday, May 13, under the authority of Sir Henry Benifield and Lord Tame. The ostensible cause of her removal was to make room for other prisoners. Richmond was the first place they stopped at, and here the princess slept, not however without much alarm at first, as her own servants were superseded by the soldiers, who were placed as guards at her chamber door. Upon representation, Lord Tame overruled this indecent stretch of power, and granted her perfect safety while under his custody.

In passing through Windsor, she saw several of her poor dejected servants waiting to see her. "Go to them," said she, to one of her attendants, "and say these words from me, tanquim ovis, that is, like a sheep to the slaughter."

The next night her Grace lodged at the house of a Mr. Dormer, in her way to which the people manifested such tokens of loyal affection that Sir Henry was indignant, and bestowed on them very liberally the names of rebels and traitors. In some villages they rang the bells for joy, imagining the princess's arrival among them was from a very different cause; but this harmless demonstration of gladness was sufficient with the persecuting Benifield to order his soldiers to seize and set these humble persons in the stocks.

The day following, her Grace arrived at Lord Tame's house, where she stayed all night, and was most nobly entertained. This excited Sir Henry's indignation, and made him caution Lord Tame to look well to his proceedings; but the humanity of Lord Tame was not to be frightened, and he returned a suitable reply. At another time, this official prodigal, to show his consequence and disregard of good manners, went up into a chamber, where was appointed for her Grace a chair, two cushions, and a foot carpet, wherein he presumptuously sat and called his man to pull off his boots. As soon as it was known to the ladies and gentlemen they laughed him to scorn. When supper was done, he called to his lordship, and directed that all gentlemen and ladies should withdraw home, marvelling much that he would permit such a large company, considering the great charge he had committed to him. "Sir Henry," said his lordship, "content yourself; all shall be avoided, your men and all." "Nay, but my soldiers," replied Sir Henry, "shall watch all night." Lord Tame answered, "There is no need." "Well," said he, "need or need not, they shall so do."

The next day her Grace took her journey from thence to Woodstock, where she was enclosed, as before in the Tower of London, the soldiers keeping guard within and without the walls, every day, to the number of sixty; and in the night, without the walls were forty during all the time of her imprisonment.

At length she was permitted to walk in the gardens, but under the most severe restrictions, Sir Henry keeping the keys himself, and placing her always under many bolts and locks, whence she was induced to call him her jailer, at which he felt offended, and begged her to substitute the word officer. After much earnest entreaty to the Council, she obtained permission to write to the queen; but the jailer who brought her pen, ink, and paper stood by her while she wrote, and, when she left off, he carried the things away until they were wanted again. He also insisted upon carrying it himself to the queen, but Elizabeth would not suffer him to be the bearer, and it was presented by one of her gentlemen.

After the letter, Doctors Owen and Wendy went to the princess, as the state of her health rendered medical assistance necessary. They stayed with her five or six days, in which time she grew much better; they then returned to the queen, and spoke flatteringly of the princess' submission and humility, at which the queen seemed moved; but the bishops wanted a concession that she had offended her majesty. Elizabeth spurned this indirect mode of acknowledging herself guilty. "If I have offended," said she, "and am guilty, I crave no mercy but the law, which I am certain I should have had ere this, if anything could have been proved against me. I wish I were as clear from the peril of my enemies; then should I not be thus bolted and locked up within walls and doors."

Much question arose at this time respecting the propriety of uniting the princess to some foreigner, that she might quit the realm with a suitable portion. One of the Council had the brutality to urge the necessity of beheading her, if the king (Philip) meant to keep the realm in peace; but the Spaniards, detesting such a base thought, replied, "God forbid that our king and master should consent to such an infamous proceeding!" Stimulated by a noble principle, the Spaniards from this time repeatedly urged to the king that it would do him the highest honor to liberate the Lady Elizabeth, nor was the king impervious to their solicitation. He took her out of prison, and shortly after she was sent for to Hampton court. It may be remarked in this place, that the fallacy of human reasoning is shown in every moment. The barbarian who suggested the policy of beheading Elizabeth little contemplated the change of condition which his speech would bring about. In her journey from Woodstock, Benifield treated her with the same severity as before; removing her on a stormy day, and not suffering her old servant, who had come to Colnbrook, where she slept, to speak to her.

She remained a fortnight strictly guarded and watched, before anyone dared to speak with her; at length the vile Gardiner with three more of the Council, came with great submission. Elizabeth saluted them, remarked that she had been for a long time kept in solitary confinement, and begged they would intercede with the king and queen to deliver her from prison. Gardiner's visit was to draw from the princess a confession of her guilt; but she was guarded against his subtlety, adding, that, rather than admit she had done wrong, she would lie in prison all the rest of her life. The next day Gardiner came again, and kneeling down, declared that the queen was astonished she would persist in affirming that she was blameless—whence it would be inferred that the queen had unjustly imprisoned her grace. Gardiner further informed her that the queen had declared that she must tell another tale, before she could be set at liberty. "Then," replied the high-minded Elizabeth, "I had rather be in prison with honesty and truth, than have my liberty, and be suspected by her majesty. What I have said, I will stand to; nor will I ever speak falsehood!" The bishop and his friends then departed, leaving her locked up as before.

Seven days after the queen sent for Elizabeth at ten o'clock at night; two years had elapsed since they had seen each other. It created terror in the mind of the princess, who, at setting out, desired her gentlemen and ladies to pray for her, as her return to them again was uncertain.

Being conducted to the queen's bedchamber, upon entering it the princess knelt down, and having begged of God to preserve her majesty, she humbly assured her that her majesty had not a more loyal subject in the realm, whatever reports might be circulated to the contrary. With a haughty ungraciousness, the imperious queen replied: "You will not confess your offence, but stand stoutly to your truth. I pray God it may so fall out."

"If it do not," said Elizabeth, "I request neither favor nor pardon at your majesty's hands." "Well," said the queen, "you stiffly still persevere in your truth. Besides, you will not confess that you have not been wrongfully punished."

"I must not say so, if it please your majesty, to you."

"Why, then," said the queen, "belike you will to others."

"No, if it please your majesty: I have borne the burden, and must bear it. I humbly beseech your majesty to have a good opinion of me and to think me to be your subject, not only from the beginning hitherto, but for ever, as long as life lasteth." They departed without any heartfelt satisfaction on either side; nor can we think the conduct of Elizabeth displayed that independence and fortitude which accompanies perfect innocence. Elizabeth's admitting that she would not say, neither to the queen nor to others, that she had been unjustly punished, was in direct contradiction to what she had told Gardiner, and must have arisen from some motive at this time inexplicable. King Philip is supposed to have been secretly concealed during the interview, and to have been friendly to the princess.

In seven days from the time of her return to imprisonment, her severe jailer and his men were discharged, and she was set at liberty, under the constraint of being always attended and watched by some of the queen's Council. Four of her gentlemen were sent to the Tower without any other charge against them than being zealous servants of their mistress. This event was soon after followed by the happy news of Gardiner's death, for which all good and merciful men glorified God, inasmuch as it had taken the chief tiger from the den, and rendered the life of the Protestant successor of Mary more secure.

This miscreant, while the princess was in the Tower, sent a secret writ, signed by a few of the Council, for her private execution, and, had Mr. Bridges, lieutenant of the Tower, been as little scrupulous of dark assassination as this pious prelate was, she must have perished. The warrant not having the queen's signature, Mr. Bridges hastened to her majesty to give her information of it, and to know her mind. This was a plot of Winchester's, who, to convict her of treasonable practices, caused several prisoners to be racked; particularly Mr. Edmund Tremaine and Smithwicke were offered considerable bribes to accuse the guiltless princess.

Her life was several times in danger. While at Woodstock, fire was apparently put between the boards and ceiling under which she lay. It was also reported strongly that one Paul Penny, the keeper of Woodstock, a notorious ruffian, was appointed to assassinate her, but, however this might be, God counteracted in this point the nefarious designs of the enemies of the Reformation. James Basset was another appointed to perform the same deed: he was a peculiar favorite of Gardiner, and had come within a mile of Woodstock, intending to speak with Benifield on the subject. The goodness of God however so ordered it that while Basset was travelling to Woodstock, Benifield, by an order of Council, was going to London: in consequence of which, he left a positive order with his brother, that no man should be admitted to the princess during his absence, not even with a note from the queen; his brother met the murderer, but the latter's intention was frustrated, as no admission could be obtained.

When Elizabeth quitted Woodstock, she left the following lines written with her diamond on the window:

> Much suspected by me,
> Nothing proved can be. Quoth Elizabeth, prisoner.

With the life of Winchester ceased the extreme danger of the princess, as many of her other secret enemies soon after followed him, and, last of all, her cruel sister, who outlived Gardiner but three years.

The death of Mary was ascribed to several causes. The Council endeavored to console her in her last moments, imagining it was the absence of her husband that lay heavy at her heart, but though his treatment had some weight, the loss of Calais, the last fortress possessed by the English in France, was the true source of her sorrow. "Open my heart," said Mary, "when I am dead, and you shall find Calais written there." Religion caused her no alarm; the priests had lulled to rest every misgiving of conscience, which might have obtruded, on account of the accusing spirits of the murdered martyrs. Not the blood she had spilled, but the loss of a town excited her emotions in dying, and this last stroke seemed to be awarded, that her fanatical persecution might be paralleled by her political imbecility.

We earnestly pray that the annals of no country, Catholic or pagan, may ever be stained with such a repetition of human sacrifices to papal power, and that the detestation in which the character of Mary is holden, may be a beacon to succeeding monarchs to avoid the rocks of fanaticism!

GOD'S PUNISHMENT UPON SOME OF THE PERSECUTORS OF HIS PEOPLE IN MARY'S REIGN

After that arch-persecutor, Gardiner, was dead, others followed, of whom Dr. Morgan, bishop of St. David's, who succeeded Bishop Farrar, is to be noticed. Not long after he was installed in his bishopric, he was stricken by the visitation of God; his food passed through the throat, but rose again with great violence. In this manner, almost literally starved to death, he terminated his existence.

Bishop Thornton, suffragen of Dover, was an indefatigable persecutor of the true Church. One day after he had exercised his cruel tyranny upon a number of pious persons at Canterbury, he came from the chapter-house to Borne, where as he stood on a Sunday looking at his men playing at bowls, he fell down in a fit of the palsy, and did not long survive.

After the latter, succeeded another bishop or suffragen, ordained by Gardiner, who not long after he had been raised to the see of Dover, fell down a pair of stairs in the cardinal's chamber at Greenwich, and broke his neck. He had just received the cardinal's blessing—he could receive nothing worse.

John Cooper, of Watsam, Suffolk, suffered by perjury; he was from private pique persecuted by one Fenning, who suborned two others to swear that they heard Cooper say, "If God did not take away Queen Mary, the devil would." Cooper denied all such words, but Cooper was a Protestant and a heretic, and therefore he was hung, drawn and quartered, his property confiscated, and his wife and nine children reduced to beggary. The following harvest, however, Grimwood of Hitcham, one of the witnesses before mentioned, was visited for his villainy: while at work, stacking up corn, his bowels suddenly burst out, and before relief could be obtained, he died. Thus was deliberate perjury rewarded by sudden death!

In the case of the martyr Mr. Bradford, the severity of Mr. Sheriff Woodroffe has been noticed—he rejoiced at the death of the saints, and at Mr. Rogers' execution, he broke the carman's head, because he stopped the cart to let the martyr's children take a last farewell of him. Scarcely had Mr. Woodroffe's sheriffalty expired a week, when he was struck with a paralytic affection, and languished a few days in the most pitiable and helpless condition, presenting a striking contrast to his former activity in the cause of blood.

Ralph Lardyn, who betrayed the martyr George Eagles, is believed to have been afterward arraigned and hanged in consequence of accusing himself. At the bar, he denounced himself in these words: "This has most justly fallen upon me, for betraying the innocent blood of that just and good man George Eagles, who was here condemned in the time of Queen Mary by my procurement, when I sold his blood for a little money."

As James Abbes was going to execution, and exhorting the pitying bystanders to adhere steadfastly to the truth, and like him to seal the cause of Christ with their blood, a servant of the sheriff's interrupted him, and blasphemously called his religion heresy, and the good man a lunatic. Scarcely however had the flames reached the martyr, before the fearful stroke of God fell upon the hardened wretch, in the presence of him he had so cruelly ridiculed. The man was suddenly seized with lunacy, cast off his clothes and shoes before the people, (as Abbes had done just before, to distribute among some poor persons,) at the same time exclaiming, "Thus did James Abbes, the true servant of God, who is saved by I am damned." Repeating this often, the sheriff had him secured, and made him put his clothes on, but no sooner was he alone, than he tore them off, and exclaimed as before. Being tied in a cart, he was conveyed to his master's house, and in about half a year he died; just before which a priest came to attend him, with the crucifix, etc., but the wretched man bade him take away such trumpery, and said that he and other priests had been the cause of his damnation, but that Abbes was saved.

One *Clark,* an avowed enemy of the Protestants in King Edward's reign, hung himself in the Tower of London.

Froling, a priest of much celebrity, fell down in the street and died on the spot.

Dale, an indefatigable informer, was consumed by vermin, and died a miserable spectacle.

Alexander, the severe keeper of Newgate, died miserably, swelling to a prodigious size, and became so inwardly putrid, that none could come near him. This cruel minister of the law would go to Bonner, Story, and others, requesting them to rid his prison, he was so much pestered with heretics! The son of this keeper, in three years after his father's death, dissipated his great property, and died suddenly in Newgate market. "The sins of the father," says the decalogue, "shall be visited on the children." John Peter, son-in-law of Alexander, a horrid blasphemer and persecutor, died wretchedly. When he affirmed anything, he would say, "If it be not true, I pray I may rot ere I die." This awful state visited him in all its loathsomeness.

Sir Ralph Ellerker was eagerly desirous to see the heart taken out of Adam Damlip, who was wrongfully put to death. Shortly after Sir Ralph was slain by the French, who mangled him dreadfully, cut off his limbs, and tore his heart out.

When Gardiner heard of the miserable end of Judge Hales, he called the profession of the Gospel a doctrine of desperation; but he forgot that the judge's despondency arose after he had consented to the papistry. But with more reason may this be said of the Catholic tenets, if we consider the miserable end of Dr. Pendleton, Gardiner, and most of the leading persecutors. Gardiner, upon his death bed, was reminded by a bishop of Peter denying his master, "Ah," said Gardiner, "I have denied with Peter, but never repented with Peter."

After the accession of Elizabeth, most of the Catholic prelates were imprisoned in the Tower or the Fleet; Bonner was put into the Marshalsea.

Of the revilers of God's Word, we detail, among many others, the following occurrence. One William Maldon, living at Greenwich in servitude, was instructing himself profitably in reading an English primer one winter's evening. A serving man, named John Powell, sat by, and ridiculed all that Maldon said, who cautioned him not to make a jest of the Word of God. Powell nevertheless continued, until Maldon came to certain English Prayers, and read aloud, "Lord, have mercy upon us, Christ have mercy upon us," etc. Suddenly the reviler started, and exclaimed, "Lord, have mercy upon us!" He was struck with the utmost terror of mind, said the evil spirit could not abide that Christ should have any mercy upon him, and sunk into madness. He was remitted to Bedlam, and became an awful warning that God will not always be insulted with impunity.

Henry Smith, a student in the law, had a pious Protesant father, of Camben, in Gloucestershire, by whom he was virtuously educated. While studying law in the middle temple, he was induced to profess Catholicism, and, going to Louvain, in France, he returned with pardons, crucifixes, and a great freight of popish toys. Not content with these things, he openly reviled the Gospel religion he had been brought up in; but conscience one night reproached him so dreadfully, that in a fit of despair he hung himself in his garters. He was buried in a lane, without the Christian service being read over him.

Dr. Story, whose name has been so often mentioned in the preceding pages, was reserved to be cut off by public execution, a practice in which he had taken great delight when in power. He is supposed to have had a hand in most of the conflagrations in Mary's time, and was even ingenious in his invention of new modes of inflicting torture. When Elizabeth came to the throne, he was committed to prison, but unaccountably effected his escape to the continent, to carry fire and sword there among the Protestant brethren. From the duke of Alva, at Antwerp, he received a special commission to search all ships for contraband goods, and particularly for English heretical books.

Dr. Story gloried in a commission that was ordered by Providence to be his ruin, and to preserve the faithful from his sanguinary cruelty. It was contrived that one Parker, a merchant, should sail to Antwerp and information should be given to Dr. Story that he had a quantity of heretical books on board. The latter no sooner heard this, than he hastened to the vessel, sought everywhere above, and then went under the hatches, which were fastened down upon him. A prosperous gale brought the ship to England, and this traitorous, persecuting rebel was committed to prison, where he remained a considerable time, obstinately objecting to recant his Anti-christian spirit, or admit of Queen Elizabeth's supremacy. He alleged, though by birth and education an Englishman, that he was a sworn subject of the king of Spain, in whose service the famous duke of Alva was. The doctor being condemned, was laid upon a hurdle, and drawn from the Tower to Tyburn, where after being suspended about half an hour, he was cut down, stripped, and the executioner displayed the heart of a traitor.

Thus ended the existence of this Nimrod of England.

CHAPTER TEN

An Account of the Life of John Wesley

J ohn Wesley was born on the seventeenth of June, 1703, in Epworth rectory, England, the fifteenth of nineteen children of Samuel and Suzanna Wesley. The father of Wesley was a preacher, and Wesley's mother was a remarkable woman in wisdom and intelligence. She was a woman of deep piety and brought her little ones into close contact with the Bible stories, telling them from the tiles about the nursery fireplace. She also used to dress the children in their best on the days when they were to have the privilege of learning their alphabet as an introduction to the reading of the Holy Scriptures.

Young Wesley was a gay and manly youth, fond of games and particularly of dancing. At Oxford he was a leader, and during the latter part of his course there, was one of the founders of the "Holy Club," an organization of serious-minded students. His religious nature deepened through study and experience, but it was not until several years after he left the university and came under the influence of Luther's writings that he felt that he had entered into the full riches of the Gospel.

He and his brother Charles were sent by the Society for the Propagation of the Gospel to Georgia, where both of them developed their powers as preachers.

Upon their passage they fell into the company of several Moravian brethren, members of the association recently renewed by the labors of Count Zinzendorf. It was noted by John Wesley in his diary that, in a great tempest, when the English people on board lost all self-possession, these Germans impressed him by their composure and entire resignation to God. He also marked their humility under shameful treatment.

It was on his return to England that he entered into those deeper experiences and developed those marvelous powers as a popular preacher which made him a national leader. He was associated at this time also with George Whitefield, the tradition of whose marvelous eloquence has never died.

What he accomplished borders upon the incredible. Upon entering his eighty-fifth year he thanked God that he was still almost as vigorous as ever. He ascribed it, under God, to the fact that he had always slept soundly, had risen for sixty years at four o'clock in the morning, and for fifty years had preached every morning at five. Seldom in all his life did he feel any pain, care, or anxiety. He preached twice each day, and often thrice or four times. It has been estimated that he traveled every year forty-five hundred English miles, mostly upon horseback.

The successes won by Methodist preaching had to be gained through a long series of years, and amid the most bitter persecutions. In nearly every part of England it was met at the first by the mob with stonings and peltings, with attempts at wounding and slaying. Only at times was there any interference on the part of the civil power. The two Wesleys faced all these dangers with amazing courage, and with a calmness equally astonishing. What was more irritating was the heaping up of slander and abuse by the writers of the day. These books are now all forgotten.

Wesley had been in his youth a high churchman and was always deeply devoted to the Established Communion. When he found it necessary to ordain preachers, the separation of his followers from the established body became inevitable. The name "Methodist" soon attached to them, because of the particular organizing power of their leader and the ingenious methods that he applied.

The Wesley fellowship, which after his death grew into the great Methodist Church, was characterized by an almost military perfection of organizaton.

The entire management of his ever-growing denomination rested upon Wesley himself. The annual conference, established in 1744, acquired a governing power only after the death of Wesley. Charles Wesley rendered the society a service incalculably great by his hymns. They introduced a new era in the hymnology of the English Church. John Wesley apportioned his days to his work in leading the Church, to studying (for he was an incessant reader), to traveling, and to preaching.

Wesley was untiring in his efforts to disseminate useful knowledge throughout his denomination. He planned for the mental culture of his traveling preachers and local exhorters, and for schools of instruction for the future teachers of the Church. He himself prepared books for popular use upon universal history, church history, and natural history. In this Wesley was an apostle of the modern union of mental culture with Christian living. He published also the best matured of his sermons and various theological works.

These, both by their depth and their penetration of thought, and by their purity and precision of style, excite our admiration.

John Wesley was of but ordinary stature, and yet of noble presence. His features were very handsome even in old age. He had an open brow, an eagle nose, a clear eye, and a fresh complexion. His manners were fine, and in choice company with Christian people he enjoyed relaxation. Persistent, laborious love for men's souls, steadfastness, and tranquillity of spirit were his most prominent traits of character. Even in doctrinal controversies he exhibited the greatest calmness. He was kind and very liberal. His industry has been named already. In the last fifty-two years of his life, it is estimated that he preached more than forty thousand sermons.

Wesley brought sinners to repentance throughout three kingdoms and over two hemispheres. He was the bishop of such a diocese as neither the Eastern nor the Western Church ever witnessed before. What is there in the circle of Christian effort—foreign missions, home missions, Christian tracts and litera-ture, field preaching, circuit preaching, Bible readings, or aught else—which was not attempted by John Wesley, which was not grasped by his mighty mind through the aid of his Divine Leader?

To him it was granted to arouse the English Church, when it had lost sight of Christ the Redeemer to a renewed Christian life. By preaching the justifying and renewing of the soul through belief upon Christ, he lifted many thousands of the humbler classes of the English people from their exceeding ignorance and evil habits, and made them earnest, faithful Christians. His untiring effort made itself felt not in England alone, but in America and in continental Europe. Not only the germs of almost all the existing zeal in England on behalf of Christian truth and life are due to Methodism, but the activity stirred up in other portions of Protestant Europe we must trace indirectly, at least, to Wesley.

He died in 1791 after a long life of tireless labor and unselfish service. His fervent spirit and hearty brotherhood still survives in the body that cherishes his name.

CHAPTER ELEVEN

An Account of the Life and Persecutions of John Bunyan

This great Puritan was born the same year that the Pilgrim Fathers landed at Plymouth. His home was Elstow, near Bedford, in England. His father was a tinker and he was brought up to the same trade. He was a lively, likeable boy with a serious and almost morbid side to his nature. All during his young manhood he was repenting for the vices of his youth and yet he had never been either a drunkard or immoral. The particular acts that troubled his conscience were dancing, ringing the church bells, and playing cat. It was while playing the latter game one day that "a voice did suddenly dart from Heaven into my soul, which said, 'Wilt thou leave thy sins and go to Heaven, or have thy sins and go to Hell?'" At about this time he overheard three or four poor women in Bedford talking, as they sat at the door in the sun. "Their talk was about the new birth, the work of God in the hearts. They were far above my reach."

In his youth he was a member of the parliamentary army for a year. The death of his comrade close beside him deepened his tendency to serious thoughts, and there were times when he seemed almost insane in his zeal and penitence. He was at one time quite assured that he had sinned the unpardonable sin against the Holy Ghost. While he was still a young man he married a good woman who bought him a library of pious books which he read with assiduity, thus confirming his earnestness and increasing his love of religious controversies.

His conscience was still further awakened through the persecution of the religious body of Baptists to whom he had joined himself. Before he was thirty years old he had become a leading Baptist preacher.

Then came his turn for persecution. He was arrested for preaching without license. "Before I went down to the justice, I begged of God that His will be done; for I was not without hopes that my imprisonment might be an awakening to the saints in the country. Only in that matter did I commit the thing to God. And verily at my return I did meet my God sweetly in the prison."

His hardships were genuine, on account of the wretched condition of the prisons of those days. To this confinement was added the personal grief of being parted from his young and second wife and four small children, and particularly, his little blind daughter. While he was in jail he was solaced by the two books which he had brought with him, the Bible and Foxe's "Book of Martyrs."

Although he wrote some of his early books during this long imprisonment, it was not until his second and shorter one, three years after the first, that he composed his immortal "Pilgrim's Progress," which was published three years later. In an earlier tract he had thought briefly of the similarity between human life and a pilgrimage, and he now worked this theme out in fascinating detail, using the rural scenery of England for his background, the splendid city of London for his Vanity Fair, and the saints and villains of his own personal acquaintance for the finely drawn characters of his allegory.

The "Pilgrim's Progress" is truly the rehearsal of Bunyan's own spiritual experiences. He himself had been the "man cloathed in Rags, with his Face from his own House, a Book in his hand, and a great Burden upon his Back." After he had realized that Christ was his Righteousness, and that this did not depend on "the good frame of his Heart"—or, as we should say, on his feelings—"now did the Chains fall off my legs indeed." His had been Doubting Castle and Sloughs of Despond, with much of the Valley of Humiliation and the Shadow of Death. But, above all, it is a book of Victory. Once when he was leaving the doors of the courthouse where he himself had been defeated, he wrote: "As I was going forth of the doors, I had much ado to bear saying to them, that I carried the peace of God along with me." In his vision was ever the Celestial City, with all its bells ringing. He had fought Apollyon constantly, and often wounded, shamed and fallen, yet in the end "more than conqueror through Him that loved us."

His book was at first received with much criticism from his Puritan friends, who saw in it only an addition to the worldly literature of his day, but there was not much then for Puritans to read, and it was not long before it was devoutly laid beside their Bibles and perused with gladness and with profit. It was perhaps two centuries later before literary critics began to realize that this story, so full of human reality and interest and so marvelously modeled upon the English of the King James translation of the Bible, is one of the glories of English literature. In his later years he wrote several other allegories, of which of one of them, "The Holy War," it has been said that, "If the 'Pilgrim's

Progress' had never been written it would be regarded as the finest allegory in the language."

During the later years of his life, Bunyan remained in Bedford as a venerated local pastor and preacher. He was also a favorite speaker in the nonconformist pulpits of London. He became so national a leader and teacher that he was frequently called "Bishop Bunyan."

In his helpful and unselfish personal life he was apostolic.

His last illness was due to exposure upon a journey in which he was endeavoring to reconcile a father with his son. His end came on the third of August, 1688. He was buried in Bunhill Fields, a church yard in London.

There is no doubt but that the "Pilgrim's Progress" has been more helpful than any other book but the Bible. It was timely, for they were still burning martyrs in Vanity Fair while he was writing. It is enduring, for while it tells little of living the Christian life in the family and community, it does interpret that life so far as it is an expression of the solitary soul, in homely language. Bunyan indeed "showed how to build a princely throne on humble truth." He has been his own Greatheart, dauntless guide to pilgrims, to many.

CHAPTER TWELVE

The Life, Sufferings, and Martyrdom of John Huss,
Who Was Burnt at Constance in Germany

J ohn Huss was a Bohemian, born in the village of Hussenitz about the year 1380. His parents gave him the best education they could bestow, and having acquired a tolerable knowledge of the classics at a private school, he was sent thence to the university of Prague, where the powers of his mind and his diligence in study soon rendered him conspicuous. In 1408 he commenced bachelor of divinity, and was after successively chosen pastor of the church of Bethlehem, in Prague, and dean, and rector of the university. These stations he discharged with great fidelity, and became at length so conspicuous for his preaching and the boldness of his truths, that he soon attracted the notice and excited the malignity of the pope and his creatures. The incident which most provoked the indignation of Huss was a papal bull, which offered remission of sin to all who would join the army of the pope in his contest with the king of Naples, who had invaded the holy see, and threatened destruction to the papal dominion.

The English reformer, Wickliffe, had so kindled the light of reformation, that it began to illume the darkest corners of popery and ignorance. His doctrines were received in Bohemia with avidity and zeal by great numbers of people; but by none so zealously as John Huss, and his friend and fellow-martyr, Jerome of Prague. The reformists daily increasing, the archbishop of Prague issued a decree to suppress the farther spreading of Wickliffe's writings. This, however, had an effect quite the reverse of what he expected, for it stimulated the converts to greater zeal, and at length almost the whole university united in promoting them. In that renowned institution the influence of

Huss was very great, not only on account of his learning, eloquence, and exemplary life; but also on account of some valuable privileges he had obtained from the king in behalf of the Bohemians.

Strongly attached to the doctrines of Wickliffe, Huss strenuously opposed the decree of the archbishop, who, notwithstanding, obtained a bull from the pope, giving him commission to prevent the publishing of Wickliffe's writings in his province. By virtue of this bull the archbishop condemned those writings: he also proceeded against four doctors who had not delivered up some copies, and prohibited them to preach. Against these proceedings Dr. Huss, with some other members of the university, protested, and entered an appeal from the sentence of the archbishop. The pope no sooner heard of this, than he granted a commission to cardinal Colonno to cite Huss to appear at the court of Rome, to answer accusations laid against him, of preaching both errors and heresies. From this Dr. Huss desired to be excused, and so greatly was he favoured in Bohemia that king Wincelaus, the queen, the nobility, and the university, desired the pope to dispense with such an appearance; as also that he would not suffer the kingdom of Bohemia to lie under the accusation of heresy, but permit all to preach the gospel with freedom in their places of worship according to their own honest convictions.

Three proctors appeared for Dr. Huss before cardinal Colonno. They pleaded an excuse for his absence, and said they were ready to answer in his behalf. But the cardinal declared him contumacious, and accordingly excommunicated him. On this the proctors appealed to the pope, who appointed four cardinals to examine the process: these commissioners confirmed the sentence of the cardinal, and extended the excommunication, not only on Huss, but to all his friends and followers. Huss then appealed from this unjust sentence to a future council, but without success; and, notwithstanding so severe a decree, and an expulsion from his church in Prague, he retired to Hussenitz, his native place, where he continued to promulgate the truth, in his writings as well as his public ministry. It was in this retirement and comparative seclusion that he compiled a treatise, in which he maintained that reading the books of protestants could not be forbidden or prevented. He wrote in defense of Wickliffe's work on the Trinity; and boldly protested against the vices of the pope, the cardinals, and the clergy of those corrupt times. In addition to these he was the author of several other productions, all of which were penned with such strength of argument as greatly facilitated the diffusion of protestant principles.

In England persecution against the protestants had been carried on for some time with relentless cruelty. They now extended to Germany and Bohemia, where Dr. Huss, and Jerome of Prague, were particularly singled out to suffer in the cause of religion. In the month of November, in the year 1414, a general council was assembled at Constance, in Germany, for the purpose of determining a dispute then existing between three persons who contended for the papal throne. These were, John, set up by the Italians; Gregory, by the French; and Benedict, by the Spaniards. The council continued four years, in which the severest laws were enacted to crush the protestants. Pope John was deposed and obliged to fly: more than forty crimes being proved against him; among which were, his attempt to poison his predecessor, his being a gamester, a liar, a murderer, an adulterer, and guilty of unnatural offences.

John Huss was first summoned to appear at the council; and to dispel any apprehension of danger, the emperor sent him a passport, giving him permission freely to come to, and return from, the council. On receiving this information, he told the persons who delivered it, that he desired nothing more than to purge himself publicly of the imputation of heresy; and that he esteemed himself happy in having so fair an opportunity for doing so as the council to which he was summoned to attend.

In the latter end of November he set out for Constance, accompanied by two Bohemian, who were among the most eminent of his disciples, and who followed him through respect and affection. He caused placards to be fixed upon the gates of the churches of Prague, in which he declared that he went to the council to answer all charges that might be made against him. He also declared, in all the cities through which he passed, that he was going to vindicate himself at Constance, and invited all his adversaries to be present. On his way he met with every mark of affection and reverence from people of all descriptions. The streets, and even the roads, were thronged with people, whom respect rather than curiosity had brought together. He was ushered into several towns with great acclamations; and he passed through Germany in a kind of triumph. "I thought," he said, "I had been an outcast. I now see my worst friends are in Bohemia."

On arriving at Constance, he immediately took lodgings in a remote part of the city. Soon after there came to him one Stephen Paletz, who was engaged by the clergy at Prague to manage the intended prosecution against him. Paletz was afterwards joined by Michel de Cassis, on the part of the court of Rome. These two declared themselves his accusers, and drew up articles against him, which they presented to the pope and the prelates of the council. Notwithstanding the promise of the emperor, to give him safe conduct to and from Constance, he regarded not his word; but, according to the maxim of the council, that "Faith is not to be kept with heretics," when it was known he was in the city, he was immediately arrested, and committed prisoner to a chamber in the palace. This breach was particularly noticed by one of Huss's friends, who urged the imperial passport: but the pope replied he never granted any such thing, nor was he bound by that of the emperor.

While Huss was under confinement, the council acted the part of inquisitors. They condemned the doctrines of Wickliffe, and in their impotent malice ordered his remains to be dug up and burnt to ashes. While these orders were executing the nobility of Bohemia and Poland used all their interest for Huss; and so far prevailed as to prevent his being condemned unheard, which appeared to have been resolved on by the commissioners appointed to try him. Before his trial took place, his enemies employed a Franciscan friar, to entangle him in his words, and then appear against him. This man of great ingenuity and subtlety, came to him in the character of an idiot and with seeming sincerity and zeal, requested to be taught his doctrines. But Huss soon detected him, and told him that his manners wore a great semblance of simplicity, but that his questions discovered a depth and design beyond the reach of an idiot. He afterwards found this pretended fool to be Didace, one of the deepest logicians in Lombardy.

At length Huss was brought before the council, when the articles exhibited against him were read: they were upwards of forty in number, and chiefly extracted from his writings. The following extract, forming the eighth article of impeachment, will give a sample of the ground on which this infamous trial was conducted. "An evil and a wicked pope is not the successor of Peter, but of Judas." Answer, "I wrote this in my treatise, if the pope be humble and meek, neglecting and despising the honour and lucre of the world; if he be a shepherd, taking his name from feeding the flock of God; if he feed the sheep with the word, and with virtuous example, and that he become even like his flock with his whole heart and mind; if he diligently and carefully labour and travel for the church, then is he without doubt the true vicar of Christ. But if he walk contrary to these virtues, so much as there is no society between Christ and Belial, and Christ himself saith, 'He that is not with me is against me,' how is he then the true vicar of Christ or Peter, and not rather the vicar of antichrist? Christ called Peter himself, Satan, when he opposed him only in one word, and that with a good affection, even him whom he had chosen his vicar, and specially appointed over his church. Why should not any other then, being more opposed to Christ, be truly called Satan, and consequently antichrist, or at least the principal minister or vicar of antichrist? Infinite testimonies of this matter are found in St. Augustine, St. Jerome, Cyprian, Chryostome, Bernard, Gregory, Remigius, Ambrose, and all the holy fathers of the Christian church."

On his examination being finished, he was taken from the court, and a resolution was formed by the council, to burn him as a heretic unless he retracted. He was then committed to a filthy prison, where, in the day-time, he was so laden with fetters that he could hardly move: and every night he was fastened by his hands to a ring against the wall. He continued some days in this situation, while many noblemen of Bohemia interceded in his behalf. They drew up a petition for his release, which was presented to the council by several of the most illustrious men of the country; notwithstanding which, so many enemies had Huss in that court, that no attention was paid to it, and the persecuted reformer was compelled to endure all the ignominy and misery inflicted on him. Shortly after the petition was presented, four bishops and two lords were sent by the emperor to the prison, in order to prevail on Huss to make a recantation. But he called God to witness, with tears in his eyes, that he was not conscious of having preached or written any thing against the truth of God, or the faith of his orthodox church. The deputies then represented the great wisdom and authority of the council; to which Huss replied, "Let them send the meanest person of that council, who can convince me by argument from the word of God, and I will submit my judgment to him." This firm and faithful answer had no effect, because he would not take the authority of the council upon trust, in opposition to the plainest reasonings of scripture. The deputies, therefore, finding they could not make any impression on him, departed, greatly astonished at the strength of his resolution.

On the 4th of July he was, for the last time, brought before the council. After a long examination he was desired to abjure, which he refused without the least hesitation. The bishop of Lodi then preached a bloody persecuting sermon, the text of which was, "Let the body of sin be destroyed." The sermon was the usual prologue to a cruel martyrdom; and when it was over his fate was fixed, his vindication rejected and judgment was pronounced. The council censured him for being obstinate and incorrigible, and ordained that he should be degraded from the priesthood, his books publicly burnt, and himself delivered to the secular power. He received the sentence without the least emotion; and at the close of it he kneeled down with his eyes lifted towards heaven, and, with all the magnanimity of a primitive martyr, thus exclaimed:

May thine infinite mercy, O my God! pardon this injustice of mine enemies. Thou knowest the iniquity of my accusations: how deformed with crimes I have been represented: how I have been oppressed by worthless witnesses, and a false condemnation: yet, O my God! let that mercy of thine, which no tongue can express, prevail with thee not to avenge my wrongs.

These excellent sentences were received as so many expressions of treason, and only tended to inflame his adversaries. Accordingly, the bishops appointed by the council stripped him of his priestly garments, degraded him, and put a paper mitre on his head, on which were painted devils, with this inscription: "A ring-leader of heretics." This mockery was received by the heroic martyr with an air of unconcern, and it seemed to give him dignity rather than disgrace. A serenity appeared in his looks, which indicated that his soul had cut off many stages of a tedious journey in her way to the realms of everlasting happiness, and when the bishops urged him to yet recant, he turned to the people, and addressed them thus:—

These lords and bishops exhort and counsel me, that I should here confess before you all, that I have erred; to which, if it were such as might be done with the infamy and reproach of man only, they might, peradventure, easily persuade me thereunto; but now truly I am in the sight of the Lord my God, without whose great displeasure, and disquietude of mine own conscience, I could by no means do that which they require of me. For I well know that I never taught any of those things which they have falsely alleged against me, but I have always preached, taught, written, and thought contrary thereunto. With what countenance then should I behold the heavens? With what face should I look upon them whom I have taught, whereof there is a great number, if through me it should come to pass that those things, which they have hitherto known to be most certain and sure, should now be made uncertain? Should I by this example astonish or trouble so many souls, so many consciences, endued with the most firm and certain knowledge of the scriptures and gospel of our Lord Jesus Christ and his most pure doctrine, armed against all the assaults of Satan? I will never do it, neither commit any such kind of offence, that I should seem more to esteem this vile carcass appointed unto death, than their health and salvation.

At this most godly speech he was forced again to hear, by the consent of the bishops, that he obstinately and maliciously persevered in his pernicious and wicked errors. The ceremony of degradation being over, the bishops delivered him to the emperor, who put him into the care of the duke of Bavaria. His books were consumed at the gates of the church; and on the 6th of July he was led to the suburbs of Constance to be burnt alive. When he had reached the place of execution, he fell on his knees, sung several portions of the Psalms, looked stedfastly towards heaven, and repeated, "Into thy hands, O Lord! do I commit my spirit: thou hast redeemed me, O most good and faithful God." As soon as the chain was put about him at the stake, he said, with a smiling countenance, "My Lord Jesus Christ was bound with a harder chain than this for my sake, why then should I be ashamed of this old rusty one?" When the fagots were piled around him, the duke of Bavaria was so officious as to desire him to abjure. His noble reply was, "No, I never preached any doctrine of an evil tendency; and what I taught with my lips I now seal with my blood." He then said to the executioner, "You are now going to burn a goose, (the name of Huss signifying goose in the Bohemian language,) but in a century you will have a swan whom you can neither roast nor boil." If this were spoken in prophecy, he must have meant Martin Luther, who shone about a hundred years after, and who had a swan for his arms—whether suggested by this circumstance or on account of family descent and heraldry is not known. As soon as the fagots were lighted, the heroic martyr sung a hymn, with so loud and cheerful a voice, that he was heard through all the crackling of the combustibles, and the noise of the multitude. At length his voice was interrupted by the flames, which soon put a period to his mortal life, and wafted his undying spirit, which no fire of earth could subdue or touch, to the regions of everlasting glory.

CHAPTER THIRTEEN

Account of the Life, Sufferings, and Martyrdom of Jerome of Prague, Who Was Burnt at Constance, in Germany for Maintaining the Doctrine of Wickliffe

This hero in the cause of truth was born at Prague and educated in its university where he soon became distinguished for his learning and eloquence. Having completed his studies, he travelled over a great part of Europe, and visited many of the seats of learning, particularly the universities of Paris, Heidelburg, Cologne, and Oxford. At the latter he became acquainted with the works of Wickliffe and, being a person of uncommon application, he translated many of them into his own language, having with great pains made himself master of the English. On his return to Prague, he openly professed the doctrines of Wickliffe; and finding that they had made considerable progress in Bohemia, from the industry and zeal of Huss, he became his assistant in the great work.

On the 4th of April, A.D. 1415, Jerome went to Constance. This was about three months before the death of Huss. He entered the town privately and, consulting with some of the leaders of his party, was easily convinced that he could render his friend no service. Finding that his arrival at Constance was publicly known and that the council intended to seize him, he prudently retired and went to Iberling, an imperial town at a short distance. While here he wrote to the emperor and avowed his readiness to appear before the council, if he would give a safe-conduct; this, however, was refused. He then applied to the council but met with an answer equally unfavourable. After this, he caused papers to be put up in all the public places of Constance, particularly on the door of the cardinal's house. In these he professed his willingness to appear at Constance in the defense of his character and doctrine, both which he said had been greatly falsified. He further declared, that if any error should be proved against him he would retract it; desiring only that the faith of the council might be given for his security.

Receiving no answer to these papers, he set out on his return to Bohemia, previously adopting the precaution to take with him a certificate signed by several of the Bohemian nobility then at Constance, testifying that he had used every prudent means in his power to procure an audience. Notwithstanding this he was seized on his way, without any authority, by an officer belonging to the duke of Sultzbach, who hoped thereby to receive commendations from the council for so acceptable a service. The duke of Sultzbach immediately wrote to the council, informing them what he had done, and asking directions how to proceed with Jerome. The council, after expressing their obligations to the duke, desired him to send the prisoner immediately to Constance. He was accordingly conveyed in irons and, on his way, was met by the elector Palatine, who caused a long chain to be fastened to Jerome, by which he was dragged like a wild beast to the cloister, whence, after some insults and examinations, he was conveyed to a tower and fastened to a block with his legs in the stocks. In this manner he remained eleven days and nights, until becoming dangerously ill, they, in order to satiate their malice still farther, relieved him from that painful state. He remained confined until the martyrdom of his friend Huss; after which he was brought forth and threatened with immediate torments and death if he remained obstinate. Terrified at the preparations of pain, in a moment of weakness, he forgot his manliness and resolution, abjured his doctrines, and confessed that Huss merited his fate, and that both he and Wickliffe were heretics. In consequence of this his chains were taken off and his harsh treatment done away. He was, however, still confined, with daily hopes of liberation. But his enemies suspecting his sincerity, another form of recantation was drawn up and proposed to him. He, however, refused to answer this, except in public, and was accordingly brought before the council, when, to the astonishment of his auditors, and to the glory of truth, he renounced his recantation, and requested permission to plead his own cause, which being refused, he thus vented his indignation:

What barbarity is this? For three hundred and forty days have I been confined in a variety of prisons. There is not a misery, there is not a want, which I have not experienced. To my enemies you have allowed the fullest scope of accusation: to me, you deny the least opportunity of defense. Not an hour will you now indulge me in preparing for my trial. You have swallowed the blackest calumnies against me. You have represented me as a heretic, without knowing my doctrine; as an enemy to the faith, before you knew what faith I professed. You are a general council: in you centre all which this world can communicate of gravity, wisdom, and sanctity: but still you are men, and men are seducible by appearances. The higher your character is for wisdom, the greater ought your care to be not to deviate into folly. The cause I now plead is not my own, it is the cause of men: it is the cause of Christians: it is a cause which is to affect the rights of posterity, however the experiment is to be made in my person.

This speech, the eloquence and force of which are worthy of the best ages, produced no effect on the obdurate foes of Jerome. They proceeded with his charge, which was reduced to five articles—That he was a derider of the papal dignity—an opposer of the pope himself—an enemy to the cardinals—a persecutor of the bishops—and a despiser of Christianity! To these charges Jerome answered with an amazing force of eloquence and strength of argument. "Now, whither shall I turn me? To my accusers? My accusers are as deaf as adders. To you, my judges? You are all prepossessed by the arts of my accusers." After this speech he was immediately remanded to his prison. The third day from this his trial was brought on, and witnesses were examined in support of the charge. The prisoner was prepared for his defense, which appears almost incredible, when we consider he had been nearly a year shut up in loathsome dungeons, deprived of day-light, and almost starved for want of common necessaries. But his spirit soared above these disadvantages.

The most bigoted of the assembly were unwilling he should be heard, dreading the effects of eloquence in the cause of truth, on the minds of the most prejudiced. This was such as to excite the envy of the greatest persons of his time. "Jerome," said Gerson, the chancellor of Paris, at his accusation, "when thou wast in Paris, thou wast thyself, by means of thine eloquence an angel; and didst trouble the whole university." At length it was carried by the majority, that he should have liberty to proceed in his defense; which he began in such an exalted strain and continued with such a torrent of elocution that the obdurate heart was seen to melt, and the mind of superstition seemed to admit a ray of conviction. He began to deduce from history the number of great and virtuous men who had, in their time, been condemned and punished as evil persons, but whom after generations had proved to have deserved honour and reward. He laid before the assembly the whole tenor of his life and conduct. He observed that the greatest and most holy men had been known to differ in points of speculation, with a view to distinguish truth, not to keep it concealed. He expressed a noble contempt of all his enemies, who would have induced him to retract the cause of virtue and truth, and upbraided his late and momentary weakness, which led him to deny himself and forget his glory. He entered on a high encomium on Huss; and declared he was ready to follow him to martyrdom. He then proceeded to defend the doctrines of the English luminary Wickliffe; and concluded with observing, that it was far from his intention to advance anything against the state of the church of God; that it was only against the abuses of the clergy he complained; and that it was certainly impious that the patrimony of the church, which was originally intended for the purpose of charity and universal benevolence, should be prostituted to sensual and sordid gratification to "the lust of the flesh, the lust of the eye, and the pride of life," which the apostle expressly declares "are not of the Father, but of the world."

The trial being ended, Jerome received the same sentence as had been passed on his martyred countryman, and was, in the usual style of popish duplicity, delivered over to the civil power; but being a layman he had not to undergo the ceremony of degradation. His persecutors, however, prepared for him a cap of paper, painted with red devils, which being put upon his head, he said, "Our Lord Jesus Christ, when He suffered death for me a most miserable sinner, did wear a crown of thorns upon His head; and I, for His sake, will wear this adorning of derision and blasphemy." Two days they delayed the execution in hopes that he would recant; meanwhile the cardinal of Florence used his utmost endeavours to bring him over: but they all proved ineffectual: Jerome was resolved to seal his doctrine with his blood.

On his way to the place of execution he sung several hymns; and on arriving at the spot, the same where Huss had suffered, he kneeled down and prayed fervently. He embraced the stake with great cheerfulness and resolution; and when the executioner went behind him to set fire to the fagots, he said, "Come here, and kindle it before my eyes; for had I been afraid of it, I had not come here, having had so many opportunities to escape." When the flames began to envelope him, he sung another hymn; and the last words he was heard to say were,

> *Hanac animam in flammis affero, Christe, tibi!*
> This soul in flames I offer, Christ, to thee!

He was of a fine and manly form and possessed a strong and healthy constitution, which served to render his death extremely painful, for he was observed to live an unusual time in the midst of the flames. He, however, sung until his aspiring soul took its flight from its mortal habitation, as in a fiery chariot, which seemed rather sent by God than prepared by man, to convey his blessed spirit from earth to heaven in the sight of a thousand witnesses.

CHAPTER FOURTEEN

*Containing Interesting Particulars of the Persecution
of Protestants in Different Foreign Countries*

SUMMARY OF PERSECUTIONS AGAINST
THE CHRISTIANS IN ABYSSINIA

About the end of the fifteenth century, some Portuguese missionaries made a voyage to Abyssinia and began to propagate the Roman Catholic doctrines among the people of that interesting country, many of whom already professed the tenets and ceremonies of a purer Christianity.

The priests gained such influence at court that the emperor consented to abolish the established rites of the Ethiopian church and to admit those of Rome; and soon after consented to receive a patriarch from the pope and to acknowledge his supremacy. This innovation, however, did not take place without great opposition. Several of the most powerful lords and a majority of the people who professed the primitive Christianity, as at first established in Abyssinia, took up arms in their defense against the emperor. Thus, by the artifices of the court of Rome and its emissaries, the whole empire was thrown into commotion, and a war commenced which was carried on through the reign of many emperors, and which ceased not for above a century and a half. All this time the Roman Catholics were strengthened by the power of the court, by means of which conjunction the primitive Christians of Abyssinia were severely persecuted, and multitudes perished by the hands of their inhuman enemies.

There is a striking contrast between the persecution in Abyssinia and those in Japan, which the careful reader will on no account overlook. In Japan they were Catholics who were the victims of pagan cruelty and suffered under a

192

superstition more gross and cruel than their own. But in Abyssinia the Catholics were, as in most other instances which have been detailed, the aggressors; and a purer class of Christians than themselves were the sufferers from their malice and policy, their jealousy and barbarity. When we witness the unrelenting and almost universal propensity of Catholics to persecute whatever classes of Christians may chance to choose to differ from them, we scarcely feel regret that they sometimes are made to drink of the bitter cup they force into the hands of others. A general lesson is, however, here taught to all—that in proportion as worldly and selfish maxims mingle themselves with religion, will that religion be perverted to an engine of mischief and misery instead of benefit and happiness.

CHAPTER FIFTEEN

*The Life and Martyrdom of John Hooper,
Bishop of Worcester and Gloucester*

J ohn Hooper, student and graduate in the university of Oxford, having made great advances in the study of the sciences, was stirred with a fervent desire to the love and knowledge of the scriptures. Advancing more and more, by God's grace, in ripeness and spiritual understanding, and shewing withal some sparks of his spirit, being then about the beginning of the six articles, in the time of king Henry VIII. fell quickly into the displeasure and hatred of certain doctors in Oxford, who soon discovered their enmity to him, until at length, by the procurement of Dr. Smith, he was compelled to quit the university. Removing from thence, he was retained in the house of Sir Thomas Arundel, in the capacity of steward, until Sir Thomas, having intelligence of his opinions and religion, which he in no case did favour, and yet exceedingly favouring the person and character of the man, found the means to send him with a message to the bishop of Winchester, writing his letter privily to the bishop, by conference of learning to do some good unto him, but in any case requiring him to send home his servant to him again. The bishop received him courteously; but after long conference with him, perceiving that neither he could do that good which he thought to him, nor that he would take any good at his hand, according to Arundel's request, sent him home again, commending his learning and wit, but yet bearing in his breast a secret enmity against him.

Not long after this, as malice is always working mischief, intelligence was given to Mr. Hooper to provide for himself, for danger was arising against him; whereupon he left Sir Thomas Arundel's house, and borrowing a horse of a friend, whose life he had saved, took his journey to the seaside to go to France, sending back the horse again by one, who indeed did not deliver him to the owner. Mr. Hooper being at Paris, remained there not long, but in a short time returned into England again, and was retained by Mr. Sentlow, until he was again molested and sought for: when he was compelled under the pretence of being captain of a ship going to Ireland, to take to the seas, and so escaped through France to the higher parts of Germany; where, commencing acquaintance with learned men, he was by them friendly and lovingly entertained, both at Basil and at Zurich: at the latter place in particular by Mr. Bullinger. Here he also married, and applied very studiously to the study of the Hebrew tongue.

At length, when God saw it good to end the bloody persecution which arose from the six articles, and to give king Edward to reign over this realm, with some peace and rest unto the church, amongst many other English exiles who then repaired homeward, was Mr. Hooper, who thought it his duty to forward the cause of God in his native country. Coming to Mr. Bullinger, and other of his acquaintance in Zurich, to give them thanks for their singular kindness towards him, his kind host thus addressed him, "Mr. Hooper, although we are sorry to part with your company for your own cause, yet much greater cause have we to rejoice, both for your sake, and especially for the cause of Christ's true religion, that you shall now return out of long banishment to your native country, where you may not only enjoy your own private liberty, but also the cause and state of Christ's church by you may fare the better, as we doubt not but it will. Another cause why we rejoice with you and for you, is this: that you shall remove not only out of exile into liberty, but leave here a barren, sour, and unpleasant country, rude and savage, and shall go into a land flowing with milk and honey, replenished with all fertility. But with this our rejoicing, one fear and care we have, lest you being absent, and so far distant from us, or else coming to such abundance of wealth and felicity, in your new welfare and plenty of all things, and in your flourishing honours, where you shall come peradventure to be a bishop, and where you shall find so many new friends, you will forget us your old acquaintance and well-wishers. If however you shall forget and shake us off, yet this persuade yourself, that we will not forget our old friend. And if you will please not to forget us, then I pray you let us hear from you."

Mr. Hooper gave Mr. Bullinger and the rest hearty thanks, for their singular good-will and undeserved affection, appearing not only now, but at all times towards him; declaring, moreover, that as the principal cause of his removing to his country was the matter of religion; so touching the unpleasantness and barrenness of that country of theirs, there was no cause therein why he could not find in his heart to continue his life there, as soon as in any place in the world, and rather than his own native country, if there were nothing else in his conscience that moved him to change. And as to the forgetting his old friends, although the remembrance of a man's country naturally delights him, and he could not deny but God had blessed his country with many great advantages; yet neither the nature of country, nor pleasure of advantages, nor newness of friends, should ever induce him to the oblivion of such benefactors, to whom he was so entirely bound; and therefore they should be sure from time to time to hear from him. But the last news of all I may not be able to write; "for there," said he, (taking Mr. Bullinger by the hand) "where I shall take most pains, there shall you hear of me to be burned to ashes: and that shall be news which I shall not be able to write unto you, but you shall hear of me from other hands."

Having thus taken his farewell of Mr. Bullinger, and his friends in Zurich, he repaired again into England, in the reign of Edward the Sixth; and coming to London, used continually to preach, most times twice, and at least once every day. In all his discourses, according to his accustomed manner, he corrected sin, and sharply inveighed against the iniquity of the world, and corrupt abuses of the church. Nor was his example less proper: his life was so pure and good, that no kind of slander could fasten any fault upon him. He was of strong body, his health whole and sound, his wit very poignant, his invincible patience able to sustain whatever adversity could inflict. He was constant of judgment, frugal of diet, spare of words, and still more so of time. In house-keeping very liberal, and sometimes more free than his living would extend unto.

After he had practised himself in this popular preaching, he was, at length, and that not without the great profit of many, called to preach before the king, and soon after made bishop of Gloucester by his majesty's commands. In that office he continued two years, and behaved himself so well, that his very enemies could find no fault in him, except in the way in which the foes of Daniel found fault with that holy prophet—"concerning the law of his God." After two years he received, in connection with Gloucester, the bishopric of the neighbouring city of Worcester.

But sinister and unlucky contention concerning the ordering and consecration of bishops, and of their apparel, with other such trifles, began to disturb the good beginning of this bishop. For notwithstanding that godly reformation of religion that arose in the church of England, besides other ceremonies more ambitious than profitable, or tending to edification, they used to wear such garments and apparel as the popish bishops were wont to do; first a chymere, and under that a white rochet; then a mathematical cap with four angles, indicative of dividing the world into four parts. These trifles tending more to superstition than otherwise, as he could never abide, so in no wise could he be persuaded to wear them. For this cause he made supplication to the king, most humbly desiring his highness, either to discharge him of the bishopric, or else to dispense with him for such ceremonial orders: which petition the king granted immediately, writing to the archbishop in his behalf. The king's letter was as follows—"Right reverend father, and right trusty and well beloved, we greet you well. Whereas we, by advice of our councils have called and chosen our right well beloved Mr. John Hooper, professor of divinity, to be our bishop of Gloucester, as well for his great knowledge, deep judgment, and long study in the scriptures; as also for his good discretion, ready utterance, and honest life; to the intent that all our loving subjects, which are in his said charge and elsewhere, might by his sound and true doctrine learn the better their duty towards God, their obedience towards us, and love towards their neighbour; from consecrating of whom we understand you to stay, because he would have you omit certain rites and ceremonies offensive to his conscience, whereby ye think ye should fall under the laws—we have thought good, by the advice aforesaid, to dispense and discharge you of all manner of dangers, penalties, and forfeitures, you shall be liable to run into by omitting any of the same. And these our letters shall be your sufficient warrant and discharge."

The earl of Warwick seconded this request of his majesty by addressing another letter to the archbishop, begging that he would dispense with Mr. Hooper's being burthened by the oath commonly used in the consecration of bishops. But these letters availed not: the bishops still stood earnestly in defence of the ceremonies, saying, it was but a small matter, and that the fault was in the abuse of the things, and not in the things themselves: adding, moreover, that Mr. Hooper ought not to be so stubborn in so light a matter, and that his wilfulness therein was not to be suffered. This being the case, Mr. Hooper at length agreed, that sometimes he should in his sermons shew himself apparelled as the other bishops were. Accordingly being appointed to preach before the king, he appeared in the objectionable habiliments. His upper garment was a long scarlet gown down to the foot, and under that a white linen rochet, that covered all his shoulders. Upon his head he had a geometrical, that is, a four-squared cap. But this private contumely and reproach, in respect of the public profit of the church, he suffered patiently. Then also very soon these differences vanished amidst the rage of persecution; and the trifling shades of opinion were lost in their unanimity of essential truths; so that, while they were in prison, several affectionate letters passed between them.[1]

After this discord, and not a little vexation, about vestures, at length Mr. Hooper entering into his diocese, there employed his time, under king Edward's reign, with such diligence as may be an example to all bishops. So careful was he in his cure, that he left neither pains untaken, nor ways unsought, how to train up the flock of Christ in the true word of salvation, continually labouring in

---

[1] The godly reconciliation of these good men appears by the following extract from bishop Ridley's letter to Mr. Hooper: "My dear brother—Forasmuch as I understand by your works, which I have yet but superficially seen, that we thoroughly agree and wholly consent together in those things which are the grounds and substantial points of our religion, against the which the world so furiously rageth in these our days, howsoever in time past, in certain bye-matters and circumstances of religion, your wisdom and my simplicity (I grant) have a little jarred, each of us following the abundance of his own sense and judgment; now, I say, be you assured that even with my whole heart, God is my witness, in the bowels of Christ I love you in the truth, and for the truth's sake which abideth in us, and as I am persuaded shall by the grace of God abide in us for evermore. And because the world, as I perceive, brother, ceaseth not to play a pageant, and busily conspireth against Christ our Saviour, with all possible force and power 'exalting high things against the knowledge of God,' let us join hands together in Christ; and if we cannot overthrow, yet to our power, and as much as in us lieth, let us shake those high altitudes, not with carnal but with spiritual weapons; and withal, brother, let us prepare for the day of dissolution, by the which, after the short time of this bodily affliction, by the grace of our Lord Jesus Christ, we shall triumph together with him in eternal glory."

the same. Other men are commonly wont, for lucre or promotion's sake, to aspire to bishoprics, some hunting for them, and some purchasing them, as men used to purchase lordships. To this class of worldly men bishop Hooper was quite contrary. He abhorred nothing more than covetousness, labouring always to save and preserve the souls of his flock. No father in his household, no gardener in his garden, nor husbandman in his vineyard, was more or better occupied, than he in his diocese amongst his flock, going about his towns and villages teaching and preaching to the people. The time that he had to spare from preaching, he bestowed either in hearing public causes, or else in private study, prayer, and in visiting schools: with his continual doctrine he adjoined due and discreet correction, not so severe to any as to those who, for abundance of riches and wealthy state, thought they might do what they pleased. And doubtless he spared no kind of people, but was indifferent to all, as well rich as poor, to the great shame of many men in these days; whereof we see so many addicted to the pleasing of the great and rich, that in the mean time they have no regard to the meaner sort whom Christ hath brought as dearly as the other.

In his personal and private character how virtuous and good he was, may be conceived and known evidently by this, that as he was hated by none but the evil, the worst of them could not reprove his life in any particular. At home, in his domestic concerns, he exhibited an example of a worthy prelate's life: bestowing the most part of his care upon the public flock and congregation of Christ, for which also he spent his blood; yet there was nothing wanting in him to bring up his own children in learning and good manners: insomuch that it is difficult to say, whether he deserved more praise for his fatherly usage at home, or his public conduct abroad. Every where he kept religion in one uniform doctrine and integrity: so that if you entered into the bishop's palace, you would suppose yourselves to have entered into some church or temple. In every corner there was the beauty of virtue, good example, honest conversation, and reading of the holy scriptures. There was not to be seen in his house any courtly rioting or idleness; no pomp, no dishonest word, no swearing, could there be heard. As to the revenues of his bishoprics, if any thing surmounted thereof, he saved nothing, but bestowed it in hospitality. Twice I was, as I remember, in his house in Worcester, where, in his common hall, I saw a table spread with good store of meat, and beset full of beggars and poor folk; and I asking his servants what this meant, they told me that every day their lord and master's manner was, to have to dinner a certain number of poor folk of the said city by course, who were served by four at a mess, with hot and wholesome meats; and, when they were served, then he himself sat down to dinner, and not before. After this sort and manner master Hooper executed the office of most careful and vigilant pastor, by the space of two years and more, so long as the state of religion in king Edward's time safely flourished. And would God that all other bishops would use the like diligence and care in their function!

After this, in the reign of queen Mary, religion being subverted and changed, this good bishop was one of the first who was sent for by a pursuivant to London. Two reasons were assigned for this step. The first, that he might answer to Dr. Heath, then re-appointed bishop of that diocese, who was deprived thereof in kings Edward's days, why he continued in an office to which he had no right? And next to render an account to Bonner, bishop of London, because he had in king Edward's time been one of his accusers. Now although he was not ignorant of the evils that should happen towards him, being admonished by certain of his friends to get away, and shift for himself, yet he would not prevent them, but remained, saying, "Once did I flee, and take me to my feet; but now, because I am called to this place and vocation, I am thoroughly persuaded to remain, and to live and die with my sheep." On reaching London, before he could see Heath or Bonner, he was intercepted, and commanded to appear before the queen and her council, to answer certain bonds and obligations, wherein he was said to be bound unto her. When he met the council, Gardiner received him very opprobriously, railing at him, and accusing him of his religion. He freely and boldly answered, and cleared himself. But he was, notwithstanding, commanded to ward, and it was declared unto him at his departure, that the cause of his imprisonment was only for certain sums of money, for which he was indebted to the queen, and not for religion. This, how false and untrue it was, shall in its place more plainly appear. Here it is enough to remark that at a second summons, such was the noise, that he could not be permitted to plead his cause, but was deprived of his bishoprics.

Before we detail the examinations of Hooper, it will be proper to let him relate the cruel captivity he endured for eighteen months in the Fleet prison.

The first of September, 1553, I was committed unto the Fleet, from Richmond, to have the liberty of the prison; and within six days after I paid five pounds sterling to the warden for fees for my liberty; who immediately upon payment thereof, complained unto the bishop of Winchester, upon which I was committed to close prison a quarter of a year in the Tower-chamber of the Fleet, and used extremely ill. By the means of a good gentlewoman, I had liberty to come down to dinner and supper, but was not suffered to speak with any of my friends; but as soon as dinner and supper were done, to repair to my chamber again. Notwithstanding, whilst I came down thus to dinner and supper, the warden and his wife picked quarrels with me, and complained untruly of me to their great friend the bishop of Winchester.

After a quarter of a year, Babington the warden, and his wife, fell out with me respecting the wicked mass: and thereupon the warden resorted to the bishop of Winchester, and obtained to put me into the wards, where I have continued a long time, having nothing appointed to me for my bed, but a little pad of straw and a rotten covering, with a tick and a few feathers therein, the chamber being vile and stinking, until by God's means good people sent me bedding to lie on. On one side of the prison is the sink and filth of the house, and on the other the town ditch, so that the stench of the house hath infected me with sundry diseases. During this time I have been sick, and the doors, bars, hasps, and chains being all closed upon me, I have mourned, called, and cried for help; but the warden when he hath known me many times ready to die, and when the poor men of the wards have called to help me, hath commanded the doors to be kept fast, and charged that none of his men should come at me, saying, "Let him alone, it were a good riddance of him." And he did this Oct. 18, 1553, as many can witness.

I paid always like a baron to the said workers, as well in fees, as for my board, which was twenty shillings a week, besides my man's table, until I was wrongfully deprived of my bishoprics; and since that time, I have paid him as the best gentleman doth in his house; yet hath he used me worse, and more vilely, than the veriest slave that even came to the common side of the prison. He hath also imprisoned my man, William Downton, and stripped him of his clothes to search for letters, and could find none, but a little remembrance of good people's names who had given me their alms to relieve me in prison; and to undo them also, the warden delivered the same bill unto Gardiner, God's enemy and mine.

I have suffered imprisonment almost eighteen months, my goods, livings, friends, and comfort taken from me; the queen owing me, by just account, fourscore pounds or more. She hath put me in prison, and giveth nothing to keep me, neither is there suffered any one to come at me, whereby I might have relief. I am by a wicked man and woman cruelly treated, so that I see no remedy, saving God's help, but I shall be cast away in prison before I come to judgment. But I commit my just cause to God, whose will be done, whether it be by life or death.

The first examination of bishop Hooper was before five bishops as commissioners—of London, Durham, Winchester, Chichester, and Landaff. On his entering their presence, Gardiner, bishop of Winchester and lord chancellor asked whether he was married. To this the good man smilingly answered, "Yes, my lord, and will not be unmarried until death unmarry me. And this is not enough to deprive me, except you do it against the law." The subject of marriage was no more talked of then for some time: but all began to make great outcries, and laughed, and used such gestures as were unseemly for the place, and for such a matter. Day, bishop of Chichester, called Hooper a hypocrite, with vehement voice, and scornful countenance. Tonstal, bishop of Durham, called him beast; so did Smith, one of the clerks of the council, and several others that stood by. At length the bishop of Winchester said, that all men might live chaste who would, and brought in this text.—"There are those that have become eunuchs for the kingdom of heaven."

To this Hooper said, the text proved not that all men could live chaste, but such to whom it was given; and read the verse before it. But again there was a clamour and cry, mocking and scorning, calling him beast, and exclaiming and the text could not be examined. Then Hooper said, that it appeared by the old canons, that marriage was not forbidden unto priests, and then named the decrees. But the bishop of Winchester sent for another part, namely, the

Clementines, or the Extravagants, and perversely, against all reason determined that he should have no other, until he was judged by these. Then began such a noise, tumult, and speaking together of a great many who favoured not the cause, that nothing was done or spoken orderly or charitably. Afterwards, judge Morgan began to rail at Hooper a long time, with many opprobrious and foul words relative to his proceedings at Gloucester, in punishing of men, and said there was never such a tyrant as he was. After that the bishop of Chichester said, that the council of Ancyra, which was before the council of Nice, was against the marriage of priests.

To this Hooper said, my lord of Chichester knoweth, that the great council of Nice, by the means of one Paphnutius, decreed, That no minister should be separated from his wife. Again such clamours and cries were used, that the council of Nice was not attended to. After alternate clamour and silence, and much illiberal speech, Tonstal, bishop of Durham, asked him whether he believed the corporeal presence of the sacrament. He said plainly, that there was none such, neither did he believe any such thing. The offended bishop would then have read out of a book; but there was such a noise and confused talk on every side, that he did not proceed. Then the bishop of Winchester asked, What authority had moved him to deny the corporeal presence? He said, the authority of God's word, and alleged this text, "Whom heaven must hold until the latter day." But the bishop of Winchester would have made that text to serve nothing for his purpose, and said, he might be in heaven, and in the sacrament also. Then Hooper would have opened the text, but all who stood about the bishop prevented his speaking with clamours and cries, so that he was not permitted to say any more against Gardiner. Whereupon they bade the notaries write, that he was married, and said that he would not go from his wife; and that he believed not the corporeal presence in the sacrament, for which he was worthy to be deprived of his bishopric.

The next examination of Hooper took place at Winchester house, rather more privately than the former, no doubt to prevent such of the noise made on that occasion. On the 22nd of January, 1555, Babington, the warden of the Fleet, was commanded to bring him before Gardiner and some other bishops to Winchester house, in St. Mary Overy's: where the latter moved Hooper earnestly to forsake the evil and corrupt doctrine preached in the days of king Edward, to return to the unity of the catholic church, and to acknowledge the pope's holiness to be head of the same church, according to the determination of the whole parliament: promising, likewise, that as they with other their brethren, had received the pope's blessing, and the queen's mercy, even so mercy was ready to be shewed to him and others, if he would arise with them, and condescend to the pope's holiness.

Master Hooper answered, that forasmuch as the pope taught doctrine altogether contrary to the doctrine of Christ, he was not worthy to be accounted as a member of Christ's church, much less to be head thereof; wherefore he would in no wise condescend to any such usurped jurisdiction. Neither esteemed he the church, whereof they call him head, to be the catholic church of Christ; for the church only heareth the voice of her spouse Christ, and flieth the strangers. "Howbeit," saith he, "if in any point to me unknown I have offended the queen's majesty, I shall most humbly submit myself to her mercy, if mercy may be had with safety of conscience, and without the displeasure of God." Answer was made, that the queen would show no mercy to the pope's enemies. Whereupon Babington was commanded to carry him to the Fleet again. He did so, and shifted him from his former chamber into another, near unto the warden's own chamber, where he remained six days; and, in the mean time, his former chamber was searched by Dr. Martin and others, for writings and books which master Hooper was thought to have made, but none were found.

One more examination, or rather effort to make Hooper recant, occurred at the same place, and before the same crafty and cruel inquisitors. Jan. 28th, the bishop of Winchester, and other commissioners, again sat in judgment at St. Mary Overy's, where Hooper appeared before them in the afternoon, and after much reasoning and disputation, was commanded aside, until Mr. Rogers, who was then come, had been examined. Examinations ended, the sheriffs were commanded, about four o'clock, to carry them to the compter in Southwark, there to remain until the following day at nine o'clock, to see whether they would relent and come home again to the catholic church. Hooper went before with one of the sheriffs, and Mr. Rogers came after with the other; and being out of the church door, Hooper looked back and stayed a little until Mr. Rogers drew near, unto whom he said, "Come, brother Rogers, must we two take this matter first in hand, and begin to fry these fagots?" "Yes, sir," said Mr. Rogers, "by God's grace." "Doubt not," said Hooper, "but God will give strength." So going forwards, there was such a press of people in the streets, who rejoiced at their constancy, that they had much ado to pass.

By the way the sheriff said to master Hooper, "I would that ye were not so hasty and quick with my lord chancellor, and did use more patience." He answered, "Master sheriff, I was nothing at all impatient, although I was earnest in my Master's cause, and it standeth me so in hand, for it goeth upon life and death; not the life and death of this world only, but also of the world to come." Then they were committed to the keeper of the compter, and appointed to different chambers, with command that they should not be suffered to speak one with another, neither was any other permitted to come to them that night.

Upon the day following, January 29th, at the hour appointed, they were brought up again by the sheriffs before Gardiner and the commissioners in the church, where they were the day before. And after long and earnest talk, when they perceived that Hooper would by no means condescend unto them, they condemned him to be degraded, and read unto him his condemnation. That done, Mr. Rogers was brought before them, and treated in like manner; and both were delivered to the secular power, two sheriffs of London, who were ordered to carry them to the Clink, a prison not far from the bishop of Winchester's house, and there to remain until night. When it became dark, Hooper was led by one of the sheriffs, with many bills and weapons, through the bishop of Winchester's house, and over London-bridge through the city to Newgate, and by the way some of the serjeants were sent before, to put out the coster-mongers' candles, who used to sit with lights in the streets; either fearing, that the people would have made some attempt to have taken him away from them by force, if they had seen him go to that prison; or else, being burdened with an evil conscience, they thought darkness to be a most fit season for such a business. But notwithstanding this device, the people having some fore-knowledge of his coming, many of them came forth to their doors with lights, and saluted him, praising God for his constancy in the true doctrine which he had taught them, and desiring God to strengthen him in the same to the end. The bishop required the people to make their earnest prayer to God for him; and so went through Cheapside to the place appointed, and was delivered as close prisoner to the keeper of Newgate, where he remained six days, nobody being permitted to come to him, saving his keepers, and such as should be appointed thereto.

During this time, Bonner, bishop of London, and others at his appointment, as Fecknam, Chedsey, and Harpsfield, resorted several times unto him, to try if by means they could persuade him to relent, and become a member of their church. All the ways they could devise, they attempted. For, besides the disputations and allegation of testimonies of the scriptures, and of ancient writers wrested to a wrong sense, according to their accustomed manner, they used also all outward gentleness and significations of friendship, with many great promises of worldly wealth; not omitting, at the same time, most grievous threatenings, if with gentleness they could not prevail; but they found him always the same man, steadfast and immovable. When they perceived that they could by no means reclaim him to their purpose, with such persuasions and offers as they used for his conversion, then went they by false rumours and reports of recantations to bring him, and the doctrine of Christ which he professed, in discredit with the people. This being spread abroad, and believed by some of the weaker sort, Hooper was greatly grieved thereat, that the people should give credit to such false rumours, having so simple a ground. Hence he was constrained to address the following letter to his fellow protestants.

The grace of our Lord Jesus Christ be with all them who unfeignedly look for the coming of our Saviour Christ. Dear brethren and sisters in the Lord, and my fellow-prisoners for the cause of God's gospel, I do much rejoice and give thanks unto God for your constancy and perseverance in affliction, unto whom I wish continuance unto the end. And as I do rejoice in your faith and constancy in afflictions that be in prison; even so do I mourn and lament to hear of our dear brethren that yet have not felt such dangers for God's truth, as we have and do feel, and are daily like to suffer more, yea, the very extreme and vile death of the fire: yet such is the report abroad, as I am credibly informed, that I, John Hooper, a condemned man for the cause of Christ, should now after sentence of death, a prisoner in Newgate, and looking daily for execution, recant and abjure that which heretofore I have preached. And that talk ariseth from this, that the bishop of London, and his chaplains resort unto me. Doubtless, if our brethren were as godly as I could wish them, they would think, that in case I did refuse to talk with him, they might have just occasion to say, that I was unlearned, and durst not speak with learned men, or else proud, and disdained to speak with them. Therefore to avoid just suspicion of both, I have, and do daily speak with them when they come, not doubting but they report that I am neither proud nor unlearned. And I would wish all men to do as I do in this point. For I fear not their arguments, neither is death terrible unto me, praying you to make true report of the same, as occasion shall serve; and that I am more confirmed in the truth which I have heretofore preached, by their coming.

Therefore, you that may send to the weak brethren, pray them that they trouble me not with such reports of recantations as they do. For I have hitherto left all things of the world, and suffered great pains and imprisonment, and I thank God I am as ready to suffer death as a mortal man can be. It were better for them to pray for us, than to credit or report such rumours that are untrue. We have enemies enough of such as know not God truly; but yet the false report of weak brethren is a double cross. I wish you eternal salvation in Jesus Christ, and also require your continual prayers, that he which hath begun in us may continue it to the end. I have taught the truth with my tongue, and with my pen heretofore; and hereafter shortly shall confirm the same, by God's grace, with my blood.

Forth of Newgate, Feb. 2, 1555.
your brother in Christ,

Upon Monday following, Bonner, bishop of London, came to Newgate, and there degraded bishop Hooper. The same Monday at night, his keeper gave Hooper a hint that he should be sent unto Gloucester to suffer death, whereat he rejoiced very much, lifting up his eyes and hands to heaven, and praising God that he saw it good to send him among the people over whom he was pastor, there to confirm with his death the truth which he had before taught them: not doubting but the Lord would give him strength to perform the same to his glory: and immediately he sent to his servant's house for his boots, spurs, and cloak, that he might be in readiness to ride when he should be called.

The day following, about four o'clock in the morning, the keeper with others came and searched him, and the bed whereon he lay, to see if he had written anything; after which, he was led by the sheriffs of London, and their officers, from Newgate to a place appointed, not far from St. Dunstan's church in Fleet-street, where six of the queen's guard were appointed to receive him to conduct him to Gloucester, there to be delivered unto the sheriff, who with the lord Chandos, Mr. Wicks, and other commissioners, were appointed to see execution done; which guard brought him to the Angel, where he brake his fast with them, eating his meat at that time more liberally than he had a good while before. About break of day he leaped cheerfully on horseback, having a hood upon his head, under his hat, that he should not be known, and so took his journey joyfully towards Gloucester; and by the way the guard inquired of him, where he was accustomed to bait or lodge, but always carried him to another inn than the one he named.

On the Thursday following he came to Cirencester, fifteen miles from

Gloucester, and there dined at a woman's house who had always hated the truth, and spoken all the evil she could of him. This woman, perceiving the cause of his coming, shewed him all the friendship she could, lamented his case with tears, confessing that she before had often reported, that if he were put to the trial, he would not stand to his doctrine. After dinner he resumed his journey, and came to Gloucester about five o'clock. At a mile without the town much people assembled, who cried and lamented his state; insomuch, that one of the guard rode post into the town, to require aid of the mayor and sheriffs, fearing lest he should have been taken from them. Accordingly, the officers and their retinue repaired to the gate with weapons, and commanded the people to keep to their houses; but there was none that gave any signification of violence. He was lodged at one Ingram's house in Gloucester; and that night, as he had done all the way, he ate his meat quietly, and slept soundly, as it was reported by the guard and others. After his first sleep, he continued in prayer until morning, and all the day, except a little time at his meals, and when conversing with such as the guard permitted to speak to him, he spent in prayer.

Sir Anthony Kingston, formerly Hooper's good friend, was appointed by the queen's letters to attend at his execution. As soon as he saw the bishop he burst into tears. Hooper did not know him at first; the knight therefore addressing him, said, "Why, my lord, do not you know me—an old friend of yours, Anthony Kingston?" "Yes," answered Hooper, "Sir Anthony Kingston; I do know you well, and am glad to see you in health, and praise God for the same." "But I am sorry to see you, my lord, in this case," replied Kingston, "for as I understand you are come hither to die. But alas! consider that life is sweet, and death is bitter. Therefore seeing life may be had, desire to live; for life hereafter may do good." "Indeed, it is true, Sir Anthony, I am come hither to end this life, and to suffer death here, because I will not gainsay the truth that I have heretofore taught amongst you in this diocese, and elsewhere; and I thank you for your friendly counsel, although it be not as I could wish. True it is that death is bitter, and life is sweet; but the death to come is more bitter, and the life to come is more sweet."

After these, and many other words, they took leave of each other, Kingston with bitter tears, Hooper with tears also trickling down his cheeks. At his departure the bishop told him, that all the trouble he had sustained in prison, had not caused him to utter so much sorrow. Then the bishop was committed by the guard into the custody of the sheriffs of Gloucester. These men, named Jenkins and Bond, with the mayor and aldermen, repaired to his lodging, and at the first meeting saluted him, and took him by the hand. He was not insensible to their apparent kindness, nor unaware of their resolution, notwithstanding, to execute the law as it now stood. His remarkable and exemplary address to them merits particular attention.

I give most hearty thanks to you, and to the rest of your brethren, that you have vouchsafed to take me a prisoner and a condemned man, by the hand; whereby, to my rejoicing, it is very apparent that your old love and friendship towards me is not altogether extinguished: and I trust also that all the things I have taught you in times past, are not utterly forgotten, when I was your bishop and pastor. For which most true and sincere doctrine, because I will not now account in falsehood and heresy, as many other men do, I am sent hither, you know, by the queen's commands, to die, and am come where I taught it, to confirm it with my blood. And now, master sheriffs, I understand by these good men, and my good friends, at whose hands I have found as much favour and gentleness on the road hither, as a prisoner could reasonably require, for which I most heartily thank them, that I am committed to your custody, as unto those that must see me brought to-morrow to the place of execution. My request to you shall be only, that there may be a quick fire, shortly to make an end; and in the mean time I will be as obedient to you as yourselves could wish. If you think I do amiss in any thing, hold up your finger and I have done. For I am not come hither as one forced or compelled to die; for it is well known, I might have had my life with worldly gain; but as one willing to offer and give my life for the truth, rather than consent to the wicked religion of the bishop of Rome, received and set forth by the magistrates in England to God's high displeasure and dishonour; and I trust, by God's grace, to-morrow to die a faithful subject to God, and a true obedient subject to the queen.

These words bishop Hooper used to the mayor, sheriffs, and aldermen, whereat many mourned and lamented. Notwithstanding, the two sheriffs went aside to consult, and were determined to have lodged him in the common gaol of the town, called Northgate, if the guard had not made earnest intercession for him; who declared at large how quietly, mildly, and patiently, he had behaved on the way; adding thereto, that any child might keep him well enough, and that they themselves would rather take pains to watch with him, than that he should be sent to the common prison. It was therefore determined that he should still remain in Robert Ingram's house; and the sheriffs, the sergeants, and other officers agreed to watch with him that night themselves. His desire was, that he might go to bed betime, saying, that he had many things to remember: accordingly he went at five o'clock, and slept one sleep soundly, then spent the rest of the night in prayer. After he had got up in the morning, he desired that no man should be suffered to come into the chamber, that he might be solitary until the hour of execution.

About eight o'clock came Sir John Bridges, lord Chandos, with a great band of men, Sir Anthony Kingston, Sir Edmund Bridges, and other commissioners appointed to see the execution. At nine, Hooper prepared himself to be in readiness, the time being now at hand. Immediately he was brought down from his chamber, by the sheriffs, who were accompanied with bills and other weapons. When he saw the multitude of weapons, he said to the sheriffs, "I am no traitor, neither needed you to have made such a business to bring me to the place where I must suffer; for if you had suffered me, I would have gone alone to the stake, and troubled none of you." Afterwards looking upon the multitude of people who were assembled, being by estimation about 7000, he spake unto those who were about him, saying, "Alas! why are these people assembled and come together? Peradventure they think to hear something of me now, as they have in times past: but alas! speech is prohibited me. Notwithstanding the cause of my death is well known unto them. When I was appointed here to be their pastor, I preached unto them true and sincere doctrine, and that out of the word of God; and because I will not now account the same to be heresy and untruth, this kind of death is prepared for me." Having said this, he went forward, led between the two sheriffs, in a gown of his host's, his hat upon his head, and a staff in his hand to rest himself upon; for the pain of the sciatica, which he had taken in prison, caused him somewhat to halt. All the way, being strictly charged not to speak, he could not be perceived once to open his mouth; but beholding the people, who mourned bitterly for him, he would sometimes lift up his eyes towards heaven, and look very cheerfully upon such as he knew; and he was never known, during the time of his being amongst them, to look with so happy and ruddy a countenance as he did then.

When he came to the place where he should die, he smilingly beheld the stake, which was near to the great elm-tree over against the college of priests, where he had been wont to preach. The place round about the houses, and the boughs of the trees, were filled with spectators: and in the chamber over the gate stood the priests of the college. Then he kneeled down (forasmuch as he could not be suffered to speak unto the people) to prayer, and beckoned six or seven times unto one whom he well knew, that he might hear his prayer, and report faithfully the same. When this person came to the bishop he poured tears upon his shoulders and in his bosom, and continued his prayer for half an hour: which prayer was drawn from the whole creed. While at his prayer a box was brought and laid before him upon a stool, with his pardon from the queen if he would recant. At the sight of this he cried, "If you love my soul, away with it." The box being taken away, the lord Chandos said, "Seeing there is no remedy, dispatch him quickly." Hooper replied, "Good, my lord; I trust your lordship will give me leave to make an end of my prayers."

When he had risen from his last devotions in this world, he prepared himself for the stake, and put off his host's gown, and delivered it to the sheriffs, requiring them to see it restored unto the owner, and put off the rest of his apparel, unto his doublet and hose, wherein he would have burned. But the sheriffs would not permit that, unto whose pleasure he very obediently submitted himself; and his doublet, hose, and waistcoat were taken off. Thus being in his shirt, he took a point from his hose himself, and trussed his shirt between his legs, where he had a pound of gunpowder in a bladder, and under each arm the like quantity delivered him by the guard. So desiring the people to say the Lord's Prayer with him, and to pray for him, he went up to the stake; when he was at it, three irons made to bind him thereto were brought: one for his neck, another for his middle, and the third for his legs. But he refusing them, said, "You have no need thus to trouble yourselves. I doubt not God will give me strength sufficient to abide the extremity of the fire without bands: notwithstanding, suspecting the frailty and weakness of the flesh, but having assured confidence in God's strength, I am content you do as you shall think good."

Then the hoop of iron prepared for his middle was brought, which being somewhat too short, he shrank and pressed in his body with his hand, until it fastened: but when they offered to have bound his neck and legs with the other hoops, he refused them, saying, "I am well assured I shall not trouble you." Being now ready he looked around on all the people, of whom he might be well seen, for he was both tall, and stood also upon a high stool, and beheld that in every corner there was nothing to be seen but weeping and sorrowful people. Then lifting up his eyes and hands to heaven he prayed in silence. By and by, he that was appointed to make the fire came to him and asked him forgiveness.

He asked why he should forgive him, saying that he never knew any offence he had committed against him. "O, sir," said the man, "I am appointed to make the fire." "Therein," said Mr. Hooper, "thou dost nothing to offend me: God forgive thee thy sins, and do thine office, I pray thee." Then the reeds were cast up, and he receiving two bundles of them in his own hands embraced them, and putting one of them under each arm, showed with his hand how the rest should be bestowed, and pointed to the place where any were wanting.

Command was now given that the fire should be kindled. But because there were not fewer green fagots than two horses could carry, it did not kindle speedily, but was some time before it took the reeds upon the fagots. At length it burned about him; but the wind having full strength in that place, and it being a lowering cold morning, it blew the flame from him, so that he was in a manner little more than touched by the fire. Endeavours were then made to increase the flame, and then the bladders of gunpowder exploded; but did him little good, being so placed, and the wind having such power. In this fire he prayed with a loud voice, "Lord Jesus, have mercy upon me! Lord Jesus, have mercy upon me! Lord Jesus, receive my spirit!" And these were the last words he was heard to utter. Yet he struck his breast with his hands, until by the renewing of the fire his strength was gone and his hand stuck fast in striking the iron upon his breast. So immediately, bowing forwards, he yielded up his spirit. Thus lingering were his last sufferings. He was nearly three quarters of an hour or more in the fire, as a lamb, patiently bearing the extremity thereof, neither moving forwards, backwards, nor to any side; but he died as quietly as a child in his bed; and he now reigneth as a blessed martyr in the joys of heaven, prepared for the faithful in Christ before the foundation of the world; for whose constancy all Christians are bound to praise God.

A POEM, BY CONRADE GESNER, ON THE MARTYRDOM OF DR. JOHN HOOPER, BISHOP OF GLOUCESTER AND WORCESTER

Hooper, unvanquish'd by Rome's cruelties,
Confessing Christ in his last moments, dies:
Whilst flames his body rack, his soul doth fly,

Inflam'd with faith, to immortality!
His Constancy on earth has rais'd his name,
And gave him entrance at the gates of fame,
Which neither storms, nor the cold north-wind's blast,
Nor all-devouring time shall ever waste:
For he whom God protects shall sure attain
That happiness, which worldlings seek in vain.

Example take by him, you who profess
Christ's holy doctrines; ne'er the world caress
In hopes of riches; or if fortune frown
With inauspicious looks, be not cast down;
For man ne'er saw, nor can his heart conceive,
What God bestows on them that righteous live.

This good bishop and servant of God whose life and martyrdom is now declared, being in prison, wrote divers books and treatises, to the number of twenty-four. Also divers letters most fruitful and worthy to be read, especially in these dangerous times, of those who seek to serve and follow the Lord through all the storms of the evil world, as by the perusal of the following to his godly wife Anne Hooper, you shall better understand.

Dearly beloved and godly wife,

Our Saviour Jesus Christ in St. Matthew's gospel said to his disciples, that it was necessary scandals should come; and that they could not be avoided, he perceived as well by the condition of those that should perish and be lost for ever, as also by their affliction they should be saved. For he saw the greatest part of the people would contemn and neglect whatsoever true doctrine should be shewn unto them, or else receive and use it as they thought good to serve their pleasures, without any profit to their souls, not caring whether they lived as they were commanded by God's word or not; but would think it sufficient to be counted to have the name of a christian, with such words and fruits of its profession as their fathers and elders, after their custom and manner, esteem and take to be good fruits and faithful works, without trying them by the word of God. These men by the just judgment of God, be delivered unto the craft and subtlety of the devil, that they may be kept by one scandalous stumbling-block or other never to come unto Christ, who came to save those that were lost; as you may see how God delivereth wicked men up unto their own lusts, to do one mischief after another, careless of coming into a reprobate mind, that forgetteth itself, and cannot know what is expedient to be done, or to be left undone, because they close their eyes, and will not see the light of God's word offered unto them: and being thus blinded, they prefer their own vanities before the truth of God's word. Where such corrupt minds, be, there are also corrupt notions of God's honour; so that the mind taketh falsehood for truth, superstitions for true religion, death for life, damnation for salvation, hell for heaven, and persecution of Christ's members for God's service and honour. And as such persons voluntarily reject the word of God; so God most justly delivereth them up to blindness of mind and hardness of heart, that they cannot understand, nor yet consent to anything that God would have preached, and set forth to his glory, after his own will and word; but they hate it mortally, and of all things most detest God's holy word. As the devil hath entered into their hearts, that they cannot or will not come to Christ, to be instructed by his holy word: even so can they not abide any other person to be a christian, and to lead his life after the word of God; but hate him, persecute him, rob him, imprison him, yea and kill him, if God suffer it. And so much are these wicked men blinded, that they regard no law, whether it be the law of God or man, but persecute such as never offended, yea, do evil to those that have prayed daily for them, and wish them God's grace.

In their blind fury they have no respect to nature. For brother persecuteth brother, and father the son: most dear friends in devilish slander and offence become most mortal enemies. And no marvel; for when they have chosen sundry masters, the one the devil, the other God, the one shall agree with the former and the other with the latter. For this cause Christ said, it is expedient and necessary that scandals should come, and many may be advised to keep the babes of Christ from the heavenly Father. But Christ saith, Woe be unto him by whom the offence cometh. Yet is there no remedy, man being of such corruption and hatred towards God, but that the evil shall be deceived, and persecute the good; and the good shall understand the truth, and suffer persecution for it unto the world's end. For "as he that was born after the flesh, persecuted in times past him that was born after the spirit, even so it is now." Therefore as we live in this life amongst so many perils and dangers, we must be well assured by God's word how to bear them, and how patiently to take them as they be sent to us from God. We must also assure ourselves, that there is no other remedy for christians in the time of trouble, than Christ himself hath appointed us. In St. Luke he giveth us this commandment, "Ye shall possess your lives in peace." In which words he giveth us both commandment what to do, and also great comfort and consolation in all troubles.

That the spirit of man may feel these consolations, the Giver of them, the heavenly Father, must be prayed unto for the merits of Christ's passion: for it is not the nature of man that can be contented, until it be regenerated and possessed with God's Spirit, to bear patiently the troubles of the mind or of the body. When the mind and heart of a man seeth on every side sorrow and heaviness, and the worldly eye beholdeth nothing but such things as be troubles and wholly bent to rob the poor of what he hath, and also to take from him his life; except we weigh these brittle and uncertain treasures with the riches of the life to come; and this life of the body, with the life in Christ's blood; and so for the love and certainty of the heavenly joys contemn all things present, doubtless we shall never be able to bear the loss of goods, life, or any other thing of this world.

Therefore St. Paul giveth a godly and necessary lesson to all in this short and transitory life, and therein sheweth how a man may best bear the iniquities and troubles of this world. "If ye be risen again with Christ, seek the things which are above, where Christ sitteth at the right hand of God the Father." Wherefore, the christian's faith must be always upon the resurrection of Christ when he is in trouble; and in that glorious resurrection he shall not only see continual and perpetual joy and consolation; but also victory and triumph over all persecution, trouble, sin, death, hell, the devil, and other tyrants and persecutors of Christ, and of Christ's people, the tears and weeping of the faithful dried up, their wounds healed, their bodies made immortal in joy, their souls for ever praising the Lord, in conjunction and society everlasting with the blessed company of God's elect in perpetual felicity. But the words of St. Paul in that place, if they be not marked, shall do little profit to the reader or hearer, and give him no peace at all in this impatient and cruel world.

When a man hath, by seeking the word of God, found out what the things above be, then must he, saith Paul, "set his affections" on them. And this commandment is more hard than the other. For men's knowledge many time seeth the best, and knoweth that here is a life to come, better than this life present, yet they set not their affections upon it: they more affect and love indeed a trifle of nothing in this that pleaseth their hearts, than the treasure of treasures in heaven, which their own judgment saith is better than all worldly things. Wherefore we must "set our affections on the things that be above;" that is to say, when any thing worse than heaven upon the earth offereth itself to be ours, if we will give our good wills to it, and love it in our hearts, then ought we to see by the judgment of God's word, whether we may have the world without offence of God, and such things as be for this worldly life without his displeasure. If we cannot, St. Paul's commandment must take place—"Set your affections on things that are above." If the riches of this world may not be gotten nor kept by God's law, neither our lives be continued without the denial of his honour, we must set our affections upon the riches and life that are above, and not upon things that are on earth. Therefore this second commandment of St. Paul requireth, that our minds judge heavenly things to be better than things upon the earth, and the life to come better than the life present; so we should choose them before the other and prefer then, and have such affection to the best, that in no case we set the worst before it, as the most part of the world doth and hath done, for they acknowledge the best and prove it, and yet follow the worst.

But these things, my godly wife, require rather thought, meditation, and prayer, than words or talk. They are easy to be spoken of, but not so easy to be used and practised. Wherefore seeing they be God's gifts, and yet they may become our privileges, we must seek them at our heavenly Father's hand, who seeth, and is privy how poor and wretched we be, and how naked, how spoiled, and destitute of all his blessed gifts we by reason of sin. He did command, therefore, his disciples, when he shewed them that they should take patiently the state of this present life full of troubles and persecution, to pray that they might well escape those troubles that were to come, and be able to stand before the Son of man. When you find yourself too much oppressed—as every one shall be sometimes with the fear of God's judgement—use the 77th psalm that beginneth, "I will cry unto God with my voice, and he shall hearken unto me." In which psalm is both godly doctrine and great consolation unto the man or woman that is in anguish of mind.

Use also in such trouble the 88th psalm, wherein is contained the prayer of one that was brought to extreme anguish and misery, and being vexed with adversaries and persecutions, saw nothing but death and hell. Yet although he felt in himself, that he had not only man, but also God angry towards him; yet he by prayer humbly resorted unto God. Remember also none of us must murmur against God, but always say his judgements are right and just, and rejoice that it pleaseth him by troubles to use us as he used heretofore such as he most loved in this world. "Be glad and rejoice, for your reward is great in heaven." His promises shall by his grace, work both consolation and patience in afflicted christians. And when our Saviour Christ hath willed men in trouble to be content and patient, because God in the end of trouble, in Christ hath ordained eternal consolation; he useth also to take from us all shame and rebuke, and make it an honour to suffer for Christ, because the wicked world doth curse and abhor such poor troubled christians. Wherefore Christ placeth all his honourably, and saith, "Even so persecuted they the prophets that were before you." We must therefore patiently suffer, and willingly attend upon God's doings, although they seem clean contrary, after our judgement, to our wealth and salvation: as Abraham did, when bid to offer his son Isaac, in whom God promised the blessing and multiplying of his seed.

And judge things indifferently, my good wife, the troubles be not yet generally, as they were in our good fathers' times, soon after the death and resurrection of our Saviour Jesus Christ, whereof he spake in St. Matthew. From which place you and I have taken many times great consolation, and especially of the latter part of the chapter, wherein is contained the last day and end of all troubles both for you and me, and for all such as love the coming of our Saviour Christ to judgement. Remember, therefore, that place, and mark it again, and you shall in this time see this consolation, and also learn much patience. Was there ever such troubles as Christ threatened upon Jerusalem? Was there since the beginning of the world such affliction? Who were then best at ease? The apostles that suffered in body persecution, and gathered of it ease and quietness in the promises of God. And no marvel, for Christ saith, "Lift up your heads, for your redemption is at hand;" that is, your eternal rest approacheth and draweth near. The world is stark blind, and more foolish than foolishness itself, and so are the people of this world: for when God saith, trouble shall come, they will have ease. And when God saith, be merry and rejoice in trouble, we lament and mourn, as though we were to be cast-away. But this our flesh (which is never merry with virtue, nor sorry with vice: never laugheth with grace, nor ever weepeth with sin) holdeth fast with the world, and letteth God slip. But, my dearly beloved wife, you know how to perceive and to beware of the vanity, and crafts of the devil well enough in Christ. And that you may the better have patience in the Spirit of God, read again the 24th of St. Matthew, and mark what difference is between the destruction of Jerusalem, and the destruction of the whole world, and you shall see, that then there were alive many offenders to repent: but at the latter day there shall be absolute judgment and sentence, never to be revoked, of eternal life and eternal death upon all men: and yet towards the end of the world *we have not so much extremity as they had then, but even as we are able to bear. So doth the merciful Father lay upon us now imprisonment, and I suppose for my part shortly death; now spoil of goods, loss of friends, and the greatest loss of all, the knowledge of God's word. His holy will be done. I wish in Christ Jesus our only Mediator and Saviour, your constancy and consolation, that you may live for ever and ever, whereof in Christ I doubt not; to whom, for his most blessed and painful passion, I commit you, Amen.*

While in prison, Hooper received a letter from his learned and pious friend Henry Bullinger, of Zurich. It was well worthy of its author and of the spirit of a saint. He exhorted him to bear with firmness that awful task to which the Lord had appointed to him, and to look beyond his troubles to the crown that awaited him.[2] One more incident amongst other memorable things worthy to be remembered in the history of Hooper, is not to be forgotten: it happened a little after the beginning of his imprisonment.

A friar came from France to England with great vaunt, asking who was the greatest heretic in England, thinking no doubt to do some great act upon him. To whom answer was made, that Dr. Hooper had then the greatest name to be the chiefest ringleader, who was then in the Fleet. The friar coming to him, asked why he was committed to prison? He said for debt. "Nay," said he, "it was for heresy;" which when Hooper had denied, "What sayest thou," quoth he, "to hoc est corpus meum?" Hooper, being partly moved at the sudden question, desired that he might ask of him another, which was this, "what remains after the consecration in the sacrament, any bread or no?" "No bread at all," said the friar. "And when you break it, what you break—whether bread or the body?" said Hooper. "No bread," said the friar; "but the body only." "If ye do so," said Hooper, "you do great injury, not only to the body of Christ, but also to the scriptures, which say, Ye shall not break of him one bone." With that the friar having nothing to answer, recoiled back, and with circles and crosses began to use exorcism as though Hooper had bewitched him!

---

[2] "Go forwards," he wrote, "constantly to confess Christ, and to defy Antichrist, being mindful of this most holy and most true saying of our Lord Jesus Christ: 'He that overcometh shall possess all things; and I will be his God, and he shall be my son.' The first death is soon overcome, although a man must burn for the Lord's sake: for they say well that do affirm this our fire to be scarcely a shadow of that which is prepared for unbelievers, and them that fall from the truth. Moreover, the Lord granteth unto us, that we may easily overcome by his power the first death, the which he himself did taste and overcome; promising withal such joys as never shall have end, unspeakable, and passing all understanding, the which we shall possess so soon as ever we do depart hence.—Therefore, seeing you have such a large promise, be strong in the Lord, fight a good fight, be faithful to the Lord unto the end. I and all my household, with my sons-in-law and kinsmen, are in good health in the Lord. They do all salute you, and pray for your constancy; being sorrowful for you and the rest of the prisoners. If there be any thing wherein I may do any pleasure to your wife and children, they shall have me wholly at commandment. The Lord Jesus preserve and deliver you from all evil, with all them that call upon his name. Farewell, and farewell eternally. You know the hand, H.B."

CHAPTER SIXTEEN

The Life and Martyrdom of Dr. Rowland Taylor

WHO SUFFERED FOR THE TRUTH OF GOD'S WORD, UNDER THE TYRANNY OF THE ROMAN BISHOPS, THE 9TH DAY OF FEBRUARY, 1555

The town of Hadley was one of the first that received the word of God in all England, at the preaching of Thomas Bilney; by whose industry the gospel of Christ had such gracious success, and took such root there, that a great number became exceedingly learned in the holy Scriptures, as well women as men. Of this parish Dr. Rowland Taylor was vicar, being doctor both in the civil and canon laws, and a right perfect divine. In addition to eminent learning, his known attachment to the pure principles of christianity recommended him to the favour and friendship of Cranmer, with whom he lived, until through his interest he obtained the vicarage of Hadley. This charge he attended with the utmost diligence, recommending and enforcing the doctrines of the gospel, not only by his judicious discourses from the pulpit, but also by the whole tenor of his life and conversation.

Dr. Taylor continued promoting the interest of the great Redeemer, and the souls of mankind, both by his preaching and example during the reign of king Edward; but on his demise, and on the succession of Mary to the throne, he could not escape the cloud that burst on the protestant community. Two of his parishioners, Foster an attorney, and Clark a tradesman, out of blind zeal, resolved that mass should be celebrated in all its superstitious forms, in the parish church at Hadley, on the Monday before Easter. They had even caused an altar to be built in the chancel for that purpose, which being pulled down by the protestant inhabitants, they erected another, and prevailed with the minister of an adjacent parish to celebrate mass in the passion-week. Taylor being employed in his study, was alarmed by the ringing of bells at an unusual time, and went to the church to inquire the cause. He found the great doors fast, but lifting up the latch of the chancel door, he entered, and was surprised to see a priest in his habit prepared to celebrate mass, and guarded by a party of men under arms, to prevent interruption.

Being vicar of the parish, he demanded of the priest the cause of such proceeding without his knowledge or consent; and how he dared profane the temple of God with abominable idolatries. Foster, the lawyer, insolently replied—"Thou traitor, how darest thou to intercept the execution of the queen's orders?" but the doctor undauntedly denied the charge of traitor, and asserted his mission as a minister of Christ, and delegation to that part of his flock, commanding the priest as a wolf in sheep's clothing to depart, nor infect the pure church of God with popish idolatry. A violent altercation then ensued, between Foster and Dr. Taylor, the former asserting the queen's prerogative, and the other the authority of the canon-law, which commanded that no mass be said but at a consecrated altar. Meanwhile the priest, intimidated by the intrepid behaviour of the protestant minister, would have departed without saying mass but Clark said to him, "Fear not, you have a super altare," which is a consecrated stone, commonly about a foot square, which the popish priests carry instead of an altar, when they say mass in gentlemen's houses. Clark then ordered him to proceed in his present duty. They then forced the doctor out of the church, celebrated mass, and immediately informed the bishop of Winchester of his behaviour, who summoned him to appear and answer the complaints alleged against him.

Dr. Taylor upon receipt of the summons cheerfully prepared to obey the same: and on some of his friends advising him to fly beyond sea, in order to avoid the cruelty of his inveterate enemies, he told them that he was determined to go to the bishop, and he accordingly repaired to London and waited on him. As soon as Gardiner saw him, according to his common custom he reviled him calling him knave, traitor heretic, with many other villanous reproaches, which Taylor, having patiently heard for some time, at last answered thus without fear or impropriety—"My lord, I am neither traitor nor heretic, but a true subject, and a faithful christian, and am according to your commandment, to know the cause of your lordship's sending for me."

"Art thou come, thou villain?" said the violent Gardiner; "how darest thou look me in the face for shame? Knowest thou not who I am?" "Yes," said Dr. Taylor, "I know who you are, Dr. Stephen Gardiner, bishop of Winchester, and lord chancellor, and yet but a mortal man. But if I should be afraid of your lordly looks, why fear you not God, the Lord of us all? How dare you for shame look any christian in the face, seeing you have forsaken the truth, denied our Saviour Christ and his word, and done contrary to your own oath and writing? With what countenance will you appear before the judgement seat of

Christ, and answer to your oath made first unto king Henry, and afterwards unto Edward, his son?"

The bishop answered, "That was Herod's oath, unlawful; and therefore worthy to be broken. I have done well in breaking it; and I thank God I am come home again to our mother, the catholic church of Rome and so I would thou shouldest do. Our holy father the pope hath discharged me of it." Then said Dr. Taylor, "But you shall not be so discharged before Christ, who doubtless will require it at your hands, as a lawful oath made to our liege and sovereign lord the king, from whose obedience no man can quit you, neither the pope nor any of his." "I see," quoth the bishop, "thou art an arrogant knave and a very fool." "My lord," saith Dr. Taylor, "I am a Christian man; and you know that 'he that saith to this brother, Raca, is in danger of a council: and he that saith, Thou fool, is in danger of hell fire.' " The bishop answered, "Ye are false and liars, all the sort of you." "Nay," quoth Dr. Taylor, "we are true men, and know that it is written, 'The mouth that lieth, slayeth the soul.' And therefore we abide by God's word, which ye deny and forsake."

"Thou has resisted the queen's proceedings," said Gardiner, "and would not suffer the parson of Aldham, (a very virtuous and devout priest,) to say mass in Hadley." Dr. Taylor answered, "My lord, I am parson of Hadley; and it is against all right, conscience, and laws, that any man should come into my charge, and presume to infect the flock committed unto me with the venom of the popish idolatrous mass." With that the bishop waxed very angry, and said, "Thou art a blasphemous heretic indeed, that blasphemest the blessed sacrament, (And put off his cap,) and speakest against the holy mass, which is made a sacrifice for the quick and the dead." Dr. Taylor answered, "Nay, I blaspheme not the blessed sacrament which Christ instituted, but I reverence it as a Christian man ought to do; and confess that Christ ordained the holy communion in the remembrance of his death and passion. Christ gave himself to die for our redemption upon the cross, whose body there offered was the propitiatory sacrifice, full, perfect, and sufficient unto salvation for all them that believe in him. And this sacrifice did our Saviour Christ offer in his own person himself once for all, neither can any priest any more offer him, nor we need any more sacrifice."

Then the bishop called his men, and said, "Have this fellow to the King's Bench, and charge that he be straitly kept." Then Taylor knelt, and held up both his hands and said, "Good Lord, I thank thee! and from the tyranny of the bishop of Rome, and all his detestable errors, idolatries, and abominations, good Lord deliver us! and God be praised for good king Edward." They carried him to prison to the King's Bench, where he was confined almost two years. Of course Gardiner's command for strict confinement was obeyed. These several particulars are mentioned in a letter that Dr. Taylor wrote to a friend of his, thanking God for his grace, at the same time that he had confessed his truth, and was found worthy for truth to suffer prison and bonds, beseeching his friends to pray for him, that he might persevere constant unto the end.

In January, 1555, Dr. Taylor, Mr. Bradford, and Mr. Saunders, were again called to appear before the bishops of Winchester, Norwich, London, Salisbury, and Durham, and being again charged with heresy and schism, a determinate answer was required, whether they would submit themselves to the Roman bishop, and abjure their errors, or hear their condemnation. Dr. Taylor and his fellows answered stoutly and boldly, that they would not depart from the truth which they had preached in king Edward's days, neither would they submit to the Romish Antichrist; but they thanked God for so great mercy, that he would call them to be worthy to suffer for his word. When the bishops saw them so boldly, constantly, and unmovably fixed in the truth, they read the sentence of death upon them, which when they heard they most joyfully gave God thanks, and stoutly said unto the bishops, "We doubt not, but God the righteous judge will require our blood at your hands; and the proudest of you all shall repent this receiving again of Antichrist, and your tyranny that ye now show against the flock of Christ."

When Dr. Taylor had lain in the Compter in the Poultry about a week, on Feb. 4, 1555, bishop Bonner, with others, came to degrade him, bringing with them such ornaments as do appertain to their massing-mummery. He called for Taylor to be brought unto him; the bishop being then in the chamber where the keeper of the Compter and his wife lay. Dr. Taylor was accordingly brought down from the chamber to Bonner. "I wish you would remember yourself, and turn to your holy mother church, so may you do well enough, and I will sue for your pardon," said Bonner. Dr. Taylor answered—"I wish that you and your fellows would turn to Christ. As for me, I will not turn to antichrist." Said the bishop, "I am come to degrade you: wherefore put on these vestures." Dr. Taylor said resolutely, "I will not." "Wilt thou not? I shall make thee, ere I go," replied Bonner. "You shall not, by the grace of God," said Taylor. Again Bonner charged him upon his obedience to do it, but he would not. Upon this he ordered another to put them upon his back; and being thoroughly furnished therewith, he set his hands to his side, walking up and down, and said—"How say you, my lord, am not I a goodly fool? How say you, my masters, if I were in Cheapside, should I not have boys to laugh at these apish toys and trumpery?" At this Bonner was so enraged, that he would have given Dr. Taylor a stroke on the breast with his crosier-staff, when his chaplain said—"My lord, strike him not, for he will certainly strike again." The bishop then laid his curse upon him, but struck him not. Dr. Taylor said, "Though you curse me, yet God doth bless me."

The night after his degradation, his wife, his son, and his servant, came to him, and were, by the keepers, permitted to sup with him: at their coming, they kneeled down and prayed. After supper, walking up and down, he gave God thanks for his grace that had so called him, and given him strength to abide by his holy word; and turning to his son he said—"My dear son, Almighty God bless thee, and give thee his Holy Spirit, to be a true servant of Christ, to learn his word, and constantly to stand by his truth all thy life long: and see that thou fear God always. Flee from all sin and wicked living: be virtuous, serve God with daily prayer, and apply to the holy book. In any wise see that thou be obedient to thy mother, love her and serve her; be ruled by her now in thy youth, and follow her good counsel in all things. Beware of the lewd company of young men that fear not God, but who follow their lusts and vain appetites. Fly from whoredom, and hate all filthy living, remembering that I, thy father, die in the defence of holy marriage. Another day, when God shall bless thee, love and cherish the poor people, and count that thy chief riches is to be rich in alms; and when thy mother is waxed old, forsake her not; but provide for her to thy power, and see that she lack nothing: for so will God bless thee, and give thee long life upon earth and prosperity, which I pray God to grant thee." And then turning to his wife, he said—"My dear wife, continue stedfast in the fear and love of God: keep yourself undefiled from popish idolatries and superstition. I have been unto you a faithful yoke-fellow, and so have you to me, for which I pray God to reward you, and doubt not but he will reward it. Now the time is come that I shall be taken from you, and you discharged of the wedlock bond towards me; therefore I will give you the counsel which I think most expedient for you. You are yet a child-bearing woman, and therefore it will be most convenient for you to marry."

On the following morning the sheriff of London with his officers, came by two o'clock, and brought him forth, and without any light led him to the Woolpack, an inn without Aldgate. Mrs. Taylor, suspecting that her husband would that night be carried away, watched all night in St. Botolph's church porch, without Aldgate, having with her two children, the one named Elizabeth, an orphan, whom the doctor had adopted at three years old; the other named Mary, his own daughter. When the sheriff and his company came against St. Botolph's church, the grateful little Elizabeth cried—"O my dear father! mother, mother, here is my father led away!" "Rowland," said his wife, "where art thou?" for it was so dark a morning, that the one could not see the other. "Dear wife, I am here," said the doctor, and stopped. The sheriff's men would have forced him on; but the sheriff said—"Stay a little, I pray you, and let him speak to his wife."

She then came to him, when he took his daughter Mary in his arms, while he, his wife, and Elizabeth, kneeled down and said the Lord's prayer. At which sight the sheriff wept much, as did several others of the company. The prayer finished, Taylor rose up and kissed his wife, and pressing her hand, he said—"Farewell, my dear wife, be of good comfort, for I am quiet in my conscience. God shall stir up a father for my children." And then he kissed his daughter Mary, and said, "God bless thee, and make thee his servant:" and kissing Elizabeth, he said, "God bless thee. I pray you all, stand strong and stedfast unto Christ and his word, and beware of idolatry." Then said his wife unto him, "God be with thee, my dear Rowland: I will, with God's grace, meet thee at Hadley."

He was then led on, while his wife followed him. As soon as he came to the Woolpack, he was put into a chamber, wherein he was kept with four yeoman of the guard, and the sheriff's men. As soon he entered the chamber, he fell on his knees, and gave himself wholly to prayer. The sheriff then seeing

Mrs. Taylor there, would in no case grant her to speak any more with her husband, but gently desired her to go to his house, and use it as her own, promising her, that she should lack for nothing, and sending two officers to conduct her thither. Notwithstanding this, she desired to go to her mother's, whither the officers led her, and charged her mother to keep her there until they came again. Meanwhile the journey to Hadley was delayed. Dr. Taylor was confined at the Woolpack by the sheriff and his company, until eleven o'clock, by which time the sheriff of Essex was ready to receive him; when they sat him on horseback within the inn, the gates being shut.

On coming out of the gates his servant John Hull stood at the rails with young Taylor. When the doctor saw them, he called them saying—"Come hither, my son Thomas." John Hull lifted the child up, and set him on the horse before his father; who then put off his hat, and said to the people— "Good people, this is mine own son, begotten in lawful matrimony: and God be blessed for lawful matrimony." Then he lifted up his eyes towards heaven and prayed for his child, placing his hat upon his head. After blessing him, he delivered him to his faithful servant, whom he took by the hand and said— "Farewell, John Hull, the most faithful servant ever man had." After this they rode forth, the sheriff of Essex, and four yeomen of the guard, and the sheriff's men leading them.

When they were come almost to Brentwood, one Arthur Faysie, a man of Hadley, who formerly had been Dr. Taylor's servant, met with them, and he, supposing him to have been at liberty, said—"Master, I am glad to see you again at liberty," and took him by the hand. "Sir," returned the sheriff, "he is a prisoner; what hast thou to do with him?" "I cry your mercy," said Arthur, "I knew not so much, and I thought it no offence to talk to a true man." The sheriff was very angry with this, and threatened to carry Arthur with him to prison; notwithstanding he bid him get quickly away. And so they rode forth to Brentwood, where they caused to be made for Dr. Taylor a close hood. This they did, that no man should know him, nor he to speak to any man; which practice they used also with others.

All the way, Dr. Taylor was joyful and merry, as one that accounted himself going to a most pleasant banquet or bridal. He spake many notable things to the sheriff and yeomen of the guard that conducted him, and often moved them to weep through his much earnest calling upon them to repent, and turn to the true religion. Of these yeomen of the guard three used him very tenderly, but the fourth, named Holmes, treated him most unkindly. The party supped and slept at Chelmsford. At supper the sheriff earnestly besought him to return to the popish religion, thinking with fair words to persuade him, and said— "Good Doctor, we are sorry for you, considering the loss of such a man as you. You would do much better to revoke your opinions, and return to the catholic church of Rome, acknowledge the pope's holiness to be the supreme head of the church, and reconcile yourselves to him. You may do well yet if you will: doubt not but you shall find favour at the queen's hands. I and all these your friends will be suitors for your pardon; this council I give you,

Doctor, of a good heart and will towards you: and therefore I drink to you."
In this joined all the rest.

When the cup was handed to him, he staid a little, as one studying what answer he might give. At last he said—"Mr. Sheriff, and my masters all, I heartily thank you for your good will; I have attended to your words, and marked well your counsels. And to be plain with you, I find that I have been deceived myself, and am like to deceive a great many of Hadley of their expectation." With that word they all rejoiced. "Yes, Doctor," said the sheriff, "God's blessing on your heart; hold you there still. It is the most comfortable word we have heard you speak yet." The cheerful man then explained himself, "I will tell you how I have been deceived, and, as I think, I shall deceive a great many. I am, as you see, a man of a very large body, which I thought should have been buried in Hadley church-yard, had I died as I hoped I should have done; but herein I was deceived; and there are a great number of worms in Hadley church yard, which would have had merry feeding upon me; but now I know we shall be deceived, both I and they; for this carcass must be burned to ashes, and they shall lose their feast." When the sheriff and his company heard him say so, they were amazed, and looking one on another, marvelled at his constant mind, that thus without fear he could speak of the torment and death now prepared for him.

At Chelmsford he was delivered to the sheriff of Suffolk, and by him conducted to Hadley. On their arrival at Lavenham, the sheriff staid there two days; and thither came to him a great number of gentlemen and justices, who were appointed to aid him. These endeavoured very much to reduce the Doctor to the Romish religion, promising him his pardon, which they said they had for him. They also promised him great promotions, even a bishopric if he would take it: but all their labour and flattery were in vain.

When they came to Hadley, and were passing the bridge, there waited a poor man with five children; who when they saw Dr. Taylor, fell down upon their knees, and holding up their hands, cried with a loud voice—"O dear father and good shepherd! God help and succour thee as thou hast many a time succoured us!" Such witness had the servant of God of his virtuous and charitable life. The streets of Hadley were crowded with men and women of the town and country, who waited to see him; and in beholding him led to death, with weeping eyes and lamenting voices they cried one to another—"Ah, good Lord! there goeth our good shepherd from us, who so faithfully hath taught us, so fatherly hath cared for us, and so godly hath governed us! Good Lord, strengthen and comfort him." Arriving over against the alms-houses, which he well knew, he cast money to the poor people, that remained out of what had been given him in the time of his imprisonment. His living of Hadley they took from him at his first going to prison, so that he was sustained by the charitable alms of good people that visited him.

At the last, coming to Aldham-common, and seeing a great multitude, he asked, "What place is this, and what meaneth it that so much people are gathered hither?" It was answered, "It is Aldham-common, the place where you must suffer; and the people are come to behold you." Then said he, "Thanked be God, I am even at home;" and so alighted from his horse, and with both his hands rent the hood from his head. When the people saw him, they cried, "God save thee, good Dr. Taylor! Jesus Christ strengthen thee and help thee; the Holy Ghost comfort thee:" with such other like godly wishes. Then desired Dr. Taylor license of the sheriff to speak; but he denied it him. Perceiving that he could not be suffered to speak, he sat down, and seeing one named Soyce, he called him, and said—"Soyce, I pray thee come and pull off my boots, and take them for thy labour: thou hast long looked for them, now take them." Then he rose up and put off his clothes unto his shirt, and gave them away. Which done, he said with a loud voice—"Good people, I have taught you nothing but God's holy word, and those lessons that I have taken out of God's blessed book, the Holy Bible: and I am come hither this day, to seal it with my blood."

On hearing his voice, the yeoman of the guard who had used him cruelly all the way, gave him a great stroke upon the head and said—"Is that keeping thy promise, thou heretic?" Then seeing they would not permit him to speak, he kneeled down and prayed, and a poor woman who was among the people stepped in and prayed with him: they endeavoured to thrust her away, and threatened to tread her down with their horses: notwithstanding this she would not remove, but abode and prayed with him. When he had finished his devotions, he went to the stake and kissed it, and set himself into a pitch barrel, which they had brought for him to stand in, and thus stood with his back upright against the stake, with his hands folded together, and his eyes towards heaven, and continually prayed. Then they bound a chain around him, and the sheriff called Richard Donningham, a butcher, and commanded him to set up the fagots; but the man refused, and said—"I am lame, sir, and not able to lift a fagot." The sheriff on this threatened to send him to prison; still he would not do it. The sheriff then compelled several worthless fellows of the multitude to set up the fagots and make the fire, which they most diligently did: and one of them cruelly cast a fagot at the martyr, which struck him on the face, and the blood ran down. He meekly said—"O friend, I have suffering enough, what needed that?"

Sir John Shelton standing by, as Dr. Taylor was speaking, and saying the psalm Miserere in English, struck him on the lips—"You knave," he said, "speak Latin, or I will make thee." At last they kindled the fire; when the martyr, holding up his hands, called upon God, and said, "Merciful Father of heaven, for Jesus Christ my Saviour's sake, receive my soul into thy hands." He then remained still without either crying or moving, with his hands folded together, until Soyce with an halberd struck him on the head so violently, that his brains fell out, and the dead corpse fell down into the fire. Thus rendered he his soul into the hands of his merciful Father, and to his most dear and certain Saviour Jesus Christ, whom he most entirely loved, faithfully and earnestly preached, obediently followed in living, and constantly glorified in death.

These severities were very hateful to the nation. It was observed that in king Edward's time, those that opposed the laws were only turned out of their benefices, and some few of them were imprisoned; but now men were put in prison on trifling pretences, and kept there until laws were made, by which they were condemned merely for their opinions, when they had acted nothing contrary to law. One piece of cruelty was remarkable—when the council sent away those who were to be burnt in the country, they threatened to cut out their tongues if they would not promise to make no speeches to the people; to which they, to avoid that butchery, consented. Those who loved the reformation were now possessed with great aversion to the popish party, and the body of the nation now detested this cruelty, and began to hate king Philip for it. Gardiner and the other counsellors had openly said, that the queen set them on to it, so that the blame of it was laid on the king, the sourness of whose temper, together with his bigotry in matters of religion, made it seem reasonable. He finding that this was likely to raise such prejudices against him as might probably spoil his design of making himself master of England, took care to vindicate himself. Accordingly his confessor, Alphonsus, a Franciscan, preached a sermon at court against taking people's lives for opinions in religion; and inveighed against the bishops for doing it; thus the blame of it was turned back on them, and this made them stop for some weeks; but at last they resolved rather to bear it avowedly, than not advance in their favourite career of blood!

At this time a petition was printed beyond sea, by which the reformers addressed themselves to the queen: they set before her the danger of being carried by a blind zeal to destroy the members of Christ, as St. Paul had done before his conversion: they reminded her of Cranmer's interposing to preserve her life in her father's time: they cited many passages out of the books of Gardiner, Bonner, and Tonstal, by which she might see that they were not actuated by true principles of conscience, but were turned as their fears or interests led them. They shewed her how contrary persecution was to the spirit of the gospel; that Christians tolerated Jews; and that Turks, notwithstanding the barbarity of their tempers, and the cruelty of their religion, yet tolerated Christians. They reminded her, that the first law for burning in England was made by Henry IV, as a reward to the bishops who had helped him to depose Richard II, and so to mount the throne. They represented to her, that God had trusted her with the sword, which she ought to employ for the protection of her people, and not to abandon them to the cruelty of wolves. The petition also appealed to the nobility and the rest of the nation, on the dangers of a Spanish yoke, and a bloody inquisition set before them. Upon this the popish authors wrote several books in justification of those proceedings. They observed that the Jews were commanded to put blasphemers to death; and said the heretics blasphemed the body of Christ, and called it only a piece of bread. Various other pleas were set up, and the nation had bitter experience in the coming years of the vigilance and industry with which they were acted upon.

CHAPTER SEVENTEEN

The Life and Martyrdom of John Bradford, Who Together with John Leaf Was Burned in Smithfield

J ohn Bradford was born at Manchester in Lancashire. His parents brought
him up in learning from his infancy and continued his education until he
attained such knowledge in the Latin tongue and such skill in writing that he
was able to gain his own living in a respectable situation. He then entered into
the service of Sir John Harrington, knight, who, in the great affairs of King
Henry VIII and Edward VI, which he had in hand when he was treasurer of the
king's camps and buildings at Boulogne, had such experience of Mr. Bradford's
activity in writing, his expertness in the art of auditors as also in his faithfulness,
that he placed great confidence in him. Thus encouraged and trusted, Mr.
Bradford continued several years in a thriving way, after course of this world,
and so would have continued if his mind could have been satisfied. But the
Lord had ordained him to more glorious and important objects: to preach the
word of God to man. He called his chosen servant to the understanding and
partaking of the gospel in which he was truly taught, that forthwith his effectual mission was perceived by the fruits. For then he forsook his worldly affairs
and, after a just account given to his master of all his doings, he departed from
him to further the kingdom of God by the ministry of his holy word and to
give himself wholly to the study of the scriptures. The better to accomplish
his design, he departed from the Temple at London and went down to the
university at Cambridge, where his diligence in study, his profiting in knowledge, and his pious conversation so pleased all men that, within a few years
after he had been there, the university gave him the degree of master of arts.

Immediately after, the master and fellows of Pembroke Hall gave him a fellowship in their college and that good man, Martin Bucer, held him not only most dear unto him but also oftentimes exhorted him to bestow his talent in preaching. To this Bradford always answered that he was unable to serve in that office through want of learning, to which Bucer was wont to reply, "If thou hast not fine wheat bread, yet give the poor people barley bread or whatsoever else the Lord hath committed unto thee." While Mr. Bradford was thus persuaded to enter into the ministry, Dr. Ridley, according to the order then in the church of England, called him to the degree of deacon. This order was not without some abuse to which Mr. Bradford would not consent, and the bishop, perceiving that he was willing to enter into the ministry, was content to ordain him deacon without any abuse, even as he desired. He then obtained for him a licence to preach and gave him a prebend in his cathedral church of St. Paul's where Mr. Bradford diligently laboured for the space of three years.

On the 13th of August, in the first year of the reign of queen Mary, Mr. Bourne, then bishop of Bath, made a sermon at Paul's Cross, which set forth the merits of popery in such sort, that it moved the people to such great indignation, that they could scarcely refrain pulling him out of the pulpit. Neither could the reverence of the place, nor the presence of bishop Bonner, nor yet the command of the lord-mayor of London, whom the people ought to have obeyed, stay their rage: but the more they spoke, the more the people were incensed. At length Mr. Bourne, seeing the violence of the people, and himself in such peril, desired Mr. Bradford, who stood in the pulpit behind him, to come forth, and to stand in his place and speak to the people. Mr. Bradford at his request obeyed, and spake to the people of godly and quiet obedience. As soon as the people heard him begin to speak unto them, they were so glad that they gave a great shout. The tumult soon ceased and in the end each departed quietly to his house.

The same Sunday afternoon, Mr. Bradford preached at Bow church in Cheapside, and reproved the people for their seditious misdemeanor. After this he abode in London, with an innocent conscience, to wait what would come to pass. He was not long at liberty, for within three days after he was sent for to the Tower, where the queen then was, to appear before the council. There he was charged with this act of saving Bourne, which they called seditious; and they also objected against him for preaching, and so by them he was committed first to the Tower, then to the King's Bench in Southwark, and after his condemnation he was sent to the Compter in the Poultry in London; in which latter places he preached twice a day continually, unless sickness hindered him. He ate but one frugal meal a day, and studied continually on his knees.

He remained in prison from August 1553, until January 1555; upon the 22nd of which month he was called before Gardiner, and other of the commissioners. On coming into the presence of the council, (who had just finished with Dr. Farrar, of whom ye have heard,) John Bradford kneeled down; but immediately, by the lord chancellor, was bidden to stand up. Then the lord chancellor spake thus to him in effect: that he had been of long time justly imprisoned for his seditious behaviour at Paul's Cross, the 13th of August, in the year 1553, for his false preaching and arrogancy, taking upon him to preach without authority. "But now," said he, "The time of mercy is come, and therefore the queen's highness, minding to offer unto you mercy, hath by us sent for you, to declare and give the same, if you will with us return: and if you will do as we have done, you shall find as we have found, I warrant you."

Mr. Bradford answered, "My lord and lords, I confess that I have been long imprisoned, and (with humble reverence be it spoken) unjustly, for that I did nothing seditiously, falsely, or arrogantly, in word or deed, by preaching or otherwise, but rather sought truth, peace, and all godly quietness, as an obedient and faithful subject, both in going about to serve the present bishop of Bath, then Mr. Bourne, the preacher at the Cross, and in preaching for quietness accordingly."

Lord Chan. I know thou hast a glorious tongue, and goodly shews thou makest; but all is lies thou speakest. And again, I have not forgotten how stubborn thou wast when thou wast before us in the Tower, whereupon thou wast committed to prison concerning religion: I have not forgotten thy behaviour and talk, for which cause thou hast been kept in prison, as some that would have done more hurt than I will speak of.

Brad. My lord, I stand as before you, so before God, and one day we shall all stand before him: the truth then will be the truth, though now ye will not so take it. Yea, my lord, I dare say, that my lord of Bath, Mr. Bourne, will witness with me, that I sought his safeguard with the peril of mine own life, I thank God there-for. I took nothing upon me undesired, and that of Mr. Bourne himself, as if he were here present, I dare say he would affirm. For he desired me both to help him to pacify the people, and also not to leave him until he was in safety. And as for my behaviour in the Tower, and talk before your honours, if I did or said any thing that did not beseem me, if your lordships would tell me wherein it was, I should and would presently make you answer.

Lord Chan. Well, to leave this matter: how sayest thou now? Wilt thou return again, and do as we have, and thou shalt receive the queen's mercy and pardon?

Brad. My lord, I desire your mercy with God's mercy; but your mercy with God's wrath, God keep me from: although, I thank God, my conscience doth not accuse, that I did speak any thing why I should need to receive the queen's mercy or pardon. For all that ever I did or spake was both agreeable to God's laws and the laws of the realm at that time, and did make much to quietness. I have not deceived the people, nor taught any other doctrine than, by God's grace, I am ready to confirm with my life. And as for its devilishness and falseness, I would be sorry you could so prove it.

Durham. What say you of the ministration of the communion, as now it is?

Brad. My lord, I must desire of your lordship and of all your honours a question, before I dare make you an answer to any question. I have been six times sworn that I shall in no case consent to the practising of any jurisdiction, or authority, on the bishop of Rome's behalf within this realm of England. Now, before God, I humbly pray your honours to tell me whether you ask me this question by his authority, or not? If you do, I dare not answer you any thing in his authority, except I would be forsworn, which God forbid. I was thrice sworn in Cambridge, when I was admitted master of arts, when I was admitted fellow of Pembroke Hall, and when I was there, the visitors came thither and sware the university. Again, I was sworn when I entered into the ministry, when I had a prebend given me, and when I was sworn to serve the king, a little before his death.

Rochester. My lords, I never knew wherefore this man was in prison before now: but I see well that it had not been good that this man had been abroad: what the cause was that he was put in prison I know not; but I now well know that not without a cause he was, and is to be kept in prison.

Sec. Bourne. Yea, it was reported this parliament time by the earl Derby, that he hath done more hurt by letters, and exhorting those that have come to him in religion, than ever he did when he was abroad by preaching. In his letters he curseth all that teach any doctrine which is not according to that he taught, and most heartily exhorteth them to whom he writeth to continue still in that they received by him, and such like as he is. How say you, Sir, have you not thus seditiously written and exhorted the people?

Brad. I have not written nor spoken any thing seditiously; neither, I thank God, have I admitted any seditious thought, nor trust ever shall do. Concerning my letters, what I have written I have written.

Lord Chan. We shall never have done with thee, I perceive now: be short, wilt thou have mercy?

Brad. My lords, if I may live as a quiet subject without a clog of conscience, I shall heartily thank you for that pardon; if otherwise I behave myself, then I am in danger of the law: in the mean season I ask no more than the benefit of a subject until I be convicted of transgression. If I cannot have this, as hitherto I have not had, God's good will be done.

Here the lord chancellor again offered mercy, and Bradford answered as before. Mercy with God's mercy should be welcome, but otherwise he would have none. Whereupon the lord chancellor rang a bell, when the under marshal came in, to whom his lordship said, "You shall take this man to you, and keep him close without conference with any man, but by your knowledge, and suffer him not to write any letters, for he is of another manner of charge to you now than he was before." And so they departed, Bradford looking as cheerfully as any man could do, declaring even a desire to give his life for the confirmation of his faith and doctrine.

The second examination of Mr. Bradford took place immediately after the excommunication of Mr. Rogers, who has been before the reader. After a long speech of Gardiner and another bishop or two, Mr. Bradford said, "My lord, and my lords all, as I now stand in your sight before you, so I humbly beseech your honours to consider, that you sit in the seat of the Lord, who (as David doth witness) is in the congregation of judges, and sitteth in the midst of them judging righteously: and as you would have your place to be by us taken as God's place, so demonstrate yourselves to follow him in your sitting; that is, seek no guiltless blood, neither hunt by questions to bring into a snare them which are out of the same. At this present I stand before you guilty or guiltless: if guilty, proceed to give sentence accordingly; if guiltless, then give me the benefit of a subject, which hitherto I could not have."

Here the lord chancellor said, that Bradford began with a true sentence—That the Lord is in the midst of them that judge. But, this and all his gesture declared but hypocrisy and vainglory. Then he endeavoured to clear himself that he sought not guiltless blood, and began a long process, stating that Bradford's fact at St. Paul's Cross was presumptuous and arrogant, and declared a taking upon himself to lead the people, which could not but turn to much disquietness, in that he was so refractory and stout in religion at that present. For which, as he was then committed to prison, so hitherto he has been kept in prison, where he has written letters to the great hurt of the queen's subjects, as was credibly declared by the earl of Derby in the parliament house. And to this he added, that Mr. Bradford did stubbornly behave himself the last time he was before them; and therefore not for any other thing did he now demand of him, but for his doctrine and religion.

Brad. My lord, where you accuse me of hypocrisy and vainglory, I must and will leave it to the Lord's declaration, who will one day open yours and my truth and hearty meanings: in the mean season, I will content myself with the testimony of my own conscience, which if it yield to hypocrisy, could not but have God to be my foe also; and so both God and man were against me. And as for my fact at St. Paul's Cross, and behaviour before you at the Tower, I doubt not but God will reveal it to my comfort. For if ever I did any thing which God used to public benefit, I think that my deed was one, and yet for it I have been and am kept a long time in prison. And as for letters and religion, I answer as I did the last time I was before you.

Lord Chan. There didst thou say stubbornly and saucily that thou wouldst maintain the erroneous doctrine in king Edward's days.

Brad. My lord, I said, the last time I was before you, that I had six times taken an oath, that I should never consent to the practising of any jurisdiction on the bishop of Rome's behalf; and therefore I dust not answer to any thing that should be so demanded, lest I should be forsworn, which God forbid. Howbeit, saving my oath, I said I was more confirmed in the doctrine set forth publicly in the days of king Edward than ever I was before I was put in prison: and so I thought I should be, and yet think still shall be found more ready to give my life as God will, for the confirmation of the same.

Lord Chan. I remember well that thou madest much ado about needless matter, as though the oath against the bishop of Rome were so great a matter. So others have done before thee; but yet not in such sort as thou hast: for thou pretendest a conscience in it, which is nothing else but mere hypocrisy.

Brad. My conscience is known to the Lord, and whether I deal herein hypocritically or no, he knoweth. As therefore I said then, my lord, so I say again now—that for fear I should be perjured I dare not answer to any thing you should demand of me, if my answering should consent to the confirming or practising of any jurisdiction for the bishop of Rome here in England. I am not afraid of death, I thank God; for I have looked for nothing else at your hands a long time: but I am afraid when death cometh, I should have matter to trouble my conscience by the guiltiness of perjury, and therefore I answer as I do.

Lord Chan. You have written seditious letters, and perverted the people thereby, and still seem as though you would defend the erroneous doctrine in king Edward's time, against all men: and now you say you dare not answer.

Brad. I have written no seditious letters, I have not perverted the people: but that which I have written and spoken, will I never deny, by God's grace. And where your lordship says, I dare not answer you; that all men may know I am not afraid, save mine oath, ask me what you will, and I will plainly make you answer, by God's grace, although I now see my life lieth thereon. But, O Lord, into thy hands I commit it, come what will: only sanctify thy name in me, as in an instrument of thy grace, Amen. Bow, ask what you will, and you shall see, I am not afraid, by God's grace, flatly to answer.

Lord Chan. Well then, how say you to the blessed sacrament? Do you not believe there Christ to be present concerning his natural body?

Brad. My lord, I do not believe that Christ is corporally present at and in the due administration of the sacrament. By 'corporally,' I mean present corporally unto faith. I have been now a year and almost three quarters in prison, and in all this time you have never questioned me hereabout, when I might have spoken my conscience frankly without peril; but now you have a law to hang up and put to death, if a man answer freely and not to your liking, and therefore you come to demand this question. Ah, my lord, Christ used not this way to bring men to faith. Nor did the prophets nor apostles. Remember what Bernard writes to Eugenius the pope—"I read that the apostles stood to be judged, but I read not, that they sat to judge."

Lord Chan. I use not this means. It was not my doing, although some there be that think this to be the best way: for I, for my part, have been challenged for being too gentle oftentimes.

Brad. My lord, I pray you stretch out your gentleness that I may feel it, for hitherto I have not.

Lord Chan. With all my heart, not only but the queen's highness would stretch out mercy, if with them you would return.

The next morning about seven o'clock, one Thomas Hussey came into the chamber wherein Mr. Bradford lay, and began a long oration, saying, that of love and acquaintance he came to speak that which he would farther utter. "You did," said he, "so wonderfully behave yourself before the lord chancellor, and other bishops yesterday, that even the greatest enemies you have, saw that they have no matter against you: and therefore I advise you, this day, to desire a time, and men to confer withal, so shall all men think it a wonderful wisdom, and piety in you; and by this means you shall escape present danger, which else is nearer than you are aware of." To this Mr. Bradford answered, "I neither can nor will make such request. For then shall I give occasion to the people, to think that I doubt of the doctrine which I confess; which I do not, for thereof I am most assured, and therefore will give no such offence."

As they were thus talking, the chamber door was opened, and Dr. Seaton entered, who after some by-talk of Mr. Bradford's age, and his country, began a gay and long discourse of my lord of Canterbury, Mr. Latimer, and Mr. Ridley, and how they at Oxford were not able to answer any thing at all; and that therefore my lord of Canterbury desired to confer with the bishop of Durham and others; all which talk tended to this end, that Mr. Bradford should make the like suit, being not to be compared in learning to Dr. Cranmer. But John Bradford kept still one answer—"I cannot, nor I will not so offend the people:" whereat master Seaton waxed hot, and called Bradford arrogant, proud, and vainglorious. Bradford answered, "Beware of judging, lest you condemn yourself." When all their talk took no such effect as they looked for, Hussey asked Bradford, "Will ye not admit conference, if my lord chancellor should offer it publicly?" To this Bradford replied, "Conference! if it had been offered before the law had been made, or if it were offered so that I might be at liberty to confer, and as safe as he with whom I should confer, then it were something: but else I see not to what other purpose conference should be offered but to defer that which at length will come, and the lingering may give more offence than do good. Howbeit, if my lord should make such an offer of his own motion, I accused Mr. Bradford with being arrogant and proud, and they soon accused Mr. Bradford with being arrogant and proud, and they soon left him. Shortly after they were gone, Mr. Bradford was led to the church and there tarried uncalled for until eleven o'clock; meanwhile the excommunication of Mr. Saunders, already related, took place.

At length the time arrived for Mr. Bradford's last examination. He was again brought before the lord chancellor and other bishops, and his lordship began to speak to this effect—that if he would answer with modesty and humility, and conform himself to the catholic church with them, he might yet find mercy, because they would be loth to use extremity. Therefore he concluded with an exhortation, that Mr. Bradford would recant his doctrine.

Bradford. As yesterday I besought your honours to set in your sight the majesty and presence of God to follow him, who seaketh not to subvert the simple by subtle questions; so I humbly beseech every one of you to do this day: for you know well enough that guiltless blood will cry for vengeance. And this I pray not your lordships to do, as one that taketh upon me to condemn you utterly herein; but that ye might be more admonished to do that, which none doth so much as he should do. For our nature is so much corrupt, that we are very forgetful of God. And last of all, as yesterday the answers I made were by protestation and saving mine oath, so shall mine answers be this day; and this I do, that when death (which I look for at your hands) shall come, I may not be troubled with the guiltiness of perjury.

At these words the lord chancellor was wroth, and said that they had given him respite to deliberate until this day, whether he would recant his errors of the blessed sacrament, which yesterday he uttered before them.

Brad. My lord, you gave me no time of any such deliberation, neither did I speak anything of the sacrament which you did disallow. For when I had declared a presence of Christ to be there to faith, you went from that matter to purge yourself, that you were not cruel, and so went to dinner.

Lord Chan. What! I perceive we must begin all again with thee. Did I not yesterday tell thee plainly, that thou madest a conscience where none should be? Did I not make it plain, that the oath against the bishop of Rome was an unlawful oath?

Brad. No, indeed, my lord: you said so, but you have not proved it yet, nor ever can do.

Lord Chan. O Lord God, what a fellow art thou! Thou wouldst go about to bring into the people's heads, that we, all the lords of the parliament house, the knights and burgesses, and all the whole realm be perjured. O what a heresy is this! Here, good people, you may see what a senseless heretic this fellow is. If I should make an oath I would never help my brother, nor lend him money in his need; were this a good answer to tell my neighbour desiring my help, that I had made an oath to the contrary? or that I could not do it?

Brad. O, my lord, discern betwixt oaths that be against charity and faith, and oaths that be according to faith and charity, as this is against the bishop of Rome.

Here a long time was spent about oaths which were good, and those which were evil—the lord chancellor captiously asking often of Bradford a direct answer concerning oaths; which Bradford would not give simply, but with a distinction. Whereat the chancellor was much offended: but Bradford still kept him at bay, that the oath against the bishop of Rome was a lawful oath, using thereto the lord chancellor's own book, of true obedience, for confirmation of his assertion.

Then came master Chamberlain of Woodstock, and told my lord chancellor, that Bradford had been a serving-man with master Harrington. To which Gardiner said—"True, and he did deceive his master of seven-score pounds: and because of this, he went to be a gospeller and a preacher, good people; and yet you see how he pretendeth conscience."

Brad. My lord, I set my foot by his, whoever he be, that can come forth, and justly vouch to my face, that ever I deceived my master. And as you are chief justicer by office in England, I desire justice upon them that so slander me, because they cannot prove it.

Here my lord chancellor and master Chamberlain were smitten blank, and said they heard it. "But," quoth Gardiner, "we have another manner of matter than this against you; for you are a heretic." "Yea," quoth the bishop of London, "he did write letters to master Pendleton, which knoweth his hand as well as his own: your honour did see the letters."

Brad. That is not true; I never did write to Pendleton since I came to prison, and therefore I am not justly spoken of.

Lord Chan. Sir, in my house the other day, you did most contemptuously despise the queen's mercy, and stoutly said that you would maintain the erroneous doctrine of king Edward's days against all men.

Brad. Well, I am glad that all men see now you have had no matter to imprison me before that day justly. Now say I, that I did not contemptuously contemn the queen's mercy; but would have had it, (though if justice might take place, I need it not,) so that I might have had it with God's mercy, that is, without doing or saying anything against God and his truth. And as for maintenance of doctrine, because I cannot tell how you will stretch this word maintenance, I well repeat again that which I spake. I said I was more confirmed in the religion set forth in king Edward's days than ever I was: and if God so would, I trusted I should declare it by giving my life for the confirmation and testification thereof. So I said then, and so I say now.

Lord Chan. Well, yesterday thou didst maintain false heresy concerning the blessed sacrament; and therefore we gave thee until to-day to deliberate.

Brad. My lord, as I said at the first, I spake nothing of the sacrament, but that which you allowed; and therefore you reproved it not, nor gave me any time to deliberate.

Lord Chan. Didst thou not deny Christ's presence in the sacrament?

Brad. No, I never denied nor taught, but that to faith, whole Christ, body and blood, was as present as bread and wine to the due receiver.

Lord Chan. Yea, but dost thou not believe that Christ's body naturally and really is there, under the forms of bread and wine?

Brad. My lord, I believe Christ is present there to the faith of the due receiver: as for transubstantiation, I plainly and flatly tell you, I believe it not. I deny not his presence to the faith of the receiver; but deny that he is included in the bread, or that the bread is transubstantiate.

Worcester. If he be not included, how is he then present?

Brad. Forsooth, though my faith can tell how, yet my tongue cannot express it; not you, otherwise than by faith, hear it, or understand it.

Here was much ado, now one doctor standing up and speaking this, and others speaking that, and the lord chancellor talking much of Luther Zuinglius,

Oecolampadius; but still Bradford kept him at this point, that Christ is present to faith; and that there is no transubstantiation not including of Christ in the bread: but all this would not save them. Therefore another bishop asked whether the wicked man received Christ's very body or no? To which Bradford answered plainly, "No." Whereat my lord chancellor made a long oration, showing how that it could not be that Christ was present, except that the evil man received it. But Bradford silenced his oration in a few words, that grace was at that time offered to his lordship, although he received it not; so that the receiving made not the presence, but God's grace, truth, and power, is the cause of the presence, which grace, the wicked that lack faith cannot receive. Bradford concluded his answer admirably, thus—"My lord, are not these words, Take, eat, a commandment? and are not these words, This is my body, a promise? If you will challenge the promise, and do not the commandment, may you not deceive yourself?"

Here the lord chancellor denied Christ to have commanded the sacrament, and the use of it. Bradford said, "Why, my lord, is it not plain to children, that Christ, in so saying, commandeth? If it be not a commandment of Christ to take and eat the sacrament, why dare any take upon them to command and make that of necessity, which God leaveth free? as you do in making it a necessary commandment, once a year for all that be of discretion, to receive the sacrament. Here the lord chancellor called him again diabolus or calumniator, and began out of these words, "Let a man prove himself, and so eat of the bread, ['yea, bread,' quoth Bradford,] and drink of the cup," to prove that it was no commandment to receive the sacrament: "for then," quoth he, "if it were a commandment, it should bind all men, in all places, and at all times."

Brad. O my lord, discern between commandments: some be general, as the ten commandments, that they bind always, in all places, and all persons; some be not so general, as this of the supper, the sacrament of baptism, of the thrice appearing before the Lord yearly at Jerusalem, of Abraham offering of Isaac, and many others.

Here my lord chancellor denied the cup to be commanded of Christ: "for then," quoth he, "we should have eleven commandments." To this Bradford said—"Indeed I think you think as you speak: for else you would not take the cup from the people, in that Christ saith, 'Drink ye all of it.' But how say you, my lords? Christ saith to you bishops especially, 'Go and preach the gospel:' 'Feed Christ's flock,' etc. Is this a commandment or no?"

Here was my lord chancellor in a chafe, and said as pleased him. Then the bishop of Durham asked Bradford when Christ began to be present in the sacrament—whether before the receiver received it, or no? Bradford answered that the question was curious, and not necessary; and further said, that as the cup was the New Testament, so the bread was Christ's body to him that received it duly; but yet so, that the bread is bread. "For," quoth he, "in all the Scripture ye shall not find this proposition, 'Non est panis,' 'There is no bread.' And he brought forth Chrysostome, 'Si in corpore essemus.' Much ado was hereabouts; they calling Bradford heretic; and he, desiring them to proceed on in God's name, looked for that which God appointed for them to do.

Lord Chan. This fellow is now in another heresy; as though all things were so tied together, that of mere necessity all things must come to pass.

Here Bradford prayed him to take things as they be spoken, and not wrest them into a contrary sense: "Your lordship," said he, "doth discern betwixt God and man. Things are not by fortune to God at any time, though to man they seem so sometimes. I speak but as the apostles did—'Lord, see how Herod and Pontius Pilate, with the prelates, are gathered together against thy Christ, to do that which thy hand and counsel hath before ordained for them to do.'"

Here the lord chancellor began to read the excommunication. And when he came to the name of John Bradford, layman; he said, art thou no priest? To which he answered, "No, nor ever was a priest, or beneficed, or married, or any preacher, before public authority had established religion, or preacher after public authority had altered religion, and yet I am thus handled at your hands: but God, I doubt not, will bless where you curse." And so he fell down on his knees, and heartily thanked God that he had counted him worthy to suffer for his name's sake; and prayed to God to give him repentance and a good mind. After the excommunication was read, he was delivered to the sheriff of London, and so had to the Clink, and afterwards to the Compter in the Poultry; this being proposed by his murderers, that he should be delivered from thence to the earl of Derby, to be conveyed into Lancashire, and there to be burned in the town of Manchester, where he was born: but their purpose concerning the place was afterwards altered, for he suffered in London. After his condemnation, which was the last day of January, Bradford being sent to prison, remained there until the 1st of July; during all which time, divers other conferences and conflicts he sustained with sundry adversaries, which repaired unto him in the prison: of whom first bishop Bonner, coming to the Compter to degrade Dr. Taylor the 4th of February, called first for John Bradford, and began to talk with him, the effect whereof here ensueth:

Bonner. Because I perceive that ye are desirous to confer with some learned men, therefore I have brought master archdeacon Harpsfield to you.

Brad. I never desired to confer with any man, nor yet do. Howbeit if ye will have one to talk with me I am ready.

Bonner. Well, master Bradford, you are well beloved; I pray you consider yourself, and refuse not charity when it is offered.

Brad. Indeed, my lord, this is small charity, to condemn a man as you have condemned me, which never brake your laws. In Turkey a man may have charity; but in England I could not yet find it. I was condemned for my faith, so soon as I uttered it at your requests, before I had committed anything against the laws. And as for conference, I am not afraid to talk with whom you will. But to say that I desire to confer, that do I not.

Bon. Well, well.—Then he called for Taylor, and Bradford went his way.

On another day of February, one master Willerton, chaplain of the bishop of London, came to confer with Bradford, and commenced by saying that he swerved from the church.

Brad. That do I not, but ye do. For the church is Christ's spouse, and Christ's obedient spouse, which your church is not, which robbeth the people of the Lord's cup, and of service in the English tongue.

Willerton. Why? It is not profitable to have the service in English; for it is written, "The lips of the priest should keep the law, and out of his mouth man must look for knowledge."

Brad. Should not the people, then, have the Scriptures? Wherefore serveth this saying of Christ, "Search the Scriptures?"

Wil. This was not spoken to the people, but to scribes and learned men.

Brad. Then the people must not have the Scriptures?

Willerton. No; for it is written, "They shall be all taught of God."

Brad. Must we learn all at the priests? Then would you bring the people to hang up Christ, and let Barabbas go; as the priests then wished.

At which words, Willerton was so offended that he had no wish to talk any more. On the 25th of February, Percival Creswell came with master Harpsfield, who, after formal salutation, make a long oration to the effect that all men, even the infidels, Turks, Jews, anabaptists, and libertines, desire felicity as well as the Christians, and that every one thinketh to attain it by his religion. To which Bradford answered that he spake not amiss.

Harps. But the way thither is not all alike: for the infidels by Jupiter and Juno, the Turk by his Alcoran, the Jew by his Talmud, do believe to come to heaven. For so may I speak of such as believe the immortality of the soul. And here is the matter, to know the way to this heaven.

Brad. We may not invent any manner of ways. There is but one way, and that is Jesus Christ, as he himself doth witness, "I am the way!"

Harps. It is true that you say, and false also. I suppose that you mean by Christ, believing in Christ.

Brad. I have learned to discern betwixt faith and Christ. Albeit, I confess, that whoso believeth in Christ, the same shall be saved.

Harps. No, not all that believe in Christ: for some shall say, "Lord, Lord, have we not cast out devils?" etc. But Christ will answer in the day of judgment to these, "Depart from me, I know you not."

Brad. You must make difference betwixt believing, and saying, I believe: as for example, if one should swear he loveth you, for all his saying ye will not believe him when you see he doeth you all the evil he can.

Harps. Well, this is not much material. There is but one way, Christ. How come we to know him? Where shall we seek to find him?

Brad. We must seek him by his word, in his word, and after his word.

Harps. Very good: but tell me how first we came into the company of them that could tell us this, but by baptism?

Brad. Baptism is the sacrament, by which outwardly we are ingrafted into Christ: I say outwardly, because I dare not exclude from Christ all that die without baptism.

Harps. Well, we agree, that by baptism then we are brought, and begotten to Christ. For Christ is our Father, and the church his spouse, is our mother. Now then tell me whether this church of Christ hath not been always?

Brad. Yes, since the creation of man, and shall be for ever.

Harps. Very good. But tell me whether this church is a visible church, or not?

Brad. It is no otherwise visible, than Christ was here on earth; that is, by no exterior pomp or shew that setteth her forth commonly: and therefore to see her we must put on such eyes, as good men put on to see and know Christ when he walked here on earth: for as Eve was of the same substance that Adam was of, so was the church of the same substance that Christ was of.

Harps. Well, this church is a multitude. Hath it not the preaching of the gospel, and the administration of the sacraments? And yet more, hath it not the power of jurisdiction? I mean by jurisdiction, admonishing one another, and so forth. It hath also succession of bishops, which I will endeavour to prove as an essential point.

Brad. You say as you would have it; for if this part fail you, all the church you go about to set up will fall down. You shall not find in all the scripture, this your essential part of succession of bishops. In Christ's church antichrist will sit. And Peter tells us, as it went in the old church before Christ's coming, so it will be in the new church since Christ's coming: that as there were false prophets, and such as bear rule were adversaries to the true prophets, so shall there be false teachers, even of such as are bishops and bear rule amongst the people.

After some further talk, Harpsfield departed, promising to come again. On the 23rd of the same month, the archbishop of York and the bishop of Chichester came to the Compter to speak with Bradford. When he was brought before them, they used him very gently: desired him to sit down, and because he would not, they also would not sit. So they all stood, and whether he would or not, they would needs have him put on his cap, saying to him, that obedience was better than sacrifice. As they were thus standing together, the archbishop of York began to tell Mr. Bradford that they came to him out of pure love and charity, without being sent; and, after commending his godly life, he concluded with this question, How he was certain of salvation and of his religion? Mr. Bradford thanked him for their good will, and answered thus, "By the word of God, even by the scriptures, I am certain of salvation and religion."

York. Very well said: but how do you know the word of God and the scriptures, but by the church?

Brad. Indeed, my lord, the church was and is a means to bring a man to know the scriptures and the word of God, as the woman of Samaria was the means by which the Samaritans knew Christ: but when they heard him speak, they said, "Now we know that he is Christ, not because of thy words, but because we ourselves have heard." So after we come to the hearing and reading of the scriptures shewed unto us, and discerned by the church, we do believe them, and know them as Christ's sheep, not because the church saith they are the scriptures, but because they be so, being assured thereof by the same Spirit who wrote and spake them.

York. You know, in the apostles' time at first the word was not written.

Brad. True, if you mean it for some books of the New Testament; but else for the Old Testament St. Peter tells us, "We have a more sure word of prophecy;" not that it is simply so, but in respect of the apostles, which being alive and subject to infirmity, attributed to the written word more weight, as wherewith no fault can be found; whereas for the infirmity of their persons men perchance might have found some fault at their preaching; although in very deed no less obedience and faith ought to have been given to the one, than to the other; for all proceedeth from one Spirit of truth.

York. That place of St. Peter is not to be understood of the word written. You know that Irenaeus and others do magnify much, and allege the church against the heretics, and not the scripture.

Brad. True, for they had to do with such heretics as denied the Scriptures, and yet did magnify the apostles; so that they were forced to use the authority of those churches wherein the apostles had taught, and which had still retained the same doctrine.

Chichester. You speak the very truth; for the heretics did refuse all Scriptures, except it were a piece of Luke's gospel.

Brad. Then the alleging of the church cannot be principally used against me, which am so far from denying of the Scriptures, that I appeal to them utterly, as to the only judge.

York. A pretty matter, that you will take upon you to judge the church! I pray you, where hath your church been hitherto? For the church of Christ is catholic and visible hitherto.

Brad. My lord, I do not judge the church when I discern it from that congregation, and those which be not the church; and I never denied the church to be catholic and visible, although at some times it is more visible than at others.

Chich. I pray you tell me where the church which allowed your doctrine was, these four hundred years?

Brad. I will tell you, my lord, or rather you shall tell yourself, if you will tell me this one thing: where the church was in Elias's time, when Elias said that he was left alone?

Chich. That is no answer.

Brad. I am sorry that you say so: but this will I tell your lordship, that if you had the same eyes wherewith a man might have espied the church then, you would not say it were no answer. The fault why the church is not seen by you, is not because the church is not visible, but because your eyes are not clear enough to see it.

Chich. You are much deceived in making this collation betwixt the church then and now.

York. Very well spoken, my lord; for Christ said, "I will build my church;" and not "I do, or I have built it;" but, "I will build it."

Brad. My lords, Peter teacheth me to make this collation, saying, as in the people there were false prophets, which were most in estimation before Christ's coming, so shall there be false teachers amongst the people after Christ's coming, and very many shall follow them. And as for your future tense, I hope your grace will not thereby conclude Christ's church not to have been before, but rather that there is no building in the church but Christ's work only: for Paul and Apollos be but waterers.

Chich. In good faith I am sorry to see you so light in judging the church.

Brad. My lords, I speak simply what I think, and desire reason to answer my objections. Your affections and sorrows cannot be my rules. If you consider the order and case of my condemnation, I cannot think but that it shall something move your honours. You know it well enough, no matter was laid against me, but was gathered upon mine own confession. Because I denied transubstantiation, and the wicked to receive Christ's body in the sacrament, therefore I was condemned and excommunicated; but not of the church, although the pillars of the church did it.

Chich. No; I heard say the cause of your imprisonment was, for that you exhorted the people to take the sword in one hand, and the mattock in the other.

Brad. I never meant any such thing, nor spake anything in that sort.

York. Yea, and you behaved yourself before the council so stoutly at the first, that you would defend the religion then; and therefore worthily were you prisoned.

Brad. Your grace did hear me answer my lord chancellor to that point. But put case I had been so stout as they and your grace make it: were not the laws of the realm on my side then? Wherefore unjustly was I prisoned: only that which my lord chancellor propounded, was my confession of Christ's truth against transubstantiation, and of that which the wicked do receive, as I said.

York. You deny the presence.

Brad. I do not, to the faith of the worthy receivers.

York. What is that other than to say that Christ lieth not on the altar?

Brad. My lord, I believe no such presence.

Chich. It seemeth that you have not read Chrysostome, for he proveth it.

Brad. I do remember Chrysostome saith, that Christ lieth upon the altar, as the seraphim with their tongs touch our lips with the coals of the altar in heaven, which is an hyperbolical locution, of which Chrysostome is full.

York. It is evident that you are too far gone; but let us come then to the church, out of which you are excommunicate.

Brad. I am not excommunicated out of Christ's church, my lord, although they which seem to be in the church, and of the church, have excommunicated me, as the poor blind man was, John ix.; I am sure Christ receiveth me. As I think you did well to depart from the Romish church, so I think you have done wickedly to couple yourselves to it again; for you can never prove that which you call the mother church, to be Christ's.

Chich. You were but a child when this matter began. I was a young man, and then coming from the university, I went with the world: but, I tell you, it was always against my conscience.

Brad. I was but a child; howbeit, as I told you, I think you have done evil. For you are come and have brought others to that wicked man which sitteth in the temple of God, that is, in the church: for it cannot be understood of Mahomet, or any out of the church, but of such as bear rule in the church.

York. See how you build your faith upon such places of scripture as are most obscure, to deceive yourself.

Brad. Well, my lord, though I might by fruits judge of you and others, yet will I not utterly exclude you out of the church. And if I were in your case, I would not condemn him utterly that is of my faith in the sacrament, knowing as you know, that at least 800 years after Christ, as my lord of Durham writeth, it was free to believe or not believe transubstantiation. Will you condemn any man that believeth truly the twelve articles of the faith, although in some points he believe not the definition of that which you call the church? I doubt not but that he which holdeth firmly the articles of our belief, though in other things he dissent from your definitions, yet he shall be saved.

"Yea," said both the bishops, "this is your divinity."

Brad. No, it is Paul's; who saith, that if they hold the foundation, Christ, though they build upon him straw and stubble, yet they shall be saved.

York. How you delight to lean to hard and dark places of the Scriptures.

Chich. I will show you how that Luther did excommunicate Zuinglius for this matter: (and so he read a place of Luther making for his purpose.)

Brad. My lord, what Luther writeth, as you mind it not, no more do I in this case. My faith is not built on Luther, Zuinglius, or Oecolampadius, in this point; and indeed I never read any of their works in this matter.

York. Well, you are out of communion of the church; for you would have the communion of it consist in faith.

Brad. Communion consisteth, as I said, in faith, and not in exterior ceremonies, as appeareth both by St. Paul, who would have one faith, and by Irenaeus to Victor, for the observation of Easter.

York. You think none are of the church but such as suffer persecution.

Brad. What I think, God knoweth: I pray your grace to judge me by my words, and mark what St. Paul saith—"All that will live godly in Christ Jesus must suffer persecution," Sometimes Christ's church hath rest here; but commonly it is not so, and specially towards the end her form will be more unseemly.

York. Well, master Bradford, we lease our labour; for ye seek to put away all things which are told you to your good: your church no man can know. I pray you, whereby can we know it?

Brad. Chrysostome says, "by the Scriptures:" and thus he often saith.

York. That of Chrysostome in Opere imperfecto may be doubted of. The thing whereby the church may be known best, is succession of bishops.

Brad. No, my lord, Lyra full well writeth upon Matthew, that "the church consisteth not in men, by reason either of secular or temporal power; but in men endued with true knowledge, and confession of faith, and of verity." Hilary, writing to Auxentius, says that the church was hidden rather in caves, than did glister and shine in thrones of pre-eminence.

After they had tarried three hours with Bradford, one of their servants came and told them that my lord of Durham waited for them at master York's house. And so, after putting up their written books, and wishing poor Bradford good in words, they went their way, and he to his prison.

Within two days following came into the Compter two Spanish friars to talk with master Bradford, sent (as they said) by the earl of Derby; of whom one was the king's confessor, the other was Alphonsus, who had before written a popish book against heresies.

Alph. What is the matter whereof you were condemned? We know not.

Brad. I have been in prison almost two years: I never transgressed any of their laws for which I might justly be imprisoned; and now I am condemned, because I frankly confessed (which I repent not) my faith concerning the sacrament, when I was demanded in these two points: one, that there is no transubstantiation; the other, that the wicked do not receive Christ's body.

Alph. Let us look a little on the first. Do you not believe that Christ is present really and corporally in the form of bread?

Brad. No, I do believe that Christ is present to the faith of the worthy receiver, as there is present bread and wine to the senses and outward man: as for any such presence of including and placing Christ, I believe not, nor dare believe.

Alph. I am sure you believe Christ's natural body is circumscriptible.

And here he made much ado of the two natures of Christ, how that the one is everywhere, and the other is in his proper place. After further talk on this subject, the friar, in a wonderful rage, spake so high that the whole house rang again; and had Bradford been anything hot, one house could not have held them. At the length he came to this point, that Bradford could not find in the Scripture baptism and the Lord's supper to bear any similitude to each other.

Brad. Be patient, and you shall see that by the Scripture I will find baptism and the Lord's supper coupled together. Paul saith, that as we are baptized into one body, so "we have drunk of one spirit," meaning the cup in the Lord's supper.

Alph. Paul hath no such words.

Brad. Yes, that he hath. Give me a Testament, and I will show you. The text is plain enough, and there are of the fathers which do so understand the place: for Chrysostome doth expound it so.

Alphonsus, who had the Testament in his hand, desirous to suppress this foil, turned the leaves until he came to the place, (1 Cor. xi.;) and there he read how that he was guilty who made no difference of the Lord's body.

Brad. Yea, but therewith he saith, "He that eateth of the bread;" calling it bread still: and that after consecration, as in 1 Cor. x., he saith, "The bread which we break," etc.

Alph. Oh, how ignorant are ye which know not that things, after their conversion, retain the same names which they had before, as Moses' rod.

Brad. Sir, there is mention made of the conversion, as well as that the same appeared to the sense; but here you cannot find it so. Find me one word how the bread is converted, and I will then say, you bring some matter that maketh for you. I do not trust my own reason, or my own interpretation; for I will bring you the fathers of the church 800 years after Christ, to confirm what I speak.

Alph. This church hath defined the contrary, and that I will prove by all the good fathers from Christ's ascension, even for 800 years at least continually, yea that the bread is turned into Christ's body. Will you believe?

Brad. Belief is God's gift, therefore I cannot promise: but I tell you I will give place: and I hope I shall believe his truth always, so good is he to me in Christ my Saviour.

Alph. I find great fault with your answer. But this I let pass, and repeat the question, if I can prove it as you said, whether you will give place?

Brad. Yes, that I will. Give me paper, pen, and ink, to write; and now suppose that I prove by the testimony of the fathers, that continually for 800 years after Christ at least, they did believe that the substance of bread doth remain in the sacrament, what will you do?

Alph. I will give place.

Brad. Then write you here that you will give place if I so prove, and I will write that I will give place if you so prove; because you are the elder you shall have the pre-eminency.

Here the friar fumed marvellously, and said, "I came not to learn at thee: are not here witnesses? be not they sufficient?" So they arose and talked no more of that matter, going away without bidding Bradford farewell. After they were gone, a priest came, and willed him not to be so obstinate.

On the 21st of March, Mr. Bradford was called down, and as soon as he entered into the hall, Dr. Weston very gently took him by the hand, and asking how he did, desired all to go out, save himself, Mr. Collier, the earl of Derby's servant, the subdean of Westminster, the keeper, Mr. Claydon, and the parson of the church near the Compter. In their presence he began to tell Mr. Bradford, that he had often intended to come unto him, being desired by the earl of

Derby: and that after he perceived that he could be contented rather to speak with him than any other, he could not but come to do him all the good in his power, without intending in the least to hurt or injure him.

Bradford. Sir, when I perceived by the report of my lord's servant, that you did bear me good will, more than any other of your sort, I told him then that I could be better content and more willing to talk with you, if you should come unto me. This did I say: otherwise I desired not your coming.

West. Well, Mr. Bradford, I am now come to talk with you: but before we begin, certain principles we must agree upon, which shall be this day's work; and the first of these is that I shall greatly desire you to put away all vainglory, and not hold any thing for the praise of the world.

Brad. Sir, St. Augustine maketh that indeed a piece of the definition of a heretic; which, if I cannot put away clean, (for I think there will be a spice of it remain in us, as long as this flesh liveth) yet I promise you by the grace of God, that I purpose not to yield to it. God, I hope, will never suffer it to bear rule in them that strive against it, and desire all the dregs of it utterly to be driven out of us.

West. I am glad to hear you say so, although, indeed, I think you do not so much esteem it as others do. And my next wish is, I would desire you to put away singularity in your judgment and opinions.

Brad. Sir, God forbid that I should stick to any singularity or private judgment in God's religion. Hitherto I have not desired it. I neither do, nor mind at any time to hold any other doctrine than is public and catholic, taking the word catholic as good men do according to God's word.

West. Very well, this is a good day's work. I hope to do you good; and therefore now I shall pray you to write me the heads of those things whereupon you stand in the sacrament, and to send them to me betwixt this and Wednesday next: until which time, yea, until I come to you again, be assured that you are without all peril of death. Of my fidelity I warrant you, therefore away with all doubts and misgivings of your safety.

Brad. Sir, I will write to you the grounds I lean upon in this matter. As for death, if it come, welcome be it; this which you require of me shall be no great hindrance to me therein.

West. You know that St. Augustine was a Manichean, yet was he converted at the length; so have I good hope of you.

Brad. Sir, because I will not flatter you, I would you should flatly know, that I am even settled in the religion wherefore I am condemned.

West. Yea, but if it be not the truth, and you see evident matter to the contrary, will you not then give place?

Brad. God forbid, but that I should always give place to the truth. And I heartily and constantly pray that he will more and more confirm me in it, as he hath done and doth.

West. Yea, but pray with a condition if you be in it already.

Brad. No, sir, I cannot pray so, because I am settled and assured of this truth.

West. Well, as the learned bishop answered St. Augustine's mother, that though he was obstinate, yet the tears of such a mother could not but win her son; so also I hope your prayers, which you offer with tears, cannot but be heard by God, though not as you would, yet as best shall please him. Do you not remember the history that I refer to?

Brad. Yea, Sir, I think it is of St. Ambrose.

West. No, that it is not. I would lay you a wager on the truth of its being St. Augustine. As you are overseen herein, so are you in other things.

Brad. Well, Sir, I will not contend with you for the name. This St. Augustine writeth in his confessions.

West. The people are too much persuaded by you to withstand the queen. Send to me the heads of the doctrine of the supper, and after Wednesday I will come unto you again. Before I depart now I drink to your health.

In the mean time, when Mr. Bradford had written his reasons and arguments, and had sent them to Dr. Weston, soon after, about the 28th of March, there came to the Compter, Dr. Pendleton, and with him Mr. Collier, some time warden of Manchester, and Stephen Bech. After salutations, Dr. Pendleton began to speak to Mr. Bradford, that he was sorry for his trouble. And further, said he, after that I knew you could be content to talk with me I made the more speed, being as ready to do you good, and serve you what I can, as you would wish. To this Bradford answered, "Sir, I remember that once you were, as far as any man might judge, of the religion that I am of at present, and I remember that you have earnestly set forth the same. Gladly, therefore, would I learn of you what thing it was that moved your conscience to alter, and gladly would I see what thing it is that you have seen since which you saw not before. The cause for which I am condemned, which you say you do not know, is no other than transubstantiation, and because I deny that wicked men do receive Christ's body: wherein I would desire you to shew me what reasons, which before you knew not, did move your conscience now to alter. For once, as I said, you were as I am in religion."

Dr. Pendleton, half amazed, began to excuse himself, as though he had not fully denied transubstantiation, although he confessed, that the word was not in scripture. He then made an endless tale of the thing that moved him to alter: but said he would gather all the places which moved him and send him them. And here he desired Mr. Bradford that he might have a copy of that which he had sent to Dr. Weston; which Bradford promised him, and Pendleton soon after went his way.

In the afternoon came Dr. Weston to Bradford; and, after gentle salutations, he desired every man to depart. After that he had thanked Bradford for his writing to him, he showed the same writing which Bradford had sent him, which contained certain reasons against transubstantiation which he had carefully collected from the fathers and the holy scriptures.

Tertullian saith:

That which is former is true; that which is later, false. But the doctrine of transubstantiation is a late doctrine, for it was not defined generally before the council of Lateran, about 1215 years after Christ's coming, under Pope Innocent, the third of that name. Before that time it was free for all men to believe, or not believe it, as the bishop of Durham doth witness in his book of the presence of Christ in his supper, lately published. Therefore the doctrine of transubstantiation is false.

The words of Christ's supper be figurative; the circumstances of the scriptures, the analogy or proportion of the sacraments, and the opinions of all the holy fathers, which were and wrote for the space of 1000 years after Christ's ascension, do teach this: whereupon it follows, that there is no transubstantiation.

The Lord gave to his disciples bread, and called it his body; the scriptures do witness. For he gave that and called it his body, which he took in his hand, whereon he gave thanks; which also he brake, and gave to his disciples, that is to say, bread; as the fathers Irenaeus, Tertullian, Origen, Cyprian, Epiphanius, Augustine, and all the residue which are of antiquity, do affirm: but inasmuch as the substance of bread and wine is another thing than the substance of the body and blood of Christ, it plainly appeareth that there is no transubstantiation.

The bread is no more transubstantiate than the wine; but that the wine is not transubstantiate, St. Matthew and St. Mark reach us: for they witness that Christ said he would drink no more of the fruit of the vine, which was not blood but wine: and therefore it follows, that there is no transubstantiation. Chrysostom upon St. Matthew, and Cyprian do affirm this reason.

The bread in the Lord's supper is not Christ's natural body, but it is his mystical body: for the same Spirit that spake of it, This is my body, said also, For we being many are one bread and one body. But now it is not the mystical body by transubstantiation, and therefore it cannot be his natural body by transubstantiation.

The words spoken over the cup in St. Luke and St. Paul are not so mighty and effectual as to transubstantiate it: for then the cup, or that which is in it, should be transubstantiated into the New Testament: therefore the words spoken over the bread, are not so mighty as to make transubstantiation.

The doctrine which agreeth with those churches which be apostolical mother churches, is to be counted for truth, because it holdeth that which these churches received of the apostles, the apostles received of Christ, and Christ received of God. But it is manifest that the doctrine taught at present by the church of Rome, concerning transubstantiation, doth not agree with the apostolic and mother churches of Greece, of Corinth, of Philippi, Colossia, Thessalonica, and Ephesus, which never taught transubstantiation; yea, it agreeth not with the doctrine of the church of Rome, as it was taught in times past.

After considerable discussion on the preceding, Bradford told Weston that he was still even as he was at the first: and until he should see matter to teach his conscience the contrary, he said he must needs so continue. And so master doctor with most gentle words took his leave for three days. On the 5th of

April, Dr. Weston came again to the Compter; and after much talk he left Bradford, saying, "If I can do you good, I will: hurt you I will not. I am no prince, and therefore cannot promise you life, except you will submit yourself to the definition of the church." Now after his departing came the keeper, master Claydon, and Stephen Bech; and they were very hot with Bradford, and spake with him in such sort as utter enemies, notwithstanding the friendship they both had hitherto pretended. God be with us, and what matter is it who be against us?

Among divers which came to master Bradford in prison, some to dispute and confer, some to give counsel, some to take comfort, and some to visit him, there was a certain gentlewoman's servant, whose mistress had been cruelly afflicted, and miserably handled in her father's house, for not coming to the mass, and like at length to have been pursued to death, had not the Lord delivered her from her father's house. The servant of this gentlewoman coming to master Bradford, and taking him by the hand, said—"God be thanked for you: how do you do?"

Bradford. Well, I thank God. For as men in sailing, which be near to the shore or haven where they would be, would be nearer; even so the nearer I am to God, the nearer I would be. Our quarrel is most just: therefore let us not be afraid. How doth your mistress now?

Servant. Well, God be praised; but she hath been sorer afflicted with her own father and mother, than ever you were with your imprisonment; and yet God hath preserved her, I trust, to his glory.

Brad. I read this day a godly history, written by Basil the Great, of a virtuous woman who was a widow, and named Juletta. She had great lands and many children, and nigh her dwelt a cormorant, who for her virtuous and pious living had great indignation against her, and of malice he took away her lands, so that she was constrained to go to law with him: and in conclusion, the matter came to trial before the judge, who demanded of this tyrant why he wrongfully withheld these lands from this woman? He made answer and said, he might so do, for the woman was disobedient to the king's proceedings: for she would in no wise worship his gods, nor offer sacrifice unto them. Then the judge hearing that, said unto her, 'Woman, if this be true, thou art not only likely to lose thy land, but also thy life, unless that thou worship our gods, and do sacrifice unto them.' This good woman hearing that, stepped forth to the judge, and said—'Is there no remedy but either to worship your false gods, or else to lose my lands and life? Then farewell suit, farewell lands, farewell children, farewell friends, yea, and farewell life too: and in respect to the true honour of the everlasting God, farewell all.' And with that saying the judge committed her to prison, and afterwards she suffered most cruel death: and being brought to the place of execution, she exhorted all women to be strong and constant. For she said they were redeemed with as dear a price as men. For although they were made of the rib of the man, yet they were all of his flesh; so that also in the case and trial of their faith towards God, they ought to be as strong. And thus died she constantly not fearing death. I pray you tell your mistress this story.

John Bradford continued in this prison until the month of July, in such labours and sufferings as he always had sustained. But when the time of his death was come, he was suddenly conveyed out of the Compter, in the night season, to Newgate; and from thence he was carried the next morning to Smithfield, where he, constantly abiding in the same truth of God which before he had confessed, earnestly exhorting the people to repent and to return to Christ, and sweetly comforting the godly young man who was burnt with him, cheerfully ended his painful life, to live with Christ.

With John Bradford was burnt one John Leaf, an apprentice to Humfrey Gawdy, tallow-chandler, of the parish of Christ-Church in London, of the age of nineteen years and above, born at Kirby-Moorside, in the county of York. Upon the Friday next before Palm-Sunday he was committed to the Compter in Bread-street, by an alderman of the ward where he dwelt. Afterwards, on coming to examination before Bonner, he gave a firm and Christian testimony of his doctrine and profession, answering to such articles as were objected to him. First, as touching his belief and faith in the sacrament of the altar, he answered, that after the words of consecration, spoken by the priest over the bread and wine, there was not the very true and natural body and blood of Christ in substance; and further did hold and believe, that the said sacrament of the altar, as it is now called, used and believed in this realm of England, is idolatrous and abominable; and also said further, that he believed, that after the words of consecration spoken by the priest over the material bread and wine, there is not the self-same substance of Christ's body and blood there contained; but bread and wine as it was before: and further said that he believed, that when the priest delivereth the said material bread and wine to the communicants, he delivereth it but only material bread and wine; and the communicants do receive the same in remembrance of Christ's death and passion, and spiritually, in faith, they receive Christ's body and blood, but not under the forms of bread and wine. He also affirmed, that he believed auricular confession not to be necessary to be made unto a priest, for it is no point of soul-health; neither that the priest hath any authority given him by the Scripture to absolve and remit any sin.

Upon these his answers and testimony of his faith, he at that time being dismissed, was bid the Monday next, being the 10th of June, to appear again in the said place, there and then to hear the sentence of his condemnation. At this time the bishop, propounding the said articles again to him as before, essaying by all manner of ways to revoke him to his own trade, that is, from truth to error, notwithstanding all his persuasions, threats, and promises, found him the same man still, so planted upon the sure rock of truth, that no words nor deeds of men could remove him.

Then the bishop, after many words to and fro, at last asked him if he had been master Rogers's scholar? To whom John Leaf answered again, granting him so to be; and that he did believe in the same doctrine of the said Rogers, and in the doctrine of bishop Hooper, Cardmaker, and others of their opinion, who of late were burned for the testimony of Christ, and that he would die in that doctrine that they died for: and on the bishop moving him again to return to the unity of the church, he with great courage answered him in these words:—"My lord, you call mine opinion heresy; but it is the true light of the word of God." And again, repeating the same, he professed that he would never forsake his staid and well-grounded opinion, while the breath should be in his body. Whereupon the bishop, being too weak either to refute his sentence or to remove his constancy, proceeded consequently to read the popish sentence of cruel condemnation: whereby this godly and constant young man, being committed to the secular power of the sheriffs there present, was then adjudged, and not long after suffered with master Bradford, confirming with his death that which he had spoken and professed in his life.

It is reported of the said John Leaf, by one that was in the Compter at the same time, and saw the thing, that after his examinations before the bishop, when two bells were sent unto him in the Compter in Bread-street, the one containing a recantation, the other his confessions, to know to which of them he would put his hand, first hearing the bill of recantation read unto him, (because he could not read nor write himself,) that he refused. And when the other was read to him, which he well liked of, instead of a pen he took a pin, and so pricking his hand, sprinkled the blood upon the said bill, willing the reader thereof to show the bishop that he had sealed the same bill with his blood already.

When Bradford and Leaf came to the stake in Smithfield to be burned, master Bradford lying prostrate on the one side, and John Leaf on the other side, they lay flat on their faces, praying to themselves the space of a minute. Then one of the sheriffs said to master Bradford, "Arise, and make an end; for the press of the people is great."

At that word they both stood up; and then master Bradford took a fagot in his hand, and kissed it, and so likewise the stake. And when he had so done, he desired of the sheriffs that his servant might have his raiment. "For," said he, "I have nothing else to give him: and besides that, he is a poor man." And the sheriff said he should have it. And so forthwith master Bradford did put off his raiment, and went to the stake; and holding up his hands, and casting his countenance up towards heaven, he said thus: "O England, England, repent thee of thy sins, repent thee of thy sins! Beware of idolatry, beware of false antichrists, take heed they do not deceive you." And as he was speaking these words the sheriff bade tie his hands, if he would not be quiet. "O master sheriff," said Bradford, "I am quiet: God forgive you this, master sheriff." One of the officers which made the fire, hearing master Bradford so speaking to the sheriff said, "If you have no better learning than that, you are but a fool, and were best hold your peace." To the which words master Bradford gave no answer; but asked all the world forgiveness, and forgave all the world, and prayed the people to pray for him, and turned his head unto the young man that suffered with him, and said, "Be of good comfort, brother; for we shall have a merry supper with the Lord this night:" and so spake no more words that any man did hear, but, embracing the reeds, he said, "Strait is the way, and narrow is the gate, that leadeth to eternal salvation, and few there be that find it." Thus they both ended their mortal lives, most like two lambs, without any alteration of their countenance, being void of all fear, hoping to obtain the price of the game they had long run at; to the which I beseech Almighty God happily to conduct us, through the merits of Jesus Christ our Lord and Saviour. Amen.

This godly Bradford and heavenly martyr, during his imprisonment wrote sundry comfortable treatises, and many godly letters: some to the city of London, Cambridge, Walden, Lancashire, and Cheshire, and divers to his private friends. By which letters it appears how this godly man occupied his time in prison, what special zeal he bare to Christ's church, how earnestly he admonished all men, how tenderly he comforted the heavy-hearted and how faithfully he confirmed those whom he had taught. The first letter (from which the following is an extract) was addressed to his mother.

I am at this present in prison, (sure enough for starting,) to confirm that I have preached unto you: as I am ready, I thank God, with my life and blood to seal the same, if God vouchsafe me worthy of that honour. For, good mother and brethren, it is a most special benefit of God, to suffer for his name's sake and gospel, as now I do: I heartily thank God for it, and am sure that with him I shall be partaker of his glory; as Paul saith, "If we suffer with him, we shall reign with him." Therefore be not faint-hearted; but rather rejoice, at the least for my sake, which now am in the right and high way to heaven: for by many afflictions we must enter into the kingdom of heaven. Now will God make known his children. When the wind doth not blow, then cannot a man know the wheat from the chaff; but when the blast cometh, then flieth away the chaff, but the wheat remaineth, and is so far from being hurt, that by the wind it is more cleansed from the chaff, and known to be wheat. God, when it is cast into the fire, is more precious; so are God's children by the cross of affliction.

Fear God, stick to his word, though all the world swerve from it. Die you must once, and when or how you cannot tell. Die, therefore, with Christ; suffer for serving him truly and after his word; for sure may we be, that of all deaths it is most to be desired to die for God's sake. This is the most safe kind of dying: we cannot doubt but that we shall go to heaven, if we die for his name's sake. And that you shall die for his name's sake, God's word will warrant you, if you stick to that which God by me hath taught you. You shall see that I speak as I think: for, by God's grace, I will drink before you of this cup, if I be put to it.

The second letter was addressed "to all that profess the gospel and true doctrine of Christ in the city of London." The following is an extract:

Cast your care on the Lord, knowing he careth for you. Depend on the providence of God, not only when you have means to help you, but when you have no means, yea, when all means are against you. Give him this honour, which of all other things he requireth at your hands—to become his children through belief in Christ his blessed Son. When you fall he will put his hand beneath you. Before you call he heareth you. Out of all evil he will finally deliver you, and bring you to his eternal joy. I would gladly have given here my body to be burned for the confirmation of the true doctrine I have taught unto you. But that my country must have; therefore I pray you take in good part this signification of my good will towards all of you. Impute the want herein to time and trouble. Pardon my mine offensive and negligent behaviour when I was amongst you. With me repent and labour to amend. Continue in the truth which I have truly taught unto you, by preaching in all places where I have come; God's name, therefore, be praised. Confess Christ when you be called, whatsoever cometh therefrom, and the God of peace be with us all, Amen.

The third letter, addressed to the University of Cambridge, we insert at full length. It is an admirable specimen of faithful remonstrance and reasoning.

To all that love the Lord Jesus and his true doctrine, being in the university and town of Cambridge, John Bradford, a most unworthy servant of the Lord, now not only imprisoned, but also condemned for the same doctrine, wisheth grace, peace, and mercy, with increase of all godliness from God the Father of all mercy, through the bloody passion of our Saviour Jesus Christ, by the lively working of the Holy Spirit for ever, Amen.

Although I look hourly when I should be had to the stake, and although the charge over me is great and strict, yet having by the providence of God secretly pen and ink, I could not but signify unto you my solicitude which I have for all of you in the Lord, though not as I would, yet as I may. You have often and openly heard the truth disputed and preached, that it is needless to do any more but only to put you in remembrance of the same; but hitherto you have not heard it confirmed, and as it were sealed up, as now you do and shall hear by me, that is, by my death and burning. For albeit I have deserved—through my uncleanness, hypocrisy, avarice, vainglory, idleness, unthankfulness, and carnality, whereof I accuse myself, to my confusion before the world, that before God through Christ I might, as my assured hope is I shall, find mercy—eternal death and hell fire, much more than this affliction and fire prepared for me: yet my dearly beloved, it is not these, or any of these things, for which the prelates do persecute me, but God's verity and truth. Yea, even Christ himself is the only cause for which I am now condemned, and shall be burned as a heretic, because I will not grant the antichrist of Rome to be Christ's vicar general and supreme head of his church here, and every where upon earth, by God's ordinance; and because I will not grant such corporeal, real, and carnal presence of Christ's body and blood in the sacrament, as doth transubstantiate the substance of bread and wine, and is received by the wicked. Also I am excommunicated and accounted as a dead member of Christ's church, as a rotten branch, and therefore shall be cast into the fire.

Therefore you ought heartily to rejoice with me, and to give thanks for me, that God the eternal Father hath vouchsafed our mother to bring up any child in whom it would please him to magnify his holy name as he doth, and I hope for his mercy and truth's sake, will do in me and by me. Oh, what such benefit upon earth can it be, as that I who deserved death by reason of my sins, should be delivered to a demonstration, a testification, and confirmation of God's verity and truth? Thou, my mother the university, hast not only had the truth of God's word plainly manifested unto thee by reading, disputing, and preaching publicly and privately; but now to make thee altogether excuseless, and as it were, almost to sin against the Holy Ghost, if thou put to thy helping hand with the Romish rout to suppress the verity, thou hast my life and blood as a seal to confirm thee, if thou wilt be confirmed: else to confound thee, and to bear witness against thee, if thou wilt take part with the prelates and clergy, which now fill up the measure of their fathers who slew the prophets and apostles, that all the righteous blood from Abel to Bradford, shed upon earth, may be required at their hands.

Of this therefore I thought good before my death, as time and liberty would suffer me, to admonish thee, good mother, and my sister the town, that you would call to mind from whence you are fallen, and study to do the first works. You know these matters of the Romish supremacy, and the antichristian transubstantiation, whereby Christ's supper is overthrown, his priesthood evacuated, his sacrifice frustrated, the ministry of his word unplaced, repentance repelled, faith fainted, piety extinguished, the mass maintained, idolatry supported, and all impiety cherished: you know, I say, that these opinions are not only beside God's word, but even directly against whom you cannot prevail.

Therefore for the tender mercy of Christ, in his bowels and blood I beseech you to take Christ's eye-salve to anoint your eyes, that you may see what you do, and have done, in admitting, as I hear you have admitted, yea, alas! authorized, the Romish rottenness which once you utterly expelled. O be not, "The dog returned to his own vomit; the sow that was washed returned to her wallowing in the mire." "Beware, lest Satan enter in with seven other spirits, and then the last shall be worse than the first." "It had been better ye had never known the truth, than after knowledge to run from it." Ah, woe to this world and the things therein, which hath now so wrought with you. Oh that ever the dirt of the devil should daub up the eye of the realm! for thou, O mother, art as the eye of the realm. If thou be light and shine, all the body shall fare the better: but if thy light be darkness, alas, how great will the darkness be! What is man, whose breath is in his nostrils, that thou shouldst thus be afraid of him!

Oh what is honour and life here! Bubbles. What is glory in this world, but shame! Why art thou afraid to carry Christ's cross? Wilt thou come into his kingdom, and not drink of his cup? Dost thou not know Rome to be Babylon? Dost thou not know that as the old Babylon had the children of Judah in captivity, so hath this Rome the true Judah, that is, the confessors of Christ? Dost thou not know, that as destruction happened unto it, so shall it do unto this? And thinkest thou that God will not deliver his people now when the time is come, as he did then? Hath not God commanded his people to come out from her? Hast thou forgotten the woe that Christ threateneth to offence-givers? Wilt thou not remember, that it were better that a mill-stone were hanged about thy neck and thou thrown into the sea, than that thou shouldst offend the little ones?

And alas, how hast thou offended! Yea, and how dost thou still offend! Wilt thou consider things according to the outward shew? Was not the synagogue more seemly and like to be the true church, than the simple flock of Christ's disciples? Hath not the whore of Babylon more costly array, and rich apparel, externally to set forth herself, than the homely housewife of Christ? Where is the beauty of the king's daughter, the church of Christ? Without or within? Doth not David say, within? O remember that as they are happy which are not offended at Christ, so are they happy which are not offended at his poor church. Can the pope and his prelates mean honestly, which make so much of the wife, and so little of the husband? The church they magnify, but Christ they contemn. If this church were an honest woman, (that is, Christ's wife) except they would make much of her husband, Christ and his word, she would not be made much of by them.

When Christ and his apostles were upon the earth, who was most like to be the true church, they or the prelates, bishops and synagogue? If a man should have followed custom, unity, antiquity, or the greater part, should not Christ and his company have been cast out of doors? Therefore Christ saith, "Search the scriptures." Good mother, shall the servant be above his master? Shall we look for better entertainment at the hands of the world, than Christ and his dear disciples found? In Noah's time who was taken for the church, poor Noah and his family, or all the others that were destroyed by the flood? Who was taken for God's church in Sodom, righteous Lot, or the others? And doth not Christ say, "As it was then, so shall it go now towards the coming of the Son of man?" What meaneth Christ when he saith, iniquity shall have the upper hand? Doth not he likewise say, that charity shall wax cold? And we plainly see the greatest scarcity of it in those, who would now be taken for Christ's true catholic church. All that fear God in this realm can tell more of this than I can write.

Therefore, dear mother, receive some admonition of one of thy poor children, now going to be burnt to ashes for the testimony of Jesus. Come again to God's truth; come out of Babylon; confess Christ and his true doctrine; repent of what is past, make amends by declaring thy repentance by the fruits. Remember the reading and preaching of God's prophet, the true preacher, Martin Bucer. Call to mind the threatenings of God against impenitent sinners. Let the exile of Leaver, Pilkington, Grindal, Haddon, Horn, Scory, Ponet, and others, awake and strengthen thee. Let the imprisonment of thy dear sons, Cranmer, Ridley, and Latimer, move thee. Consider the martyrdom of thy intimate friends, Rogers, Saunders, and Taylor. And now cast not away my poor admonition, that am now going to be burnt and to receive the like crown of glory with my fellows. Take to heart God's calling by us. Be not as Pharaoh was, that it may not happen unto thee as it did unto him. What is that? Hardness of heart. And what then? Destruction eternally both of body and soul. Ah, therefore, good mother, awake, awake, repent, repent, and make haste to turn to the Lord. For otherwise it shall be more easy for Sodom and Gomorrah in the day of judgment than for thee. O harden not your hearts; O stop not your ears to-day in hearing God's voice, though it be by a most unworthy messenger. O fear the Lord, for his anger is begun to kindle. Even now the axe is laid to the root of the tree.

You know I prophesied truly before the sweating sickness came, what would come, if you repented not your carnal preaching. And now I tell you before I depart hence, that the ears of men shall tingle to hear the vengeance of God that will fall upon you all, both town and university, if you repent not, if you leave not your idolatry, if you turn not speedily to the Lord, if you still be ashamed of Christ's truth which you know.

O, Perne, repent; O, Thompson, repent! O, doctors, bachelors, and masters, repent! O, mayor, aldermen, and town-dwellers, repent, repent, repent, that you may escape the approaching vengeance of the Lord! Rend your hearts and make haste to come unto the Lord. Let us all say, "We have sinned, we have done wickedly, we have not hearkened to thy voice, O Lord. Deal not with us after our deserts, but be merciful unto our iniquities, for they are great. O pardon our offences. In thine anger remember thy mercy. Turn us unto thee, O Lord God of hosts, for the glory of thy name's sake. Spare us and be merciful unto us. Let not the wicked people say, Where is now their God? O for thine own sake, for thy name's sake, deal mercifully with us. Turn thyself unto us, and us unto thee, and we shall praise thy name for ever."

If in this sort, my dearly beloved, in heart and mouth we come unto our Father, and prostrate ourselves before the throne of his grace, then surely we shall find mercy. Then shall the Lord look tenderly upon us, for his mercy's sake in Christ; then shall we hear him speak peace unto his people. For he is gracious and merciful, of great pity and compassion: he cannot be chiding for ever: his anger cannot last long to the penitent. Though we weep in the morning, yet at night we shall have our sorrow to cease. For he is merciful, and hath no pleasure in the death of a sinner: he would rather have him turn from his wickedness and live.

Oh turn ye now and repent, yet once again, I humbly beseech you, and then the kingdom of heaven shall draw nigh. The eye hath not seen, the ear hath not heard, nor is the heart of man able to conceive the joys prepared for us, if we repent, amend our lives, and heartily turn to the Lord. But if you repent not, but be as ye are, and go forwards with the wicked, following the fashion of the world, the Lord will lead you on with wicked doers, you shall perish in your wickedness, your blood will be upon your own heads, your parts shall be with hypocrites, where shall be weeping and gnashing of teeth; you shall be cast from the face of the Lord for ever and ever; eternal shame, sorrow, woe, and misery, shall be both in body and soul to you world without end. Oh, therefore, right dear to me in the Lord, turn you, turn you, repent you, repent you, amend, amend your lives, depart from evil, do good, follow peace, and pursue it. Come out from Babylon, cast off the works of darkness, put on Christ, confess his truth, be not ashamed of his gospel, prepare yourselves for the cross, drink of God's cup before it come to the dregs, and then shall I with you and for you, rejoice in the day of judgment, which is at hand; and therefore prepare yourselves

251

thereto, I heartily beseech you. And thus I take my farewell for ever of you in this present life, mine own dear hearts in the Lord. The Lord of mercy be with us all, and give us a joyful and sure meeting in his kingdom, Amen.

Your own in the Lord for ever,

JOHN BRADFORD.

Mr. Bradford's fourth letter was addressed to the people of Lancashire and Cheshire, among whom he had laboured with fidelity and success. The fifth he wrote to the inhabitants of Walden in Essex, now generally called Saffron Walden, where he had many friends, whom he earnestly exhorted to be "steadfast and unmoveable, always abounding in the work of the Lord." The sixth he calls a letter to his loving brethren, their wives, and families; but the initials only of those brethren appear. The seventh he addressed to a friend named Erkinalde Rawlins, and this contains a passage not to be omitted. "You have cause to rejoice for those days because they are days of trial, wherein you yourselves and all true believers shall know that you belong not unto the world, but are the favourites and friends of God. Before these days came, Lord God! how many thought themselves in God's bosom, and so were taken and would be taken by the world. But now we see whose they are. For whom we obey his servants we be. If we obey the world, then are we the world's, but if we obey God then are we God's; which thing these days have declared to all of us better than we ever knew it before."

The eighth letter of this devoted saint was addressed to a suffering lady of the reformed faith, named Warcup; to whom the thirty-fifth letter was also inscribed, and to whose husband, with herself and some mutual friends of the name of Wilkinson, he addressed the thirteenth in the collection. From the thirty-fifth an extract will appear in due order; at present we must return to the ninth, inscribed to his fellow sufferer Mr. Laurence Saunders, who was then in the Marshalsea prison, and containing allusions to Dr. Taylor and Mr. Philpot, which we have no means at hand of explaining. In conclusion he says, "God, our Father and gracious Lord, make perfect the good work he hath begun in us. He will do it, my brother, my dear brother, whom I have in my inward bowels to live and die with." The tenth letter is also addressed to Lawrence Saunders, and contains little else than a repetition of the preceding.

The eleventh letter is addressed "to my dear Fathers, Dr. Cranmer, Dr. Ridley, and Mr. Latimer;" and is here given almost entire:

Jesus Immanuel. My dear fathers in the Lord, I beseech God our sweet Father through Christ, to make perfect the good he hath begun in us all. I had thought that every one of your staves had stood next the door, but now it is otherwise perceived. Our dear brother Rogers hath broken the ice valiantly, as this day, I think, or to-morrow at the uttermost, hearty Hooper, sincere Saunders, and trusty Taylor, end their course, and receive their crown. The next am I, which hourly look for the porter to open me the gates after them, to enter into the desired rest. God forgive me mine unthankfulness for this exceeding great mercy, that amongst so many thousands it pleaseth his mercy to choose me to be one, in whom he will suffer. For although it be most true, that I justly suffer, (for I have been a great hypocrite, and a grievous sinner, the Lord pardon me,) yet he hath done it, he hath done it indeed; yet what evil hath he done? Christ whom the prelates persecute, his verity which they hate in me, hath done no evil, nor deserved death. Therefore ought I most heartily to rejoice of this tender kindness of the Lord towards me, which useth a remedy for my sin as a testimonial of his covenant, to his glory, to my everlasting comfort, to the edifying of his church, and to the overthrowing of antichrist and his kingdom.

Out of prison in haste, looking for the tormentor,
February 8th, 1555
JOHN BRADFORD.

The fourteenth letter was written to Sir James Hales, then a prisoner, like his estimable correspondent for the truth as it is in Jesus Christ. Mr. Bradford was, as he says, "unknown to him both by face and name;" yet he knew him to suffer for righteousness' sake, and therefore would not content himself with calling daily to God in his behalf. His style of writing in this letter is somewhat chastened, yet characteristic, as the following extract will shew. "Look, good master Hales, on your vocation: not many judges, not many knights, not many landed and rich men, hath God chose to suffer for his sake as he hath done you. Certainly, I dare say, you think not so of yourself, as though God were bound to prefer you, or had need of you; but rather attribute this as all things to the free mercy of God in Christ. Being a wise man you do judge of things wisely; that is concerning this your cross, you judge of it not after the world, which is the great master of error; nor after the judgment of the world's wisdom, which is foolishness to faith; nor after the present sense, to which it seemeth not to be joyous but grievous; but after the word of God, which tells you that the cross is the path way to glory, felicity, and heaven."

In the fifteenth letter the writer conjures Dr. Hill, a protestant physician of celebrity in that day, to abide in the true faith for which he had begun to suffer, and to fear God as the best preservative to the fear of man. In the sixteenth, he entreats a pious gentlewoman, whose initials only he gives us, to make God's glory shine in all her words and works. The eighteenth is addressed to a faithful and pious woman, more exposed to inward than outward distress, and to whom, in a long and excellent letter, he thus writes, "Do you not hunger and thirst after righteousness? and I pray you, saith not he who cannot lie, that happy are such? How should God wipe away the tears from your eyes in heaven, if now on earth you shed no tears? How could heaven be a place of rest, if on earth you find it? How could you desire to be at home, if in your journey you find no difficulty, distress, or grief? How could you be made like unto Christ in joy, if in sorrow you never sobbed with him? If you will sit at Christ's table in his kingdom, you must first abide with him in his temptations. If you will drink of his cup of glory, despise not his cup of ignomy. If you were a market sheep, you should go in more fat and grassy pasture. If you were for the fair, you should be stall fed, and want no wealth; but because you are God's own occupying, therefore you must pasture on the bleak and barren heath, abiding the storms and tempests that he may send down upon that and upon you."

Most of the martyrs of this melancholy reign were more or less comforted, and some of them wholly supported as to their mortal frame, by the noble lady Vane. Several of the letters of Mr. Philpot and Mr. Trehern were addressed to her. She was also one of good Mr. Bradford's correspondents, and to her the nineteenth and twentieth and twenty-ninth letters in this collection were inscribed. They chiefly relate to certain important and intricate queries which she had in writing or in conversation proposed to him; but are not of sufficient importance to merit the preference of insertion.

In the twenty-third letter he writes to some persons, whose names are not mentioned, but of whose piety he has a good opinion, while what he says implies some apprehension of their fainting in the day of final trial. In the twenty-fourth, a class of rather different persons, whose integrity he suspects, and of consequence stands in great doubt of their stability even in an outward profession of just sentiments, are faithfully admonished in the following terms. "You promised to fight under Christ's standard. You learned his cross before you learned your alphabet. Go forward then, and pay your vows to the Lord. Fight like men, and valiant men too under the standard of Christ. Take up the cross and follow your Master unto death—as your brethren Hooper, Rogers, Taylor, and Saunders, have already done; and as now your brethren Cranmer, Latimer, Ridley, Farrar, and Bradford, are ready to do."

The twenty-fifth letter was addressed to his "good brother" John Careless, then a prisoner in the King's Bench. It was in answer to one of which he says— "I never received so much consolation by any thing since I came into prison as I have by your last letter." It would appear that either Bradford had been too unmindful of this friend, or was in a state of depression when he wrote very unusual with him; for notwithstanding is the letter very brief, but almost full of misgiving and self-accusation. It concludes thus, "It is not one or two drops that maketh the stone hollow; but the perpetual dropping; so if with hearty prayer for them, and by good example gently working upon them, we may at length see the operation of God, we shall in the end rejoice. I beseech God to make perfect all the good he hath begun in us all."

Letters the twenty-sixth and seventh are addressed to Mr. John Hall and his wife, then prisoners in Newgate, and contain, with nothing remarkable, his usual flow of consolatory reflection and benevolent admonition and advice. The twenty-eighth is in answer to a woman who desired to know of him if she might be present at the popish matins, provided she were absent from the mass? His reasons against her proposals are—that they were idolatrous, and therefore sinful—and that her example might greatly influence and injure others, for whom she would be called to judgment.

The thirtieth letter was addressed to the sheriff of Coventry, Mr. Richard Hopkins, who to avoid danger and preserve unmolested the observance of the true faith and worship, fled with his family to Basle, where he remained until

Mary's death. In the thirty-second letter there is this admirable passage, in answer to the inquiry of a friend, how he was to reply to his adversaries? "When you shall come before the magistrates, to give a reason for the hope that is in you, do it with all reverence and simplicity: and if you are afraid of their power and cruelty, set before you the example of the good father Moses; for he set the invisible God before the eyes of his faith, and with them he looked upon his glorious majesty and power, as with the eyes of his body he saw Pharaoh and all his frightful terrors. So do you, my dearly beloved, let your inward eyes give light unto you, that while you are before the magistrates, so and much more are you and they present before the face of God, who will give you such wisdom and strength as your enemies will be amazed at."

The thirty-fourth is a remarkably serious and spiritual letter addressed to Mr. George Eaton. In the thirty-sixth he strongly urges a young lady, persecuted by her parents for not going to mass, to be steadfast in the true faith, and to reject with firmness and perseverance the papal system. The thirty-seventh is a letter of warm and honest thanks to all the friends from whom he had received comfort and relief during his long imprisonment. The good man's hour was now drawing near, when he fully apprehended, or rather anticipated, that he should pass through the fire of earth to the felicity of heaven. Letters forty-one and forty-two are to his mother, intimating this expectation as likely soon to be fulfilled. The latter is his final farewell to his venerable parent, and thus expresses his perfect confidence and calmness in the almost immediate view of death. "My most dear mother, I heartily pray and beseech you to be thankful for me to God, who now taketh me unto himself. I die not as a criminal, but as a witness of Christ, the truth of whose gospel I have hitherto confessed, and now am willing to confirm by fire. I have nothing to give you, or to leave behind me for you; only I pray God my Father, for Christ's sake, to bless you and to keep you from all evil. May he make you patient and thankful that he will take the fruit of your womb to witness his truth; wherein I confess to the whole world that I die, and depart this life in hope of a much better, which I look for at the hands of God my Father, through the merits of his Son Jesus Christ. Thus, my dear mother, I take my last farewell of you in this life, beseeching the Almighty and eternal Father by Christ, to grant us to meet in the life to come, where we shall give him continual thanks and praise for ever and ever, Amen." The forty-third letter, the last but one in the collection, was addressed to the queen, her council, and the whole parliament. Let those who but imagine it possible that John Bradford should have made these high powers his resort at last in hope of forgiveness, or, still more, should have attempted to conciliate them by flattery, or propitiate them by compromise and recantation, read the letter, and confess their suspicion, or fear, or whatever else it might be, unfavourable to his pre-eminent reputation for courage and constancy, to have been both premature itself and an offense against him.

In most humble wise complaineth unto your majesty and honours, a poor subject, persecuted for the confession of Christ's verity; which verity deserveth at your hands to be maintained and defended, as the thing by which you reign, and have your honours and authorities. Although we that be professors, and, through the grace of God, the constant confessors of the same, are, as it were, the out-sweepings of the world; yet I say, the verity itself is a thing not unworthy for your ears to hear, for your eyes to see, and for your hands to handle, help, and succour as the Lord hath made you able, and placed you where you are for the same purpose. Your highness and honours ought to know, that there is no innocency in words or deeds, where it is enough and sufficient only to accuse. It behoveth kings, queens, and all that be in authority, to know, that in the administration of their kingdoms they are God's ministers. It behoveth them to know, that they are not kings, but plain tyrants, who reign not to this end, that they may serve and set forth God's glory after true knowledge; and therefore it is required of them that they would be wise, and suffer themselves to kiss their Sovereign, lest they perish; as all those potentates, with their principalities and dominions, cannot long prosper, but perish indeed, if they and their kingdoms be not ruled with the scepter of God, that is, with his word; which whoso honoureth not, honoureth not God; and they that honour not the Lord, the Lord will not honour them, but bring them into contempt, and at length take his own cause, which he hath chiefly committed to them to care for, into his own hands, and so overthrow them, and set up his own truth gloriously: the people also perishing with the princes, where the word of prophecy is wanting, much more is suppressed, as it is now in this realm of England, over which the eyes of the Lord are set to destroy it, your highness and all your honours, if in time you look not better to your office and duties herein, and not suffer yourselves to be slaves and hangmen to antichrist and his prelates, who have already brought your highness and honours in the mind to let Barabbas loose, and to hang up Christ. This by the grace and help of God I shall make apparent, if first it would please your excellent majesty, and all your honours, to take to heart God's doctrine, which rather through the malice of the pharisees, I mean the bishops and prelates, than your consciences, is oppressed; and not for our contemptible and execrable state in the world to pass the less of it. For this doctrine is higher, and of more honour and majesty than all the whole world. It standeth invincible above all power, being not our doctrine, but the doctrine of the ever-living God, and of his Christ, whom the Father hath ordained king, to have dominion from sea to sea, and from the river unto the end of the world. And truly so he doth and will reign, that he will shake all the earth with his iron and brazen power, with his golden and silver brightness, only by the rod of his mouth, to shivers, in such a manner as though they were pots of clay, according to what the prophets write of the magnificence of his kingdom. And thus much for the doctrine, and your duties to hearken, to propagate, and defend the same.

But now will our adversaries mainly cry out against us, because no man be admitted once to speak against them, that we pretend falsely the doctrine and word of God, calling us the most wicked contemners of it, and heretics, schismatics, traitors, &c. All which their sayings, how malicious and false they are, though I might refer to that which is written by those men whose works

they have condemned, and all that retain any of them, publicly by proclamation;
yet here will I occasion your majesty and honours by this my writing, to see that
it is far otherwise than they report of us. God our Father, for his holy name's
sake, direct my pen to be his instrument to put into your eyes, ears, and hearts,
that which most may make to his glory, in the safeguard of your souls and
bodies, and preservation of the whole realm. Amen.

In the month of May before, mention was made of certain letters directed
from the king and queen to Bonner. Besides which letters, certain others had
been directed a little before from the council to the said bishop; by occasion
of which letters. Bonner not long after caused a certain declaration to be made
unto the people at Paul's cross, by Dr. Chedsey, to purge himself from the
general suspicion of cruelty, which was spread abroad of him among the common
people. The words of which declaration were in part as follow:

And whereas by these letters, coming from the king's and queen's majesties, it
appeareth that their majesties do charge my lord bishop of London, and the rest
of the bishops, with remissness and negligence in instructing the people infected
with heresy, if they will be taught, and in punishing them if they will be
obstinate and wilful, ye shall understand that my lord bishop of London, for his
part, offereth himself ready to do therein his duty to the uttermost:—and that he
will travail and take pains with all that be of his jurisdiction for their
amendment; and sorry he is that any are in prison for any such matter. And he
willed me to tell you, that he is not so cruel or hasty to send men to prison as
some be—slanderous and wilful to do naught, and lay their faults on other men's
shoulders.

CHAPTER EIGHTEEN

History and Martyrdom of Bishop Ridley and Bishop Latimer

On the 16th of October, 1555, those two pillars of Christ's church, Dr. Nicholas Ridley, bishop of London, and Mr. Hugh Latimer, some time bishop of Worcester, were burnt in one fire at Oxford. Men ever memorable for their piety, learning, and incomparable ornaments and gifts of grace, joined with no less commendable sincerity of life.

Dr. Ridley was born in the county of Northumberland, and was descended from a most respectable family. He received the rudiments of his education at Newcastle; and, when a child, discovered great promptness in learning. From Newcastle he was removed to the university of Cambridge, where in a short time he became so famous, that for his singular aptness, he was called to higher functions and offices of the university, by degrees pertaining thereunto, and was at length placed at the head of Pembroke-hall, and there made doctor of divinity. After this, departing from thence he travailed to Paris, and at his return was made chaplain to king Henry VIII and promoted afterwards to the bishopric of Rochester, and from thence, in king Edward's days, translated to the more important bishopric of London.

In his several offices he so diligently applied himself by preaching and teaching the true and wholesome doctrine of Christ that no good child was more singularly loved by his dear parents, than he by his flock and diocese. Every holiday and Sunday he preached in one place or other, except he were otherwise hindered by weighty affairs and business; and to his sermons the people resorted in great numbers, swarming about him like bees; and so faithfully did his life portray his doctrines, that even his very enemies could not reprove him in anything. His learning, moreover, was superior, his memory was great, and he had attained such reading withal, that he deserved to be compared to the best men of his age, as his works, sermons, and sundry disputations in both the universities well testified. He was also wise of counsel, deep of wit, and very politic in all things doings. He was anxious to gain the papists from their erroneous opinions, and sought by gentleness to win them to the truth, as his gentleness and courteous treatment of Dr. Heath, who was prisoner in his house a whole year, sufficiently proved. In fine, he was in all points so good, pious, and spiritual a man, that England never saw his superior.

He was comely in his person, and well proportioned. He took all things in good part, bearing no malice nor rancor against any one, but straightways forgetting all injuries and offences done against him. He was very kind and faithful to his relations; and yet not bearing with them any otherwise than right would require, giving them always for general rule, yea to his own brother and sister, that they doing evil should look for nothing at his hand, but should be as strangers and aliens to him, and that to be his brother and sister in deed and in truth, they must be children of God, disciples of Christ, and live towards all men in peace and love.

He used all kinds of ways to mortify himself, and was much given to prayer and contemplation: for duly every morning, as soon as he was dressed, he went to his chamber, and there upon his knees prayed for half an hour; which being done, immediately he went to his study where he continued until ten o'clock, and then came to the common prayer daily used in his house. These being done he went to dinner; where he talked little, except where occasion required, and then it was sober, discreet, and wise, and sometimes merry if reasonable cause allowed and justified it. The dinner done, which was not very long, he used to sit an hour, or thereabouts, talking, or playing at chess: he then returned to his study, and there would continue, except visitors or business abroad prevented him, until five o'clock, when he would come to common prayer, as in the forenoon; which being finished, he went to supper, behaving himself there as at his dinner before. After supper he recreated himself again at chess, after which he would return again to his study; continuing there until eleven o'clock at night, which was his common hour of going to bed, after saying his prayers upon his knees as in the morning when he rose. When at his manor of Fulham, he used to read daily a lecture to his family at the common prayer, beginning at the Acts of the Apostles, and so going through all the epistles of St. Paul, giving to every man that could read a New Testament, rewarding them also with money, for learning by heart certain principal chapters; being marvelously careful over his family, that they might be a pattern of all virtue and honesty to others. In short, as he was godly and virtuous himself, so nothing but virtue and godliness reigned in his house, feeding them with the food of our Saviour Jesus Christ.

The following is a striking instance of the benevolence of his temper, shewn to Mrs. Bonner, mother of Dr. Bonner, bishop of London. When at his manor of Fulham he always sent for Mrs. Bonner, who dwelt in a house adjoining his own, to dinner and supper, with Bonner's sister. She was always placed in the chair at the head of the table, being as gently treated and welcomed as his own mother, and he would never have her displaced from her seat, although the king's council had been present; saying, when any of them were there, "By your lordship's favor, this place of right and custom is for my mother Bonner." How well he was recompensed for this singular kindness and gentle pity afterwards at the hands of Dr. Bonner, is too well known. For who afterwards was a greater enemy to Dr. Ridley than Dr. Bonner? Who went more about to seek his destruction than he? Recommencing his gentleness with extreme cruelty; as well appeared by the severity against Dr. Ridley's own sister and her husband: whereas the gentleness of the other permitted Bonner's mother, sister, and others of his kindred, not only quietly to enjoy all that which they had from bishop Bonner, but also entertained them in his house, shewing much courtesy and friendship daily unto them; while, on the other side, Bonner being restored again, would not suffer the brother and sister of bishop Ridley, and other of his friends, to enjoy that which they had by their brother, but also churlishly, without all order of law or honesty, wrested from them all the livings they had in their own right.

Dr. Ridley was first called to the favoring of Christ and his gospel, by the reading of Bertram's book of the sacrament; and the conference with archbishop Cranmer, and with Peter Martyr, did not a little confirm him in that belief. Being now, by the grace of God, thoroughly won and brought to the true way, as he was before blind and zealous in his old ignorance, so was he constant and faithful in the right knowledge which the Lord had opened unto him, and so long he did much good, when power and authority defended the gospel, and supported the peace and happiness of the church. But after it pleased God to bereave us of our stay, in taking from us king Edward, the whole state of the church of England was left desolate and open to the enemy's hand: so that bishop Ridley, after the coming in of queen Mary, was one of the first upon whom they laid their hands, and committed to prison, as hath been sufficiently declared; first in the Tower, and from thence conveyed with archbishop Cranmer and bishop Latimer, to Oxford, and with them enclosed in the common prison of Bocardo; but at length being separated from them, he was committed to custody in the house of one Irish, where he remained until the day of his martyrdom, which was upwards of eight months.

While he continued in prison with his fellow-sufferer Latimer, they would sometimes confer together by letter, when they could not with safety converse with the tongue. The following is a specimen of this kind of prison conversation.

Ridley says, "In writing again you have done me an unspeakable pleasure, and I pray that the Lord may requite it you in that day. For I have received great comfort at your words: but yet I am not so filled withal, but that I thirst much more now than before, to drink more of that cup of yours, wherein you mingle unto me profitable with pleasant. I pray you, good father, let me have one draught more to comfort my stomach. For surely, except the Lord assist me with his gracious aid, in the time of his service, I know I shall play but the part of a whitelivered knight. But truly my trust is in Him, that in mine infirmity He should try Himself strong, and that He can make the coward in His cause to fight like a man. I now begin almost every day to look when Diotrephes with his warriors shall assault me: wherefore I pray you, good father, for that you are an old soldier, and an expert warrior, and God knoweth I am but a young soldier, and as yet of small experience in these feats, help me, I pray you, to buckle my harness. And now I would have you to think, that these darts are cast at my head by some one of Diotrephes' or Antonius; soldiers."

Latimer answers, "'Except the Lord help me,' ye say. Truth it is: 'for without Me,' saith he, 'ye can do nothing;' much less suffer death of our adversaries, through the bloody law now prepared against us. But it followeth, 'If you abide in me, and my word abide in you, ask what you will, and it shall be done for you.' What can be more comfortable? Sir, you make answer yourself so well, that I cannot better it. Sir, I begin now to smell what you mean by travelling thus with me; you use me as Bilney did once, when he converted me, pretending as though he would be taught by me, he sought ways and means to teach me, and so do you. I thank you therefore most heartily. For indeed you minister armor unto me, whereas I was unarmed before and unprovided, saving that I give myself to prayer for my refuge.

The objector, whose darts Ridley apprehended, visited both these good men in prison, and thus assailed them.

Obj. All men marvel greatly, why you, after the liberty granted unto you, more than the rest, do not go to mass, which is a thing much esteemed by all men, yea, of the queen herself.

Rid. Because no man that layeth hand on the plough and looketh back is fit for the kingdom of God, and also for the self-same cause why St. Paul would not suffer Titus to be circumcised, which is that the truth of the gospel might remain with us incorrupt. And also, "If I build again the things which I destroyed, I make myself a trespasser." This is likewise another cause: lest I should seem by outward fact to allow the thing, which I am persuaded is contrary to sound doctrine, and so should be a stumbling-block unto the weak. But "woe be unto him by whom offence cometh: it were better for him that a mill-stone were hanged about his neck, and he cast into the midst of the sea."

Obj. What is it then that offendeth you so greatly in the mass, that you will not vouchsafe once either to hear or see it? And from whence cometh this new religion upon you? Have you not been used in times past to say mass yourself?

Rid. I confess my fault and ignorance; but know you that for these matters I have done penance long ago, both at St. Paul's Cross, and also openly in the pulpit at Cambridge, and I trust that God hath forgiven me this mine offence: for I did it ignorantly. But if you be desirous to know, and will vouchsafe to hear what things offend me in the mass, I will rehearse those which be most clear, and seem most manifestly to impugn God's word, and they are these— The strange tongue; the want of the shewing of the Lord's death; the breaking of the Lord's commandment of having a communion; the sacrament is not communicated to all under both kinds, according to the word of the Lord; the sign is servilely worshipped for the thing signified; Christ's passion is injured, forasmuch as this mass-sacrifice is affirmed to remain for the purging of sins; to be short, the manifold superstitions, and trifling fooleries which are in the mass, and about the same.

Lat. Better a few things well pondered, than to trouble the memory with too much; you shall prevail more with praying, than with studying, though mixture be best, for so one shall alleviate the tediousness of the other. I intend not to contend much with them in words, after a reasonable account of my faith given: for it will be but in vain. They will say as their fathers said, when they have no more to say—"We have a law, and by our law he ought to die." "Be you steadfast and immovable, abounding in the work.—Stand fast." How oft is this repeated—"If you abide in Me, and in My word." But we shall be called obstinate, sturdy, ignorant, heady, and what not; so that a man hath need of much patience, having to do with such men.

Obj. But you know how great a crime it is to separate yourself from the communion of fellowship of the church, and to make a schism, or division. You have been reported to have hated the sect of the anabaptist, and always to have impugned the same. Moreover, this was the pernicious error of Novatus, and of the heretics called Cathari, that they would not communicate with the church.

Rid. I know that the unity of the church is to be retained by all means, and the same is necessary to salvation. But I do not take the mass, as it is at this day, for the communion of the church, but a popish device, whereby both the commandment and the institution of our Saviour, for the oft frequenting of the remembrance of his death, is eluded, and the people of God are miserably deluded. The sect of the anabaptists, and the heresy of the Navatians, ought of right to be condemned, forasmuch as without any just or necessary cause, they wickedly separated themselves from the communion of the congregation; for they did not allege that the sacraments were unduly administered; but turning their eyes from themselves, and casting their eyes ever upon others, they always reproved something, for which they abstained from the communion, as from an unholy thing.

Lat. I remember that Calvin beginneth to confute the Interim after this sort, with this saying of Hilary—"The name of peace is beautiful, and the opinion of unity is fair: but who doubteth that to be the true and only peace of the church, which is Christ's?" I would you had that little book, there would you see how much is to be given to unity. St. Paul, when he requireth unity, joineth with it, according to Jesus Christ, no further. Diotrephes now of late, did always harp upon unity. Yea, Sir, said I, but in verity, not popery. Better is diversity, than unity in popery.

Obj. But admit there be in the mass what peradventure might be amended, or at least made better; yea, seeing you will have it so, admit there be a fault; if you do not consent thereto, why do you trouble yourself in vain? Do you not know both by Cyprian and Augustine, that communion of sacraments doth not defile a man, but consent of deeds?

Rid. If it were any one trifling ceremony, or if it were some one thing of itself indifferent, for the continuance of the common quietness I could be content to bear it. But forasmuch as things done in the mass tend openly to the overthrow of Christ's institution, I judge that by no means either in word or deed I ought to consent unto it. As for that which is objected out of the fathers, I acknowledge it to be well spoken, if it be well understood. But it is meant of them which suppose they are defiled, if any secret vice be either in the ministers, or in them that communicate with them; and is not meant of them which suppose they are defiled, if any secret vice be either in the ministers, or in them that communicate with them; and is not meant of them which abhor superstition, and wicked traditions of men, and will not suffer the same to be thrust upon themselves, or upon the church, instead of God's word and the truth of the gospel.

Lat. The mass is altogether detestable, and by no means to be borne withal; so that of necessity, the mending of it is to abolish it forever. For if you take away ablation and adoration, which hang upon consecration and transubstantiation, most of the papists will not set a button by the mass, as a thing which they esteem not, but for the gain that followeth thereon. For if the English communion, which of late was used, were as gainful to them as the mass hath been heretofore, they would strive no more for their mass: from thence groweth the grief.

Obj. Consider into what dangers you cast yourself, if you forsake the church; and you cannot but forsake it, if you refuse to go to mass. For the mass is the sacrament of unity; without the ark there is no salvation. The church is the ark and Peter's ship. You know this saying well enough—"He shall not have God to be his Father, which acknowledgeth not the church to be his mother." Moreover, without the church, as Augustine saith, be the life ever so well spent, none shall inherit the kingdom of heaven.

Rid. The holy catholic or universal church, which is the communion of saints, the house of God, the city of God, the spouse of Christ, the body of Christ, the pillar and stay of truth; this church I believe according to the creed; this church I do reverence and honor in the Lord. But the rule of this church is the word of God, according to which rule we go forward unto life. "And as many as walk according to this rule," I say with St. Paul, "peace be upon them, and upon Israel, which pertaineth unto God." The guide of this church is the Holy Ghost. The marks whereby this church is known unto me in this dark world, and in the midst of this crooked and forward generation, are—the sincere preaching of God's holy word, the due administration of the sacraments, charity, and faithful observing of ecclesiastical discipline, according to the word of God. And that church or congregation which is garnished with these marks, is in very deed that heavenly Jerusalem, which consisteth of those that be born from above. This is the mother of us all, and by God's grace I will live and die the child of this church. Out of this, I grant, there is no salvation; and I suppose the rest of the places objected are rightly to be understood of this church only. 'In times past, there were many ways to know the church of Christ, that is to say, by good life, by miracles, by chastity, by doctrine, by administering the sacraments. But from the time that heresies took hold of the church, it is only known by the scriptures which is the true church. They have all things in outward show, which the true church. To that which they say, that the mass is the sacrament of unity, I answer—The bread which we break, according to the institution of the Lord, is the sacrament of the unity of Christ's mystical body. "For we being many, are one bread and one body, forasmuch as we are all partakers of one bread." But in the mass, the Lord's institution is not observed; for we are not all partakers of one bread, but one devoureth all. So that it may seem a sacrament of singularity, and of a certain special privilege for one sect of people, whereby they may be discerned from the rest, rather than a sacrament of unity, wherein our knitting together in one is represented.[1]

Lat. Yea, what fellowship hath Christ with antichrist? Therefore it is not lawful to bear the yoke with papists. "Come forth from among them, and separate yourselves from them," saith the Lord. It is one thing to be the church indeed, another thing to counterfeit it. Would to God it were well known what is the forsaking of the church. In king Edward's days, who was the church of England? The king and his favorers, or mass-mongers in corners? If the king and the favourers of his proceedings, why were we not now the church, abiding in the same proceeding? If private mass-mongers might be of the church, and yet contrary to the king's proceedings, why may we not be of the church contrary to the queen's proceedings? Not all that are covered with the title of the church, are the church indeed. Separate thyself from them that are such, saith St. Paul. From whom? The text hath before—"If any man follow other doctrines, he is puffed up and knoweth nothing." Weigh the whole text, that you may perceive what is the fruit of contentious disputations. But wherefore are such men said to know nothing, when they know so many things? You know the old verses—

> *Hoc est nescire, sine Christo plurima scire:*
> *Si Christum bene scis, sutis est, si cetera nescis.*[2]

---

[1] This passage of Ridley—this definition of the true church, and of the certain marks by which it may be known—this distinction between the method of ascertaining the church before and after it became Roman and papal—merits the utmost attention, and deserves to be written in letters of gold. If Ridley had never written or spoken any thing else, this would have been sufficient to convince the world that, on every thing relating to the evidences of religious truth and sacred scriptural worship, he would have been equal as a disputant to the most enlightened who ever opened his lips or employed his pen in such a cause.

[2] To give full effect to these admirable lines, we present the reader with the following rather free, but still fair and faithful translation.

> *To know all things here, and yet not Christ to know,*
> *Is ignorance deep as the deepest below:*
> *To know the Lord Jesus, and know nothing more,*
> *Is knowledge the highest to which we can soar.*

Therefore would St. Paul know nothing but Jesus Christ and him crucified. As many as are papists and mass-mongers, they may well be said to know nothing. For they know not Christ, forasmuch as in their massing, they take much away from the benefit and merit of Christ.

Obj. That church when you have described to me is invisible, but Christ's church is visible and known. For else why should Christ have said, "Tell it unto the church?" For He had commanded in vain to go unto the church, if a man cannot tell which it is.

Rid. The church which I have described is visible, it hath members which may be seen; and also I have before declared, by what marks and tokens it may be known; but if either our eyes be so dazzled, that we cannot see, or that Satan hath brought such darkness into the world, that it is hard to discern the church, that is not the fault of the church, but either of our blindness, or of Satan's darkness. But yet in this most deep darkness, there is one most clear lamp, which of itself alone is able to put away all darkness. "Thy word is a lamp unto my feet, and a light into my steps."

Obj. The church of Christ is a catholic or universal church, dispersed throughout the whole world; this church is the great house of God, in which are good men and evil mingled together, goats and sheep, corn and chaff: it is the net which gathereth all kinds of fishes. This church cannot err, because Christ hath promised it His Spirit, which shall lead it into all truth, and that the gates of hell shall not prevail against it; that He will be with it unto the end of the world; whatsoever it shall loose or bind upon earth shall be loosed or bound in heaven. This church is the pillar and stay of truth; this is it for which St. Augustine saith, he believeth the gospel. But this universal church alloweth the mass, because the greater part of the same alloweth it.

Rid. I grant that the name of the church is taken after three diverse manners in the Scripture. Sometimes for the whole multitude of them who profess the name of Christ, of which they are also named Christians. But as St. Paul saith of the Jews, not everyone is a Jew, that is so outwardly; neither yet all that be of Israel are counted the seed; even so, not everyone that is a Christian outwardly is a Christian indeed. For if any man have not the spirit of Christ, the same is none of His. Therefore that church which is His body, and of which Christ is the head, standeth only on living stones, and true Christians, not only outwardly in name and title, but inwardly in heart and in truth. But forasmuch as this church, as touching the outward fellowship, is contained within the great house, and hath with the same outward society of the sacraments and ministry of the word, many things are spoken of that universal church which cannot truly be understood, but only if that pure part of the church. So that the rule of Ticonius concerning the mingled church, may here well take place; where there is attributed unto the whole church that which cannot agree to the same, but by reason of the one part thereof; that is, either for the multitude of good men, which is the very true church indeed; or for the multitude of evil men, which is the malignant church and synagogue of

Satan. And there is also a third taking of the church; of which although there be seldom mention in the scriptures in that signification, yet in the world, even in the most famous assemblies of Christendom, this church hath borne the greatest sway. This distinction pre-supposed of the three sorts of church, it is an easy matter, by a figure called synecdoche, to give to the mingled and universal church that which cannot truly be understood, but only of the one part thereof. But if any man will affirm that universality doth so pertain unto the church, that whatsoever Christ hath promised to the church, it must needs be understood of that, I would gladly know of the same man where that universal church was in the times of the patriarchs and prophets, of Noah, Abraham, and Moses, of Elias, and Jeremiah, of Christ and the apostles, in the time of Arius, when Constantius was emperor, and Felix, bishop of Rome, succeeded Liberius. It is worthy to be noted, what Lyra writeth upon Matthew—"The church doth not stand in men by reason of their power or dignity, whether it be ecclesiastical or secular. For princes and popes, and other inferiors, have been found to have fallen away from God. Therefore the church consisteth in those persons, in whom is true knowledge and confession of the faith, and of the truth. Evil men are in the church in name, and not in deed." And St. Augustine saith—"Whoever is afraid to be deceived by the darkness of this question, let him ask counsel at the same church of it; which church the scripture doth point out without any doubtfulness." All my notes which I have written and gathered out of such authors as I have read in this matter, and such like, are come into the hands of such as will not let me have the least of all my written books; wherein I am enforced to complain of them unto God: for they spoil me of all my labors, which I have taken in my study these many years. My memory was never good, for help whereof I have used for the most part, to gather out notes of my reading, and so to place them, that thereby I might have had the use of time when the time required. But who knoweth whether this be God's will, that I should be thus ordered, and spoiled of the poor learning I had in store, to the intent that I, now destitute of that, should from henceforth with St. Paul learn only to know Christ and him crucified? The Lord grant me herein to be a good young scholar, and to learn this lesson so well, that neither death nor life, wealth nor woe, make me ever to forget it.

Lat. I have no more to say in this matter for yourself have said all that is to be said. The strong saying of St. Augustine—I would not believe the gospel, but as the church declareth it—was wont to trouble many men; as I remember, I have read it well qualified by Philip Melancthon. This it is in effect: the church is not a judge but a witness. There were some in his time that lightly esteemed the testimony of the church, and the outward ministry of preaching, and rejected the outward word itself, cleaving only to their inward revelations. Such rash contempt of the word provoked and drove St. Augustine into that excessive vehemency. In which, after the bare sound of the words, he might seem to such as do not attain unto his meaning, that he preferred the church far before the gospel, and that the church hath a free authority over the same;

but that pious man never thought so. It were a saying worthy to be brought forth against the Anabaptists, who thought the open ministry to be a thing not necessary, if they any thing esteemed such testimonies. I would not hesitate to affirm, that the most part of the whole universal church may easily err. And again I would not hesitate to affirm, that it is one thing to be gathered together in the name of Christ, and another thing to come together with a mass of the Holy Ghost going before. For in the first, Christ ruleth; in the latter, the devil beareth the sway; and how can anything be good which they thus go about? From this latter shall our six articles come forth again into the light, they themselves being very darkness. But it is demanded, whether the sounder or better part of the catholic church may be seen of men. St. Paul saith—"The Lord knoweth them that are his." What manner of speaking is this in commendation of the Lord, if we knew as well as he who are his? Well, thus is the text—"the sure foundation of God standeth still, and hath this seal, The Lord knoweth them that are His; and let every man that nameth the name of Christ depart from iniquity." Now how many are there of the whole catholic church of England who depart from iniquity? How many of the noblemen, how many of the bishops or clergy, how many of the rich men, or merchants, how many of the queen's counsellors, yea, how many of the whole realm? In how small room then, I pray you, is the true church within the realm of England? And where is it? And in what state?

Obj. General councils represent the universal church, and have this promise of Christ—"Where two or three be gathered together in my name, there am I in the midst of them." If Christ be present with two or three, then much more where there is so great a multitude. But in general councils mass hath been approved and used.

Rod. Of the universal church which is mingled of good and bad, thus I think—Whensoever they which be chief in it, which rule and govern the same, and to whom the whole mystical body of Christ doth obey, are the lively members of Christ, and walk after the guiding and rule of his word, and go before the flock to everlasting life, then undoubtedly councils gathered together of such guides and pastors of the Christian flock, do indeed represent the christian church; and being so gathered in the name of Christ, they have a promise of the gift and guiding of his Spirit into all truth. But that any such council hath at any time allowed the mass, such an one as ours was of late, in a strange tongue, and stuffed with so many absurdities, errors, and superstitions; that I utterly deny, and affirm it to be impossible. For like as there is no agreement betwixt light and darkness, betwixt Christ and Belial; so surely superstition and the sincere religion of Christ, will-worship and the pure worshipping of God, such as God requireth of His, in spirit and truth, never can agree together. You will say, where so great a company is gathered together it is not credible but there are two or three gathered in the name of Christ. I answer, If there be one hundred good, and two hundred bad, what can the less number of voices avail? It is a known thing, and a common proverb, oftentimes the greater part overcometh the better.

Lat. As touching general councils, at this present I have no more to say than you have said. Only I refer you to your own experience, to think of our country parliaments and convocations, how and what you have seen and heard. The greater part in my time did bring forth six articles: for then the king would have it so, being seduced of certain. Afterward the greater part did repel the same, our good Josias willing to have it so. The same articles gain another great but worse part hath restored. O what an uncertainty is this! But after this manner most commonly are men's proceedings. God be merciful unto us! Who shall deliver us from such torments of mind? Therefore is death the best physician unto the faithful, whom he together and at once delivereth from all griefs.

Obj. If the matter should go thus, that in general councils men should not stand to the greater number of the multitude, then should no certain rule be left unto the church, by which controversies in weighty matters might be determined: but it is not to be believed, that Christ would leave His church destitute of so necessary a help and safeguard.

Rid. Christ, who is the most loving spouse of His church, who also gave Himself for it, that He might sanctify it unto Himself, did give unto it abundantly all things which are necessary to salvation; but yet so, that the church should declare itself obedient unto Him in all things and keep itself within the bounds of His commandments, and not to seek any thing which He teacheth not, as necessary unto salvation. Now for determination of all controversies in His religion, Christ Himself hath left unto the church not only Moses and the prophets, whom He willeth in all doubts to go unto, and ask counsel at, but also the gospels, and the rest of the body of the New Testament; in which whatsoever is heard of Moses and the prophets, and whatsoever is necessary to be known unto salvation, is revealed and opened. So that now we have no need to say—"Who shall climb up into heaven, or who shall go down into the depth," to tell us what is needful to be done? Christ hath done both, and hath commended us to the word of faith, which also is abundantly declared to us; so that hereafter, if we walk earnestly in this way to the searching out of the truth, it is not to be doubted but through the certain benefit of His Spirit, which He hath promised unto us, we may find it, and obtain everlasting life. Should men ask counsel of the dead for the living? saith Isaiah. Let them go rather to the law and to the testimony. Christ sendeth them that be desirous to know the truth unto the scriptures, saying—"Search the scriptures." I remember a like thing well spoken of St. Jerome—"Ignorance of the scriptures is the mother and cause of all errors." and in another place, as I remember, in the same author—"The knowledge of the scriptures is the food of everlasting life." But now methinks I enter into a very broad sea, in that I begin to show, either out of the scriptures themselves, or out of the ancient writers, how much the holy Scripture is of force to teach the truth of our religion. But this is it that I am now about, that Christ would have the church, his spouse, in all matters of doubt to ask counsel at the word of his Father, written and faithfully left, and commended unto it in both Testaments. Neither do we read, that

Christ in any place hath laid so great a burden upon the members of His spouse, that He hath commanded them to go to the universal church. "Whatsoever things are written, are written for our learning." Christ gave unto His church, "some apostles, some prophets, some evangelists, some shepherds and teachers, to the edifying of the saints, until we come all to the unity of the faith." But that all men should meet together out of all parts of the world, to define the articles of our faith, I neither find it commanded by Christ, nor written in the word of God.

Lat. There is difference between things pertaining to God or faith, and politic and civil matters. For in the first we must stand only to the scriptures, which are able to make us all perfect and instructed unto salvation, if they be well understood. And they offer themselves to be well understood only to them, which have good-wills, and give themselves to study and prayer. Neither are there any men less apt to understand them, than the prudent and wise men of the world. But in the other, that is, in civil and politic matters, oftentimes the magistrates tolerate a less evil for avoiding a greater. And it is the property of a wise man to dissemble many things, and he that cannot dissemble, cannot rule. In which they betrayed themselves, that they do not earnestly weigh what is just, and what is not. Wherefore for as much as man's laws, if they be but in this respect only, that they be devised by men, are not able to bring anything to perfection, but are enforced of necessity to suffer many things out of square, and are compelled sometimes to wink at the worst things; seeing they know not how to maintain the common peace and quiet otherwise, they do ordain that the greater part shall take place. You know what these kind of speeches mean; I speak after the manner of men; you walk after the manner of men; all men are liars. St. Augustine well saith—"If ye live after man's reason, ye do not live after the will of God."

Obj. If you say that councils have sometimes erred, or may err, how then should we believe the catholic church? since councils are gathered by the authority of the catholic church.

Rid. From "may be," to "be indeed," is no good argument; but from "being," to "may be," no man doubteth but it is a most sure argument. That councils have sometimes erred, it is manifest. How many were there in the eastern world, which condemned the Nicene council? and all those who would not forsake the same, they called by a slanderous name, Homousians. Were not Athanasius, Chrysostom, Cyril, and Eustachius, men very well learned, and of godly life, banished and condemned as famous heretics, and that by evil councils? How many things are there in the canons and institutions of the councils, which the papists themselves do much dislike? But here peradventure one man will say unto me, We will grant you this in provincial councils, or councils of some one nation, that they may sometimes err, forsomuch as they do not represent the universal church; but it is not to be believed, that the general and full councils have erred at any time. I will recite one place only out of St. Augustine which, in my judgment, may suffice in this matter instead of many. "Who knoweth not that the holy scripture is so set before us, that it is not lawful to doubt of it; and that the letters of bishops may be reproved by other men's words, and by councils; and that the councils themselves which are gathered by provinces and countries, do give place to the authority of the general and full councils; and that the former and general councils are amended by the latter, when as by some experience of things, either what was shut up is opened, or that which was hid is known?" Thus much out of St. Augustine. But I will plead our Antonian, upon matter confessed. Here with us as we popery reigned, I pray you how doth that book, which was called, "The bishop's book," composed in the time of king Henry VIII whereof the bishop of Winchester is thought to be either the first father, or chief gatherer; how doth it sharply reprove the Florentine council, in which was decreed the supremacy of the bishop of Rome, and that with the consent of the emperor of Constantinople, and of the Grecian heads? So that in those days our learned ancient fathers and bishops of England did not hesitate to affirm, that a general council might err. But methinks I hear another man despising all that I have brought forth, and saying—"These which you have called councils, are not worthy to be called councils, but rather assemblies and conventicles of heretics." I pray you, Sir, why do you judge them worthy of so scandalous a name? Because they decreed things heretical, contrary to sound doctrine and true godliness, and against the faith of true religion? The cause must be weighty, for which they ought of right so to be called. But if it be so that all councils ought to be despised which decree anything contrary to sound doctrine. and the true word, which is according to godliness, forsomuch as the mass such as we had here of late, is openly against the word of God; forsooth, it must of necessity follow, that all such councils as have approved such masses, ought to be shunned and despised, as conventicles and assemblies that stray from the truth.

Another man alleged unto me the authority of the bishop of Rome, without which, neither can the councils be lawfully gathered, nor being gathered, determine anything concerning religion. But this objection is only grounded upon the ambitious and shameless maintenance of the Romish tyranny and usurped dominion over the clergy; which tyranny we Englishmen long ago, by the consent of the whole realm, have expelled and abjured. And how rightly we have done it, a little book set forth of both the powers doth clearly show. I grand that the Romish ambition hath gone about to challenge itself, and to usurp such a privilege of old time. But the council of Carthage, in the year of our Lord 457, did openly withstand it, and also the council at Melevite, in which St. Augustine was present, did prohibit any applications to be made to bishops beyond the sea.

Obj. St. Augustine saith, the good men are not to be forsaken for the evil; but the evil are to be borne withal for the good. You will not say that in our congregations all be evil.

Rid. I speak nothing of the goodness or badness of your congregations; but I fight in Christ's quarrel against the mass, which doth utterly take away and overthrow the ordinance of Christ. Let that be taken quite away, and then the partition wall that made the strife shall be broken down. Now to the place of St. Augustine, for bearing with the evil for the good's sake, there ought to be added other words, which the same writer hath expressed in other places; that is, if those evil men do cast abroad no seeds of false doctrine, nor lead others to destruction by their example.

Obj. It is perilous to attempt any new thing in the church, which lacketh of good men. How much more so is it to commit any act, unto which the examples of the prophets, of Christ, and of the apostles, are contrary? But unto this your fact, in abstaining from the church by reason of the mass, the examples of the prophets, of Christ, and of the apostles, are clean contrary. The first part of the argument is evident, and the second part I prove thus, In the times of the prophets of Christ, and his apostles, all things were most corrupt. The people were miserably given to superstition, the priests despised the law of God; and yet notwithstanding we read not that the prophets made any schisms or divisions; and Christ Himself frequented the temple, and taught in the temple of the Jews. Peter and John went up into the temple at the ninth hour of prayer. Paul after the reading of the law, being desired to say something to the people, did not refuse to do it. Yea further, no man can shew that either the prophets, or Christ, or His apostles, did refuse to pray together with others, to sacrifice, or to be partakers of the sacrament of Moses' law.

Rid. I grant the former part of your argument; and to the second part I say, that although it contain many true things, as of the corrupt state in the times of the prophets, and the apostles; and of the temple being frequented by Christ and His apostles; yet the second part of your argument is not sufficiently proved. For you ought to have proved, that either the prophets, or Christ, or His apostles, did in the temple communicate with the people in any kind of worshipping which is forbidden by the law of God, or repugnant to the word of God. But that can no where be shewed. And as for the church, I am not angry with it, and I never refused to go to it, and to pray with the people, to hear the word of God, and to do all other things whatsoever, that may agree with the word of God. St. Augustine, speaking of the ceremonies of the Jews, although he grants they grievously oppressed that people, both for the number and bondage of the same, yet he calleth them burdens of the law, which were delivered unto them in the word of God; not presumptions of men, which notwithstanding, if they were not contrary to God's word, might in some measure be borne withal. But now, seeing they are contrary to such things as are written in the word of God, whether they ought to be borne by any Christian, let him judge who is spiritual, who feareth God more than man, and loveth everlasting life more than this short and transitory one. To that which was said, that my fact lacketh example of the godly fathers that have gone before, the contrary is most evident in the history of Tobit; of whom it is said, that when all others went to the golden calves, which Jeroboam the king of Israel had made, he himself alone fled from their company, and got him to Jerusalem unto the Lord, and there worshipped the Lord God of Israel.

Did not the man of God threaten grievous plagues both unto the priests of Bethel, and to the altar which Jeroboam had there made after his own fantasy? Which plagues king Josias, the true minister of God, did execute at the time appointed. And where do we read, that the prophets or the apostles did agree with the people in their idolatry? For what cause, I pray you, did the prophets rebuke the people so much, as for their false worshipping of God after their own minds, and not after God's word? For what was so much war in Israel as for that? Wherefore the false prophets ceased not to accuse the true prophets of God: therefore they beat them, and banished them. How else, I pray you, can you understand what St. Paul allegeth, when he saith, "What concord hath Christ with Belial? or what part hath the believer with the infidel? Or how agreeth the temple of God with idols? For ye are the temple of the living God, as God Himself hath said; I will dwell among them, and will be their God, and they shall be my people. Wherefore, come out from among them, and separate yourselves from them, and touch no unclean thing; so will I receive you, and be a Father unto you, and you shall be My sons and daughters, saith the Lord God Almighty."

Judith, that holy woman, would not suffer herself to be defiled with the meats of the wicked. All the saints of God, which truly feared God, when they have been provoked to do any thing which they knew to be contrary to God's laws, have chose to die rather than forsake the laws of their God. Wherefore the Maccabees put themselves in danger of death for the defense of the law, and at length died manfully in the defense of the same. If we praise the Maccabees, and that with great admiration, because they did stoutly stand even unto death, for the law of their country; how much more ought we to suffer all things for our baptism, for the sacrament of the body and blood of Christ, and for all the points of his truth? As to the supper of the Lord, such a one as Christ commanded us to celebrate, the mass utterly abolisheth, and corrupteth most shamefully.

Lat. Who am I, that should add anything to this which you have spoken? Nay, I rather thank you, you have vouchsafed to minister so plentiful an armour to me, being otherwise altogether unarmed, saving, that he cannot be left destitute of help, who rightly trusteth in the help of God. I only learn to die in reading of the New Testament, and am always praying unto my God, that he will be an helper unto me in the time of need.

Obj. Seeing you are obstinately set against the mass, as you affirm, because it is done in a tongue not understood by the people, and for other causes, I cannot tell you what; therefore it is not the true sacrament ordained of Christ. I begin to suspect you, that you think not catholicly of baptism also. Is our baptism which we use in a tongue unknown to the people, that true baptism of Christ, or not? If it be, then the strange tongue doth not hurt the mass. If it be not the baptism of Christ, tell me how you were baptized. Or will you have, as the anabaptists insist, all which were baptized in Latin, baptized again in the English tongue?

Rid. Although I would wish baptism to be given in the vulgar tongue, for the people's sake which are present, that they may the better understand their own profession, and also be more able to teach their children the same, yet, notwithstanding, there is not like necessity of the vulgar tongue in baptism, as in the Lord's supper. Baptism is given to children, who, by reason of their age, are not able to understand what is spoken to them, whatsoever it be. The Lord's supper is and ought to be given to them that are at years of maturity. Moreover, in baptism, which is accustomed to be given to children in the Latin tongue, all the substantial points which Christ commanded to be done, are observed. And therefore I judge your baptism to be a true baptism: and that it is not only not needful, but also not lawful, for any man so baptized, to be baptized again. But yet they ought to be taught the catechism of the Christian faith, when they come to years of discretion: which catechism whosoever despiseth, or will not desirously embrace and willingly learn, in my judgment he playeth not the part of a Christian. But in the popish mass are wanting certain substantials, that is to say, things commanded by the word of God, to be observed in the ministration of the Lord's supper; of which there is sufficient declaration made before.

Lat. Where you say, "I would wish," surely I would wish that you had spoken more strongly, and to have said, It is of necessity that all things in the congregation should be done in the vulgar tongue, for the edifying and comfort of them that are present, notwithstanding that the child itself is sufficiently baptized in the Latin tongue.

Obj. Forasmuch as I perceive you are so wedded to your opinion, that no gentle exhortations, no wholesome counsels, can call you home to a better mind, there remaineth that which in like cases was wont to be the only remedy against stubborn persons, that you must be hampered by the laws, and compelled to obey; or else suffer that which a rebel to the laws ought to suffer. Do you not know, that whosoever refuseth to obey the laws of the realm betrayeth himself to be an enemy to his country? Do you not know, this is the readiest way to stir up sedition and civil war? It is better that you should bear your own sin, than through the example of your breach of the common laws, the common quiet should be disturbed. How can you say you will be the queen's true subjects, when you openly profess that you will not keep her laws?

Rid. O heavenly Father, the Father of all wisdom, understanding, and true strength, I beseech thee, for thy only Son our Saviour Christ's sake, look mercifully upon me, wretched creature, and send Thine Holy Spirit into my breast, that not only I may understand according to Thy wisdom how this pestilent and deadly dart is to be borne off, and with what answer it is to be beaten back, but also when I must join to fight in the field for the glory of Thy name, that then I, being strengthened with the defense of Thy right hand, may manfully stand in the confession of Thy faith, and of truth, and continue in the same unto the end of my life, through the same our Lord Jesus Christ. Amen.

Now to the objection. I grant it to be reasonable, that he, which by words and gentleness cannot be made to yield to that which is right and good, should be bridled by the strait correction of the laws: that is to say, He that will not be subject to God's word, must be punished by the laws. It is true that is commonly said, "He that will not obey the gospel, must be tamed and taught by the rigor of the law." But these things ought to take place against him who refuseth to do that which is right and just according to true godliness, not against him who cannot quietly bear superstitions, but doth hate and detest from his heart such kind of proceedings, and that for the glory of the name of God. To that which you say, a transgressor of the common laws betrayeth himself to be an enemy of his country, surely a man ought to look unto the nature of the laws, what manner of laws they be which are broken: for a faithful Christian ought not to think alike of all manner of laws. But that saying ought only truly to be understood of such laws as are not contrary to God's word. Otherwise, whosoever love their country in truth, they will always judge, if at any time the laws of God and man be the one contrary to the other, that a man ought rather to obey God than man. And they that think otherwise, and pretend a love to that country, forasmuch as they make their country to fight as it were against God, in whom consisteth the only stay of their country, surely I think such are to be judged most deadly enemies and traitors to their country. For they that fight against God, who is the safety of their country, what do they else but go about to bring upon their country a present ruin and destruction!

But this is the readiest way, you say, to stir up sedition, to trouble the quiet of the commonwealth; therefore are these things to be repressed in time by force of law. Behold, Satan doth not cease to practice his old guiles and accustomed subtleties. He hath ever his dart in readiness to hurl against his adversaries, to accuse them of sedition, that he may bring them, if he can, in danger of the higher powers. For so hath he by his ministers always charged the prophets of God. Ahab said unto Elias, "Art thou he that troubleth Israel?" The false prophets also complained to their princes of Jeremy, that his words were seditious, and not to be suffered. Did not the scribes and pharisees falsely accuse Christ as a seditious person, and one that spake against Caesar? Did they not at last cry, "If thou let this man go, thou art not Caesar's friend"? The orator Tertullus, how doth he accuse Paul before Felix the high deputy? "We have found this man a pestilent fellow, and stirrer of sedition, unto all the Jews in the whole world." But, I pray you, were these men, as they were called, seditious persons? Christ, Paul, and the prophets? God forbid but they were by false men falsely accused. And for what, I pray you, but because they reproved before the people their guiles, superstition, and deceits? For that which was objected last, that he cannot be a faithful subject to his prince, who professeth openly that he will not observe the laws which the prince hath made; here I would wish that I might have an impartial judge, and one that feareth God, to whose judgment in this cause I promise I will stand. I answer, therefore, a man ought to obey his prince, but in the Lord, and never against the Lord. For he that knowingly obeyeth him against God, doth not a duty to the prince, but is a deceiver, and a helper unto him to work his own destruction. He is also unjust who giveth not to the prince that which is the prince's, and to God that which is God's. Here cometh to my remembrance that notable saying of Valentinian the emperor, for choosing the bishop of Milan—"Set him in the bishop's seat, to whom, if we, as men, do offend at any time, we may submit ourselves." Polycarp the most constant martyr, when he stood before the chief rulers, and was commanded to blaspheme Christ, and to swear by the fortune of Caesar, answered with a mild spirit—"We are taught to give honour unto princes, and those powers which be of God; but such honour as is not contrary to God's religion."

THUS THE ANSWERS TO THE OBJECTOR APPEAR AT PRESENT TO END: WHAT FOLLOWS SEEMS TO HAVE BEEN ADDRESSED BY RIDLEY TO LATIMER IN A MORE PRIVATE CONFERENCE

Hitherto you see, good father, how I have in word only made, as it were, a flourish before the fight, which I shortly look for, and how I have begun to prepare certain kinds of weapons to fight against the adversary of Christ, and to muse with myself how the darts of the old enemy may be borne off, and after what manner I may smite him again with the sword of the Spirit. I learn also to accustom myself to armor, and to try how I can go armed. In Tynedale, where I was born, not far from the borders of Scotland, I have known my countrymen to watch night and day in their harness, such as they had, and their spears in their hands, especially when they had any private warning of the coming of the Scots. And so doing, although at every such bickering some of them spent their lives, yet by such means, like valiant men, they defended their country. And those that so died, I think that before God they died in a good quarrel, and their offspring sake. And in the quarrel of Christ our Saviour, in the defense of his own divine ordinances, by which He giveth unto us life and immorality; yea, in the quarrel of faith and the Christian religion, wherein resteth our everlasting salvation, shall we not watch? Shall we not go always armed? Always looking when our adversary shall come upon us by reason of our slothfulness? Yea, and woe be unto us if he can oppress us unawares, which undoubtedly he will do, if he find us sleeping. Let us awake, therefore; for if the good man of the house knew at what hour the thief would come, he would surely watch, and not suffer his house to be broken up. Let us awake, therefore, I say: let us not suffer our house to be broken up. "Resist the devil, and he will fly from you." Let us resist him manfully, and taking the cross upon our shoulders, let us follow our captain Christ, who, by His own blood, hath dedicated and hallowed the way which leadeth unto the Father, that is, to the light which no man can attain, the fountain of everlasting joys. Let us follow, I say, whither He calleth and inviteth us, that after these afflictions, which last but for a moment, whereby He trieth our faith, as gold by the fire, we may everlastingly reign and triumph with Him in the glory of the Father, and that through the merit of our Lord and Saviour Jesus Christ; to whom, with the Father and the Holy Ghost, be all honor and glory, now and forever, Amen. Amen.

Good father, forasmuch as I have determined with myself to pour forth these my cogitations into thy bosom, here, methinks, I see you suddenly lifting up your head towards heaven, after your manner, and then looking upon me with your prophetical countenance, say, "Trust not, my son, to these word-weapons; for the kingdom of God is not in word, but in power." And remember always the words of the Lord: "Do not imagine beforehand, what and how you will speak; for it shall be given you in the same hour what ye shall speak. For it is not you that speak, but the spirit of your Father which speaketh in you." I pray you, therefore, father, pray for me, that I may cast my whole care upon him, and trust upon him in all perils. For I know, and am surely persuaded, that whatsoever I can imagine or think beforehand it is nothing, except He assist me with His Spirit when the time is. I beseech you therefore father, pray for me, that such a complete harness of the Spirit, such a boldness of mind, may be given unto me, that I may out of a true faith say with David, "I will not trust in my bow, and it is not my sword that shall save me. For He hath no pleasure in the strength of an horse: but the Lord's delight is in them that fear him, and put their trust in His mercy." I beseech you pray, pray that I may enter this fight only in the name of God, and that when all is past, I being not overcome, through his gracious aid, may remain and stand fast in Him until that day of the Lord, in which to them that obtain the victory shall be given the lively manna to eat, and a triumphant crown for evermore. Now, father, I pray you to help me to buckle on this harness a little better. For you know the deepness of Satan, being an old soldier, and you have collared with him ere now; blessed be God, who hath ever aided you so well. I suppose he may well hold you at the bay. But truly he will not be so willing, I think, to join with you as with us youngsters. Sir, I beseech you, let your servant read this unto you, and now and then, as it shall seem unto you best, let your pen run in my book: spare not to blot my paper; I give you good leave.

To this admirable communication of Ridley, Latimer returned the following characteristic answer.

Sir, I have caused my man not only to read your armor unto me, but also to write it out, for it is not only solid armor, but also well buckled armor. I see not how it could be better. I thank you even from the bottom of my heart for it, and my prayers you shall not lack, trusting that you do the like for me; for indeed there is the "help in time of need." And if I were learned as well as St. Paul, I would not bestow much amongst them, further than gall them, and spur-gall too, when and where occasion were given, and matter came to mind; for the law shall be our sheet-anchor, stay, and refuge. Therefore there is no remedy, now when they have the master-bowl in their hand, but patience. Better is it to suffer what cruelly they will put upon us, than to incur God's high indignation. Wherefore, my good lord, be of good cheer in the Lord, with due consideration what He requireth of you, and what He doth promise you. Our common enemy shall do no more than God will permit him. God is faithful, who will not suffer us to be tempted above our strength. Be at a point what you will stand unto; stick unto that, and let them both say and do what they list. They can but kill the body, which otherwise is of itself mortal. Neither yet shall they do that when they list, but as God will suffer them, when the hour appointed is come. It will be but in vain to use many words with them, now they have a bloody and deadly law prepared for you.

The number of the criers under the altar must needs be fulfilled: if we be separated thereunto, happy be we. That is the greatest promotion that God giveth in this world, to be such Philippines, "to whom it is given not only to believe, but also to suffer for the sake of Christ." But who is able to do these things? Surely all our ability, all our sufficiency is of God. He requireth and promiseth. Let us declare our obedience to His will when it shall be requisite in the time of trouble, yea, in the midst of the fire. When the number that cry under the altar is fulfilled which I suppose will be shortly, then have at the papists, when they shall say, Peace, all things are safe, when Christ shall come to keep His great parliament to redress all things that are amiss. But He shall not come as the papists feign Him, to hide Himself, and to play bo-peep as it were under a piece of bread; but he shall come gloriously, to the terror and fear of all His enemies and to the great consolation and comfort of all that will here suffer for Him. Comfort yourselves and one another with these words.

Lo, Sir, here have I blotted your paper vainly, and played the fool egregiously; but so I thought better than not to fulfil your request at this time. Pardon me, and pray for me; pray for me I say, pray for me. For I am sometimes so fearful, that I would creep into a mouse-hole; sometimes God doth visit me again with His comfort. So He cometh and goeth, to teach me to feel and to know mine infirmity, to the intent to give thanks to Him that is worthy, lest I should rob Him of His due, as so many do, and almost all the world. What belief is to be given to papists may appear by their racking, writing, wrenching, and monstrously injuring of God's holy scripture, as appeareth in the pope's law. But I dwell here now in a school of forgetfulness. Fare you well once again, and be you steadfast and unmoveable in the Lord. Paul loved Timothy marvellously well, notwithstanding he saith unto him—"Be thou partaker of the afflictions of the gospel;" and again, "Harden thyself to suffer afflictions. Be faithful unto death, and I will give thee a crown of life."

THE FOLLOWING LETTER IS AN INTERESTING COMMUNICATION FROM RIDLEY TO BRADFORD AND HIS PRISON-FELLOWS IN THE KING'S BENCH, SOUTHWARK, 1554

Well beloved in Christ our Saviour, we all with one heart wish to you, with all those that love God in deed and truth, grace and health, and especially to our dearly beloved companions which are in Christ's cause, and the cause of both of *their brethren and of their own salvation, to put their neck willingly under the yoke of Christ's cross. How joyful it was to us to hear the report of Dr. Taylor, and of his godly confession, I assure you it is hard for me to express. Blessed be God, which was and is the giver of that, and of all godly strength and support in the time of adversity. As for the rumors that have or do go abroad, either of our relenting or massing, we trust, that they which know God and their duty towards their brethren in Christ, will not be too easy of belief. For it is not the slanderer's evil tongue, but a man's evil deed that can with God defile a man; and, therefore, with God's grace, you shall never have cause to do otherwise than you say you do, that is, not to doubt but that we will by God's grace continue steadfast and unmoveable. Like rumors as you have heard of our coming to London, have been here spread of the coming of certain learned men prisoners hither from London; but as yet we have known no certainty which of these rumors is or shall be more true. Know you that we have you in our daily remembrance, and which you all the rest of our foresaid companions well in Christ.*

It would much comfort us, if we might have knowledge of the state of the rest of our most dearly beloved, which in this troublesome time do stand in Christ's cause, and in the defense of the truth thereof. We have heard somewhat of Mr. Hooper's matter, but nothing of the rest. We long to hear of father Crome, Dr. Sands, Mr. Saunders, Veron, Beacon, Rogers, and others. We are in good health, thanks be to God, and yet the manner of using us doth change as sour ale in summer. It is reported to us by our keepers, that the university beareth us heavily. A coal happened to fall in the night out of the chimney, and burnt a hole in the floor, and no more harm was done, the bailiff's servant sitting by the fire. Another night there chanced, as the bailiffs told us, a drunken fellow to multiply words, and for the same he was set in Bocardo. Upon these things, as is reported, there is a rumor risen in the town and country about, that we would have broke the prison with such violence, as that if the Bailiffs had not played the pretty men, we should have made an escape. We had out of our prison a wall that we might have walked upon, and our servants had liberty to go abroad in the town or fields, but now both they and we are restrained from both.

My lord of Worcester passed through Oxford, but he did not visit us. The same day our restraint began to be more close, and the book of the communion was taken from us by the bailiffs at the mayor's command, as the bailiffs did report to us. No man is licensed to come unto us; before they might, that would see us upon the wall, but that is so grudged at, and so evil reported, that we are not restrained. Blessed be God, with all our evil reports, grudges, and restraints, we are merry in God, all our care is and shall be, by God's grace, to please and serve him, of whom we look and hope, after these temporal and momentary miseries, to have eternal joy and perpetual felicity with Abraham, Isaac, and Jacob, Peter, and Paul, and all the heavenly company of the angels in heaven, through Jesus Christ our Lord. As yet there has no learned man, nor any scholar, been to visit us since we came into Bocardo, which now in Oxford may

*be called a college of Quondams. For as you know we are no fewer than three,[3]
and I dare say everyone well contented with this portion, which I do reckon to be
our heavenly Father's good and gracious gift. Thus fare you well. We shall, by
God's grace, one day meet together, and be merry. The day assuredly
approacheth apace; the Lord grant that it may shortly come. For before that day
come, I fear the world will wax worse and worse. But then all our enemies shall
be overthrown and trodden under foot: righteousness and truth then shall have
the victory, and bear the bell away, whereof the Lord grant us to be partakers,
and all that love truly the truth.*

*We all pray you, as we can, to cause all our commendations to be made unto
all such as you know did visit us and you when we were in the Tower, with their
friendly remembrances and benefits. Mrs. Wilkinson and Mrs. Warcup[4] have not
forgotten us, but ever since we came to Bocardo, with their charitable and
friendly benevolence have comforted us: not that else we did lack, (for God be
blessed, he hath always sufficiently provided for us) but that is a great comfort,
and an occasion for us to bless God, when we see that he maketh them so
friendly to tender us, whom some of us were never familiarly acquainted withal.*

A selection only of letters of Ridley can be made. The next deserving
special attention is one addressed generally to all his suffering brethren through
the country.

*Grace, peace, and mercy, be multiplied among you. What worthy thanks can we
render unto the Lord for you, my brethren; namely, for the great consolation
which, through you, we have received in the Lord, who, notwithstanding the
rage of Satan, that goeth about by all manner of subtle means to beguile the
world, and also busily laboureth to restore and set up his kingdom again, that of
late began to decay and fall to ruin; you remain yet still immoveable, as men
surely grounded upon a strong rock. And now, albeit that Satan by his soldiers
and wicked ministers, daily draweth numbers unto him, so that it is said of him,
that he plucketh the very stars out of heaven, while he driveth into some men the
fear of death, and loss of all their goods, and showeth to others the pleasant baits
of the world; namely, riches, wealth, and all kinds of delights and pleasures, fair
houses, great revenues, fat beneficies, and what not; and all to the intent that
they should fall down and worship, not the Lord, but the dragon, the old serpent,
which is the devil, that great beast and his image, and should be enticed to
commit fornication with the strumpet of Babylon, together with the kings of the
earth, with the lesser beast, and with the false prophets, and so to rejoice and be
pleasant with her, and go get drunk with the wine of her fornication: yet blessed*

---

[3] Cranmer was the other individual of the three; and though nothing is hinted of his taking a share
in the correspondence of these illustrious prisoners, it is evident, by the incidental mention of
him in this place, that he had not yet become shaken, nor that he yet thought of recanting.
[4] Two excellent women to whom some of Bradford's best letters were addressed. It would appear
from their ministrations to the Oxford as well as London prisoners, that they devoted themselves
to a general attention to the wants of the martyrs of that day.

be God the Father of our Lord Jesus Christ, which hath given unto you a manly courage, and hath so strengthened you in the inward man, by the power of His Spirit, that you can contemn so well all the allurements of the world, esteeming them as vanities, mere trifles, and things of nought; who hath also wrought, planted, and surely established in your hearts, so steadfast a faith and love of the Lord Jesus Christ, joined with such constancy, that by no engines of antichrist, be they ever so terrible or plausible, you will suffer any other Jesus, or any other Christ, to be forced upon you, besides him whom the prophets have spoken of before, the apostles have preached, the holy martyrs of God have confessed and testified with the effusion of their blood.

In this faith stand you fast, my brethren, and suffer not yourselves to be brought under the yoke of bondage and superstition anymore. For you know, brethren, how our Saviour warned us before hand, that such should come as would point unto the world another Christ, and would set him out with so many false miracles, and with such deceivable and subtle practices, that even the very elect, if it were possible, should thereby be deceived: such strong delusion to come did our Saviour give warning of before. But continue you faithful and constant, and be of good comfort, and remember that our great captain hath overcome the world: for He that is in us is stronger than he that is in the world, and the Lord promiseth us, that for the elect's sake, the days of wickedness shall be shortened. In the mean season abide you and endure with patience as you have begun: "Endure," I say, and "reserve yourselves unto better times," as one of the heathen poets said; cease not to shew yourselves valiant soldiers of the Lord, and help to maintain the travailing faith of the gospel.

"You have need of patience, that after you have done the will of God you may receive the promises. For yet a very little, and he that shall come, will come, and will not tarry; and the just shall live by faith: but if any withdraw himself, My soul shall have no pleasure in him." These are the words of the living God. "But we are not they which do withdraw ourselves unto damnation, but they which believe unto the salvation of the soul." Let us not suffer these words of Christ to fall out of our hearts by any manner of terror, or threatenings of the world. "Fear not them which kill the body," the rest you know. For I write not unto you, as men which are ignorant of the truth, but who know the truth; and to this end only, that we agreeing together in one faith, may comfort one another, and be more confirmed and strengthened thereby. We never had a better, or more just cause either to contemn our life, or shed our blood; we cannot take in hand the defense of a more certain, clear, and manifest truth. For it is not any ceremony for which we contend; but it toucheth the very substance of our whole religion, yea, even Christ himself. Shall we, or can we receive any other Christ instead of him, who is alone the everlasting Son of the everlasting Father, and is the brightness of the glory, and a lively image of the substance of the Father, in whom only dwelleth corporeally the fulness of the Godhead, who is the only way, the truth, and the life? Let such wickedness, let such horrible wickedness be far from us. For although there be that be called gods, whether in heaven or in earth, as there may be many gods, and many lords, yet unto us there is but one

God, who is the Father, of whom are all things, and we by Him; but every man hath not knowledge. This is life eternal, that they know Thee to be the only true God, and Jesus Christ whom Thou hast sent. If any therefore would force upon us any other God, besides him who Paul and the apostles have taught, let us not hear him, but let us fly from, and hold him accursed.

Brethren, you are not ignorant of the deep and profound subtleties of Satan; for he will not cease to range about you, seeking by all means possible whom he may devour: but you play you the men, and be of good comfort in the Lord. And although your enemies and the adversaries of the truth, armed with all worldly force and power that may be, do set upon you: yet be you not faint-hearted, and shrink not therefore, but trust unto your captain Christ, trust unto the Spirit of truth, and trust to the truth of your cause; which as it may by the malice of Satan be darkened, so can it never be clean put out. For we have most plainly, evidently, and clearly on our side, all the prophets, all the apostles, and undoubtedly all the ancient ecclesiastical writers which have written, until of late years past.

Let us be hearty and of good courage therefore, and thoroughly comfort ourselves in the Lord. Be in no wise afraid of your adversaries; for that which is to them an occasion of perdition, is to you a sure token of salvation, and that of God. For unto you it is given, that not only you should believe on Him, but also suffer for His sake. And when you are railed upon for the name of Christ, remember that by the voice of Peter, yea, and of Christ our Saviour also, ye are counted with the prophets, with the apostles, and with the holy martyrs of Christ, happy and blessed for ever: for the glory and Spirit of God resteth upon you. On their part our Saviour Christ is evil spoken of, but on your part He is glorified. For what can they else do unto you by persecuting you, and working all cruelty and villany against you, but make your crowns more glorious, yea beautify and multiply the same, and heap upon themselves the horrible plagues and heavy wrath of God? and therefore, good brethren, though they rage ever so fiercely against us, yet let us not wish evil unto them again, knowing that while for Christ's cause they vex and persecute us, they are like mad-men, most outrageous and cruel against themselves, heaping hot burning coals upon their own heads: but rather wish well unto them, knowing that we are thereunto called in Christ Jesus, that we should be heirs of the blessing. Let us pray therefore unto God, that He would drive out of their hearts this darkness of errors, and make the light of His truth to shine unto them, that they acknowledging their blindness, may with all humble repentance be converted unto the Lord, and with us confess Him to be the only true God, which is the Father of light, and His only Son Jesus Christ, worshipping Him in spirit and truth. The Spirit of our Lord Jesus Christ comfort your hearts in the love of God, and patience of Christ, Amen. Your brother in the Lord, whose name this bearer shall signify unto you, ready always by the grace of God to live and die with you.

Grindal, afterwards archbishop of Canterbury, was at this time an exile in the city of Frankfort. Thence he addressed a letter to bishop Ridley, lamenting his sufferings, and entreating him to be constant and valiant for the truth. In the course of the letter he desires to know the mind of Ridley in regard to printing a manuscript of his on the subject of transubstantiation. Ridley answers that he does not think it worth while to translate or print the work until it is seen how he, the author, is likely to be disposed. There is nothing in the other parts of his answer to Grindal that is remarkable, unless it be the following paragraph, which shews him to have been a man of humor and wit as well as true wisdom and virtue: "Of us three prisoners at Oxford, I am kept most strict; because the man in whose house I am a prisoner is governed by his wife—a morose superstitious old woman, who thinks she shall merit by having me closely confined. The man himself, whose name is Irish, is civil enough to all, but too much ruled by his wife. Though I never had a wife, yet from this daily usage I begin to understand how great and intolerable a burden it is to have a bad one. The wise man says rightly—a good wife is the gift of God, and he who has a good wife is a blessed man."

Having commenced this chapter with a sketch of the life of Ridley, it will now be proper to review the leading incidents in the history of Latimer. He was the son of Hugh Latimer, of Thurcaster, in the county of Leicester, a husbandman in good repute, with whom he was brought up until he was about four years old: when his parents, seeing him to be of a ready, prompt, and sharp wit, purposed to train him up to literature; wherein he so profited in the common schools of his own country, that at fourteen years of age he was sent to the university of Cambridge: where, after some continuance in the exercise of other things, he devoted himself to the school divinity of that age. Zealous he was then in the popish religion, and therewith so scrupulous, as himself confessed, that being a priest, and officiating at the mass, he was so servile an observer of the Romish decrees, that he thought he had never sufficiently mingled his massing wine with water; and moreover, that he should never be damned, if he were once a professed friar, with many such superstitious fantasies. And in this blind zeal his was a great enemy to the professors of Christ's gospel; as both his oration, when he commenced bachelor of divinity, against Melancthon, and his other works, plainly declared. He also was strongly excited against Mr. Stafford, reader of the divinity lectures in Cambridge, at whom he most spitefully railed, and persuaded the youth of Cambridge in no wise to believe him.

Notwithstanding, such was the purpose of God, that when he saw his good time, by which he thought utterly to have defaced the professors of the gospel, and true church of Christ, he was himself by a member of the same caught in the blessed net of God's word. For Mr. Thomas Bilney, seeing Mr. Latimer to have a zeal, although not according to knowledge, felt a brotherly pity towards him, and began to consider by what means he might win this zealous ignorant brother to the truth. Wherefore, after a short time, he came to Mr. Latimer's study, and desired him to hear his confession, which he willingly did; when he was, by the good Spirit of God, so touched, that immediately he forsook the study of the School-doctors, and other such fopperies, and became an earnest student in true divinity. So that whereas before he was an enemy, and almost a persecutor of Christ, he was now a zealous seeker after him, changing his old manner of cavilling and railing, into a diligent kind of conferring, both with Mr. Bilney and others, and went also to Mr. Stafford before he died, and desired his forgiveness.

After his own conversion, he was not satisfied without endeavoring to bring about that of others. He therefore became both a public preacher, and a private instructor to the rest of his brethren within the university, for the space of three years, spending his time partly in the Latin tongue among the learned, and partly amongst the simple people in his native language. But the Prince of darkness soon found a means to disturb this happy state. There was an Augustine friar, who took occasion upon certain sermons of Mr. Latimer, which he preached about Christmas, 1529, as well in the church of St. Edward, as also in that of St. Augustine, within the university of Cambridge, to inveigh against him, because Mr. Latimer in the said sermons, according to the common usage of the season, gave the people certain cards out of the 5th, 6th, and 7th chapters of St. Matthew, whereupon they might, not only then, but at all other times, occupy their time. For the chief triumph in the cards he limited the heart, as the principal thing they should serve God withal, whereby he quite overthrew all hypocritical and external ceremonies, not tending to the necessary furtherance of God's holy word and sacraments. For the better attaining hereof, he wished the scriptures to be in English, in order that the common people might be better enabled to learn their duty to God and to their neighbors. His treatment of this subject was so apt for the time, and so pleasantly applied by him, that it not only declared the wit and dexterity of the preacher, but also wrought in the hearers much fruit, to the overthrow of popish superstition.

This happened on the Sunday before Christmas-day; on which day coming to the church, he entered the pulpit, taking his text the words of the gospel aforesaid, "Who art thou?" And in delivering the cards as above mentioned, he made the heart to be triumph,[5] exhorting and inviting all men thereby to serve the Lord with inward heart and true affection, and not with outward ceremonies: adding moreover, to the praise of that Triumph, that though it were ever so small, yet it would take up the best court card beside in the bunch, yea, though it were the king of clubs: meaning thereby how the Lord would be worshipped and served in simplicity of heart and verity, wherein consisteth true Christian religion, and not in the outward deeds of the letter only, or in the glittering shew of man's traditions, or pardons, pilgrimages, ceremonies, vows, devotions, voluntary works, and works of supererogation, foundations, oblations, the pope's supremacy, so that all these either were needless, where the other is present; or else were of small estimation, in comparison of the other. As these sermons were so important in their consequences, we here

---

[5] The word trump, as now used, is a corruption from triumph—the triumph card.

present the reader with the following beautiful extract from one of them, written in Cambridge about the year of our Lord 1529:—

Tu quis es? Which words are as much as to say in English, "Who art thou?" These be the words of the Pharisees, which were sent by the Jews unto John the Baptist in the wilderness, to have knowledge of him who he was; which words they spake unto him of an evil intent, thinking that he would have taken on him to be Christ, and so they would have had him done by their good wills, because they knew that he was more carnal and given to their laws, than Christ indeed should be, as they perceived by their old prophecies: and also, because they marvelled much at his great doctrine, preaching, and baptizing, they were in doubt whether he was Christ or not: wherefore they said unto him, "Who art thou?" Then answered John, and confessed that he was not Christ. Now here is to be noted the great and prudent answer of John the Baptist unto the Pharisees, that when they required of him who he was, he would not directly answer of himself, what he was himself; but he said he was not Christ, by which saying he thought to put the Jews and Pharisees out of their false opinion and belief towards him, in that they would have had him to exercise the office of Christ, and so declared further unto them of Christ saying—"He is in the midst of you, and amongst you, whom ye know not, the latchet of whose shoe I am not worthy to unloose." By this you may perceive that St. John spake much in the praise of his master Christ, professing himself to be in no wise like unto Him. So likewise it shall be necessary unto all men and women of this world, not to ascribe unto themselves any goodness of themselves, but all unto our Lord God, as shall appear hereafter, when this question Who art thou? shall be moved unto them: not as the Pharisees did unto John, from an evil purpose, but of a good and simple mind, as may appear hereafter.

Now then, according to the preacher, let every man and woman, of a good and simple mind, contrary to the Pharisees' intent, ask this question— Who art thou? This question must be moved to themselves, what they be of themselves, on this fashion—What art thou of thy only and natural generation between father and mother, when thou camest into the world? What substance, what virtue, what goodness art thou of thyself? Which question, if thou rehearse oftentimes to thyself, thou shalt well perceive and understand, how thou shalt make answer to it: which must be made in this wise: I am of myself, and by myself, coming from my natural father and mother, the child of the anger and indignation of God, the true inheritor of hell, except I have better help of another, than I have of myself. Now we may see in what state we enter into this world, that we be of ourselves the true and just inheritors of hell, the children of the ire and indignation of Christ, working all towards hell, whereby we deserve of ourselves perpetual damnation, by the right judgment of God and the true claim of ourselves: which unthrifty state that we be born unto is come unto us for our own deserts, as proveth well this example following.

Let it be admitted for the probation of this, that it might please the king's grace now being, to accept into his favor a mean man, of simple degree and birth, not born to any possessions; whom the king's grace favoreth, not because this person hath of himself deserved any such favour, but that the king casteth his favor unto him of his own mere motion and fancy: and because the king's grace will more declare his favor unto him, he giveth unto this said man a thousand pounds in lands, to him and his heirs, on this condition, that he shall take upon him to be the chief captain and defender of his town of Calais, and to be true and faithful to him in the custody of the same, against the Frenchmen especially above all other enemies. This man then taketh on him this charge, promising this fidelity thereunto; it chanceth in process of time, that by the singular acquaintance and frequent familiarity of this captain with the Frenchmen, these Frenchmen give unto the said captain of Calais a great sum of money, so that he will be but content and agreeable, that they may enter into the said town of Calais by force of arms, and so thereby possess the same unto the crown of France. Upon this agreement the Frenchmen do invade the said town of Calais, only by the negligence of this captain.

Now the king hearing of this invasion, cometh with a great puissance to defend this his said town, and so by good policy of war overcometh the said Frenchmen, and entereth again into his town of Calais. Then he being desirous to know how these enemies of his came thither, maketh strict search and inquiry by whom this treason was conspired; by this search it was known and found his own captain to be the very author and the beginner of the betraying it. The king seeing the great infidelity of this person, dischargeth this man of his office, and taketh from him and his heirs this thousand pounds' possessions. Think you not that the king doth use justice unto him, and all his posterity and heirs? Yes truly, the said captain cannot deny himself but that he had true justice, considering how unfaithfully he behaved himself to his prince, contrary to his own fidelity and promise: so likewise it was of our first father Adam. He had given unto him the spirit and science of knowledge, to work all goodness therewith; this said spirit was not given only to him, but unto all his heirs and posterity. He had also delivered him the town of Calais, that is to say, paradise in earth, the most strong and fairest town in the world, to be in his custody: he nevertheless, by the instigation of these Frenchmen, that is, the temptation of the fiend, did consent unto their desire, and so he broke his promise and fidelity, the commandment of the everlasting King his master.

Now then, the king seeing this great treason in his captain, dispossessed him of the thousand pounds' of lands, that is to say, from everlasting life and glory, and all his heirs and posterity: for likewise as he had the spirit of science and knowledge for him and his heirs; so in like manner when he lost the same, his heirs also lost it by him, and in him. So now this example proveth, that by our father Adam we had once in him the very inheritance of everlasting joy; and by him, and in him again we lost the same. The heirs of the captain of Calais could not by any manner of claim ask of the king the right and title of their father in the thousand pounds, by reason the king might answer and say unto them, that although their father deserved not of himself to enjoy so great possessions, yet he deserved by himself to lose them, and greater, committing so high treason as he did, against his prince's commandment; whereby he had no wrong to lose his title, but was unworthy to have the same, and had therein true justice; let not you think, which be his heirs, that if he had justice to lose his possessions, you have wrong to lose the same.

In the same manner it may be answered unto all men and women now in being, that if our father Adam had true justice to be excluded from his possessions of everlasting glory in paradise, let us not think the contrary that be his heirs, but that we have no wrong in losing also the same; yea, we have true justice and right. Then in what miserable estate we are, that of the right and just title of our own deserts have lost the everlasting joy, and claim of ourselves to be true inheritors of hell! For he that committeth deadly sin willingly, bindeth himself to be an inheritor of everlasting pain: and so did our forefather Adam willingly eat of the apple forbidden. Wherefore he was cast out of the everlasting joy in paradise, into this corrupt world among all vileness, whereby of himself he was not worthy to do anything laudable or pleasant to God, evermore bound to corrupt affections and beastly appetites, transformed into the uncleanest and most variable nature that was made under heaven, of whose seed and disposition all the world is lineally descended; insomuch that this evil nature is so much diffused and shed from one into another, that at this day there is no man or woman living, who can of themselves wash away this abominable vileness: and so we must needs grant ourselves to be in like displeasure unto God, as our father Adam was; by reason hereof, as I said, we are of ourselves the very children of the indignation of God, the true inheritors of hell, and working all towards hell, which is the answer to this question, made to every man and woman by themselves—Who art thou?

And now the world standing in this damnable state, cometh in the occasion of the incarnation of Christ; the Father in heaven perceiving the frail nature of man, that he by himself and of himself could do nothing for himself, by His prudent wisdom sent down the second person in the Trinity, His Son Jesus Christ, to declare unto man His pleasure and commandment: and so at the Father's will, Christ took on Him human nature, being willing to deliver man out of this miserable way, and was content to suffer cruel passion in shedding His blood for all mankind, and so left behind for our safeguard, laws and ordinances, to keep us always in the right path unto everlasting life, as the gospels, the sacraments, the commandments; which if we do keep and observe according to our profession, we shall answer better unto this question—"Who art thou?" than we did before: for before thou didst enter into the sacrament of baptism, thou wert by a natural man or our natural woman; as I might say, a man, a woman; but after thou takest on thee Christ's religion, thou hast a longer name; for then thou art a Christian man, a Christian woman. Now then, seeing thou art a Christian man, what shall be the answer of this question—"Who art thou?"

The answer of this question is, when I ask it unto myself, I must say that I am a Christian man, a Christian woman, the child of everlasting joy, through the merits of the bitter passion of Christ. This is a joyful answer. Here we may see how much we are bound and indebted unto God, that hath revived us from death of life, and saved us that were condemned; which great benefit we cannot well consider unless we remember what we were of ourselves before we meddled with him or his laws: and the more we know our feeble nature, and set less by it, the more we shall conceive and know in our hearts what God hath done for us: and the more we know what God hath done for us, the less we shall set by ourselves, and the more we shall love and please God; so that in no condition we shall either know ourselves or God, except we utterly confess ourselves to be mere vileness and corruption. Well now it is come unto this point, that we are Christian men, Christian women, I pray you, what doth Christ require of a Christian man, or of a Christian woman? Christ requireth nothing else of a Christian man or woman, but that they will observe his rules.

To relate at full the alarm the preaching of this and the other sermons occasioned at Cambridge, would require too much time and space. And prior of Black Friars, named Buckenham, attempted to prove that it was not expedient for the scripture to be in English, lest the ignorant and vulgar sort, through the occasion thereof, might be brought in danger of leaving their vocations, or else of running into some inconvenience. As an example he said, "The ploughman, when he heareth this in the gospel, "No man that layeth his hand on the plough and looketh back, is meet for the kingdom of God,' might peradventure cease from his plough. Likewise the baker, when he hears that a little leaven corrupteth a whole lump of dough, may perchance leave our bread unleavened, and so our bodies shall be unseasoned. Also the simple man, when he heareth in the gospel, 'If thine eye offend thee, pluck it out and cast it from thee,' may make himself blind, and so fill the world with beggars." These, with some others, this clerkly friar brought out, to prove his purpose of keeping Scripture in a strange tongue, and from the common people!

Mr. Latimer hearing the sermon of Buckenham, came shortly after the church to answer him. To hear him came a multitude, as well of the university as of the town, both doctors and other graduates, with great expectation to learn what he could say: among whom also, directly in the face of Latimer, underneath the pulpit, sat Buckenham, with his black friar's cowl about his shoulders. Then Latimer, first repeating the reason of Buckenham, whereby he would prove it a dangerous thing for the vulgar to have the scriptures in their own tongue, so refuted the friar, so answered to his objections, so ridiculed his bald reason of the ploughman looking back, of the baker leaving his bread unleavened, and of the simple man plucking out his eye, that the vanity of the friar might to all men appear, well proving and declaring to the people, that there was no such danger from the scriptures being in English. And proceeding moreover in his sermon, he began to discourse of the mystical speeches and figurative phrases of the scriptures; which he said were not so diffuse and difficult as pretended.

Besides this Buckenham, there was also another railing friar, a doctor and a foreigner, named Venetus, who likewise in his sermons railed and raged against Mr. Latimer, calling him a mad and brainless man, and persuading the people not to believe him. To whom Mr. Latimer answering again, took for his ground the words of our Saviour Christ, "Thou shalt not kill, and whosoever shall kill shall be in danger of the judgment. But I say unto you, Whosoever is angry with his neighbour shall be in danger of judgment; and whosoever shall say unto his neighbour Raca, shall be in danger of judgment; and whosoever shall say unto his neighbour Raca, shall be in danger of the council: and whosoever shall say to his neighbour, Fool, shall be in danger of hell-fire." The discussing of which, first he divided the offense of killing into three branches, one to be with hand, the other with heart, the third with word. With hand, when we use any weapon drawn, to spill the blood of our neighbour. With heart, when we be angry with him. With word, when we disdainfully rebuke our neighbour, or despitefully revile him.

But why should we here decipher the names of his adversaries, when whole swarms of friars and doctors flocked against him on every side, almost through the whole university, preaching against the abusing him? Amongst whom was Dr. Watson, master of Christ's college, whose scholar Latimer had been. In short, almost as many as were heads of houses, so many were the enemies of this worthy standard-bearer of Christ's gospel. At last came Dr. West, bishop of Ely, who preaching against him at Barnwell-abby, forbade him within the churches of that university to preach anymore. Not withstanding, so the Lord provided, that Dr. Barnes, prior of the Augustine friars, did license Mr. Latimer to preach in his church of the Augustines, and he himself preached at St. Edward's church, which was the first sermon of the gospel that Dr. Barnes preached, being Sunday and Christmas Eve. Whereupon certain articles were gathered out of his sermon, and brought against him by Mr. Tyrell fellow of the King's-hall, and so by the vice-chancellor they were presented to the cardinal.

Thus Mr. Latimer being baited by the friars, doctors, and masters of that university, about the year 1529, notwithstanding the malice of these malignant adversaries, continued yet in Cambridge preaching for about three years together, with favor and applause of the godly, also with such admiration of his enemies who heard him, that the bishop himself coming in, and witnessing his merit, wished himself to have the like, and was compelled to commend him upon it. After this, Mr. Latimer and Mr. Bilney continued in Cambridge for some time, where they so frequently conferred together, that the field wherein they usually walked was long after called the heretics' hill. As their intimacy was much noted by many of the university, so was it full of many good examples, to all who would follow them, both in visiting the prisoners, and relieving the needy. The following interesting story will exemplify the benevolence of Mr. Latimer. It happened that, with Mr. Bilney, he went to visit the prisoners in the tower of Cambridge, and being there, among others was a woman who was accused of having killed her own child, which act she plainly and steadfastly denied. Whereby it gave them occasion to search for the matter, and at length they found that her husband loved her not, and therefore sought all means to destroy her. The particulars were thus:—

A child of hers had been sick a whole year, and at length died in harvest time, as it were in a consumption: which when it was gone, she sought her neighbors to help her at the burial, but all being abroad in the harvest, she was forced with heaviness of heart, to prepare the child alone for the burial. Her husband coming home, accused her of murdering the child. This was the cause of her trouble; and Mr. Latimer, by earnest inquisition of conscience, thought the woman not guilty. Immediately after this he was called to preach before king Henry VIII at Windsor, and after his sermon the king sent for him, and talked familiarly with him. At which time Mr. Latimer, finding an opportunity, kneeled down, opened the whole matter to the king, and desired her pardon, which he granted, and gave it to him at his return home. In the meantime the woman was delivered of a child in the prison, to which Mr. Latimer stood godfather. But all the while he would not tell her of the pardon, but labored to have her confess the truth of the matter. At length the time came when she expected to suffer, and Mr. Latimer came as he was wont, to instruct her; when she made great lamentations, to be purified before her suffering, for she thought she must be damned if she died without purification. Mr. Bilney being with Mr. Latimer, told her, that law was made for the Jews, and not for us, and that women were as well in the favor of God before they be purified as after: and that it was appointed for a civil and politic law. They then argued with her until they had better instructed her, and at length shewed her the king's pardon, and liberated her.

Besides this, many other actions equally benevolent, were known to originate from this zealous Christian; insomuch, that the enemies of truth, instigated by envy, soon sought a means to interrupt the harmony of him and his friend. So much virtue provoked envy in many. Among the rest of this number was Dr. Redman, a man favouring more of superstition than of true religion, after the zeal of the Pharisees, yet not so malignant or hurtful, but of a mild disposition, and also liberal in well doing, so that few poor scholars were in that university who fared not the better by his purse. He was a man of great authority in the university of Cambridge, and perceiving the boldness of Mr. Latimer, in publishing in sincerity the genuine truths of the gospel, endeavoured by a letter to persuade him from his manner of preaching. To this Mr. Latimer wrote the following laconic answer.

Reverend Mr. Redman, it is even enough for me, that Christ's sheep hear no man's voice but Christ's: and as for you, you have no voice of Christ against me; whereas for my part, I have a heart that is ready to hearken to any voice of Christ that you can bring me. Thus fare you well, and trouble me no more from talking with the Lord my God.

Mr. Latimer having thus labored in preaching and teaching in Cambridge about three years, was at length called up to Cardinal Wolsey for heresy, by the procurement of some of the university, where he was content to subscribe and grant to such articles as they then propounded to him. After that he again returned to the university, where shortly after, by the means of Dr. Butts, the king's physician, a singular good man, he was placed in the number of those who labored in the cause of the king's supremacy. On this he went to the court, where he remained a certain time in Dr. Butts's chamber, and preached very often in London. At last being weary of the court, and having a benefice offered by the king, at the suit of the lord Cromwell and Dr. Butts, he gladly accepted it, and withdrew from the court, wherewith in no case he could agree.

The royal gift was at West Kingston, in Wiltshire, in the diocese of Sarum. Here this good preacher exercised himself with much diligence, teaching his flock and all the country about. In fine, his diligence was so great, his preaching so powerful, the manner of his teaching so zealous, that there also he could not escape enemies. So true it is what St. Paul foretelleth us—"Whosoever will live godly in Christ shall suffer persecution." It so happened, that as he was preaching upon the Virgin Mary, and reserving all honor to Christ our only Saviour, certain popish priests being therewith offended, sought and created much trouble against him, drawing out articles and impositions which they falsely and uncharitably imputed unto him—That he should preach against our Lady, for that he reproved in a sermon the superstitious rudeness of certain blind priests, who taught that she never had any sin, and that she was not saved by Christ—that he should say, that saints were not to be worshipped—that Ave Maria was a salutation only, and no prayer—that there was no material fire in hell—and that there was no purgatory, trifling with the subject and saying, that he had rather be in purgatory than in Lallard's Tower.

The chief enemies and molesters of him, besides these country priests, were Dr. Powel, of Salisbury, Dr. Wilson, sometime of Cambridge, a Mr. Hubberdin, and Dr. Sherwood. Of whom some preached and some wrote against him; insomuch that by their procurement he was cited up, and called to appear before Warham, archbishop of Canterbury, and Stokesly, bishop of London, January 29th, 1531. Against which citation, although Mr. Latimer did appeal to his own ordinary, yet notwithstanding that, he was brought to London before Warham and Stokesly, where he was greatly molested, and detained a long time from his cure at home, being called thrice every week before the bishops, to make answer for his preaching, and had certain articles or propositions drawn out and laid to him, whereunto they required him to subscribe. At length he not only perceiving their practical proceedings, but being also much grieved with their troublesome unquietness, who neither would preach themselves, nor yet suffer him; he wrote to the archbishop, partly excusing his infirmity, whereby he could not appear at their commandment, partly expostulating with them for so troubling and detaining him from doing his duty, and that for no just cause, but only for preaching the truth against certain vain abuses crept into religion, much needful to be spoken against. The letter is as follows.

MOST REVEREND GOVERNOR,

Had not sickness prevented me, I had myself waited on you at your palace; but these fresh troubles have brought on me a sharp return of an old distemper, so that I can't be able to wait on you today without great pain; but that your lordship might no longer in vain expect my coming, I have sent these lines scribbled with mine own hand to your grace, as to a most upright judge, of my excuse, in which I wish I had more time or more judgment to frame a just expostulation with your grace for detaining me so long against my will from my cure, and that so unseasonably, at a time when it most behoves every pastor to be with his flock. But what shall I say, if it is lawful for so mean a prisoner to plead with so great a father? If we esteem a priest good for doing his duty, who, while he remains in this earthly tabernacle, never ceaseth to teach and admonish his congregation, and so much the more as he draws nearer his last home, what must we think of those who neither preach themselves now, nor permit those who are desirous to do it, unless they are bound to do and say nothing but what they please. At first I thought it safe to submit myself entirely to your clemency, but now it seems as safe to justify myself a little, since one thing was pretended in the beginning, but now another, and what will be the end I have great room to doubt; but I hope truth only will be used. First I was sent to London, where I was before the court of Canterbury; then all was stopped that had been done, and the matter had bounds and limits set to it by him who sent me; but so the business was handled and brought into doubt, that at length there seemed no end of it, but that it must be infinitely prolonged. For while, without either method or design, I was questioned of one thing after another, whether pertinent or impertinent, now by one and then by another, if I gave them no answer, or if I answered them to the purpose—which I thought was not imprudent sometimes to put an end to the dispute—I was equally uncivil; while one answer to many and of many things, he may inadvertently say something that may prejudice the most righteous cause. None ought to judge me wicked for what at most they can call but an error of conscience; and to remember all things, it behoves a man to remember the foundation of the other world. When a man acts against conscience, he doth it to gain, to maintain, or defend his own; but what they charge me with is far different, and I believe without example, wickedly requesting to know the cause of my confinement. If any person is disposed to attack my sermons, that they are obscure, or not cautiously enough worded, I am prepared either to explain or vindicate them, for I never preached anything against the truth, against the councils of the fathers, or the catholic faith. All that my adversaries or detractors truly charge me with, is what I have long desired, and do desire, namely, the improving the common people's judgment. I heartily desired that all men might know and comprehend the disagreement of things, the worth, place, time, degrees, and order proper for each, and how much they are concerned in those things which God has prepared for them to walk in: every man ought to be very diligent in doing the works of his calling; after which, many things indifferent may be done with equal diligence, amongst which are all things which no law has forbid, unless we forbid them to ourselves. It is lawful to use images, to go on pilgrimages, to invocate saints, to remember the souls in purgatory, but these which are voluntary acts are to be so restrained, that they diminished not the just esteem of the precepts of God, which bestow eternal life on those who follow them: them who use them otherwise, are so far from gaining the love of God, that they rather incur His hatred. The true love of God is to keep His commandments, as our Saviour says, "He who heareth my words and doeth them, he it is who loveth me." Let no man then have so mean an opinion of the laws of God, as to make them equal to the fancies of men, since by those at the last day before the tribunal of Christ we shall all be judged, and not by these; as Christ says, "The word that I speak, that shall judge you at the last day:" and what man is able to make amends for the breach of one of those commandments, by any or all of these specious additions? O that we would be but as ready, as diligent, as devoted to do his will, as we are to follow our own empty notions! Many things done with an upright heart God accepts of, making allowances for our infirmities, though he has not commanded or required them; but these things ought to be taken away when they begin to have the force of commands, lest while we do these we omit those that are absolutely necessary; and what can be more absurd than to revere as ordinances of God, the idle fancies of men, whilst his true ordinances are neglected: whence I in behalf of the commandments of God stand hitherto immoveable, not seeking my own but Christ's gain, not my own but God's glory: and whilst I live I will stand steadfast.

Thus all the German divines have hitherto complained of the intolerable abuse of these things, that no man desirous of the glory of Christ can accept of the ministry without doing what is against his conscience, and if some have submitted to this hardship purely to do good, yet what doth the Christian religion suffer by it? unless we are so miserably blinded as to think that these things are to be dispensed with for our own filthy gain, though they are not for the honor of God. Now who can justify the constant practise of such things which in themselves are highly criminal? Some things are constantly performed which ought never, while others are omitted which ought always to be done: now who cannot see this manifest abuse? And who sees, and does not grieve? And who grieves, that would not labour to remove it? And when shall it be removed, while it is constantly preached and commended? Why, it is hardly possible for it not to be universal. It is one thing barely to permit, and another to enforce as law. "Go," says Christ, "and teach the people whatsoever I have commanded you." Let us therefore, by the help of God, go and do this: let us employ our whole strength to preach the sincere word of God, not to flatter or cook up our sermons to men's depraved taste, then shall we be true preachers of God's word. Careless as men are in what relates to God, they are diligent enough in what relates to themselves, to this they want no spurs; but they are miserably deceived by an unjust esteem of things, and an early superstition received in their tender years from their forefathers, which we are hardly able to remember by any preaching, how frequent, how earnest, how sincere and pure soever, which God doth now permit; for in these evil days they who ought to preach themselves, forbid them to preach who are willing and able, and on the contrary, compel timeservers, who damnably detain the miserable people in superstition and false confidence; but the Lord have mercy upon us, and grant we may know his way upon earth, not to be found amongst those to whom he says, "My ways are not your ways, neither are my thoughts your thoughts." Hence I dare not subscribe to these propositions, most honored father, because I would no ways be accessary to the longer continuance of these popular superstitions, lest I should be the author of my own damnation. Were I worthy, I would even give you some advice, but that impertinent thing, the heart, can do little else than guess, none knowing the things of a man but the spirit of a man which is in him. It is not any pride that hinders me from subscribing to these propositions; on the contrary, I am very sorry I cannot wholly perform your request. I know how great a crime it is to disobey God rather than man.

My head aches so much; and my body is so weak, that I can neither come, nor write over again and correct these lines; but your lordship I hope, will approve, if not the judgment, yet the endeavors of your lordship's devoted servant.

The several articles which he was required by the bishops to subscribe were these—"I believe that there is a purgatory to purge the souls of the dead after this life; that the souls in purgatory are holpen with the masses, prayers, and alms of the living; that the saints do pray as mediators now for us in heaven; that they are to be honoured by us in heaven; that it is profitable for Christians to call upon the saints, that they may pray as mediators for us unto God; that pilgrimages and oblations done to the sepulchers and relics of saints are meritorious; that they which have vowed perpetual chastity may not marry, nor break their vow, without the dispensation of the pope; that the keys of binding and loosing, delivered to Peter, do still remain with the bishops of Rome his successors, although they live wickedly, and are by no means, nor at any time, committed to laymen; that men may merit and deserve at God's hand by fasting, prayer, and other good works of piety; that they which are forbidden by the bishop to preach, as suspected persons, ought to cease until they have purged themselves before the said bishop, or their superiors, and be restored again; that the fast which is used in Lent and other fasts prescribed by the canons, and by custom received of the Christians, are to be observed and kept;

that God in every one of the seven sacraments giveth grace to a man, rightly receiving the same; that consecrations, sanctifyings, and blessings, by use and custom received in the church, are laudable and profitable; that it is laudable and profitable, that the venerable images of the crucifix and other saints should be had in the churches as a remembrance, and to the honor and worship of Jesus Christ and his saints; that it is laudable and profitable to deck and to clothe those images, and set up burning lights before them to the honor of the said saints."

To these articles, whether he did subscribe or not, it is uncertain. It appears by his letter above, that he durst not consent to them; for he says—"I dare not subscribe to these propositions, because I would no ways be accessary to the longer continuance of these popular superstitions, lest I be the author of my own damnation." But whether he was compelled afterwards to agree, through the cruel dealings of the bishops, remains a doubt. By the words and the title in Tonstal's register prefixed before the articles, it may seem that he did subscribe. The words of the register are these—"Hugh Latimer, bachelor of divinity, of the university of Cambridge, in a convocation held at West-minster before the lord archbishop of Canterbury, the lord bishop of London, and the rest of the clergy, has acknowledged and made the following confession of his faith, as in these articles, March 21st, 1531." If these words be true, it may be thought that he subscribed. But it ought to be received with great doubt, considering the subtlety, artifice, and want of candour, that prevailed amongst the Romish party. The following curious incident was related by himself in a sermon preached at Stamford, October 9th, 1550.

I was once in examination before five or six bishops, where I had much trouble: thrice every week I came to examinations, and many snares and traps were laid to get something. Now God knoweth I was ignorant of the law, but that God gave me wisdom what I should speak; it was God indeed, or else I had never escaped them. At last I was brought forth to be examined into a chamber hung with arras, where I was wont to be examined: but now at this time the chamber was somewhat altered. For whereas before there was wont always to be a fire in the chimney, now the fire was taken away, and an arras hung over the chimney, and the table stood near the fire-place. There was amongst the bishops who examined me, one with whom I had been very familiar, and took him for my great friend, an aged man, and he sat next to the table's end. Then amongst other questions he put forth a very subtle and crafty one, and such an one indeed, as I could not think so great danger in. And when I should make answer, one said, "I pray you, Mr. Latimer, speak out, I am very thick of hearing, and here may be many that sit far off." I marvelled at this that I was bid to speak out, and begun to suspect, and give an ear to the chimney; and there I heard a pen writing in the chimney behind the cloth. They had appointed one there to write all mine answers, for they made sure that I should not start from them: there was no starting from them. God was my good Lord, and gave me answer, I could never else have escaped it.

The question then and there objected to him was—Whether he thought in his conscience that he had been suspected of heresy? This was a captious question. There was no holding of peace; for that was to grant himself faulty. To answer it was every way full of danger. But God, who always giveth in need what to answer, helped him, or else he had never escaped their bloody hands. Although what was his answer he doth not there express.

Amongst these hard and dangerous straits, it had been hard for him, and almost impossible to have escaped and continued so long, had not the almighty helping hand of the Highest preserved him through the power of his prince; who with much favor embraced him, and with his mere power sometimes rescued and delivered him out of the crooked claws of his enemies. Moreover, at length, also through the interest of Dr. Butts and lord Cromwell, he advanced him to the dignity of a bishop, namely, bishop of Worchester. It were too long to stand particularly upon such things as might be brought to the commendation of this pious prelate; but the days then were so dangerous and variable, that he could not in all things do what he would. Yet what he could do, that he performed to the utmost of his strength, so that although he was not utterly able to extinguish all the sparkling relics of superstition, yet he so wrought that they were, in a great measure, lessened of their evil. As for example, in this thing, and diverse others, it appeared that when it could not be avoided, but that holy water and holy bread must needs be received, yet so he prepared and instructed them of his diocese, with such informations and lessons, that in receiving thereof superstition should be excluded, and some remembrance taken thereby, teaching and charging the ministers of his diocese, in delivering the holy water and the holy bread, to use these forms. On giving the water, which had been blessed, they were to say to the people—

> Remember your promise in baptizing;
> Christ, his mercy and blood-shedding,
> By whose most holy sprinkling,
> Of all your sins you have free pardoning.

And on giving the people the consecrated bread, they were to say—

> Of Christ's body this is a token,
> Which on the cross for our sins was broken:
> Wherefore of your sins you must be foresakers,
> If of Christ's death you will be partakers.

Thus this good man behaved himself in his diocese. But still, both in the university and at his benefice, he was tossed and troubled by wicked and evil disposed persons; so in his bishopric also, he was not free from some that sought his trouble. As among many other evil willers, one especially there was, and he no small person, who accused him then to the king for his sermons. He thus explained himself in another discourse—"In the king's days that is dead, a great many of us were called together before him, to speak our minds in certain matters. In the end one kneeleth down and accuseth me of having preached seditious doctrine. A heavy salutation, and a hard point of such a man's doing, as if I should name you would not think. The king turned to me and said—'What say you to that, Sir?' Then I kneeled down, and turned first to my accuser, and asked him—'Sir, what form of preaching would you appoint me in preaching before a king? Would you have me preach nothing as concerning a king in a king's sermon? Have you any commission to appoint me what I shall preach?' Besides this, I asked him diverse other questions, and he would make no answer to any of them all; he had nothing to say.

"Then I turned to the king, and submitted myself to his grace, and said—'I never thought myself worthy, nor did I ever sue to be a preacher before your grace, but I was called to it, and would be willing to give place to my betters; for I grant that there be a great many more worthy of the room than I am. And if it be your grace's pleasure so to allow them for preachers, I could be content to carry they books after them. But if your grace allow me for a preacher, I would desire you to give me leave to discharge my conscience, and thus to frame my doctrine according to my audience. I had been a very blockhead to have preached so at the borders of your realm, as I preach before your grace.' And I thank Almighty God that my sayings were well accepted of the king; for like a gracious lord he turned into another communication. It is even as the scripture saith—'The Lord directeth the king's heart.' Some of my friends came to me with tears in their eyes, and told me, they expected I should have been in the Tower the same night."

Besides this, diverse other conflicts and combats this godly bishop sustained in his own country and diocese, in taking the cause of right and equity against oppression and wrong. Thus he continued in his laborious function of a bishop until the coming of the six articles. Then being distressed through the straitness of time, he must either sacrifice a good conscience, or else forsake his bishopric; the latter of which he freely did, and Dr. Shaxton, bishop of Salisbury, resigned likewise with him. At which time he threw off his rochet in his chamber among his friends, and suddenly gave a leap for joy, on being discharged of such a heavy burden. However, he was not so lightened, but that troubles and labours followed him wheresoever he went. For a little after he renounced his bishopric, he was much bruised by the fall of a tree: then coming up to London for remedy, he was molested and troubled by the bishops, and was at length sent to the Tower, where he remained prisoner until the king Edward came to the crown, by which means the golden mouth of this preacher, long shut up before, was not opened again. He continued all the reign of Edward laboring in the Lord's harvest most fruitfully, discharging his talent at Stamford, and before the duchess of Suffolk, and many other places in this realm, as at London in the Convocation-house, and especially before the king at the court. In the inner garden, which had been applied to lascivious and courtly pastimes, there he dispensed the fruitful word of the glorious gospel of Jesus Christ, preaching before the king and his whole court, to the edification of many; for the most part twice every Sunday, although being so bruised by the fall of a tree, and above sixty-seven years of age.

As the diligence of this man of God never ceased all the time of king Edward, to profit the church both publicly and privately, so it is likewise to be observed, that the same good Spirit of God who assisted and comforted him in preaching the gospel, did also enable him to foretell all those plagues which afterwards ensued; if England ever had a prophet, he seemed to be one. And for himself, he ever affirmed that the preaching of the gospel would cost him his life, to which he no less cheerfully prepared himself; for after the death of king Edward, and not long after Mary was proclaimed queen, a pursuivant was sent down into the country to call him up, of whose coming, although Mr. Latimer lacked no forewarning, being informed thereof about six hours before by one John Careless, yet he was so far from endeavoring to escape, that he prepared himself for his journey before the officer came to his house.

At this the pursuivant marvelled, when Mr. Latimer said unto him—"My friend, you are a welcome messenger unto me. And be it known unto you and to all the world, that I go as willingly to London at this present, being called by my prince to render a reckoning of my doctrine, as ever I was at any place in the world. I doubt not but that God, as he hath made me worthy to preach his word before two excellent princes, so will he able me to witness the same unto the third, either to her comfort or discomfort eternally." When the pursuivant had delivered his letters, he departed, affirming that he had command not to wait for him. By this it was manifest that they would not have had him appear, but rather to have fled out of the realm, knowing that his constancy would deface them in their popery, and confirm the godly in the truth.

Coming up to London, and entering by Smithfield he merrily said, that Smithfield had long groaned for him. He was then brought before the council, where he patiently bearing all the mocks and taunts given him by the scornful papists, was again sent to the Tower: there being assisted by the heavenly grace of Christ, he meekly endured imprisonment a long time, notwithstanding the cruel and unmerciful usage of his enemies, who then thought their kingdom would never fall; yet he showed himself not only patient, but also merry and cheerful, above all that they could work against him: yea, such a valiant spirit the Lord gave him, that he was able not only to despise the terrors of prisons and torments, but also to deride and laugh to scorn even the cruel proceedings of his enemies. It is well known to many what answer he made to the lieutenant when he was in the Tower. For when the lieutenant's man upon a time came to him, the aged father, kept without fire in the frosty winter, and well nigh starved with cold, bade the man tell his master, that if he did not look better after him, perchance he might deceive him—meaning by a premature death.

The lieutenant hearing this, and not knowing what to make of so odd a speech, and fearing that he would in earnest make his escape, began to look more strictly to his prisoner, and so coming to him, charged him with his words, at the same time reciting them. His answer was—"So I said, for I suppose you expect that I should burn; but except you let me have some fire,

I am like to deceive your expectation, for I am in danger of starving here with cold." Thus this good man passing a long time in the Tower, with as much patience as a man in his case could do, from thence was carried to Oxford, with Cranmer and Ridley, there to dispute upon articles sent down from Gardiner, bishop of Winchester as before mentioned: the manner and order of which disputations between them and the university doctors, having been sufficiently expressed. Where also is declared, how and by whom Mr. Latimer, with his fellow-prisoners, were condemned after disputations, and so committed again to the prison, where they continued from the month of April until October, occupied either with brotherly conference, fervent prayer, or fruitful writing.

Mr. Latimer, by reason of the feebleness of his age, wrote least of all the distinguished martyrs of the day, especially in the latter time of his imprisonment; but in prayer he was fervently occupied, earnestly sending up to the throne of grace the following among numerous other petitions—That as God had appointed him to be a preacher of his word, so also He would give him grace to stand to his doctrine until his death. That God of His great mercy would restore His gospel to England once again. That of His good providence he would preserve the lady Elizabeth, whom in his prayer he used to name, and even with tears desiring God to make her a comfort to England. The answer to this prayer especially reminds us that "the prayer of a righteous man availeth much." So it appeared in the present case: indeed all the requests of this faithful servant were fully granted. His letters were equally to his prayers. Many of them were written in Latin; and they are so numerous and so long, that our limits will not admit of their insertion.

THE FOLLOWING IS A LETTER OF MASTER LATIMER TO MASTER MORRICE, CONCERNING THE ARTICLES WHICH WERE FALSELY AND UNTRULY LAID AGAINST HIM:—

Right worshipful and mine own good master Morrice, health in Christ Jesus. And I thank you, for all hearty kindness, not only heretofore shewed unto me, but also that now of late you would vouchsafe to write unto me, so poor a wretch, to my great comfort among all these my troubles, I trust and doubt nothing in it, but God will reward you for me, and abundantly supply my inability. Mr. Morrice, you would wonder to know how I have been treated at Bristol, I mean by some of the priests, who first desired me, welcomed me, made me cheer, heard what I said, and allowed my saying in all things while I was with them; but when I was gone home to my benefice, perceiving that the people favored me so greatly, and that the mayor had appointed me to preach at Easter, privily they procured in inhibition for all them that had not the bishop's license, which they knew well enough I had not, and so craftily defeated master mayor's appointment, pretending they were sorry for it, procuring also certain preachers to rail against me, as Hubberdin and Powel, with others; whom when I had brought before the mayor, and the wise council of the town, to know what they could lay to my charge, wherefore they so declaimed against me, they said they spake as they were informed. However no man could be brought forth that could stand to anything: so that they had place and time to belie me shamefully, but they had no place or time to lay to my charge when I was present and ready to make them answer. God amend them, and assuage their malice, that they have against the truth and me.

They did belie me to have said that our Lady was a sinner, when I had said nothing of the sort; but to reprove certain, both priests and beneficed men, which do give so much to our Lady, as though she had not been saved by Christ, a whole Saviour, both of her, and of all that be or shall be saved. I did reason after this manner, that either she was a sinner, or no sinner; if a sinner, then she was delivered from sin by Christ; so that He saved her, either by delivering or preserving her from sin, so that without Him neither she nor any other could be saved.⁶ And to avoid all offense, I showed how it might be answered, both to certain scriptures, which maketh all generally sinners, and also unto Chrysostom and Theophylact, who make her namely and specially a sinner. But all would not serve, their malice was so great; notwithstanding that 500 honest men can and will bear record. When they cannot reprove that thing that I do say, then will they belie me to say that thing which they can reprove; for they will needs appear to be against me.

THIS WAS NOT THE ONLY SUBJECT OF CALUMNY WHICH LATIMER'S ENEMIES TOOK UP. HE PROCEEDS THUS TO DESCRIBE THEM.

So they lied when I had shewn certain divers significations of this word "saints" among the vulgar people: First, images of saints are called saints, and so they are not to be worshipped: take worshipping of them for praying to them; for they are neither mediators by way of redemption, nor yet by way of intercession. And yet they may be well used when they be applied to the uses for which they were ordained, to be laymen's books for remembrance of heavenly things, exciting the living to "follow them who through faith and patience inherit the promises." Take saints for inhabitants of heaven, and worshipping of them, for praying to them; I never denied, but that they might be worshipped, and be our mediators,

---

⁶Mary was indeed, according to the salutation of Elizabeth, highly blessed among women in bearing that sacred body wherein her God became incarnate; but still she was a daughter of Adam, and consequently not without sin, and needing the atoning blood of Christ and his righteousness, as many as any of her fellow creatures—a fact indirectly conveyed by the words of Christ himself, who, when a certain woman exclaimed—"Blessed is the womb that bare thee, and the paps which thou hast sucked!"—answered "Yea, rather blessed are they who hear the word of God and keep it." Nothing can be clearer than that a humble believer in Christ is superior to the virgin as such, and that her chief excellence consists in her own humble and holy faith in his salvation.

though not by way of redemption, in which Christ alone is a whole Mediator, both for them and for us; yet by the way of intercession.[7]

Although they have charged me with denying pilgrimage, I never denied it. And yet I have said that much scurf must be pared away, ere ever it can be well done: superstition, idolatry, false faith, and trust in the pilgrimage, unjust estimation of the thing, setting aside God's ordinances for doing of the thing; debts must be paid, restitution made, wife and children must be provided for, duty to our neighbours discharged. And when it is at the beast, before it be vowed, it need not be done, for it is neither under the command of God nor man to be done. And wives must advise with their husbands, and husbands and wives with curates, before it be vowed to be done.

As for the Ave Maria,[8] *who can think that I would deny it? I said it was a heavenly greeting or saluting of our blessed Lady, wherein the angel Gabriel, sent from the Father of heaven, did annunciate and shew unto her the good-will of God towards her, what He would with her, and to what He had chosen her. But I said it was not properly a prayer as the Pater Noster, which our Saviour Christ himself made for a proper prayer, and bid us to say it for a prayer, not adding that we should say ten or twenty Ave Marias withal: and I denied not but that we may well say Ave Maria also, but not so that we shall think that the Pater Noster is not good, a whole and perfect prayer, and cannot be well said without Ave Maria: so that I did not speak against the well saying of it, but against the superstitious saying of it, and of the Pater Noster too; and yet I put a difference betwixt it, and that which Christ made to be said for a prayer.*

Whoever could think or say that I alleged that there was no fire whatever in hell? However, good authors do make a difference betwixt suffering in the fire with bodies, and without bodies. The soul without the body is a spiritual substance, which they say cannot receive a corporal quality; and some make it a spiritual fire, and some a corporeal fire. And as it is called a fire, so it is called a worm, and it is thought of some not to be a material worm, that is, a living reptile, but it is a metaphor, but that is nothing to the purpose; for a fire it is, a worm it is, pain it is, torment it is, anguish it is, a grief, a misery, a sorrow, a heaviness inexplicable and intolerable, whose nature and condition in every point, who can tell, but he that is of God's privy council? God give us grace rather to be diligent to keep us out of it, than to be curious to discuss the property of it; for certain we be, that there is little ease, yea, none at all, but weeping, wailing, and gnashing of teeth, which be the effects of extreme pain, rather certain token what pain there is, than what manner of pain there is.

---

[7] This may seem a harmless opinion; but no warrant for it can be drawn from scripture. We see neither in the Prophets nor the Apostles any examples of praying to saints. All requests are to be made known unto God through Christ, Psa. xlv. 17; lxxii. 15; Acts iv. 12; Phil ii 9—11; 1 Tim. ii 5, 6; Heb. ix. 14, 15.

[8] To speak with the least harshness of this, it was certainly a work of supererogation and of will worship. Mr. Latimer, in these answers, doubtless discovers an apprehension of speaking the simple truth, which many of his brother martyrs were quite free from. This, however, was in an early part of his career; as he advanced he became more firm and clear, until all obscurity vanished.

THE SUBJECT OF PURGATORY HAS ALREADY BEEN BEFORE THE READER IN REFERENCE TO LATIMER. HE WRITES THUS—

He that sheweth the state and condition of it, doth not deny it. But I had rather be in it than Lollard's Tower, that bishop's prison, for diverse reasons. In this I might die bodily for lack of meat and drink; in that I could not. In this I might die spiritually for fear of pain, or lack of good counsel; there I could not. In this I might be in extreme necessity; in that I could not, if it be peril of perishing. In this I might lack charity; there I could not. In this I might lose my patience; in that I could not. In this I might be in danger of death; in that I could not. In this I might be without surety of salvation; in that I could not. In this I might dishonour God; in that I could not. In this I might murmur and grudge against God; in that I could not. In this I might displease God; in that I could not. In this I might be displeased with God; in that I could not. In this I might be judged to perpetual prison, as they call it; in that I could not. In this I might be craftily handled; in that I could not. In this I might be brought to bear a fagot; in that I could not. In this I might be discontented with God; in that I could not. In this I might be separated and dissevered from Christ; in that I could not. In this I might be a member of the devil; in that I could not. In this I might be an inheritor of hell; in that I could not. In this I might pray out of charity, and in vain; in that I could not. In this my lord and his chaplains might manacle me by night; in that they could not. In this they might strangle me, and say that I hanged myself; in that they could not. In this they might have me to the consistory, and judge me after their fashion; from thence they could not. Therefore I had rather to be there than here. For though the fire be called ever so hot, yet if the bishop's two fingers can shake away a piece, a friar's cowl another part, and "scali coeli" altogether, I will never found abby, college, nor chauntry, for that purpose. For seeing there is no pain that can break my charity, break my patience, cause me to dishonor God, to displease God, to be displeased with God, cause me not to joy in God, nor that can bring me to danger of death, or to danger of desperation, or from surety of salvation, that can separate us from Christ, or Christ from us, I care the less for it. Chrysostom saith, the greatest pain that damned souls have, is to be separate and cut off from Christ for ever: which pain the souls in purgatory neither have nor can have.

Consider, Mr. Morrice, whether provision for purgatory hath not brought thousands to hell. Debts have not been paid; restitution of evil-gotten lands and goods hath not been made; Christian people whose necessities we see, to whom whatsoever we do Christ reputeth done to himself, to whom we are bound under pain of condemnation to do for, as we would be done for ourselves, are neglected and suffered to perish; last wills unfulfilled and broken; God's ordinance set aside; and also for purgatory, foundations have been taken for sufficient satisfaction; so we have trifled away the ordinances of God and restitutions. Thus we have gone to hell with masses, dirges, and ringing of many a bell. And who can pull pilgrimages from idolatry, and purge purgatory from robbery, but he shall be in peril to come in suspicion of heresy with them? so that they may fleece one with pilgrimage, and spoil with purgatory. And verily the abuse of them cannot be taken away, but great lucre and advantage shall fall away from them, who had rather have profit with abuse, than lack the same with use; and that is the wasp that doth sting them, and maketh them to swell. And if purgatory were purged of all that it hath gotten, by setting aside restitution, and robbing of Christ, it would be but a poor purgatory; so poor, that it should not be able to feed so fat, and trick up so many idle and slothful lubbers.

I take God to witness, I would hurt no man, but it grieveth me to see such abuse continue without remedy. I cannot understand what they mean by the pope's pardoning of purgatory, but by way of suffrage: and as for suffrage, unless he do his duty, and seek not his own, but Christ's glory, I had rather have the suffrage of Jack of the scullery, who in his calling doth exercise both faith and charity, but for his mass. And that is as good of another simple priest as of him. For, as for authority of keys, it is to loose from guiltiness of sin and eternal pain, due to the same, according to Christ's word, and not to his own private will. And as for pilgrimage, you will wonder what juggling there is to get money withal. I dwell within half a mile of the Foss-way; and you would wonder to see how they come by flocks out of the west country to many images, but chiefly to the blood of Hayles. And they believe verily that it is the very blood that was in Christ's body, shed upon the mount of Calvary for our salvation; and that the sight of it with their bodily eye doth certify them, and putteth them out of doubt, that they be clean in life, and in state of salvation without spot of sin, which doth bolden them to do many things. For you would wonder if you should commune with them both coming and going what faith they have: for, as for forgiving their enemies, and reconciling their Christian brethren, they cannot away withal; for the sight of that blood doth requite them for a time.

I read in Scripture of two certifications; one to the Romans: "We being justified by faith have peace with God." If I see the blood of Christ with the eye of my soul, that is true faith, that his blood was shed for me. Another in the epistle of St. John: "We know that we are translated from death to life, because we love the brethren." But I read not that I have peace with God, or that I am translated from death to life, because I see with my bodily eye the blood of Hayles. It is very probable, that all the blood that was in the body of Christ, was united and knit to His Divinity, and then no part thereof shall return to His corruption. And I marvel that Christ shall have two resurrections. And if it were that they did violently and injuriously pluck it out of His body when they scourged Him and nailed Him to the cross, did see it with their bodily eye, yet they were not in can life. And we see the self-same blood in form of wine, when we have consecrated, and may both see it, feel it, and receive it to our damnation, as touching bodily receiving. And many do see it at Hayles without confession, as they say. God knoweth all, and the devil in our time is not dead.

Christ hath left a doctrine behind Him, wherein we be taught how to believe, and what to believe; He doth suffer the devil to use his craftiness, for our trial and probation. It were little thank-worthy to believe well and rightly, if nothing should move us to false faith, and to believe superstitiously. It was not in vain that Christ said, "Beware of false prophets." But we are secure and careless as though false prophets could not meddle with us, and as if the warning of Christ were no more earnest and effectual, than is the warning of mothers when they trifle with their children. Lo, Sir, how I run at riot beyond measure. When I began, I was minded to have written but half a dozen lines; but thus I forget myself, whenever I write to a trusty friend, who will take in worth my folly, and keep it from mine enemy.

As for Dr. Wilson, I know not what I should say: but I pray God endue him with charity. Neither he nor any of his countrymen did ever love me, since I did inveigh against their factions, and partiality in Cambridge. Before that, who was more favored of him than I? That is the bile that may not be touched. A certain friend showed me, that Dr. Wilson is gone now into his country, about Beverley in Holderness, and from thence he will go a journey through Yorkshire, Lancashire, Cheshire, and so from thence to Bristol. What he intendeth by this progress God knoweth, and not I. If he come to Bristol, I shall hear.

As for Hubberdin he is a man of no great learning, nor yet of stable wit. He is here servus hominum; for he will preach whatsoever the bishops will bid him. Verily in my mind they are more to be blamed than he. He doth magnify the pope more than enough. As for our Saviour Christ and Christian kings, they are little beholden to him. No doubt he did miss the cushion in many things. Howbeit, they that did send him, men think, will defend him; I pray God amend him and them both. They would fain make matter against me, intending so either to deliver him by me, or else to rid us both together, and so they would think him well bestowed.

As touching Dr. Powel, how highly he took upon him in Bristol, and how little he regarded the sword, which representeth the king's person, many can tell you. I think there is never an earl in this realm that knoweth his obedience by Christ's commandment to his prince, and knoweth what the sword doth signify, that would have taken upon him so stoutly. However, master mayor, as he is a profound wise man, did flout him prettily; it were too long to write all. Our pilgrimages are not a little beholden to him, in favor of which he alleged this text: "Whoever leaveth father, house, wife, kindred, and his own life also for me, shall be my disciple." But that you may perceive his hot zeal and crooked judgment. Because I am so belied, I could wish that it would please the king's grace to command me to preach before his highness a whole year together every Sunday, that he himself might perceive how they belie me, saying, that I have neither learning nor utterance worthy thereunto. I pray you pardon me, I cannot make an end.

Besides his letter to master Morrice, and two epistles in Latin, he also wrote other letters, as two to sir Edward Baynton, which contain much fruitful matter and worthy to be known, albeit space can here be had only for a few extracts. The letter from which these are given was an answer to one from Baynton, the purport of which is shown in Latimer's reply:

Either I am certain or uncertain that it is truth that I preach. If it be truth, who may not I say so, to courage my hearers to receive the same more ardently, and ensue it more studiously? If I be uncertain, why dare I be so bold to preach it? And if your friends, in whom ye trust so greatly, be preachers themselves, after their sermon I pray you to ask them whether they be certain and sure that they taught you the truth or no; and send me word what they say, that I may learn to speak after them. If they say they be sure, ye know what followeth: if they say they be unsure, when shall you be sure, that have so doubtful teachers and unsure? And you yourselves, whether are you certain or uncertain that Christ is your Saviour? And so forth of other articles that ye be bounden to believe.

Our knowledge here, you say, is but "per speculum in enigmate:" what then? ergo, it is not certain and sure. I deny your argument; yea, if it be by faith, it is much sure, "because the certainty of faith is the most surest certainty;" there is a great discrepance between certain knowledge and clear knowledge, for that may be of things absent that appear not, this requireth the presence of the object, I mean of the thing known; so that I certainly and surely know the thing which I perfectly believe, though I do not clearly and evidently know it. I know your school subtleties as well as you, which dispute as though enigmatical knowledge, that is to say, dark and obscure knowledge, might not be certain and sure knowledge, because it is not clear, manifest, and evident knowledge; and yet there have been which have had a zeal, but not after knowledge. True it is there have been such, and yet are too many to the great hinderance of Christ's glory, which nothing doth more obscure, than a hot zeal accompanied with great authority without right judgment. There have been also, which have had knowledge without any zeal of God, who holding the verity of God in unrighteousness, shall be beaten with many stripes, while they knowing the will of God do nothing thereafter. I mean not among Turks and Saracens that be unchristened, but of them that be christened. And there have been also, they that have lost the spiritual knowledge of God's word which they had before, because they have not followed after it, nor promoted the same, but rather with their mother's wits have impugned the wisdom of the Father, and hindered the knowledge thereof, which therefore hath been taken away from them; that Christ may be justified in his sayings, and overcome when he is judged: threatening to him that hath not, that also which he hath (that is, that which he seemeth to have) shall be taken from him: because to abuse that which a man hath, or not use it well, is as not to have it; and also seeing it is true, that God's wisdom will not dwell in a body subject to sin, albeit it abound in carnal wisdom too much: for the mere carnal and philosophical understanding of God's Scriptures is not the wisdom of God, which is hid from the wise, and is revealed to little ones. And if to call this or that truth requireth a deep and profound knowledge, then every man hath either a deep and profound knowledge, or else no man can call this or that truth; and it behoveth every preacher to have this deep and profound knowledge, that he may call this or that truth, which this or that he taketh in hand to preach for the truth; and yet he may be ignorant and uncertain in many things, as Apollos was; but which things he will not attempt to preach for the truth. As for myself, I trust in God I have my senses well enough exercised to discern good and evil in those things, which (being without deep and profound knowledge in many things) I preach not: yea, there be many things in Scripture, nor yet with help of all interpreters that I have, no content myself and others in all scrupulosity that may arise; but in such I am wont to wade no further into the stream, than that I may either go over or else return back again, having ever respect, not to the ostentation of my little wit, but to the edification of them that hear me, as far forth as I can, neither passing mine own nor yet their capacity.

And such manner of argumentations might well serve the devil contra pusillanimes, to occasion them to wonder and waver in the faith, and to be uncertain in things in which they ought to be certain: or else it may appear to make and serve against such preachers as will define great subtleties and high matters in the pulpit, which no man can be certain and sure of by God's word to be truth, unless a man had a superlative sense to discern good and evil.—Such arguments might appear to make well against such preachers, not against me, which simply and plainly utter true faith and the fruits of the same, which be the good works of God, that he hath prepared for us to walk in, every man to do the thing that pertaineth to his office and duty in his degree and calling, as the word appointeth, which thing a man may do with soberness, having a sense but indifferently exercised to discern good and evil. For it is but foolish humility, willingly to continue always an infant in Christ and in infirmity. In reproof of which it was said—"Ye have need of milk and not of strong meat." For St. Paul saith not—"Be ye humble, so as to deceive yourselves by ignorance." For though he would not that we should think arrogantly of ourselves, and above what it becometh us to think of ourselves, but so to think of ourselves that we may be sober and modest; yet he biddeth us so to think of ourselves, as God hath distributed to every one the measure of faith. For he that may not with meekness think in himself what God hath done for him, and of himself as God hath done for him, how shall he, or when shall he give due thanks to God for his gifts? And if your friends will not allow the same, I pray you inquire of them, whether they may with sobriety and modesty follow St. Paul's advice, where he saith unto us all—"Be not children in understanding, but in maliciousness be ye infants." God give us all grace to keep the mean, and to think of ourselves neither too high nor too low, but so that we may restore unto him who hath sent abroad his gifts again, with good use of the same, so that we do our part with the same, to the glory of God.

I pray you what mean your friends by a Christian congregation? All those who have been baptized? But many of those be in a worse condition, and shall have greater damnation, than many unbaptized. For it is not enough to a Christian congregation that is of God, to have been baptized: but it is to be considered what we promise when we are baptized, to renounce Satan, his works, his pomps. Which things if we busy not ourselves to do, let us not boast that we profess Christ's name in a Christian congregation in one baptism. And whereas they add, "in one Lord," I read in Matt. xvii., "Not every one that saith Lord, Lord." And in Luke the Lord Himself complaineth and rebuketh such professors and confessors, saying to them, "Why call you me Lord, Lord, and do not that I bid you?" Even as though it were enough to a Christian man, or to a Christian congregation, to say every day, "Domine, dominus noster," and to salute Christ with a double "domine." But I would your friends would take the pains to read over Chrysostome, super Matthaeum, hom. 49. cap. 24, to learn to know a Christian congregation, if it will please them to learn at him. And whereas they add, "in one faith." St. James saith boldly, "show me thy faith by thy works." And St. Jerome, "If we believe, we show the truth in working." And the Scripture saith, "He that believeth God, attendeth to His commandments:" And the devils do believe to their little comfort. I pray God to save you and your friends from believing congregation, and from that faithful company!

But now your friends have learned of St. John, that "everyone that confesseth Jesus Christ in flesh, is of God:" and I have learned of St. Paul, that there have been, not among the heathen, but among the Christians, which confess Christ with their mouth, and deny Him with their acts: so that St. Paul should appear to expound St. John, saving that I will not affirm anything as of myself, but leave it to your friends to show you, "utrum qui factis negant Christum et vita sint ex Deo necne per solam oris confessionem:" for your friends to know well enough by the same St. John, "qui ex Deo est, non peccat:" and there both have been and be now too many, "which with mouth only confess Christ to be come in the flesh;" but will not effectually hear the word of God, by consenting to the same, notwithstanding that St. John saith— "He who is of God, heareth God's word; you hear not, because you are not of God." And many shall hear, "I never knew you," which shall not alonely be christened, but also shall "prophetare," and do puissant things in the name of Christ. St. Paul said, there would come ravening wolves, which would not spare the flock: meaning of them who should with their lips confess Christ in the flesh, and yet usurp the office; which Christ biddeth us beware of, saying, "They shall come in sheep's clothing;" not feeding, but smiting their fellows, eating and drinking with the drunken, which shall have their portion with hypocrites. They are called servants, I suppose, because they confess Christ in the flesh; and naughty they are called, because they deny him in their deeds, not giving meat in due season, and exercising mastership over the flock. And yet your friends reason as though there could none bark and bite at true preachers, but they that be unchristened, notwithstanding that St. Augustine, upon the same epistle of St. John, calleth such confessors of Christ, antichrist; and so making division, not between christened and unchristened, but between Christians and antiChristians, when neither tongue nor pen can divide the antiChristian from their blind folly.

Sir, I have had more business in my little cure since I spake with you, what with sick folks, and what with matrimonies, than I have had since I came to it, or than I would have thought a man should have in a great cure. I wonder how men can go quietly to bed, who have great and many cures, and yet peradventure are in none of them all. But I pray you tell none of your friends that I spake so foolishly, lest I make a dissension in a Christian congregation, and divide a sweet and peaceable union, or as many as may rest with this in such an age. Sir, I had just made an end of this scribbling, and was beginning to transcribe it more correctly, but there came a man of my lord of Farley's, with a citation to appear before my lord of London in haste, to be punished for such excesses as I committed at my last being there, so that I could not perform my purpose; I doubt whether you can read it as it is. If you can, well be it; if not, I pray you send it me again, and that you so do, whether you can read it or not. Jesus, mercy, what a world is this, that I should be put to so great labor and pains, besides great charges, above my power, for preaching a poor simple sermon! But I think our Saviour Christ said true, I must needs suffer: so dangerous a thing it is to live virtuously with Christ, yea, in a Christian congregation. God make us all Christians, after the right fashion, Amen.

Master Latimer growing in some favor with the king, and seeing the great decay of Christ's religion by reason of proclamations forbidding the reading of God's holy Scriptures, and touched therefore with the zeal of conscience, directed unto king Henry a long letter, thereby intending by all means possible to persuade the king's mind to set open again the freedom of God's holy word amongst his subjects. The whole letter would well repay perusal, but space will only serve to exhibit the following extracts:

To the most mighty prince, king of England, Henry the Eighth, grace, mercy, and peace from God the Father, by our Lord Jesus Christ. The holy doctor, St. Augustine, in an epistle which he wrote to Casalandus saith, that he which for fear of any power hideth the truth, provoketh the wrath of God to come upon him, for he feareth men more than God. And according to the same, the holy St. John Chrysostom saith, that he is not only a traitor to the truth, which openly for truth teacheth a lie; but he also which doth not freely pronounce and show the truth that he knoweth. These sentences, most redoubted king, when I read now of late, and marked them earnestly in the inward parts of mine heart, they made me sore afraid, troubled, and vexed me grievously in my conscience; and at the last drove me to this strait, that either I must show forth such things as I have read and learned in Scripture, or else be of that sort who provoke the wrath of God upon them, and be traitors unto the truth: the which thing, rather than it should happen, I had rather suffer extreme punishment.

First, and before all things, I will exhort your grace to mark the life and process of our Saviour Christ, and his apostles, in preaching and setting-forth of the gospel; and to note also the words of our master Christ, which he said to his disciples when he sent them forth to preach his gospel; and to these have ever in your mind the golden rule of our master Christ, "The tree is known by the fruit;" for by the diligent marking of these, your grace shall clearly know and perceive who be the true followers of Christ, and teachers of His gospel, and who be not. And concerning the first, all Scripture showeth plainly, that our Saviour Jesus Christ's life was very poor.

But this he did to show us that his followers and vicars should not regard and set by the riches and treasures of this world, but after the saying of David we ought to take them, which saith thus: "If riches, promotions, and dignity happen to a man, let him not set his affiance, pleasure, trust, and heart upon them." So that it is not against the poverty in spirit, which Christ preacheth in the gospel of St. Matthew, chapter v., to be rich, to be in dignity and in honor, so that their hearts be not fixed and set upon them so much, that they neither care for God nor good men. But they be enemies to this poverty in spirit, have they never so little, that have greedy and desirous minds to the goods of this world, only because they would live after their own pleasures and lusts. And they also be privy enemies (and so much the worse) which have professed, as they have say, willful poverty, and will not be called worldly men; and they have lords' lands, and kings' riches. Yea, rather than they would lose one jot of that which yea, between the king and his subjects, and cause rebellion against the temporal power, to the which our Saviour Christ Himself obeyed, and paid tribute as the gospel declareth; unto whom the holy apostle St. Paul teacheth every Christian man to obey: yea, and beside all this, they will curse and ban, as much as in them lieth, even into the deep pit of hell, all that gainsay their appetite, whereby they think their goods, promotions, or dignities should decay. And although I named the spiritualty to be corrupt with this unthrifty ambition, yet I mean not all to be faulty therein, for there be some good of them: neither will I that your grace should take away the goods due to the church, but take away such evil persons from the goods, and set better in their stead.

The holy apostle St. Paul saith, that "every man that will live godly in Christ Jesus, should suffer persecution." And also he saith further, in the Epistle written to the Philippians, in the first chapter, that "it is not only given to you to believe in the Lord, but also to suffer persecution for his sake." Wherefore take this for a sure conclusion, that there, where the word of God is truly preached, there is persecution, as well of the hearers as of the teachers: and where is quietness and rest in worldly pleasure, there is not the truth. For the world loveth all that are of the world, and hateth all things that are contrary to it. And, to be short, St. Paul calleth the gospel the word of the cross, the word of punishment. And the holy Scripture doth promise nothing to the favorers and followers of it in this world, but trouble, vexation, and persecution, which these worldly men cannot suffer, nor away withal. Therefore pleaseth it your good grace to return to this golden rule of our Master and Saviour Jesus Christ, which is this, "By their fruits you shall know them."

But as concerning this matter, other men have showed your grace their minds, how necessary it is to have the Scripture in English. The which thing also your grace hath promised by your last proclamation: the which promise I pray God that your gracious highness may shortly perform, even to-day, before to-morrow.—Seeing that our Saviour Christ hath sent His servants, that is to say, His true preachers, and His own word also, to comfort our weak and sick souls, let not these worldly men make your grace believe that they will cause insurrections and heresies, and such mischiefs as they madly imagine, lest that He be avenged upon you and your realm, as He hath ever upon them which have obstinately withstood His word.

Wherefore, gracious king, remember yourself, have pity upon your soul; and think that the day is even at hand, when you shall give account of your office, and of the blood that hath been shed with your sword. In the which day that your grace may stand steadfastly, and not be ashamed, but be clear and ready in your reckoning, and to have (as they say) your "quietus eat" sealed with the blood of our Saviour Christ, which only serveth at that day, is my daily prayer to him that suffered death for our sins, which also prayeth to his Father for grace for us continually. To whom be all honor and praise for ever, Amen. The Spirit of God preserve your grace.—Anno Domini *1530.* Prom. die Decembris.

In this letter of master Latimer we have to consider his good conscience to God, his good-will to the king, the duty of a right pastor unto truth, and his tender care to the church of Christ. Further, we may note the subtle practices of prelates in abusing the name and authority of kings, to set forth their own malignant proceedings; and also the great boldness of this man, who durst, in defense of Christ's gospel, so freely and plainly counsel that which no other durst once speak of. And yet God so wrought with His servant's bold adventure that no danger nor displeasure rose to him thereby, but rather thanks and good-will of His prince, who soon after advanced him to the bishopric of Worchester.

During the time that the said master Latimer was prisoner in Oxford, we read not of much that he did write besides his conference with Dr. Ridley, and his protestation at the time of his disputation. Otherwise of letters we find very few, or none, save only these few lines, which he wrote to one Mrs. Wilkinson of London, a godly matron, and an exile afterward for the gospel's sake: who, so long as she remained in England, was a singular patroness to the good saints of God, and learned bishops, as to Hooper, to the bishop of Hereford, to Coverdale, to Latimer, to Cranmer, and many others. The copy of his letter to Mrs. Wilkinson here followeth:

If the gift of a pot of cold water shall not be in oblivion with God, how can God forget your manifold and bountiful gifts, when he shall say to you, "I was in prison, and you visited me?" God grant us all to do and suffer, while we be here, as may be his will and pleasure.—Yours, Hugh Latimer.

Touching the memorable acts and doings of this worthy man, among many others this is not to be neglected, what a bold enterprise he attempted in sending to king Henry a present, the manner whereof is this. There was then, and remaineth still, an ancient custom received from the old Romans, that upon New-year's day, every bishop with some handsome New-year's gift should gratify the king; and so they did, some with gold, some with silver, some with a purse full of money, and some one thing, some another. But master Latimer, being bishop of Worchester then, among the rest, presented a New Testament for his New-year's gift, with a napkin having this posy about it, *"Fornicators et adulteros judicabit Dominus."*

And thus thou hast, gentle reader, a sketch of the life both of master Ridley and of master Latimer severally by themselves set forth and described, with their chief proceedings from time to time until this present month of October 1555: in the which month they were brought forth together to their final examination and execution. Wherefore as they were together joined both in one cause and martyrdom, we will, by the grace of Christ, so prosecute the rest that remaineth concerning their latter examination, degrading, and constant suffering.

First, after the appearing of Thomas Cranmer, archbishop of Canterbury, before the pope's delegate, and the queen's commissioners, in St. Mary's church at Oxford, about the 12th of September, (whereof more shall be said, by God's grace, when we come to the death of the said archbishop;) shortly after, on the 28th of the said month, was sent down to Oxford another commission from cardinal Pole, legate a latere, to John White, bishop of Lincoln, to Dr. Brooks, bishop of Glouchester, and Dr. Holyman, bishop of Bristol. The contents and virtue of which commission were, that the said bishops should have full power and authority to cite, examine, and judge master Latimer and Dr. Ridley, for diverse and sundry erroneous opinions, which the said Hugh Latimer and Nicholas Ridley did hold and maintain in open disputations had in Oxford, in the months of May, June, and July, in the year of our Lord 1554, as long before, in the time of perdition, and since. Which opinions, if they would now recant, giving and yielding themselves to the determination of the universal and catholic church planted by Peter in the blessed see of Rome, that then the deputed judges, by the authority of their commission, should have power to receive the penitent persons, and forthwith administer unto them the reconciliation of the holy father the pope. But if they would stoutly and stubbornly maintain their erroneous opinions, then the said lords by their commission should proceed in form of judgment, according to the law of heretics; that is, degrade them from their promotion and dignity of bishops, priests, and all other ecclesiastical orders, pronounce them as heretics, cut them off from the church, and deliver them up to receive the punishment due to such heresy and schism.

Wherefore, the last of September, Nicholas Ridley and Hugh Latimer were cited to appear before the said lords, in the divinity school at Oxford, at eight of the clock. At which time thither required the lords, placing themselves in the high seat made for public lectures and disputations, according to the usage of that school. And after the said lords were placed and set, the said Latimer and Ridley were sent for; and first appeared Dr. Ridley, and anon master Latimer. But because it seemed good severally to examine them, Latimer was kept back until master Ridley was thoroughly examined. Therefore, soon after the coming of Ridley into the school, the commission was published by an appointed notary, and openly read. Ridley at first stood bareheaded, but as soon as he had heard the cardinal named, and the pope's holiness, he put on his cap. Wherefore after the commission was published, the conference thus proceeded.

Lincoln. Mr. Ridley, although neither I, nor yet my lords here, in respect of our own persons, look for cap or knee, yet because we bear and represent such persons as we do, that is, my lord cardinal's grace, legate a latere to the pope's holiness, as well in that he is of a noble parentage (here Dr. Ridley moved his cap with low obeisance) descending from the royal blood, as in that he is a man worthy to be reverenced with all humility, for his great knowledge and learning, noble virtues and godly life, it would have become you at this name to have uncovered your head. Wherefore except you will of your ownself take the pains to put your hand to your head, and at the nomination, as well of the said cardinal, as of the pope's holiness, uncover the same, you will cause us to oblige some man to pluck off your cap.

Rid. Respecting what you said, my lord, that you of your own persons desire no cap or knee, but only require it in consideration of your representing the cardinal's grace, I would have you know, that I put on my cap at the naming of him, not for any contumacy that I bear towards your own persons, nor for any derogation of honor towards the lord cardinal. For I know him to be a man worthy of all humility, reverence, and honor, in that he came of the most regal blood, and in that he is a man endued with manifold graces of learning and virtue; and as touching these virtues and points, I, with all humility (here he put off his cap and bowed his knee) and obeisance, reverence, and honor his grace. But as he is a legate to the bishop of Rome (and therewith put on his cap) whose usurped supremacy and abused authority I utterly refuse and renounce, I may in no wise give obeisance or honor unto him, lest my so doing might be prejudicial to mine oath, and a derogation to the verity of God's words: therefore that I might not only by confession profess the truth, in not reverencing the renounced authority, contrary to God's word, but also in gesture, in behavior, and all my doings, express the same, I have put on my cap, and for this consideration only, and not for any contumacy to your lordships, neither contempt of this worshipful audience, or derogation of honor due to the cardinal's grace.

Lin. Mr. Ridley, you excuse yourself of that with which we pressed you not, in that you protest you keep on your cap, neither for any contumacy towards us, nor for any contempt of this audience; which although justly they may, yet in this case do not require any such obeisance of you; neither in derogation of any honor due to my lord cardinal for his regal descent (at which word Dr. Ridley moved his cap) and excellent qualities; for although in all the premises honor be due, yet in these respects we require none of you, but only in that my lord cardinal's grace is here in England, deputy of the pope's holiness, (at which word the lords and others put off their caps, and Dr. Ridley put on his) and therefore we say unto you the second time, that except you take the pains yourself, to put your hand to your head, and put off your cap, you shall put us to the pains to cause some man to take it from you, except you allege some infirmity and sickness, or other more reasonable cause, upon the consideration whereof we may do as we think good.

Rid. The premises I said only for this end, that it might as well appear to your lordships, as to this worshipful audience, why and for what consideration I sued such kind of behavior, in not humbling myself to your lordships with cap and knee: and as for my sickness, I thank my Lord God, that I am as well at east as I have been this long time; and therefore I do not pretend that which is not, but only this, that it might appear by this my behavior, that I acknowledge in no point that usurped supremacy of Rome, and therefore contemn and utterly despise all authority coming from him.

Then the bishop of Lincoln, after the third admonition, commanded one of the beadles to take his cap from his head. Dr. Ridley bowing his head to the officer, gently permitted him to take it away. After this the bishop of Lincoln, in a long oration, exhorted Ridley to recant, and submit himself to the universal faith of Christ, endeavoring to prove the right of supremacy in the church of Rome, charging him also, with having formerly been favorable to their doctrines and ceremonies. Ridley heard him patiently, and when he had concluded, desired his patience to suffer him to speak somewhat of the premises, lest the multitude of things might confound his memory; and having leave granted him, he thus spake:

I most heartily thank your lordship, as well for your gentleness, as for your good and favorable zeal in this learned exhortation, in which I have marked especially three points, by which you sought to persuade me to leave my doctrine and religion, (which I perfectly know to be grounded, not upon man's imaginations and decrees, but upon the infallible truth of Christ's gospel,) and to return to the Romish see. First, the first point is this, that the see of Rome taking its beginning from Peter, upon whom you say Christ hath builded his church, hath in all ages lineally, from bishop to bishop, been brought to this time. Second, that even the holy fathers have in their writings confessed the same. Third, that I myself was of the same opinion, and altogether with you I did acknowledge the same.

First, as touching the saying of Christ, from whence your lordship gathereth the foundation of the church upon Peter, truly the place is not to be understood as you take it, as the circumstance of the place will declare. For after Christ had asked His disciples whom men judged Him to be, and they answered, that some had said He was a prophet, some Elias, some one thing, some another; then he said, "Whom say ye that I am?" Then Peter answered, "I say that Thou art Christ the Son of God." To whom Christ answered, "I say thou art Peter, and upon this stone I will build My church;" that is to say, Upon this stone, not meaning Peter himself, as though he would have constituted a mortal man, so frail and brittle a foundation of his stable and infallible church: but upon this rickstone, that is, this confession of thine, that I am the Son of the living God, I will build My church. For this is the foundation and beginning of all Christianity, with word, heart, and mind, to confess that Christ is the Son of God. Here we see upon what foundation Christ's church is built, not upon the frailty of man, but upon the stable and infallible word of God.

As touching the lineal descent of the bishops in the see of Rome, true it is, that the patriarchs of Rome in the apostles' time, and long after, were great maintainers of Christ's glory, in which, above all other countries and regions, there especially was preached the true gospel, the sacraments were most duly administered; and as, before Christ's coming, it was a city so valiant in prowess, and martial affairs, that all the world was in a manner subject to it; and after Christ's passion divers of the apostles there suffered persecution for the gospel's sake: so after that the emperors, their hearts being illuminated, received the gospel, and became Christians, the gospel there, as well for the fame of the place, flourished most, whereby the bishops of that place were had in more reverence and honor, most esteemed in all councils and assemblies, not because they acknowledge them to be their head, but because the place was most reverenced and spoken of, for the great power and strength of the same. As now here in England, the bishop of Lincoln, in sessions and sittings, hath the pre-eminence of other bishops, not that he is the head and ruler of them; but for the dignity of the bishopric. Wherefore the doctors in their writings have spoken most reverently of this see of Rome, and in their writings preferred it; and this is the prerogative which your lordship did rehearse the ancient doctors to give to the see of Rome. In the same manner I cannot nor dare but commend, reverence, and honor the see of Rome, so long as it continued in the promotion and setting forth of God's glory, and in due preaching of the gospel, as it did many years after Christ, but after that the bishops of that see, seeking their own pride, and not God's honor, began to set themselves above kings and emperors, challenging to them the title of God's vicars, the dominion and supremacy over all the world, I cannot but with St. Gregory, a bishop of Rome also, confess that place is the very true Antichrist, whereof St. John speaketh by name of the whore of Babylon; and say, with Gregory, "He that maketh himself a bishop over all the world, is worse than Antichrist."

Whereas you say St. Augustine should seem not only to give such a prerogative, but also supremacy to the see of Rome, in that he saith all the Christian world is subject to the church of Rome, and therefore should give to that see a certain kind of subjection; I am sure that your lordship knoweth, that in Augustine's time there were four patriarchs, of Alexandria, Constantinople, Antioch, and Rome, which patriarchs had under them certain countries; as in England the archbishop of Canterbury hath under him certain bishoprics in England and Wales, to whom he may be said to be their patriarch. Also your lordship knoweth right well, that at the time Augustine wrote that book he was then bishop in Africa. Farther, you are not ignorant, that between Europe and Africa lieth the sea called the Mediterranean Sea, so that all the countries in Europe to him which is in Africa, may be called countries beyond the sea. Hereof Augustine saith,

"All the Christian countries beyond the seas and remote regions, are subject to the see of Rome." If I should say all countries beyond the sea, I do except England, which to me now, being in England, is not beyond the sea. In this sense, Augustine saith, "All the countries beyond the sea are subject to the see of Rome;" declaring thereby that Rome was one of the sees of the four patriarchs, and under it Europe. By what subjection I pray you? only for a pre-eminence; as we here in England say, that all the bishoprics are subject to the archbishoprics.

For this pre-eminence also the other doctors say, that Rome is the mother of churches, as the bishopric of Lincoln is mother to the bishopric of Lincoln, and they were once both one; and so is the archbishopric of Canterbury mother to the other bishoprics which are in her province. In like manner the archbishopric of York, is mother to the north bishoprics; and yet no man will say, that Lincoln, Canterbury, or York, is supreme head to the other bishoprics; neither then ought we to confess the see of Rome to be supreme head, because the doctors, in their writings, confess the see of Rome to be mother of churches.

Where you say, I was once of the same religion as you are of, the truth is, I cannot but confess the same. Yet so was St. Paul a persecutor of Christ. But in that you say, I was one of you not long ago, in that I, in doing my message to my lord of Winchester, should desire him to stand stout in that gross opinion of the supper of the Lord: in very deed I was sent, as your lordship said, from the council to my lord of Winchester, to exhort him also to receive the true confession of justification; and because he was very refectory, I said to him, "What make you so great a matter herein? you see many anabaptists rise against the sacrament of the altar; I pray you, my lord, be diligent in confounding of them!" for at that time my lord of Winchester and I had to do with two anabaptists in Kent. In this sense I willed my lord to be stiff in the defense of the sacraments against the detestable errors of anabaptists, and not in the confirmation of that gross and carnal opinion now maintained.

In like manner, respecting the sermon which I made at St. Paul's Cross, you shall understand, that there were at St. Paul's, and divers other places, fixed railing bills against the sacrament, terming it Jack of the Box, the Sacrament of the Halter, round Robin, with other unseemly terms; for which causes, to rebuke irreverent behaviour of certain evil-disposed persons, I preached as reverently of that matter as I might, declaring what estimation and reverence ought to be given to it, what danger ensued the mishandling thereof; affirming in that sacrament to be truly and verily the body and blood of Christ, effectually by grace and spirit; which words the unlearned understanding not, supposed that I had meant of the gross and carnal being which the Romish decrees set forth, that a body having life and motion should be indeed under the shapes of bread and wine.

Lin. Well, Dr. Ridley, thus you wrest places to your own pleasure. I could bring many more places of the fathers for a confirmation of what I have advanced; but we came not hither to dispute with you, but only to take your answers to certain articles; and used this in the way of disputation, in which you interrupted me: wherefore I will return thither again. You must, first of all, consider that the church of Christ lieth not hid, but is a city on the mountain, and a candle in the candlestick. The church of Christ is catholic, and universally spread throughout the world. Wherefore, for God's love, be you not singular; acknowledge with all the realm the truth, it shall not be prejudicial to the crown; for their majesties the king and queen have renounced that usurped power taken of their predecessors, and justly have renounced it. I am sure you know there are two powers, the one declared by the sword, the other by the keys. The sword is given to kings and rulers of countries; the keys were delivered by Christ to Peter, and of him left to all the successors.

Consider your state, remember your former degrees, spare your body; especially consider your soul, which Christ so dearly bought with His precious blood. Do not rashly cast away that which was precious in God's sight; enforce us not to do all that we may do, which is not only to publish you to be none of us, but to cut you off from the church. We do not, nor can we condemn you to die, (as most untruly hath been reported of us) but that is the office of the temporal judges; we only declare you to be not of the church, and then you must, according to the tenor of them, and pleasure of the rulers, abide their determination, so that we, after we have given you up to the temporal rulers, have no further to do with you. But I cannot help to hope and trust, Dr. Ridley, we shall not have occasion to do what we may. I trust you will suffer us to rest in that point of our commission, which we most heartily desire, that is, upon recantation and repentance to receive, to reconcile you, and again to join you to the unity of the church.

Rid. My lord, I acknowledge an unspotted church of Christ, in which no man can err, without which no man can be saved, which is the congregation of the faithful; neither do I bind the same to any one place as you said, but confess the same to be universal; and where Christ's sacraments are duly administered, His gospel truly preached and followed there doth Christ's church shine as a city upon a hill, and as a candle in the candlestick: but rather it is such as you that would have the church of Christ bound to a place, who appoint the same to Rome, that there and no where else is the foundation of Christ's church. But I am fully persuaded that Christ's church is every where founded, in every place where His gospel is truly received, and effectually followed. And in that the church of God is in doubt, I use herein the counsel of Vincentius Lyrinensis, whom I am sure you will allow, who giving precepts how the catholic church may be in all schisms and heresies known, writeth it this manner, "When one part is corrupted with heresies, then prefer the whole world before that one part; but if the greatest part be infected, then prefer antiquity." In like manner now, when I perceive the greatest part of Christianity to be infected with the poison of the see of Rome, I repair to the usage of the primitive church, which I find quite contrary to the pope's decrees: as in that the priest receiveth alone, that it is made unlawful to the laity to receive in both kinds, and such like: wherefore it requireth, that I prefer the antiquity of the primitive church before the novelty of the Romish.

Lin. Dr. Ridley, these faults which you charge the see of Rome withal, are indeed no faults. For first, it was never forbid the laity, but that they might, if they demanded, receive under both kinds. You know also, that Christ after His resurrection, at the time He went with His apostles to Galilee, opened Himself by breaking of bread.—So that the church seemeth to have authority by the Holy Ghost, whom Christ said He would send after His ascension, which should teach the apostles all truth, to have power to alter such points of the scriptures, ever reserving the foundation. But we came not, as I said before, to reason the matter with you, but we have certain instructions ministered unto us, according to which we must proceed, proposing certain articles, unto which we require your answer directly, either denying or granting them, without further disputations, which articles you shall hear now; and tomorrow we will require and take your answers, and then according to the same proceed. If you require a copy of them, you shall have it, pen, ink, and paper; also such books as you shall demand, if they be to be gotten.

The articles referred to were then jointly and severally ministered to Dr. Ridley and master Latimer, by the pope's deputy: they were these—"In the name of God, Amen. We John Lincoln, James Gloucester, and John Bristol, bishop: (1.) We do object to thee, Nicholas Ridley, and to thee, Hugh Latimer, jointly and severally; first, that thou Nicholas Ridley, in this high university of Oxford, anno 1554, in the months of April, May, June, and July, or in some one or more of them, hast affirmed and openly defended and maintained, and in many other times and places besides, that the true and natural body of Christ, after the consecration of the priest, is not really present in the sacrament of the altar. (2.) That in the said year and months aforesaid, thou hast publicly affirmed and defended, that in the sacrament of the altar remaineth still the substance of bread and wine. (3.) That in the said year and months thou hast openly affirmed and obstinately maintained, that in the mass is no propitiatory sacrifice for the quick and the dead. (4.) That in the year, place, and months aforesaid, these thy foresaid assertions solemnly have been condemned by the scholastical censure of this school, as heretical and contrary to the catholic faith, by the worshipful Dr. Weston, prolocutor then of the convocation-house, as also by other learned men of both the universities. (5.) That all and singular the premises be true, notorious, famous, and openly known by public fame, as well to them near hand, as also to them far off."

All these articles I thought good here to place together, that, as often as hereafter rehearsal shall be of any of them, the reader may have recourse hither, and so not trouble the story with several repetitions thereof. After these articles were read, the bishops took counsel together. At the last the bishop of Lincoln said, "These are the very same articles which you, in open disputation here in the university, did maintain and defend. What say you unto the first? I pray you answer affirmatively, or negatively."

Rid. Why, my lord, I supposed that you would have given me until to-morrow, that upon good advice I might bring a determinate answer.

Lin. Yea, master Ridley, I mean not that your answers now shall be prejudicial to your answers to-morrow. I will take your answers at this time, and yet notwithstanding it shall be lawful for you to add, diminish, alter, and change these answers to-morrow what you will.

Rid. Seeing you appoint me a time to answer to-morrow, and yet would take mine answers out of hand, I require the notaries to take and write my protestation, that in no point I acknowledge your authority, or admit you to be my judges, in that point that you are authorized from the pope. Therefore, whatsoever I shall say or do, I protest I neither say nor do it willingly, thereby to admit the authority of the pope: and if your lordship will give me leave, I will show the cause which move me thereunto.

Lin. No, we have instructions to the contrary. We may not suffer you.

Rid. I will be short: I pray you suffer me to speak but three words.

Lin. To-morrow you shall speak forty. The time is far past; therefore we require your answer determinately. What say you to the first article?

Rid. I answer, that in the sacrament is the very true and natural body and blood of Christ even that which was born of the Virgin Mary, which ascended into heaven, which sitteth on the right hand of God the Father, which shall come from thence to judge the quick and the dead, only we differ in *modo,* in the way and manner of being: we confess all one thing to be in the sacrament, and dissent in the manner of being there. I, being fully by God's word persuaded, confess Christ's natural body to be in the sacrament indeed by spirit and grace, because that whosoever receiveth worthily that bread and wine, receiveth effectuously Christ's body, and drinketh His blood, (that is, he is made effectually partaker of His passion;) and you make a grosser kind of being, enclosing a natural, a lively, and a moving body, under the shape or form of bread and wine. Now, this difference considered, to the question thus I answer, that in the sacrament of the altar is the natural body and blood of Christ *vere et realiter,* indeed and really, for spiritually, by grace and efficacy; for so every worthy receiver receiveth the very true body of Christ. But, if you mean really and indeed, so as to include a lively and a movable body under the forms of bread and wine, then, in that sense, is not Christ's body in the sacrament.

This answer taken, the bishop of Lincoln proposed the second article.

Rid. In the sacrament is a certain change, in that, that bread, which was before common bread, is now made a lively presentation of Christ's body. Notwithstanding this sacramental mutation, the true substance and nature of bread and wine remaineth: with the which the body is in like sort nourished, as the soul is by grace and Spirit with the body of Christ.

Then the notaries penned that he answered affirmatively to the second article; and the bishop recited the third, and required a direct answer.

Rid. Christ, as St. Paul writeth, made one perfect sacrifice for the sins of the whole world, neither can any man reiterate that sacrifice of His, and yet is the communion an acceptable sacrifice to God of praise and thanksgiving. But to say that thereby sins are taken away (which wholly and perfectly was done by Christ's passion, of the which the communion is only a memory) that is a great derogation of the merits of Christ's passion; for the sacrament was instituted, that we, receiving it, and thereby recognizing and remembering his passion, should be partakers of the merits of the same. For otherwise doth this sacrament take upon it the office of Christ's passion, whereby it might follow that Christ died in vain.

The notaries penned this his answer to be affirmatively. And then the bishop of Lincoln recited the fourth article; to the which Ridley answered, that in some part it was true, and in some part false: true, in that those his assertions were condemned as heresies, although unjustly: false, in that it was said they were condemned *sicentia scholastica,* in that the disputations were in such sort ordered, that it was far from any school act. This answer penned of the notaries, the bishop of Lincoln rehearsed the fifth article. To the which Ridley answered, that the premises were in such sort true, as in these his answers he had declared. Whether that all men spake evil of them he knew not, in that he came not much abroad. This answer also written, the bishop said: "To-morrow you shall appear before us in St. Mary's church; and because we cannot well agree upon your answer to the first article, you may, if it please you, write your answer."

Now master Latimer, being also brought to the divinity school, there tarried until they called him; and after that Ridley was committed to the mayor, the bishop of Lincoln commanded the bailiffs to bring him in, who eftsoons as he was placed said to the lords: "My lords, if I appear again, I pray you not to send for me until you be ready: for I am an old man, and it is great hurt to mine old age to tarry so long gazing upon the cold walls." Then said the bishop of Lincoln, "Master Latimer, I am sorry you are brought so soon, although it is the bailiff's fault, and not mine: but it shall be amended." Then Latimer bowed his knee down to the ground, holding his hat in his hand, having a kerchief on his head, and upon it a night-cap or two, and a great cap, (such as townsmen use, with two broad flaps to button under the chin,) wearing an old threadbare Bristol frieze-gown girded to his body with a penny leather girdle, at the which hanged by a string of leather his Testament, and his spectacles without case, depending about his neck upon his breast. After this the bishop of Lincoln began a long oration, in the which, as he has by Dr. Ridley, he declared their commission, charged him which his errors; spake of the unity and infallibility of their church, entreated him back to the same, and if stubbornly perverse, threatened him with the consequences. After the bishop had somewhat paused, Latimer lifted up his head, (for before he leaned on his elbow;) and asking whether his lordship had done, said, "Then will you give me leave to speak a word or two?"

Lin. Yea, so you use a modest kind of talk, without railing or taunts.

Lat. I beseech your lordship, license me to sit down.

Lin. At your pleasure, Mr. Latimer, take as much ease as you will.

Lat. Your lordship gently exhorted me in many words to come to the unity of the church. I confess, my lord, a catholic church, spread throughout all the world, in which no man may err, without which unity of the church no man can be saved; but I know perfectly by God's word, that this church is in all the world, and hath not its foundation in Rome only, as you say; and me thought your lordship brought a piece out of the scriptures to confirm the same, that there was a jurisdiction given to Peter, in that Christ bade him govern His people. Indeed, my lord, St. Peter did his office well and truly, in that he was bid to govern; but since, the bishops of Rome have taken a new kind of government. Indeed they ought to govern, but how, my lord? not as they will themselves; but this government must be hedged and ditched in. They must rule, only according to the word of God. But the bishops of Rome have turned the rule according to the word of God into the rule according to their own pleasures, and as it pleaseth them best; as there is a book set forth which hath diverse points in it, and, amongst others, this point is one, which your lordship went about to prove; and the argument which he bringeth forth for the proof of that matter is taken out of Deuteronomy, where it is said, "If there ariseth any controversy among the people, the priests of the order of Levi shall decide the matter according to the law of God, so it must be taken." This book, perceiving this authority to be given to the priests of the old law, taketh occasion to prove the same to be given to the bishops and others the clergy of the new law: but, in proving this matter, whereas it was said there, as the priests of the order of Levi should determine the matter "according to God's law," that "according to God's law" is left out, and only is recited, as the priests of the order of Levi shall decide the matter so it ought to be taken of the people; a large authority I assure you, what gelding of Scripture is this? what clipping of God's coin? This is much like the "ruling" which your lordship talked of. Nay, nay, my lords, we may not give such authority to the clergy, to rule all things as they will. Let them keep themselves within their commission. I trust, my lord, I do not rail yet.

Lin. No, master Latimer, your talk is more like taunting than railing; but in that I have not read nor know the book, I can say nothing therein.

Lat. The book is open to be read, my lord; it is by one who is bishop of Gloucester, whom I never knew, neither did see to my knowledge.

With that the people laughed, because the bishop of Gloucester sat there in commission. Then the bishop stood up, and said it was his book.

Lat. Was it yours, my lord? Indeed I knew not your lordship, neither ever did I see you before, nor yet now, through the brightness of the sun shining betwixt you and me. (Then the audience laughed again.) Why, my masters, this is no laughing matter: I answer upon life and death.

The bishop of Lincoln commanded silence, and then said, "Master Latimer, if you had kept yourself within your bounds, if you had not used such scoffs and taunts, this had not been done." After this Gloucester said, in excusing this book, "Hereby every man may see what learning you have."

Lat. Lo, you look for learning at my hands who have gone so long to the school of oblivion, making the bare walls my library, keeping me so long in prison without book, or pen and ink; and now you let me loose to come and answer to articles. You deal with me as though two were appointed to fight for life and death, and over night the one through friends and favor, is cherished, and hath good counsel given him how to encounter with his enemy. The other, for envy or lack of friends, all the whole night is set in the stocks. In the morning when they shall meet, the one is in strength and lusty; the other is stiff in his limbs, and almost dead for feebleness. Think you, that to run through this man with a spear is not a goodly victory?

Glou. I went not about to recite any places of Scripture in that place of my book; for then if I had not recited faithfully, you might have had just occasion of reprehension: but I only in that place formed an argument a majore, in this sense; that if in the old law the priests had power to decide matters of controversy, much more then ought the authority to be given to the clergy in the new law: and I pray you, in this point what availeth their rehearsal, according to the law of God?

Lat. Yes, my lord, very much. For I acknowledge authority to be given to the spiritualty to decide matters of religion; and as my lord said even now, to rule; but they must do it according to the word and law of God, and not after their own wills, imaginations, and fantasies.

Then Lincoln said they came not to dispute, but to take his answers; and so began to propose to master Latimer the same articles as proposed to Ridley, requiring his answer to the first. Then Latimer, making his protestation that notwithstanding his answers it should not be taken that thereby he would acknowledge any authority of the bishop of Rome, saying that he was their majesties' subject, and not the pope's, neither could serve two masters at one time; required the notaries to take his protestation, that whatsoever he should say or do, it should not be taken as though he did thereby agree to any authority that came from the bishop of Rome.

Lin. Your protestation shall be so taken; and I require you to answer briefly, affirmatively or negatively, to the first article.

Lat. I do not deny, my lord, that in the sacrament by spirit and grace is the very body and blood of Christ; because that every man by receiving bodily that bread and wine, spiritually receiveth the body and blood of Christ, and is made partaker thereby of the merits of Christ's passion: but I deny that the body and blood of Christ is in such manner in the sacrament as you would have it.

Lin. Then you answer affirmatively; and what say you, Mr. Latimer, to the second article?

Lat. There is, my lord, a change in the bread and wine, and such a change as no power but the omnipotency of God can make, in that that which before was bread, should now have the dignity to exhibit Christ's body; and yet the bread is still bread, and the wine still wine; for the change is not in the nature, but the dignity, because now that which was common bread hath the dignity to exhibit Christ's body: for whereas it was common bread, it is now no more common bread, neither ought it to be so taken, but as holy bread sanctified by God's word.

Lin. Lo, Mr. Latimer, see what steadfastness is in your doctrine. That which you abhorred and despised most, you now most establish: for whereas you most railed at holy bread, you now made your communion holy bread. Is not this your answer, that the substance of bread and wine remaineth after the words of consecration?

Lat. Yes, verily, it must needs be so. For Christ Himself calleth it bread; St. Paul calleth it bread; the doctors confess the same; the nature of a sacrament confirmeth the same; and I call it holy bread: not in that I make no difference between your holy bread and this, but for the holy office which it beareth, that is, to be a figure of Christ's body, and not only a bare figure but effectually to represent the same.

Lin. What say you to the third question?

Lat. Christ made one perfect sacrifice for all the whole world, neither can any man offer him again, neither can the priest offer up Christ again for the sins of man, which He took away by offering Himself once for all upon the cross: neither is there any propitiation for our sins saving His cross only.

Lin. What say you to the fourth? Do you not hear me?

Lat. Yes, but I do not understand what you mean thereby.

Lin. Marry, only this, that these your assertions were condemned by Dr. Weston as heresies; is it not so, master Latimer?

Lat. Yes, I think they were condemned. But how unjustly, he that shall be Judge of all knoweth.

So the notaries took his answer to this article to be affirmatively, as they did also to the other three before recited.

Lin. What say you, master Latimer, to the fifth article?

Lat. I know not what you mean by these terms. I am no lawyer; I wish you would propose the matter plainly.

Lin. In that we proceed according to the law, we must use their terms also. The meaning only is this, that these your assertions are notorious, evil spoken of, and yet common and frequent in the mouths of the people.

Lat. I cannot tell how much, nor what men talk of them. I come not so much among them, for I have been secluded a long time. What men report of them I know not, and care not.

Lin. Mr. Latimer, we mean not that these your answers shall be prejudicial to you. To-morrow you shall appear before us again, and then it shall be lawful for you to alter and change what you will. We give you respite until then, trusting that after you have pondered well all things against that time, you will not be ashamed to confess the truth.

Lat. Now, my lord, I pray you give me license in three words to declare the causes why I refused the authority of the pope.

Lin. Nay, Mr. Latimer, to-morrow you shall have license to speak forty words.

Lt. Nay, my lords, I beseech you to do with me now as it shall please your lordships. I require no respite, for I am at a point; you shall give me respite in vain: therefore I pray you let me not trouble you to-morrow.

Lin. Yes, for we trust God will work with you against to-morrow. There is no remedy, you must needs appear again to-morrow at eight o'clock in St. Mary's church.

And forthwith the bishop charged the mayor with master Latimer, and dismissed him: he then brake up their sessions for that day, at one o'clock. The next day (the first of October) the said lords repaired to St. Mary's; and after they were set in a high throne, then appeared Ridley, who was set at a framed table a good space from the bishop's feet, and the place was encompassed about in a quadrate form, partly for gentlemen who repaired thither, and for the heads of the university to sit, and partly to keep off the press of the audience: for the whole body, as well of the university as of the town, came to see the end of these two persons. After Dr. Ridley's appearance, and the silence of the audience, the bishop of Lincoln commenced speaking.

Lin. Mr. Ridley, yesterday we took your answers to certain articles, which we then proposed unto you: but because we could not be thoroughly satisfied with your answer then to the first article, neither could the notaries take any determinate answer of you, we granted you license to bring your answer in writing, and thereupon command the mayor that you should have pen, paper, and ink, yea, any books also that you would require, if they were to be good: we licensed you then also to alter your former answers this day at your pleasure: therefore we are now come hither, to see if you are in the same mind now, that you were yesterday, or contrary, contented to revoke your former assertions, and in all points consent to submit yourself to the determination of the universal church; and I for my part most earnestly exhort you, not because my conscience pricketh me, as you said yesterday, but because I see you a rotten member, and in the way of perdition. Now, Dr. Ridley, what say you to the first article? If you have brought your answer in writing, we will receive it: but if you have written any other matter, we will not receive it.

Then Ridley took a sheet of paper out of his bosom, and began to read that he had written: but Lincoln ordered the beadle to take it from him.

Rid. Why, my lord, will you require my answer, and not suffer me to publish it? I beseech you, let the audience bear witness in this matter.

Lin. Well, Dr. Ridley, we will first see what you have written, and then if we shall think it good to be read, you shall have it published; but, except you will deliver it first, we will take none at all from you.

With that, master Ridley, seeing no remedy, delivered it to an officer, who immediately delivered it to the bishop of Lincoln; who, after he had secretly communicated it to the other two bishops, declared the sense, but would not read it as it was written, saying, that it contained words of blasphemy; therefore he would not fill the ears of the audience therewithal, and so abuse their patience. Notwithstanding, Ridley desired very instantly to have it published; saying that, except a line or two, there was nothing contained but the ancient doctors' sayings, for the confirmation of his assertions. After the said bishops had secretly perused the whole, then the bishop of Lincoln said, "In the first part, master Ridley, is nothing contained but your protestation, that you would not have these your answers to be taken as though you seemed thereby to consent to the authority or jurisdiction of the pope's holiness."

Rid. No, my lord: pray read it out, that the audience may hear it.

This the bishop of Lincoln would in no wise grant; but recited the first article, and required Ridley's answer to it. Then Ridley said his answer was there in writing, and desired it might be published: but the bishop would not read the whole, but here and there a piece of it. And when he had read what he pleased, he recited the second article, and required an answer. Dr. Ridley again referred him to his answer in writing exhibited now, and also before at the time of disputation: and like answers were taken to all the rest of the articles. The bishop of Gloucester then addressed him thus.

If you would once empty your stomach, captivate your senses, subdue your reason, and, together with us, consider what a feeble ground of your religion you have, I do not doubt but you might easily be brought to acknowledge one church with us, to confess one faith with us, and to believe one religion with us. For what a weak and feeble stay in religion is this, I pray you? Latimer leaneth to Cranmer, Cranmer to Ridley, and Ridley to the singularity of his own wit: so that if you overthrow the singularity of Ridley's wit, then must needs the religion of Cranmer and Latimer fall also. You remember well, Dr. Ridley, that the prophet speaketh most truly, saying—"Woe be to them which are singular and wise in their own conceits."

But you will say here, it is true that the prophet saith; but how know you that I am wise in mine own conceit? Yes, Dr. Ridley, you refuse the determination of the catholic church; you must needs be singular and wise in your own conceit, for you bring scripture for the proof of your assertions, and we also bring scripture: you understand them in one sense, and we in another. How will you know the truth herein? If you stand to your own interpretation, then you are singular in your own conceit: but if you say you will follow the minds of the doctors and ancient fathers, likely you understand them in one meaning, and we take them in another: how then will you know the truth herein? If you stand to your own judgment, then are you singular in your own conceit—then cannot you avoid the woe which the prophet speaketh of.

Wherefore if you have no stay but the catholic church in matters of controversy, except you will rest upon the singularity and wisdom of your own brain, if the prophet most truly saith, "Woe, woe be to them that are wise in their own conceit:" then for God's love, Dr. Ridley, stand not singular, be not you wise in your own conceit, please not yourself overmuch. How were the Arians, the Manichees, Eutychians, with other heretics suppressed and convinced? By reasoning and disputations? No, truly, the Arians had no more places of Scripture for confirming their heresy than the catholics for the defense of the truth. How, then, were they convinced? Only by the determination of the church. And indeed, except we do constitute the church our foundation, stay, and judge, we can have no end of controversies, no end of disputations. For in that we all bring scriptures and doctors for the proof of our assertions, who should be judge of this our controversy? If we ourselves be singular and wise in our own conceits, then cannot we avoid the woe that the prophet speaketh of.

To this oration of the bishop of Gloucester, by which he endeavored to persuade Dr. Ridley to turn and forsake his religion, the latter answered, That he said most truly with the prophet, "Woe be to him that is wise in his own conceit:" but that he acknowledged no such singularity, nor knew any cause why he should attribute so much to himself. And whereas he said that archbishop Cranmer leaned to him, that was most untrue, in that he was but a young scholar in comparison of Dr. Cranmer; for when he was but a novice, Mr. Cranmer was then a doctor; so that he confessed he might have been his schoolmaster for many years. He would have spoke more, but the bishop of Gloucester interrupted him, saying: "Why, Dr. Ridley, it is your own confession, for Mr. Latimer, at the time of his disputation, confessed his learning to lie in Dr. Cranmer's books, and Dr. Cranmer also said that it was your doing."

The bishop of Lincoln likewise with many words, and holding his cap in his hand, desired him to turn. But Dr. Ridley made a determinate answer— That he was fully persuaded the religion which he defended was grounded upon God's word, and therefore without great offense towards God, great peril and damage of his soul, he could not forsake his God; but desired the bishop to perform his grant, in that his lordship said the day before, that he should have license to shew his cause, why he could not with a safe conscience admit the authority of the pope. But the bishop of Lincoln said, that whereas then he had demanded license to speak three words, he was contented then that he should speak forty, and that grant he would perform. Then Dr. Weston, who sat by, stepped forth and said, "Why, my lord, he hath spoken four hundred already." Dr. Ridley confessed he had, but they were not of his prescribed number, neither of that matter. The bishop of Lincoln bade him take his license:

but he should speak but forty, and he would tell them upon his fingers. And so before Ridley had ended half a sentence, the doctors said that his number was out: and with that he was put to silence.

Lin. You will not suffer us to stay in that point of our commission which we most desired: for indeed (I take God to witness) I am sorry for you.

Rid. I believe it, my lord, for one day it will be burdenous to your soul.

Lin. Nay, not so, master Ridley, but because I am sorry to see such stubbornness in you, that by no means you may be persuaded to acknowledge your errors, and receive the truth. But seeing it is so, because you will not suffer us to persist in the first, we must of necessity proceed to the other part of our commission. Therefore I pray you hearken to what I say.

And forthwith he did read the sentence of condemnation, which was written in a long process. The effect of it was as this: "That forasmuch as the said Nicholas Ridley did affirm, maintain, and stubbornly defend certain opinions, assertions, and heresies, contrary to the word of God and the received faith of the church, as in denying the true and natural body of Christ, and his natural blood to be in the sacrament of the altar; secondarily, in affirming the substance of bread and wine to remain after the words of consecration; thirdly, in denying the mass to be a lively sacrifice of the church for the quick and the dead, and by no means would be induced and brought from these his heresies: they therefore (the said John of Lincoln, James of Gloucester, John of Bristol) did judge and condemn the said Nicholas Ridley as a heretic, and so adjudged him presently both by word and also in deed, to be degraded from the degree of a bishop, from priesthood, and all ecclesiastical order; declaring, moreover, the said Nicholas Ridley to be no member of the church: and therefore committed him to the secular powers, of them to receive due punishment; and further excommunicate him by the great excommunication." This sentence being published by the bishop of Lincoln, Ridley was committed to the mayor, and Latimer was sent for; who so soon as he appeared laid his hat, which was an old felt, under his elbows, and spake immediately to the commissioners, saying:

Lat. My lords, I beseech you to set a better order here at your entrance: for I am an old man, and have a very evil back, so that the press of the multitude doth me much harm.

Lin. I am sorry for your hurt: at your going, we will see to better order.

With that Latimer thanked his lordship, making a very low curtsey. After this the bishop of Lincoln began on this manner:

Lin. Although yesterday, after we had taken your answers to those articles which we proposed, we might have justly proceeded to judgment against you, especially in that you required the same; yet having a good hope of your returning, desiring not your destruction, but rather that you would recant, revoke your errors, and turn to the catholic church, deferred farther process until this day; and now according to the appointment we have called you before us, to hear whether you are content to revoke your heretical assertions, and submit yourself to the determination of the church, as we most heartily desire, and for my part as I did yesterday, do most earnestly exhort you, or to know whether you persevere still the man that you were, for which we would be sorry.

On this Latimer spoke, "Your lordship doth often repeat the catholic church, as though I should deny the same. No, my lord, I confess there is a catholic church, to the determination of which I will stand; but not the church which you call catholic, which ought rather to be termed diabolic. And whereas you join together the Romish and catholic church, stay there, I pray you. For it is one thing to say the Romish church, and another thing to say catholic church. I must use here in this mine answer the counsel of Cyprian, who when cited before certain bishops, who gave him leave to take deliberation and counsel, to try and examine his opinion, answered them thus, 'In adhering to, and persevering in the truth there must no counsel or deliberation be taken.' And again, being demanded of them sitting in judgment, which was most like to be of the church of Christ, whether he who was persecuted, or they who did persecute? 'Christ,' said he, 'hath foreshowed, that he that doth follow Him, must take up His cross. Christ gave knowledge that His disciples should have persecution and trouble.' How think you then, my lords, is it likely that the see of Rome, which hath been a continual persecutor, is rather the church, or that small flock which hath continually been persecuted by it, even to death? Also 'the flock of Christ hath been but few in comparison of the residue, and ever in subjection:' which he proved, beginning at Noah's time, even to the apostles."

Lin. Your cause and St. Cyprian's is clean contrary: for he suffered for Christ's sake and the gospel. You are in trouble for your errors and false assertions, contrary to God's word and the received truth of the church.

Lat. Yes verily, my cause is as good as St. Cyprian's; for his was for the word of God, and so is mine.

Lin. Also at the beginning and foundation of the church, it could not be but that the apostles should suffer great persecution. Further, before Christ's coming, continually there were few which truly served God; but after His coming began the time of grace. Then began the church to increase, and was continually augmented, until it came unto this perfection, and now hath justly that jurisdiction which the unchristian princes before by tyranny did resist: there is a diverse consideration of the state of the church now in the time of grace, and before Christ's coming. But, Mr. Latimer, although we had instructions given us determinately to take your answer to such articles as we should propose, without any reasoning or disputations, yet we hoping by talk somewhat to prevail with you, appointed you to appear before us in the divinity-school, a place for disputations. And whereas then notwithstanding you had license to speak your mind, and were answered to every matter, yet you could not be brought from your errors; we thinking that from that time you would with good conversation ponder your state, gave you a respite until this time, and now have called you again in this place, by your answers to learn whether you are the same man as before? Therefore we ill propose unto you the same articles which we did then, and require of you a determinate answer, without further reasoning.

Lat. Always my protestation saved that, by these mine answers it should not be thought that I did condescend and agree to your lordships' authority, in that you are legaced by the pope, so that thereby I might seem to consent to his jurisdiction: To the first article I answer as I did yesterday, that in the sacrament the worthy receive the very body of Christ, and drink His blood by the Spirit and grace. But after a corporeal being, which the Romish church prescribeth, Christ's body and blood is not in the sacrament under the forms of bread and wine.

The notaries took his answer to be affirmatively. For the second article he referred himself to his answers made before. After this the bishop of Lincoln recited the third article, and required a determinate answer.

Lat. Christ made one oblation and sacrifice for the sins of the whole world, and that a perfect sacrifice; neither needeth there to be any other, nor can there be any other, propitiatory sacrifice.

The notaries took his answer to be affirmatively. In like manner did he answer to the other articles, not varying from his answers made the day before. After his answers were penned of the notaries, and the bishop of Lincoln had exhorted him in like sort to recant, as he did master Ridley, and revoke his errors and false assertions, and Latimer had answered that he neither could nor would deny his master Christ and his verity, the bishop of Lincoln desired him to hearken to him: and then master Latimer, hearkening for some new matter and other talk, the bishop of Lincoln read his condemnation; after the publication of which the said three bishops brake up their sessions, and dismissed the audience. Latimer required the bishop of Lincoln to perform his promise in saying, the day before, that he should have license briefly to declare the cause why he refused the pope's authority. But the bishop said that now he could not hear him, neither ought to talk with him. Then Latimer asked him, whether it were not lawful for him to appeal from this his judgment. And the bishop asked him again to whom he would appeal. "To the next general council," quoth Latimer, "which shall be truly called in God's name." With that appellation the bishop was content; but he said it would be a long season before such a convocation as he meant would be called. Then the bishop committed master Latimer to the mayor, saying, "Now he is your prisoner, master mayor." And because the press of the people was not yet diminished, each man looking for further process, the bishop of Lincoln commanded avoidance, and desired Latimer to tarry until the press were diminished, lest he should take hurt at his egression as he did at his entrance. And so continued bishop Ridley and master Latimer in durance until the 16th day of the said month of October.

In the mean season upon the 15th day of the same month in the morning, Dr. Brooks, bishop of Gloucester, and the vice-chancellor of Oxford, Dr.

Marshal, with diverse others of the chief and heads of the same university, and many others accompanying them, came unto master Irish's house, then mayor of Oxford, where Dr. Ridley, late bishop of London, was close prisoner. And when the bishop of Gloucester came into the chamber where the said Dr. Ridley did lie, he told him for what purpose their coming was unto him, saying, that yet once again the queen's majesty did offer unto him, by them, her gracious mercy, if that he would receive the same, and come home again to the faith which he was baptized in, and revoke his erroneous doctrine that he of late had taught abroad to the destruction of many. And further said, that if he would not recant, and become one of the catholic church with them, then they must needs (against their wills) proceed according to the law, which they would be very loth to do, if they might otherwise. "But," saith he, "we have been oftentimes with you, and have requested that you would recant this your fantastical and devilish opinion, which hitherto you have not, although you might in so doing win many, and do much good. Therefore, good master Ridley, consider with yourself the danger that shall ensue both of body and soul, if you so willfully cast yourself away in refusing mercy offered unto you at this time." "My lord," quoth Dr. Ridley, "you know my mind fully herein; and as for the doctrine which I have taught, my conscience assureth me that it was sound, and according to God's word, (to His glory be it spoken;) the which doctrine, the Lord God being my helper, I will maintain so long as my tongue shall wag, and breath is within my body, and in confirmation thereof seal the same with my blood."

Brooks. Well, you were best, master Ridley, not to do so, but to become one of the church with us: for you know this well enough, that whosoever is out of the catholic church cannot be saved. Therefore I say once again, that while you have time and mercy offered you, receive it and confess with us the pope's holiness to be the chief head of the same church.

Ridley. I marvel that you will trouble me with any such vain and foolish talk. You know my mind concerning the usurped authority of that Romish antichrist. As I confessed openly in the schools, so do I now, that both by my behavior and talk I do no obedience at all unto the bishop of Rome, nor to his usurped authority, and that for good and godly considerations.

And here Dr. Ridley would have reasoned with the said Brooks of the bishop of Rome's authority, but could not be suffered; and yet he spake so earnestly against the pope therein, that the bishop told him if he would not hold his peace he should be compelled against his will. "And seeing," saith he, "that you will not receive the queen's mercy, now offered unto you, but stubbornly refuse the same, we must, against our wills, proceed according to our commission to degrading, taking from you the dignity of priesthood. For we take you for no bishop, and therefore we will the sooner have done with you. So, committing you to the secular power, you know what doth follow."

Ridley. Do with me as it shall please God to suffer you, I am well content to abide the same with all my heart.

Brooks. Put off your cap, master Ridley, and put on this surplice.

Ridley. Not I, truly.

Brooks. But you must.

Ridley. I will not.

Brooks. You must make no more ado, but put this surplice upon you.

Ridley. Truly if it come upon me, it shall be against my will.

Brooks. Will you not do it upon you?

Ridley. No, that I will not.

Brooks. It shall be put upon you by one or other.

Ridley. Do therein as it shall please you, I am well contented with that, and more than that: "the servant is not above his Master." If they dealt so cruelly with our Saviour Christ, as the Scripture saith, and He suffered the same patiently, how much more doth it become us His servants!

And in saying of these words, they put upon the said Dr. Ridley the surplice, with all the trinkets appertaining to the mass. And as they were putting on the same, Dr. Ridley did vehemently inveigh against the Romish bishop, and all that foolish apparel, calling him antichrist, and the apparel foolish and abominable, yea, too fond for a vice in a play, insomuch that bishop Brooks was exceeding angry, and said, "Well, you were best to hold your peace, lest your mouth be stopped. At which words one Edridge, the reader then of the Greek lecture, standing by, said to Dr. Brooks, "Sir, the law is he should be gagged; therefore let him be gagged." At which words Dr. Ridley, looking earnestly upon him that so said, shook his head at him, but made no answer. When they came to that place where Dr. Ridley should hold the chalice and the wafer-cake, called the singing-bread, they bade him hold the same in his hands. And Dr. Ridley said, "They shall not come in my hands; for, if they do, they shall fall to the ground for all me." Then there was one appointed to hold them in his hand, while bishop Brooks read a certain thing in Latin, touching the degradation of spiritual persons according to the pope's law.

Afterward they put a book in his hand, and withal read another thing in Latin, the effect whereof was: "We do take from you the office of preaching the gospel," etcetera. At which words Dr. Ridley gave a great sigh, looking up towards heaven, saying—"O Lord God, forgive them this their wickedness!"

When all this their abominable and ridiculous degradation was ended very solemnly, Dr. Ridley said unto Dr. Brooks, "Have you done? If you have done, then give me leave to talk with you a little concerning these matters." Brooks answered, "Master Ridley, we may not talk with you; you be out of the church; and our law is, that we may not talk with any that be out of the church." Then master Ridley said—"Seeing that you will not suffer me to talk, neither will vouchsafe to hear me, what remedy but patience? I refer my cause to my heavenly Father, who will reform things that be amiss, when it shall please Him." At which words they would have been gone, but Ridley said, "My lord,

I would wish that you would vouchsafe to read over and peruse a little book of Bertram's doings, concerning the sacrament. I promise you, you shall find much good learning therein, if you will read the same with an indifferent judgment." Dr. Brooks made no answer, but was going away. Then said Dr. Ridley, "Oh, I perceive that you cannot away with this manner of talk. Well! in boots not, I will say no more, I will speak of worldly affairs. I pray you therefore, my lord, hear me, and be a mean to the queen's majesty, in the behalf of a great many poor men, and especially for my poor sister and her husband which standeth there. They had a poor living granted unto them by me, whiles I was in the see of London, and the same is taken away from them by him that now occupieth the same room, without all law or conscience. Here I have a supplication to her majesty in their behalfs. You shall hear the same read, so shall you perceive the matter the better." Then he read the same; and when he came to the place in the supplication that touched his sister by name, then he wept; so that for a little space he could not speak for weeping. After that he had left off weeping, he said, "This is nature that moveth me, but I have now done;" and with that read out the rest and delivered the same to his brother, commanding him to put it up to the queen's majesty, and to sue, not only for himself, but also for such as had any leases or grants by him, and were put from the same by Dr. Bonner, then bishop of London. Whereunto Brooks said, "Indeed, master Ridley, your request in this supplication is very lawful and honest: therefore I must needs in conscience speak to the queen's majesty for them."

Ridley. I pray you, for God's sake, do so.

Brooks. I think your request will be granted, except one thing let it, and that is, I fear, because you do not allow the queen's proceedings, but obstinately withstand the same, that it will hardly be granted.

Ridley. What remedy? I can do no more but speak and write. I trust I have discharged my conscience therein; and God's will be done.

Brooks. I will do what lieth in me.

This degradation being past, and all things finished, Dr. Brooks called the bailiffs, delivering to them master Ridley with this charge, to keep him safely from any man speaking with him, and that he should be brought to the place of execution when they were commanded. Then Ridley, in praising God, burst out with these words, "God, I thank Thee, and to Thy praise be it spoken, there is none of you all able to lay to my charge any open or notorious crime: for if you could, it should surely be laid in my lap, I see very well." Whereunto Brooks said, he played the part of a proud Pharisee, exalting and praising himself. But master Ridley said, "No, no, no; as I have said before, to God's glory be it spoken. I confess myself to be a miserable wretched sinner, and have great need of God's help and mercy, and do daily call and cry for the same: therefore, I pray you, have no such opinion of me." Then they departed; and in going away, a certain warden of a college, of whose name I am not very sure, bade Dr. Ridley repent him, and forsake that erroneous opinion. Whereunto Ridley said, "Sir, repent you, for you are out of the truth. And I pray God (if it be his blessed will) have mercy upon you, and grant you the understanding of his word." Then the warden, being in a passion thereat, said, "I trust that I shall never be of your devilish opinion, either yet to be in that place whither you shall go: thou art the most obstinate and willful man that I ever heard talk since I was born."

On the night before he suffered, his beard was washed and his legs; and as he sat at supper, at the house of Mr. Irish, his keeper, he invited his hostess, and the rest at the table, to his marriage: for, said he, tomorrow I must be married, and so showed himself to be as merry as ever he had been before. And wishing his sister at his marriage, he asked his brother sitting at the table, whether she could find in her heart to be there or no. He answered, "Yea, with all her heart." At which word, he said he was glad to hear of her so much therein. At this talk Mrs. Irish wept. But Dr. Ridley comforted her, saying, "O Mrs. Irish, you love me not, I see well enough; for in that you weep, it doth appear you will not be at my marriage, neither are content therewith. Indeed you are not so much my friend as I thought you had been. But quiet yourself, though my breakfast shall be somewhat sharp and painful, yet I am sure my supper will be more pleasant and sweet."

When they arose from the table, his brother offered to stay all night with him. But he said, "No, no, that you shall not. For I intend, God willing, to go to bed, and to sleep as quietly tonight as ever I did." On this his brother departed, exhorting him to be of good cheer, and to take his cross quietly, for his reward was great in heaven.

Upon the north side of the town, in the ditch over against Balliol college,[9] the place of execution was appointed: and for fear of any tumult that might arise, to let the burning of them, the lord Williams was commanded, by the queen's letters, and the householders of the city, to be there assistant, sufficiently appointed. And when everything was in readiness, the prisoners were brought forth by the mayor and bailiffs. Master Ridley had a fair black gown furred, and faced with foins, such as he was wont to wear, being bishop, and a tippet of velvet furred likewise about his neck, a velvet night-cap upon his head, and a corner cap upon the same, going in a pair of slippers to the stake, and going between the mayor and an alderman, etcetera. After him came master Latimer, in a poor Bristol frieze frock all worn, with his buttoned cap, and a kerchief on his head, all ready to the fire, a new long shroud hanging over his hose down to the feet: which at the first sight stirred men's hearts to rue upon them, beholding on the one side the honor they sometime had, and on the other the calamity whereunto they were fallen.

Dr. Ridley, as he passed toward Bocardo, looked up where Dr. Cranmer did lie, hoping to have seen him at the glass-window, and to have spoken to

---

[9] "Not many weeks since, some workmen, who were employed in making a drain in Broadstreet, opposite the door of the master of Balliol's lodgings, found, at the depth of about three feet from the present surface, such a quantity of ashes and burnt sticks, as plainly indicated that they had discovered the spot on which the martyrs suffered."—Christian Observer, June 1838.

him. But then Cranmer was busy with friar Soto and his fellows, disputing together, so that he could not see him, through that occasion. Then Ridley looking back, espied master Latimer coming after, unto whom he said, "Oh, be ye there?" "Yea," said Latimer, "have after as fast as I can follow." So he, following a pretty way off, at length they came both to the stake, the one after the other where first Dr. Ridley entering the place, marvellous earnestly holding up both his hands, looked towards heaven. Then shortly after espying Latimer, with a wonderous cheerful look he ran to him, embraced, and kissed him; and, as they that stood near reported, comforted him, saying, "Be of good heart, brother, for God will either assuage the fury of the flame, or else strengthen us to abide it."

With that went he to the stake, kneeled down by it, kissed it, and effectually prayed; and behind him master Latimer kneeled, as earnestly calling upon God as he. After they arose, the one talked with the other a little while, until they which were appointed to see the execution removed themselves out of the sun. What they said I can learn of no man.

Then Dr. Smith (of whose recantation in king Edward's time ye have heard) began his sermon to them upon this text of St. Paul, in 1 Cor. xiii., "If I yield my body to the fire to be burned, and have not charity, I shall gain nothing thereby." Wherein he alleged, that the goodness of the cause, and not the order of death, maketh the holiness of the person: which he confirmed by the examples of Judas, and of a woman in Oxford who of late hanged herself, for that they and such like as he recited, might then be adjudged righteous, which desperately separated their lives from their bodies, as he feared that those men that stood before him would do. But he cried still to the people to beware of them, for they were heretics and died out of the church. He ended with a very short exhortation to them to recant and come home again to the church, and save their lives and souls, which else were condemned. His sermon scarcely lasted a quarter of an hour.

Dr. Ridley said to master Latimer, "Will you begin to answer the sermon, or shall I?" Latimer said, "Begin you first, I pray you," "I will," said Ridley. Then, the wicked sermon being ended, they both kneeled down upon their knees towards my lord Williams of Thame, the vicechancellor of Oxford, and divers other commissioners appointed for that purpose, who sat upon a form thereby, unto whom master Ridley said, "I beseech you, my lord, even for Christ's sake, that I may speak but two or three words." And whilst my lord bent his head to the mayor and vice-chancellor, to know (as it appeared) whether he might give him leave to speak, the bailiffs and Dr. Marshal, vicechancellor, ran hastily unto him, and with their hands stopped his mouth, and said, "Master Ridley, if you will revoke your erroneous opinions, and recant the same, you shall not only have liberty so to do, but also the benefit of a subject; that is, have your life." "Not otherwise?" asked Ridley. "No," quoth Dr. Marshal. "Therefore if you will not so do, then there is no remedy but you must suffer for your deserts." "Well," quoth Ridley, "so long as the breath is in my body, I will never deny my Lord Christ, and His known truth. God's will be done in me!" And with that he rose up, and said with a loud voice, "Well, then, I commit our cause to Almighty God which shall differently judge all." To whose saying master Latimer added his old posy—"Well! there is nothing hid but it shall be opened." And he said he could answer Smith well enough, if he might be suffered.

Incontinently they were commanded to make them ready, which they with all meekness obeyed. Dr. Ridley took his gown and his tippet, and gave to his brother-in-law, master Shipside, who all his time of imprisonment, although he might not be suffered to come to him, lay there at his own charges to provide him necessaries, which from time to time he sent him by the serjeant that kept him. Some other of his apparel he also gave away; other the bailiffs took. He gave away besides, divers other small things to gentlemen standing by, and divers of them pitifully weeping, as to sir Henry Lee he gave a new groat; and to divers of my lord Williams's gentlemen, some napkins, some nutmegs, and rases of ginger; his dial, and such other things as he had about him, to everyone that stood next him. Some plucked the points off his hose, and happy was he who could get the least trifle of him.

Master Latimer gave nothing, but very quietly suffered his keeper to pull off his hose, and his other array, which was very simple; and being stripped to his shroud, he seemed as comely a person to them that were there present as one could well see. Then master Ridley, standing as yet in his truss, said to his brother, "It were best for me to go in my truss still." "No," quoth his brother, "it will put you to more pain: and the truss will do a poor man good." Whereunto Ridley said, "Be it, in the name of God:" and so unlaced himself. Then, being in his shirt, he stood upon the foresaid stone, and held up his hand and said, "O heavenly Father, I give unto Thee most hearty thanks, for that Thou hast called me to be a professor of Thee, even unto death. I beseech thee, Lord God, take mercy upon this realm of England, and deliver the same from all her enemies." Then the smith took a chain of iron, and brought the same about both their middles: and as he was knocking in a staple, Dr. Ridley took the chain in his hand, and shaked the same, for it did gird in his belly, and looking aside to the smith said, "Good fellow, knock it in hard, for the flesh will have its course." Then the smith's brother did bring him a bag of gunpowder, and would have tied the same about his neck. Dr. Ridley asked what it was; and on being told it was gunpowder, he said, "I will take it to be sent of God. And have you any for my brother?" meaning Latimer. "Yea, sir, that I have," said the man. "Then give it unto him betime," said Ridley, "lest ye come too late." So the man carried of the same gunpowder unto master Latimer.

In the mean time Dr. Ridley spake unto my lord Williams, and said, "My lord, I must be a suitor unto your lordship in the behalf of divers poor men, and specially in the cause of my poor sister: I have made a supplication to the queen in their behalfs. I beseech your lordship, for Christ's sake, to be a means to her grace for them. My brother here hath the supplication, and will resort to your lordship to certify you hereof. There is nothing in all the world troubleth my conscience, I praise God, this only excepted. Whilst I was in the see of London, divers poor men took leases of me, and agreed with me for the same. Now I hear that the bishop who occupieth the same room will not allow my grants unto them made: but, contrary to all law and conscience, hath taken from them their livings, and will not suffer them to enjoy the same. I beseech you, my lord, be a mean for them: you shall do a good deed, and God will reward you."

Then they brought a lighted fagot, and laid the same down at Ridley's feet; upon which Latimer said, "Be of good comfort, master Ridley, and play the man. We shall this day light such a candle, by God's grace, in England, as I trust shall never be put out." And so the fire being given unto them, when Dr. Ridley saw the fire flaming up towards him, he cried with a wonderful loud voice, *"In manus tuas, Domine, commendo spiritum meum? Domine recipe spiritum meum."* And after repeated this latter part often in English, "Lord, Lord, receive my spirit!" Master Latimer cried as vehemently, on the other side, "O Father of heaven, receive my soul!" who received the flame as it were embracing it. After that he had stroked his face with his hands, and as it were bathed them a little in the fire, he soon died (as it appeareth) with very little pain or none. And thus much concerning the end of this old and blessed servant of God, master Latimer, for whose laborious travails, fruitful life, and constant death, the whole realm hath cause to give great thanks to Almighty God.

But Dr. Ridley, by reason of the evil making of the fire unto him, because the fagots were laid about the gorse, and overhigh built, the fire burned first beneath, being kept down by the wood: which when he felt he desired them, for Christ's sake, to let the fire come unto him. Which when his brother-in-law heard, but not well understood, intending to rid him out of his pain, (for the which cause he gave attendance,) as one in such sorrow not well advised what he did, heaped fagots upon him, so that he clean covered him, which made the fire more vehement beneath, that it burned all his nether parts before it once touched the upper; and that made him leap up and down under the fagots, and often desire them to let the fire come to him, saying, "I cannot burn." Which indeed appeared well: for, after his legs were consumed by reason of his struggling through the pain, (whereof he had no release, but only his contentation in God,) he showed that side towards us clean, shirt and all untouched with flame. Yet in all this torment he forgot not to call upon God, still having his mouth. "Lord have mercy upon me," intermingling he cry, "let the fire come unto me, I cannot burn!" In which pangs he labored until one of the standers by with his bill pulled the fagots off above; and where he saw the fire flame up, he wrestled himself unto that side. And when the flame touched the gunpowder, he was seen to stir no more, but burned on the other side, falling down at master Latimer's feet. In beholding of which horrible sight hundreds were moved to tears, and signs of sorrow there were on every side.

Some took it grievously to see their deaths, whose lives they held full dear. Some pitied their persons, who thought their souls had no need thereof. But the sorrow of his brother moved many men, whose attempt to put a speedy end to his sufferings had so miserably prolonged them. But whoso considered their preferments in time past, the places of honor that they some time occupied in this commonwealth, the favor they were in with their princes, and the opinion of learning they had in the university where they studied, could not choose but sorrow with tears, to see so great dignity, honor, and estimation, so necessary members sometimes accounted, so many godly virtues, the study of so many years, such excellent learning, to be put into the fire, and consumed in one moment. Well! dead they are, and the reward of this world they have already. What reward remaineth for them in heaven, the day of the Lord's glory, when He cometh with his saints, shall shortly, I trust, declare.

Albeit the same Nicholas Ridley (a man so reverenced for his learning and knowledge in the Scriptures that even his very enemies report well of him) wrote divers treatises, letters, and exhortations, containing fruitful admonition and wholesome doctrines, much of which we here pass over for want of space; as long farewell to all his true and faithful friends in God, concluding with a sharp reproof unto the papists, and specially to the higher house of Parliament, of which he says, "As you have banqueted and lain by the whore in the fornication of her whorish dispensations, pardons, idolatry, and such like abominations; so shall ye drink with her, except ye repent betimes, of the cup of the Lord's indignation and everlasting wrath, which is prepared for the beast, his false prophets, and all their partakers. For he that is partner with them in their plagues, and in the latter day shall be thrown with them into the burning lake. Thus fare ye well, my lords all. I pray God give you understanding of His blessed will and pleasure, and make you to believe and embrace the truth. Amen."

Another farewell of Bishop Ridley to the prisoners in Christ's gospel's cause, and to all them which for the same cause are exiled and banished out from their own country, choosing rather to leave all worldly commodity than their master Christ:—

Farewell, my dearly beloved brethren in Christ, both you my fellow-prisoners, and you also that be exiled and banished out of your country, because you will rather forsake all worldly advantages, than the gospel of Christ. Farewell all you together in Christ: for you know that the trial of your faith bringeth forth patience, and patience shall make us perfect, whole, and sound on every side, and such, after trial, ye know shall receive the crown of life, according to the promise of the Lord made to His dearly beloved; let us therefore be patient unto the coming of the Lord. As the husbandman abideth patiently the former and latter rain for the increase of his crop, so let us be patient, and pluck up our hearts, for the coming of the Lord approacheth apace. Let us, my dear brethren, take example of patience in tribulation of the prophets, who likewise spake God's word truly in his name. Let Job be to us an example of patience, and the end which the Lord suffered, which is full of mercy and pity.

We know, my brethren, by God's word, that our faith is much more precious than any corruptible gold, and yet that is tried by the fire: even so our faith is therefore tried likewise in tribulations, that it may be found when the Lord shall appear, laudable, glorious, and honorable. For if we for Christ's cause do suffer, that is grateful before God; for thereunto are we called, that is our state and vocation, wherewith let us be content. Christ, we know, suffered for us afflictions, leaving us an example that we should follow His footsteps; for He committed no sin, neither was there any guile found in His mouth: when He was railed upon, and reviled, He railed not again: when He was evil intreated, He did not threaten, but committed the punishment thereof to Him that judgeth aright.

Let us ever have in fresh remembrance those wonderful comfortable sentences spoken by the mouth of our Saviour Christ—"Blessed are they which suffer persecution for righteousness' sake, for theirs is the kingdom of heaven. Blessed are ye when men revile you, persecute you, and speak evil against you for my sake: rejoice and be glad, for great is your reward in heaven; for so did they persecute the prophets that were before you." Christ, our master, hath told us beforehand, that the brother should put the brother to death, and the father the son, and the children should rise against their parents and kill them, and that Christ's true apostles should be hated of all men for His name's sake; but he that abideth patiently unto the end shall be saved. Let us then endure in all troubles patiently, after the example of our master Christ, and be contented therewith, for he suffered, being our Master and Lord: how doth it not then become us to suffer! for the disciple is not above his master, nor the servant above his lord. It may suffice the disciple to be as his master, and the servant to be as his lord. If they have called the Father of the family, the Master of the household, Beelzebub, how much more shall they call them so of his household? Fear them not (saith our Saviour) for all hidden things shall be made plain; there is now nothing secret, but it shall be showed in light. Of Christ's words let us neither be ashamed nor afraid to speak; for so Christ commandeth us, saying—"What I tell you privily, speak openly abroad, and what I tell you in your ear, preach upon the house top. And fear not them which kill the body, for the soul they cannot kill; but fear him which can cast both body and souls into hell-fire."

Know ye that our heavenly Father hath ever a gracious eye, and respect toward you, and a fatherly providence for you, so that without his knowledge and permission nothing can do you harm. Let us therefore cast all our care upon Him, He shall provide that which shall be best for us. For if of two small sparrows, which both are sold for a mite, one of them lighteth not on the ground without your Father, and all the hairs of our head are numbered, fear not them (saith our master Christ) for you are more worth than many small sparrows. And let us not shrink to confess Me before men, him shall I confess before My Father which is in heaven: but whosoever shall deny Me, him shall I likewise deny before My Father which is in heaven." Christ came not to give us here a carnal amity, and a worldly peace, or to knit His unto the world in ease and peace, but rather to separate and divide from the world, and to join them unto Himself: in whose cause we must, if we will be His, forsake father and mother, and stick unto Him. If we forsake Him or shrink from Him for trouble or death sake, which He calleth His cross, He will none of us, we cannot be His. If for

His cause we shall lose our temporal lives here, we shall find them again, and enjoy them for evermore: but if, in this cause, we will not be contented to leave nor lose them here, then shall we lose them so, that we shall never find them again, but in everlasting death. What though our troubles here are painful for the time, and the sting of death bitter and unpleasant; yet we know that they shall not last, in comparison of eternity, no not the twinkling of any eye, and that they patiently taken in Christ's cause, shall procure and get us unmeasureable heaps of heavenly glory, unto which these temporal pains of death and troubles compared, are not to be esteemed, but to be rejoiced upon. "Wonder not"—saith St. Peter—"as though it were any strange matter that ye are tried by the fire," he meaneth of tribulation, "which thing is done to prove you; nay, rather in that ye are partners of Christ's afflictions rejoice, that in his glorious revelation ye may rejoice with merry hearts. If ye suffer rebukes in Christ's name, happy are ye, for the glory and Spirit of God resteth upon you. Of them God is reviled and dishonoured, but of you He is glorified."

Let no man be ashamed of that which he suffereth as a Christian, and in Christ's cause: for now is the time that judgment and correction must begin at the house of God: and if it begin at us, what shall be the end of those which believe not the gospel? And if the righteous shall hardly be saved, the wicked and the sinner, where shall they appear? Wherefore they which are afflicted according to the will of God, let them lay down and commit their souls to him by well doing, as to a trusty and faithful Maker. This, as I said, may not seem strange to us, for we know that all the whole fraternity of Christ's congregation in this world is served with the like, and by the same is made perfect. For the fervent love that the apostles had unto their master Christ, and for the great advantages and increase of all godliness which they felt by their faith to insure of afflictions in Christ's cause, and also for the heaps of heavenly joys which the same do get unto the godly, which shall endure in heaven for evermore; for these causes the apostles did joy of their afflictions, and rejoiced in that they were had and accounted worthy to suffer contumelies and rebukes for Christ's name. And St. Paul, as he glorieth in the grace and favor of God, whereunto he was brought and stood in by faith; so he rejoiced in his afflictions for the heavenly and spiritual profits which he numbered to rise upon them: yea, he was so far in love with what the carnal man loathed so much, that is, with Christ's cross, that he judged himself to know nothing else but Christ crucified: he will glory, he saith, in nothing else but in Christ's cross, yea, and he blesseth all those as the only true Israelites, with peace and mercy, which walk after that rule, and after no other.

O Lord, what a wonderful spirit was that which made St. Paul, in setting forth of himself against the vanity of Satan's false apostles, and in his claim there, that he, in Christ's cause, did excel and surpass them all! What wonderful spirit was that, I say, that made him to reckon up all his troubles, his labors, his beatings, his whippings and scourgings, his shipwrecks, his dangers and perils by water and by land, his famine, hunger, nakedness, and cold, with many more, and the daily care of all the congregations of Christ, among whom every man's pain did pierce his heart, and every man's grief was grievous unto him! O Lord, is this Paul's primacy whereof he thought so much good that he did excel others? Is not this Paul's saying unto Timothy his own scholar? and doth it not pertain to whosoever will be Christ's true soldiers? Bear thou, saith he, affliction, like a true soldier of Jesus Christ. This is true; if we die with Christ, we shall live with Him; if we suffer with Him, we shall reign with Him; if we deny Him, He shall deny us; if we be faithless, He remaineth faithful, He cannot deny Himself. This, Paul would have known to everybody; for there is no other way to heaven but Christ and His way; and all that will live godly in Christ, shall suffer persecution. By this way went to heaven the patriarchs, the prophets, Christ our master, His apostles, His martyrs, and all the godly since the beginning. And as it hath been of old, that he which was born after the flesh, persecuted him who was born after the Spirit, for so it was in Isaac's time, so said St. Paul, it was in his time also. And whether it be so now or no, let the spiritual man, the self-same man I mean, that is endued with the Spirit of Almighty God, let him be judge. Of the cross of the patriarchs, as ye may read in their stories, if ye read the book of Genesis, ye shall perceive. Of others St. Paul in a few words comprehendeth much matter, speaking in a generality of the wonderful afflictions, death, and torments which the men of God in God's cause, and for the truth's sake, willingly and gladly did suffer. After much particular rehearsal of many, he saith—"Others were racked and despised, and would not be delivered, that they might obtain a better resurrection. Others were tried with mockings and scourgings, and moreover with bonds and imprisonments; they were stoned, hewn asunder, tempted, slain upon the edge of the sword; some wandered to and fro in sheep skins, in goat skins, forsaken, oppressed, afflicted, such godly men as the world was unworthy of, wandering in wildernesses, in mountains, in caves, and in dens, and caves of the earth, destitute, afflicted and tormented." And yet they abide for us the servants of God, and for those their brethren which are to be slain as they were for the word of God's sake, that none be shut out, but that we may all go together to meet our master Christ in the air at His coming, and so be in bliss with Him in body and soul for evermore.

Therefore seeing we have so much occasion to suffer, and to take afflictions for Christ's name's sake patiently, so many advantages thereby, so weighty causes, so many good examples, so great necessity, so sure promises of eternal life and heavenly joys of Him that cannot lie: let us throw away whatever might hinder us, all burden of sin, and all kind of carnality, and patiently and constantly let us run the race that is set before us, ever having our eyes upon Jesus Christ, the author and perfecter of our faith, "who for the joy that was set before Him endured the cross, not minding the shame and ignominy thereof, and is set now at the right hand of the throne of God. Consider this, that He suffered such strife of sinners against Himself, that ye should not give over nor faint in your minds. As yet we have not withstood unto death fighting against sin." Let us never forget, dear brethren, for Christ's sake, that fatherly exhortation of the wise man that speaketh unto us, as unto his children, the godly wisdom of God, saying thus—"My son, despise not the correction of the

Lord, nor fall from Him when thou art rebuked of Him; for whom the Lord loveth, him doth He correct, and scourgeth every child whom He receiveth. What child is he whom the father doth not chasten? If ye be free from chastisement, whereof all are partakers, then are ye bastards and no children. Seeing then, when as we not be much more be subject unto our spiritual Father that we might live? And they for a little time have taught us after their own mind but this Father teacheth us to our own advantage, to give unto us His holiness. All chastisement for the present time appeareth not pleasant, but painful; but afterwards it rendereth the fruit of righteousness on them which are exercised in it. Wherefore let us be of good cheer, good brethren, and let us pluck up our feeble members that were fallen or begun to faint, heart, hands, knees, and all the rest, and let us walk upright and straight, that no limping nor halting bring us out of the way. Let us not look upon the things that be present, but with the eyes of our faith let us steadfastly behold the things that be everlasting in heaven, and so choose rather in respect of that which is to come, with the chosen members of Christ to bear Christ's cross, than for this short life-time to enjoy all the riches, honors, and pleasures of the broad world. Why should we Christians fear death? Can death deprive us of Christ which is all our comfort, our joy and our life? Nay forsooth. But contrary, death shall deliver us from this mortal body, which loadeth and beareth down the spirit, that it cannot so well perceive heavenly things; in which so long as we dwell, we are absent from God.

Wherefore understand our state in that we be Christians, that if our mortal body, which is our earthly house, were destroyed, we have a building, a house not made with hands, eternal in the heavens, therefore we are of good cheer, and know that when we are in the body, we are absent from God; for we walk by faith and not by sight. Nevertheless we are bold, and had rather be absent from the body, and present with God. Wherefore we strive, whether we be present at home, or absent abroad, that we may always please Him: and who that hath true faith in our Saviour Christ, whereby he knoweth somewhat truly what Christ our Saviour is, that He is the eternal Son of God, life, light, the wisdom of the Father, all goodness, all righteousness, and whatsoever is good that heart can desire, yea infinite plenty of all these, above what man's heart can either conceive or think; and also that he is given us of the Father, and made of God to be our wisdom, our righteousness, our holiness, and our redemption: who then is he that believeth this indeed, that would not gladly be with his master Christ? Paul for this knowledge coveted to have been loosed from the body, and to have been with Christ, for he counted it much better for himself, and had rather be loosed than to live. Therefore the words of Christ to the thief on the cross, who asked of Him mercy, were full of comfort and solace—"This day thou shalt be with Me in paradise." To die in the defense of Christ's gospel, it is our bounden duty to Christ, and also to our neighbor. To Christ, because He died for us, and rose again that He might be Lord over all. And seeing He died for us, we also should hazard, yea give our life for our brethren, and this kind of giving and losing, is getting and winning indeed: for he that giveth or loseth his life thus, getteth and winneth it for evermore. Blessed are they therefore that die in the

Lord, and if they die in the Lord's cause, they are most happy of all. Let us not then fear death, which can do us no harm, otherwise than for a moment to make the flesh to smart: but that our faith, which is fastened and fixed upon the word of God, telleth us that we shall be anon after death in peace, in the hands of God, in joy, in solace, and that from death we shall go straight unto life. For St. John saith, He that liveth, and believeth in Me, shall never die. And in another place, He shall depart from death unto life. And therefore this death of the Christian is not to be called death, but rather a gate or entrance into everlasting life. Therefore Paul calleth it but a dissolution and change, and both Peter and Paul, a putting off this tabernacle or dwelling house: meaning thereby the mortal body, as wherein the soul or spirit doth dwell here in this world for a small time. Yea, this my death may be called, to the Christian, an end of all miseries. For so long as we live here, we must pass through many tribulations before we can enter into the kingdom of heaven. And now, after that death hath shot his bolt, all the Christian man's enemies have done what they can; after that they have no more to do. What could hurt or harm poor Lazarus that lay at the rich man's gate? his former penury and poverty? his misery, beggary, and horrible wounds and sickness? No; as soon as death had struck him with his dart, so soon came the angels, and carried him straight up into Abraham's bosom. What lost he by death, who from misery and pain is conducted, by the ministry of angels, to a place of joy and felicity?

Farewell, dear brethren, farewell; let us comfort our hearts in all troubles, and in death, with God's word, for heaven and earth shall perish, but the word of the Lord endureth for ever. Farewell Jesus Christ's dearly beloved spouse, here wandering in this world in a strange land, encompassed about with deadly enemies, who seek thy destruction. Farewell, farewell to you, O ye the whole universal congregation of the chosen of God here living upon earth, the true church militant of Christ, the true mystical body of Christ, the very household and family of God and the sacred temple of the Holy Ghost, farewell. Farewell, O thou little flock of the high heavenly pastors of Christ, for to you it hath pleased the heavenly Father to give an everlasting and eternal kingdom. Farewell thou spiritual house of God, thou holy and royal priesthood, thou chosen generation, thou holy nation, thou won spouse. Farewell, farewell.

The next month after the burning of Ridley and Latimer, which was the month of November, Stephen Gardiner, bishop and chancellor, a man hated of God and all good men, ended his wretched life. He was born in the town of Bury in Suffolk, and brought up most part of his youth in Cambridge: his wit, capacity, memory, and other endowments of nature were not to be complained of, if he had well used and rightly applied the same. He profited not a little in such studies as he gave his head unto; as in civil law, languages, and such other like, especially in those arts and faculties which had the prospect of dignity and preferment. But to those gifts were joined great vices, which not so much followed him as overtook him, not so much burdened him as made him burdenous to the whole realm. He was of a proud stomach and high-minded; in wit, crafty and subtle; towards his superiors, flattering and fair spoken; to his inferiors, fierce; against his equals, stout and envious, as appeared between the good lord Cromwell and him in the reign of king Henry. Upon his estimation and fame he stood too much, more than was meet for a man of his coat and calling, whose profession was to be crucified unto the world.

As touching divinity, he was so variable, wavering with time, that no constant censure can be given what to make of him. If his doings and writings were according to his conscience, no man can rightly say whether he was a right protestant or a papist; and if he wrote otherwise than he thought, then was he a double dissembler before God and man. For first in the beginning of Anne Boleyn's time, who was so forward or busy in the matter of the king's divorce as Stephen Gardiner, who was first sent to Rome, and then to the emperor with Edward Foxe, as chief agent in the behalf of lady Anne? by whom also he was preferred to the bishopric of Winchester. Again, at the abolishing of the pope, who so ready to swear or so vehement to write against he pope as he, as not only by his sermons but also by his book *"De Obedientia"* may appear? in which book, lest any should think him drawn thereunto otherwise than by his own consent, he plainly declareth how not rashly nor upon a sudden, but in a long deliberation and advertisement in himself about the matter, he at length uttered his judgment. And moreover so he uttered his judgments in writing against the usurped supremacy of the pope, that coming to Louvain afterward he was there accounted as excommunicate and schismatic, insomuch that he was not permitted in their church to say mass, and in their public sermons they openly cried out against him.

And thus long continued he firm and forward, so that who but Winchester during all the time of queen Anne? After her fall, by little and little he was carried away, until at length the emulation of Cromwell's estate, and especially for his so much favouring of Bonner, whom Winchester at that time could in no case abide, made him an utter enemy against the said Cromwell and also his religion. Again, in king Edward's days, he began a little to rebate from certain points of popery, and somewhat to smell of the gospel, as appears by his sermon before the king, and also by his subscribing to certain articles. This was a half turn of Stephen Gardiner from popery again to the gospel, and no doubt he would have further turned had not the unlucky decay of the duke of Somerset clean turned him away from true divinity to plain popery, wherein he continued a cruel persecutor to his dying day. And thus much concerning the trade and profession of Stephen Gardiner.

Touching the death of the foresaid Stephen Gardiner, and the manner thereof, I would they which were present thereat would testify unto us what they saw; notwithstanding I thought not to overpass a certain hearsay openly reported in the house of a worthy citizen bearing yet office in this city: "The same day, when bishop Ridley and master Latimer suffered at Oxford, there came into the house of Stephen Gardiner the duke of Norfolk, with his secretary, master Munday. The duke there waiting and tarrying for his dinner, the bishop being not yet disposed to dine, deferred the time to three or four of the clock at afternoon. At length, about four of the clock cometh his servant, posting in all possible speed from Oxford, bringing intelligence to the bishop what he had heard and seen; of whom the said bishop diligently inquiring the truth of the matter, and hearing by his man that fire was most certainly set unto them, cometh out rejoicing to the duke—'Now,' saith he, 'let us go to dinner:' whereupon they being set down, meat immediately was brought, and the bishop began merrily to eat. But what followed? The bloody tyrant had not eaten a few bits, but the sudden stroke of God's terrible hand fell upon him in such sort as immediately he was taken from table, and so brought to his bed; where he continued the space of fifteen days in intolerable anguish and torments: a spectacle worthy to be noted and beholden of all such bloody burning persecutors."

I could name the man who, being then present, and a great doer about the said Winchester, reported to us concerning the said bishop, that when Dr. Day, bishop of Chichester, came to him, and began to comfort him with the words of God's promise, and with the free justification in the blood of Christ our Saviour, repeating the Scriptures to him, Winchester cried out, "What, my lord, will you open that gap now? Then farewell altogether. To me, and such others in my case, you may speak it; but open this window to the people, then farewell altogether!" Having given this brief sketch of Gardiner's story, leaving him to his Judge, we shall return, (by the grace and leave of the Lord,) as the course of these doleful days shall lead us, to prosecute the residue of Christ's martyrs.

The political and ecclesiastical state of the realm at this period has been summed up by a former editor of this work in the following comprehensive and judicious manner. "The parliament was now assembled, and it appeared that the nation was much turned in their affections. It was proposed to give the queen a subsidy. This was the first aid that the queen had asked, though she was now in the third year of her reign; and what was now desired, was no more than what she might have exacted at her first coming to the crown; and since she had forgiven so much at her coronation, it seemed unreasonable to deny it now: yet great opposition was made to it. Many said, she was impoverishing the crown, and giving away the abbey-lands, and therefore she ought to be supplied by the clergy, and not turn to the laity: but it was answered, that the convocation had given her 6s. in the pound, but that would not serve her present occasions; so the debate grew high; but to prevent further heats, the queen sent a message, declaring that she would accept the subsidy, upon which it was granted. The queen sent for the speaker of the house of commons, and told him she could not with a good conscience exact the first-fruits of the clergy, since they were given to her father to support his unlawful dignity, of being the supreme head of the church: she also thought that all tithes, and impropriations were the patrimony of the church, and therefore was resolved to resign such of them as were in her hands. The former part passed easily in the house, but great opposition was made to the latter part of her motion: for it was looked on as a step to the taking all the impropriations out of the hands of the laity: upon a division of the house, one hundred and twenty-six were against it, and one hundred and ninety-three were for it; so it was carried by sixty-seven voices. An bill was put in against the duchess of Suffolk, and several others that favored the reformation, and had gone beyond sea that they might freely enjoy their consciences; requiring them to return, under severe penalties: the lords passed it, but the commons threw it out: for they began now to repent of the severe laws they had already consented to, and resolved to add no more. They also rejected another bill, for incapacitating some to be justices of peace who were complained on for their remissness in prosecuting heretics. An act was put in for debarring one Bennet Smith, who had hired some assassins to commit a most detestable murder, from the benefit of the clergy; which, by the course of the common law, would have saved him. This was an invention of the priests, that if any who was capable of entering into orders, and had not been twice married, or had not married a widow, could read, and vow to take orders, he was to be saved in many criminal cases. And it was looked on as part of the ecclesiastical immunity; which made divers of the bishops oppose this act; yet it passed, though four of them and five temporal lords protested against it. There was such a heat in the house of commons in this parliament, that Sir Anthony Kingston called one day for the keys of the house; but for this temerity, in the dissolution of parliament, he was sent to the Tower: he was, however, soon after set at liberty; but next year he and six others were accused of a design of robbing the exchequer. Sir Anthony died before he was brought up to London; the other six were executed; but the evidence against them does not appear on record.

Cardinal Pole, about this time, called a convocation, having first procured a licence from the queen, empowering them both to meet and to make such canons as they should think fit. This was done to preserve the prerogatives of the crown, and to secure the clergy, that they might not be afterwards brought under a praemunire. In it several decrees were proposed by Pole, and assented to by the clergy: For observing the feast of the reconciliation made with Rome, with great solemnity. For condemning all heretical books, and receiving that exposition of the faith which pope Eugenius sent from the council of Florence to the Armenians. For the decent administration of the sacraments, and the putting down the yearly feasts in the dedications of churches. For requiring all bishops and priests to lay aside secular cares, and to give themselves wholly to the pastoral charge: and all pluralists to resign all their benefices except one, within two months, otherwise to forfeit all. For bishops to preach often, and to provide good preachers for their dioceses, to go over them as their visitors. For the pomp and luxury of the tables, servants, and families of the bishops to cease, and the money to be laid out on works of charity. For orders to be granted only after strict examination. For personal partiality in bestowing benefices no longer to prevail. For the abolition of simony. For schools to be connected with every cathedral, chargeable on its revenues—and for some other inferior purposes. In these, the politic temper of cardinal Pole may well be discerned. He thought the people were more wrought on by the scandals they saw in the clergy, than by the arguments which they heard from the reformers; and therefore reckoned that if pluralities and non-residences, and the other abuses of churchmen, could have been removed, and if he could have brought the bishops to life better, and labor more, to be stricter in giving orders, and more impartial in conferring benefices, and if he could have established seminaries in cathedrals, heresy might have been driven out of the nation by gentler means that racks and fires. In one thing, however, he showed the meanness of his spirit, namely that though he himself condemned cruel proceedings against heretics, yet he both gave commissions to other bishops and archdeacons to try them, and suffered a great deal of cruelty to be exercised in his own diocese: but he had not courage enough to resist pope Paul IV, who thought of no other way for bearing down heresy, than that of setting up courts of inquisition every where. He had imprisoned cardinal Marone, Pole's great friend, upon suspicion of heresy; and would very probably have used himself so, if he had got him at Rome.

About this time the Jesuits were beginning to grow considerably; they were restrained, besides their other vows, by an absolute obedience to the see of Rome: and set themselves every where to open free-schools, for the education of youth, and to bear down heresy. They were excused from the hours of the quire, and were consequently looked on as a mongrel order, between the regulars and the seculars. They proposed to cardinal Pole, that since the queen was restoring the abbey-lands, it would be to little purpose to give them again to the Benedictine order, which was not rather a clog than a help to the church: and therefore they desired that houses might be assigned to them, for maintaining schools and seminaries; and they did not doubt but they should quickly drive out heresy and recover the church-lands. Cardinal Pole would not listen to this, for which the Jesuits much censured him. It is not certain whether he foresaw that disorder which they were likely to bring into the church, and that corruption of morals that hath since emanated from their schools.

CHAPTER NINETEEN

An Account of the Persecutions in the Netherlands

The light of the Gospel having successfully spread over the Netherlands, the pope instigated the emperor to commence a persecution against the Protestants; when many thousand fell martyrs to superstitious malice and barbarous bigotry, among whom the most remarkable were the following:

Wendelinuta, a pious Protestant widow, was apprehended on account of her religion, when several monks, unsuccessfully, endeavored to persuade her to recant. As they could not prevail, a Roman Catholic lady of her acquaintance desired to be admitted to the dungeon in which she was confined, and promised to exert herself strenuously towards inducing the prisoner to abjure the reformed religion. When she was admitted to the dungeon, she did her utmost to perform the task she had undertaken; but finding her endeavors ineffectual, she said, "Dear Wendelinuta, if you will not embrace our faith, at least keep the things which you profess secret within your own bosom, and strive to prolong your life." To which the widow replied, "Madam, you know not what you say; for with the heart we believe to righteousness, but with the tongue confession is made unto salvation." As she positively refused to recant, her goods were confiscated, and she was condemned to be burnt. At the place of execution a monk held a cross to her, and bade her kiss and worship God. To which she answered, "I worship no wooden god, but the eternal God who is in heaven." She was then executed, but through the before-mentioned Roman Catholic lady, the favor was granted that she should be strangled before fire was put to the fagots.

Two Protestant clergymen were burnt at Colen; a tradesman of Antwerp, named Nicholas, was tied up in a sack, thrown into the river, and drowned; and Pistorius, a learned student, was carried to the market of a Dutch village in a fool's coat, and committed to the flames.

Sixteen Protestants, having received sentence to be beheaded, a Protestant minister was ordered to attend the execution. This gentleman performed the function of his office with great propriety, exhorted them to repentance, and gave them comfort in the mercies of their Redeemer. As soon as the sixteen were beheaded, the magistrate cried out to the executioner, "There is another stroke remaining yet; you must behead the minister; he can never die at a better time than with such excellent precepts in his mouth, and such laudable examples before him." He was accordingly beheaded, though even many of the Roman Catholics themselves reprobated this piece of treacherous and unnecessary cruelty.

George Scherter, a minister of Salzburg, was apprehended and committed to prison for instructing his flock in the knowledge of the Gospel. While he was in confinement he wrote a confession of his faith; soon after which he was condemned, first to be beheaded, and afterward to be burnt to ashes. On his way to the place of execution he said to the spectators, "That you may know I die a true Christian, I will give you a sign." This was indeed verified in a most singular manner; for after his head was cut off, the body lying a short space of time with the belly to the ground, it suddenly turned upon the back, when the right foot crossed over the left, as did also the right arm over the left: and in this manner it remained until it was committed to the flames.

In Louviana, a learned man, named Percinal, was murdered in prison; and Justus Insparg was beheaded, for having Luther's sermons in his possession.

Giles Tilleman, a cutler of Brussels, was a man of great humanity and piety. Among others he was apprehended as a Protestant, and many endeavors were made by the monks to persuade him to recant. He had once, by accident, a fair opportunity of escaping from prison, and being asked why he did not avail himself of it, he replied, "I would not do the keepers so much injury, as they must have answered for my absence, had I gone away." When he was sentenced to be burnt, he fervently thanked God for granting him an opportunity, by martyrdom, to glorify His name. Perceiving, at the place of execution, a great quantity of fagots, he desired the principal part of them might be given to the poor, saying, "A small quantity will suffice to consume me." The executioner offered to strangle him before the fire was lighted, but he would not consent, telling him that he defied the flames; and, indeed, he gave up the ghost with such composure amidst them, that he hardly seemed sensible of their effects.

In the year 1543 and 1544, the persecution was carried on throughout all Flanders in a most violent and cruel manner. Some were condemned to perpetual imprisonment, others to perpetual banishment; but most were put to death either by hanging, drowning, immuring, burning, the rack, or burying alive.

John de Boscane, a zealous Protestant, was apprehended on account of his faith, in the city of Antwerp. On his trial, he steadfastly professed himself to be of the reformed religion, which occasioned his immediate condemnation. The magistrate, however, was afraid to put him to death publicly, as he was popular through his great generosity, and almost universally beloved for his inoffensive life, and exemplary piety. A private execution being determined on, an order was given to drown him in prison. The executioner, accordingly, put him in a large tub; but Boscane struggling, and getting his head above the water, the executioner stabbed him with a dagger in several places, until he expired.

John de Buisons, another Protestant, was, about the same time, secretly apprehended, and privately executed at Antwerp. The numbers of Protestants being great in that city, and the prisoner much respected, the magistrates feared an insurrection, and for that reason ordered him to be beheaded in prison.

A.D. 1568, three persons were apprehended in Antwerp, named Scoblant, Hues, and Coomans. During their confinement they behaved with great fortitude and cheerfulness, confessing that the hand of God appeared in what had befallen them, and bowing down before the throne of his providence. In an epistle to some worthy Protestants, they expressed themselves in the following words: "Since it is the will of the Almighty that we should suffer for His name, and be persecuted for the sake of His Gospel, we patiently submit, and are joyful upon the occasion; though the flesh may rebel against the spirit, and hearken to the council of the old serpent, yet the truths of the Gospel shall prevent such advice from being taken, and Christ shall bruise the serpent's head. We are not comfortless in confinement, for we have faith; we fear not affliction, for we have hope; and we forgive our enemies, for we have charity. Be not under apprehensions for us, we are happy in confinement through the promises of God, glory in our bonds, and exult in being thought worthy to suffer for the sake of Christ. We desire not to be released, but to be blessed with fortitude; we ask not liberty, but the power of perseverance; and wish for no change in our condition, but that which places a crown of martyrdom upon our heads."

Scoblant was first brought to his trial; when, persisting in the profession of his faith, he received sentence of death. On his return to prison, he earnestly requested the jailer not to permit any friar to come near him; saying, "They can do me no good, but may greatly disturb me. I hope my salvation is already sealed in heaven, and that the blood of Christ, in which I firmly put my trust, hath washed me from my iniquities. I am now going to throw off this mantle of clay, to be clad in robes of eternal glory, by whose celestial brightness I shall be freed from all errors. I hope I may be the last martyr to papal tyranny, and the blood already spilt found sufficient to quench the thirst of popish cruelty; that the Church of Christ may have rest here, as his servants will hereafter." On the day of execution, he took a pathetic leave of his fellow prisoners. At the stake he fervently said the Lord's Prayer, and sung the Fortieth Psalm; then commending his soul to God, he was burnt alive.

Hues, soon after died in prison; upon which occasion Coomans wrote thus to his friends: "I am now deprived of my friends and companions; Scoblant is martyred, and Hues dead, by the visitation of the Lord; yet I am not alone, I have with me the God of Abraham, of Isaac, and of Jacob; He is my comfort, and shall be my reward. Pray unto God to strengthen me to the end, as I expect every hour to be freed from this tenement of clay."

On his trial he freely confessed himself of the reformed religion, answered with a manly fortitude to every charge against him, and proved the Scriptural part of his answers from the Gospel. The judge told him the only alternatives were recantation or death; and concluded by saying, "Will you die for the faith you profess?" To which Coomans replied, "I am not only willing to die, but to suffer the most excruciating torments for it; after which my soul shall receive its confirmation from God Himself, in the midst of eternal glory." Being condemned, he went cheerfully to the place of execution, and died with the most manly fortitude, and Christian resignation.

William of Nassau fell a sacrifice to treachery, being assassinated in the fifty-first year of his age, by Beltazar Gerard, a native of Ranche Compte, in the province of Burgundy. This murderer, in hopes of a reward here and hereafter, for killing an enemy to the king of Spain and an enemy to the Catholic religion, undertook to destroy the prince of Orange. Having procured firearms, he watched him as he passed through the great hall of his palace to dinner, and demanded a passport. The princess of Orange, observing that the assassin spoke with a hollow and confused voice, asked who he was, saying that she did not like his countenance. The prince answered that it was one that demanded a passport, which he should presently have.

Nothing further passed before dinner, but on the return of the prince and princess through the same hall, after dinner was over, the assassin, standing concealed as much as possible by one of the pillars, fired at the prince, the balls entering at the left side, and passing through the right, wounding in their passage the stomach and vital parts. On receiving the wounds, the prince only said, "Lord, have mercy upon my soul, and upon these poor people," and then expired immediately.

The lamentations throughout the United Provinces were general, on account of the death of the prince of Orange; and the assassin, who was immediately taken, received sentence to be put to death in the most exemplary manner, yet such was his enthusiasm, or folly, that when his flesh was torn by red-hot pincers, he coolly said, "If I was at liberty, I would commit such an action over again."

The prince of Orange's funeral was the grandest ever seen in the Low Countries, and perhaps the sorrow for his death the most sincere, as he left behind him the character he honestly deserved, viz., that of father of his people.

To conclude, multitudes were murdered in different parts of Flanders; in the city of Valence, in particular, fifty-seven of the principal inhabitants were butchered in one day, for refusing to embrace the Romish superstition; and great numbers were suffered to languish in confinement, until they perished through the inclemency of their dungeons.

CHAPTER TWENTY

The Life, State, and Martyrdom of the Reverend Pastor and Prelate, Thomas Cranmer, Archbishop of Canterbury

A s concerning the life and estate of Thomas Cranmer, late archbishop of Canterbury, it is first to be noted and considered that the same Thomas Cranmer, coming of an ancient parentage, from the conquest to be deducted, was born in a village called Aslacton, in Nottinghamshire. Being from his infancy kept at school, and brought up not without much good civility, he came in process of time unto the university of Cambridge; and there prospering in right good knowledge amongst the better sort of students, was chosen fellow of Jesus college in Cambridge. It was at that time, when all good authors and fine writers being neglected, filthy barbarousness was embraced in all schools and universities. The names and numbers of liberal arts did only remain, the arts themselves were clean lost; and divinity was fallen into the state, that being laden with articles and distinctions, it served rather for the gain of a few than for the edification of many. At length the tongues and other good learning began, by little and little, to spring up again, and the books of Faber and Erasmus began to be much occupied and had in good estimation, with a number of good authors besides: in whom the said Cranmer took no small pleasure. At length, when Martin Luther was risen up, the more bright and happy days of God's knowledge did waken men's minds to truth; at which time, he being about thirty years old, gave his whole mind to discuss matters of religion.

So Cranmer, being master of arts, and fellow of Jesus college, it chanced that he married a gentleman's daughter, by which he lost his fellowship, and became a reader in Buckingham college. In order that he might with the more diligence apply himself to his office of reading, he placed his wife at an inn, in Cambridge, the mistress of which was a relation of hers. On account of his frequent visits he was much noticed by some popish merchants: on this arose the slanderous noise and report against him, after he was preferred to the archbishopric of Canterbury. He continued reader in Buckingham college until his wife died in child birth. After this the masters and fellows of Jesus college, desirous of their old companion, for his eminent learning, chose him again fellow of the same college. Remaining at his study, he became in a few years reader of the divinity lecture, and in such estimation was he held by the whole university, that when doctor of divinity, he was commonly appointed to examine such as yearly proceed in commencement, either bachelors or doctors, and by whose approbation the whole university licensed them to proceed unto their degree, or by whose non-approbation the university retained them until they were better furnished with knowledge and qualified for advancement.

Dr. Cranmer, ever favouring the knowledge of the scripture, would not permit any to proceed in divinity, unless they were substantially versed in the history of the Bible: by which certain friars and other religious persons, who were principally brought up in the study of school-authors, without regard to the authority of the scriptures, were commonly rejected by him, so that he was greatly hated; yet it came to pass in the end, that many of them, thus compelled to study the scriptures, became afterwards very learned; insomuch, that when they became doctors of divinity, they could not too much extol Cranmer's goodness towards them, who for a time had put them back, to initiate them in better knowledge. His merit soon spreading abroad, he was much solicited by Dr. Capon, to be one of the fellows in the foundation of Cardinal Wolsey's college in Oxford, which he refused, not without danger of offending. While he continued in Cambridge, the important cause of Henry's divorce with the lady Katherine came into question; which being many ways, for the space of two or three years amongst the canonists, civilians, and other learned men, diversely disputed and debated, it came to pass that Dr. Cranmer, on account of the plague being in Cambridge, resorted to Waltham-Abbey, to the house of Mr. Cressey, whose wife was his relation, and whose two sons he brought with him from Cambridge, they being his pupils.

During this summer, cardinals Campeius and Wolsey, being in commission from the pope, to hear and determine the great cause in controversy between the king and queen, delayed until the month of August in hearing the cause debated. When August was come, the cardinals little caring to proceed to give sentence, took occasion to finish their commission, and to determine no further therein, pretending that it was not permitted by the laws to keep courts of ecclesiastical matters in harvest time. This sudden interruption so much enraged the king, that taking it as a mock at the cardinals' hands, he commanded the dukes of Norfolk and Suffolk to dispatch immediately to Rome cardinal Campeius: and in haste removed himself to Waltham for a night or two, while his household removed to Greenwich: by which means it happened that the harbingers, Dr. Stephen Gardiner, secretary, and Dr. Foxe, almoner, came to lodge in the house of Mr. Cressey, where Dr. Cranmer resided. When supper-time came, the three doctors met together; Gardiner and Foxe were very much surprised at Cranmer being there. He declared the cause, namely, because the plague was in Cambridge: and as they were old acquaintance, the secretary and the almoner very well entertained Dr. Cranmer, intending to learn his opinion concerning the great business they had in hand. And as this occasion served, while they were at supper, they conferred with Dr. Cranmer concerning the king's cause, requesting him to give his opinion of it.

Cranmer answered, That he could say little to the matter, as he had not studied nor looked for it. Notwithstanding, in his opinion they made more ado in prosecuting the ecclesiastical law than needed. It were better, he thought, that the question—Whether a man may marry his brother's wife, or no? were discussed by the divines, and by the authority of the word of God, whereby the conscience of the prince might be better satisfied and quieted, than thus from year to year, by unnecessary delays, to prolong the time, leaving the very truth of the matter unsettled. There was but one truth in it, which the scripture will soon make manifest, being by learned men well handled, and that may be as well done in England in the universities here, as at Rome, or elsewhere in any foreign nation, the authority whereof will soon compel any judge to come to definitive sentence: and therefore as he took it, they might that way have made an end of the matter long since. When Dr. Cranmer had thus ended his tale, the other two liked well his device and wished they had proceeded so before, and thereupon conceived some matter of council to instruct the king with, who was then thinking to send to Rome again for a new commission.

Now the next day, when the king removed to Greenwich, recollecting in himself, how he had been used by the cardinals, in thus deferring his cause, his mind was very uneasy, and desirous to see an end of this long and tedious suit, he called unto him the two principal managers of his cause, Gardiner and Foxe, who related their conference with Dr. Cranmer, and told the king the plan he had suggested for a more speedy termination of the affair. The king accordingly sent for Dr. Cranmer, approved and adopted his scheme, received him into favour, and advanced him, on the death of archbishop Warham, to the see of Canterbury, anno 1530.

Although the said Cranmer was now exalted to so great dignity and honour, still was he compassed about by mighty enemies, and by many crafty trains impugned; yet, through God's mighty providence working in the king's heart to favour him, he rubbed out all king Henry's time; and under the government and protection of his son king Edward (to whom Cranmer was godfather) his state was rather more advanced. Afterward, this king Edward falling sick, and perceiving that his death was at hand, and knowing that his sister Mary was wholly wedded unto popish religion, bequeathed the succession of the realm to the lady Jane Grey, by consent of all his council and lawyers. When all the nobles of the realm, states and judges, had subscribed to this testament, they sent for the archbishop, and required that he also would subscribe. Cranmer refused at the first; but after that he had spake with the king, and when they all agreed that by law of the realm it might be so, with much ado he subscribed. Well, not long after this king Edward died, A.D. 1553, being almost sixteen years of age, to the great sorrow but greater calamity of the whole realm.

At the oppression of the good lord Cromwell, in king Henry's time, it was fully determined that Cranmer also should be committed to prison; but he privily obtaining speech of the king, there upon his knees declared his innocence in the matter of which he was accused; and the king delivered him his signet, saying, "Go thy ways! if thou deceive me, I will never trust thy bald pate again while I live." And thus he escaped that present danger. Here also may be noted the saying which is constantly affirmed of divers persons, that the said archbishop, with the lord Wriothesley, saved the life of queen Mary, the king being determined to have off her head for certain causes of stubbornness; whereupon the king afterward said that Cranmer made intercession for her, which would his destruction, and would trouble them all.

After king Edward's decease immediately it was commanded that the lady Jane should be proclaimed queen; but Mary, hearing of the death of her brother, was established in the possession of the realm by the assistance of the commons as ye heard before. This queen Mary, coming to London, caused the duke of Northumberland and the duke of Suffolk to be executed, and likewise the lady Jane, together with her husband. The rest of the nobles, paying fines, were forgiven, the archbishop of Canterbury only excepted; for as yet the old grudge against Cranmer, for the divorcement of her mother, remained hid in the bottom of her heart; and besides she remembered the state of religion changed, the cause whereof was imputed to him.

Not long after Cranmer was condemned of treason, and committed to the Tower; and when the queen could not honestly deny him his pardon, seeing all the rest were discharged, she released to him his action of treason, and accused him only of heresy. Thus stood the cause of Cranmer, until at length it was determined by the queen and the council that he should be removed from the Tower to Oxford, there to dispute with the doctors and divines, to whom word was sent privily to prepare themselves. After these said disputations were finished in Oxford, between the doctors of both universities, and the three worthy bishops, Cranmer, Ridley, and Latimer, ye heard then how sentence condemnatory was ministered against them by Dr. Weston and others of the university; whereby they were judged to be heretics, and so committed to the mayor and sheriffs of Oxford. But forasmuch as the sentence given against them was void in law, (for, at that time, the authority of the pope was not yet received into the land,) therefore was a new commission sent from Rome, and a new process framed for the conviction of these reverend and learned men aforesaid.

At the coming down of the said commissioners, which was upon Thursday the 12th of September, 1555, there was erected a solemn scaffold in the east end of the church of St. Mary, over against the high altar, with cloth of state very richly and sumptuously adorned, for bishop Brooks was pope's legate, apparelled in pontificalibus, representing the pope's person. On the right hand beneath him sat Dr. Martin, and on the left hand Dr. Storey, the king and queen's commissioners, which were both doctors of the civil law; and underneath them other doctors, scribes, and pharisees also, with the pope's collector, and a rabblement of such other like.

And thus these bishops being placed in their pontificalibus, the bishop of Canterbury was sent for to come before them. He came forth of the prison to the church of St. Mary, set round with bills and glaves for fear he should start away, being clothed in a fair black gown, with his hood on both shoulders, such as doctors of divinity in the university use to wear, and in his hand a white staff. After he was come into the church, and did see them sit in their pontificalibus, he did not put off his cap to any of them, but stood still until that he was called. And anon one of the proctors for the pope, or else his doctor, called, "Thomas archbishop of Canterbury! appear here, and make answer to that shall be laid to thy charge; that is to say, for blasphemy, incontinency, and heresy; and make answer here to the bishop of Gloucester, representing the pope's person!"

Upon this, Cranmer being brought more near unto the scaffold, where the foresaid bishop sat, he first well viewed the place of judgment, and spying where the king and queen's majesties' proctors were, putting off his cap, he (first humbly bowing his knee to the ground) made reverence to the one, and after to the other. That done, beholding the bishop in the face, he put on his bonnet again; making no manner of token of obedience towards him at all: whereat the bishop, being offended, said that it might beseem him right well, weighing the authority he did represent, to do his duty unto him. Whereunto Dr. Cranmer answered, that he had once taken a solemn oath, never to consent to the admitting of the bishop of Rome's authority into this realm of England again; that he had done it advisedly, and meant by God's grace to keep it; and therefore would commit nothing either by sign or token which might argue his consent to the receiving of the same; and so he desired the said bishop to judge of him. He did it, he said, not for any contempt to his person, which he could have been content to have honoured as well as any of the others, if his commission had come from as good an authority as theirs. When, after many means used, they perceived that the archbishop would not move his bonnet, the bishop of Gloucester proceeded with studied eloquence and painted art in his oration; and after he had finished, Dr. Martin took the matter in hand. After that Dr. Martin had ended his oration, the archbishop said, "My lord, I do not acknowledge this session of yours, nor yet you, my mislawful judge; neither would I have appeared this day before you, but that I was brought hither as a prisoner. And therefore I openly here renounce you as my judge, protesting that my meaning is not to make any answer, as in a lawful judgment, (for then would I be silent,) but only for that I am bound in conscience to answer every man of that hope which I have in Jesus Christ, by the counsel of St. Peter; and lest by my silence many of those who are weak, here present, might be offended. And so I desire that my answers may be accepted as extra judicialia." When he had ended his protestation he said, "Shall I then make answer?" To whom Dr. Martin answered, "As you think good; no man shall let you." And here the archbishop, kneeling down on both knees towards the west, said first the Lord's Prayer; then rising up, he reciteth the articles of the creed; which done he entereth on his profession of faith.

Toward the close of the session, Dr. Martin demanded of Dr. Cranmer, who was supreme head of the church of England? "Marry," quoth my lord of Canterbury, "Christ is head of this member, as he is of the whole body of the universal church." "Why," quoth Dr. Martin, "you made king Henry the eighth supreme head of the church." "Yea," said the archbishop, "of all the people of England, as well ecclesiastical as temporal." "And not of the church?" said Martin. "No," said he; "for Christ only is the head of his church, and of the faith and religion of the same. The king is head and governor of his people, which are the visible church." "What," quoth Martin, "you never durst tell the king so." "Yes, that I durst," quoth he; "and in the publication of his style, wherein he was named supreme head of the church, there was never other thing meant." A number of other fond and foolish objections were made, with repetition whereof I thought not to trouble the reader.

After that they had received his answers to all their objections, they cited him to appear at Rome within fourscore days, to make there his personal answers; which he said, if the king and queen would send him, he would be content to do. And so thence he was carried to prison again, where he continually remained, notwithstanding that he was commanded to appear at Rome. Furthermore, though the said archbishop was detained in strait prison, so that he could not appear, (as was notorious both in England and also in the Romish court,) yet in the end of the said fourscore days was that worthy martyr decreed "contumax," that is, sturdily, frowardly, and wilfully absent, and in pain of the same his absence condemned and put to death.

And as touching the said executory letters of the pope sent to the king and queen, by virtue of that commission, the bishop of Ely, and Bonner bishop of London, were assigned by the king and queen to proceed in the execution thereof upon the 14th day of February. These two coming to Oxford upon St. Valentine's day, as the pope's delegates with a new commission from Rome, by the virtue thereof commanded the archbishop aforesaid to come before them, in the choir of Christ's church, before the high altar; where they sitting (according to their manner) in their pontificalibus, first began to read their commission, the which came from the pope, "plenitudine potestatis;" supplying all manner of defects in law or process committed in dealing with the archbishop, and giving them full authority to proceed to deprivation and degradation of him, and so upon excommunication to deliver him up to the secular power, "omni appellatione remota." When the commission was read they proceeded thereupon to his degradation; and when they would have taken his crosier-staff out of his hand, he held it fast, and refused to deliver the same; and withal, imitating the example of Martin Luther, pulled an appeal out of his left sleeve, which he there and then delivered unto them, saying, "I appeal to the next general council; and herein I have comprehended my cause and form of it, which I desire to be admitted;" and prayed divers of the standers by, name to be witnesses, and especially master Curtop.

This appeal being put up to Thirleby the bishop of Ely, he said, "My lord, our commission is to proceed against you, 'omni appellatione remota,' and therefore we cannot admit it. But," he added, "if it may be admitted, it shall," and so received it of him. Then began he to persuade earnestly with the archbishop to consider his state, promising to become a suitor to the king and queen for him. Afterward, they proceeded with his degradations; and whilst they were thus doing Cranmer said, "All this needed not; I had myself done with this gear long ago." Last of all they stripped him out of his gown into his jacket, and put upon him a poor yeoman-beadle's gown, full bare and nearly worn, a townsman's cap on his head, and so delivered him to the secular power.

While the archbishop was thus remaining in durance, (whom they had kept now in prison almost three years,) the doctors and divines of Oxford busied themselves all that ever they could, to have him recant, essaying by all crafty practices and allurements they might devise how to bring their purpose to pass, specially Henry Sydal and John de Villa Garcia. First, they set forth how acceptable it would be both to the king and queen, and especially how gainful to him, and for his soul's health. They added how the council and noble men bare him good will; and put him in hope that he should not only have his life, but also be restored to his ancient dignity, saying, it was but a small matter and so easy that they required him to do, only that he would subscribe to a few words with his own hands; which, if he did, there should be nothing in the whole realm that the queen would not easily grant him, whether he would have riches or dignity; or else if he had rather live a private life in quiet rest, in whatsoever place he listed, without all public ministry, only that he would set his name in two words to a little leaf of paper. But if he refused there was no hope of health and pardon, for the queen was so purposed that she would have Cranmer a catholic, or else no Cranmer at all. Moreover, they exhorted him that he would look to his wealth, his estimation and quietness, saying that he was not so old but that many years yet remained in this his so lusty age; and if he would not do it in respect of the queen, yet he should do it for respect of his life, and not suffer that other men should be more careful for his health than he was himself. Finally, if the desire of life did nothing move him, yet he should remember that to die is grievous in all ages, and especially in these his years and flower of dignity it were more grievous; but to die in the fire and such torments is most grievous of all.

With these and like provocations, these fair flatterers ceased not to solicit and urge to their side; whose force his manly constancy did a great while resist. But at last, when they made no end of calling and crying upon him, the archbishop being overcome, whether by their importunity, or by his own imbecility, or of what mind I cannot tell, at length gave his hand, though it was against his conscience. But so it pleaseth God, that so great virtues in this archbishop should not be had in too much admiration of us without some blemish, or else that the falsehood of the popish generation by this means might be made more evident, or else to minish the confidence of our own strength, that in him should appear an example of man's weak imbecility.

This recantation was soon caused by the doctors and prelates to be imprinted, and set abroad in all men's hands. All this while Cranmer was in uncertain assurance of his life, although the same was faithfully promised to him by the doctors; but after that they had their purpose, the rest they committed to all adventure, as became men of that religion to do. The queen received his recantation very gladly, but of her purpose to put him to death she would nothing relent. And now was Cranmer's cause in a miserable taking, who neither inwardly had any quietness in his own conscience, nor yet outwardly any help in his adversaries.

In the meantime, while these things were adoing in the prison among the doctors, the queen taking secret counsel how to dispatch Cranmer out of the way, appointed Dr. Cole, and secretly gave him in commandment, that against the 21st of March he should prepare a funeral sermon for Cranmer's burning. Soon after, the lord Williams of Thame, and the lord Chandos, sir Thomas Bridges, and sir John Brown were sent for, with other worshipful men and justices, and commanded in the queen's name to be at Oxford at the same day, with their servants and retinue, lest Cranmer's death should raise there any tumult.

Cole the doctor, having this lesson given him before, and charged by her commandment, returned to Oxford ready to play his part; who, two days before the execution, came into the prison to Cranmer, to try whether he abode in the catholic faith wherein before he had left him. To whom, when Cranmer had answered, that by God's grace he would daily be more confirmed in the catholic faith; Cole, departing for that time, the next day repaired to the archbishop again, giving no signification as yet of his death that was prepared. In the morning appointed for his execution, the said Cole, coming to him, asked him if he had any money; to whom when Cranmer answered that he had none, he delivered him fifteen crowns to give to the poor to whom he would; and so exhorting him so much as he could to constancy in faith, departed thence about his business.

By this partly, and other like arguments, Cranmer began more and more to surmise what they went about. Then there came to him the Spanish friar, John de Villa Garcia, witness of his recantation, bringing a paper with articles which Cranmer should openly profess in his recantation before the people. But the archbishop, thinking that the time was at hand in which he could no longer dissemble the profession of his faith with Christ's people, put secretly into his bosom his prayer with his exhortation, which he minded to recite to the people, before he should make the last profession of his faith, fearing lest, if they had heard the confession of his faith first, they would not afterward have suffered him to exhort the people.

Soon after, about nine of the o'clock, the lord Williams, sir Thomas Bridges, sir John Brown, and the other justices, with certain other noblemen that were sent of the queen's council, came to Oxford with a great train of waiting men. Also of the multitude on every side (as is wont in such a matter) was made a great concourse, and greater expectation. Cranmer at length cometh from the prison of Bocardo into St. Mary's church, (the chief church in the university,) with the mayor and aldermen, walking between two friars. There was a stage set over against the pulpit, where Cranmer had his standing, waiting until Cole made him ready to his sermon. He that was late archbishop, metropolitan, and primate of all England, and the king's privy councillor, being now in bare and ragged gown, and ill-favouredly clothed, with an old square cap, exposed to the contempt of all men, did admonish men not only of his own calamity, but also of their state and fortune. In this habit, when he had stood a good space upon the stage, turning to a pillar near adjoining thereunto, he lifted up his hands to heaven, and prayed unto God once or twice, until at the length Dr. Cole coming into the pulpit began his sermon. Proceeding a little from the beginning, he took occasion by and by to turn his tale to Cranmer, and with many hot words reproved him, that once he, being indued with the favour and feeling of wholesome and catholic doctrines, fell into the contrary opinion of pernicious error.

All this meantime, with the greatest grief, Cranmer stood hearing his sermon: one while lifting up his hands and eyes unto heaven, and then again for shame letting them down to the earth, while the tears gushed from his eyes. Great commiseration and pity moved all men's hearts, that beheld so heavy a countenance, and such abundance of tears in an old man of so reverend dignity. Cole having ended his sermon, he called back the people that were ready to depart. "Brethren," said he, "lest any man should doubt of this man's earnest conversion and repentance, you shall hear him speak before you; and therefore I pray you, Mr. Cranmer, to perform that now which you promised not long ago; namely, that you would openly express the true and undoubted profession of your faith, that you may take away all suspicion from men and that all men may understand that you are a catholic indeed."

To this Cranmer, rising up and uncovering his head, replied thus: "I will do it, and that with a good will. Good people, my dearly beloved brethren in Christ, I beseech you most heartily to pray for me to Almighty God, that he will forgive me all my sins and offences, which are without number, and great above measure. But yet one thing grieveth my conscience more than all the rest, whereof, God willing, I intend to speak more hereafter. But how great and how many soever my sins be, I beseech you to pray to God of his mercy to pardon and forgive them all." And here kneeling down he said the following prayer.

O Father of heaven, O Son of God, Redeemer of the world, O Holy Ghost, three persons and one God, have mercy upon me, most wretched caitiff and miserable sinner. I have offended both against heaven and earth, more than my tongue can express. Whither then may I go, or whither shall I flee; to heaven I may be ashamed to lift up mine eyes, and in earth I find no place of refuge or succour. To thee, therefore, O Lord, do I run; to thee do I humble myself. O Lord my God, my sins be great, but yet have mercy upon me for thy great mercy. The great mystery that God became man was not wrought for little or few offences. Thou didst not give thy Son, O heavenly Father, unto death for small sins only, but for all the greatest sins of the world, so that the sinner return to thee with his whole heart, as I do at this present. Wherefore have mercy on me, O God, whose property is always to have mercy; have mercy upon me, O Lord, for thy great mercy. I crave nothing for mine own merits, but for thy name's sake, that it may be allowed thereby, and for thy dear Son Jesus Christ's sake. And now, therefore, our Father of heaven, hallowed be thy name, etc.

Rising he said—

Every man, good people, desireth at the time of his death to give some good exhortation, that others may remember the same before their death, and be the better thereby: so I beseech God grant me grace that I may speak something at this my departing, whereby God may be glorified, and you edified. It is a heavy cause to see that so many folk so much dote upon the love of this false world, and be so careful for it, that of the love of God, or the world to come, they seem to care very little or nothing. Therefore this shall be my first exhortation, that you set not your minds overmuch upon this deceitful world, but upon God, and upon the world to come, and to learn to know what this lesson meaneth which St. John teacheth, that the love of this world is hatred against God.

Next unto God, you obey your king and queen willingly and gladly without murmuring or grudging; not for fear of them only, but much more for the fear of God; knowing that they be God's ministers, appointed by God to rule and govern you: and, therefore, whosoever resisteth them, resisteth the ordinance of God. Then I further entreat that you love altogether like brethren and sisters. For, alas! pity it is to see what contention and hatred one christian man beareth to another, not taking each other as brother and sister, but rather as strangers and mortal enemies. But I pray you learn and bear well away this one lesson, to do good unto all men, as much as in you lieth, and to hurt no man, no more than you would hurt your own natural loving brother or sister. For this you may be sure of, that whosoever hateth any person, and goeth about maliciously to hinder or hurt him, surely, and without all doubt, God is not with that man, although he think himself ever so much in God's favour.

I exhort them that have great substance and riches of this world, that they will well consider and weigh three sayings of the scripture: one is of our Saviour himself, who saith, "It is hard for a rich man to enter into the kingdom of heaven." A sore saying, and yet spoken by him who knoweth the truth. Another is of St. John, whose saying is this—"He that hath the substance of this world, and seeth his brother in necessity, and shutteth up his mercy from him, how can he say that he loveth God?" One more saying I wish you to remember is of St. James, who speaketh to the covetous rich man, after this manner—"Weep you and howl for the misery that shall come upon you: your riches do rot, your clothes be moth-eaten, your gold and silver doth canker and rust, and their rust shall bear witness against you, and consume you like fire; you gather a hoard or treasure of God's indignation against the last day." Let them that be rich ponder well these three sentences: for if they ever had occasion to shew their charity, they have it now at this present, the poor people being so many, and victuals so dear.

And now forasmuch as I am come to the end of my life, whereupon hangeth all my life past, and all my life to come, either to live with my Master Christ for ever in joy, or else to be in pain for ever with wicked devils in hell, and I see before mine eyes presently either heaven ready to receive me, or else hell ready to swallow me up: I shall therefore declare unto you my very faith how I believe, without any colour of dissimulation; for now is no time to dissemble, whatsoever I have said or written in times past.

He then recited the creed, and added—

I believe every article of the catholic faith, every word and sentence taught by our Saviour Christ, his apostles and prophets, in the New and Old Testament.

And now I come to the great thing which so much troubleth my conscience, more than any thing that ever I did or said in my whole life, and that is the setting abroad of a writing contrary to the truth; which now I here renounce and refuse, as things written with my hand contrary to the truth which I thought in my heart, and written for fear of death, and to save my life if it might be; and that is, all such bills and papers which I have written or signed with my hand since my degradation, wherein I have written many things untrue. And forasmuch as my hand hath offended, writing contrary to my heart, therefore my hand shall first be punished; for when I come to the fire, it shall be first burned. As for the pope, I refuse him, as Christ's enemy and antichrist, with all his false doctrine. As for the sacrament, I believe as I have taught in my book against the bishop of Winchester, which my book teacheth so true a doctrine of the sacrament, that it shall stand at the last day before the judgment of God, where the papistical doctrine contrary thereto shall be ashamed to shew her face.

Here the standers-by were all astonished and amazed, and looked upon one another, whose expectation he had so notably deceived. Some began to admonish him of his recantation, and to accuse him of falsehood. Briefly, it was a world to see the doctors beguiled of so great a hope; for they looked for a glorious victory by this man's retractation. As soon as they heard these things they began to rage, fret, and fume: and so much the more, because they could not revenge their grief; for they could no longer threaten or hurt him. For the most miserable man in the world can die but once; whereas of necessity he must needs die that day. And so when they could do nothing else to him, yet lest they should say nothing, they ceased not to object unto him his falsehood and dissimulation. To this he replied—"Ah, my masters, do not you take it so. Always since I lived hitherto, I have been a hater of falsehood, and a lover of simplicity, and never before this time have I dissembled." In saying this he wept bitterly. And when he began to speak more of the sacrament and of the papacy, some of them began to cry out and bawl, especially Cole, who cried out, "Stop the heretic's mouth and take him away!"

Then Cranmer being pulled down from the stage, was led to the fire, accompanied by those friars, vexing, troubling, and threatening him most cruelly. "What madness," say they, "has brought thee again into this error, by which thou will draw innumerable souls with thee into hell?" To whom he answered nothing, but directed all his talk to the people, saving that to one troubling him in the way he spake, and exhorted him to get home to his study, and apply to his book diligently; saying, if he did earnestly call upon God, by reading more, he should get knowledge. But the other, raging and foaming was almost out of his wits, always having this in his mouth, Non fecisti? Didst thou it not?

When he came to the place where the holy bishops and martyrs of God, Latimer and Ridley, were burnt before him for a confession of the truth, kneeling down he prayed to God; and not long tarrying in his prayers, putting off his garments to his shirt, he prepared himself to death. His shirt was made long, down to his feet, which were bare; likewise his head, when both his caps were off, was so bare that one hair could not be seen upon it. His beard was so long and thick, that it covered his face, and his reverend countenance moved the hearts both of his friends and enemies. Then the Spanish friars, John and Richard, began to exhort him, and play their parts with him afresh; but Cranmer, with steadfast purpose, abiding in the profession of his doctrine, gave his hand to certain old men and others that stood by, bidding them farewell. When he had thought to have done so likewise to Mr. Ely, the latter drew back his hand and refused, saying, it was not lawful to salute heretics, and especially such an one as falsely returned to the opinions he had forsworn. And if he had known before that he would have done so, he would never have used his company so familiarly, and chid those serjeants and citizens who had not refused to give him their hands. This Mr. Ely was a student in divinity, and had been lately made a priest, being then one of the fellows in Brazen-nose college.

Then was an iron chain tied about Cranmer, whom when they perceived to be more steadfast than that he could be moved from his sentence, they commanded the fire to be set unto him. And when the wood was kindled and the fire began to burn near him, stretching out his arm, he put his right hand into the flame, which he held so steadfast and unmovable, (saving that once with the same hand he wiped his face,) that all men might see his hand burned before his body was touched. His body did so abide the burning of the flame with such constancy and steadfastness, that standing always in one place without moving his body, he seemed to move no more than the stake to which he was bound; his eyes were lifted up into heaven, and oftentimes he repeated "his unworthy right hand," so long as his voice would suffer him; and using often the words of Stephen, "Lord Jesus, receive my spirit," in the greatness of the flames he gave up the ghost, in the sixty-seventh year of his age.

And this was the end of this learned archbishop, whom, lest by evil subscribing he should have perished, by well recanting God preserved; and lest he should have lived longer with shame and reproof, it pleased God rather to take him away, to the glory of his name and profit of his church. So good was the Lord to his church, in fortifying the same with the blood and testimony of such a martyr; and so good also to the man with this cross of tribulation, to purge his offences in this world, not only of his recantation, but also of his standing against John Lambert and master Allen, or if there were any other with whose burning and blood his hands had been before anything polluted. Thus have you the story of the life and death of this reverend archbishop and martyr of God, and also of divers other the learned sort of Christ's martyrs burned in queen Mary's time, of whom Cranmer was the last, being burned about the very middle time of the reign of that queen, and almost the very middle man of all the martyrs which were burned in all her reign besides.

Divers books, treatises, and letters the said Thomas Cranmer wrote, both in prison and out of prison, the which we have no space here to insert, saving an extract from a letter to queen Mary, which here followeth:

I learned by Dr. Martin, that on the day of your majesty's coronation, you took an oath of obedience to the pope of Rome, and at the same time you took another oath to this realm, to maintain the laws, liberties, and customs of the same. And if your majesty did make an oath to the pope, I think it was according to the other oaths which he useth to administer to princes; which is, to be obedient to him, to defend his person, to maintain his authority, honour, laws, lands, and privileges. And if it be so, then I beseech your majesty to look upon your oath made to the crown and realm, and to compare and weigh the two oaths together, to see how they do agree, and then do as your majesty's conscience shall direct you: for I am surely persuaded, that willingly your majesty will not offend, nor do against your conscience for any thing.

But I fear there are contradictions in your oaths, and that those who should have informed your grace thoroughly, did not their duties therein. And if your majesty ponder the two oaths diligently, I think you shall perceive you were deceived; and then your highness may use the matter as God shall put in your heart. Furthermore, I am kept here from the company of learned men, from books, from counsel, from pen and ink, except at this time, to write unto your majesty, which were all necessary for a man in my case. Wherefore I beseech your majesty that I may have such of these as may stand with your majesty's pleasure. And as for my appearance at Rome, if your majesty will give me leave, I will appear there. And I trust that God shall put in my mouth to defend his truth there as well as here. But I refer it wholly to your majesty's pleasure.

CHAPTER TWENTY-ONE

Containing Farther Accounts of the Persecutions in Various Parts

ACCOUNT OF THE PERSECUTIONS
IN BOHEMIA AND GERMANY

The severity exercised by the Roman catholics over the churches of the Bohemians, induced them to send two ministers and four laymen to Rome, in the year 977, to seek relief from the pope. After some delay their request was granted and their grievances redressed. Two things in particular were permitted them, namely to have divine service in their own language and to give the cup in the sacrament to the laity. The disputes, however, soon broke out again, the succeeding popes exerting all their power to fetter their prejudices on the minds of the Bohemians; and the latter with great spirit aiming to preserve their religious liberties. Some friends, zealous of the gospel, applied to Charles, king of Bohemia, A.D. 1375, to call a council for enquiry respecting the abuses which had crept into the church and to make a through reformation. Charles, at a loss how to proceed, sent to the pope for advice; the latter incensed at the affair, only replied, "Punish severely those presumptuous and profane heretics." The king accordingly banished every one who had been concerned in the application, and to shew his zeal for the pope, imposed additional restraints on the religious liberties of the country.

The martyrdom of John Huss and Jerom of Prague—two great men brought to the light of the truth by reading the doctrines of our countryman, John Wickliffe, who, like the morning star of the reformation, first burst from the dark night of popish error, and illuminated the surrounding world—greatly increased the indignation of the believers, and gave animation to their cause.

362

These two distinguished reformers were condemned by order of the council of Constance, when fifty-eight of the principal Bohemian nobility interposed in their favour. Nevertheless they were burnt; and the pope, in conjunction with the council of Constance, ordered the Romish clergy, everywhere, to excommunicate all who adopted their opinions or pitied their fate. In consequence of these orders great contentions arose between the papists and reformed Bohemians, which produced a violent persecution against the latter. At Prague it was extremely severe, until at length the reformed, driven to desperation, armed themselves, attacked the senate-house, and cast twelve of its members with the speaker out of the windows. The pope hearing of this, came to Florence, and publicly excommunicated the reformed Bohemians, exciting the emperor of Germany, and all other kings, princes, dukes, &c. to take up arms in order to extirpate the whole race; promising, by way of encouragement, full remission of all sins to every one who should kill a Bohemian protestant. The result of this was a bloody war; for several popish princes undertook the extirpation, or at least expulsion, of the proscribed people: while the Bohemians, arming themselves, prepared to repel the assault in the most vigorous manner. The popish army prevailing against the protestant forces at the battle of Cuttenburgh, they conveyed their prisoners to three deep mines near the town, and threw several hundred into each, where they perished in a miserable manner.

A bigoted popish magistrate, named Pichel, seized twenty-four protestants, among whom was his daughter's husband. On their all confessing themselves of the reformed religion, he sentenced them to be drowned in the river Abbis. On the day of the execution a great concourse of people attended, among whom was Pichel's daughter. Seeing her husband prepared for death, she threw herself at her father's feet, bedewed them with tears, and implored him to commiserate her sorrow, and pardon her husband. The obdurate magistrate sternly replied, "Intercede not for him, child; he is a heretic, a vile heretic." To which she nobly answered, "Whatever his faults may be, or however his opinions may differ from yours, he is still my husband, a name which, at a time like this, should alone employ my whole consideration." Pichel flew into a violet passion, and said, "You are mad! Cannot you, after his death, have a much worthier husband?" "No, Sir," she replied, "my affections are fixed upon him, and death itself shall not dissolve my marriage vow." Pichel, however, continued inflexible, and ordered the prisoners to be tied with their hands and feet behind them, and in that manner thrown into the river. This being put into execution, the young lady watched the opportunity, leaped into the waves, and embracing the body of her husband, both sank together.

The emperor Ferdinand, whose hatred to the protestants was unlimited, not thinking he had sufficiently oppressed them, instituted a high court of judges, upon the plan of inquisition, with this difference, that the new court was to remove from place to place, and always to be attended by a body of troops. The greater part of this court consisted of Jesuits, from whose decisions there was no appeal. This bloody tribunal, attended by its ferocious guard, made the tour of Bohemia, and seldom examined or saw a prisoner; but suffered the soldiers to murder the protestants as they pleased, and then to make report of the matter in their own manner and time.

The first who fell a victim to their barbarity was an aged minister, whom they killed as he lay sick in bed. Next day, they robbed and murdered another, and soon after shot a third while preaching in his pulpit. The soldiers abused the daughter of a protestant before his face, and then tortured her father to death. They tied a minister and his wife back to back and burnt them. Another minister they hung upon a cross beam, and making a fire under him, broiled him to death. One gentleman they hacked into small pieces; and filled a young man's mouth with gunpowder, and setting fire to it, blew his head to atoms. But their principal rage was directed against the clergy. They seized a pious protestant minister, whom they tormented daily for a month. They placed him amidst them, derided and mocked him.

They hunted him like a wild beast, until ready to expire with fatigue, they made him run the gantlet, each striking him with a twig, their fists, or with ropes. They scourged him with wires; they tied him up by the heels until the blood started out of his nose and mouth; they hung him up by the arms until they were dislocated, and then had them set again. Burning papers, dipped in oil, were placed to his feet; his flesh was torn with red-hot pincers; he was put to the rack, and mangled by every cruel device. Even boiling lead was poured upon his feet; and, lastly, a knotted cord was twisted about his forehead in such a manner as to force out his eyes. In the midst of these enormities, particular care was taken lest his wounds should mortify, and his sufferings be shortened; until the last day, when forcing out his eyes proved fatal.

At length, winter being far advanced, the high court of judges, with their military ruffians, thought proper to return to Prague; but on their way meeting with a protestant pastor, they could not resist the temptation of feasting their barbarous eyes with a new kind of cruelty. It was to strip him naked, and to cover him alternately with ice and burning coals. This novel mode of tormenting a fellow-creature was immediately put in practice, and the unhappy victim expired beneath the torments, which seemed to delight his inhuman persecutors. Sometime after a secret order was issued by the emperor, for apprehending all noblemen and gentlemen who had been principally concerned in supporting the protestant cause, and in nominating Frederic, elector Palatine of the Rhine, to be king of Bohemia. Fifty of these were seized in one night and brought to the castle of Prague; while the estates of those who were absent were confiscated, themselves made outlaws, and their names fixed upon a gallows as a mark of public ignominy. The court afterwards proceeded to try those who had been apprehended, and two apostate protestants were appointed to examine them. Their examiners asked many unnecessary and impertinent questions, which so exasperated one of the noblemen, that he exclaimed, opening his breast at the same time, "Cut here; search my heart; you shall find nothing but the love of religion and liberty: these were the motives for which I drew my sword, and for these I am willing to die."

As none of the prisoners would renounce their faith or acknowledge themselves in any error, they were all pronounced guilty: the sentence was, however, referred to the emperor. When that monarch had read their names, and the accusations against them, he passed judgment on all, but in a different manner; his sentences being of four kinds, viz. death, banishment, imprisonment for life, and imprisonment during pleasure. Twenty, being ordered for execution, were informed they might send for Jesuits, monks, or friars, to prepare for their awful change, but that no communication with protestants would be permitted them. This proposal they rejected, and strove all they could to comfort and cheer each other upon the solemn occasion. The morning of the execution being arrived, a cannon was fired as a signal to bring the prisoners from the castle to the principal market-place, in which scaffolds were erected and a body of troops drawn up to attend. The prisoners left the castle, and passed with dignity, composure, and cheerfulness, through soldiers, Jesuits, priests, executioners, attendants, and a prodigious concourse of people assembled to see the act of these devoted martyrs. They were executed in the following order:

I. Lord Schilik, a nobleman about the age of fifty. He possessed great abilities, natural and acquired. On being told that he was to be quartered, and his parts scattered in different places, he smiled with great serenity, and said, "The loss of a sepulchre is but a trifling consideration." A friend stood by, crying, "Courage, my lord." He replied, "I possess the favour of God, which is sufficient to inspire anyone with courage: the fear of death does not trouble me. I have faced him in fields of battle to oppose Antichrist." After repeating a short prayer, he told the executioner he was ready, who cut off his right hand and head, and then quartered him. His hand and head were placed upon the high tower of Prague, and his quarters distributed in different parts of the city.

II. Lord Viscount Winceslaus, a venerable nobleman, exalted by his piety, who had attained the age of seventy, and was esteemed equally for his learning and hospitality. He was so little affected by the loss of worldly riches, that on his house being broken into, his property seized, and his estates confiscated, he only said with great composure, "The Lord hath given, and the Lord hath taken away." Being asked why he could engage in a cause so dangerous as that of attempting to support the elector palatine Frederic against the power of the emperor, he replied, "I acted according to the dictates of my conscience, and, to this day, acknowledge him as my king. I am not full of years, and which to lay down my life, that I may not be witness of the evils which await my country. You have long thirsted for my blood: take it, and God will be my avenger." He then approached the block, stroked his grey beard, and said, "Venerable hairs, the greater honour now attends you; a crown of martyrdom is your portion." Then laying down his head, it was severed from his body, and afterwards placed upon a pole in a conspicuous part of the town.

III. Lord Harant was a gentleman whose natural abilities were much refined and improved by travelling, having visited the principal places in Europe,

Asia, and Africa. The accusations against him were his being a protestant and having taken an oath of allegiance to Frederic, the elector palatine of the Rhine, as king of Bohemia. When he ascended the scaffold, he said, "I have travelled through many countries and traversed many barbarous nations, yet have I never found so much cruelty as at home. I have escaped innumerable perils both by sea and land and have surmounted all to suffer innocently in my native place. My blood is likewise sought by those for whom I and my ancestors have hazarded our lives and fortunes: but, Almighty God! forgive them, for they know not what they do." Then approaching the block, he kneeled down and exclaimed with great energy, "Into thy hands, O Lord, I commend my spirit; in thee have I always trusted; receive me, therefore, my blessed Redeemer." The fatal stroke was soon given.

IV. Lord Frederic De Bile suffered as a protestant and an instigator of the war: he met his fate with firmness, and only said he wished well to the friends whom he left behind, forgave his enemies, denied the authority of the emperor in that country, acknowledged Frederic to be the only true king of Bohemia, and trusted for salvation in the merits of his Redeemer.

V. Lord Henry Otto on first coming upon the scaffold seemed greatly agitated, and said, as if addressing himself to the emperor, "Thou tyrant Ferdinand, thy throne is established in blood; but if you kill my body and disperse my members, they shall still rise up in judgment against you." He was then silent; and having walked about awhile, recovered his fortitude, and growing calm, said to a gentleman, "A few minutes I was greatly discomposed, but now I feel my spirits revive; seem to invite me to participate of some unknown joys." Then kneeling before the block, he said, "Almighty God! to Thee I commend my soul, receive it for the sake of Christ, and admit it to the glory of Thy presence." The pains of his death must have been severe, the executioner making several strokes before his head was separated from his body.

VI. The earl of Rugenia was distinguished for his great accomplishments and unaffected piety. On the scaffold he said, "We who drew our swords fought only to preserve the liberties of the people and to keep our consciences sacred. As we were overcome, however, I am better pleased at the sentence of death than if the emperor had given me life; for I find that it pleases God to have his truth defended, not by our swords, but by our blood." He then went boldly on the block, saying, "I shall now soon be with Christ," and was almost instantly launched upon the ocean of eternity and glory.

VII. Sir Gasper Kaplitz was a nobleman eighty-six years of age. On coming to the place of execution, he addressed the principal officer thus: "Behold an unworthy and ancient man, who hath often entreated God to take him out of this wicked world, but could not until now obtain his desire; for God reserved me until these years to be a spectacle to the world and a sacrifice to Himself: therefore God's will be done." An officer told him that in consideration of his great age, if he would only ask pardon, he would immediately receive it. "Ask pardon!" exclaimed he, "I will ask pardon of God whom I have frequently offended, but not of the emperor whom I never injured. Should

I sue for pardon, it might be justly suspected I had committed some crime for which I deserved this fate. No, no; as I die innocent, and with a clear conscience, I would not be separated from these noble companions who have proceeded me to heaven: so saying, he cheerfully resigned his neck to the block.

VIII. Procopius Dorzecki said on the scaffold, "We are now under the emperor's judgment; but in time he shall be judged, and we shall appear as witnesses against him." Then taking a gold medal from his neck, which was struck when the elector Frederic was crowned king, he presented it to one of the officers with these words—"As a dying man I request, that if ever king Frederic be restored to the throne of Bohemia, you will give him this medal. Tell him, for his sake I wore it until death, and that now I willingly lay down my life for God and my king." He then cheerfully submitted to the fatal blow.

IX. Dionysius Zervius was a gentleman fifty-six years of age and had been educated as a Roman Catholic; but had embraced the reformed religion for some years. Just before his death the Jesuits used their utmost endeavours to make him recant and return to his former faith, but he gave not the least heed to their exhortations. Kneeling down, he said, "They may destroy my body, but cannot injure my soul; that I commend to my Redeemer."

X. Valentine Cockan was a gentleman of great fortune and eminent for piety and uprightness. His talents and acquirements were of an inferior order; yet his imagination seemed to brighten, and his faculties to improve on death's approach; and just before he was beheaded, he expressed himself with such eloquence, energy and precision, as amazed his hearers. This is one of innumerable instances in which unusual wisdom follows the acquisition of eminent piety.

XI. Tobias Steffick was remarkable for his affability and, upon the approach of death, displayed the greatest serenity. A few minutes before he died, he said, "I have received, during the course of my life, many favours from God; ought I not therefore cheerfully to take one bitter cup, when He thinks proper to present it? or rather, ought I not to rejoice that it is His will I should give up a corrupted life for that of immortality?"

XII. Dr. Jessenius, a learned student of physic, who had been accused of speaking disrespectful words of the emperor, of treason in swearing allegiance to the elector Frederic, and of heresy in being a protestant. For the first accusation he had his tongue cut out; for the second he was beheaded; and for the third and last he was quartered, and the several parts of his body exposed on poles.

XIII. Christopher Chober no sooner stepped upon the scaffold, than he said, "I come in the name of God to die for his glory. I have fought the good fight, and finished my course; so, executioner, do your office." On this he instantly received the crown of martyrdom.

XIV. John Shultis was by all who knew him beloved in life and regretted at his death. The only words he spoke before his martyrdom were, "The righteous seem to die in the eyes of fools, but they only go to rest. Lord Jesus!

thou hast promised that those who come to thee shall not be cast out. Behold, I am come; look on me, pity me, pardon my sin, and receive my soul."

XV. Maximilian Hostialick was celebrated for his learning, piety, and humanity. When he first came on the scaffold he seem terrified at the approach of death. Soon after he said, "Christ will wash me from my crimes." He then told the officer he should repeat the song of Simeon; at the conclusion of which the executioner might do his duty. He accordingly said, "Lord! now let thy servant depart in peace, according to thy word, for mine eyes have seen Thy salvation:" at which words his head, at one blow, was severed from his body.

XVI. John Kutnaur, not having been born independent, but having acquired a fortune by a mechanical employment, was ordered to be hanged. Just before he was turned off he said, "I die, not for having committed any crime, but for following the dictates of my conscience and defending my country and religion."

XVII. Simeon Sussickey was father-in-law to Kutnaur and was ordered to be executed in the same manner. He appeared impatient to be gone, saying, "Every moment delays me from entering into the kingdom of Christ."

XVIII. Nathaniel Wodnianskey, a gentleman, was hanged for having supported the protestant cause and the election of Frederic to the Bohemian throne. At the gallows the Jesuits used all their persuasions to make him renounce his faith. Finding their attempts unavailing, one of them said, "If you will not abjure your heresy, at least repent of your rebellion." To which Wodnianskey replied, "You take away our lives under a pretended charge of rebellion; and, not content with that, seek to destroy our souls: glut yourselves with blood and be satisfied, but tamper not with our consciences." His son then approached the gallows, and said, "Sir, if life should be offered to you on condition of apostasy, I entreat you to remember Christ." To this the father replied, "It is very acceptable, my son, to be exhorted to constancy by you, but suspect me not; rather endeavour to confirm in their faith your brothers, sisters, and children, and teach them to imitate my constancy." He had no sooner concluded these words than he received his fate with great fortitude.

XIX. Wenceslaus Gisbitzkey, throughout his imprisonment, had great hopes given him, from which his friends became very apprehensive for the safety of his soul. He, however, continued stedfast in his faith, prayed fervently at the gallows, and met his end like a Christian hero.

XX. Martin Foster was an unfortunate cripple; the chief accusations against him were his being charitable to heretics and his advancing money to the elector Frederic. It is supposed, however, that his great wealth was the principal cause of his death; as it no doubt was the ground on which many of the preceding gentlemen and noblemen were cruelly slain.

CHAPTER TWENTY-TWO

Anecdotes and Sayings of the Martyrs

W hen sentence was given against Jerome of Prague, a great and long mitre of paper was brought unto him, painted about with red devils, which, when he beheld, throwing away his hood upon the ground amongst the prelates, he took and put upon his head, saying, "Our Lord Jesus Christ, when He should suffer death for me, most wretched sinner, did wear a crown of thorns upon His head, and I, for His sake, instead of that crown, will willingly wear this mitre and cap."—Constance, 1416.

There came unto George Carpenter a certain schoolmaster of St. Peter saying, "My friend, George! Dost thou not fear the death and punishment which thou must suffer? If thou wert let go, wouldst thou return to thy wife and children?" Whereunto he answered, "If I were set at liberty, whither should I rather go, than to my wife and well-beloved children?" Then said the schoolmaster, "Revoke your former sentence and opinion, and you shall be set at liberty." Whereunto George answered, "My wife and my children are so dearly beloved unto me that they cannot be bought from me for all the riches and possessions of the Duke of Bavaria, but, for the love of my Lord God, I will willingly forsake them."—Munich, 1527.

And so going forth they came to the place of execution, where Anthony Peerson, with a cheerful countenance, embraced the post in his arms, and kissing it said, "Now welcome mine own sweet wife! For this day shalt thou and I be married together in the love and peace of God." And pulling the straw unto him, he laid a good deal thereof upon the top of his head, saying, "This is God's hat; now am I dressed like a true soldier of Christ, by Whose merits only I trust this day to enter into His joy."—Windsor, 1543.

As Giles Tilleman was brought to the place of burning, where he saw a great heap of wood piled, he required the greater part thereof to be taken away, and to be given to the poor: a little (Said he) would suffice him. Also seeing a poor man coming by, as he went, that lacked shoes, he gave his shoes unto him; better (said he) so to do, than to have his shoes burnt, and the poor to perish for cold. Standing at the stake, the hangman was ready to strangle him before; but he would not, saying that there was no such need that his pain should be mitigated; "for I fear not," said he, "the fire; do thou therefore as thou art commanded." And thus the blessed martyr, lifting up his eyes to heaven in the middle of the flame, died, to the great lamentation of all that stood by.—Brussels, 1544.

Peter Miocius was let down into a deep dungeon, under the castle-ditch, full of toads and filthy vermin. Shortly after, the senate began to examine him of certain articles of religion. To whom, as he was about to answer boldly and expressly to every point, they, interrupting him, bade him say in two words, either yea or nay. "Then," said he, "If ye will not suffer me to answer for myself in matters of such importance, send me to my prison again, among my toads and frogs, which will not interrupt me, while I talk with my Lord and my God."—Dornick, 1545.

Master Wingfield said to Kerby, "Remember the fire is hot, take heed of thine enterprise, that thou take no more upon thee, than thou shalt be able to perform. The terror is great, the pain will be extreme, and life is sweet. Better it were betimes to stick to mercy, while there is hope of life, than rashly to begin, and then to shrink."

To whom Kerby answered, "Ah, Master Wingfield! Be at my burning, and you shall say, there standeth a Christian soldier in the fire. For I know that fire and water, sword and all other things, are in the hands of God, and He will suffer no more to be laid upon us, than He will give us strength to bear."—Ipswich, 1545.

When the rope was put about Ann Audebert, she called it her wedding-girdle wherewith she should be married to Christ; and as she should be burned upon a Saturday, upon Michaelmas-even; "Upon a Saturday," said she, "I was first married, and upon a Saturday I shall be married again."—Orleans, 1549.

About ten of the clock cometh riding the sheriff, with a great many other gentlemen and their retinue appointed to assist him, and with them Christopher Wade, riding pinioned, and by him one Margery Polley of Tunbridge; both singing of a psalm: which Margery, as soon as she espied afar off the multitude gathered about the place where he should suffer, waiting his coming, said unto him very loud and cheerfully, "You may rejoice, Wade, to see such a company gathered to celebrate your marriage this day."

Wade, coming straight to the stake, took it in his arms, embracing it, and kissed it, setting his back unto it, and standing in a pitchbarrel.

As soon as he was thus settled, he spake, with his hands and eyes lifted up to heaven, with a cheerful and loud voice, the last verse of Psalm 86: "Show some good token upon me, O Lord, that they which hate me, may see it, and be ashamed; because Thou, Lord, hast helped me, and comforted me." The sheriff, often interrupted, saying, "Be quiet, Wade! And die patiently." "I am," said he, "I thank God, quiet, master sheriff! And so trust to die." Then the reeds being set about him, Wade pulled them, and embraced them in his arms, always with his hands making a hold against his face, that his voice might be heard, which they perceiving that were his tormentors, always cast faggots at the same hole, which notwithstanding, he still, as he could, put off, his face being hurt with the end of a faggot cast thereat. Then fire being put unto him, he cried unto God often, "Lord Jesus! Receive my soul," without any token of sign or impatiency in the fire.—Dartford, 1555.